Frontiers of Pattern Recognition

THE PROCEEDINGS OF THE INTERNATIONAL CONFERENCE ON FRONTIERS OF PATTERN RECOGNITION

Jointly Sponsored by
Pattern Recognition Committee, IEEE Computer Society
Pattern Recognition Committee, IEEE Systems, Man and Cybernetics Group
and the University of Hawaii
Held at Honolulu, January 18-20, 1971

Organizing Committee

Conference Chairman	C. K. Chow
Coordination	Laveen Kanal
Program	Azriel Rosenfeld
Local Arrangements	Satosi Watanabe
N. S. F.	Morris S. Ojalvo
Secretary	Charlotte S. Oser

ACADEMIC PRESS RAPID MANUSCRIPT REPRODUCTION

Frontiers of Pattern Recognition

Edited by

Satosi Watanabe

University of Hawaii
Honolulu, Hawaii

Academic Press • New York • London • 1972

ACADEMIC PRESS, INC.
111 Fifth Avenue, New York, New York 10003

United Kingdom Edition published by
ACADEMIC PRESS, INC. (LONDON) LTD.
24/28 Oval Road, London NW1

LIBRARY OF CONGRESS CATALOG CARD NUMBER: 77-159610

PRINTED IN THE UNITED STATES OF AMERICA

CONTENTS

CONTENTS

CONTRIBUTORS

A. P. Ambler (Scotland)
H. G. Barrow (Scotland)
A. W. Biermann (United States)
R. M. Burstall (Scotland)
B. Chandrasekaran (United States)
H. Chernoff (United States)
C. K. Chow (United States)
T. M. Cover (United States)
S. Csibi (Hungary)
J. A. Feldman (United States)
K. S. Fu (United States)
D. A. Glaser (United States)
L. Kanal (United States)
S. Kaneff (Australia)
T. Kaneko (United States)
T. Kasvand (Canada)
Y. Kaya (Japan)
M. G. Kendall (England)
K. Kobayashi (Japan)
D. G. Lainiotis (United States)
D. J. Langridge (Australia)
A. Lerner (U. S. S. R.)
H. Nishio (Japan)
S. Noguchi (Japan)
E. A. Patrick (United States)
T. Pavlidis (United States)
J. M. Richardson (United States)
A. Rosenfeld (United States)
A. C. Shaw (United States)
J. W. Snively, Jr. (United States)
C. W. Swonger (United States)
S. Tomita (Japan)
Y. Z. Tsypkin (U. S. S. R.)
J. R. Ullmann (England)
C. B. Ward (United States)
S. Watanabe (United States)
T. Watanabe (Japan)
P. H. Winston (United States)
S. S. Yau (United States)

PREFACE

Pattern recognition is a fast-moving and proliferating discipline. It is not easy to form a well-balanced and well-informed summary view of the newest developments in this field. It is still harder to have a vision of its future progress. Thirty authorities originating from eleven different countries were therefore requested to contribute papers to describe the frontiers of pattern recognition viewed from diverse angles. It is hoped that the reader will find this volume helpful in putting order in his collection of knowledge and in finding incentive and hints for his future research work.

This volume is the Proceedings of the International Conference on Frontiers of Pattern Recognition which took place on January 18 through 20, 1971, at the University of Hawaii, Honolulu.* This conference will be remembered as the first joint conference of the two Committees on Pattern Recognition in the IEEE, one belonging to the Computer Society and the other to the Systems, Man and Cybernetics Group. The third sponsor of the conference was the University of Hawaii. The funds that made this conference possible came from the National Science Foundation and were administered by this University. The entire conference was planned by the Organizing Committee, with Dr. C. K. Chow as the Conference Chairman. Since there was also a specialized conference on pattern recognition in 1968 at Honolulu, this book may be considered as a sister volume of the Proceedings of that conference, published under the title: *Methodologies of Pattern Recognition,* Academic Press, 1969. All the secretarial chores connected with the planning, invitation, meeting, and editing were very ably carried out by Mrs. Charlotte S. Oser. The beautiful typing is the work of Miss Priscilla Piano. There are many others who in different capacities contributed to the successful meeting and to the completion of this compilation. To all of them

Mahalo

Satosi Watanabe

---

*Two authors from the U.S.S.R., Dr. Ya. Z. Tsypkin and Dr. A. Lerner, could not attend the meeting but were kind enough to send their articles. Dr. A. Guzman, of Mexico, and Dr. A. Hamburgen, of the United States, who presented papers at the conference could not find time to complete the manuscripts.

Frontiers of Pattern Recognition

SOME TECHNIQUES FOR RECOGNISING STRUCTURES IN PICTURES

H. G. Barrow, A. P. Ambler and R. M. Burstall

DEPARTMENT OF MACHINE INTELLIGENCE AND PERCEPTION
UNIVERSITY OF EDINBURGH

Introduction

Scope

The task to which this paper is addressed is that of scene analysis, that is, of deducing from a single two-dimensional image the organisation of the scene which it depicts, in terms of objects and their interrelationships.

The aim of our research is to develop techniques whereby a machine may observe its surroundings and then use its observations to achieve goals in an effective and efficient manner. To fulfill such requirements the machine will inevitably use 'knowledge' gained from past experience and observation to plan its activities, and also to interpret its sensory data.

In the present early stages of development of picture analysis and Artificial Intelligence (the two are inevitably and inextricably linked) we are not yet close to achieving an analysis system of reasonable power and versatility. The rest of this paper describes some steps in what we think may be the right direction.

We shall treat the task of scene analysis as primarily that of describing the picture and matching the description against models.

The purpose of the paper is to discuss the idea of a finite relational structure, that is a set of elements with given properties and relations between them, as a useful mathematical tool for describing pictures, and to describe general techniques for matching such structures against each other. These may be used to recognise known objects in a picture, without dependence upon special properties of objects or the environment.

A number of experiments are described in which these ideas and techniques are applied to picture interpretation. In particular, a program is described which is used in conjunction with an on-line T.V. camera to recognise such simple, but irregular objects as cups and spectacles (Barrow and Popplestone 1971). The T.V. picture is first converted into a set of regions of uniform brightness and properties of those regions (compactness, triangularity) and relations between them (adjacency, leftof) are determined. This structure of regions with given properties and relations is then matched against standard structures previously stored. Other programs have been written embodying more sophisticated techniques which match relational structures with as many as 40 elements, but these have not yet been used on structures derived from actual T.V. pictures.

The methods of this paper might also have application in the fields of inferential systems, problem solving and question answering.

Representation of Pictures

The starting point in our investigations is the description of the picture and object models in relational terms. We do not here advocate any particular set of elements or properties or relations. We have experimented with descriptions couched in terms of straight lines, of areas and of boundary curves, using a variety of properties and relations. For example Figure 1 shows a picture *'Bear on rug with ball'*, and Figure 2 shows the relational structure which corresponds to it using regions as elements, the property *circular* and two-place relations *adjacent, immediately-inside* and *left-of* (abbreviated to *circ, adj, ins* and *left*). This relational structure leaves a great deal unspecified, for example the arms could be just above the legs and the mouth could be above the eyes. Introducing extra relations such as *above* and *larger-than* would make the description more precise. Figure 3 shows the relational structure defining the known object *'Bear'*, a substructure of the one for *'Bear on rug with ball'*. By using only a limited number of relations and perhaps not specifying all possible instances of these we enable a wide class of pictures to be recognised as bears; evidently we must try to be neither too strict nor too lax in our definition.

Clowes (1971) has endeavoured to focus attention on the distinction between a 2-dimensional picture and a 3-dimensional scene and he and Huffman (1971) improve on ideas of Guzman (1968) to give effective methods for deducing the 3-dimensional structure of polyhedra from pictures, using local clues (they do not deal with irregular shapes). This gives us two alternatives:

A. (i) Analyse picture into regions, lines points or whatever.
(ii) Convert into a relational structure.
(iii) Match this relational structure with stored structures describing views of known objects.
(iv) Use knowledge of 3-dimensional structure of the objects

found to deduce the 3-dimensional structure of the scene.

B. (i) Analyse the picture into regions, lines, points or whatever.

(ii) Use local clues or stereo information to determine 3-dimensional analysis of scene.

(iii) Express this 3-dimensional analysis as a relational structure (now using relations like *behind*).

(iv) Match this relational structure with stored structures describing known objects.

Indeed we can think of the picture and its subpictures as relational structures using one set of properties and relations and one kind of element, and the 3-dimensional objects and their parts as relational structures using another set of properties and relations and another kind of element.

The Barrow and Popplestone program proceeds by (A), but both alternatives are worth pursuing, and both involve a matching step (Aiii, Biv), to find what *known* objects are depicted.

Why do we use relational structures as representations? The object recognition process is essentially one of abstraction, where we say that a number of pictures all represent the same object, or possibly objects forming a class such as cups or chairs. Thus we must discard most of the information in the picture, and it is plausible that we should discard the *metric* information and keep only properties and interrelationships of parts of the picture. Thus the distance between two lines may not be important but the fact that they are parallel may be. This approach has been taken by people who have worked with 'logical' descriptions of pictures (Evans 1964, Burstall 1968, Clowes 1971). In the 2-dimensional recognition case this means storing relational descriptions of a small number of characteristic views of each object, since small rotations leave the relationships intact.

The element set and relations are usually carefully selected so that the 'useful' information is retained while the 'noise' is discarded. The notion of noise is here extended to mean not only an extra spurious quantity mixed with the original correct signal, but also variations in the picture which are not useful in analysing and interpreting.

In practice throwing away *all* the numerical information may be too rash. As a compromise we may extend the notion of relational structure slightly so that instead of a relation which takes n-tuples of elements to truth values we use a function which takes n-tuples of elements to real numbers. The Barrow and Popplestone program does this. A relational structure is not, however, an efficient representation for all mathematical structures, e.g. representation of the spatial organisation of an array as a relational structure requires many statements of positional information, perhaps one for each pair of points.

The matching process for relational structures attempts to find whether one structure "occurs in" or is a substructure of another structure. More precisely we need a function which assigns to each element of the first structure a distinct element of the second structure in such a way as to preserve the properties and relations which subsist in the first structure. (If a 'kluge' is a round region on top of a square region, then if the picture shows a kluge it must have a round region on top of a square region.) Such a function is called a *monomorphism* from one relational structure to the other, that is a homomorphism which is one-to-one. In the next section we will give more precise definitions.

Relational Structures As Picture Descriptions

In this section we will define the notions of relational structure and monomorphism, giving examples of their use for describing pictures and solid objects.

Definition. A *predicate set* is a set of predicates each having a given number of arguments.

Definition. A *relational structure* over a given predicate set is a set X, called the *carrier*, and an assignment to each n-argument predicate of an n-ary relation, i.e. a subset of X^n, the set of all n-tuples of elements in X. (We will call a 1-ary relation a property.)

Definition. Given two relational structures R and S over the same predicate set and carriers X and Y, we say that a function $f: X \longrightarrow Y$ is *homomorphism* if for any predicate p, $p(f(x_1), \ldots, f(x_n))$ holds in S whenever $p(x_1, \ldots, x_n)$ holds in R. We write $f: R \longrightarrow S$ if f is a homomorphism.

Definition. A *monomorphism* is a homomorphism which is one to one (or "injective") i.e. $f(x_1) = f(x_2)$ implies $x_1 = x_2$.

Definition. The homomorphism (or monomorphism) f is said to be *full* if, for any p, $p(f(x_1), \ldots, f(x_n))$ holds in S if and only if $p(x_1, \ldots, x_n)$ holds in R.

Definition. A relational structure R is said to be a *substructure* of a relational structure S if there is a monomorphism $f: R \longrightarrow S$.

We may sometimes allow a set of *operators* each denoting a function in $X^n \longrightarrow X$ and extend the definition of homomorphism to require that $g(f(x_1), \ldots, f(x_n)) = f(g(x_1, \ldots, x_n))$ for any operator g.

Relational structures are used to give the semantics of first order logic, see, for example, Schoenfield (1967) or Cohn (1965) for details. A sentence of first order logic *denotes* a class of relational structures, namely all those which satisfy it.

If R is a relational structure describing a view of a known object and S is a relational structure describing a picture which is presented for analysis we translate the question "Is the object in the picture?" to the question "Is there a monomorphism $f: R \longrightarrow S$?". Similarly given a repertoire of relational structures $R_1, \ldots, R_n$ representing views of known objects, we wish to find all monomorphisms from the R_i to S.

The choice of elements of the carrier of the relational structure and of the predicates is left free. The elements may be points, lines, regions in the two dimensional case, or vertices, edges, surfaces and solid regions in three dimensions.

For example in Figure 2, 'Bear on rug with ball' we had a relational structure which used predicates *circular* (one place) and *adjacent, immediately-inside* and *left-of* (two place). The same predicate set is used in Figure 3 'Bear', but the two relational structures are different, with different carriers and different relations. Thus the relations for 'Bear on rug with ball' have the following sets of n-tuples.

circ: (1), (5), (6), (7), (8), (9), (10)

adj: (2,11),(2,14),(2,15),(3,5),(4,5),(5,11),(11,12),(11,13),(11,14), (11,15),(11,2) etc. for symmetric pairs

ins: (1,2), (6,5), (7,6), (8,5), (9,5), (10,9)

left: (3,4),(6,9),(6,10),(7,9),(7,10),(12,13),(14,15)

The relations for 'Bear' have

circ: (3), (4), (5), (6), (7), (8)

adj: (1,3),(2,3),(3,9),(9,10),(9,11),(9,12),(9,13),(3,1) etc. for symmetric pairs

ins: (4,3), (5,4), (6,3), (7,3), (8,7)

left: (1,2),(4,7),(4,8),(5,7),(5,8),10,11),(12,13)

'Bear' is a substructure of 'Bear on rug with ball' since there is a monomorphism f:

$f(1) = 3,\ f(2) = 4,\ f(3) = 5,\ f(4) = 6,\ f(5) = 7,\ f(6) = 8,\ f(7) = 9,$

$f(8) = 10,\ f(9) = 11,\ f(10) = 12,\ f(11) = 13,\ f(12) = 14,\ f(13) = 15.$

(Note: Because we have omitted the relation *above*, and hence have not specified that arms must be above legs, there is a second monomorphism, f_2:

$f_2(1) = 3,\ f_2(2) = 4,\ f_2(3) = 5,\ f_2(4) = 6,\ f_2(5) = 7,\ f_2(6) = 8,$

$f_2(7) = 9,\ f_2(8) = 10,\ f_2(9) = 11,\ f_2(10) = 14,\ f_2(11) = 15,$

$f_2(12) = 12,\ f_2(13) = 13.$)

An alternative way of looking at a relational structure, at least so long as only unary or binary predicates are involved is to think of it as a graph, with labels or 'colours' associated with the nodes and arcs. This point of view connects the problem of finding monomorphisms between relational structures with work on Graph Isomorphism (Unger 1964, Sussenguth 1965, Corneil and Gottlieb 1970).

We would like to point out one way in which the notion of relational structure might be improved on as a picture description tool. If we take points, lines and regions as the elements the distinction between these classes is more fundamental than predicates such as vertical or straight. Similarly the "boundary operator" which takes a line onto its endpoints and a region onto its bounding lines is a fundamental relation. We may think of a relational structure whose carrier is not a set but a complex, in the sense of algebraic topology. One may speculate that taking account of this particular form of the structures might lead to more efficient algorithms, and we have some tentative ideas along these lines.

Methods of Matching Relational Structures

The methods considered

We wish to match a known relational structure R against another structure S derived from the picture, that is we wish to know whether there is any monomorphism from R to S so showing that R is a substructure of S. We will first outline each method briefly and later give a fuller description.

A naive strategy would be to generate all possible one-to-one functions from R to S and check each of them to see whether it is a monomorphism. One improvement on this has been used in the Barrow and Popplestone object recognition program. The function is built up pair by pair by taking an element from R and one from S. As each pair is added it is checked to see that any relations holding in R for its first element hold for the corresponding element in S. A mismatch causes consideration of all functions which could be constructed by extending the current partial function to be deferred, and another pair of corresponding elements is tried, thus generating a search tree. By always developing the tree in the most promising direction the best possible match can be found.

Another strategy is to progress systematically through the structures from some initial pair of nodes, adding new pairs which have elements related to some already specified pair. This is analogous to the notion of parsing a string of characters from left to right and this analogy has been exploited in the QUAC program (Ambler and Burstall 1969) which uses relational search techniques for question-answering and for some matching of picture relational structures.

For complex structures, such generative approaches usually lead to consideration of an unnecessarily large number of candidates. It is more efficient to guide the search process in some way. Unger (1964) proposed a technique for matching graphs which has been extended by Rastall (1969) following some suggestions by Burstall. This technique uses the given properties and relations to classify the elements of R and S. For example, a class of elements of R may consist of all elements with a certain property which are related by a certain relation to two other elements. The corresponding class of S elements will consist of all elements with that property which are related by that relation to *at least* two other elements. The only functions which could possibly be monomorphisms are those which carry elements of an R class into elements of the corresponding S class. Alternating classification and enumerative choices are used to produce all monomorphisms.

Another approach, suggested by Barrow and programmed by D. Milner (1971) is that of hierarchical synthesis. In this method we not only specify a set of known structures representing objects which might occur in the picture but also specify a hierarchy of substructures of these. The recognition proceeds by first finding the smaller substructures and then checking combinations of them to recognise larger known substructures in the picture. This process may be extended over several stages. This process has been described and programmed in more algebraic terms by Burstall and Barrow.

We will first describe these methods in more detail and then make some comments about their respective merits and demerits. In the following section we will point out some connections with logical inference systems.

An object recognition program using a simple matching algorithm

When we had successfully connected a T.V. camera as a peripheral to our I. C. L. 4130 computer, we started to tackle the problem of object recognition with everyday objects including curved and irregular objects, rather than rely too heavily upon the neat projective properties of polyhedra. A program was accordingly written to recognise single irregular objects in pictures (cups, spectacles). It is reported in full elsewhere (Barrow and Popplestone 1971), so only an outline is given here.

The work of Brice and Fennema (1970) upon region analysis was shown to us, and Popplestone suggested describing a picture in terms of properties of and relations between the significant regions, matching the resulting relational structure against models.

The first stage of the program is based upon the concepts of region analysis, but is intended to be much faster and more economical than Brice and Fennema's algorithm, sacrificing the exhaustiveness to do so. Starting from 256 points regularly spaced over the picture, the program tries to find an area of approximately constant brightness round each. Since several points may lie within one region, regions are recognised by their centroid co-ordinates, area, perimeter and average contrast across their boundaries. Thus only one copy of each region is retained; the regions may at this stage over-lap. The next step is to coalesce adjacent regions if the average contrast a-cross their common boundary is less than a threshold value. When this pro-cess can no longer be performed, the picture has been partitioned into areas of significant size and with strong contrast at their boundaries.

The description phase is then entered. In this program the notion of a relational structure has been extended. Relations (and properties) are not simply true or false, but may take a real value, that is, they are functions to real numbers. For each region several Fourier coefficients are calculated as a measure of the shape of the region. Thus seven property measures for each region are determined. Relational measures computed include the adjacency of two regions, which contains topological information, a measure of the (normalised) distance between the centroids of two regions, which contains geometrical information about relative position, and a measure of convexity of common boundary. The properties and relations are computed exhaus-tively to form the description, but only as a matter of experimental conven-ience.

Models of views of objects are stored as relational structures with the same relation set. The extension to real values results in storage of a mean and standard deviation for each relation measure. Picture and model rela-tions are taken to agree if the picture value lies within 3 standard deviations of the mean.

The final phase of the program is the matching. Matching is performed in an incremental fashion by building up correspondences, one pair at a time. A partial match is evaluated by determining how many of the relations in the model structure agree with their corresponding picture relations. Only relations involving elements in the new pair need be considered.

At any stage of the process many partial correspondences will exist and the program selects for incrementing that which is most promising (accord-ing to a function computed from number of agreements etc.). In fact the partial matches for all the models are mixed together, so the program at-tempts to extend the most promising match of all at each step.

The result of the process is the best match, according to the evaluation function, that can be found between the picture and any object model. Such a match need not necessarily be complete i.e. the best result may be the match of part of the picture with part of the model. Thus the program can be used even if not all the object is visible, or the picture is 'dirty', producing errors in the description.

The program has a repertoire of nine objects; ball, pencil, doughnut, wedge, cylinder, hammer, tube, cup and spectacles. It can correctly recognise these objects about 85% of the time taking from one to ten minutes, depending upon the complexity of the picture.

One limitation of the existing program is that the description in terms of regions is too global in nature, and is easily affected by partial occlusion. More local information, and redundancy are required. However, this would increase the number of elements upon which the description is based and would exacerbate the second limitation, which is that the matching process, while being more efficient than an exhaustive, naive strategy, takes a time which increases rapidly with the number of elements. It is after all a tree search. Much time is taken if there are more than about six regions.

Relational composition search

This technique grow out of a relational question answering project along the lines of Raphael's SIR (1964) but with means of defining new relations as compositions, unions, intersections, inverses, etc. of old ones, based on an analogy with context-free grammars. The program 'QUAC' is described in Ambler and Burstall (1969), and it was used to recognise some objects from relational structure descriptions of them, as well as to answer questions in a small subset of English using a relational data base.

Consider again our friend the bear (Figure 3). If we use $.$ to denote composition of relations, $\cup$ and $\cap$ to denote union and intersection (considered as operations on their pairs) and $^{-1}$ to denote inversion we can say that the defined relation

$$\text{adj} \cap (\text{left} \,.\, \text{adj})$$

holds between 1 and 3. Also

$$(\text{ins} \,.\, (\text{ins} \cap (\text{left} \,.\, \text{ins})) \cap \text{left} \,.\, \text{ins} \,.\, \text{ins}))\ \text{ins}^{-1}$$

holds between 5 and 6.

Given any element and such a definition of a relation it is easy to find all elements so related to it, using a recursive top to bottom 'parsing' technique. Starting from such a given element the existence of such a related element defines the intermediate structure, so that we have a representation of the relational structure, or at least some paths through it, basically in terms of relational composition. The definitions are a little awkward and unnatural but the program succeeded in recognising a 'cube' (9 elements in 9) in about 60 seconds and the 'bear' in 8 seconds.

The technique does not seem appropriate for large structures but may be useful for detecting local structure in large pictures, when used in combination with another method such as the hierarchical one described below. It does seem to use the adjacency of nodes in a natural way.

Relational structure matching using extensions of graph isomorphism techniques

The problem of finding monomorphisms from one relational structure to another is a generalisation of the better known problem of finding isomorphisms between graphs. In this context, by "graph" we mean a set of nodes N (the carrier) together with a binary relation $R \subseteq N \times N$ defined over them. In the relational structure case we have many relations, not necessarily binary, and for monomorphisms the structures will not necessarily have the same number of nodes. What is more we are not just looking for *full* monomorphisms. Relations of 3 or more arguments can be converted into sets of binary relations, and unary relations (properties) present no problems.

Techniques for finding (full) isomorphisms of graphs have been described by Unger (1964), by Sussenguth (1965), and Corneil and Gottlieb (1970). Sussenguth also deals with monomorphisms. It is possible to generalise Unger's techniques to find monomorphisms of relational structures (Rastall 1969). In essence Unger uses the structure of a graph to derive additional properties of the nodes of the graph and hence to classify the nodes. For example, the number of arcs leaving each node may be used as an extra property for classification. We want a function from the nodes of the first graph onto nodes of the second. Unger classifies the nodes of each graph and so restricts the number of possible functions since a node in a certain class of the first graph must correspond to some node in the same class of the second graph. For example, a node with two arcs leaving it can only be mapped onto a node with two arcs leaving it. He uses the resulting classes to define further properties and thus refine the classification, and so on until either it has been shown that no isomorphism is possible, or until one has been found, or until no further refinement is possible, at which stage an enumerative choice is made and the classification phase is repeated.

To refine a classification Unger determines for each node how many neighbours it has in each of the classes. Two nodes in the same class may differ in the distribution of their neighbours among the other classes and this will yield a refinement of the classification. Schematically:

procedure examine (classification);

begin

```
refine:  try to refine classification;
         if inconsistent then exit;
         if each class has just one node then check for isomorphism
            and exit;
         if no refinement was possible then
            enumerate: for new classification := choice_1,...,choice_n do
                               examine (new classification)
         else goto refine
end;
examine (initial classification);
```

Example

The non-directed graphs in Figure 4 can be initially classified by number of neighbours thus:

Graph 1. A: (1,3), B:(5,6,7) C:(2,8) D:(4)

Graph 2. A: (5,7) B:(1,4,3) C:(6,8) D:(2)

This reduces the initial 8! functions to 24 functions consistent with the classification. We now note the classes of the neighbours of each node.

Graph 1	Graph 2
1 CC	5 CC
3 CD	7 CD
5 BBD	1 BBC
6 BBD	4 BBD
7 BBC	3 BBD
2 AACD	6 AACD
8 ABCD	8 ABCD
4 ABBCC	2 ABBCC

This yields a refined classification with only two possible functions

Graph 1 E:(1) F:(3) G:(7) H:(5,6) I:(2) J:(8) K:(4)

Graph 2 E:(5) F:(7) G:(1) H:(4,3) I:(6) J:(8) K:(2)

Repeated examination of neighbours fails to distinguish the nodes in H (in fact there is an automorphism carrying 5 into 6 and 4 into 3, so they are indistinguishable). We enumerate, putting 5 into a class of its own, say L, and *either* 4 *or* 3 into L in the second graph. Both alternatives give isomorphisms without further processing.

Corneil and Gottlieb have a means of further refining the classification before enumerating, but this does not seem extendable to the monomorphism case.

Turning now to relational structure monomorphisms the main difficulty in extending the graph isomorphism techniques is not in dealing with a number of relations. It is that the image element in the picture structure may have relations to a larger number of elements than does the source element in the structure describing the known object. Thus element 9 in 'Bear' (Figure 3) has only 5 elements adjacent to it whilst its image 11 in 'Bear on rug with ball' (Figure 2) has 6. This occurs even if we seek only *full* monomorphisms since an element in the substructure may be related to the elements outside it. Thus if we classify the source ('Bear') elements and make the classes of target ('Bear on rug with ball') elements which might correspond to each of these, the latter classes will be overlapping rather than disjoint. Rastall's method is to follow the same general scheme of computation as in the *'procedure'* given about but to allow overlapping classes of target elements.

Consider finding monomorphisms from R, 'Bear', to S, 'Bear on rug with ball'. Let us use the property *circ* to get an initial classification

Structure R. A: (1,2,9,10,11,12,13) B: (3,4,5,6,7,8)

Structure S. A: (1,2,3,4,5,6,7,8,9,10,11,12,13,14,15) B: (1,5,6,7,8,9,10)

Class A in R does not have *circ*, class B has. The corresponding class A in S contains both non-*circ* elements and *circ* elements, whilst B contains only *circ* elements, since if an element is *circ* its image must be *circ*.

We now refine the classification using the relations *adj, ins* and *left* successively to get classes

Structure R. C:(1) D:(2) E:(9) F:(10,12) G:(11,13) H:(4) I:(5)

Structure S. C:(3,4) D:(4) E:(11) F:(3,12,14) G:(4,13,15) H:(6) I:(6,7)

Structure R continued J:(6) K:(8) L:(7) M:(3)

Structure S continued J:(6,7,8,9,10) K:(9,10) L:(9) M:(5)

For example elements 1, 2 and 9 of R have a circular node adjacent to them and so can only go into nodes 3, 4 or 11 of S. Using the other relations eliminates some of these possibilities to give the classification shown above. At this stage we notice that 4 of S is committed to element 2 of R, so that we can remove it from classes C and G of S. Such observations lead to

Structure R. C:(1) D:(2) E:(9) F:(10,12) G:(11,13) H:(4) I:(5)

Structure S. C:(3) D:(4) E:(11) F:(12,14) G:(13,15) H:(6) I:(7)

Structure R continued J:(6) K:(8) L:(7) M:(3)

Structure S continued J:(8) K:(10) L:(9) M:(5)

Further attempts to refine this are fruitless so we make a pair of enumerative choices, say 10 goes to 12 *or* 10 goes to 14. Each of these on refinement immediately leads to an unambiguous classification which is a monomorphism.

In practice, Rastall's program starts off with an initial partition based on a property-relation-property classification (circles adjacent to circles, etc.) or a still stricter one and reaches a solution even more quickly. Going from isomorphisms to monomorphisms reduces the power of the classification method somewhat, but the program has recognised such things as a description of a cube in a collection of objects (9 elements in 40, 32 seconds) and a 'cat' in a 'cat on table' (10 elements in 18, 257 seconds). Times are rather variable depending both on the nature of the structures and on certain parameter settings which control the effort expended in various parts of the search. The general impression is that refined combinatorial analysis, in the spirit of say Corneil and Gottlieb (1970), is less important than avoidance of tedious attempts at classification which do not pay off. The program needs more flexibility in its choice between refinement and enumeration. It is restricted to dealing with properties and 2-place relations, but n-ary relations can be translated into sets of 2-place ones with some loss of efficiency.

In general the method is quite fast. Unfortunately we see no simple way of extending it to deal with 'dirty' or incomplete pictures with missing nodes or instances of relations, nor will it easily cope with 'real-valued' properties and relations (that is, functions).

Recognition by hierarchical synthesis

Suppose a relational structure, S, has N elements, and we wish to match it against another structure, R, with n elements. A simple combination generating-checking approach will involve testing of the order of N^n combinations (assuming $N >> n$). It will be clear that in practice such approaches become unworkable if n is larger than about 10.

We now make the following observation. In general, for substructures of non-trivial complexity, the number of occurrences of a particular substructure in S will be of the order of N. (This is not a law; but it provides a useful heuristic technique.) Suppose we break R into k substructures of r_i elements ($i = 1, \ldots k, k < n$). We now first identify all occurrences of each substructure in S: there will be of the order of N for each of these. Then we generate and test combinations of the substructures, searching for combinations which match R. The number of combinations will be of the order of N^k. Thus the total number of checking operations will be of the order of

$$N^k + \sum_{i=1}^{k} N^{r_i}$$

which will be much less than $N^n = N^{\sum_i r_i} = \prod_i N^{r_i}$.

Thus, if we can break up the model structure into suitable substructures, we can reduce considerably the amount of work required in matching. In fact, we can apply this procedure recursively to make very great economies of time and effort.

This principle has been used in practice, in a program written by D. Milner which endeavours to find complex objects in pictures. The data in this case is provided by hand, and is, arbitrarily, a description in terms of regions: we have not yet connected the program to the real picture analysis routines.

Each object that the program 'knows about' is composed of several sub-objects, and these may be composed of smaller sub-objects, in a hierarchy with picture regions at the bottom-most level. See for example Figure 5 which shows a hierarchical structure for 'Bear' (many other hierarchical decompositions would be possible).

The program is written in a modular fashion, for each object there is a module, and the interrelations of the modules form a network. It is the job of each module to produce a set of all the objects of a certain type in the picture. It does this by accepting similar sets from the modules associated with its sub-objects, generating combinations of sub-objects and checking them. At the lowest level, modules accept as their input the set of all regions of the picture, and produce sets of regions of particular shapes. (At present, it seems that the lowest level requires the bulk of the picture processing time, as every member module checks all the picture regions. A more subtle classification technique could easily be used here.)

Regions are classified into about 40 categories but there are only 3 relations *adjacent, above, left-of*. Once more, however, *adjacency* is a real-valued measure, and not a strictly binary predicate. About a dozen objects are defined at present, the most complex possessing 12 regions and 5 levels of sub-object.

The program performs encouragingly well. It takes only seconds to recognise objects compared with minutes for even simple objects with the previous single-level matching program. A 10-region man-figure is recognised in 10 seconds, while for a 37-region picture (Figure 6) containing a man, a car and a house, only 26 seconds are required to identify all three objects. The program is in a high-level language and could be speeded up by machine coding.

Having described the organisation of the network, it is perhaps now worthwhile to describe the organisation of the operations. A module may be activated, or remain dormant. If it is activated and all the modules upon which it depends have produced their results, it performs its task of generation and testing. When it has produced its set of results, it then makes a request for activation of all modules which accept its results as data. If the module is activated and it is unable to function because it lacks data, it requests that the offending lower level modules be activated. At every stage, the most popular module is activated, and since some modules never become activated at all operating efficiency is secured.

The program can be run 'bottom-up' or 'top-down'. If a particular object module is activated, it will call only those modules upon whose results it depends. Thus a search for a particular object in the picture may be carried out. Alternatively, if all the lowest level modules are activated, activity will spread up the hierarchy to modules which might be able to produce results. Thus all objects in the picture may be recognised.

The remaining problem of this approach is that of setting up the modules and network automatically in a 'learning phase'. At present we have not attempted to tackle this problem. The ideas of Winston (1970) about learning descriptions in the form of relational structures may be relevant.

A mathematical discussion of the hierarchical matching method may be of interest both to understand it better and make it easier to program; we give such a discussion in the Appendix. We separate the idea into two parts, one of which is dependent on the notion of relational structures and their monomorphisms, and the other is a more general algebraic notion of a hierarchical descriptive system couched in category theoretic terminology, and hence allowing other interpretations of the notion of morphism and structures other than relational structures, (see Cohn 1965 or Maclane and Birkhoff 1967 for the terminology used). This extra freedom might have practical significance in cases where metric or topological structure turned out to be more significant than relational structures. It can be used to cope with the case where the relations are replaced by real-valued functions and approximate matches are desired.

The method as described in the Appendix has been programmed to check that there are no snags. It ran more slowly than Milner's version, but it did recognise a small structure 'House' (see Appendix) in 17 seconds and "Bear" in 68 seconds and should run faster if more tightly coded.
The program is simple and is made up almost entirely of general functions which could be used in other programs about algebras and relational structures.

At first sight, hierarchical synthesis may appear to be a picture grammar by another name. In fact it has some similarities but is in reality a different approach. The idea that it does take over from grammars is the notion of *constituency:* that a symbol (substructure) consists of a collection of lower-order symbols, i.e. that a substructure may itself possess substructures. However, in the formulation in terms of relational structures, the constituent substructures need not necessarily be disjoint.

Comparison of methods

The methods described above have been applied to a large variety of problems. Table 1 gives results for some that were definable in a form which enabled all the methods to be used. There are types of problem to which not all methods are applicable (e.g. those involving numerical information or incomplete data). We wish to emphasize that the times given in Table 1 should not be taken too seriously, since a different representation of the data was required for each method. (All times in this paper are for programs written in the POP-2 language on an ICL 4130, a machine roughly similar to the IBM 7090.)

The tree-search method of building up a monomorphism one pair at a time is robust, enabling one to handle 'real-valued' properties and relations, imperfect matches, and simultaneous matching against many models. It was used successfully with actual T.V. pictures. But it seems to be too combinatorially inefficient to handle structures of any great size.

The relational composition search is quite fast, but the construction of definitions of objects is unnatural. It uses definitions of paths through a relational structure, rather than the relational structure itself. This means that the definition of "parallelepiped" is very cumbersome. It can only look for one object at a time, but since it can memorize sub-paths (i.e. sub-objects) that it finds in the course of its search, the labour involved in looking for a second object that shares some structure with the first, is reduced. The relational composition search method cannot cope with incomplete data. We feel that, used in conjunction with other methods, something along along the lines of relational composition search should be useful for finding local structures in larger pictures.

The method based on Unger's graph isomorphism technique suffers from its generality. There is at present no way of giving it extra information about the type of picture to be processed (in the way that the sub-objects of hierarchical synthesis method represent such special information). As demonstrated by the Picture example, it is badly affected by irrelevant data. In this case it has spent most of the time in processing completely useless information (e.g. that region 35 is to the left of region 20, or that region 6 is

TABLE 1

	Tree Search	Relational Composition	Extended Graph Isomorphism	Hierarchical Synthesis
Flower (5 elements in 5)	680 secs	2 secs	3 secs	0.85 secs
Maid (8 elements in 11)	10^6 secs (by extrapolation)	10 secs	36 secs	2 secs
Parallelepiped (9 elements in 9)	10^{10} secs (by extrapolation)	65 secs	408 secs	22.5 secs
Bear (13 elements in 15)	10^{10} secs (by extrapolation)	8 secs	17 secs	5 secs
Picture (6, 11, 12 elements in 37)	–	–	4000 secs (estimate)	26 secs

Description of problems

Flower. A 5 element object to be recognised in a 5 element picture, with properties "petal-shaped", "leaf-shaped", "stalk-shaped" and "circular", and with relations ""left", "adjacent" and "above".

Maid. An 8 element object to be recognised in an 11 element picture, with properties "circular", "elliptical", "toppart", "line" and "skirt", and with binary relations "ontop", "onleft", "onright", "onrightbottom", "onleftbottom" and the tertiary relation "aligned".

Parallelepiped. A 9 element object to be recognised in a 9 element picture. This is a line picture of a cube as described in Burstall (1968) but using only the binary relation "parallel" and the tertiary "between" and not using "equidistant". Recognition of this object was expected to be difficult for all of the methods, because the definition is highly symmetrical. There is a six-fold automorphism (three rotations and a reflection) and hence six parallelepipeds must be found.

Bear. A 13 element object to be found in a 15 element picture, properties and relations as described elsewhere in this paper.

Picture. 12 objects to be looked for in a 37 element picture containing three objects: Man (11 elements), Car (12 elements) and House (6 elements). This is the Picture of Figure 6, with 42 shape properties and the binary relations "adjacent", "above", "below", "left" and "right".

below region 37). Furthermore, it can only look for one object at a time. Since twelve were to be sought, this irrelevant work had to be done twelve times. The Parallelepiped example took a long time because of the tertiary relation "between". The program has recognised such a line drawing of a parallelepiped, but using the binary relations "meets" and "parallel" in 17 secs.

The method of hierarchical synthesis is quite fast. Moreover, since objects have sub-objects in common and basic elements may be sorted by property, it is possible to search for a number of objects in parallel with much greater efficiency than searching for them in sequence. Real-valued relations may be used in descriptions and they may be evaluated when required, rather than in advance. Since it builds up structures via their parts it offers hope of guissing at partly occluded objects. It can be used either to look for a given object (top-to-bottom) or to say which of a repertoire of known objects occur in a picture without checking each one separately (bottom-to-top).

Hierarchical synthesis thus seems to be the most promising method of those investigated.

Connection with Logical Inference

Given a description of a picture using certain predicates and definitions of objects which might occur in it using the same predicates, instead of talking in terms of relational structures we can set up the recognition problem as a proof problem in first-order logic in the obvious way. We will need constants to denote the elements (points, lines, etc.) in the picture. The picture description will be a set of sentences, each of which states that a predicate applies to an n-tuple of these constants. The object definitions will be clauses involving universally quantified variables. For example, with a similar decomposition to Figure 5, we may define a bear in first-order logic using the basic predicates *circular, adjacent, inside, leftof* and auxiliary predicates *head, eyes, body* and *triple* (we omit universal quantifiers by convention):

$$\mathrm{head}(x_1, \ldots, x_8) \,\&\, \mathrm{body}(x_9, \ldots, x_{13}) \,\&\, \mathrm{adj}(x_3, x_9) \Rightarrow \mathrm{bear}(x_1, \ldots, x_{13})$$

$$\mathrm{triple}(x_1, x_3, x_2) \,\&\, \mathrm{circ}(x_3) \,\&\, \mathrm{eyes}(x_4, x_5, x_7, x_8) \,\&\, \mathrm{circ}(x_6) \,\&\, \mathrm{ins}(x_4, x_3) \\ \&\, \mathrm{ins}(x_6, x_3) \,\&\, \mathrm{ins}(x_7, x_3) \Rightarrow \mathrm{head}(x_1, \ldots, x_8)$$

$$\mathrm{circ}(x_1) \,\&\, \mathrm{circ}(x_2) \,\&\, \mathrm{circ}(x_3) \,\&\, \mathrm{circ}(x_4) \,\&\, \mathrm{ins}(x_2, x_1) \,\&\, \mathrm{ins}(x_4, x_3) \\ \&\, \mathrm{left}(x_3, x_1) \Rightarrow \mathrm{eyes}(x_1, x_2, x_3, x_4)$$

$$\mathrm{triple}(x_2, x_1, x_3) \,\&\, \mathrm{triple}(x_4, x_1, x_5) \Rightarrow \mathrm{body}(x_1, \ldots, x_5)$$

$$\mathrm{adj}(x_2, x_1) \,\&\, \mathrm{adj}(x_3, x_1) \,\&\, \mathrm{left}(x_2, x_3) \Rightarrow \mathrm{triple}(x_2, x_1, x_3)$$

The picture 'bear on rug with ball' to be recognised would be represented by variable-free sentences, in terms of constants $a_1, \ldots, a_{15}$ denoting regions of the picture.

$\mathrm{circ}(a_1)$. $\mathrm{circ}(a_5)$. $\mathrm{circ}(a_6)$. $\mathrm{circ}(a_7)$. $\mathrm{circ}(a_8)$. $\mathrm{circ}(a_9)$. $\mathrm{circ}(a_{10})$.

$\mathrm{adj}(a_2, a_{11})$. . . . $\mathrm{adj}(a_{11}, a_{15})$.

$\mathrm{ins}(a_1, a_2)$. . . . $\mathrm{ins}(a_{10}, a_9)$

$\mathrm{left}(a_3, a_4)$. . . . $\mathrm{left}(a_{14}, a_{15})$

Now we can prove there is a bear in the picture i.e. $\mathrm{bear}(a_3, \ldots, a_{15})$ using the usual logical inference rules of instantiation and modus ponens. Thus from the eyes definition and the sentences

$\mathrm{circ}(a_6)$. $\mathrm{circ}(a_7)$. $\mathrm{ins}(a_7, a_6)$. $\mathrm{circ}(a_9)$. $\mathrm{circ}(a_{10})$. $\mathrm{ins}(a_{10}, a_9)$

we infer

$\mathrm{eyes}(a_6, a_7, a_9, a_{10})$.

similarly we obtain $\mathrm{triple}(a_3, a_5, a_4)$ from $\mathrm{adj}(a_3, a_5)$. $\mathrm{adj}(a_4, a_5)$ and $\mathrm{left}(a_3, a_5)$ and use this with some of the original sentences to obtain $\mathrm{head}(a_3, \ldots, a_{10})$, and so on to get $\mathrm{bear}(a_3, \ldots, a_{15})$.

If we think of the resolution method of mechanical theorem proving (Robinson, 1965a) we see that this proof, easy though it is, involves a large number of resolution steps. However the inferences using a definition each correspond to a single *hyper-resolution* inference (Robinson, 1965b), and only 5 such 'macro' inference steps are required. But we still need a more efficient method of finding a set of unit ground clauses than the very tedious one of comparing the literals on the left of the definition one by one with the data clauses in a tree-search manner until a match is found. This is impracticable if the definition has more than half a dozen or so literals on its left hand side.

To deal with larger definition clauses we may use one of the techniques for finding monomorphisms between relational structures. We are dealing with the restricted kind of hyper-resolution inference where the definition clause (the 'nucleus' or negative clause) contains only predicates applied to variables and where picture clauses (the 'electrons' or positive clauses) are unit clauses consisting of a predicate applied to some constants.

Suppose we wish to hyper-resolve the 'head' definition clause with the original picture clauses together with $\mathit{eyes}(a_4, a_5, a_7, a_8)$ and $\mathit{triple}(a_3, a_5, a_4)$. Then we must find a unifying substitution σ, that is a function from the variables $x_1, \ldots, x_8$ in the 'head' clause to the constants $a_1, \ldots, a_n$, such that if $p(x_{i_1}, \ldots, x_{i_n})$ occurs in the definition then $p(\sigma x_{i_1}, \ldots, \sigma x_{i_n})$ occurs as a ground unit clause. Clearly we need a monomorphism $\sigma: R \rightarrow S$, where (i) R is the relational structure whose carrier is the variable symbols $x_1, \ldots, x_8$ and whose predicates *circular, adjacent, inside, leftof* and *eye* hold for some n-tuple of x's just if this n-tuple and predicate occurs as a literal on the left hand side of the definition clause and (ii) S is the relational structure whose carrier is the constant symbols $a_1, \ldots, a_{15}$ and whose predicates hold for some n-tuple of a's just if this n-tuple and predicate occurs as a unit clause in the picture description.

A hyper-resolution theorem prover was written by Ambler, and the Rastall relational structure monomorphism program was incorporated to find the unifying substitutions for the hyper-resolution inferences. This was indeed much faster for long clauses than the naive method of matching literals one at a time, which was only used for short clauses. The matching was generalised a little to allow ground terms in the picture clauses as well as constants and terms in the definition clauses. In one example "Maid", with 8 nodes and 18 literals on the left hand side of the definition, the naive hyper-resolution method took 50 minutes, whilst the hyper-resolution using the monomorphism program took 20 seconds (the hyper-resolution was not very efficiently programmed but even so the difference is quite startling). The Rastall monomorphism program was only written to cope with unary and binary relations, so that some pains had to be taken at the interface between the theorem prover and the monomorphism tester to convert n-ary relations $(n \geq 3)$ to a number of binary ones; this slowed up the program somewhat.

One pleasing feature of this approach is that it connects the relational structure matching techniques which are quite efficient with logical inference techniques which are more general in their application and might be necessary for making deductions about non-pictorial aspects of the situation. The connection between relational structure monomorphism finding and hyper-resolution is not confined to picture processing problems, although it is only of any practical interest where long clauses are encountered.

Appendix

Mathematical discussion of the hierarchical method

Our task is to compare a hierarchy of structures with a given picture structure and find all monomorphisms from the structures in the hierarchy to the picture structure. Such monomorphisms 'describe' the picture by saying that some known object occurs in it. We think of the hierarchy with its monomorphisms as a *category*, i.e. a collection of 'objects' (structures) and, morphisms,(monomorphisms from one structure to another) with an associative composition operation for morphisms and an identity morphism for each object (Cohn 1965, Maclane and Birkhoff 1967). Indeed the hierarchy is a subcategory of a larger category containing also all possible picture structures. For generality we will not at first restrict the category to be one of relational structures and their monomorphisms, only introducing this specialisation when necessary. We think of an object in the hierarchy being constructed out of lower objects in the hierarchy and for each such construction give a rule for trying to find the higher object in the picture when the lower objects have been found. Such a step forms an operation of a general algebra whose elements are monomorphisms from objects of the hierarchy to the picture. We start off with monomorphisms from the lowest objects to the picture and try to find monomorphisms from the higher objects be repeatedly applying these operations, that is by closing the initial subset of this algebra.

Let $\mathcal{C}$ be a category and $\mathcal{V}$ be a subcategory of $\mathcal{C}$ (the vocabulary of objects to be used in descriptions). Let V_o be a subset of the objects of $\mathcal{V}$. By a description of an object c of $\mathcal{C}$ we will mean a morphism $h: b \rightarrow c$ where be is an object of $\mathcal{V}$.

By a construction of b from a_i, where b and the a_i are all objects of $\mathcal{V}$, $i = 1, \ldots, n$, we mean an n-tuple of morphisms, f, where $f_i: a_i \rightarrow b$ for $i = 1, \ldots, n$. Let F be a set of such constructions. (The number n may vary from one construction in F to another.)

Definition. We will call $(\mathcal{V}, V_o, F)$ a hierarchical descriptive system for $\mathcal{C}$ if the following conditions hold.

(i) For any construction f in F with $f_i: a_i \rightarrow b, i = 1, \ldots, n$, with a_i and b in $\mathcal{V}$ and any n-tuple g with $g_i: a_i \rightarrow c, i = 1, \ldots, n$, with c in $\mathcal{C}$ there exists at most one $h: b \rightarrow c$ such that the diagram

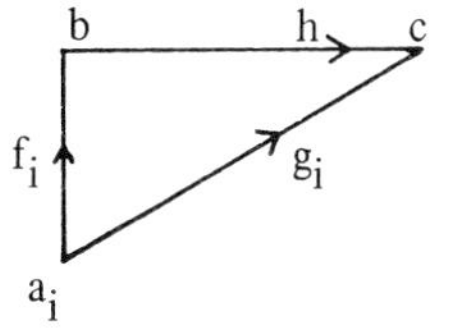

commutes for all i.

We denote this h by $\alpha_f(g_1, \ldots, g_n)$, considering, α_f as a partial function in $\mathrm{Hom}(a_1, c) \times \ldots \times \mathrm{Hom}(a_n, c) \rightarrow \mathrm{Hom}(b, c)$.

(ii) For any b in $\mathcal{V}$ either b in V_o or else there exists a construction f in F with $f_i: a_i \rightarrow b$, for some a_i.

(iii) There is a partial ordering $\leq$ over the objects $\mathcal{V}$ such that if f is in F with f_i: $a_i \longrightarrow b$ then $a_i < b$ for each i.

(iv) Hom(b,c) is finite for any b in $\underline{V}$ and c in $\underline{C}$.

(v) F is finite (and hence so is the set of objects of $\underline{V}$, by condition ii above).

If $(\mathcal{V}, V_o, F)$ is a hierarchical descriptive system for $\mathcal{C}$ we may associate with it a partial algebra $\mathcal{F}$ whose carrier is the set of all morphisms g: b$\rightarrow$c, for b in $\mathcal{V}$, and which has an operation α_f associated with each f in F.

By the closure of a subset of the carrier of $\mathcal{F}$ we mean the least subalgebra containing that set.

Our algorithm derives from the fact that, under the above assumptions, we can describe an object c in forms of the vocabulary $\mathcal{V}$ by starting with descriptions of c in terms of the basic objects in V_o and then applying the operations of $\mathcal{F}$ repeatedly to get descriptions in terms of higher objects. i.e. compute the closure of the set of initial descriptions. Any description, h, of c can be obtained in this way. Formally we have:

Theorem. For any h: b c where b is in $\mathcal{V}$, h is in G_c where

$$G_c = \text{Closure}_{\mathcal{F}}\left(\bigcup_{a \in V_o} \text{Hom}(a,c)\right)$$

Proof. By induction on $\leq$ we have immediately

(i) If b is in V_o then h is in Hom(b,c), which is a subset of G_c

(ii) Otherwise, suppose the theorem holds for all $b' < b$. There exists f in F with f_i: $a_i \rightarrow b$. Put $g_i = f_i \,.\, h$. Then since $a_i < b$ we have g_i is in G_c for each i, and since $h = \alpha_f(g_1, \ldots, g_n)$ h is in gG_c.

This theorem gives us 'completeness' of the closure process (it com putes all descriptions of c). Each element of the closure is clearly a morphism to c from some b, by the definition of F, so the process is 'sound'. Since $\underline{V}$ has finitely many objects, each with finitely many morphisms to c, the closure is finite and the process of computing it must terminate.

Hierarchical descriptive systems for relational structures

Let us take as the category $\mathcal{C}$ the category of finite relational structures over a particular predicate set and their monomorphisms. We take as $\mathcal{V}$ the subcategory of structures representing meaningful objects and substructures of these which are likely to be useful for recognising them.

If c is the relational structure obtained from the picture to be described then G_c is the set of descriptions, with the maximal elements under $\leq$ being the "most comprehensive" descriptions, the largest identifiable substructures. We take V_o as some easily obtainable initial structures e.g. all single nodes of c, or perhaps some or all of the n-tuples occurring in the relations of c.

For the constructions in F we take n-tuples of monomorphisms $f_i: a_i \rightarrow b$ such that the union of the images of the a_i is the whole carrier of b.

To define $h = \alpha_f(g_1, \ldots, g_n)$, such that $f_i \cdot h = g_i$, $i = 1, \ldots, n$ we note that since f_i is a monomorphism it has an inverse, say f_i^{-1}, which is a partial injection, composing this with g_i, considered as an injection, we get the partial injection $f_i^{-1} \cdot g_i$. Taking the union of these we get $\bigcup_i (f_i^{-1} \cdot g_i)$: $b \rightarrow c$ which is total, but may or may not be single valued and injective. If it is a total injection it still may not be a homomorphism. If it is a homomorphism $\bigcup_i (f_i^{-1} \cdot g_i)$ is the required unique monomorphism h. If it fails to be single valued, injective or a homomorphism then $\alpha_f(g_1, \ldots, g_n)$ is undefined.

To save some of the labour of checking that $\bigcup_i (f_i^{-1} \cdot g_i)$ is a homomorphism from b to c, we may express b as the 'superimposition' of a pair of structures b_1 and b_2 on the same carrier as b, such that any relation holding in b holds either in b_1 or in b_2 but not in both; also a relation holds for $x_1, \ldots, x_k$ in b_1 iff it holds for $f_i^{-1}(x_1), \ldots, f_i^{-1}(x_k)$ in a_i for some i. Thus b_1 is the image of the f_i, and b_2 represents the extra structure in b, not contained in the a_i. Now to ensure that $\bigcup_i (f_i^{-1} \cdot g_i)$ is a homomorphism we need only check the relations in b_2 since those in b_1 are automatically satisfied.

Example. Suppose V consists of the following, using one binary directed relation.

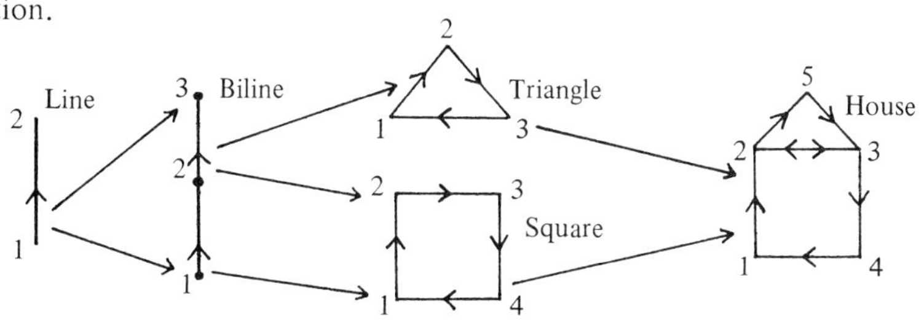

Then denoting the function $f:\ \{1,..,m\} \longrightarrow \{1,..,n\}$

$f(1) = i_1, \ldots, f(m) = i_m$

by $(i_1,..,i_m)$ we have constructions

Line, Line $\longrightarrow$ Biline	$f_1 = (1,2),\ f_2 = (2,3)$
Biline $\longrightarrow$ Triangle	$f_1 = (1,2,3)$
Biline, Biline $\longrightarrow$ Square	$f_1 = (1,2,3),\ f_2 = (3,4,1)$
Triangle, Square $\longrightarrow$ House	$f_1 = (2,5,3),\ f_2 = (1,2,3,4)$

If we take

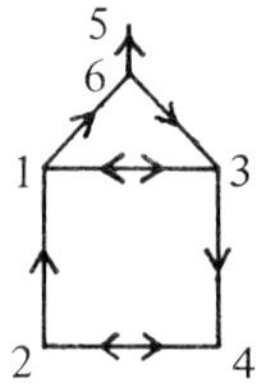

Picture

The required h: House $\longrightarrow$ Picture is $h = (2,1,3,4,6)$ which is obtained from g_1: Triangle $\longrightarrow$ House, $g_1 = (1,6,3)$ and g_2: Square $\longrightarrow$ House, $g_2 = (2,1,3,4)$, which are obtained eventually from g_{10}: Line $\longrightarrow$ House, $g_{10} = (2,1)$, g_{11}: Line $\longrightarrow$ House, $g_{11} = (1,6)$ etc.

Computing closures for an algebra

Having shown how to compute the individual operations α_f it remains to explain how the closure of the starting set of monomorphisms with respect to these operations is to be computed. There are some obvious techniques. We can start with the initial elements and apply each operation to all possible n-tuples of them repeating the process with the new elements added to the set. This process can be much improved by noticing that the operation α_f with $f_i: a_i \longrightarrow b$ only applies to $g_i: a_i \longrightarrow b$, so that the object a_i may be thought of as the 'sort' or 'type' of the ith argument. By collecting elements of the same sort together it is no longer necessary to generate all n-tuples, but only those which have the correct sorts. Better still if F is large is to keep a table showing which constructions in F require arguments of a given type a, and only apply a construction in F when a suitable argument for it has been generated.

Alternatively if we are looking for a particular object b in the picture c we may proceed from "top to bottom" and use V and F to explore only the possible constructions of b.

A further improvement might be gained by looking for an object d before using f such that

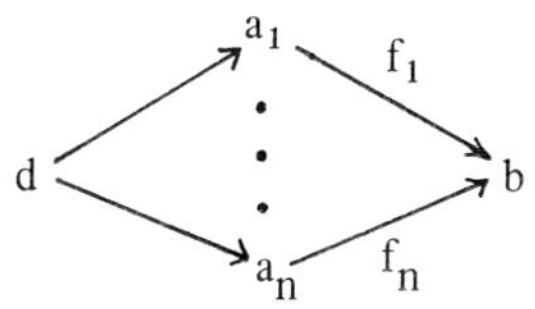

Application of f will not succeed unless $g: d \longrightarrow c$ has already been found and $d < a_i$ for each i. This again cuts down the number of n-tuples $g_i: a_i \longrightarrow c$ which need be tried. In the above example we only need try injections of triangles and squares which have a line in common.

Thus the distinction between computing the results of the operations α_f and closing the algebra breaks up the computation into two parts each capable of refinements for efficiency.

Acknowledgements

This work has been carried out at Edinburgh University with the help of a grant from the Science Research Council. We would like to thank Professor D. Michie for his encouragement of the vision work, Mr. Steve Salter for building the equipment and Miss Eleanor Kerse for her speedy and accurate typing of the paper. We are grateful to Mr. John Rastall and Mr. David Milner for allowing us to describe their contributions to this research which were carried out as student projects.

REFERENCES

1. Ambler, A. P. and Burstall, R. M. (1969) Question-Answering and Syntax Analysis, *Experimental Programming Reports: No.18,* Department of Machine Intelligence and Perception, University of Edinburgh.
2. Barrow, H. G. and Milner D. (1971) A Hierarchical Picture Interpretation System with Directed Search. *MIP - R - 85,* Department of Machine Intelligence and Perception, University of Edinburgh.
3. Barrow, H. G. and Popplestone, R. J. (1971) Relational Descriptions in Picture Processing. *Machine Intelligence 6* (eds. B. Meltzer and D. Michie) Edinburgh: University Press, pp. 377-396.
4. Brice, C. R. and Fennema, C. L. (1970) Scene Analysis Using Regions, *Artificial Intelligence 1,* 205-226.
5. Burstall, R. M. (1968) Computer Recognition of Rectilinear Solids from an Imperfect T.V. Picture. *MIP-R-40,* Department of Machine Intelligence and Perception, University of Edinburgh.
6. Clowes, M. B. (1971) On Seeing Things. *Artificial Intelligence 2,* 1, 79-116.

7. Cohn, P. M. (1965) *Universal Algebra.* New York: Harper and Row.
8 Corneil, D. G. and Gottlieb, C. C. (1970) An Efficient Algorothm for Graph Isomorphism. *J. Assoc. Comput. Mach.,* 17, 51-64.
9. Evans, T. G. (1964) A Heuristic Program to Solve Geometric-Analogy Problems. *AFIPS Spring Joint Comput. Conf., 25,* 327-338.
10. Green, C. (1969) The Application of Theorem-Proving to Question-Answering Systems. *A. I. Technical Memo. No. 8, S.R.I. Project 7494,* Stanford Research Institute.
11. Guzman. A. (1968) Decomposition of a Visual Scene into Three-Dimensional Bodies. *AFIS Proc. Fall Joint Comput. Conf.,* 33, 291-304.
12. Huffman, D. A. (1971) Impossible Objects as Nonsense Sentences. *Machine Intelligence 6* (eds. B. Meltzer and D. Michie) Edinburgh: University Press, pp. 295-324.
13. MacLane, S. and Birkhoff, G. (1967) *Algebra.* New York: Macmillan.
14. Raphael, B. (1964) SIR: A Computer Program for Semantic Information Retrieval. *MAC-TR2, Project MAC,* Massachusetts Institute of Technology. Cambridge: Massachusetts.
15. Rastall, J. (1969) Graph-Family Matching. *MIP-R-62,* Department of Machine Intelligence and Perception, University of Edinburgh.
16. Robinson, J. A. (1965a) A Machine-Orientated Logic Based on the Resolution Principle. *J. Assoc. Comput. Mach., 12,* 23-41.
17. Robinson, J. A. (1965b) Automatic Deduction with Hyper-Resolution. *Internat. J. Assoc. Comput. Math., 1,* 227-234.
18. Schoenfield, J. R. (1967) *Mathematical Logic.* Reading, Massachusetts: Addison -Wesley.
19. Sussenguth, E. H. (1965) A Graph-Theoretic Algorithm for Matching Chemical Structures, *J. of Chem. Documentation, 5,* 36-43.
20. Unger, S. H. (1964) GIT - A Heuristic Program for Testing Pairs of Directed Line Graphs for Isomorphism. *Comm. Assoc. Comput. Mach., 7,* 26-34.
21. Winston, P. H. (1970) Learning Structural Descriptions From Examples. *MAC-TR-76, Project MAC,* Massachusetts Institute of Technology. Cambridge: Massachusetts.

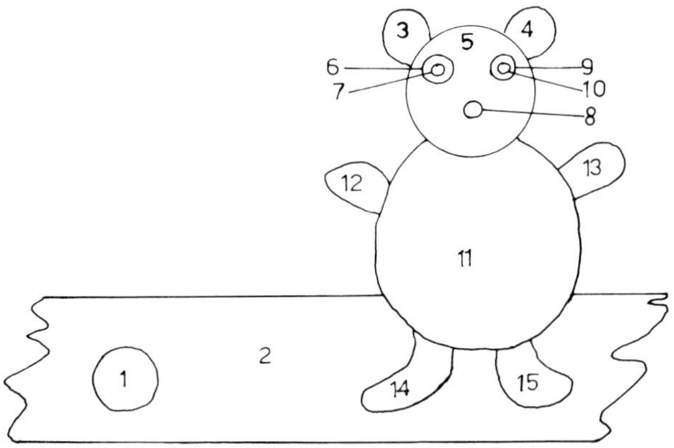

Figure 1. 'Bear on rug with ball'

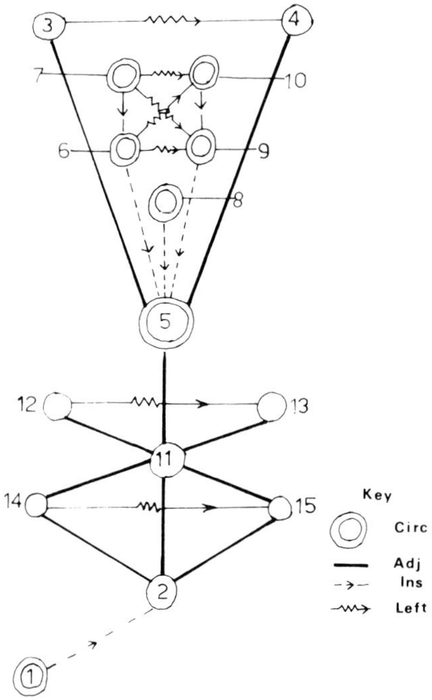

Figure 2. 'Bear on rug with ball' relational structure

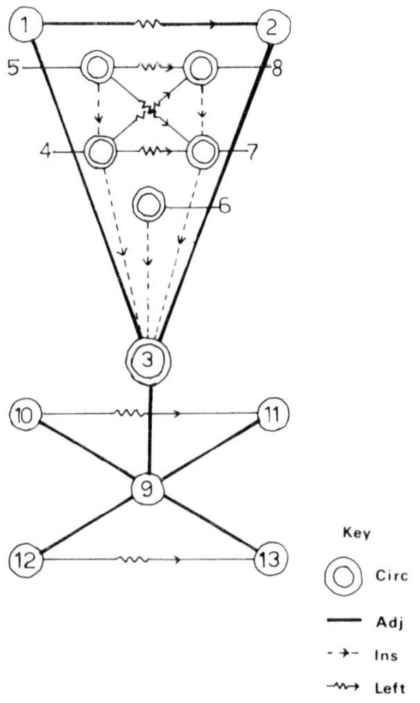

Figure 3. 'Bear' relational structure

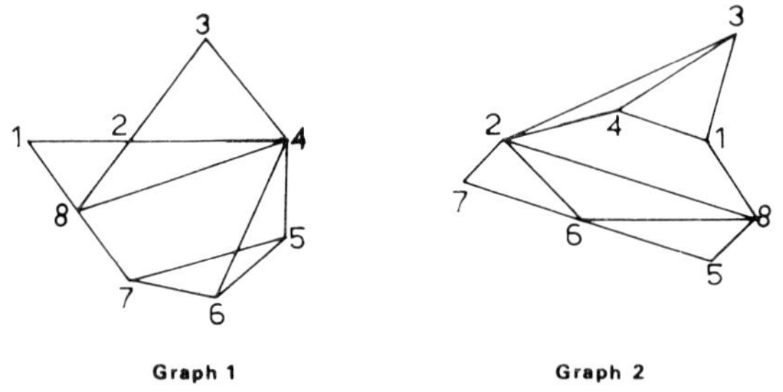

Figure 4

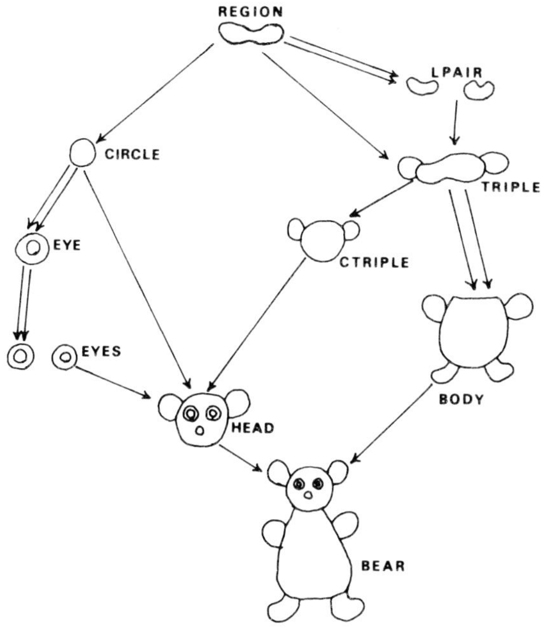

Figure 5. Hierarchical synthesis of 'Bear'

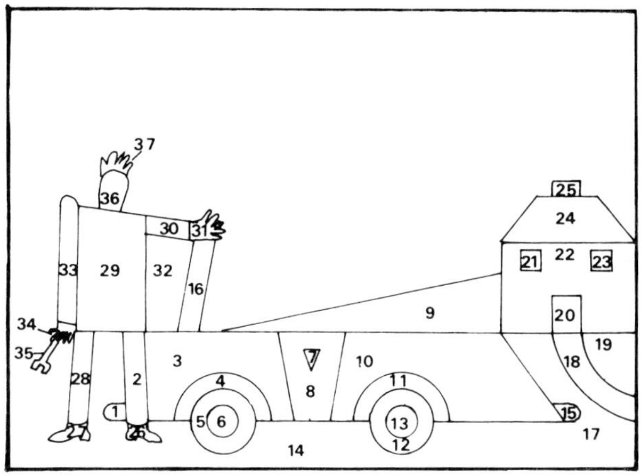

Figure 6. Picture

A SURVEY OF RESULTS IN GRAMMATICAL INFERENCE

A. W. Biermann

DEPARTMENT OF COMPUTER AND INFORMATION SCIENCE
OHIO STATE UNIVERSITY
COLUMBUS, OHIO

J. A. Feldman

DEPARTMENT OF COMPUTER SCIENCE
STANFORD UNIVERSITY
STANFORD, CALIFORNIA

I. Introduction

The grammatical inference problem can be described as follows: a finite set of symbol strings from some language L and possibly a finite set of strings from the complement of L are known, and a grammar for the language is to be discovered. Precisely the same problem arises in trying to choose a model or theory to explain a collection of sample data. This is one of the most important information processing problems known and it is surprising that there has been so little work on its formalization.

The grammatical inference problem and its solution have implications for pattern recognition research for two reasons. First, considerable research has been invested in recent years into the development of linguistic methods for picture description and analysis, and the discovery of grammars for these systems has posed a problem. Various researchers [17, 27, 38] have indicated a need for improved methods for grammar discovery and it appears that the results discussed here will be useful for their applications. (See Evans [8] for an example.) Secondly, if pattern recognition is a search for structure in information space, then grammatical inference can be considered to be an example of pattern recognition in itself. In this case, the observed data is the pattern to be analyzed, and the inferred grammar can be thought of as its description or classification.

Any attempt to formalize the grammatical inference problem must include precise formulations of several concepts left vague in the first paragraph. The four central notions are: the hypothesis space, the measure of adequacy, the rules by which the samples are drawn, and the criterion for success in the limit of the inference process. For this paper, the hypothesis spaces will be subsets of the general rewriting systems* [10] such as the context-free or finite-state grammars. The measures of adequacy will be discussed in Section III but the minimal requirement on a grammar will be that it generate all of the known strings in the language L and none of the known non-strings. In the model which we consider here, a string of symbols is presented at each time $t = 1,2,3, \ldots$ together with an indication of whether or not the string is in the source language, and a grammar is inferred at each time on the basis of all observed information. Except where noted, it will always be assumed that every possible string will appear at some time, and our guess of the source grammar should improve in quality as more and more information becomes available.

The source of information about a language L will be an *information sequence* I(L) which is an infinite sequence of strings from the set

$$T = \{+y | y \epsilon L\} \cup \{-y | y \notin L\}$$

with the property that every element of T appears somewhere in I(L). Some of the algorithms which will be discussed will use only *positive information sequences* $I_+(L)$ which contain at least one occurrence of every string in L and no other strings. The set of all possible information sequences for language L will be denoted $\mathcal{I}(L)$ (or for the set of all positive information sequences, $\mathcal{I}_+(L)$). The first t elements of a (positive) information sequence which an inference system has observed at time t will be called the *presentation*, denoted S_t, and the strings which are in and not in the source language, respectively, will be called the *positive* and *negative information*.

This paper will describe some of the major developing results on grammatical inference and will indicate where the interested reader can look further. The next section will discuss the limiting properties of the inference process, several definitions of learnability, and the importance of having both positive and negative information available. The following section will discuss the intermediate behavior of inference algorithms and criteria for choosing a grammar on the basis of a finite amount of information. In Section IV, we will describe a number of methods which have been developed for inferring grammars and evaluate some of their properties, and in the final section, we will make some concluding remarks. We give some examples of grammars which were inferred by computer in the Appendix. The reader is assumed to have some familiarity with formal language theory, and rigorous definitions and proofs will not be included. The original sources should be consulted for a more detailed treatment.

---

*The general rewriting systems are grammars for the recursively enumerable sets.

II. Grammatical Inference in the Limit

One of the first questions one might ask about the inference problem is whether one can ever expect to discover a grammar for the source language and if not, what limiting performance can be expected over time. Much of the early work on this problem was done by Gold [16] in connection with his work on limiting recursion [15].

Consider a class $\mathcal{C}$ of grammars and a machine $M_{\mathcal{C}}$. Suppose some $G \epsilon \mathcal{C}$ and some I in $\mathcal{I}(L(G))^*$ are chosen for presentation to the machine $M_{\mathcal{C}}$. We suppose that $M_{\mathcal{C}}$ can form a guess $A_t = M_{\mathcal{C}}(S_t)$ on the basis of the observed finite presentation S_t at each time t, and we define successively weaker formalizations of the notion of the machine $M_{\mathcal{C}}$ learning the grammar G.

The machine $M_{\mathcal{C}}$ is said to *identify* the grammar G *in the limit* if there is a τ such that $t > \tau$ implies both $A_t = A_\tau$ and $L(A_\tau) = L(G)$. If $M_{\mathcal{C}}$ is such that $t > \tau$ implies $L(A_t) = L(G)$, then $M_{\mathcal{C}}$ is said to *match* G in the limit.

Intuitively, $M_{\mathcal{C}}$ identifies G if it eventually guesses only one grammar and that grammar generates exactly L(G). This does not imply that $M_{\mathcal{C}}$ can effectively choose one grammar and stop considering new data. The machine $M_{\mathcal{C}}$ will match the grammar G if it eventually guesses only grammars of L(G), albeit different ones. These notions are closely related and both require that $M_{\mathcal{C}}$ find the correct language in finite time. We would also like to consider a weaker form of learning in which the guesses A_t are ever better approximations to the grammar G. One can imagine placing a metric on the class $\mathcal{C}$ of grammars and using convergence as the criterion, but this has not yet been done. We will discuss some non-metric ideas on approximations of grammars after presenting the basic results on identifiability.

The main results by Gold [16] deal with the great difference in learnability effected by allowing information sequences with negative instances rather than just positive instances of the languages. He shows that for any enumerable class $\mathcal{C}$ of decidable** grammars there is a machine $M_{\mathcal{C}}$ such that for any $G \epsilon \mathcal{C}$ and any $I \epsilon \mathcal{I}(L(G))$, G will be identified in the limit by $M_{\mathcal{C}}$. To see this, consider the machine $M_{\mathcal{C}}$ which sequences through an enumeration $\mathcal{G}$ of $\mathcal{C}$. At each time t there is a first $G \epsilon \mathcal{G}$ which is compatible with the observed set of strings S_t, and it is the guess A_t of $M_{\mathcal{C}}$. Since I contains every possible string on the alphabet, any A such that $L(A) \neq L(G)$ will eventually be incompatible with some S_t, either by generating a $-y \epsilon S_t$

*L(G) denotes the set of strings generated by grammar G.

**G is decidable if it is decidable for every string w whether G generates w.

or failing to generate a $+y \epsilon S_t$. At some time τ, A_τ will be such that $L(A_\tau) = L(G)$. Then A_τ will be compatible with the remainder of the information and will be the constant result of M_C.

Thus with complete positive and negative information available, a very wide class of grammars can be identified in the limit. By restricting the information to only $I \epsilon \mathcal{I}_+(L)$, we give up identifiability in the limit almost entirely as shown by the following result.

If $I \epsilon \mathcal{I}_+(L(G))$ and G is from a class of languages which contains all the finite languages and any one infinite language L_∞, then there is no machine for the class which can be guaranteed to match G in the limit. This can be proven by showing that for any M_C, there is a sequence $I \epsilon \mathcal{I}_+(L_\infty)$ which will make M_C change the inferred language an infinite number of times. Since M_C must be able to infer all finite languages, there is a sample which causes it to yield a grammar for some finite language L_1 such that $L_1 \subset L_\infty$. Now consider an information sequence which then presents some string $x \epsilon L_\infty - L_1$ repeatedly. At some time t, $M_C(S_t)$ must be a grammar of $L_1 \cup \{x\} = L_2$ because all finite languages are inferred. This construction can be repeated indefinitely, yielding an information sequence $I \epsilon \mathcal{I}_+(L_\infty)$ which will change the value of M_C an infinite number of times. Since each L_i is finite, the machine M_C chooses an A_t such that $L(A_t) \neq L_\infty$ an infinite number of times.

The weaker notions of learnability which have been defined require M_C to choose grammars which have languages increasingly like the target language. The following definitions were developed by Feldman [10] for studying limiting behavior for the classes of general rewriting systems and decidable rewriting systems. In the former class of grammrs, it is possible to enumerate the strings of the language but not necessarily possible to decide whether any arbitrary string is in the language. In the latter class, membership in the language is decidable.

The machine M_C is said to *approach* the grammar G if the following two conditions hold

a) For any $y \epsilon L(G)$ there is a time τ such that $t > \tau$ implies $y \epsilon L(A_t)$.

b) For any H such that $L(H) - L(G) \neq \varphi$ there is a time τ such that $t > \tau$ implies $A_t \neq H$.

M_C will be said to *strongly approach* G if the following additional condition holds.

c) There is an A such that $L(A) = L(G)$ and for any positive S_t there is an information sequence $I \epsilon \mathcal{I}_+(L(G))$ such that $S_t \subset I$ and an n such that $S_{t+n} \subset I$ and $A_{t+n} = A$.

This definition of approachability is asymmetric with regard to L(G) and its complement. This asymmetry arises from the fact that there is no procedure for enumerating the complement of L(G) for a general rewriting system (grs) G. If one strengthened condition b) to parallel condition a), no machine could approach arbitrary grs grammars. One could weaken a) in parallel to b) but this allows trivial guesses to satisfy the definition. For example, a machine M_C which simply chose a different A_t at each t would approach G.

In addition to the limiting requirement of approaching G, we would like to require that the A_t bear some resemblance to G, and this is the goal of the probability and complexity measures described in Section III. In the absence of such considerations, condition c) of the above definition forces M_C to choose A_t with some care. Thus a machine which chose A_t so that $L(A_t) = S_t$ (guessed exactly the sample) could approach, but not strongly approach, a grammar. We next present the basic result on approachability in the absence of complexity considerations as given in [10].

For any class C of decidable rewriting systems (drs), there is a machine $M_C(S)$ such that for any $G \epsilon C$ and $I \epsilon \mathcal{I}_+(L(G))$, G is strongly approachable through I. A machine which satisfies this requirement and the stronger requirements discussed below can be constructed as follows. The machine $M_C(S)$ will employ an enumeration G of C and an auxiliary function $N_k(G)$, the number of strings of length **k** or less generated by the grammar G. For any drs, $N_k(G)$ is computable. It will also employ an increasing computable bounding function f(k) with the property that $f(k) > \sum_{i=0}^{k} m^i + k$ for an infinite number of values of the integer k. (m is the number of symbols which may appear in the languages L(G) in C.) At each time t, the machine computes the smallest integer k such that $f(k) > t$. It then guesses A_t as the first* grammar G which is compatible with S_t and minimizes $N_k(G)$. The compatibility requirement guarantees that (a) of the definition will be satisfied, and the minimization of $N_k(G)$ for increasing k insures that (b) will be satisfied. This algorithm can be made to choose the first grammar in the enumeration for the source language by including in the presentation all of the strings of length k or less for k large enough. The magnitude requirement of f makes it possible to do this so (c) is also satisfied.

The proof of this theorem also yields the following additional result. The machine M_C will identify G through any $I \epsilon \mathcal{I}_+(L(G))$ if there is a τ such that for all $t > \tau$ the following condition holds: if j is the smallest

*At any given time, the device considers only the first i grammars, but i is always growing.

integer such that $f(j) > t$ then all of the strings in $L(G)$ of length j or less are in S_t. The basic idea here is that M_C assumes that it has seen every sample y of length k or less by the time t such that $f(k) > t > f(k-1)$. If this is true, M_C will identify G, and if not, M_C will still strongly approach G. The machine M_C can use a very large bounding function and identify the grammar for any sequence ordered by a smaller function. The problem is that such a machine will be slow to reject overbroad grammars. Further, if M_C has chosen a bounding function which is too small, it will eventually discover that fact. There will appear some y_t such that $f(\ell(y_t)) < t$. At this time M_C can switch to a larger bounding function. There is, however, no way to construct an M_C which will identify G through arbitrary information sequences, because there is no computable enumeration of the computable bounding functions [30].

There are, in [10] a number of related theorems on decidability in the absence of a complexity measure. It is shown that with a mild condition on C the basic approachability result applies to the general rewriting systems. It is also shown that no one machine can identify grammars with complete negative information and simultaneously approach them if some negative strings are missing. Thus the existence of a bounding function f is a stronger condition than the appearance of each positive and negative string.

The results presented above make very weak requirements on the individual guesses A_t. In Section III we discuss measures of fit which can be used to require A_t to be a "good" grammar for the sample S_t. There are in [10] and [23] a number of decidability results on learning the "best" grammar. The basic theorem states conditions under which it is possible to choose the best A_t for a finite sample S_t. There are additional results describing when a machine which always guesses the best grammar can be known to approach or match the target grammar. These results all apply to the general rewriting systems and give rise to the hope that grammatical inference can be extended to other domains.

III. Inference from a Finite Presentation, Probability and Complexity Measures

While reasonably satisfactory results can be obtained on the limiting properties of inference algorithms, the intermediate behavior of these algorithms is much harder to measure. There are an infinite number of grammars which are capable of generating any given set of strings, and one can imagine them being ordered on a "fit" spectrum with the grammars which generate the largest languages (poor fit) on the left and those which give a "tighter" representation (good fit) of the positive presentation on the right.

At the extreme left would be a grammar for the largest language which excludes the negative presentation, and at the other extreme would be a grammar which generates only the finite positive presentation. In the typical inference situation, the grammars which are of interest will tend to be more complex if they are nearer the right end of the spectrum and so the decision as to which grammar to choose rests on the questions of how tight a fit is required and how much complexity can be tolerated. Furthermore, these quantities may not vary greatly from grammar to grammar making the final decision seem that much more arbitrary. Three possible methods for producing an inference are to

(1) set up a probabilistic model which provides a technique for computing the most probable grammar,

(2) design a complexity measure for the grammars and their derivations and find the least complex explanation for the data, or

(3) develop a constructive algorithm which converges on a correct answer at the fastest practicable rate and let its intermediate behavior be what it will be.

Horning [23] has given an example of a probabilistic model and shown how enumeration can be used to discover the optimum (most probable) answer. His technique requires that it be possible to assign a probability $P(w|G)$ to each string w generated* by grammar G, and the suggested method is to assign probabilities to the rules of the grammar, assume the rules are independently chosen according to those probabilities, and compute $P(w|G)$ by multiplying together the probabilities** of the rules required in the derivation of w. The strings of the presentation S are assumed to be independently generated so that $P(S|G) = \prod_{w \in S} P(w|G)$. A method for assigning probabilities $P(G)$ to the grammars under consideration is also needed, and this is done by representing the grammars themselves as strings of symbols and using a stochastic "grammar-grammar" to generate the grammars and assign them probabilities. The availabilities of these probabilities makes it possible to apply Bayes' Theorem to compute

$$P(G_i|S) = \frac{P(G_i) \cdot P(S|G_i)}{\sum_j P(G_j) \cdot P(S|G_j)}$$

for each grammar G_i.

The algorithm for computing the most probable grammar for a finite

*$P(w|G) = 0$ if G does not generate w.

**Horning does not consider ambiguous grammars although their inclusion yields only a minor modification to the procedure.

set of strings S proceeds as follows. We need an enumeration $G_1, G_2, G_3, \ldots$ of the class of grammars of interest with a corresponding computable function $T(\zeta)$ which has the property $i > T(\zeta)$ implies $P(G_i) < \zeta$. Then we find the first grammar G_k which generates S and search the finite number of grammars G_i where $k \leq i \leq T(P(G_k))$ for the grammar with the highest probability. Horning shows that this algorithm yields the most probable grammar for the given S and that in the learning situation the probability of identifying the source language approaches unity.

This analysis has the desirable property that its decisions are based on the well founded concepts of probability theory. The main criticism is usually that the a priori probabilities are often unknown and must be chosen in some kind of arbitrary manner. Also, many applications are not probabilistic and should not be treated as such. A partial rebuttal to these objections is that the alternative to a probabilistic model may be even more arbitrary.

Another approach is to view the whole problem in terms of complexities. The best explanation for a phenomenon is perhaps the least complex. This principle must be carefully applied, however, because the least complex grammar for generating S is often a grammar for the universal language so as Solomonoff [37] points out, the complexity of the derivation of S using grammar G must be included as part of the measure of G's acceptability.

An example of a complexity measure of a grammar or string is the amount of information contained therein, that is, the negative of the logarithm of its probability. Interestingly enough, a complete complexity model for the grammatical inference problem can be obtained by simply taking the negative of the logarithm of all the probabilistic quantities in the above model. Thus we obtain a complexity associated with each rule of the grammar G and can compute the complexity $C(w|G)$ of any string w which G generates by adding up the complexities of the individual rules needed to generate w. In an analogous way, $C(S|G) = \sum_{w \in S} C(w|G)$, $C(G)$ can be computed, and the complexity of G for generating S is $C(G_i|S) = C(G_i) + C(S|G_i) + (\text{function of } S)$. Carrying the analogy to its logical conclusion, we can produce an enumerative algorithm which is guaranteed to compute the grammar G with the smallest possible complexity $C(G|S)$ for generating the presentation S.

Feldman [10] has shown that for a large class of complexity functions it is possible to find the least complex grammar for a finite set of strings S for very general classes of grammars. The only stipulations are that it be possible to enumerate the grammars of the class and the language of each grammar, and he does not require that membership in the grammar's language be decidable. The requirements on the complexity measure are

(1) that it is a computable unbounded increasing function

$\gamma(c(G,\mathcal{C}),d(S,G))$ of $c(G,\mathcal{C})$ the *intrinsic complexity* of G in class $\mathcal{C}$ and of $d(S,G)$ the *derivational complexity* of S with respect to G,

(2) that $c(G,\mathcal{C})$ be a positive computable unbounded effectively approximately ordered* function of the number of symbols required to write G down on the given alphabet, and

(3) that $d(S,G)$ is a positive function which is defined when $S \subset L(G)$ and which has the property that $d(S,G) < m$ is decidable for all m.

In order to find the minimal complexity grammar, one enumerates at each instant of time (1) a new grammar and (2) one step of a string generation on each previously enumerated grammar until a grammar is found which generates the strings S. This gives an upper bound γ_B on the complexity γ for the least complex grammar, and the effectively approximately ordered property makes it possible to limit the search to the finite number of grammars which can be written down with $f_c(C')$ symbols or less (where $\gamma_B = \gamma(C',0)$). Of the grammars which are left, those whose derivational complexity $d(S,G)$ is either too high or not defined can be eliminated, and for the remaining grammars, $d(S,G)$ can be computed. Thus γ can be computed for the remaining grammars and the least complex one can be chosen.

A number of other measures on grammars and languages have been studied in various contexts. Gruska [19] has studied mappings in general from the set of context-free grammars into the non-negative numbers. Snively [35] has studied three particular measures on phrase structure grammars: the length of the longest member in any rule, the vocabulary size, and the number of rules. Feldman et al. [11] define several size measures for languages and discuss their properties. Of course, there is considerable other literature on computational complexity available with implications for our study, and the reader may consult [2] and [21] for a survey of this work.

IV. Methods for Inferring Grammars

One of the first techniques suggested for grammatical inference was simple enumeration of all possible grammars in the class of interest until a suitable grammar is found. Historically, the concept of enumeration has provided a proof technique for many theorems and has greatly aided in our understanding of these problems. Enumerative techniques have the advantage that they can often be shown to produce an optimum answer on the

*There is a computable function f_c which finds for each possible complexity value the largest number of symbols required to write down any grammar of that complexity value or less.

basis of minimal information. Gold [16] has pointed out that in the learning situation where a new string is presented and a new grammar is guessed at each instant of time, that no other algorithm can uniformly reach a steady correct guess in less time for all grammars in the class and for all information sequences.

On the pragmatic side, however, the combinatorics involved are extremely discouraging and so enumeration is impractical for many applications. If we consider finite-state grammars, for example, with rules of the form $v_i \to Av_j$ and $v_i \to A$ which have m terminal symbols and n nonterminals, there exist approximately $2^{mn(1+n)}$ different grammars to examine. Since each grammar must be generated and checked for its acceptability, it is not hard to imagine a machine spending hours or even years trying to solve problems of only moderate size. Fortunately a number of methods have been developed for increasing enumerative efficiency by eliminating large classes of grammars from the search.

First of all, the particular application will often include special requirements which enable one to restrict the amount of enumeration which must be done. Only grammars of the desired form need be considered and often they can be enumerated in a fashion which eliminates the generation of an unnecessarily large number of equivalent grammars. Thus one might choose to search for a context-free grammar in Chomsky [5], Greibach [18], or some other standard form.

Secondly, the only grammars which need be examined are those which are compatible with the presentation and many incompatible grammars can be eliminated without ever being created. This is often carried out by deleting classes of incompatible grammars on the basis of a test on one of them. In order to show how this can be done, we introduce the concept of grammar "coverage".

Let f be a function which maps each nonterminal in grammar G_2 into a nonterminal in grammar G_1. Further suppose that f maps the initial nonterminal of G_2 into the initial nonterminal of G_1 and that the set of rules in G_1 are exactly the rules obtained if f is applied to all the nonterminals in G_2. Then G_1 will be said to *cover* G_2 [29] and furthermore $L(G_2) \subseteq L(G_1)$. This result enables us to discard all grammars which are covered by G if G does not generate all of the known strings in the language because the covered grammars will have the same fault. On the other hand, if G generates some strings which are known to be outside of the language, then all grammars which cover G will be similarly inadequate. Consequently, the discovery that some particular grammar in an enumeration is not compatible with the presentation makes it possible to eliminate from consideration that grammar and possibly a whole class of other grammars.

Horning [23] has written an enumerative inference program which uses the above result as follows: he thinks of the class of grammars as being organized into a tree where each grammar G with n nonterminals represents a node on the tree and each grammar G' with $n + 1$ nonterminals which is covered by G is associated with a branch grown downward from G. (Actually, he eliminates some redundancy in the tree by requiring that each G' be obtained from a "canonical split" of G: that is, the initial and last nonterminals in an ordered list of the nonterminals of G' are obtained by "splitting" the initial nonterminal of G.) Thus each grammar in the tree covers all of the grammars below it. Horning's search for a grammar begins at the top of the tree and moves downward creating a grammar at each node and examining its compatibility with the presentation. If any grammar fails to produce all of the known strings in the language, it can be eliminated along with all of its dependent nodes. Also if a grammar is found to be reducible (either some nonterminal is never generated from the initial nonterminal or some nonterminal generates no strings of terminal symbols), it can be eliminated along with its dependent nodes if only irreducable grammars are desired.

Horning did some experimental tests to measure the effectiveness of his pruning techniques and in one example mentioned generating 440 two nonterminal, two terminal finite-state grammars and finding 363 of them either not reduced or not able to generate the string B. It thus appears that his techniques speed the search perhaps by orders of magnitude. The Appendix gives examples of grammars inferred by this program and some of the other programs discussed below.

Pao [28] has developed a finite search algorithm for finite-state grammar inference which employs the grammar covering concept as a pruning technique. She constructs the simplest finite-state machine which accepts exactly the finite number of strings which are known to be in the language, and she assumes that the machine to be identified can be found by merging states of this machine. Thus she creates the set of all such machines and orders them in a finite lattice such that each machine at one level of the lattice is connected to each machine at a higher level which can be obtained by merging states of the first machine. Therefore the grammar associated with the machine at one node on the lattice will cover the grammars associated with its connected lower nodes on the lattice and the above mentioned pruning techniques are applicable. In her method, two distinct machines on the lattice are chosen and a string is found which is accepted by one machine but not the other. The algorithm then asks a "teacher" whether the string in question is in the language, and depending on whether the answer is yes or no, it either deletes the second machine and all its connected lower machines or it deletes the first machine and all of its connected higher machines. The algorithm continues asking questions and deleting machines until only one machine (or several equivalent machines) is left and it yields the associated grammar as its inference.

In contrast to the exhaustive search methods which produce optimum performance often at the cost of an astronomical computational effort, a few constructive inference procedures have been developed, which produce useful if not optimal grammars in a reasonable length of time.

As an example of a nonenumerative inference, consider the problem of finding a context-free grammar for the set of strings in Figure 1.

a c a c a
a b c b a c a
a b b c b b a c a
a c a b c b a
a b c b a b c b a
a b b c b b a b c b a

Figure 1

It appears that the recursive rule $v \rightarrow bvb$ has been used in the generation of these strings and that the parse of these strings might be as indicated by the parentheses in Figure 2.

a(c)a(c)a
a(b(c)b)a(c)a
a(b(b(c)b)b)a(c)a
a(c)a(b(c)b)a
a(b(c)b)a(b(c)b)a
a(b(b(c)b)b)a(b(c)b)a

Figure 2

So the set of strings S can be written as $S = a\alpha_1 a\alpha_2 a$, $\alpha_1 = \{c, bcb, bbcbb\}$, and $\alpha_2 = \{c, bcb\}$. Then, we could infer that α_1 and α_2 are simply the short strings of some larger sets, possibly the same larger set $\alpha = \{b^i c b^i | i = 0,1,2, \ldots\}$ and thus arrive at the grammar $v_1 \rightarrow av_2 av_2 a$, $v_2 \rightarrow bv_2 b$, $v_2 \rightarrow c$.

Most of the constructive inference algorithms which we will discuss go through steps similar to those in this example.

(1) Attempt to discover the syntactic structure of the known strings

by whatever means is possible.

(2) Determine what sublanguages make up the language which is being analyzed.

(3) Look for equivalences between the various sublanguages and note them.

(4) Produce the inferred grammar.

Discussing each of these steps in order, we first note that step (1) is trivial for finite-state languages because they can be generated by either a right linear or a left linear grammar. For linear languages, it appears that the method indicated in the example will effectively determine the string structure. For certain special classes of languages like the operator precedence languages, the terminal symbols themselves indicate something about how the string was generated. Crespi-Reghizzi [7] assumes that a complete structural description like that in Figure 2 is included with the presentation, thus eliminating step (1). He does this because he wants to infer a grammar which is structurally equivalent to the source grammar and because the additional information makes it possible to solve much more difficult problems.

In step (2), the goal is to collect the set

$$S_{w_1,w_2} = \{x | w_1 x w_2 \text{ is in the presentation}\}$$

for each possible context w_1,w_2 where the rightmost symbol of w_1 is a left parenthesis and the leftmost symbol of w_2 is the matching right parenthesis. This step may also include the inference that S_{w_1,w_2} is a finite-subset of some specified infinite language L_{w_1,w_2}. There may be evidence that some of the sublanguages L_{w_1,w_2} are equivalent to each other and if the evidence is sufficient, such equivalences are inferred in step (3). Finally, the resulting grammar is assembled in step (4).

There are algorithms in the literature for finite-state grammar inference by Chomsky and Miller [6], Feldman et al. [11], and Biermann and Feldman [4] which work approximately as described above, and we will briefly describe the latter one. This method requires an integer parameter k as input along with the presentation. The sublanguages S_w are created where

$$S_w = \{x | wx \text{ is in the positive presentation}\}$$

and two sublanguages are considered to be equivalent only when they are exactly identical for all strings of length k or less. A grammatical rule $v_i \to av_j$ is produced if there exists a string w such that S_w is the i-th sublanguage and S_{wa} is the j-th sublanguage. The rule $v_i \to a$ is produced if there is a string w such that S_w is the i-th sublanguage and wa is in the presentation. This algorithm has been programmed and works quite well when aided by a certain amount of preprocessing and postprocessing. This algorithm has been shown to identify any finite-state language in the limit from positive information only if an upper bound is known to the number of states required to accept the language or if the presentation is weakly ordered.* The exactness of the grammar produced for any given presentation can be adjusted by varying k from 0 up to the length of the longest string, and the inferred languages vary correspondingly from something close to the universal language to the presentation itself.

We have a linear grammar inference program currently under development which also follows the above outline. The program searches for strings $w_1, w_2, w_3, x,$ and y such that $w_1 x^i w_2 y^i w_3$ is in the presentation for $i = 0,1,2, \ldots, k$ and k is a prespecified constant. This analysis is designed to find a reasonable parse for the strings and makes it possible to construct the S_{w_1,w_2} sets which have the following form. Each such set has an associated set of matching pairs of strings $P = \{(x_i,y_i) | i = 1,2, \ldots, n\}$ and a *core* C such that each "short" string of the form $w_1 x_{i_1} x_{i_2} \ldots x_{i_\ell} z y_{i_\ell} \ldots y_{i_2} y_{i_1} w_2$ with $(x_{i_j},y_{i_j}) \epsilon P$ and $z \epsilon C$ is in the presentation. The cores C which are produced in this way are reanalyzed to obtain more $S_{w_1;w_2}$ sets and their cores are analyzed etc. until the process terminates. These sets S_{w_1,w_2} which are constructed are equated if they are similar for short strings and finally a grammar is produced in a straightforward manner. It appears that the technique which we are using is close to what Solomonoff had in mind in [36].

Special techniques can be developed in more highly structured situations which allow very efficient inferences; the doctoral dissertation [7] by Crespi-Reghizzi provides a good example. He was interested in inferring operator precedence grammars [12] from sets of strings some of which have a complete structural description. He used the given structural descriptions to determine a precedence matrix for the terminal alphabet and from this constructed the "free" operator precedence grammar which is associated with the matrix. The special nature of the free operator precedence grammars makes it possible to obtain very strong properties such as identifiability in the limit with positive information only. Finally, he showed that his method can be used as a part of an enumerative algorithm which will identify any operator precedence grammar in the limit from positive and negative information.

We will very briefly mention some other efforts in grammatical inference. Solomonoff [36, 37] discussed several approaches to the problem and gave a number of examples to illustrate his ideas. He did not give

*A presentation is *weakly ordered* if it has an associated bounding function as described in Section II.

precise algorithms but his papers served as an important source for later researchers. Gips [11] wrote a program for finding "pivot" grammars which are a slight generalization of linear grammars. Miller [26] has written an interactive program for the inference of finite-state machines. Each of these efforts used heuristic techniques and no proofs were given guaranteeing their effectiveness.

Pao [28] has produced an inference algorithm for the class of "delimited" languages which use only context-free rules of the general form $v_{i_0} \rightarrow A_{i_1} v_{i_1} A_{i_2} v_{i_2} \ldots A_{i_m}$. This inference algorithm requires that a "teacher" be available to provide certain "cues" such as the "delimiter sequences" $(A_{i_1}, A_{i_2}, \ldots, A_{i_m})$ which are associated with the rules to be learned. Using these rather strong assumptions, she gives a proof that her method will, indeed, always converge to the correct answer.

Klein and his associates [24, 25] have done extensive work on the problem of finding grammars for natural language and have stated that their goal is to develop a program to "duplicate the functions of a human linguist in working with a live informant". Their program uses heuristic techniques to produce transformational grammars and operates interactively with a human speaker of the unknown language. They give examples taken from various spoken languages.

We are aware of one effort in grammatical inference by Evans [8] which is concerned with picture grammars rather than the model we have discussed here. Evans' grammars employ picture primitives as terminal symbols and the grammatical generations are partially governed by predicates which indicate spatial relationships between the various parts of the picture. He produces a grammar for a set of pictures by first finding a grammar for each individual picture and then merging the set of grammars into one using various heuristic techniques. The generality of his methods is demonstrated by several examples, one of which involves the inference of a finite state grammar for a set of strings. Evans' work is important because he has shown how many of the ideas discussed in this paper can be used in a distinctly different setting.

There is not a lot of information available on the performance of the various programs discussed above but it usually takes a large amount of string information to do a correct inference. If a finite-state language is accepted by an n state machine with k-distinguishable states [13] and with m terminal symbols, it takes at most $\sum_{i=0}^{k+1} m^i$ strings to characterize each state and its successors so about $n\sum_{i=0}^{k+1} m^i$ positive and negative strings are required to do the inference.* Most of the constructive inference programs which we are familiar with need approximately this many strings or more to do a correct inference. From another point of view, there are about $n^{nm}(2^n - 2)$ different such finite-state machines so that it would appear that $\log_2(n^{nm}(2^n - 2))$ strings might be enough to make the correct choice since we get one bit of information from each string. A look at the ratio of the two figures indicates that one could hope for much better performance than has thus far been achieved with constructive algorithms. This is especially true for large machines as can be seen in the table of Figure 3.

Number of states	Approximate number of strings required to identify an n-state machine	Theoretical minimum number of required strings
n	$n \sum_{i=0}^{n-1} m^i$	$\log_2(n^{nm}(2^n - 2))$
1	1	–
2	6	5
3	21	13
4	60	20
5	155	29

An estimate of number of strings required to do an inference for an n-state machine with two input symbols ($m = 2$).

Figure 3

The amount of computer time required to do an inference varies greatly with the method used, and we give some information on this in the Appendix. Typical run times for our finite-state and linear language programs vary between one second and one minute for grammars of five or ten variables and five or ten terminal symbols.

In our experience with inference programs, we have found that interactive programs are often the easiest to use. Such a program usually requires an initial presentation and then asks questions about the unknown language in the form of strings which the user must classify as either in or not in the language. A well designed program will ask a minimal number of questions and the user is spared from typing a large presentation.

One criticism that can be leveled at most constructive inference programs is that their performance is very poor if very many "short" strings are

*This estimate is actually a little high because the same string may be part of the characterization of several states.

missing. One would hope that if string information is liberally available except for a few scattered short strings that the inference could still be expeditiously performed. This is not true for known methods, however, and it may may be that constructive techniques which seek low complexity grammars can be developed to help overcome the problem.

Finally, it should be pointed out that the various algorithms mentioned above differ dramatically in their incremental abilities, that is, their ability to to revise a previously inferred grammar on the basis of a small amount of new information. If the algorithm involves setting up an information structure which is stored in memory, as is the case with most of the constructive methods, the addition of new strings can often be accounted for by making minor erasures and additions in the existing structure. This can even be done for enumerative algorithms if the enumeration can be saved. However, some methods such as the search methods require branching decisions during the computation and deletion of much of the previously generated information so that the complete computation must be repeated after each change in the presentation. Some examples of algorithms with excellent incremental abilities are those described in [4] and [7].

V. Comments

This paper has surveyed developing results in a theory of learning behavior. In concentrating on the limiting behavior, the optimization of intermediate behavior, and the development of practical inference algorithms, we have discussed some but not all of the important aspects that such a study should contain. We have few results which indicate how much information must be obtained from a language before it can be learned using any of our criteria for learnability. Thus except for simple classes of languages, we do not know how long it is likely to take a device to learn a language. We do not have any methods for inferring to which class a language may belong so that if algorithms are available for learning various classes of grammars, there is no method for deciding which one to use.* Also, the inference techniques which exist do not use special information which may be available about the language such as the meanings of the symbols or the form of the desired grammar.

The usefulness of existing grammatical inference programs has been investigated in several domains. Crespi-Reghizzi [7] was concerned with producing precedence grammars for programming languages and demonstrated

*There are some decidability results which are relevant to this problem in [14] and [32]. For example, it is recursively unsolvable to decide whether a given context-free grammar has an equivalent finite-state grammar.

his program by producing grammars for some classes of arithmetic expressions. In our laboratory, we have used our programs to infer integer sequences and to solve mazes. A grammar for a maze is a description of all the possible successful paths through the maze and is inferred from a finite set of successful paths. We are currently investigating the possibility of discovering grammars for early child language. In most of these applications, we have found that the programs were slower to produce a correct grammar than one might expect because the algorithms were not able to use all of the available information about the problem to be solved. It appears that for optimum performance an algorithm must be restyled for each new application to account for and take advantage of its own special constraints.

Despite these practical problems, the grammatical inference model serves as an abstract model of learning or inferential behavior. It has provided a concrete basis for a study of learnability, rates of learning, and methods of learning and has sharpened our understanding of the problems that any theory of inference must face. Furthermore, it has yielded solutions to at least a few problems and perhaps can be extended to solve others.

VI. Acknowledgement

The authors are indebted to Dr. Irving Traiger for many helpful comments concerning this paper.

Appendix

SOME EXAMPLES OF GRAMMARS INFERRED BY COMPUTERS

Horning's enumerative program was capable of generating and testing several thousand grammars per minute (using an IBM 360). But even with his pruning techniques he was only able to discover fairly simple grammars such as those given in Figure A1. The discovery of such grammars usually took several minutes of computer time and required five or ten strings from the unknown language.

$$v_1 \to B \ / \ Bv_1 \ / \ Av_2$$
$$v_2 \to A \ / \ Bv_2 \ / \ Av_1$$

$$v_1 \to A \ / \ Av_2$$
$$v_2 \to Av_1$$

Grammars inferred by Horning's enumerative program
on the basis of minimum complexity
Figure A1

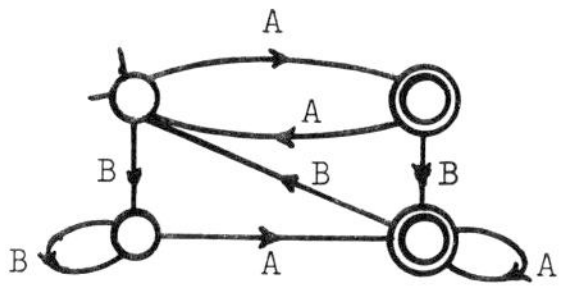

Time	Strings given to the machine	Questions asked by the machine	Answers to questions	Grammars Inferred
1	+A			
2	+AB			
3	+BA			
4	+BBA			
5	-AA			
6	-B			
7		(string of length zero)	-	
8				$v_1 \rightarrow Av_2/A/Bv_1$ $v_2 \rightarrow Bv_2/B$
9	+AAA			
10				$v_1 \rightarrow Av_2/A/Bv_1$ $v_2 \rightarrow Av_1/Bv_2/B$
11	+ABA			
12		ABAB	-	
13		ABAA	+	
14				$v_1 \rightarrow Av_2/A/Bv_1$ $v_2 \rightarrow Av_1/Bv_3/B$ $v_3 \rightarrow Av_3/A$
15	+BBAA			
16		BAB	-	
17		AAAB	+	
18		AABA	+	
19		BAAA	+	
20		BAA	+	
21		BBBA	+	
22		ABBA	+	
23		BABA	+	
24		BB	-	
25		ABAAA	+	
26		ABABA	+	
27		ABBAB	+	
28		ABBBA	+	
29				$v_1 \rightarrow Av_2/A/Bv_3$ $v_2 \rightarrow Av_1/Bv_4/B$ $v_3 \rightarrow Av_4/A/Bv_3$ $v_4 \rightarrow Av_4/A/Bv_1$

Figure A2

Figure A2 shows a demonstration of our interactive program for finite-state grammars. A grammar represented by the automaton shown was to be learned by the machine. The program accepts strings of symbols (second column), and then asks questions about other strings of symbols (column three) which the environment must answer. When the machine printed out an incorrect grammar, it was given additional strings indicating the inadequacy of the grammar. It took about six seconds of CPU time to do this example on a PDP-10 time-sharing system. The program gives similar performance on all problems of this difficulty.

The linear grammar inference program described in this paper is demonstrated by the example of Figure A3. The 39 strings shown were input to the machine and the grammar was printed out after 25 seconds of CPU time.

1. ADDRFF	14. AGTU	27. ASSDSRF
2. ADDSRFF	15. AHGTUL	28. ASSDYUF
3. ADDYUFF	16. AHHTLL	29. ASSR
4. ADRF	17. AHTL	30. ASSSDRF
5. ADSDRFF	18. AR	31. ASSSR
6. ADSRF	19. ASDDRFF	32. ASSSSR
7. ADSSRF	20. ASDRF	33. ASSSSSR
8. ADSSSRF	21. ASDSRF	34. ASSSSYU
9. ADSSYUF	22. ASDSSRF	35. ASSSYU
10. ADSYUF	23. ASDSYUF	36. ASSYU
11. ADYUF	24. ASDYUF	37. ASYU
12. AGGTUU	25. ASR	38. AT
13. AGHTLU	26. ASSDRF	39. AYU

The strings

$$v_1 \rightarrow A\ v_2\ /\ A\ v_3$$

$$v_2 \rightarrow D\ v_2\ F\ /\ S\ v_2\ /\ R\ /\ YU$$

$$v_3 \rightarrow G\ v_3\ U\ /\ H\ v_3\ L\ /\ T$$

The grammar

Figure A3

Finally, we exhibit an example from Crespi-Reghizzi's dissertation. His program produced operator precedence grammars from strings of symbols which are marked to indicate their structure. The terminal symbols in this case are A, +, (, and) and the brackets ⟨ and ⟩ define the correct parse of strings. He indicated that this example was completed in less than four seconds of CPU time.

⟨⟨A⟩+⟨⟨A⟩+⟨A⟩⟩⟩
⟨⟨(⟨⟨A⟩+⟨A⟩⟩)⟩+⟨A⟩⟩
⟨⟨(⟨(⟨⟨A⟩+⟨⟨A⟩+⟨A⟩⟩⟩)⟩)⟩+⟨⟨A⟩+⟨(⟨⟨A⟩+⟨A⟩⟩)⟩⟩⟩
⟨(⟨(⟨⟨A⟩+⟨⟨(⟨⟨A⟩+⟨A⟩⟩)⟩+⟨A⟩⟩⟩)⟩)⟩
⟨(⟨⟨(⟨⟨A⟩+⟨A⟩⟩)⟩+⟨(⟨⟨(⟨⟨A⟩+⟨A⟩⟩)⟩+⟨A⟩⟩)⟩⟩)⟩
⟨⟨A⟩+⟨(⟨⟨(⟨⟨A⟩+⟨A⟩⟩)⟩+⟨A⟩⟩)⟩⟩
⟨⟨(⟨⟨A⟩+⟨A⟩⟩)⟩+⟨⟨(⟨⟨A⟩+⟨A⟩⟩)⟩+⟨A⟩⟩⟩
⟨⟨A⟩+⟨⟨A⟩+⟨(⟨⟨A⟩+⟨A⟩⟩)⟩⟩⟩
⟨(⟨⟨A⟩+⟨(⟨⟨A⟩+⟨A⟩⟩)⟩⟩)⟩
⟨⟨A⟩+⟨⟨(⟨⟨A⟩+⟨A⟩⟩)⟩+⟨⟨(⟨⟨A⟩+⟨A⟩⟩)⟩+⟨(⟨⟨A⟩+⟨A⟩⟩)⟩⟩⟩⟩
⟨⟨(⟨⟨A⟩+⟨A⟩⟩)⟩+⟨⟨A⟩+⟨A⟩⟩⟩

The strings

N1 → A
N2 → N1 + N1
N2 → N1 + N2
N3 → (N2)
N3 → (N3)
N2 → N3 + N1
N2 → N3 + N2
N2 → N1 + N3
N2 → N3 + N3
S → N2
S → N3

The grammar

A grammar inferred by Crespi-Reghizzi's program

Figure A4

Acknowledgement of Financial Support

The research reported here was done partly in the Computer Science Department, Stanford University and was supported by the Advanced Research Projects Agency of the Office of the Secretary of Defense (SD-183). Part of the work was done in the Computer and Information Science Department at the Ohio State University and was supported by Grant Number GN 534.1 from the Office of Science Information Service, National Science Foundation.

REFERENCES

[1] S. Amarel, "Representations and Modeling in Problems of Program Formation," Technical Report No. 4, Department of Computer Science, Rutgers University, July 1970.

[2] M. A. Arbib, *Theories of Abstract Automata,* Prentice-Hall, Inc., Englewood Cliffs, N. J., 1969.

[3] A. W. Biermann, "A Grammatical Inference Program for Linear Languages," Fourth Hawaii International Conference on System Sciences, Honolulu, Hawaii, Jan. 12-14, 1971.

[4] A. W. Biermann and J. A. Feldman, "On the Synthesis of Finite-State Acceptors," A. I. Memo No. 114, Computer Science Department, Stanford University, April 1970.

[5] N. Chomsky, "On Certain Formal Properties of Grammars," *Information and Control,* Vol. 2, pp. 137-167, 1959.

[6] N. Chomsky and G. A. Miller, *Pattern Conception,* Report No. AFCRC-TN-57-57, August 7, 1957. (ASTIA Document No. AD 110076).

[7] S. Crespi-Reghizzi, "The Mechanical Acquisition of Precedence Grammars," Report No. UCLA-ENG-7054, School of Engineering and Applied Science, University of California at Los Angeles, June 1970.

[8] T. G. Evans, "Grammatical Inference Techniques in Pattern Analysis," Third International Symposium on Computer and Information Sciences, Miami Beach, Florida, Dec. 18-20, 1969.

[9] J. A. Feldman, "First Thoughts on Grammatical Inference," A. I. Memo No. 55, Computer Science Department, Stanford University, August 1967.

[10] J. A. Feldman, "Some Decidability Results on Grammatical Inference and Complexity," A. I. Memo No 93.1, Computer Science Department, Stanford University, May 1970.

[11] J. A. Feldman, J. Gips, J. J. Horning, S. Reder, "Grammatical Complexity and Inference," Technical Report No. CS 125, Computer Science Department, Stanford University, June 1969.

[12] R. W. Floyd, "Syntactic Analysis and Operator Precedence," *Journal of the Association for Computing Machinery,* Vol. 10, pp. 316-333, 1963.

[13] A. Gill, *Introduction to the Theory of Finite-State Machines,* McGraw-Hill Book Co., Inc., New York, 1962.

[14] S. Ginsburg, *The Mathematical Theory of Context-Free Languages,* McGraw-Hill Book Co., Inc., New York, 1966.

[15] M. Gold, "Limiting Recursion," *Journal of Symbolic Logic*, 30 pp. 28-48, 1965.

[16] M. Gold, "Language Identification in the Limit," *Information and Control,* Vol. 10, pp. 447-474, 1967.

[17] A. Grasselli, Editor, *Automatic Interpretation and Classification of Images,* Academic Press, New York, 1969.

[18] S. A. Greibach, "A New Normal-Form Theorem for Context-Free Phrase Structure Grammars," *Journal of the Association for Computing Machinery*, Vol. 12, No. 1, pp. 42-52, 1965.

[19] J. Gruska, "Some Classifications of Context-Free Languages," *Information and Control,* Vol. 14, pp. 152-179, 1969.

[20] M. A. Harrison, *Introduction to Switching and Automata Theory,* McGraw-Hill Book Co., Inc., New York, 1965.

[21] J. Hartmanis and J. E. Hopcroft, "An Overview of the Theory of Computational Complexity," Technical Report No. 70-59, Department of Computer Science, Cornell University, April 1970.

[22] J. E. Hopcroft and J. D. Ullman, *Formal Languages and their Relation to Automata,* Addison-Wesley, Reading, Mass., 1969.

[23] J. J. Horning, "A Study of Grammatical Inference," Technical Report No. CS 139, Computer Science Department, Stanford University, August 1969.

[24] S. Klein, W. Fabens, R. G. Herriot, W. J. Katke, M. A. Kuppin, A. E. Towster, "The Autoling System," Technical Report No. 43, Computer Science Department, University of Wisconsin, September 1968.

[25] S. Klein and M. A. Kuppin, "An Interactive Heuristic Program for Learning Transformational Grammars," Technical Report, Computer Science Department, University of Wisconsin, 1970.

[26] G. A. Miller, "Finite-State Machine Induction," M. S. Thesis, The Moore School of Electrical Engineering, University of Pennsylvania, May 1969.

[27] W. F. Miller and A. C. Shaw, "Linguistic Methods in Picture Processing–A Survey," *Proceeding AFIPS Fall Joint Computer Conference,* pp. 279-290, 1968.

[28] T. W. L. Pao, "A Solution of the Syntactical Induction-Inference Problem for a Non-Trivial Subset of Context-Free Languages," Report No. 70-19, The Moore School of Electrical Engineering, University of Pennsylvania, August 1969.

[29] J. C. Reynolds, "Grammatical Covering," Technical Memorandum No. 96, Applied Mathematics Division, Argonne National Laboratory, March 1968.

[30] H. Rogers, Jr., *Recursive Functions and Effective Computability,* McGraw-Hill, New York, 1967.

[31] A. Rosenfeld, H. K. Huang, and V. H. Schneider, "An Application of Cluster Detection to Text and Picture Processing," Technical Report No. 68-68, Computer Science Center, University of Maryland, June 1968.

[32] E. Shamir, "A Remark on Discovery Algorithms for Grammars," *Information and Control,* Vol. 5, pp. 246-251, 1962.

[33] A. C. Shaw, "A Formal Picture Description Scheme as a Basis for Picture Processing Systems," *Information and Control,* Vol. 14, pp. 9-52, 1969.

[34] A. C. Shaw, "Parsing of Graph Representable Pictures," *Journal of the Association for Computing Machinery,* Vol. 17, pp. 453-481, 1970.

[35] J. W. Snively, Jr., "Bounds on the Complexity of Grammars," Technical Report No. 70-114, Computer Science Center, University of Maryland, May 1970.

[36] R. Solomonoff, "A New Method for Discovering the Grammars of Phrase Structure Languages," *Information Processing,* pp. 258-290, June 1959.

[37] R. Solomonoff, "A Formal Theory of Inductive Inference," *Information and Control,* Vol. 7, pp. 1-22, pp. 224-254, 1964.

[38] P. H. Swain, K. S. Fu, "Nonparametric and Linguistic Approaches to Pattern Recognition," Technical Report No. TR-EE 70-20, School of Electrical Engineering,

Purdue University, June 1970.
[39] S. Watanabe, *Knowning and Guessing,* John Wiley and Sons, Inc., New York, 1969.
[40] S. Watanabe, *Methodologies of Pattern Recognition,* Academic Press, New York, 1969.

THE SELECTION OF EFFECTIVE ATTRIBUTES FOR DECIDING BETWEEN HYPOTHESES USING LINEAR DISCRIMINANT FUNCTIONS

Herman Chernoff
DEPARTMENT OF STATISTICS
STANFORD UNIVERSITY
STANFORD, CALIFORNIA

Abstract

Let X be a multidimensional random variable, whose components are called attributes, with mean μ_i and covariance matrix Σ_i under H_i, $i = 1,2$. The ability to discriminate between H_1 and H_2 using a linear discriminant function is measured by $S = \max|b'(\mu_1 - \mu_2)|[(b'\Sigma_1 b)^{1/2} + (b'\Sigma_2 b)^{1/2}]$. As a consequence of a result of Anderson and Bahadur it is seen that the problem of selecting additional variables or attributes involves increasing the Mahalanobis Distance $\delta'\Sigma^{-1}\delta$ where $\delta = \mu_1 - \mu_2$ and Σ is an appropriate weighted average of Σ_1 and Σ_2. Thus our problem is related to problems in regression theory. Some simple examples illustrate that if Σ_1 is in some sense much smaller than Σ_2, there is a premium on adjoining additional attributes for which the variance under H_1 is relatively small.

1. Introduction

Let X be a univariate random variable with mean μ_i and variance σ_i^2 under hypothesis H_i, $i = 1,2$. Becker [3] proposed the use of

$$S = |\mu_1 - \mu_2|/(\sigma_1 + \sigma_2) \tag{1.1}$$

as a measure of separability or of the effectiveness of X for distinguishing between the two hypotheses. This proposal was suggested by his conjecture that if both hypotheses are equally likely, the probability, that a single observation on X used with an optimal one sided test will lead to accepting the wrong hypotheses, is bounded by $[2(1 + S^2)]^{-1}$. Becker showed that this bound is attained by presenting appropriate two point distributions with the specified means and variances. Chernoff [4] proved the validity of the conjecture. Becker used the measure S to help select a "best" among available attributes, i.e., univariate random variables, for discriminating between hypotheses.

In the cases Becker studied and in many practical problems the typical random variable X is approximately normally distributed. In such cases a more relevant justification for the use of S as a measure of separability lies in the fact that the error probability for a one-tailed test based on X is, for large S, of the order of magnitude of

$$\Phi(-S) \approx (2\pi S^2)^{-1/2} \exp(-S^2/2)$$

where Φ is the standard normal cumulative distribution function. This amount is substantially smaller than the bound $[2(1+S^2)]^{-1}$.

In many applications it is important to compare the effectiveness of groups of random variables. The measure S is easily extended to the multivariate case. Suppose now that X has mean vector μ_i and positive definite covariance matrix Σ_i under H_i. Then if b is a non-zero vector of the same dimensionality as X, we let S(b) represent the S measure applied to the scalar random variable $b'X$, i.e., $b'X$ has mean $b'\mu_i$ and variance $b'\Sigma_i b$ under H_i and hence

$$S(b) = |b'\delta| / ((b'\Sigma_1 b)^{1/2} + (b'\Sigma_2 b)^{1/2}) \tag{1.2}$$

where

$$\delta = \mu_1 - \mu_2 \,. \tag{1.3}$$

Now let

$$S = \sup_b S(b) \,. \tag{1.4}$$

Then S roughly measures how well one can discriminate between H_1 and H_2 by use of linear discriminant functions if X has approximately a multivariate normal distribution.

The measure S has been applied to multivariate problems previously. In particular it was studied in some detail by Clunies-Ross and Riffenburgh [5] and by Anderson and Bahadur [2] who pointed out its connection in the multivariate normal problem to the test based on linear discriminant functions which minimizes the maximum error probability.

Our object is to illustrate with a few simple examples how these results relate to the problem of helping select effective attributes. The essential mathematics was carried out in the above mentioned papers whose main result characterizing S will be restated here.

2. Characterization of S in the Multivariate Case

The following theorem is essentially a restatement of some of the results of [2] and [5] and its proof will not be presented.

Theorem 1.

$$S^2 = t(1-t)\delta'\Sigma^{-1}\delta \tag{2.1}$$

where

$$\Sigma = t\Sigma_1 + (1-t)\Sigma_2 \tag{2.2}$$

and t *is the unique solution between* 0 *and* 1 *of*

$$R(t) = \delta'\Sigma^{-1}(t^2\Sigma_1 - (1-t)^2\Sigma_2)\Sigma^{-1}\delta = 0\,. \tag{2.3}$$

The optimal value of b *is given by*

$$b = \Sigma^{-1}\delta \tag{2.4}$$

and is unique up to a multiplicative constant. For this optimal value of b

$$|b'\delta| = \delta'\Sigma^{-1}\delta = S^2/t(1-t) \tag{2.5}$$

and

$$t^2 b'\Sigma_1 b = (1-t)^2 b'\Sigma_2 b = S^2\,. \tag{2.6}$$

The fact that

$$\frac{dR}{dt} = 2\delta'\Sigma^{-1}(t\Sigma_1+(1-t)\Sigma_2)\Sigma^{-1}\delta - 2\delta'\Sigma^{-1}(\Sigma_1-\Sigma_2)\Sigma^{-1}(t^2\Sigma_1 - (1-t)^2\Sigma_2)\Sigma^{-1}\delta$$

$$\frac{dR}{dt} = 2\delta'\Sigma^{-1}[(t\Sigma_1+(1-t)\Sigma_2)\Sigma^{-1}(t\Sigma_1+(1-t)\Sigma_2)-(\Sigma_1-\Sigma_2)\Sigma^{-1}(t^2\Sigma_1-(1-t)^2\Sigma_2)]\Sigma^{-1}\delta$$

$$\frac{dR}{dt} = 2\delta'\Sigma^{-1}\Sigma_1\Sigma^{-1}\Sigma_2\Sigma^{-1}\delta \tag{2.7}$$

(which is positive for $\delta \neq 0$) can be used to solve $R(t) = 0$ numerically by the Newton Iterative technique where an approximation t^* to t is improved to $t^{**} = t^* - (dR(t^*)/dt)^{-1} R(t^*)$.

Theorem 1 presents S^2 as a multiple of $\delta'\Sigma^{-1}\delta$ which may be regarded as a Mahalanobis distance with respect to the inverse of the weighted average Σ of the two covariance matrices Σ_1 and Σ_2. To study the effect of adjoining additional components to a vector X we are largely concerned with the effect of such a change on the distance. Thus let δ be decomposed into two subvectors δ_1 and δ_2 and Σ correspondingly decomposed into $\Sigma_{11}, \Sigma_{12}, \Sigma_{21}$ and Σ_{22}. Then a classical result implicit in [1, p. 28] gives

$$\delta'\Sigma^{-1}\delta = \delta_1'\Sigma_{11}^{-1}\delta_1 + \nu_2 W_{22}^{-1}\nu_2 \tag{2.8}$$

where

$$\nu_2 = \delta_2 - \Sigma_{21}\Sigma_{11}^{-1}\delta_1 \tag{2.9}$$

and

$$W_{22} = \Sigma_{22} - \Sigma_{21}\Sigma_{11}^{-1}\Sigma_{12} \ . \tag{2.10}$$

The terms ν_2 and W_{22} have a standard interpretation in terms of regression. If we assume that Y, which decomposes into Y_1 and Y_2, has a multivariate normal distribution with mean vector δ and covariance matrix Σ then

$$Z_2 = Y_2 - \Sigma_{21}\Sigma_{11}^{-1}Y_1 \tag{2.11}$$

has mean ν_2 and covariance matrix W_{22} and is independent of Y_1. Hence, assuming that t does not change much when X_2 is adjoined to X_1, the increment in distance due to adjoining X_2 is itself a Mahalanobis distance corresponding to that part of Y_2 unexplained by the regression of Y_2 on Y_1. In cases where the additional components of X_2 do not contribute enormously to the ability to discriminate, one expects their influence on the appropriate value of t to be small and the increase in S^2 close to

$$\Delta S^2 = t(1-t)\nu_2' W_{22}^{-1}\nu_2 \ . \tag{2.13}$$

3. Examples

A couple of simple examples involving a vector X whose components are independent may add some insight. Assume that X_i has mean μ_{1i} and variance v_i under H_1 and mean μ_{2i} and variance w_i under H_2. In the case of independence there is no loss of generality in assuming that the differences $\delta_i = \mu_{1i} - \mu_{2i}$ are all one since a scale multiplication of the ith component can be used to achieve this aim. Then

$$S^2 = t(1-t) \sum_{i=1}^{n} (tv_i + (1-t)w_i)^{-1}$$

where t is the unique solution of

$$R(t) = \Sigma(tv_i + (1-t)w_i)^{-2}(t^2 v_i - (1-t)^2 w_i) = 0$$

and the optimal vector $b = (b_1, b_2, \ldots, b_n)$ where $b_i = (tv_i + (1-t)w_i)^{-1}$. Suppose now that X_o is an additional component with variances v_o and w_o which are not too small. Then t is barely changed and S^2 is changed by

$$\Delta S^2 \approx (t(1-t)(tv_o + (1-t)w_o)^{-1}.$$

Thus the effectiveness of the incremental attribute X_o is determined by $(tv_o + (1-t)w_o)^{-1}$. If the vector $X = (X_1, \ldots, X_n)$ has yielded $t = .9$, one must be concerned with adjoining new components for which v is especially small.

The following special examples emphasize that if previously selected components have w_i larger than v_i, there is a premium on selecting additional components, where v_i *continues* to be relatively small rather than to attempt a balance.

Example 1. Let $v_i = 1$ and $w_i = 9$ for $i = 1, 2, \ldots, n$. The equation $R = 0$ yields $t = .75$ and then $S^2 = n/16$.

Example 2. Let $v_i = 1$ and $w_i = 9$ for $i = 1, 2, \ldots, n$ and $v_i = 9$ and $w_i = 1$ for $i = n+1, \ldots, 2n$. By symmetry $t = 1/2$ and $S^2 = n/10$.

In Example 2 each component contributes .05 to S^2 which is somewhat, though not enormously, smaller than the 1/16 for Example 1.

The author believes that this lackluster difference and possibly also the above mentioned premium on not attempting a balance are due to the restriction that linear discriminant functions be used. It is quite probable that different results would apply when the relative variances under the two populations fluctuate considerably and the statistician is permitted to use nonlinear discriminant functions.

REFERENCES

[1] Anderson, T.W., (1958). *Introduction to Multivariate Analysis,* Wiley, New York.

[2] Anderson, T.W. and Bahadur, R.R. (1962). "Classification into two multivariate normal distributions with different covariance matrices," *Ann. Math. Statist.,* 33, 420-431.

[3] Becker, P. (1968). "Recognition of Patterns," Polyteknisk Forlag, Copenhagen.

[4] Chernoff, H. (1970). "A bound on the classification error for discrimination between populations with specified means and variances," *Stanford Tech. Report, No. 66,* 1-13.

[5] Clunies-Ross, C.W. and Riffenburgh, R.H. (1960). "Geometry and linear discrimination," *Biometrika,* 47, 185-189.

BOUNDARY DETECTION OF RADIOGRAPHIC IMAGES BY A THRESHOLD METHOD

C. K. Chow and T. Kaneko

IBM THOMAS J. WATSON RESEARCH CENTER
YORKTOWN HEIGHTS, NEW YORK

Abstract

A threshold method based on statistical principles and heuristics is developed to detect boundaries in radiographic images. Each local region of the image containing a portion of boundary is characterized by a mixture of two (normal) intensity distributions. Thresholds are set dynamically according to local, rather than global, characteristics estimated from the observed intensity histograms. A program to implement the method has been written. Experimental results on cardioangiograms are presented to successfully demonstrate the feasibility of the method for low quality images. The method is insensitive to shading or gradually varying interference.

I. Introduction

The image pattern recognition, one of the most difficult steps is to extract objects from an irrelevant background. The degree of difficulties involved varies greatly with the quality of the picture and the nature of the object. The object extraction problem has been recognized to be the most difficult task in the bio-medical engineering areas of chromosome analysis [1,2], blood cell identification [3], bacterial colony analysis [4], brain scintigram analysis [5,6]; and heart image extraction from a cardiac cineangiogram [7,8]. The main reason is that pictures in these fields are often noisy and object images are poorly defined.

A cardiac cineangiogram, an X ray motion picture of a heart image, has been one of the most important means for cardiologists to diagnose a patient. The picture shown in Figure 1 is a frame of a cardioangiogram. Quantitative information is obtainable. The interest has been focused on the determination of left ventricular volume. In recent experiments [8,9] technicians trace around the chamber image with an electronic digitizer to feed into a digital computer which computes the volume. The task to extract the left ventricle chamber requires human assistance at the present time.

This paper presents a method to detect boundaries in radiographic images. The method is also applicable to other object extraction in low quality pictures. Although our ultimate goal is computer measurement of a left stet chamber volume, attention will be restricted to the most essential problem of extracting the heart image.

II. Boundaries and Detection Methods

Regions between objects and background are called boundaries. Therefore the object extraction can be considered to be a problem of finding boundaries between two categories, the object and background. Unfortunately, there is as yet no operational definition of boundaries that is universally applicable. However, methods to recognize boundaries have been devised based upon such properties as:

(1) that photometric intensities at or near boundaries change faster than other regions, and

(2) that boundaries are located between two categories, namely regions of higher and lower intensity.

When the first property is emphasized one generally applies spatial differentiations such as the gradients and Laplacians to pictures to detect the boundaries. But these operations rarely work for low quality pictures because spatial differentiations enhance high spatial components, where noise is usually dominant. In methods based upon the second property, the prime concern is to determine an optimal threshold to separate the two categories. A threshold may be obtained by the percentile method [10] or a context oriented method by Harlow et al [6]. Their use is also limited. More widely used is the mode method [10], which first computes the intensity histogram of a picture, and in the simplest form tacitly assumes the observed histogram to be bi-modal. It then identifies the intensity level corresponding to the valley point in the histogram as the threshold. Mendelsohn et al [2] used the mode method to determine threshold for a chromosome picture. Young [16] and Green [3] have applied it to blood cell analysis, although Green has modified the method in determining the location of the valley.

However, no available method is found suitable for the task under consideration. For images of low quality, it is not feasible to set a single threshold for the entire picture in order to reliably separate objects from the background. Instead, the value of threshold should be set dynamically according to the local characteristics and consequently may vary from point to point.

In the following section a dynamic threshold method based on statistical principles is described.

III. The Dynamic Threshold Method

A. *A Statistical Approach*

Due to statistical fluctuation, the intensity seldom remains constant over any region in the picture. The intensity variation over any region is characterized by a statistical distribution. In our analysis, the fundamental assumption, which is empirically verified, is that the probability distribution of the intensity for any small region of the picture consisting solely of the object or the background is uni-modal.

Now consider a small region in the picture which contains a boundary, for example, the region marked by A in Figure 2. There are two uni-modal distributions, one for the object and one for the background. These two distributions generally overlap. In this application, due to the presence of a contrast agent, the object is usually brighter than the background, i.e. the distribution of the object has a larger mean than that of the background as indicated in Figure 3. The overall distribution of this small region is consequently a mixture of two uni-modal distributions and is generally bi-modal. The histogram for this region will therefore generally exhibit two peaks and a valley as shown in Figure 3. The problem of determining the boundary reduces to that of ascertaining which distribution each individual image point belong to.

In the mode method, the valley point in the observed histogram of the mixture determines the threshold that separates the object and the background. However, it is not always optimal. By the principle of maximum likelihood an optimal threshold can be readily obtained once the two component distributions are determined. However, in determining the component distributions two questions arise: the functional form of the uni-modal distributions and identifiability, i.e. the question whether it is possible to determine two distributions uniquely from their mixture.

The estimation of the parameters to characterize distribution functions has been extensively studied [11], and is a prime problem in unsupervised learning [12]. It is known that all finite mixtures of either normal or Poisson distributions are identifiable [13]. For convenience, in this paper we assume that the distributions for the object and for background are both normal. Only two parameters, mean and variance, are needed to specify a normal distribution and a mixture of two normal distributions is known to be identifiable and is characterized by five parameters.

B. *Procedure*

The method consists of the following major steps:

(1) divide the entire picture into a set of smaller, overlapping regions,
(2) compute the histogram for each region,
(3) select histograms with large variances,
(4) for each selected histogram estimate the component distributions and coefficient of mixture using a curve fitting algorithm,
(5) test the resultant mixtures of estimated distributions for bi-modality,
(6) for every histogram with appreciable bi-modality calculate the threshold from the estimated distributions by the method of maximum likelihood,
(7) interpolate from the thresholds calculated in (6) thresholds for all image points,
(8) perform the binary decision for each image point using the threshold obtained in (7).

Details are given in Section IV.

C. *Analysis*

The logarithmic operation, log (•), is a commonly used nonlinear operation in dealing with photometric images. Its use has been motivated by the technical reason [14] that it transforms a skewed intensity distribution to a somewhat uniform intensity distribution. However, our use of the logarithmic transform is based on the physical reason that it restores the exponential operation caused by the radioactive absorption. Therefore, if the logarithm of an image is taken, the detected boundary corresponds more closely to the real dimension of the image. It is also supported by physiological evidence [15] that the human visual system perceives according to the logarithm of incoming images. From these reasons, the logarithmic transformation is first operated on the images in this paper. The boundaries obtained by applying the method directly to the images without the logarithmic transformation differ appreciably with human recognition. Figure 4 is the logarithmic image of the picture shown in Figure 1.

Let the density function of the r-th region be

$$f_r(x) = \sum_{k=1}^{2} \frac{p_{kr}}{\sqrt{2\pi}\,\sigma_{kr}} \text{Exp}\left\{-\frac{(x-\mu_{kr})^2}{2\,\sigma_{kr}^2}\right\} \qquad (1)$$

where p_{1r} and p_{2r} are the theoretical fractions of areas of the r-th region occupied by the background and the object respectively; μ_{1r} and σ_{1r} are the mean and variance of the distribution associated with the background in the r-th region while μ_{2r} and σ_{2r} are the corresponding parameters of the object. $p_{1r} + p_{2r} = 1$ and either may be zero.

It can be readily shown that the mean and variance of the mixture are:

$$\mu_r = p_{1r}\,\mu_{1r} + p_{2r}\,\mu_{2r} \tag{2}$$

$$\sigma_r^2 = p_{1r}\,\sigma_{1r}^2 + p_{2r}\,\sigma_{2r}^2 + p_{1r}\,p_{2r}\,(\mu_{2r}-\mu_{1r})^2 \tag{3}$$

The above relations are always valid whether the component distributions are normal or not.

Since for our pictures the observed image in the region of the object is a sum of the heart chamber and the injected contrast agent, the following relations can be assumed:

$$\mu_{2r} = \mu_{1r} + \mu_{cr} \tag{4}$$

$$\sigma_{2r}^2 = \sigma_{1r}^2 + \sigma_{cr}^2 \tag{5}$$

and $\mu_{1r}, \mu_{2r}, \mu_{cr} > 0$

where μ_{cr} represents the mean density of the contrast agent contained in the object. By substituting Eqs. (4) and (5) into Eqs. (2) and (3), we have

$$\mu_r = \mu_{1r} + p_{2r}\,\mu_{cr} > \mu_{1r} \tag{6}$$

$$\sigma_r^2 = \sigma_{1r}^2 + p_{2r}\,\sigma_{cr}^2 + p_{1r}\,p_{2r}\,\mu_{cr}^2 > \sigma_{1r}^2 \tag{7}$$

It is evident from Eqs. (6) and (7) that the mean and variance increase after the contrast agent is injected. The mean increases linearly with p_{2r}, the fraction of the area occupied by the object, and the variance increases quadratically with p_{2r}. Eq. (7) can be rewritten as

$$\sigma_r^2 = -\mu_{cr}^2\,\{p_{2r} - (\frac{1}{2} + \frac{\sigma_{cr}^2}{2\,\mu_{cr}^2})\}^2 + \sigma_{1r}^2 + \frac{(\sigma_{cr}^4 + \mu_{cr}^2)^2}{4\,\mu_{cr}^2} \tag{8}$$

Since for our picture we have $\sigma_{cr}^2 << \mu_{cr}^2$, in general the variance first increases and then decreases to $\sigma_{2r}^2 = \sigma_{1r}^2 + \sigma_{cr}^2$ as p_{2r} increases. A larger variance indicates that the number p_{2r} is closer to 1/2. However, it should be noted that the conclusion holds not only for the comparison before and after the injection of the contrast agent in a given region, but also is valid for comparing different regions with or without a boundary provided that the variances σ_{1r}^2 and σ_{2r}^2 do not vary significantly from region to region. Therefore the magnitude of σ_r^2 can be used as a crude indication of whether the region r contains a boundary or not.

IV. Experimental Results

To demonstrate the feasibility of the method for low quality images, experimental results on two 35 mm cardioangiograms, Figures 1 and 9 are presented. Each cardioangiogram is scanned by a flying spot scanner controlled by an IBM 1800 and converted into a 256 x 256 array of 8 bit words. This array was stored on a magnetic disc to be accessed and processed by a IBM System 360/91 computer.

A. *Computation of Histograms*

The logarithmic operation is first performed. The entire area is then divided into 7 x 7 regions with 50% overlap as shown in Figure 5. An intensity histogram is computed over each region. To compute histograms, we first determine the range in intensities of the entire picture and then delete scattered extreme values. The resultant range in gray levels is normalized to [0,1] and divided into 50 equal domains. A histogram is thus a list of the numbers of the image intensities in each domain. Figure 6 is a histogram which does not exhibit clear bi-modal shape.

Figures 7(a) and 7(b) are the histograms of the same picture over the regions denoted by A and B on Figure 2 respectively; it should be noted here that intensities are log-transformed. The histogram Figure 7(a) has a very clear bi-modal shape, implying that the region contains a boundary crossing in the middle of the region. On the other hand, the histogram Figure 7(b) is uni-modal, and there is no boundary seen in the region B. The dynamic threshold method does take advantage of the fact that there are quite a few regions whose histograms show clear bi-modal shapes even though there is no apparent bi-modality in the histogram computed over the entire region.

B. *Selection of Histograms for Estimation*

The variance is computed for each of 49 regions. Table I lists the variances for the angiogram of Figure 1. It is interesting to note that larger variances occur near the boundary to be detected. In this example 30 histograms with larger variances are selected and treated at this stage as mixtures of two normal distributions, Eq. (1). To each of these histograms, Eq. (1) is least square fitted by adjusting the five parameters p_{1r}, μ_{1r}, μ_{2r}, σ_{2r} and σ_{2r}. The algorithm used is a hill climbing method employing conjugate gradients. The program, called "FMCG", is available in the IBM System/360

Scientific Subroutine Package. An example is shown in Figure 7(a), where "x" and "o" points are the starting and final points respectively.

The histograms on which the curve fitting procedure was applied are not necessarily bi-modal. We therefore further examine the shape of the sum of two resultant normal curves. The bi-modality is tested by the difference in means, $\mu = \mu_{2r} - \mu_{1r}$, ratio of variances $\epsilon = \sigma_{1r}/\sigma_{2r}$ and the "valley to peak" ratio, δ = (minimum value of f( ) in $[\mu_{1r}, \mu_{2r}]$/Min $[f(\mu_{1r}), f(\mu_{2r})]$. They are listed in Table II(a), (b), and (c). With $\mu > 0.2$, $1/3 < \epsilon < 3$ and $\delta < 0.8$, only 8 of the 30 histograms survive this test. As is expected, their locations are along the boundary.

Finally for these 8 histograms the thresholds are computed according to the following quadratic formula derived from the method of maximum likelihood for the value of t_r which minimizes the probability of misclassification:

$$\left(\frac{1}{\sigma_{1r}^2} - \frac{1}{\sigma_{2r}^2}\right) t_r^2 + 2\left(\frac{\mu_{2r}}{\sigma_{2r}^2} - \frac{\mu_{1r}}{\sigma_{1r}^2}\right) t_r + \frac{\mu_{1r}^2}{\sigma_{1r}^2} - \frac{\mu_{2r}^2}{\sigma_{2r}^2} + 2\,\ell n \frac{p_{2r}}{p_{1r}} = 0 \qquad (9)$$

The computed thresholds are listed in Table III.

C. *Interpolations*

At this stage, some regions are not assigned thresholds. Their thresholds are obtained as weighted averages of the computed thresholds of their neighboring regions. The averaging process also applied to the original computed thresholds to insure a more gradual transition. Table IV gives the 49 thresholds so obtained for the angiogram of Figure 1. A second interpolation is carried out in a pointwise manner, to ensure continuity in the boundary at the border of two neighboring regions with different thresholds. The two interpolation procedures are straightforward and will not be elaborated here.

At the end of the interpolations, all the 256 x 256 points are assigned their thresholds, which are represented by a 256 x 256 matrix $\{T_{i,j}\}$, $1 \leq i,j \leq 256$.

D. *Binary Decision*

Finally a binary decision is carried out for each point of the picture $\{I_{i,j}\}$, $1 \leq i, j \leq 256$:

$$O_{i,j} = \begin{cases} 1 & \text{if } I_{i,j} \geq T_{i,j} \\ 0 & \text{otherwise} \end{cases} \qquad (10)$$

And $\{O_{i,j}\}$ is the output image.

A computer program to implement this method has been written in FORTRAN IV. Figure 8 shows the flow chart of the program. It takes about twenty seconds to obtain the final binary output on an IBM 360/91 computer. The processed image is outputed on a tape and converted into a photographic image using the same flying spot scanner as that used at the in-input step.

The two frames taken from a cardiac cineangiogram are depicted in Figure 1 and Figure 9. Their respective logarithmic transforms are shown in Figures 4 and 10. Figure 11 is the histogram for the entire region of the picture shown in Figure 10. There is again no bi-modal shape. Figures 12 and 13 show the final binary images for the pictures shown in Figures 1 and 9 respectively. Figures 14 and 15 depict the original angiograms, Figure 1 and 9 respectively, with the computed boundaries superimposed on them. The results show that the detected boundaries are in good agreement with human recognition.

E. *Insensitivity to Shading*

The present method is insensitive to shading or gradually changing interference. For a small region, intensities of a shade vary little and therefore its distribution is close to a delta function. An image with superimposed shade has approximately the same distribution as the image without the shade except a shift in the intensity scale due to convolution with the delta function. Therefore the resultant threshold shifts by that value which eliminates the effect of the shade. This effect can be demonstrated by adding an artificially constructed shade: 0.2 at the top (or bottom) and gradually tapering down linearly to zero at the bottom (or top). Note that 0.2 stands for 20% of the difference between the maximum and minimum intensities of the pictures. The final processed image is shown in Figure 16.

Although the size of the region is fixed in this paper, one can readily adopt the method to variable size in search for a segment of the boundary. A useful modification would be to expand the region until a clear indication of bi-modality in the histogram is obtained or some reasonable limit is exceeded. One can also use region shapes other than a square.

VI. Summary

This paper develops a threshold method based on statistical principles and heuristics to detect object boundaries by a digital computer. Thresholds are dynamically set according to local rather than global characteristics. The entire region of a picture is divided into a set of smaller regions. Histograms are computed for all the regions. Thresholds are estimated for selected ones of these histograms. These thresholds are then interpolated twice, first regionwise and then pointwise, to obtain a threshold for each and every image point. Finally a binary decision is executed for all the points of the picture.

A program to implement the method has been written in FORTRAN IV. Experimental results on two different frames of a cardiac cineangiogram are described. An artificially created shade is added to the pictures to demonstrate insensitivity of our method to shading or gradually varying interference. Feasibility of the method in detecting boundaries in cardiac cineangiograms is demonstrated.

Acknowledgement

The authors wish to thank Professor A. Papoulis of Polytechnic Institute of Brooklyn for valuable comments and suggestions, and Dr. J. H. Siegel of Einstein College of Medicine for suggesting the problem and for providing the cardiac cineangiograms.

REFERENCES

1. M. L. Mendelsohn, B. H. Mayall, and B. H. Perry, "Generalized Grayness Profiles as Applied to Edge Detection and the Organization of Chromosome Images," the Second International Conference on Medical Physics, Boston, Mass., August 15, 1969.
2. M. L. Mendelsohn, B. H. Mayall, and J. M. S. Prewitt, "Approaches to the Automation of Chromosome Analysis," *Image Processing in Biological Science,* University of California Press, Berkeley and Los Angeles, pp. 119-136, 1968.
3. J. E. Green, "Computer Methods for Erythrocyte Analysis", IEEE Conference Record of the Symposium on Feature Extraction and Selection in Pattern Recognition, pp. 100-109, October 5-7, 1970.
4. D. A. Glazer, "An Automated System for Growth and Analysis of Bacterial Colonies," *Image Processing in Biological Science,* University of California Press, San Francisco and Los Angeles, pp. 57-74, 1968.
5. S. M. Pizer and H. G. Vetter, "Perception and Processing of Medical Radioisotope Scans," *Pictorial Pattern Recognition,* Thompson Book Company, Washington, D. C., pp. 147-156, 1968.
6. C. Harlow, P. Cardill, J. Lehr, and R. Parkey, "On Image Analysis," Proc. of the UMR-Mervin J. Kelly Communications Conference, Oct. 5-7, 1970, University of Missouri-Rolla, Rolla, Missouri, pp. 6-4-1 to 6-4-6, 1970.
7. H. T. Dodge, H. Sandler, D. W. Ballen, and J. D. Lord, "The Use of Biplane Angiocardiography for the Measurement of Left Ventricular Volume in Man," *American Heart Journal,* Vol. *60*, No. 5, Nov. 1960.
8. A. H. Gott, "Cooperative Heart Study Cardiac Volume Analysis," *S. P. I. E. Journal,* Vol. *8,* pp. 233-236, Sept. 1970.

9. H. Dominic Covvey, "Measuring the Human Heart with a Real-time Computing System," *Data Processing Magazine*, pp. 27-32, May 1970.
10. A. Rosenfeld, "Picture Processing by Computer," Academic Press, New York, pp. 132-133, 1969.
11. See, for example, T. Y. Young and G. Coraluppi, "Stochastic Estimation of a Mixture of Normal Density Functions Using an Information Criterion," *IEEE Trans. on Information Theory,* Vol. *IT-16,* No. 3, pp. 258-263, May 1970.
12. D. B. and P. N. Cooper, "Nonsupervised Adaptive Signal Detection and Pattern Recognition," *Information & Control,* Vol. 7, pp. 416-444, 1964.
13. H. Teicher, "Identifiability of Finite Mixtures," *Ann. Math. Stat.,* Vol. *34*, pp. 1265-1269, 1963.
14. See, for example, E. L. Hall, R. P. Kruger, S. J. Dwyer, III, G. S. Lodwick and D. A. Audherman, "Measurement Selection Techniques Applied to Digital Images," IEEE Conference Record of the Symposium on Feature Extraction and Selection in Pattern Recognition, pp. 78-89, October 1970.
15. S. S.Stevens, "Handbook of Experimental Psychology," John Wiley, New York, pp. 921-984, 1951.
16. I. T. Young, "Automated Leukocyte Recognition," Ph.D. Thesis, MIT, June 1969.

TABLE I. Variances of the 49 histograms

n \ m	1	2	3	4	5	6	7
1	.070	.113	.122	.138	.123	.054	.075
2	.094	.122	.134	.157	.092	.040	.072
3	.112	.111	.152	.146	.048	.048	.079
4	.117	.187	.184	.114	.040	.078	.084
5	.128	.216	.116	.050	.123	.128	.080
6	.161	.177	.058	.114	.192	.124	.058
7	.203	.151	.193	.234	.188	.129	.064

TABLE II(a). Valley Level, δ

n \ m	1	2	3	4	5	6	7
1		1.00	1.00	1.00	1.00		
2		1.00	1.00	0.50			
3	0.84		0.78	0.88			
4	1.00	0.95	0.12	0.89			
5	0.92	0.29	0.89		0.87	0.45	
6	0.58	0.66		1.00	0.70	1.00	
7	0.13	1.00	0.74	0.03	0.88	0.26	

TABLE II(b). Difference in means, μ

n \ m	1	2	3	4	5	6	7
1		.18	.18	.12	.17		
2		.16	.14	.29			
3	.20		.28	.22			
4	.09	.36	.36	.18			
5	.23	.41	.18		.20	.23	
6	.27	.27		.09	.29	.11	
7	.39	.19	.30	.50	.22	.25	

TABLE II(c). Ratio of Variances, ϵ

n \ m	1	2	3	4	5	6	7
1		.52	1.95	.30	2.09		
2		1.77	.81	1.24			
3	2.24		.62	3.21			
4	2.28	.46	1.15	2.02			
5	.50	2.25	3.53		2.53	1.70	
6	.48	3.63		1.25	4.01	2.42	
7	.37	1.82	4.51	.60	.21	3.13	

TABLE III. Computed Thresholds

n \ m	1	2	3	4	5	6	7
1							
2				.737			
3			.621				
4			.677				
5		.765				.831	
6	.429						
7	.428			.528			

TABLE IV. Interpolated Thresholds

n \ m	1	2	3	4	5	6	7
1	.670	.679	.688	.688	.688	.687	.721
2	.690	.673	.679	.686	.684	.719	.739
3	.688	.649	.674	.679	.718	.730	.724
4	.634	.688	.687	.649	.726	.791	.732
5	.597	.635	.721	.684	.677	.718	.732
6	.532	.501	.647	.687	.680	.701	.713
7	.429	.429	.537	.675	.658	.679	.693

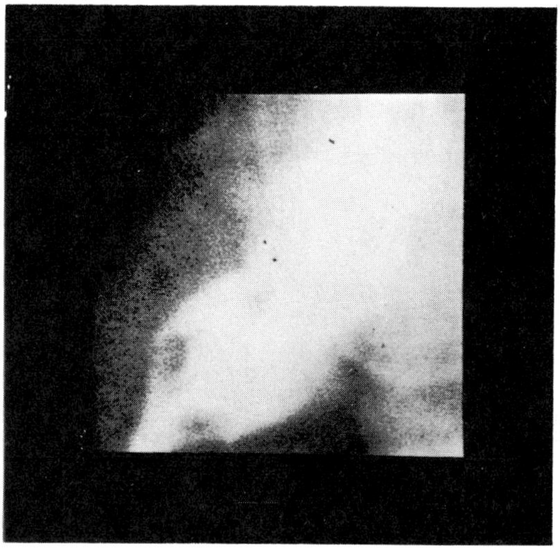

Figure 1. Cardioangiogram No. 1

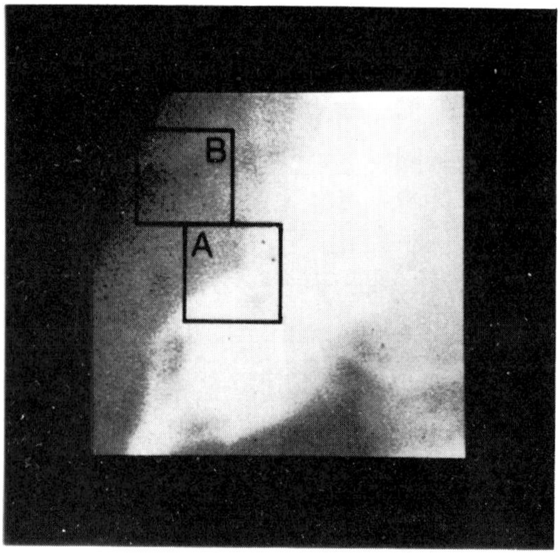

Figure 2. Regions A and B on Cardioangiogram No. 1

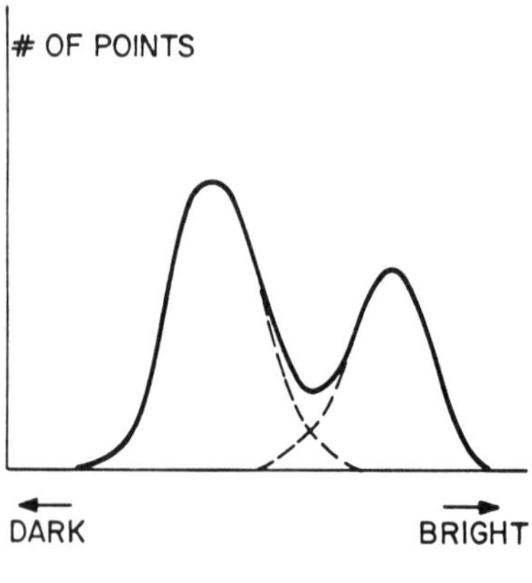

Figure 3. The histogram of a region containing boundary

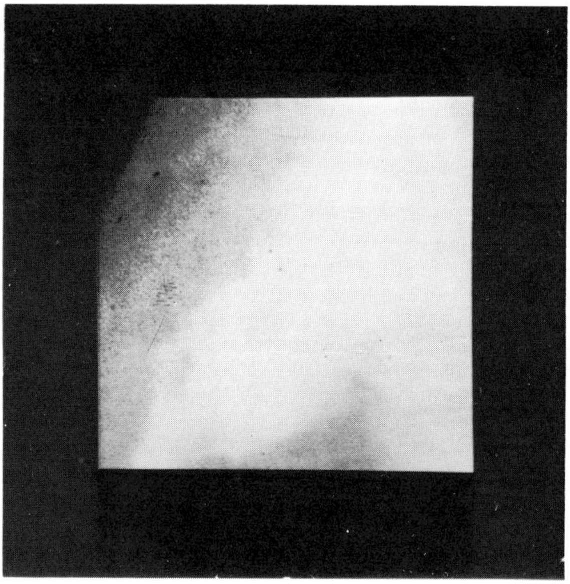

Figure 4. The logarithmic image of the cardioangiogram No. 1

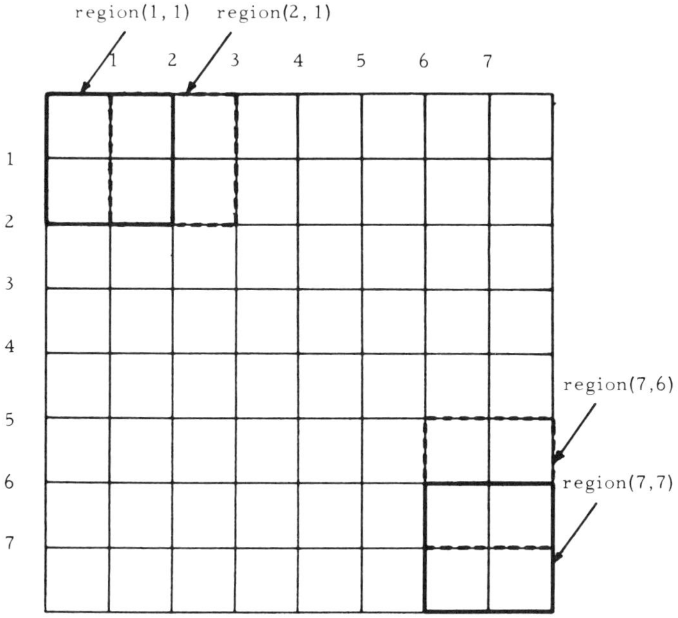

Figure 5. Assignment of 49 regions

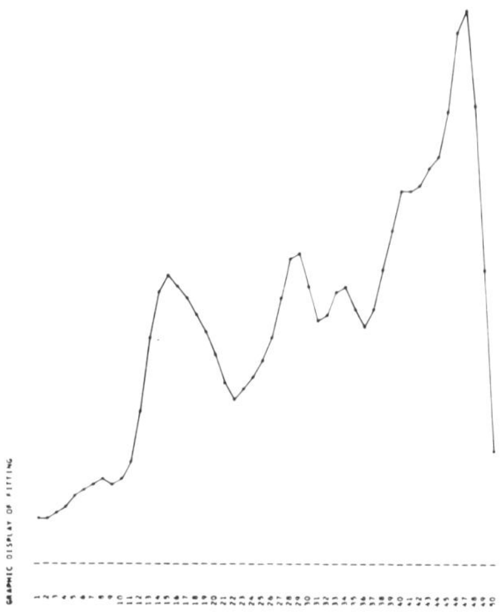

Figure 6. The histogram for the entire cardioangiogram No. 1

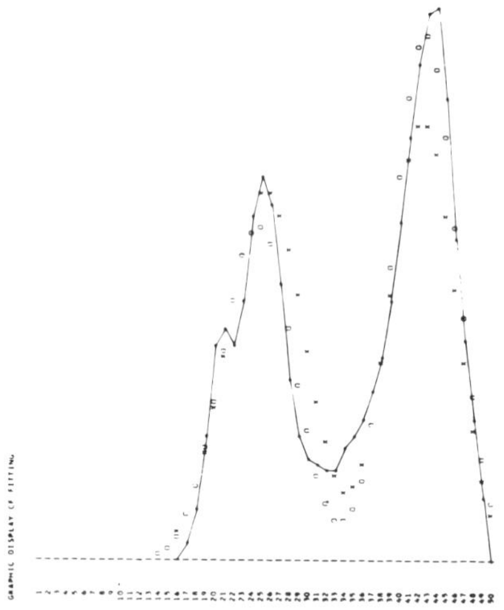

Figure 7. (a) The histogram for the region A in Figure 2

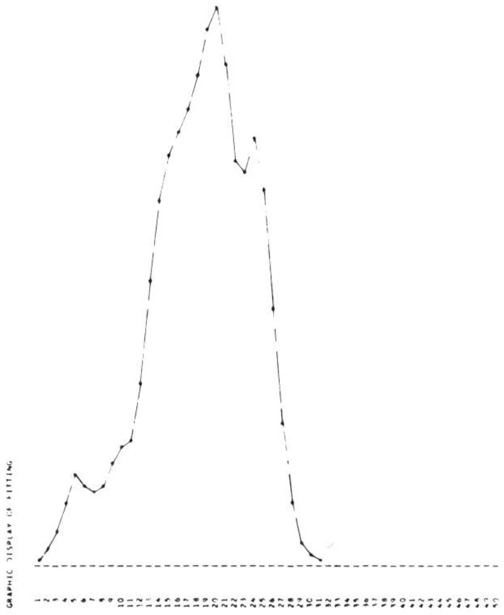

Figure 7. (b) The histogram for the region B in Figure 2

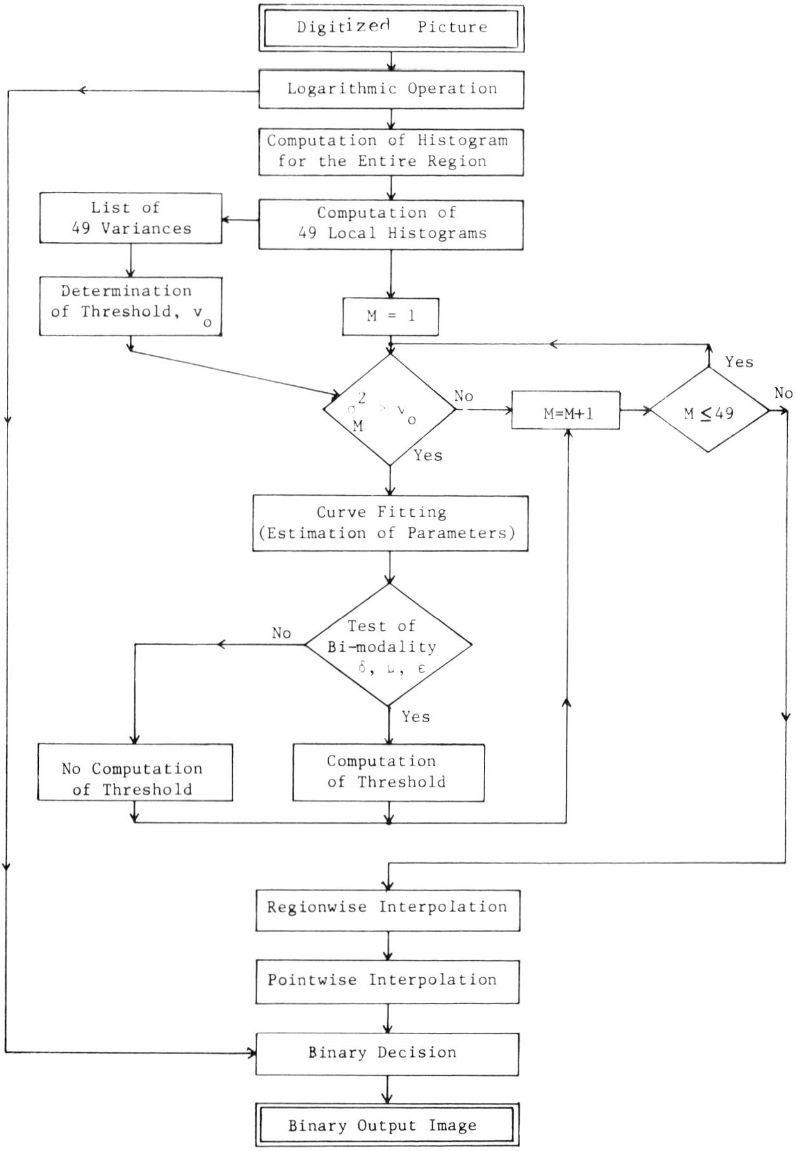

Figure 8. Flow chart of the computer program

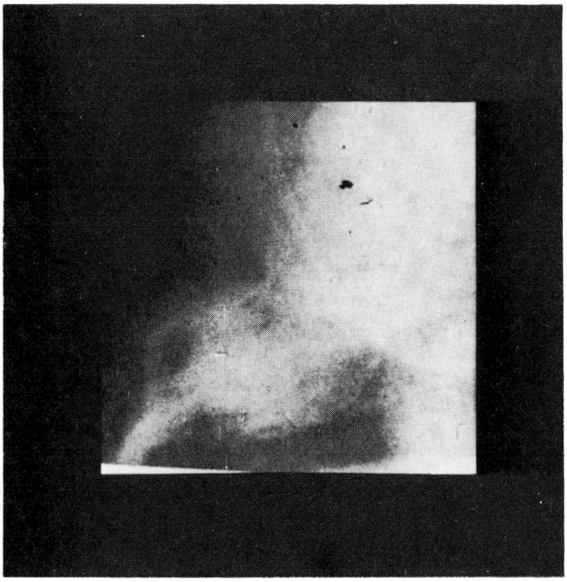

Figure 9. Cardioangiogram No. 2

Figure 10. The logarithmic image of the cardioangiogram No. 2

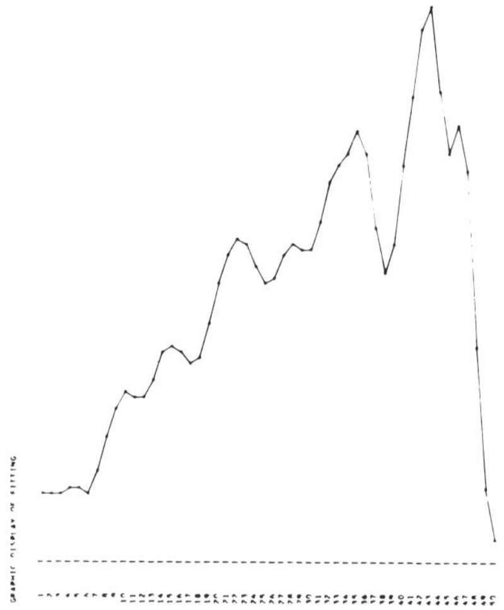

Figure 11. The histogram for the entire cardioangiogram No. 2

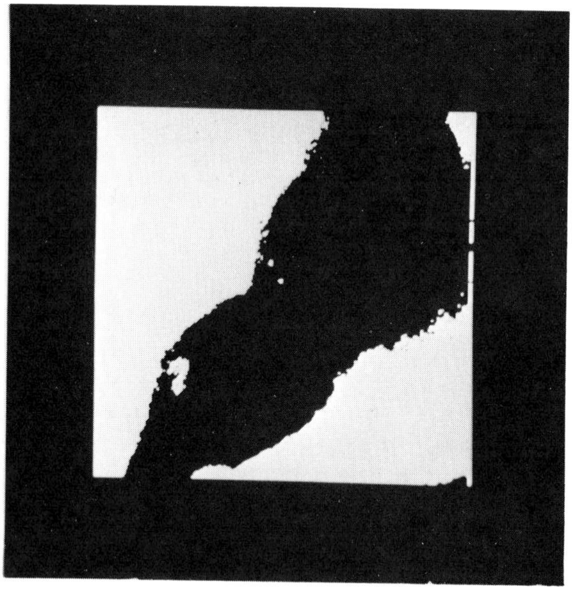

Figure 12. The binary image extracted from angiogram No. 1

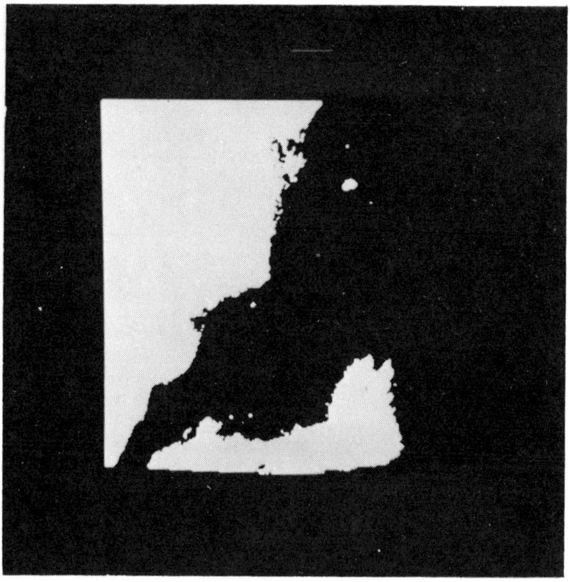

Figure 13. The binary image extracted from angiogram No. 2

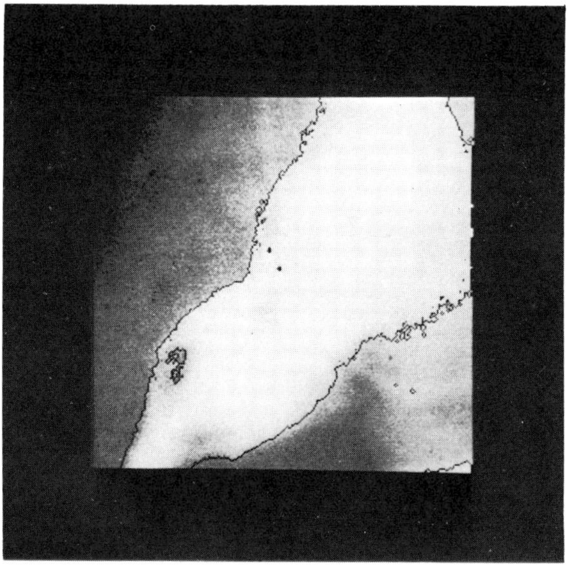

Figure 14. The binary image extracted from the image obtained by superimposing an artificial shade on angiogram No. 1

Figure 15

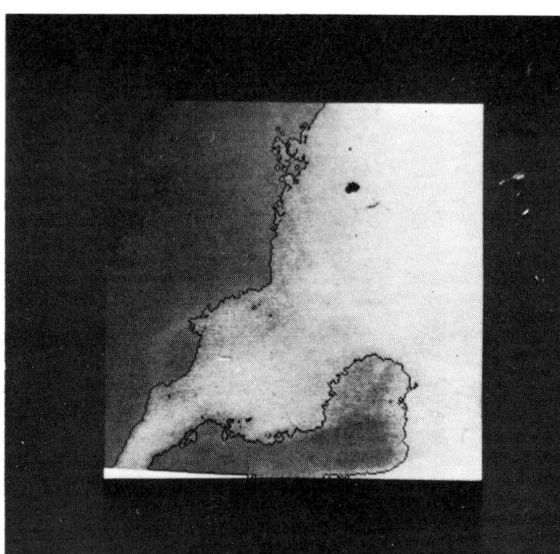

Figure 16

A HIERARCHY OF PROBABILITY DENSITY FUNCTION ESTIMATES

Thomas M. Cover

DEPARTMENT OF ELECTRICAL ENGINEERING
& STATISTICS
STANFORD UNIVERSITY

1. Abstract and Summary

The purpose of this paper is to consider a hierarchy of probability density function estimation procedures. The discussion will culminate in a speculation about a universal procedure. First the histogram approach will be investigated. We shall then consider the orthogonal function expansion approach, of which the histogram approach is a special case. Next in complexity is the slightly more complicated window function approach suggested by Parzen and Rosenblatt. One degree of freedom more is found in the approach of Loftsgaarden and Quesenberry in which the window size itself is allowed to be a function of the data.

Finally we ask ourselves what is meant by large, small and medium size samples. How should the number of degrees of freedom of the fitting densities grow with the size of the sample? What is the notion of intrinsic complexity of the underlying true distribution?

2. Introduction

Let $x_1, x_2, x_3, \ldots$ be a sequence of independent identically distributed random variables drawn according to some unknown underlying density function $f(x)$. It is desired to form a sequence of probability density function estimates $\hat{f}_n(x)$ depends only on $x_1, x_2, \ldots, x_n$. An excellent survey of various probability density function estimation procedures together with the modes of convergence, and in some cases the rates of convergence, may be found in Wegman [77] and Rosenblatt [57]. A fairly extensive list of references is also provided at the end of this paper [1-87].

3. The Histogram Approach

To fix ideas we shall consider only univariate random variables. The literature contains the multivariate extensions. In the histogram approach we have a partition of the real line into sets $S_1, S_2, \ldots$. A good estimate $\hat{f}_n(x)$ is given by letting $\hat{f}_n(x)$ be a constant over region S_i, where the constant is given by the proportion of the x_j's among $x_1, x_2, \ldots, x_n$ which fall in set S_i. Thus if g_i is the indicator function for the set S_i, we may write

$$\hat{f}_n(x) = \frac{1}{n}\sum_{j=1}^{n} g_i(x_j)\, g_i(x)$$

We may then readily verify that

$$\underset{x_1, x_2, \ldots, x_n}{E}\ \hat{f}_n(x) = \int_{S_i} f(x')dx', \quad \text{for } x \in S_i, \quad i = 1,2,\ldots,n.$$

Moreover, the variance of $\hat{f}_n(x)$ tends to zero as $1/n$.

The problems with this procedure are many. First, the partitioning of the space gives an undesirable quantization of the probability distribution--thus yielding estimates which are piecewise constant over the partitioning sets. Unless by some chance the true distribution were piecewise constant over these sets, there would be no hope of asymptotic convergence. Next, the partitioning has to be designed before the data is seen. This allows the possibility that almost all of the probability mass of the underlying distribution may lie in just one cell of the histogram partitioning and therefore that no useful density estimate will be obtained. Attempts to refine the partition as the number of observations tends to infinity are possible but are very clumsy in this framework. We shall see that the subsequent schemes due to Parzen, Rosenblatt, Loftsgaarden and Quesenberry are superior for this purpose.

4. The Orthogonal Function Approach

Let $\psi_1(x), \psi_2(x), \psi_3(x), \ldots$ be a sequence of orthonormal functions defined on the real line. Based on the sample $x_1, x_2, \ldots$ we wish to find a probability density function estimate $f_n(x)$ of the form

$$\hat{f}_n(x) = \sum_{i=1}^{k} c_i^{(n)}\ \psi_i(x)$$

In practice, the orthonormal functions are sometimes chosen to be the

Hermite polynomials, an apt choice when the underlying density is basically Gaussian with perhaps some correction terms. See for example the work by Schwartz [62-64] and also the review by Wegman [77].

Now let

$$J_n = \int \left(f(x) - \hat{f}_n(x) \right)^2 dx$$

Suppose first, for the sake of argument, that the underlying density is known, and it is desired to find the set of coefficients $c_1, c_2, \ldots c_k$ minimizing J_n. Setting to zero the partial derivatives of J_n with respect to c_i, we find that

$$c_i^* = \int f \psi_i = E \psi_i(X).$$

Now, since in fact f is not really known, a wise procedure would be to estimate the optimal coefficients from the data $X_1, X_2, \ldots, X_n$. Since the optimal coefficient c_i^* is equal to $E \psi_i(X)$, we estimate the expected value by

$$\hat{c}_i^* = \frac{1}{n} \sum_{j=1}^{n} \psi_i(x_j).$$

Note in particular that

$$E \hat{c}_i^* = \frac{1}{n} \sum_{j=1}^{n} E \psi_i(x_j) = c_i^*$$

Thus the estimate of the coefficients is unbiased. Moreover, since the $\psi_i(x_j)$ are independent random variables, the variance of the sum is the sum of the variances. Thus

$$\text{Var } \hat{c}_i^* = \frac{1}{n} \quad n \left(\text{Var } \psi_i(x) \right) = \sigma_i^{\,2}/n,$$

which tends to zero in the limit as n tends to infinity. Thus $\hat{c}_i^*$ is a consistent estimate of the optimal coefficient c_i^*.

Writing out the estimate $\hat{f}_n(x)$ using the estimates of the optimal coefficients, we have the nice formula

$$\hat{f}_n(x) = \frac{1}{n} \sum_{i=1}^{k} \sum_{j=1}^{n} \psi_i(x_j) \, \psi_i(x).$$

This expression if very reminiscent of the potential function formulation of

Aizerman, Braverman and Rozonoer.

Continuing, for known f we find that the mean squared error is now given by

$$J_n = \int f^2 - \int \hat{f}^2,$$

where $\hat{f}$ represents the projection of f onto the linear space spanned by $\psi_1, \ldots, \psi_k$. In case of unknown f with $x_1, x_2, \ldots, x_n$ known, we find that

$$E\,J_n = E\int (f-\hat{f}_n)^2 = E\int (f-\hat{f})^2 + E\int (\hat{f}-f_n)^2 = \int f^2 - \int \hat{f}^2 + \frac{1}{n}\sum_{i=1}^{n} \sigma_i^2$$

Thus we find that the expected value of J_n is equal to the projection error plus a statistical error. Luckily the statistical error tends to zero in the limit as $n \to \infty$. But a basic deficiency of this procedure, at least for a finite number of orthonormal functions is that there is a steady state projection error.

We wish to make the following comments on pdf estimation by orthogonal functions: 1) This approach is simply a generalized histogram approach. We see that the histogram approach can be expressed as an orthogonal function expansion by letting the ψ's be indicator functions for the cells S_i. 2) There is often the possibility that the orthogonal function $\hat{f}_n(x)$ expansion will be negative for some values of x and therefore not a possible probability density function. 3) There will be, in general, a steady-state projection error. 4) The scale of the ψ_i must be selected before the data is observed. Thus it may happen that all of the true density f lies in one cell of the histogram, so to speak; or, to put it another way, that the major part of f lies outside of the linear space spanned by the ψ_i. In any case, it would be nice to "peek" at the data before selecting the orthogonal functions for the expansion. One may actually observe a few observations in order to set the scale and translation parameters before one applies the procedure. However, in this case, the analysis which we have undertaken is invalid because all of the critical parameters such as ψ_i now depend on the data in a way not taken into account. For this reason, we need more sophisticated procedures where the data plays a larger role in the selection of the estimator function. Although extensions of the orthogonal functions approach have been made, we shall drop this approach for the time being.

5. Rosenblatt Estimator

Now let us consider an improvement on the histogram approach, sometimes called the naive pdf estimator. The Rosenblatt [53] estimate is of the form

$$\hat{f}_n(x) = \left(F_n(x+h) - F_n(x-h)\right) /2h,$$

where F_n is the empirical cdf of $x_1, x_2, \ldots, x_n$. In other words, the estimate of $f(x)$ at the point x, based on $x_1, x_2, \ldots, x_n$, is given by the proportion of hits of the x_i's in the window of width $2h$ centered at x. This proportion is then divided by $2h$ to form the estimate. Certainly the estimate appears to be good, since the proportion of hits in the cell is an estimate of the probability content of the cell and $2h$ is the total content of the cell. The ratio as $h \to 0$ is the probability density.

Another way of expressing $\hat{f}_n(x)$ is to define the indicator function

$$\psi_x(x') = \begin{cases} 1, & x' \epsilon \; [x-h, \; x+h] \\ 0, & \text{otherwise} \end{cases}$$

Then $\hat{f}_n(x)$ is equal to

$$\frac{1}{2nh} \sum_{i=1}^{n} \psi_x(x_i) \, .$$

Following Rosenblatt, let us calculate the expected value and variance of $\hat{f}_n$. First,

$$E\left(\hat{f}_n\right) = \frac{1}{2nh} \sum_{i=1}^{n} E \; \psi_x(x_i) \, .$$

But the $\psi_x(x_i)$'s are Bernoulli random variables taking on the values 1 and 0 with the probabilities

$$F(x+h) - F(x-h) \text{ and } 1 - F(x+h) + F(x-h)$$

respectively. Thus

$$E \; \hat{f}_n(x) = \frac{1}{2h} \left(F(x+h) - F(x-h)\right) .$$

Expanding this in a Taylor series expansion, and assuming the existence of the necessary derivatives, we obtain

$$E \; f_n(x) = f(x) + \frac{h^2}{6} \; f''(x) + 0(h^4).$$

Thus, for a window size h tending to zero, the bias of this estimate tends to zero.

In fact, these calculations hold for any sample size $n = 1,2,3, \ldots$ Thus we see that we can make the bias as small as we wish, even in the single sample case. Of course, the single sample case would result in a probability density function estimate which was extremely large a very small proportion of the time. Unbiased, yes, but the variance would be tremendous.

Now we calculate the variance of $\hat{f}_n(x)$,

$$\operatorname{Var} \hat{f}_n(x) = \operatorname{Var} \frac{1}{2nh} \sum_{i=1}^{n} \psi_x(X_i)$$

$$= \frac{1}{4n^2h^2} \left(n \operatorname{Var} \psi_x(X_i) \right)$$

$$= \frac{p(1-p)}{4nh^2} \quad ,$$

because, for independent random variables, the variance of the sum is the sum of the variances, and

$$p = \Pr\{ \psi_x(X_i) = 1 \} = 2hf + \frac{2h^3 f''(x)}{6} + 0(h^5) \; .$$

Collecting iterms, we have

$$E \left(\hat{f}_n(x) - f(x) \right)^2 = E \left(E \, \hat{f}_n(x) - \hat{f}_n(x) \right)^2 + \operatorname{Var} \hat{f}_n(x)$$

$$= \frac{f(x)}{2hn} + \frac{h^4}{36} \, | \, f''(x) \, |^2 + o\left(\frac{1}{hn} + h^4 \right) .$$

Thus the squared error of the approximation can be made to go to zero as long as h tends to zero and hn tends to infinity. Letting $h = kn^{\alpha}$, we see that the dominant terms can be minimized by setting the exponents equal, thus resulting in $h = kn^{-1/5}$ as the optimal rate of decrease of the window size. More careful analysis shows that the constant k should be $k = \left(9f(x)/2|f''(x)|^2\right)^{1/5}$.

6. Parzen Estimators

Parzen, at about the same time, investigated a general class of density estimation procedures based on his work on the estimation of spectral density functions from finite data. Consider

$$\hat{f}_n(x) = \frac{1}{h(n)} \sum_{i=1}^{n} K\left(\frac{x - x_i}{h(n)} \right).$$

For analysis of the behavior of this family of estimates, we will need the following lemma due to Bochner.

Lemma: Let K be bounded, absolutely integrable, and let

$|xK(x)| \to 0$ as $|x| \to \infty$. Let g be absolutely integrable and define

$$g_n(x) = \frac{1}{h(n)} \int K\left(\frac{x-y}{h(n)}\right) g(y)\, dy .$$

Then

$$g_n(x) \to g(x) \int K(y)\, dy, \text{ as } h(n) \to 0 ,$$

at every point of continuity of g.

The proof of Bochner's theorem is repeated in Parzen's 1965 paper [43]. Examples of kernal functions K which satisfy the hypotheses of Bochner's lemma are: a) the window function of Rosenblatt, b) $e^{-|x|}$, c) the normal density, d) the Cauchy density, and e) $(\sin^2 x)/x^2$.

We obtain the consistency of $\hat{f}_n(x)$ by applying Bochner's lemma twice. First, using the identical distribution of the X_i's,

$$\begin{aligned} E\ \hat{f}_n(x) &= \frac{1}{n} \sum_{i=1}^{n} E \frac{1}{h(n)} K\left(\frac{x-X_i}{h(n)}\right) \\ &= E \frac{1}{h(n)} K\left(\frac{x-X_i}{h(n)}\right) \\ &= \int \frac{1}{h(n)} K\left(\frac{x-y}{h(n)}\right) f(y)\, dy \\ &\to f(x) \int K(y)\, dy \\ &= f(x) \end{aligned}$$

if $\int K(y)\, dy = 1$.

Thus $\hat{f}_n(x)$ is asymptotically unbiased as $h(n) \to 0$. This result holds even when the X_i's are dependent random variables with marginal pdf $f(x)$.

Secondly, since the X_i's are independent,

$$\begin{aligned} \text{Var } \hat{f}_n(x) &= \text{Var } \frac{1}{n} \sum \frac{1}{h(n)} K\left(\frac{x-X_i}{h(n)}\right) \\ &= \frac{1}{n^2}\ n\ \text{Var } \frac{1}{h(n)} K\left(\frac{x-X_i}{h(n)}\right) \\ &\le \frac{1}{n} E\left(\frac{1}{h(n)} K\left(\frac{x-X_i}{h(n)}\right)\right)^2 \end{aligned}$$

$$= \frac{1}{nh(n)} \int \frac{1}{h(n)} K^2\left(\frac{x-y}{h(n)}\right) f(y)\, dy$$

Now,

$$\int \frac{1}{h(n)} K^2\left(\frac{x-y}{h(n)}\right) f(y)\, dy \to f(x) \int K^2(y)\, dy < \infty.$$

Thus

$$\operatorname{Var} \hat{f}_n(x) \to 0 \quad \text{as} \quad nh(n) \to \infty \cdot$$

Hence

$$E\left(f_n(x) - f(x)\right)^2 \to 0$$

if $h(n) \to 0$ (thus sending the squared bias term to zero) and $nh(n) \to \infty$ (thus sending the variance term to zero). Thus $\hat{f}_n(x)$ is a consistent estimate of $f(x)$ at every point of continuity of x if $h(n) \to 0$ and $nh(n) \to \infty$.

We note in particular that the obvious choice of scale $h(n) = \frac{1}{n}$ leaves a residual variance in the limit as $n \to \infty$. This is due to the fact that we are not smoothing the data enough. Similarly if $h(n)$ is equal to a constant, we are left with a steady-state bias term due to the over-smoothing of the density function.

We know by the Cramer-Rao lower bound that the expected squared error must be greater than or equal to $\frac{1}{nI}$ where I is an appropriate information measure. Parzen estimates can be chosen to converge at rates arbitrarily close to the rate $\frac{1}{n}$ if sufficient differentiability of f is assumed.

7. The Method of Loftsgaarden and Quesenberry

One of the problems with the two previous methods is that the scale parameters cannot be easily set. For example, in the Parzen procedure, the smoothing at time n corresponds to the scale parameter $h(n)$. Now if it just so happens that the range of the observations x_1 through x_n is less than or equal to $h(n)$, the smoothing will be much too great and the answer will be ridiculous. Parzen's theorem guarantees only that as n tends to infinity, $h(n)$ and n will bear a nice relationship guaranteeing a consistent estimate.

In practice we should cheat when applying Parzen's estimate. At time n, we should look at the data, estimate the amount of smoothing that it will tolerate, adjust $h(n)$ accordingly, and then calculate the Parzen estimate of the density. The trouble with all of this is that the analysis has been made under the assumption that $h(n)$ is a deterministic function independent of the data. Thus, the entire analysis would be invalidated by such a procedure and we would necessarily be forever suspicious of its convergence properties.

The method of Loftsgaarden and Quesenberry [36] effectively allows $h(n)$ to depend on the data. Their method is as follows. Suppose that $f(x)$ is to be estimated at the point x on the real line and that $x_1, x_2, \ldots, x_n$ are i.i.d. random variables drawn according to $f(x)$. Let k_n be some integer less than or equal to n. And let $h(n)$ be the distance to the k_nth closest point to x among the samples $x_1, x_2, \ldots, x_n$. Thus $h(n)$ is a random variable depending on the data. Now the length of the interval $[x-h(n), x+h(n)]$ is $2h(n)$. An estimate of the probability content of this interval is just the proportion of samples which fall in it, which we already know to be k_n/n. Thus it is reasonable to use

$$\hat{f}_n(x) = (k_n/n)/2h(n) = \frac{k_n}{2nh(n)}$$

as an estimate of the probability density function $f(x)$. Since we wish a local estimate of the pdf, choose k_n so that the proportion k_n/n tends to zero. If $k_n \to \infty$, $k_n/n \to 0$, it comes as no surprise that $\hat{f}_n(x)$ can be shown to be a consistent estimate of $f(x)$ at every point of continuity of x. This is shown on the paper by Loftsgaarden and Quesenberry [36] and will not be shown here.

This procedure offers several refinements over the usual histogram approach. First, we are "peeking" at the data in order to center the histogram cell about the desired point x; secondly, we are scaling the size of the histogram cell in such a manner that it contains neither too many nor too few data points. Too many would give over-smoothing and low variance; too few would give under-smoothing and high variance. Presumably, k_n is chosen so that the number of samples is just right in proportion to n. $k_n = \sqrt{n}$ is often used in practice.

8. Further Refinements

The existence of a succession of probability density function estimation procedures which takes into account ever more refined properties of the underlying density functions suggests that we may continue the refining process.

One problem with a more sophisticated approach is that it usually requires a larger sample size to yield good estimates. Ultimately, however, we can expect a more sophisticated procedure to converge faster and over a wider class of underlying densities.

The three factors at work in determining the appropriate degree of sophistication of the pdf estimator are 1) the number of degrees of freedom of the estimator, 2) the expected number of degrees of freedom of the underlying density, and 3) the number of degrees of freedom of the data, i.e., the sample size n.

It is useful to consider the parametric density function estimation problem for a moment. Suppose that $x_1, x_2, \ldots, x_n$ are independent, identically distributed according to a normal distribution $N(\mu, 1)$ with unknown mean μ. The estimation which is usually performed in this case is to estimate μ by some good estimator such as $\bar{x}_n$ and then estimate the density by $N(\bar{x}_n, 1)$. This works well because we are dealing with a parametric family of distributions, and a good estimate of the parameter yields a good estimate for the density (obviously if we had parametrized the distributions in a terrible and discontinuous way, this statement would not hold).

It is probably possible to classify the family of all pdf's by their complexity. The low complexity density functions would include, for example, the uniform distributions over fixed intervals, finite unions of uniform distributions, and normal distributions, and other distributions which have very simple descriptions. Next in complexity would come the distributions which are highly multimodal but relatively smooth. Obviously, these distributions will require a large number of samples before we are in any position to estimate the distribution precisely. For example, if the underlying density has n modes, it would certainly be foolish to expect that we could identify the position of these modes before we had observed roughly n samples or more. So we see quickly that for any sample size n it is very easy to come up with a probability density function that will be poorly estimated by n samples. For example, we might have a uniform distribution except for a spike of width ϵ^2 and height $\frac{1}{\epsilon}$. Thus the sample size necessary to detect the position of this spike would be at least $\frac{1}{\epsilon^2}$, and until $n \geq 1/\epsilon^2$, the estimate of the pdf would differ in sup-norm form from the true pdf by at least $\frac{1}{\epsilon}$.

We wish to have a hierarchy of pdf estimators of increasing complexity. For example, if the true underlying density function is a normal distribution with unknown mean, but this is not known a priori, then after observing a sufficiently large number of samples, we would begin to suspect that this is indeed the case, that in fact the underlying density function is a normal distribution--which is what often happens in practice. In this situation we would then simply estimate the mean and variance and correction terms. This procedure would look for small correction terms to the normal distribution and would be extremely effective. Certainly additional samples might throw some doubt on our tentative conclusion that the underlying density function is essentially normal. Then we would be free to jump to some other conclusion and adapt our procedure about it.

The question is whether this disorderly jumping around from procedure to procedure on the basis of some peeking at the data will still allow convergence. Practically speaking, we know that convergence will continue to hold, although the theoretical justification will probably be quite difficult. However, what is more to the point is whether we can actually converge to the true pdf as fast as a person who has a great deal more a priori knowledge and who realizes that the unknown pdf is a member of some parametric family. All that would be necessary for our convergence rate to equal that of the parametric pdf estimator would be that we would eventually be able to guess that we belonged in the appropriate parametric family.

Therefore I propose the following approach. First, let us enumerate all finite algorithms generating probability density functions. Next, at time n calculate the likelihoods of $x_1, x_2, \ldots, x_n$ under each of this infinite collection of pdfs. Among the first $\tau(n)$ pdfs choose that one for which $x_1, x_2, \ldots, x_n$ is most likely. This in some sense is the likeliest, simplest pdf. We shall let $\tau(n)$ be a function growing slowly with n. Certainly all density functions like the normal and the Cauchy and the union of uniforms will lie somewhere on this list and $\tau(n)$ will eventually grow without bound and include any particular density function on the list. And if, in fact, this density function is the true one, the likelihood of $x_1, x_2, \ldots, x_n$ under this density will soon dominate all the other likelihoods.

And just so long as $\tau(n)$ does not grow so fast that spurious candidates for pdfs have extremely high likelihoods on insufficiently small samples of data, we are guaranteed to be in the position of essentially guessing the parametric family and then estimating the underlying parameters. We have a chance of doing extremely well; certainly better than the procedures mentioned in the previous sections.

This program is far from precise and it is by no means clear whether the details and theoretical analysis could be carried out in practice. In any case, the practical applications of such an ultimate procedure would not be very great. However, in defense of these comments it should be said that all of empirical physics, chemistry and science has been accomplished more in the spirit of this last section than in the spirit of the previous sections. Thus we "know" that noise distributions on measurements are Gaussian and we "know" that the laws of physics read $F = ma$ and not $F = ma^{1.000001}$. A kernal function estimator would treat 1.0000 . . . . . and 1.00001 much the same and would miss forever the thrill of leaping from conviction to conviction to conviction.

REFERENCES

1. Aizerman, M. A., E. M. Braverman, and L. I. Rozonoer, "The Probability Problem of Pattern Recognition Learning and the Method of Potential Functions", Automation & Remote Control, Vol. 26, 1964.
2. Anderson, Gary (1969), "A comparison of probability density estimates," Presented at the Institute of Mathematical Statistics Annual Meeting, August 19-22, New York.
3. Bartlett, M. S. "Periodogram analysis and continuous spectra" Biometrika 37, 1950, 1-16.
4. Bartlett, M. S. (1963), "Statistical estimation of density functions," *Sankhyā (A), 25,* pp. 245-254.
5. Bhattacharya, P. K. (1967), "Estimation of a probability density function and its derivatives", *Sankhyā (A), 29,* part 4, pp. 373-382.
6. Brillinger, D. R. and Rosenblatt, M.,"Asymptotic theory of estimates of kth order spectra" *Advanced Seminar on Spectral Analysis of Time Series* (ed. B. Harris) 1967, 153-188.
7. Brillinger, D. R. and Rosenblatt, M., "Computation and interpretation of kth order spectra" *Advanced Seminar on Spectral Analysis of Time Series* (ed. B. Harris) 1967, 189-232.
8. Brillinger, D. R. "The spectral analysis of stationary interval functions" Proc. 6th Berkeley Symposium on Probability and Math. Stat.
9. Cacoullos, Theophiles (1966), "Estimation of a multivariate density," *Annals of the Institute of Statistical Mathematics, 18,* pp. 178-189.
10. Čencov, N. N. (1962), "Evaluation of an unknown distribution density from observations," *Soviet Math., 3,* pp. 1559-1562.
11. Cramér, H. and Leadbetter, M. R. *Stationary and Related Processes* 1967, John Wiley.
12. Craswell, W. J. (1965), "Density estimation in a topological group," *Ann. Math. Statist., 36,* pp. 1047-1048.
13. Daniels, H. "Saddlepoint approximations in statistics" Ann. Math. Statist. 25, 1964, 631-650.
14. Edgeworth, F. Y. (1904), "The law of error," *Trans. Camb. Phil. Soc., 20,* pp. 36 and 113.
15. Elderton, W. P. and Johnson, N. L. (1969), *Systems of Frequency Curves,* Cambridge University Press.
16. Elkins, T. A. (1968), "Cubical and Spherical estimation of a multivariate probability density," *JASA, 63,* pp. 1495-1513.
17. Epanechnikov, V. A. "Nonparametric estimates of a multivariate probability density" Theor. Prob. Appl. 14, 1969, 153-158.
18. Farrell, R. H. (1967), "On the lack of a uniformly consistent sequence of estimators of a density function in certain cases," *Ann. Math. Statist., 38,* pp. 471-474.
19. Fisher, L. and J. W. Van Ness, "Distinguishability of Probability Measures", Ann. Math. Stat., Vol. 40, pp. 381-392, 1969.

20. Fisher, R. A. (1912), "On an absolute criterion for fitting frequency curves," *Mess. of Math., 41,* pp. 155-160.
21. Fix, Evelyn and Hodges, J. L., Jr. (1951), "Nonparametric discrimination: consistency properties." Report Number 4, Project Number 21-49-004, USAF School of Aviation Medicine, Randolph Field, Texas, February, 1951.
22. Frenkiel, F. N. and Klebanoff, P. S. "Two-dimensional probability distribution in a turbulent field" Phys. Fluids 8, 1965, 2291-2293.
23. Gessaman, M. P. (1970), "A consistent nonparametric multivariate density estimator based on statistically equivalent blocks," to appear *Ann. Math. Statist.,* August, 1970.
24. Grenander, Ulf (1956), "On the theory of mortality measurement, Part II," *Skan. Aktuarieltidskr., 39,* pp. 125-153.
25. Grenander, U. and Rosenblatt, M. *Statistical Analysis of Stationary Time Series* 1957, John Wiley.
26. Hasselman, K., Munk, W. and MacDonald, G. "Bispectra of ocean waves" *Time Series Analysis* (ed. M. Rosenblatt) 1963.
27. Hodges, J. L. Jr. and Lehmann, E. L. "The efficiency of some nonparametric competitors of the t-test" Ann. Math. Statist. 27, 1956, 324-335.
28. Huber, P. J., Kleiner, B., Gassep, Th. and Dumermuth, G. "Statistical methods for investigating phase relations in stationary stochastic processes" to appear in the IEEE Transactions on Audio and Electroacoustics.
29. Kashyap, R. L., and C. C. Blaydon, "Estimation of Probability Density and Distribution Functions", IEEE Trans. on Info. Theory, Vol. IT-14, pp. 459-556, 1968.
30. Kendall, M. G. (1948), *The Advanced Theory of Statistics,* Vol. 1, Charles Griffin and Co., Ltd., London.
31. Kendall, M. G. and Stewart, A. (1958), *The Advanced Theory of Statistics,* Vol. 1, Charles Griffin and Co., Ltd., London.
32. Kolmogorov, A. "On the approximation of distributions of sums of independent summands by infinitely divisible distributions" Sankhya Ser. A 25, 1963, 159-174.
33. Kowalski, C. and Tarter. M. (1968), "On the simultaneous estimation of density and distribution functions with application to C-type density estimation," an unpublished manuscript.
34. Kronmal, R. and Tarter, M. (1968), "The estimation of probability densities and cumulatives by Fourier Series methods," *JASA, 38,* pp. 482-493.
35. Leadbetter, M. R. (1963), "On the non-parametric estimation of probability densities," Technical Report No. 11, Research Triangle Institute. (Doctoral dissertation at the University of North Carolina at Chapel Hill.)
36. Loftsgaarden, D. O. and Quesenberry, C. P. (1965), "A Nonparametric Estimate of a Multivariate Density Function", Ann. Math. Stat., Vol. 38, pp. 1261-1265.
37. Loftsgaarden, D. O. and Quesenberry, C. P. (1965), "A non-parametric estimate of a multivariate density function," *Ann. Math. Statist., 38,* pp. 1261-1265.
38. Moore, P. S. and Henrichon, E. G. (1969), "Uniform consistency of some estimates of a density function," *Ann. Math. Statist., 40,* pp. 1499-1502.

39. Murthy, V. K. (1965), "Estimation of probability density," *Ann. Math. Statist., 36,* pp. 1027-1031.
40. Nadaraya, É. A. (1963), "On estimation of density functions of random variables" *Soobach. Akad. Nauk. Grugin SSR, XXXII, 2,* pp. 277-280. (In Russian.)
41. Nadaraya, É. A., (1965), "On non-parametric estimates of density functions and regression curves," *Theory Prob. Appl., 10,* pp. 186-190.
42. Parzen, E. "Mathematical considerations in the estimation of spectra" Technometrics 3, 1961, 167-190.
43. Parzen, E. (1962), "On the estimation of a probability density function and the mode," *Ann. Math. Statist., 33,* pp. 1065-1076.
44. Pearson, E. S. (1969), "Some historical reflections traced through the development of the use of frequency curves," Technical Report 38, Department of Statistics, Southern Methodist University.
45. Pearson, K. (1902), "On the systematic fitting of curves to observations and measurements, I," *Biometrika, 1,* pp. 265-303.
46. Pearson, K. (1902), "On the systematic fitting of curves to observations and measurements, II," *Biometrika, 2,* pp. 1-23.
47. Pickands, J. (1969), "Efficient estimation of a probability density function," *Ann. Math. Statist., 40,* pp. 854-864.
48. Quesenberry, C. P. and Scheult, A. H. (1969), "On unbiased estimation of density function," Abstracted *Ann. Math. Statist., 40,* pp. 2224.
49. Rao, B. L. S. P. (1969), "Estimation of a unimodal density," *Sankhyā (A)*, 31, pp. 26-36.
50. Révész, Pal (1968), *The Laws of Large Numbers,* Academic Press.
51. Robertson, T. (1967), "On estimating a density which is measurable with respect to a σ lattice," *Ann. Math. Statist., 38,* pp. 482-493.
52. Robertson, T., Cryer, J. D., and Rogg, R. V. (1968), "On non-parametric estimation of distributions and their modes," an unpublished manuscript.
53. Rosenblatt, M. (1956), "Remarks on some nonparametric estimates of a density function," *Ann. Math. Statist., 27,* pp. 832-837.
54. Rosenblatt, M. "Statistical analysis of stochastic processes with stationary residuals" *H. Cramér Volume* (ed. U. Grenander) 1959, 246-275.
55. Rosenblatt, M. "Conditional probability density and regression estimates" *Multivariate Analysis Vol. 2* (ed. Krishnaiah) 1969, 25-31.
56. Rosenblatt, M. "Density estimates and Markov sequences" *Nonparametric Techniques in Statistical Inference* (ed. M. Puri) 1970, 199-210.
57. Rosenblatt, M.,"Curve Estimates", presented at the Institute of Mathematical Statistics Meeting, August 25-27, 1970, Laramie, Wyoming.
58. Roussas, G. "Nonparametric estimation in Markov processes" Ann. Inst. Statist. Math. 1969, 21, 73-87.
59. Sazanov, V. V. "On the multidimensional central limit theorem" Sankhya Ser. A. 30, 1968, 181-204.
60. Schuster, E. F. (1969), "Estimation of a probability density function and its derivatives," *Ann. Math. Statist., 40,* pp. 1187–1195.

61. Schuster, E. F. (1970), "Note on the uniform convergence of density estimates," *Ann. Math. Statist.*, Vol. *41*, August, 1970, 1347-48.
62. Schwartz, S. C. (1967), "Estimation of a probability density by an orthogonal series," *Ann. Math. Statist.*, *38*, pp. 1261-1265.
63. Schwartz, Stewart (1969), "Estimation of density functions by orthogonal series and an application to hypothesis testing," Presented at the Institute of Mathematical Statistics Annual Meeting, August 19-22, New York.
64. Schwartz, S., "An Example of Nonsupervised Adaptive Pattern Classification", IEEE Transactions on Automatic Control, Vol. AC-13, pp. 107-108, 1968.
65. Sclove, S. L. and Van Ryzin, J., "Estimating the Parameters of a Convolution", Journal of the Royal Statistical Society, Series B, Vol. 31, No. 1, pp. 181-191, 1969.
66. Tarter, M. E., Holcomb, R. L., and Kronmal R. A. (1967), "A description of new computer methods for estimating the population density," *Proc. A. C. M.*, Thompson Book Company, *22*, pp. 511-519.
67. Tarter, M. and Kronmal, R. (1970), "On multivariate density estimates based on orthogonal expansions," *Ann. Math. Statist.*, 41, pp. 718 -722.
68. Tsypkin, Y. Z., "Use of the Stochastic Approximation Method in Estimating Unknown Distribution Densities from Observations", Automatika i Telemekhanika, Vol. 27, No. 3, pp. 44-96, 1966.
69. Tukey, J. W. "An introduction to the measurement of spectra" *H. Cramér Volume* (ed. U. Grenander) 1959, 300-330.
70. Van Ness, J. "Asymptotic normality of bispectral estimates" Ann. Math. Statist. 37, 1966, 1257-1272.
71. Van Ryzin, J. (1969), "On strong consistency of density estimates," *Ann. Math. Statist.*, *40*, pp. 1765-1772.
72. Van Ryzin, J. (1970) "On a histogram method of density estimation," Presented at the Institute of Mathematical Statistics Meeting, April 8-10, Dallas, Tech. Report #226, Dept. of Stat., Univ. Wisconsin.
73. Venter, J. H. (1967), "On estimation of the mode," *Ann. Math. Statist.*, *38*, pp. 1446-1455.
74. Wahba, Grace (1970), "A polynomial algorithm for density estimation," submitted to *Ann. Math. Statist.*
75. Watson, G. S. and Leadbetter, M. R. (1963), "On estimating a probability density, I," *Ann. Math. Statist.*, *34*, pp. 480-491.
76. Watson, G. S. (1969), "Density estimation by orthogonal series," *Ann. Math. Statist.*, *40*, pp. 1496-1498.
77. Wegman, E. J. (1969), "Nonparametric probability density estimation," invited paper at the Institute of Mathematical Statistics meeting, April 8-10, 1970, Dallas; submitted to *JASA*.
78. Wegman, E. J. (1969), "A note on estimating unimodal density," *Ann. Math. Statist.*, *40*, pp. 1661-1667.
79. Wegman, E. J. (1970), "Maximum likelihood estimation of a unimodal density function," *Ann. Math. Statist.*, 41, pp. 457-471.

80. Wegman, E. J. (1969),"Maximum likelihood histograms," Institute of Statistics Mimeo Series #629, University of North Carolina at Chapel Hill.
81. Wegman, E. J. (1970), "Maximum likelihood estimation of a unimodal density, II" to appear *Ann. Math. Statist.*, December, 1970.
82. Weiss, L. and Wolfowitz, J. (1967), "Estimation of a density at a point," *Zeitschrift für Wahrscheinlichkeitstheorie und verwandte Gebiete, 7,* pp. 327-335.
83. Whittle, P. (1958), "On smoothing of probability density functions," *JRSS (B), 20,* pp. 334-343.
84. Woodroofe, M. (1967), "On the maximum deviation of the sample density," *Ann. Math. Statist., 38,* pp. 475-481.
85. Woodroofe, M. (1968), "On choosing a delta sequence," Technical Report No. 10, Department of Statistics, Carnegie-Mellon University, Pittsburgh, Pennsylvania. (Abstracted, *Ann. Math. Statist., 39,* pp. 700.)
86. Yaglom, A. M. "The influence of fluctuations in energy dissipationoon the shape of turbulence characteristics in the inertial interval" Soviet Physics–Doklady 11, 1966, 26-29.
87. Yakowitz, S., "A Consistent Estimator for the Identification of Finite Mixtures", Ann. Math. Stat., Vol. 40, p. 1728, 1969.

ON EMBEDDING HEURISTICS AND INCLUDING COMPLEXITY CONSTRAINTS INTO CONVERGENT LEARNING ALGORITHMS*

Sándor Csibi

TELECOMMUNICATION RESEARCH INSTITUTE
BUDAPEST, HUNGARY

Abstract

In this paper we are concerned with learning algorithms which are, in a sense, between series and parallel processing. More distinctly, such iterative learning procedures are considered which may also include a fairly broad class of complex (and even partly heuristically defined) processing steps. Constraints are set up under which such procedures do precisely learn discriminant functions. It is shown, how may one, while retaining convergence, confine the iteration to some fixed search domain, and also keep the required storage under control. These topics are of interest e.g., if (because of complexity) neither completely simultaneous nor subsequent, one by one, handling of the observations appears to be feasible.

Techniques of this sort offer in compound machine learning further possibilities to combine, what may be called, mid- and end- procedures.

1. Comments on Various Ways of Handling Data

Let us confine ourselves, for the sake of simplicity, to learning with a teacher.

Assume that pairs $(\omega_0, \Theta(\omega_0)), \ldots (\omega_t \Theta(\omega_t))$ of labelled samples are presented either at the same time or after another. Let the objects $\omega_0, \ldots \omega_t$ be drawn from, say, some Euclidean space Ω, and assume $\Theta(\omega_\vartheta)$ to take real values, by which each object $\omega_\vartheta (\vartheta = \overline{0,1})$ may, in some way, be associated with a given hypothesis H (e.g., (i) the sign of $\Theta(\omega_\vartheta)$ may indicate whether a hypothesis H is true or not, or (ii) the value, $\Theta(\omega_\vartheta)$ takes, may

*Presented at the International Conference on Frontiers of Pattern Recognition, Honolulu, Hawaii, January 1971.

express a grade of membership. For instance $\Theta(\omega_\vartheta)$ may, if confined to $[0,1]$, specify the a posteriori probability of H, given ω_ϑ.)

Posing the problem in this way, the task of machine learning appears as estimating, by means of a set $\Lambda_t = \{\omega_\vartheta, \Theta(\omega_\vartheta); \vartheta = \overline{0,t}\}$ of labelled samples, the discriminant function $\Theta = \{\Theta(\omega), \omega \in \Omega\}$.

We denote by $Z_t = \{Z_t(\omega), \omega \in \Omega\}$ that very estimate of Θ we propose after having observed the set Λ_t of all labeled samples, up to t. It is, of course, a question of principal interest how does, as $t \to \infty$, Z_t approach to Θ. Nevertheless, one is also very much interested to keep as $t \to \infty$, the amount of computations and storage, required at any step, under appropriate control. One is particularly interested in so doing, if learning Θ apparently needs excessive efforts.

Obviously, nothing is done for this sake, when all available data Λ_t, observed up to t, are stored at the same time; though this approach offers most freedom to include into Z_t all what we know, up to t. It seems quite natural to term, in what follows, this way of handling data parallel processing.

While parallel processing offers obvious advantages when implementable, these sort of procedures usually run out of storage if (i) either the amount of observations is excessive or (ii) observations have to be prolonged indefinitely. Anyhow also, in involved data processing, parallel processing offers a good tool to start with.

Another well known way of data handling is to introduce $\omega_t (t=0,1,\ldots)$ into computations after another, creating, at each instant t, an estimate of Θ by some iteration rule of the following form:

$$Z_{t+1} = \Psi(Z_t, \omega_t, \Theta(\omega_t)). \tag{1}$$

(Here Ψ stands for a mapping from $A \times \Omega \times (-\infty,\infty)$ onto A, A denotes the space of admitted classification functions and estimates. We take as an initial estimate some $Z_0 \in A$.)

Unfortunately, just by adopting iteration, one does not necessarily get rid of parallel processing. To show this we borrow a well known example from Cover[7], concerning the Wagner-Wolverton learning algorithm[38] in iterative form:

$$Z_{t+1}(\omega) = \frac{t}{t+1} Z_t(\omega) + \frac{\operatorname{sign}\Theta(\omega_t)}{(t+1)h_t} \; k\left(\frac{\omega - \omega_t}{h_t}\right) \tag{2}$$

for all $\omega \in \Omega$. (Here k stands for some window function and h_t a scaling coefficient of the sort introduced already in Parzen's probability density estimates[26].)

As a matter of fact (2) may be rewritten as follows:

$$Z_{t+1}(\omega) = \frac{t}{t+1} \sum_{\vartheta=1}^{t} \frac{\sin\Theta(\omega_\vartheta)}{h_\vartheta} \; k \left(\frac{\omega - \omega_\vartheta}{h_\vartheta}\right) + Z_o(\omega) \qquad (13)$$

It is obvious from (3) that, in order to obtain Z_{t+1}, one may have to store all samples in Ω_t: if this is the case iteration rule (2) represents a sort of parallel processing.

A way out of this is to constrain further the class of admitted estimates. This may be done if there is, also for Θ, some appropriate further constraint evident.

Assume, specifically, the space of admitted classification functions to be a Hilbert space (e.g., of finite, but excessive, dimensions). Assume Θ to be confined to some subspace $\bar{A} \subset A$ of some feasible dimension $\tilde{n}$, and let us constrain all estimates $Z_t (t = 0,1, \ldots)$ also to $\bar{A}$. Denote for any $\eta \in A$, by $\bar{\Psi}(\eta)$ the projection of $\Psi(\eta)$ to $\bar{A}$.

Then one may constrain, for all t the estimate Z_t, to a subspace of fixed finite dimension $\tilde{n}$, provided (1) is replaced by

$$Z_{t+1} = \bar{\Psi}(Z_t, \omega_t, \Theta(\omega_t)) \qquad (4)$$

(We have to start this time, of course, at some $Z_o \in \bar{A}$.)

Confining, however, the statistics Z_t to some fixed finite dimension does not yet settle the problem of storage constraint. We refer this time again to Cover[6,5] and Hellmann and Cover[21], who pointed out a number of basic aspects of this problem, and also showed interesting techniques how to get, in specific cases of hypothesis testing, also theoretically more close to what is actually needed.

A well known trivial transition to finite (i.e. finite range) statistics is by rounding-off which, however, needs a control of cumulated rounding-off errors. We impose, in Section 2, a constraint on how should, as $t \to \infty$, the rounding-off steps decay, in order to retain convergence also for a sort of random rounded-off iterations.[32,15] While this is a very rough approach, it still gives some insight how may one keep the transition from finite-dimensional to finite statistics within the scope of an irrelevant perturbation. (The needed storage may be, of course, specified in this case only after having adopted some sort of termination, which is an obvious drawback, one may, however, accept when adopting rounded-off iterations.)

Keeping this in mind, we will consider, in what follows, finite dimensional estimates of Θ, as first rough steps toward introducing storage constraints,and handling really the data one by one. We will therefore view, in the sequel, (4) as a prototype of series processings.

However, in actual situations, generating at $t+1$ the new estimate Z_{t+1}, as we did in (1) and (4), just by means of the most recent labeled sample $(\omega_t, \Theta(\omega_t))$ and estimate Z_t, may lead to excessively slow approximation. It is, therefore, of interest to master the learning capabilities of broader and more efficient classes of iterative processes also. Such procedures may be written as

$$Z_{t+1} = \overline{\Psi}(Z^t, \omega^t, \Theta^t) . \tag{5}$$

(Here $Z^t = \{Z_\vartheta, \vartheta \leq t\}$, $\omega^t = \{\omega_\vartheta, \vartheta \leq t\}$ and $\Theta^t = \{\Theta(\omega_\vartheta), \vartheta \leq t\}$.)

Obviously, concerning (5), only iteration rules, depending (exactly, or at least essentially) on a finite past, prior to t, are of actual interest. (We refer in another paper, to such iteration rules as rules with weak memory[9].)

A number of specific procedures in machine learning[31], deterministic optimation[27,25] and stochastic approximation[32], show that by governing iteration processes in this way, by some appropriate more global overview (including also previous data, as admitted by (5)) remarkable acceleration may be achieved.

On the other hand Dvoretzky[14], and, more recently Braverman and Rozonoer[4] and Györfi[18] in a more general context, proved convergence constraints for fairly general iterative procedures including also capabilities of this sort.

We show, in the sequel, how may one essentially broaden the class of such learning procedures while keeping convergence under control.

We obtain in this way additional new possibilities to (i) embed also complex (and even partly heuristically defined) processing steps and (ii) introduce constraints on storage and search domain in a fairly simple way.

2. An Approach to the Embedding Problem

We confine ourselves to estimates Z_t of Θ, generated by iteration with a priori weighted corrections. Viz., we set $Z_t = X_t$ (at each $t \in T = (0,1,\ldots)$), where the process $X_t = \{X_t, t \in T\}$ is defined successively, starting at some arbitrary $X_0 \in A_\Theta \subset \overline{A}$, by

$$X_{t+1} = \Phi(X_t + \alpha_t W_t). \tag{6}$$

Here (i) $\alpha = \{\alpha_t\}_{t=0}^{\infty}$ stands for an a priori fixed sequence of positive numbers by which the correction term in (6) may, also a priori, be held under control, (ii) Φ denotes a truncation (to be specified in the sequel) by which the range of X is kept, for all $t \in T$, within some given $A_\Theta \subset \overline{A} \subset A$.

The iteration is governed, at any t, by W_t, what we call in the sequel regulator. This is an a priori fixed function of ω^t, Θ^t and Z^t, which takes its values from A. I.e. the regulator W is a member of the set A of admissible discriminating functions. (See examples in the sequel.) The iteration rule (6) is obviously a specific case of rules of the form (5).

In order to retain, in a natural and simple way, convergence also for truncated iterations, we confine A_Θ to be, specifically, a parallelepiped, spanned by some base $\{e_i\}_{i=0}$ in A, and adopt a truncation operator Φ which causes, what may be called, limiting at the surface of this parallelepiped. More precisely: (i) We assume that $A_\Theta = \{a_i \leq \langle \eta, e_i \rangle \leq b_i; i = 1,2, \ldots\}$ $(-\infty \leq a_i \leq b_i \leq \infty$ denoting the vertex-coordinates. We let $a_i < b_i$ only for at most $\tilde{n} \leq \dim A$ different i, by which A_Θ is actually kept within some subspace $\bar{A}$ of dimensions $\tilde{n}$.) (ii) We define the truncation operator Φ precisely, by:

$$\Phi(\eta) = \eta, \quad \text{if } \eta \in A_\Theta,$$

$$\langle \Phi(\eta), e_i \rangle = \begin{cases} b_i, & \text{if } \langle \eta, e_i \rangle > b_i, \\ a_i, & \text{if } \langle \eta, e_i \rangle < a_i. \end{cases} \tag{7}$$

This sort of truncation has the specific property that it is uniformly norm-reducing in the following sense: $\|X_{t+1} - \eta\| \leq \|\hat{X}_{t+1} - \eta\|$, for all $\eta \in A$ and t. ($\hat{X}_{t+1} = X_t + \alpha_t W$ stands for what would be produced by the untruncated iteration.) By this property one may by a simple overbound, within a broad class of learning problems, immediately reduce convergence-studies to that of the associated untruncated iteration.

Observe also that Φ is just the sort of truncation one usually adopts when confining computations to finite intervals. (It is also a multivariate extention of the well known procedure usually adopted[2] for confining probability estimates to the interval [0,1].)

Let $\alpha_t = C_o t^{-1}$, for all $t \geq t_0 \geq 1, C_o$ and t_0 being arbitrary positive constants. (We may impose also a looser set of constraints[9] on α , similar, but somewhat more involved, to that well known in classical stochastic approximation and related topics,[33,30,22,13,29] which explicitly shows that just the global behavior of α effects the convergence.)

Having, in this way, specified in (6) all apriori fixed data, we may impose a fairly simple and general set of constraints on W, under which the iteration learns, as $t \to \infty$, precisely any discriminant function Θ in A_Θ, taught by the presented stream $\{(\omega_t, \Theta(\omega_t), t = 0,1, \ldots\}$ of labelled samples.

More distinctly, if the regulator W meets certain constraints (to be described in the sequel) the iteration process X precisely learns the taught discriminant function Θ, in the sense that it converges almost surely to Θ with respect to either of the following errors:[9] (i) $d = \|X_t - \Theta\|$ or (ii) $\tilde{d} = E(|X_t(\omega_t) - \Theta(\omega_t)\| X^t)$. (Here and in what follows $\langle \eta_1, \eta_2 \rangle$

denotes the inner product, and $\|\eta_1\| = <\eta_1, \eta_1>^{1/2}$ the norm for any $\eta_1, \eta_2 \in A$. E stands for expectation and $\widetilde{d}$ is a conditional expection, given the past X^t of the iteration process.)

There is an alternative of constraints by which convergence may be guaranteed in terms of d and $\widetilde{d}$, respectively, which we will specify, in what follows, in more details.

Constraints on W may be divided into loose and significant ones, respectively. The loose constraints, while being relevant for the convergence mechanism itself, are trivially met by almost any regulator W of actual interest. In contrast to these, the significant constraints actually confine (i) the scope of problems which may be treated and (ii) are met only by specific regulators; i.e. these impose true design restrictions.

Concerning the loose constraints, the regulator W_t has to have, at any t, (i) a uniform bound for conditional second moments (given Z^t), (ii) either finite or (at a given rate) decaying memory and (iii) variations with a uniform linear overbound (defined precisely in [9]), only for the very case for which $Z_\vartheta \in A_\Theta$, for all $\vartheta \leq t$.

We impose on W just two kinds of significant constraints. One assumes a sort of conditional stationarity in the sense:

$$E(W_t | Z^t = f_\xi^t) = m(\xi), \tag{8}$$

for any $\xi \in A_\Theta$. ($f_\xi^t = \{f_\vartheta = \xi, \vartheta \leq t\}$. (8) refers, specifically to that particular case when all previously proposed estimates equal some given admissible discriminant function $\xi \in A_\Theta$.)

By (8), learning of time-varying classification functions is obviously excluded.) (Here we only refer to such extentions of the model by which slowly varying classifications may also be pursued[16].)

The second type of significant constraints is imposed specifically, on m. We give a pair of alternatives for this case, related to d and $\widetilde{d}$, respectively.

Convergence with respect to d holds if the regulator W is such that, for some Θ and any $\varepsilon > 0$, we have:

$$\inf_{\varepsilon < \|\xi - \Theta\| < \varepsilon^{-1}} < \xi - \Theta, m(\xi) > < \Theta \tag{9}$$

(We show in Section 3 that regulators, derived specifically from cost functions do, in the case of unimodality, obviously meet constraint (9), even if memory is involved, with respect to the set Z^t of previous estimates.)

On the other hand, we get, specifically for untruncated iterations, convergence in terms of $\widetilde{d}$ if the regulator W is such that (i) $|W_t(\omega)| < C$, for all ω and, (ii) for some Θ and a constraint C_0, we have

$$< \xi - \Theta, m(\xi) > = - C_o E(|Z_t(\omega) - \Theta(\omega)||Z^t = f^t_\xi). \qquad (10)$$

We show in Section 4 that for a relevant class of potential function type learning procedures, the adopted principles obviously guarantee constraint (10) to hold, even in the more general case if, for W, memory is also admitted, with respect to previous estimates.

Observe that we imposed by (8) - (10) constraints only on such properties of the regulator W_t which appear also when, specifically, all previous estimates $Z_\vartheta, \vartheta \leq t$ are set to be equal. (This specific property is an interesting consequence of the way how the considered sort of algorithms work.)

This is the very point which provides considerable freedom for embedding also complex (and, even heuristically defined) processing steps into such sort of convergent iterative procedures. Viz., one may obviously modify the regulator of any convergent iterative learning algorithm, retaining its convergence, provided by this m is left unchanged.

To show how readily may embedding problems be overviewed, by the approach described just now, we take as a well known typical example a specific reinforcement technique proposed by Saridis[31]. (Here we confine the original scheme only to iterations with decaying weights α, and also slightly modify it, in order to be able to use the previously introduced notions.)

Assume we already have introduced a regulator W for which one of the previously described set of alternative constraints hold. I.e., updating the iteration process by the regulator W, Θ is precisely learned.

Obviously, this property is still retained if, in (6), the regulator W_t is replaced by a new one $\widetilde{W}_t = P_t W_t$ defined as follows: P_t is a linear operator mapping A onto A, given, with respect to some arbitrary base $\{\widetilde{e}_i\}_{i=1}$ in A, by a diagonal matrix

$$P_t = \begin{bmatrix} p_t^{(1)} & & & O \\ & \cdot & & \\ & & \cdot & \\ O & & & p_t^{(n)} \end{bmatrix} n.$$

$(O \leq p_t^{(i)} \leq 1, p_o^{(i)} = n^{-1}, i = \overline{1,n}.$ Assume an A which is bounded and $n < \infty$.)

The elements of this matrix are also generated by iteration. Viz.,

$$p_{t+1}^{(i)} = \mu p_t^{(i)} + (1-\mu)\lambda_t^{(i)}.$$

Here $O < \mu < 1$, and $\lambda_n^{(i)} = \tau_n^{(i)} / \Sigma_{j=1}^n \tau_n^{(j)}$.

Let

$$\tau_t^{(i)} = \begin{cases} (\vartheta^{(i)} + \kappa^{(i)})/2\kappa^{(i)} & \text{if } \vartheta_t^{(i)} > \kappa^{(i)}, \\ & \text{if } |\vartheta_t^{(i)}| \leq \kappa^{(i)}, \\ O & \text{if } \vartheta_t^{(i)} < -\kappa^{(i)}, \end{cases}$$

for some a priori specified $\kappa^{(i)} > O$ ($i =\ \ ,n$), and $\vartheta_n^{(i)} = (Z_{t+1}^{(i)} - Z_t^{(i)})(Z_t^{(i)} - Z_{t-1}^{(i)})$ $(Z_t^{(i)} = \langle Z_t, e_i \rangle$, and Z_{t+1} stands for the estimate computed from (6), adopting W.)

The assertion may readily be verified. To do so we have to observe that the loose constraints, if met by W, are also met by $\widetilde{W}$. In addition the moments $m(\xi) = E(W_t | Z^t = f_\xi^t)$ and $\widetilde{m}(\xi) = E(\widetilde{W}_t | Z^t = f_\xi^t)$, subject to the significant constraints, are for any ξ equal. (This latter property follows from the fact that, by the previous definitions, $P_t = I$ for $Z_\vartheta = \xi$, for all $\vartheta \leq t$. (I is the idem operator.)

Detailed experimental evidence is given in the cited paper[31] for typical problems, in the solving of which a remarkable acceleration is achieved by these techniques.

By an inspection of these and other [1,11,38] specific algorithms, one may readily point out a number of further heuristic ideas, in order to meet various specific objectives. For all these cases, by keeping $m = \widetilde{m}$, we have a simple tool to embed also these ideas, while retaining convergence.

We still owe with showing how round-off may be kept within admissible limits. For round-off, we adopt the following well known[32,15] random choice:

Let the round-off value $\langle \overline{X}_t, e_i \rangle$ of $\langle X_t, e_i \rangle$ be $\lfloor \langle X_t, e_i \rangle \rfloor$ with a conditional probability $\lceil \langle X_t, e_i \rangle \rceil - \langle X_t, e_i \rangle$, and $\lceil \langle X_t, e_i \rangle \rceil$ with a conditional probability $\langle X_t, e_i \rangle - \lfloor \langle X_t, e_i \rangle \rfloor$ given X_t. (We assume, the round-off values, with respect to the coordinates, are completely independent.) Obviously $E(\overline{X}_t | X^t) = X_t (\lfloor x \rfloor = C_t^{-1} \operatorname{ent} C_t x$ and $\lceil x \rceil = C_t^{-1}(\operatorname{ent} C_t x + 1)$, for any real x, and a C_t, given, for any t, by the round-off rule.

For rounding-off, replace, at instant t, X_t by $\overline{X}_t$. By so doing, convergence of the iteration to Θ will be retained, if the sequence of round-off errors $\rho_t = X_t - \overline{X}_t$ meets the requirement: $\Sigma_{t=0}^{\infty} \|s_t\|^2 < \infty$. This gives some rough insight, with what precision may one actually, in terminated procedures, keep the rounding-off within acceptable limits.

3. The Embedding Problem for Iterations Governed by Cost Functions

In many actual applications of machine learning one may, at any instant t, evaluate the performance of the learning procedure by some meaningful cost function $\widetilde{Y}_t$ (i.e., an appropriate function taking non-negative values.) E.g., when learning with a teacher, such cost may be: $|Z_t(\omega_t) - \Theta(\omega_t)|^2;$

for all $\omega \epsilon \Omega$.

For the embedding problem, we are going to consider, it does not much matter whether this cost depends only on the most recent estimate Z_t (as in the aforementioned example), or on some collection of estimates $Z_\vartheta, \vartheta \leq t$. Anyhow, we imply, in what follows, also the latter case, since costs with such a memory, are also of actual interest, e.g., because of (i) the inertia actual devices may have and (ii) the cumulative evaluation criteria actual observers may follow, (and also similar other reasons).

Observe that, within a wide scope of actual learning problems, the estimation is revised only within some finite training period, and one has actually to use the recognizer only at such instants t, at which the after-effects of this period have long disappeared; and at such instants we may, therefore, well replace Z^t by $f^t_{Z_t}$ [9,8].

Assume also $\tilde{Y}$ to be conditionally stationary, at least in the sense that $E(\tilde{Y}_t | Z^t = f^t_\xi) = R(\xi)$ does not depend on t. Then, in the course of the learning procedure, we obviously have to search for such a classification function ξ, for which $R(\xi) = \min!$. (Particularly for learning with a teacher, a necessary condition for the cost to be appropriate is that Θ has to be, at least within some A_Θ, a unique minimum of R. (Convexity guarantees in many cases, for instance also in the previous example, this to happen, for any $\xi \epsilon A_\Theta$).

In machine learning, one usually has an a priori knowledge of the entire cost function $\tilde{Y}$ (and not only that of its samples) and prefers, therefore, to replace this minimization problem by seeking for the root of some associate equation, which holds for some sort of gradient-like function. It is well known how to arrive at such an equation (and construct some simple iterative procedure for its solution), provided the cost is without memory, with respect to the previously proposed estimates.

However, to formulate this problem also in a more general case, some further considerations are needed: Nevertheless, by so doing, we arrive also at a promising systematic approach to the embedding problem specifically for iterations governed by cost.

In order to do this we relate to $\tilde{Y}$ (we exactly know) a function Y, taking values in A, only through that very specific situation, for which all estimates $Z_\vartheta, \vartheta \leq t$ are the same. More distinctly, we impose on Y just the following two constraints: (i) $E(Y_t | Z^t = f^t_\xi) = r(\xi)$ independently of t, and (ii) $r(\xi) = \text{grad}_\xi R$ (if it exists, or taking instead of this an appropriate gradient like quantity).

The first of these two relations imposes, for Y also, a sort of conditional stationarity. The second constraint enables one, this time in a more specific context, to introduce also more involved heuristic ideas, when associating some Y with a given $\widetilde{Y}$. (Observe that in this very case one may find Θ among the roots of the regression function r.)

Now, if we have the chance of using a cost function $\widetilde{Y}$, for which R is unimodal at least within some A_Θ, then

$$\inf_{\varepsilon < \|\xi - \Theta\| < \varepsilon^{-1}} < \xi - \Theta, r(\xi) > > 0 \tag{11}$$

for any $\varepsilon > 0$. Observe that (11) turns out to be the same as the constraint (9), provided r is replaced by $-m$, (i.e. Y by $-W$).

This means, however, that we may simply use, taking $Y = -W$, the iteration rule (6) for learning the discriminant function Θ, in this specific context.

Putting it in another way, learning problems related to cost functions provide an application for constraint (9).

Examples for the efficient use of these sort of procedures may be found, e.g., also in the aforementioned paper by Saridis[31], and in further studies on stochastic approximation[14], and deterministic optimization[27,25];

Several other heuristic ideas may also be checked and, if necessary, appropriately modified, by using the just described approach.

An example for heuristic algorithms, not meeting in there original form, all significant constraints, is the global search, well known in optimization, considering at the same time costs at the vertices of a simplex in A_Θ[25]. It is also an interesting exercise to try out a number of useful ways to bring this procedure also within the scope of the previously explained convergence constraints. A number of learning procedures, with a broadly surveying initial period and an analytically controlled end game, may be devised in this way.

4. Embedding Problems for Potentials Function Type Learning Procedures

Let us consider, as a further illustration of embeddings, an extension of of potential function type learning procedures.

Let us adopt, for defining the regulator W, for simplicity, a single potential function,[1,3,24,22] more distinctly an extention of this to a more general class of positive definite functions[17]. Accordingly, let us define the regulator W by means of a positive definite function $K = \{K(\omega,\widetilde{\omega}); \omega,\widetilde{\omega} \in \Omega\}$ (i) which takes its values from A, and (ii) for which $\Theta \in H(K) = A$ holds. (H(K) stands for the reproducing kernel Hilbert space generated by K.) Let $|K(\omega,\widetilde{\omega})| < C_1$.

Let us define, specifically, the regulator as

$$W_t = (\Sigma_{\vartheta \in \Delta} r_\vartheta(t)) K_t . \quad (12)$$

Here $r_\vartheta(t) = \text{sign}(\Theta(\omega_t) - Z_\vartheta(\omega_t)), K_t = K(,\omega_t), \Delta \subset [t-\tau_o, t]$, τ_o denoting some a priori fixed positive integer.)

It follows from the definition of W, and from the reproducing property of the potential function K that

$$< \xi - \Theta, m(\xi) > = - C_o E(|Z_t(\omega_t) - \Theta(\omega_t)||Z^t = f^t_\xi), \quad (13)$$

which is the same as constraint (10) in Section 2. Observe that the other constraints which have to be simultaneously met also hold. Thus, adopting iteration rule (6) and this very regulator, the discriminating function Θ will be actually learned. (We remove ambiguity by setting $Z_\vartheta = O$, for all $\vartheta < O$.)

We have chosen regulator (12) just for illustration. However, by some inspection, already this specific choice gives some insight, how heuristic steps may be embedded into potential function type learning procedures.

The regulator as given by (12) enables one to evaluate each learning sample, with respect to not just the current estimate, but also a number of previously proposed ones. Observe, that also additional evaluations may be introduced, to select a time-varying set Δ at each instant t, empirically.

However, we do not enter here into a further pursue of devising, specifically for potential functions of this sort, a regulator with memory, appropriately. The purpose of the presented example was only to show what sort of freedom we have for so doing.

5. Concluding Remarks

We have outlined, considering an interesting though obviously specific class of iterative learning, how may one make extentions for embedding also complex (even heuristically defined) processing steps, while retaining the convergence of the algorithm.

Stability of iteration processes of some readily specifiable simple structure, have been extensively studied in the past fifteen years[28,23,33,30,10,11,13,16,29,8,32]. The insight obtained, and the scope of algorithms mastered in this way are of considerable interest, and the techniques are being widely used and developed in appropriate areas of communication and control,[34,35,11,31,32]. However, people working on more complex learning models frequently find this scope of algorithms too restrictive. Furthermore there is also, with obvious reasons, some fear to disregard fruitful ideas, when studies are a priori bound to some well mastered, however, specific and closed disciplines.

On the other hand, it is fairly desirable to keep, even for complex models, the final behavior of the learning process under control, as we do this in more simple situations.

It seems, therefore, to be a question of increasing interest to develop some good algorithmic framework which, while having controlled stability properties, offers considerable freedom for embedding various sort of other kind of theoretical or just heuristic ideas. Obvious efforts for so doing appear in several more recent studies.

A systematic approach to a still modestly involved class of these sort of problems was pursued previously. The class of problems we treat in this paper is of course strongly limited by the actual knowledge and current interests of the author.

Observe the problems we consider are within a class, which may be treated in a fairly unified way, by using interesting ideas in stability theory.

In the present paper we have, intentionally, not entered into a discussion of the underlying mathematical ideas, following the aims of this very meeting. We refer in this respect to a companion paper, we have precisely referred to already in the text[9]. This work extends the techniques by Braverman and Rozonoer[4] on random processes to problems, for which there is, because of memory properties, a priori no evidence for meeting the convergence constraints.

In this paper we have made some specific comments on embedding complex steps into convergent iterations. The author is interested to hear about further views, concerning the discussed ideas as well as other approaches to the subject.

REFERENCES

1. Aĭzerman, M. A.; Braverman, E. M.; Rozonoer, L.I., "Teoretičeskie osnovy metoda potencial'nyh funkciĭ v zadače ob obučenii avtomatov razdelniju vhodnyh situacii na klassy" *Avtomatika i Telemehanika,* No. 6, 1964, pp. 917-936.
2. Aĭzerman, M. A.; Braverman, E. M.; Rozonoer, L. I., "Verojatnostnaja zadača ob obučenii avtomatov raspoznavaniju klassov i metod potencialnyh funkciĭ" *Avtomatika i Telemehanika,* No. 9, 1964, pp. 1307-1323.
3. Aĭzerman, M.A., "Remarks on two problems connected with pattern recognition" in Watanabe, M. S. (ed) *Methodologies of pattern recognition,* Academic Press, 1969, pp. 1-10.
4. Braverman, E. M.;Rozonoer L. I., "Shodimost' slučainyh processov v teorii obučenija masin. *I" Avtomatika i Telemechanika,* No. 1, 1969, pp. 57-77, (amendment, ibid. No. 2, 1970, pp. 182.)
5. Cover, T. M., "Hypothesis testing with finite statistics" *Ann. Math. Statist.* No. 3, Vol. 40, 1969, pp. 828-835.
6. Cover, T. M., "Learning in pattern recognition", in Watanabe, M. S. (ed.) "*Methodologies of pattern recognition*", Academic Press, 1969, pp. 111-132.

7. Cover, T. M., Discussion, Wolverton, Ch. T.; Wagner, T. J., "Asympotically optimal discriminant functions for pattern recognition", IEEE Trans. on Information Theory, Val. IT-15, No. 2, March 1969.
8. Csibi, S., "On continuous stochastic approximation", *Proc. of the Colloquium on Information Theory,* Bolyai Mathematical Society, 1967.
9. Csibi, S., "On iteration rules with memory in machine learning" to be submitted to *Control and Information Theory;* also *Colloquia Series (Preprint),* Telecommunication Research Institute, Budapest, 1970; partly appeared in the *Proceedings of Fourth International Conference on System Sciences,* University of Hawaii, 1971, Sec. B-8.
10. Cypkin, Ja. Z., "Adaptacija i obučenie v avtomatičeskih sistemah", *Avtomatika i Telemehanika,* Vol. 27, No. 1, 1966.
11. Cypkin, Ja. Z., *"Osnovy teorii obučajuščihsja sistem"*, Nauka, 1970.
12. Davisson, L. D., "Convergence probability bounds for stochastic approximation", *Tech. Rep.,* University of Southern California, 1969.
13. Driml, M.; Nedoma, J., "Stochastic approximation for continuous random processes", *Trans. 2nd Prague Conf., Inform. Theory, Statist., Decision Functions, and Random Processes,* Czech, Acad. Sci., Prague, 1960, pp. 145-158.
14. Dvoretzky, A., "On stochastic approximation" in *Proc. 3rd Berkeley Symp. on Math. Statist. and Prob.,* Univ. of Calif. Press, 1959, Vol. 1, pp. 39-55.
15. Fabian, V., "Zufalliges Abrunden und die Konvergenz des linearen (Seidelschen) Iterationsverfahrens", *Math Nachr.,* Vol. 16, 1957, pp. 256-279.
16. Fu, K. S., *"Sequential methods in pattern recognition and machine learning"*, Academic Press, 1968.
17. Gulyas, O., "Ob obobščenii algoritma obučenija potencialnyh funkcií io skorosti shodimosti", to be submitted to *Control and Information Theory;* also *Colloquia Series (Preprint),* Telecommunication Research Institute, Budapest, 1970.
18. Györfi, L.,"Iteration rules without memory in machine learning", *Colloquia Series (Preprint),* Telecommunication Research Institute, Budapest, 1970.
19. Has'minskij, R. Z., *Ustočnivost' sistem differencial'nyh uravnenií pri slučaĭnih vozmuščenijah ih parametrov",* Nauka, 1969.
20. Has'minskij, R. Z.; Nevel'son, M. B., "O nepreryvnyh procedurah stohastičeskoĭ aproksimacii", *Problemy Peredači Informacii* (to appear).
21. Hellman, M.E.; Cover, T. M., "Optimal learning with finite memory" (Abstract), *Ann. Math. Statist.,* Vol. 39, No. 5. October 1968, pp. 1793-1794.
22. Ho, Y. C.; Agrawala, A. K., "On pattern classification algorithms. Introduction and Survey," *Proc. IEEE,* Vol. 56, No. 12, December 1968.
23. Kiefer, J., and Wolfowitz, J.,"Stochastic approximation of the maximum of a regression function", *Ann. Math. Statist.,* Vol. 23, 1952, pp. 462-466.
24. Nagy, G., "State of the art in pattern recognition", *Proc. IEEE,* Vol. 56, No. 5, May 1968, pp. 836- 862.
25. Nelder, J. A.; Mead, R., "A simplex method for function minimization", *Computer Journal,* No. 4, 1965, pp. 308-313.
26. Parzen, E., "On estimation of probability density and mode,"*Ann.MathStatist.,* Vol. 33, 1962, pp. 1065-1076.
27. Pierre, D. A., *"Optimization theory with applications"*, Wiley, 1969.

28. Robbins, H.; Monro, A., "A stochastic approximation method", *Ann. Math. Statist.,* Vol. 122, pp. 400-407, 1951.
29. Sakrison, D. J., "A continuous Kiefer Wolfowitz Procedure for random processes", *Ann. Math. Statist.,* Vol. 35, 1964, pp. 590-599.
30. Sakrison, D. J., "Stochastic approximation. A recursive method for solving regression problems", *Advances in Communication Systems,* Vol. 2, Academic Press, 1956.
31. Saridis, G. N., "Learning applied to successive approximation algorithms", *IEEE Trans. on System Science and Cybernetics,* Vol. SSC-6, No. 2, April 1970.
32. Schmetterer, I., "Stochastic approximation", Proc. 4th Berkeley *Symp. on Math Statist. and Prob.,* Univ. of Calif. Press, 1962, pp. 587-609, Sec. 7.
33. ibid., Sec. 5.
34. Schönfeld, T. J.; Schwartz, M., "A rapidly converging first order training algorithm rithm for an adaptive equalizer", *Tech. Rep.,* Polytechnic Institute of Brooklyn, 1970.
35. Schönfeld, T. J.; Schwartz, M., "Rapidly converging second order algorithm for adaptive equalization", *Tech. Rep.,* Politechnic Institute of Brooklyn, 1970.
36. Watanabe, M. S. (ed.), *"Methodologies of pattern recognition",* Academic Press, 1969.
37. Wolfowitz, J., "On stochastic approximation methods", *Ann. Math. Statist.,* Vol. 27, 1956, pp. 1151-1156.
38. Wolverton, Ch. T.; Wagner, T. J., "Asympotically optimal discriminant functions for pattern classification", *IEEE Trans. on Information Theory,* Vol. IT-15, No. 2, March 1969, pp. 258-265.

ON SYNTACTIC PATTERN RECOGNITION AND STOCHASTIC LANGUAGES

K. S. Fu

PURDUE UNIVERSITY
LAFAYETTE, INDIANA

I. Introduction

The many different techniques used to solve pattern recognition problems may be grouped into two general approaches; namely, decision-theoretic (or discriminant) approach and syntactic (or linguistic) approach. In the decision-theoretic approach, a set of characteristic measurements (called features) are extracted from the patterns; the recognition of each pattern (assignment to a pattern class) is usually made by partitioning the feature space [1,2]. Once a pattern is transformed through feature extraction to a point or a vector in the feature space, its characteristics are expressed only by a set of numerical values. The information about the structure of each pattern is either ignored or not explicitly represented in the feature space.* Most of the developments in pattern recognition research during the past decade deal with the decision-theoretic approach. Various estimation (training or learning) techniques and decision rules have been applied to estimate the pattern characteristics of each class or directly estimate the partitioning (decision) boundary in the feature space. Successful applications of this approach to practical problems include character recognition, medical diagnosis, crop classification, etc.

In some pattern recognition problems, the structure information to describe each pattern is important, and the recognition process includes not only the capability of assigning the pattern to a class (to classify it) but also the capacity to describe aspects of the pattern which, for example, make it inelligible for assignment to a particular class. A typical example of this

*It should be mentioned that the structural relationships of patterns in the same class are usually described by a probability distribution or density function.

class of recognition problems is picture processing or, more generally speaking, scene analysis. For these problems, the decision-theoretic approach has not been very effective or efficient. The number of features and/or possible descriptions is usually very large making it impractical to regard each (high-dimensional) description as defining a class. In order to represent the (hierarchical) structure information of each pattern, the syntactic approach has been proposed [3-5]. The approach draws an analogy between the structure of patterns and the syntax of languages. Pattern primitives are first selected and their relations in the patterns are described by a set of syntactic rules (or a grammar). Since only languages with string-like sentences have been studied so far in mathematical linguistics, the relation expressed in the pattern description languages is primarily limited to the concatenation. The recognition process is accomplished by performing a syntactic analysis (or parsing) to the sentence describing the given pattern. Initial applications of the syntactic approach to the recognition of pictorial patterns have given quite promising results.

Compared with the decision-theoretic approach, the syntactic approach has not been as extensively investigated. The feature extraction and selection problem in the decision-theoretic approach and the primitive selection problem in the syntactic approach are similar in nature. Further research effort is definitely needed for both problems [6]. However, the mathematical linguistics needed for the syntactic approach is not as well developed and therefore not as useful as the statistical estimation and decision theory for the decision-theoretic approach. Very few practical results have been obtained in the study of grammatical inference–learning the grammar from the observation of the sentences in a language [9-11]. Most techniques suggested for the syntactic approach so far are rather heuristic and only for special classes of problems. The performance of the recognition system can hardly be conclusively evaluated. A general formulation of this approach is not yet available.

Since in the syntactic approach, abstract primitive elements are usually selected, effects of noise and distortion in the measurement of patterns can be reduced only through extensive preprocessing. From the viewpoint of real-data processing, noise and distortion are, in general, unavoidable in the actual practice. In order to take the noise and distortion into consideration, the use of stochastic languages for pattern description have recently been proposed as a possible solution [4]. In this paper a brief introduction of stochastic languages is first given. Some preliminary results from the study of using stochastic languages for pattern description are then presented. Initial investigations for the grammatical inference problem of stochastic languages are also discussed.

II. Stochastic Languages

A stochastic grammar is a 5-tuple

$$G_S = (V_N, V_T, P, S, D) \qquad (1)$$

where

V_N is a finite set of nonterminals

V_T is a finite set of terminals $(V_N \cap V_T = \phi)$

P is a finite set of productions

$S \epsilon V_N$ is the start symbol

D is a probability measure (assignment) over P

It is noted that from this definition a stochastic grammar is simply a non-stochastic (phrase-structure) grammar with a probability measure over its productions. Let $x \epsilon L(G_S)$ be a string of terminals generated by a stochastic grammar G_S using the sequence of productions $r_1, r_2, \ldots, r_n$. The generation process can be represented as

$$S \overset{r_1}{\Longrightarrow} \gamma_1 \overset{r_2}{\Longrightarrow} \gamma_2 \Longrightarrow \cdots \overset{r_n}{\Longrightarrow} \gamma_n = x \qquad (2)$$

where $r_i \epsilon P$ and $\gamma_i \epsilon (V_N \cup V_T)^*$. The probability associated with the generation of x is defined to be the product of conditional probabilities

$$p(x) = p(r_1)p(r_2|r_1) \cdots p(r_n|r_1, \ldots, r_{n-1}) \qquad (3)$$

If the string x can be generated by m distinct sequences of productions, then the probability associated with the generation of x is defined as

$$g(x) = \sum_1^m p(x) = \sum_1^m p(r_1)p(r_2|r_1) \cdots p(r_n|r_1, \ldots, r_{n-1}) \qquad (4)$$

where the sum is taken over the distinct generations of x. The stochastic language generated by the stochastic grammar consists of all the strings $x \epsilon L(G_S)$ and the probability information p(x).

A production probability assignment D is consistent provided

$$\sum_{x \epsilon L(G_S)} g(x) = 1 \qquad (5)$$

Necessary and sufficient conditions for D to be consistent in the finite-state and context-free languages are given in [12-15]. All stochastic grammars considered herein will be assumed to have consistent production probability assignments. In a special case where, for all production sequences,

$$p(r_i | r_1, \ldots, r_{i-1}) = p(r_i) \tag{6}$$

D is called an unrestricted production probability assignment.

Example 1: $G_S = (V_N, V_T, P, S, D)$ is a stochastic finite-state grammar, where

$V_N = \{S, A, B, C\}$
$V_T = \{a, b\}$

P	D
$S \rightarrow aA$	$\alpha \; (0 < \alpha < 1)$
$S \rightarrow bB$	$1 - \alpha$
$A \rightarrow bA$	$\beta \; (0 < \beta < 1)$
$A \rightarrow bC$	$1 - \beta$
$B \rightarrow aC$	1
$C \rightarrow a$	1

The language generated is

$$\begin{aligned} L(G_S) &= \{aba, baa, abba, abbba, \ldots\} \\ &= \{baa \cup ab(b)^* a\} \end{aligned} \tag{7}$$

The probabilities associated with the generation of, say, baa and $ab^k a$ are given respectively by

$$\begin{aligned} g(baa) &= 1 - \alpha \\ g(ab^k a) &= \alpha \, \beta^{k-1}(1 - \beta) \end{aligned}$$

D is an unrestricted production probability assignment and is also consistent since

$$\sum_{x \in L(G_S)} g(x) = (1 - \alpha) + \alpha(1 - \beta) \sum_{k=1}^{\infty} \beta^{k-1} = 1 \tag{8}$$

Notice that stochastic grammars are no more powerful in terms of the languages generated than their non-stochastic counterparts. For example, stochastic finite-state grammars still generate only finite-state languages [16]. The effect of the added probabilistic mechanism is to impress a probability distribution on the sentences of the languages generated, which, in turn, would be very useful in, say, describing noisy patterns, and modeling information retrieval and data communication systems. Stochastic finite-state and context-free languages and their corresponding acceptors (stochastic finite automata and stochastic pushdown automata) have recently been studied [16-20]. It has been shown that stochastic finite automata may accept some non-finite-state languages, and stochastic pushdown automata may accept non-context-free languages. Therefore, with respect to the acceptors, the stochastic versions seem to be more powerful in terms of the languages accepted than their non-stochastic counterparts.

The programmed grammar, which is a powerful and convenient formalism for generating a relatively broad class of languages, has recently been studied [21]. A programmed grammer is a 5-tuple $G_p = (V_N, V_T, P, J, S)$ where V_N, V_T, P, S are the same as defined before, and J is a finite set of production labels. Each production consists of a label $r \in J$, a core production of the phrase-structure type, and a success branch field and a failure branch field each consisting of elements from J. A generation or derivation in G_p proceeds as follows: the first (labelled) production is applied to the start symbol S; thereafter, if production r is applied to the current sentential form γ to rewrite a substring ω and if γ contains at least one occurrence of ω, then the leftmost ω is rewritten by the core of production r and the next production label is selected from the success branch field of r; if the current sentential form does not contain ω, then the core of production r cannot be used and the next production label is selected from the failure branch field of r; if the applicable branch field is empty, the generation halts.

If the core of a programmed grammar is in a context-free form, the grammar is called context-free programmed grammar. It is known that the set of languages generated by context-free programmed grammars properly contains the set of context-free languages and is properly contained within the set of context-sensitive languages. Writing a context-free programmed grammar is very much like writing a computer program and is a rather straightforward logical process compared with the task of writing a context-sensitive grammar. However, experience indicates that the class of languages generated by context-free programmed grammars includes interesting context sensitive languages.

An extension of the context-free programmed grammar is to add the desired probabilistic mechanism while retaining its basic simplicity and power. This combination of features appears to make the resulting formalism even more attractive for possible applications in syntactic pattern recognition. One obvious possibility to make a context-free programmed grammar probabilistic is to assign branch probabilities in cases where the prescribed branch field contains more than one choice (in the non-stochastic case, the selection of the next production label is nondeterministic) [22]. The following example is used to illustrate this proposal.

Example 2: $G_{Sp} = (V_N, V_T, P, J, S, D)$ is a stochastic context-free programmed grammar where

$V_N = \{S, A, B, C, D\}$

$V_T = \{a, b, c, d\}$

$J = \{1, 2, 3, 4, 5, 6, 7\}$

	P			D	
Label	Core	Success Branches	Failure Branches	Success Branch Probabilities	Failure Branch Probabilities
1	$S \rightarrow aAB$	$\{2,3\}$	ϕ	$\{\alpha, 1-\alpha\}$	1
2	$A \rightarrow aAC$	$\{2,3\}$	ϕ	$\{1-\beta, \beta\}$	1
3	$A \rightarrow D$	$\{4\}$	ϕ	1	1
4	$C \rightarrow d$	$\{5\}$	$\{6\}$	1	1
5	$D \rightarrow bDc$	$\{4\}$	ϕ	1	1
6	$B \rightarrow d$	$\{7\}$	ϕ	1	1
7	$D \rightarrow bc$	ϕ	ϕ	1	1

A generation of the string abcd can be expressed as

$$S \overset{1}{\Longrightarrow} aAB \overset{3}{\Longrightarrow} aDB \overset{6}{\Longrightarrow} aDd \overset{7}{\Longrightarrow} abcd \tag{9}$$

and $p(abcd) = 1 - \alpha$. Similarly, $p(a^n b^n c^n d^n) = \alpha\beta(1-\beta)^{n-2}$, $n = 2, 3, \ldots,$ and

$$\sum_{x \in L(G_{Sp})} g(x) = (1-\alpha) + \sum_{n=2}^{\infty} \alpha\beta(1-\beta)^{n-2} = 1 \tag{10}$$

Hence, D is a consistent probability assignment.

III. Stochastic Languages for Pattern Description

In this section, examples are given to demonstrate the potential for using stochastic languages for the description of distorted and noisy patterns. The approach taken is perhaps quite ad hoc, and the results are only preliminary.

Example 3: An equilateral triangle and eight other distorted versions are shown in Figure 1. The pattern primitives selected are given in Figure 2. Each triangle is described by a string of length 3. Suppose that, from the a priori knowledge or actual observations, the probabilities of the generation of these nine different triangles are known or can be estimated, say, from the relative frequencies of occurrences,of these triangles. This information is listed in Table 1. The stochastic finite-state grammar which will generate these strings with associated probabilities is

$$G_S = (V_N, V_T, P, S, D)$$

where

$$V_N = \{S, A_1, A_2, A_3, A_4\}$$
$$V_T = \{a, b_1, b_2, b_3, c_1, c_2, c_3\}$$

and

P	D
$S \to aA_1$	1
$A_1 \to b_1 A_2$	$\frac{1}{6}$
$A_1 \to b_2 A_3$	$\frac{2}{3}$
$A_1 \to b_3 A_4$	$\frac{1}{6}$
$A_2 \to c_1$	$\frac{1}{6}$
$A_2 \to c_2$	$\frac{1}{3}$
$A_2 \to c_3$	$\frac{1}{2}$
$A_3 \to c_1$	$\frac{1}{24}$

P	D
$A_3 \rightarrow c_2$	$\frac{21}{24}$
$A_3 \rightarrow c_3$	$\frac{1}{12}$
$A_4 \rightarrow c_1$	$\frac{1}{2}$
$A_4 \rightarrow c_2$	$\frac{1}{3}$
$A_4 \rightarrow c_3$	$\frac{1}{6}$

It should be noted that the grammar G_S not only generates the sentences to describe these nine triangles, but also carries the probability information p(x), which might be quite important and useful in describing real-world patterns.

Example 4: A right-angled triangle and eight other distorted versions are shown in Figure 3. Based on the pattern primitives shown in Figure 2 and probabilistic information listed in Table 2, the corresponding stochastic finite-state grammar is

$$G'_S = (V'_N, V'_T, P', S, D')$$

where

$$V'_N = \{S, A_1, A_2, A_3, A_4\}$$
$$V'_T = \{a, b_o, b_1, b_2, c_2, c_3, c_4\}$$

and

P′	D′
$S \rightarrow aA_1$	1
$A_1 \rightarrow b_o A_2$	$\frac{2}{3}$
$A_1 \rightarrow b_1 A_3$	$\frac{1}{6}$
$A_1 \rightarrow b_2 A_4$	$\frac{1}{6}$
$A_2 \rightarrow c_2$	$\frac{1}{24}$
$A_2 \rightarrow c_3$	$\frac{1}{12}$

P′	D′
$A_2 \rightarrow c_4$	$\frac{21}{24}$
$A_3 \rightarrow c_2$	$\frac{1}{6}$
$A_3 \rightarrow c_3$	$\frac{2}{3}$
$A_3 \rightarrow c_4$	$\frac{1}{6}$
$A_4 \rightarrow c_2$	$\frac{1}{3}$
$A_4 \rightarrow c_3$	$\frac{1}{2}$
$A_4 \rightarrow c_4$	$\frac{1}{6}$

It is noted that the strings ab_1c_2, ab_1c_3, ab_2c_2, and ab_2c_3 in Table 2 are also listed in Table 1. If we consider the strings (triangles) in Table 1 as forming the pattern class I and the strings in Table 2 as forming the pattern class II, then the four strings ab_1c_2, ab_1c_3, ab_2c_2, and ab_2c_3 fall into both classes. In the decision-theoretic approach, the classification problem with "overlapping" classes can be solved by applying statistical decision theory [2]. A similar idea is also applied here. The probability information $p(x)$ of the strings belonging to each pattern class plays an important role in the classification problem. For example, suppose that the input pattern (a triangle) is represented by the string ab_1c_2. With the assumption of equal a priori probabilities (of the occurrences of each class), the information $p(x)$ can be used for the maximum-likelihood classification rule. That is, in this case, ab_1c_2 should be classified as belonging to class I since

$$p_I(x) = \frac{2}{36} > \frac{1}{36} = p_{II}(x) \tag{11}$$

Similarly, classification rules can also be formulated with known a priori probabilities and/or given loss functions.

Since the probability information $p(x)$ is used in the classification rule, the computation of $p(x)$ for any given x (a string) at the time of classification becomes an important problem. In an extremely simple problem such as that in Example 4, the information in Table 1 and Table 2 (which can also be easily derived from the two corresponding stochastic grammars) can be directly stored in the machine. A "table look-up" procedure will provide the necessary information for classification. In general, the number of strings generated by a grammar is often very large or infinite. The advantage of using the grammar to describe the structure of a language is that such a finite representation can be used instead of listing all the strings in the language. In order to recognize whether or not a string (a pattern) belongs to the language generated by a particular grammar (a pattern class), the notion of acceptors (or recognizers) has been introduced.

It is known that, for a given stochastic finite-state grammar, a stochastic finite automaton can be synthesized to accept only those strings with their associated generation probabilities, p(x) [16]. For the problem in Example 4, two stochastic finite automata, M and M′, can be synthesized,† corresponding to G_S and G'_S, respectively. These strings listed in Table 1 will be accepted by the automaton M (corresponding to G_S), and the strings listed in Table 2 accepted by the automaton M′ (corresponding to G'_S). For each string x applied to an automaton, the probability associated with the generation of x, p(x), can be easily computed from the transition probability matrices of the automaton. For example, if ab_1c_2 is the input string (pattern), it will be accepted by both automata, but the information p(x) computed from the two automata is different (i.e., $\frac{2}{36}$ and $\frac{1}{36}$, respectively). If ab_0c_3 is the input string, then it will be accepted only by the automaton corresponding to G'_S and rejected (or, say, accepted with probability zero) by the automaton corresponding to G_S. That is, the pattern described by ab_0c_3 would be classified as belonging to class II.

Example 5:†† A stochastic grammar was developed to describe "noisy squares," for example, the squares drawn on a CRT input device or a RAND tablet. The following assumptions were made to keep the grammar simple but interesting.

(1) The squares were to have their side length geometrically distributed with mean length $\frac{1}{\alpha}(0 < \alpha < 1)$.

(2) The squares were to be drawn horizontal/vertical and the operator was assumed skillful enough so that the "noise" could be considered primarily the quantization error resulting from input through a digital or finite-state device.

(3) The "target aiming" effect, which could come into play as a square is about to be closed and would assist in ensuring closure, was ignored.

A generator program for languages generated by stochastic context-free

†For detailed synthesis procedure, see [16].

††For a more detailed discussion of this example, see [22].

programmed grammars was written for a PDP-9 digital computer with a Model 339 Graphical Display. The program generates strings in a stochastic manner using any specified stochastic context-free programmed grammar as input "data" and displays a pictorial interpretation of the generation process. The generation and display capabilities permit the user to observe the grammar at work, to interactively improve the grammar, and to qualitatively assess its stochastic properties.

For this example, a language with tails was used.† A typical noisy square generated is shown in Figure 4, and the stochastic context-free programmed grammar appears in Table 3. "Reasonable" values were selected for the branch probabilities in the grammar. If a hand-drawn "training set" were available for analysis in terms of the grammatical model, these probabilities could be more closely adjusted to the actual physical situation.

IV. Stochastic Languages in Grammatical Inference

In Section III, examples are given to demonstrate the possibility of using stochastic languages for the description of noisy patterns. However, nothing has been said about how to obtain a stochastic grammar from a set of strings which describe noisy patterns. A problem similar in nature in the decision-theoretic approach is the learning (or estimation) problem. Recent results in the study of grammatical inference seems to be quite promising [9]. There is no doubt that, in dealing with real-world patterns, the structural information should be obtained directly from actual data. In the following, an inference procedure is presented, which is a modified version of the procedure proposed in [11] for the non-stochastic case. The reason for choosing the procedure (although it may be heuristic) is primarily due to its simplicity in implementation. Again, it should be pointed out that the purpose here is to demonstrate the potential application rather than presenting conclusive results in the inference of stochastic grammar.

Similar to the approach used in [11], for a finite set of strings over the set of symbols Σ

$$X = \{x_1, \ldots, x_n\}, \qquad x_i \in \Sigma^* , \tag{12}$$

†Let L_1 be a language over the terminals V_T and L_2 be a language over $V_T \cup \{s,t\}$ where $s,t \notin V_T$ such that $L_2 = \{xst^{\ell} | x \in L_1$ and ℓ depends on $x\}$. Then L_2 is said to be of the form L_1 with tails. The x portion is referred to as the body of the string, s as the tail delimiter, and t^{ℓ} as the tail. In general, the tail is found to be a convenient place to perform any book-keeping functions (as a counter in this example) necessary for the generation of the language.

let the given probability information be

$$R = \{f_1, \ldots, f_n\}, \qquad 0 \leq f_i \leq 1 \tag{13}$$

where f_i is the probability or the relative frequency of occurrence of the string x_i. After (x_i, f_i) has been observed, let†

$$h(z,X,k) = \{(w,f_i) \mid zw = x_i \in X \text{ and } |w| \leq k\} \tag{14}$$

where $|w|$ denotes the length of the string w and $k \geq 0$. Based on the information (X,R), a stochastic automaton can be defined as

$$M(X,R,k) = (\Sigma, Q, \delta, q_o, F) \tag{15}$$

where Σ is the same set of input symbols,

$$Q = \{h(z,X,k) \mid z \in \Sigma^*\}$$

is the set of states,

$$q_o = h(\lambda, X, k) \qquad (\lambda \text{ is the empty string})$$

is the initial state, and

$$F = \{h(z,X,k) \mid h(z,X,k) = \{(\lambda, f_i)\} \text{ for some } f_i \in R\}$$

is the set of final states. Let

$$Q' = \{h(z,X,k) \mid (\lambda, f_i) \in h(z,X,k) \text{ for some } f_i \in R\}$$

be the set of states of which each serves at least as a final state and possibly also as a transition state. The transition from state $q = (w,f_i) = h(z,X,k)$ to state $q' = (w',f_i) = h(za,X,k)$, $a \in \Sigma$, is defined as

$$\delta(q,a) = \begin{cases} (q',p), \text{ if } q' \in (Q - Q') \text{ or } q' = q_f \in F \\ \{(q',p_1), (q_f,p_2) \mid q_f \in F\}, \text{ if } q' \in (Q' - F) \end{cases} \tag{16}$$

where p, p_1 and p_2 are transition probabilities which will be calculated from the relations

$$\delta(q_o, x_i) = (q_f, f_i), \qquad i = 1, \ldots, n \tag{17}$$

†The formalism presented here, which is equivalent to, but more concise than, the one originally proposed [27], is suggested by A. W. Biermann (private communication after the conference). The $w \in \Sigma^*$ in (14) is essentially the k-tail of a string z with respect to X defined in [11].

It is anticipated that for a sufficiently large value of k (e.g., $k \geq \max |x_i|$), the above relations will give a unique solution of all the transition probabilities. In this case, the number of states would also be large enough so that the automaton would accept all the strings in X. Then the following condition may be realized:

$$L(M(X,R,k)) = (X,R)\ , \qquad \sum_{i=1}^{n} f_i = 1 \tag{18}$$

That is, the language accepted by the stochastic automaton M(X,R,k) will be exactly the same as X with the associated probability information R. However, if $\sum_{i=1}^{n} f_i < 1$, there is a certain probability $1 - \sum_{i=1}^{n} f_i$ that other strings will also be accepted.† Since there is no additional information available, the set of other strings accepted by the automaton seems to be rather arbitrary as long as the normalization conditions imposed on the transition probabilities are satisfied. Nevertheless, the quantity $\sum_{i=1}^{n} f_i$ may serve as a measure of confidence for the grammar inferred. In the following, without going through any further theoretical treatment, an example is given to illustrate the proposed procedure.††

Example 6: The strings and their associated probabilities listed in Table 1 are given as the input information; i.e.,

$$(X,R) = \{(ab_1c_1, \tfrac{1}{36}),\ (ab_1c_2, \tfrac{2}{36}),\ (ab_1c_3, \tfrac{3}{36}),\ (ab_2c_1, \tfrac{1}{36}),$$
$$(ab_2c_2, \tfrac{21}{36}),\ (ab_2c_3, \tfrac{2}{36}),\ (ab_3c_1, \tfrac{3}{36}),\ (ab_3c_2, \tfrac{2}{36}),$$
$$(ab_3c_3, \tfrac{1}{36})\}$$

Let

$$M(X,R,k) = (\Sigma, Q, \delta, q_o, F)$$

where

$$\Sigma = \{a, b_1, b_2, b_3, c_1, c_2, c_3\}.$$

---

†This is also one of the reasons that, instead of $\{p(x_1), \ldots, p(x_n)\}$, the notation $R = \{f_1, \ldots, f_n\}$ is used in this section.

††For other related discussions of the procedure, see [23].

For k = 3,

$z = \lambda, \quad q_0 = \{(ab_1c_1, \frac{1}{36}), (ab_1c_2, \frac{2}{36}), (ab_1c_3, \frac{3}{36}), (ab_2c_1 \frac{1}{36}),$

$(ab_2c_2, \frac{21}{36}), (ab_2c_3, \frac{2}{36}), (ab_3c_1, \frac{3}{36}), (ab_3c_2, \frac{2}{36}),$

$(ab_3c_3, \frac{1}{36})\}$

$z = a, \quad q_1 = \{(b_1c_1, \frac{1}{36}), (b_1c_2, \frac{2}{36}), (b_1c_3, \frac{3}{36}), (b_2c_1, \frac{1}{36}),$

$(b_2c_2, \frac{21}{36}), (b_2c_3, \frac{2}{36}), (b_3c_1, \frac{3}{36}), (b_3c_2, \frac{2}{36}),$

$(b_3c_3, \frac{1}{36})\}$

$z = ab_1, \quad q_2 = \{(c_1, \frac{1}{36}), (c_2, \frac{2}{36}), (c_3, \frac{3}{36})\}$

$z = ab_2, \quad q_3 = \{(c_1, \frac{1}{36}), (c_2, \frac{21}{36}), (c_3, \frac{2}{36})\}$

$z = ab_3, \quad q_4 = \{(c_1, \frac{3}{36}), (c_2, \frac{2}{36}), (c_3, \frac{1}{36})\}$

$z = ab_1c_1, \quad q_5 = \{(\lambda, \frac{1}{36})\}$

$z = ab_1c_2, \quad q_6 = \{(\lambda, \frac{2}{36})\}$

$z = ab_1c_3, \quad q_7 = \{(\lambda, \frac{3}{36})\}$

$z = ab_2c_2, \quad q_8 = \{(\lambda, \frac{21}{36})\}$

$z = ab_2c_1, \quad q_9 = q_5$

$z = ab_2c_3, \quad q_{10} = q_6$

$z = ab_3c_1, \quad q_{11} = q_7$

$z = ab_3c_2, \quad q_{12} = q_6$

$z = ab_3c_3, \quad q_{13} = q_5$

$$Q = \{q_0, q_1, q_2, q_3, q_4, q_5, q_6, q_7, q_8\}$$

$$F = \{\{(\lambda, \frac{1}{36})\}, \{(\lambda, \frac{2}{36})\}, \{(\lambda, \frac{3}{36})\}, \{(\lambda, \frac{21}{36})\}\}$$

$$Q' = \{q_5, q_6, q_7, q_8\}$$

$$\delta(q_0,a) = (q_1,p_1), \qquad \delta(q_3,c_1) = (q_5,p_8)$$
$$\delta(q_1,b_1) = (q_2,p_2), \qquad \delta(q_3,c_2) = (q_8,p_9)$$
$$\delta(q_1,b_2) = (q_3,p_3), \qquad \delta(q_3,c_3) = (q_6,p_{10})$$
$$\delta(q_1,b_3) = (q_4,p_4), \qquad \delta(q_4,c_1) = (q_7,p_{11})$$
$$\delta(q_2,c_1) = (q_5,p_5), \qquad \delta(q_4,c_2) = (q_6,p_{12})$$
$$\delta(q_2,c_2) = (q_6,p_6), \qquad \delta(q_4,c_2) = (q_6,p_{12})$$
$$\delta(q_2,c_3) = (q_7,p_7),$$

The transition diagram of the stochastic automaton is given in Figure 5.† From Figure 5 and the information (X,R), the following relations can be established:

$$p_1 p_2 p_5 = \frac{1}{36}$$
$$p_1 p_2 p_6 = \frac{2}{36}$$
$$p_1 p_2 p_7 = \frac{3}{36}$$
$$p_1 p_3 p_8 = \frac{1}{36}$$
$$p_1 p_3 p_9 = \frac{21}{36}$$
$$p_1 p_3 p_{10} = \frac{2}{36}$$
$$p_1 p_4 p_{11} = \frac{3}{36}$$
$$p_1 p_4 p_{12} = \frac{2}{36}$$
$$p_1 p_4 p_{13} = \frac{1}{36}$$

and the normalization conditions are:

$$p_1 = 1$$
$$p_2 + p_3 + p_4 = 1$$
$$p_5 + p_6 + p_7 = 1$$
$$p_8 + p_9 + p_{10} = 1$$
$$p_{11} + p_{12} + p_{13} = 1$$

From

$$p_1 p_2 (p_5 + p_6 + p_7) = \frac{1}{36} + \frac{2}{36} + \frac{3}{36} = \frac{1}{6}$$

†The transition diagram can be simplified by merging all the final states into one state.

and

$$p_5 + p_6 + p_7 = 1$$

we obtain

$$p_2 = \frac{1}{6}, \quad p_5 = \frac{1}{6}, \quad p_6 = \frac{1}{3}, \quad p_7 = \frac{1}{2}$$

Similarly,

$$p_3 = \frac{2}{3}, \quad p_8 = \frac{1}{24}, \quad p_9 = \frac{21}{24}, \quad p_{10} = \frac{1}{12}$$

$$p_4 = \frac{1}{6}, \quad p_{11} = \frac{1}{2}, \quad p_{12} = \frac{1}{3}, \quad p_{13} = \frac{1}{6}$$

It should be noted that in this example $\sum_{i=1}^{9} f_i = 1$. The value of k (=3) has been selected such that the resulting automaton will accept exactly the strings in X. If, for example, the information regarding the last two strings, $(ab_3c_2, \frac{2}{36})$, $(ab_3c_3, \frac{1}{36})$, is not available, then the transition from q_4 is only partially specified (i.e., only the transition from q_4 to q_7). Under such a situation, the transition from q_4 to other states (including itself) except q_7 can be rather arbitrarily specified as long as the normalization conditions are satisfied. Of course, the arbitrarily specified transitions would affect the additional strings (and their associated probabilities) accepted by the automaton.†

After the stochastic automaton is synthesized, a corresponding stochastic finite-state grammar can be constructed using a procedure similar to the non-stochastic case [24]. Associated with the initial state, the start symbol S is assigned. For the remaining states in Q, assign a non-terminal for each of the states. Then, with the set of terminals $V_T = \Sigma$,

$S \to aA$	p	if $\delta(q_0,a) = (q,p)$, $a \in \Sigma$, where A is the nonterminal associated with the state q and $q \in F$.
$A_1 \to aA_2$	p	if $\delta(q_1,a) = (q_2,p)$, $a \in \Sigma$ where A_1 and A_2 are the nonterminals associated with the states q_1 and q_2, respectively, and $q_2 \in F$.
$A \to b$	p	if $\delta(q,b) = (q_f,p)$, $b \in \Sigma$ and $q_f \in F$ where A is the nonterminal associated with the state q.

Based on the construction procedure sketched, the stochastic finite-state grammar corresponding to the stochastic finite automaton in Figure 5

†This might be interpreted as the generalization or the inductive part of the inference (learning) process.

is†

$$G_S = (V_N, V_T, P, S, D)$$

where

$$V_N = \{S, A_1, A_2, A_3, A_4\}$$
$$V_T = \Sigma$$

and

	P	D
$\delta(q_0, a) = (q_1, 1)$	$S \to aA_1$	1
$\delta(q_1, b_1 = (q_2, \frac{1}{6})$	$A_1 \to b_1 A_2$	$\frac{1}{6}$
$\delta(q_1, b_2) = (q_3, \frac{2}{3})$	$A_1 \to b_2 A_3$	$\frac{2}{3}$
$\delta(q_1, b_3) = (q_4, \frac{1}{6})$	$A_1 \to b_3 A_4$	$\frac{1}{6}$
$\delta(q_2, c_1) = (q_5, \frac{1}{6})$	$A_2 \to c_1$	$\frac{1}{6}$
$\delta(q_2, c_2) = (q_6, \frac{1}{3})$	$A_2 \to c_2$	$\frac{1}{3}$
$\delta(q_2, c_3) = (q_7, \frac{1}{2})$	$A_2 \to c_3$	$\frac{1}{2}$
$\delta(q_3, c_1) = (q_5, \frac{1}{24})$	$A_3 \to c_1$	$\frac{1}{24}$
$\delta(q_3, c_2) = (q_8, \frac{21}{24})$	$A_3 \to c_2$	$\frac{21}{24}$
$\delta(q_3, c_3) = (q_6, \frac{1}{12})$	$A_3 \to c_3$	$\frac{1}{12}$
$\delta(q_4, c_1) = (q_7, \frac{1}{2})$	$A_4 \to c_1$	$\frac{1}{2}$
$\delta(q_4, c_2) = (q_6, \frac{1}{3})$	$A_4 \to c_2$	$\frac{1}{3}$
$\delta(q_4, c_3) = (q_5, \frac{1}{6})$	$A_4 \to c_3$	$\frac{1}{6}$

V. Conclusion and Further Remarks

Some preliminary thoughts regarding the potential applications of stochastic languages to syntactic pattern recognition are discussed in this paper. Emphasis is on the description of noisy and/or distorted patterns and the

†It should be noted that, for this example, the nonterminals associated with the final states q_5, q_6, q_7 and q_8 are not needed since (from the transition diagram, there is no transitions from these states to other states) there is no productions involving these nonterminals.

learning of grammar (structural description) from the actual pattern samples. It has been demonstrated by several very simple examples and sometimes with rather heuristic justifications, that the use of probability information in syntactic pattern recognition would make the syntactic approach more flexible and attractive. It is expected that the use of probability information in syntactic analysis (recognition), though not discussed in this paper, would probably improve the efficiency and flexibility of the analysis procedure. The materials presented in this paper may appear to be incomplete and premature for presentation. The reason for doing so is the hope that the preliminary ideas discussed will stimulate more interest and research effort in this area. Furthermore, this perhaps also suits the main purpose of this conference.† The area of syntactic pattern recognition, though very promising, is still in its infancy. Many problems, such as primitive selection, flexible and powerful pattern description techniques, and efficient analysis and inference procedures still need to be solved [26].

Acknowledgements

The author would like to thank T. Huang and A. W. Biermann for many helpful discussions. The work was supported by the National Science Foundation Grant GK-18225 and AFOSR Grant 69-1776.

†Quote from the announcement and invitation of the Conference Organizing Committee: "The purpose of the conference is to help to form a bird's eye view of the diverse and fast-moving developments and to explore the new horizon of the field. We are more interested in ideas and suggestions than mathematical formulae and numerical data."

REFERENCES

1. N. J. Nilsson, *Learning Machines,* McGraw-Hill, 1965.
2. K. S. Fu, *Sequential Methods in Pattern Recognition and Machine Learning,* Academic Press, 1968.
3. W. F. Miller and A. C. Shaw, "Linguistic Methods in Picture Processing–A Survey," Proc. Fall Joint Computer Conference, 1968.
4. K. S. Fu and P. H. Swain, "On Syntactic Pattern Recognition, " COINS-69 Symposium, published in *Software Engineering,* Vol. II, ed. by J. T. Tou, Academic Press, 1971.
5. N. V. Zavalishin and I. B. Muchnik, "Linguistic (Structural) Approach to the Pattern Recognition Problem (Review)," *Automation and Remote Control,* No. 8, pp. 1263-1291, August 1969.
6. Symposium Record, IEEE Symposium on Feature Extraction and Selection in Pattern Recognition, October 5 - 7, 1970 (Argonne, Illinois).
7. V. A. Kovalevsky, "Sequential Optimization in Pattern Recognition and Pattern Description," *Information Processing 68,* pp. 1603-1607, North-Holland Publ. Co., 1969.
8. U. Grenander, "A Unified Approach to Pattern Analysis," *Advances in Computers,* Vol. 10, Academic Press, 1970.
9. A. W. Biermann and J. A. Feldman, "A Survey of Results in Grammatical Inference," International Conference on Frontiers of Pattern Recognition, Jan. 18-20, 1971, Honolulu, Hawaii.
10. T. G. Evans, "Grammatical Inference Techniques in Pattern Analysis," COINS-69 Symposium, published in *Software Engineering,* Vol. II, ed. by J. T. Tou, Academic Press, 1971.
11. A. W. Bierman and J. A. Feldman, "On the Synthesis of Finite-State Acceptors," Stanford Artificial Intelligence Project MEMO AIM-114, Stanford University, April 1970.
12. U. Grenander, "Syntax-Controlled Probabilities," Tech. Rept., Division of Applied Mathematics, Brown University, Providence, R. I., 1967.
13. T. L. Booth, "Probabilistic Representation of Formal Languages," Conf. Record, IEEE Tenth Annual Symposium on Switching and Automata Theory, October 1969.
14. T. Huang and K. S. Fu, "On Stochastic Context-Free Languages," *Information Sciences,* Vol. 3, July 1971.
15. S. E. Hutchins, "Stochastic Sources for Context-Free Languages," Ph.D. Thesis, Dept. of Applied Physics and Information Science, University of California, San Diego, June 1970.
16. K. S. Fu and T. J. Li, "On Stochastic Automata and Languages," *Information Sciences,* Vol. 1, October 1969.
17. A. Paz, "Some Aspects of Probabilistic Automata," *Information and Control,* Vol. 9, 1965.
18. A. Salomaa, "On Languages Accepted by Probabilistic and Time-Variant Automata," Proc. Second Annual Princeton Conference on Information Sciences and

Systems, March 1968.
19. P. Turakainen, "On Stochastic Languages," *Information and Control,* Vol. 12, 1968.
20. C. A. Ellis, "Probabilistic Languages and Automata," Rept. No. 355, Dept. of Computer Science, University of Illinois, October 1969.
21. D. J. Rosenkrantz, "Programmed Grammars–A New Device for Generating Formal Languages," Conference Record, IEEE Eighth Annual Symposium on Switch Switching and Automata Theory, October 1967.
22. P. H. Swain and K. S. Fu, "Stochastic Programmed Grammars for Syntactic Pattern Recognition," *PATTERN RECOGNITION,* Special Issue on Syntactic Pattern Recognition, Vol. 3, 1971.
23. T. Huang and K. S. Fu, "On Stochastic Languages and Their Applications to Pattern Recognition," Tech. Rept., School of Electrical Engineering, Purdue University, 1971.
24. J. E. Hopcroft and J. D. Ullman, *Formal Languages and Their Relation to Automata,* Addison-Wesley, 1969.
25. Satoshi Watanabe, *Knowing and Guessing; A Quantitative Study of Inference and Information,* Wiley, 1969.
26. Special Issue of *PATTERN RECOGNITION* (The Journal of the Pattern Recognition Society) on Syntactic Pattern Recognition, Vol. 3, Pergamon Press, 1971.
27. K. S. Fu, "On Syntactic Pattern Recognition and Stochastic Languages," Tech. Rept. TR-EE 71-21, School of Electrical Engineering, Purdue University, 1971.

TABLE 1

x	p(x)
ab_1c_1	$\frac{1}{36}$
ab_1c_2	$\frac{2}{36}$
ab_1c_3	$\frac{3}{36}$
ab_2c_1	$\frac{1}{36}$
ab_2c_2	$\frac{21}{36}$
ab_2c_3	$\frac{2}{36}$
ab_3c_1	$\frac{3}{36}$
ab_3c_2	$\frac{2}{36}$
ab_3c_3	$\frac{1}{36}$

TABLE 2

x	p(x)
ab_0c_2	$\frac{1}{36}$
ab_0c_3	$\frac{2}{36}$
ab_0c_4	$\frac{21}{36}$
ab_1c_2	$\frac{1}{36}$
ab_1c_3	$\frac{4}{36}$
ab_1c_4	$\frac{1}{36}$
ab_2c_2	$\frac{2}{36}$
ab_2c_3	$\frac{3}{36}$
ab_2c_4	$\frac{1}{36}$

TABLE 3

Stochastic Grammar Describing the Noisy Squares

$V_N = \{S,A,X,Q,A,M,W,C,E,R,T,B,V\}$

$V_T = \{-,0,+,*,\$\}$

$J = \{1,2,...,37\}$

0 : unit segment in direction of current side
+ : unit segment with slope + 1 relative to current side
− : unit segment with slope − 1 relative to current side
* : corner (change direction by + 90°)
$: tail delimiter (final string only)

Label	Core	Success Branches and Branch Probabilities	Failure Branches and Branches Probabilities
1	$S \longrightarrow FXVQ$	$\{2,4,7\}$, $\{1-2\alpha,\alpha,\alpha\}$	$\{\emptyset\}$, $\{1\}$
2	$F \longrightarrow OFA$	$\{3\}$, $\{1\}$	$\{\emptyset\}$, $\{1\}$
3	$X \longrightarrow XXX$	$\{10\}$, $\{1\}$	$\{\emptyset\}$, $\{1\}$
4	$F \longrightarrow +FA$	$\{5\}$, $\{1\}$	$\{\emptyset\}$, $\{1\}$

TABLE 3
(cont.)

Label	Core	Success Branches and Branch Probabilities	Failure Branches and Branches Probabilities
5	$M \longrightarrow XXX$	{10}, {1}	{6}, {1}
6	$X \longrightarrow WXX$	{10}, {1}	{∅}, {1}
7	$F \longrightarrow -FA$	{8}, {1}	{∅}, {1}
8	$W \longrightarrow XXX$	{10}, {1}	{9}, {1}
9	$X \longrightarrow MXX$	{10}, {1}	{∅}, {1}
10	$W \longrightarrow W$	{2,4,7,12}, $\{p_1, p_2, p_3, \beta\}$	{11}, {1}
11	$M \longrightarrow M$	{2,4,7,12}, $\{p_1, p_3, p_2, \beta\}$	{2,4,7,12}, $\{p_4, p_3, p_3, \beta\}$
12	$F \longrightarrow *F$	{13}, {1}	{∅}, {1}
13	$Q \longrightarrow R$	{16}, {1}	{14}, {1}
14	$R \longrightarrow S$	{16}, {1}	{15}, {1}
15	$S \longrightarrow T$	{16}, {1}	{36}, {1}
16	$B \longrightarrow A$	{16}, {1}	{17}, {1}
17	$A \longrightarrow B$	{18}, {1}	{20}, {1}
18	$E \longrightarrow C$	{17}, {1}	{19}, {1}
19	$V \longrightarrow CV$	{17}, {1}	{∅}, {1}
20	$W \longrightarrow X$	{21}, {1}	{22}, {1}
21	$C \longrightarrow E$	{20}, {1}	{∅}, {1}
22	$M \longrightarrow X$	{23}, {1}	{25,26,29}, $\{1-2\alpha, \alpha, \alpha\}$
23	$E \longrightarrow C$	{22}, {1}	{24}, {1}
24	$V \longrightarrow CV$	{22}, {1}	{∅}, {1}
25	$F \longrightarrow OF$	{32}, {1}	{∅}, {1}
26	$F \longrightarrow +F$	{27}, {1}	{∅}, {1}
27	$M \longrightarrow X$	{32}, {1}	{28}, {1}
28	$X \longrightarrow W$	{32}, {1}	{∅}, {1}
29	$F \longrightarrow -F$	{30}, {1}	{∅}, {1}
30	$W \longrightarrow X$	{32}, {1}	{31}, {1}
31	$X \longrightarrow M$	{32}, {1}	{∅}, {1}
32	$C \longrightarrow E$	{33}, {1}	{∅}, {1}
33	$C \longrightarrow C$	{34}, {1}	{12}, {1}
34	$W \longrightarrow W$	{25,26,29}, $\{1-\alpha-\alpha^2, \alpha^2, \alpha\}$	{35}, {1}
35	$M \longrightarrow M$	{25,26,29}, $\{1-\alpha-\alpha^2, \alpha, \alpha^2\}$	{25,26,29}, $\{1-2\alpha, \alpha, \alpha\}$
36	$T \longrightarrow \$$	{37}, {1}	{∅}, {1}
37	$F \longrightarrow F$	{∅}, {1}	{∅}, {1}

$p_1 = (1-\alpha-\alpha^2)(1-\beta)$, $p_2 = \alpha^2(1-\beta)$, $p_3 = \alpha(1-\beta)$, $p_4 = (1-2\alpha)(1-\beta)$

The noisy square shown in Figure 4 is the pictorial representation of the string:

−000000000−00+−000000+00000000000+0000*
00000−000000000000000000000000000000000*
00+000000000000000−00+000000000−0000000*
0000000000000000000000+000000000000000*$ (tail omitted)

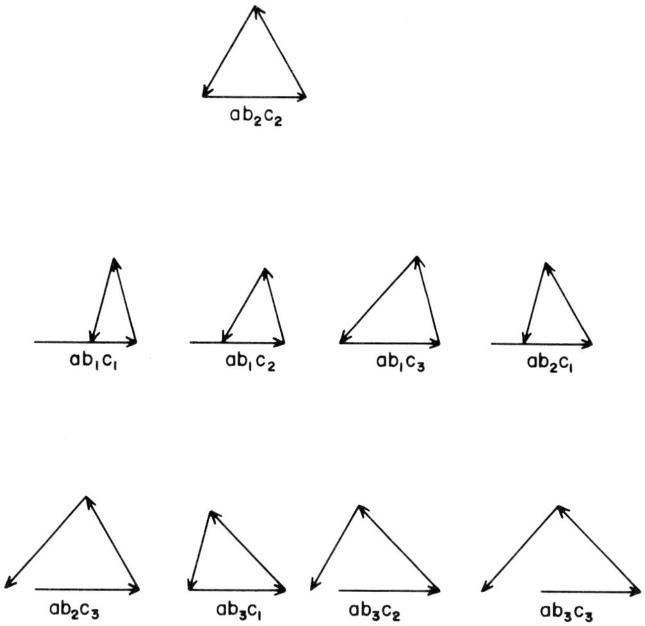

Figure 1

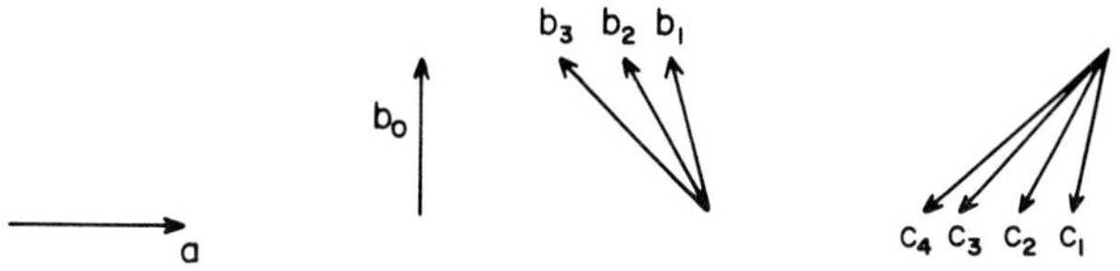

Figure 2

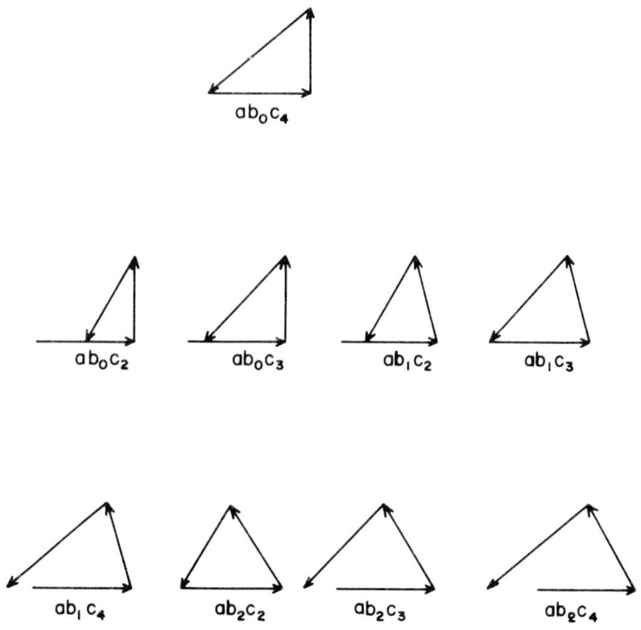

Figure 3

SCALE: 1/8" PER UNIT LENGTH
α = 0.05, β = 0.05

Figure 4

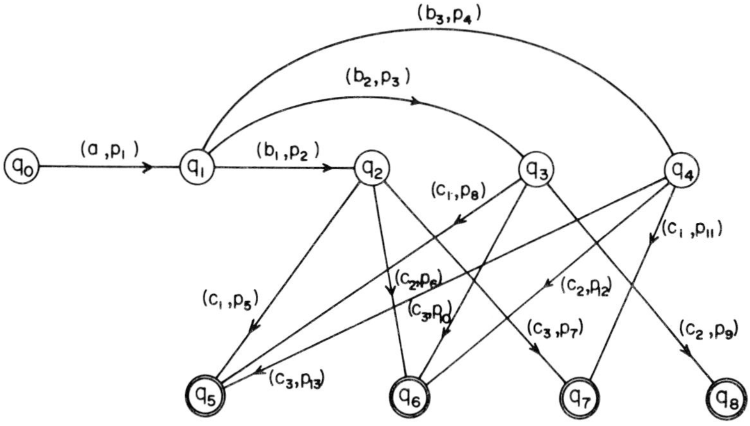

Figure 5

COMPUTER IDENTIFICATION OF BACTERIA BY COLONY MORPHOLOGY

D. A. Glaser and C. B. Ward

VIRUS LABORATORY
UNIVERSITY OF CALIFORNIA
BERKELEY

Abstract

Species of bacteria important in medical diagnosis, public health surveys, industrial applications, and biological research can often be identified by the appearance of colonies they form when growing on solid agar. Colonies are located and counted automatically by flying spot scanner examination of photographs. Measurements of colony diameter and optical density profiles on colony diameters permit identification that is better than 90% correct for eight strains already characterized. Extending the library to 50 strains with accuracies exceeding 90% seems quite feasible.

For more than a century physicians and biologists have studied the growth of microorganisms such as bacteria, yeast and fungi because of their importance as agents of disease, their value as industrial tools, and their intrinsic interest as simple living organisms. In most assay applications the purpose is to detect the presence of known organisms and establish their response to various nutrients or to treatment with drugs or heat. In health applications one wants to know how many organisms of each kind are present in a sample taken from a patient or from a contaminated food or water supply and also what drugs or other treatments would be most effective in destroying the harmful organisms. Single organisms or small numbers of them can be identified partially under the microscope by their shape and tendency to be stained by various dyeing procedures. When a suspension of single cells is spread on the surface of nutrient agar gel in a petri dish and incubated at a suitable temperature the cells grow and divide every hour or so under typical circumstances, to produce in 24 hours a colony several millimeters in diameter. Figures 1 through 3 illustrate the development of a colony of *Staphlococcus albus* in 24 hours and Figures 4 through 6 show the same development for a colony of *Bacillus subtilis*. One expects the shape and the size of the colony to depend on the shape and size of the individual cell, its mode of division, its tendency to clump or form long chains of cells, its mobility on the agar surface, its sensitivity to nutrient concentration, oxygen deprivation, self-secreted poisons and a great variety of other factors that are only partially understood. The interplay of these factors accounts for the final characteristics of the mature colony in a complicated way that can be used as a "fingerprint" for identifying the organism provided the colony morphology is highly reproducible, even though its causes are not understood. In fact when pure cultures of identical microorganisms are used to inoculate the petri dish the mature colonies do appear remarkably alike. Visual inspection by an experienced technician is often sufficient for identification of the strain of bacteria although absolutely positive identification requires detailed biochemical, serological and microscopic staining techniques. These supplemental operations require that a number of organisms be picked from a suspicious colony, recultured in a liquid suspension, usually overnight, and subjected to additional tests done by hand which may require 1 or 2 days for completion. The total process usually takes about 3 days. Variations of these methods are used in diagnosis of infectious disease, in analysis of contaminated food, water and medical supplies, in the measurement of contamination levels in sewage subjected to various degrees of treatment, and in detection of possible contamination carried by spacecraft. With the recent flowering of molecular biology, bacteria as well as some yeast and fungi have been the subject of intensive study aimed at understanding their basic growth and reproduction processes. A critical step in many experiments in molecular biology is counting the number of colonies of a certain particular type of genetic mutant which arises from some parental type as a result of controlled treatment with radiation, drugs or other mutagenic agents.

The general purpose of the present work is to use methods of automatic pattern recognition to make rapid and automatic quantitative analysis of the appearance of colonies of growing microorganisms in the hope that such quantitative measurements will be sufficiently accurate to identify species and strains of microorganisms without the need for the time consuming and expensive additional tests conventionally used. We were encouraged to undertake this study by the opinion of many microbiologists who claim that qualitative visual inspection of colonies by a trained technician allows correct identification of microorganisms in about 70% of the cases encountered in most practical applications. If quantitative analysis of the appearance of colonies could raise the accuracy of identification to over 90% it would be sufficient for a wide range of applications and would permit a dramatic reduction in the time and cost of carrying out the identifications. Furthermore, a number of large scale epidemiological surveys, monitoring of daily changes in contamination levels of water supplies, and extensive evolutionary experiments with microorganisms would become feasible for the first time.

To study the morphology of growing colonies of bacteria a drop of suspension containing 10 or 20 organisms is spread uniformly over the surface of nutrient agar gel in the bottom of a flat 100-mm diameter dish. The dishes are covered and incubated usually at 37°C. Thirty-five millimeter photographs on black and white film are made after 24 hours of incubation, sometimes with color filters which may aid in the identification of the colony.

A typical petri dish containing a small number of colonies is shown in Figure 7. In order for the colony to exhibit its characteristic shape and not be distorted by nearby colonies competing for nutrient, dishes must be sparsely inoculated as shown here. For counting very large numbers of organisms of known identity, heavy inoculations can be made so that the plates may contain a few hundred colonies each.

Figures 8 through 10 are photographs of 24 hour colonies of 3 strains of bacteria that are identified in our system. Figure 11 shows a dish of organisms cultivated from a drop of pond water showing modest contamination levels due to a variety of different organisms. These photographs were made with an incubator-camera apparatus which we call the "Candid camera" in which the dish is illuminated by a very well collimated parallel beam of light from below and photographed from above while being incubated in a sterile, constant temperature glove box. Figure 12 shows the Candid camera with some single colony photographs on the wall behind it. Typical experiments in molecular biology generate hundreds to thousands of petri dishes in a batch and these can be photographed rapidly in a device called the "Roundabout" shown in Figure 13. Dishes are presented to the machine in plastic cartridges containing 20 dishes and photographed at the rate of about one a second. For large scale experiments in microbial evolution as well as for carrying out medical diagnosis and contamination surveys on a large scale, we are constructing a large machine to handle 10,000 petri dishes in one batch. Figure 14 shows the design of this "Dumbwaiter" machine as it is called. The petri dishes are carried on frames about 1 meter square shown stacked in the left elevator of the machine. The frames rise one at a time to the top horizontal duct, move across the duct past stations where they can be photographed and manipulated and then arrive on the stack on the right which lowers them to the bottom cross duct where they again pass manipulation stations and photography stations to re-enter the original stack on the left. The Dumbwaiter can accomodate conventional petri dishes or large sheets of agar contained in glass trays carried two per frame in the machine. Figure 15 shows an engineering test model of one of these frames.

Photographs taken by any of these cameras are analyzed by a flying-spot scanner with a resolution of 4000 lines and the ability to measure 64 levels of gray. The first pattern recognition task is to locate the colonies, count them, and identify and select those which are suitable for morphological analysis. Counting the colonies is easy in uncrowded plates but in crowded plates the colonies frequently overlap when they reach a diameter of 2 or 3 mm. A pattern recognition strategy for resolving multiple overlaps is shown in Figure 16 in which the boundary points of a figure are shown on the display scope of the computer together with averaged tangents laid down around the perimeter. Discontinuities in the second derivative of the curve of the boundary are used to identify cusps and portions of arcs between adjacent cusps are analyzed by a least squares program which finds the center of each arc, as shown in Figure 17. Each center thus determined is taken to indicate the presence of a single colony in the overlapping configuration except when two centers are closer than some predetermined distance. Then the centers are considered to belong to arcs that are parts of the same colony and are counted as one, as shown in Figure 18. Here the computer has decided that there are three colonies, as indicated by the three centers shown. A more difficult case is shown in Figure 19. Figure 20 shows centers of arcs found by the computer which draws lines on the display connecting those centers that are going to be fused according to its error criterion. Figure 21 shows the final decision of the computer indicating that this figure contains six colonies. At the present time the computer requires about a minute to carry out this counting operation for dishes containing one to two hundred colonies. The present accuracy is about 3% when calibrated against the results of a trained technician. These figures can probably be improved considerably.

Identification of bacterial species by this method depends on quantitative analysis of shape, color, graininess, turbidity, and other features that can be recorded relatively simply by photography. The principle basis of the identification depends on the observation that the colonies are not simple flat discs but have complicated contours of ridges and valleys that vary considerably from one strain to another. In principle these topographical features could be recorded by stereo photography or holography but computer analysis of such pictures would be quite difficult and costly. We have therefore relied on a strategy which depends on the optical lens-like quality of the colony. When illuminated by parallel light the pattern of ridges and valleys will cause a set of bright point and halo images to be formed in the space above and below the colony. By photographing the colonies with a camera with shallow depth of field and focussed at various heights above the colony we are able to record these images as illustrated in Figure 22, showing a single *Pseudomonas fluorescens* colony photographed in the middle top of the slide with some combination of reflected and transmitted light that would be typical of ordinary viewing with the naked eye. For comparison we see three other pictures taken with the camera sharply focussed on the agar surface and at distances of 0.1 and 0.5 inches above the agar. These photographs were all taken with a lens opening of about f/2.5, using a 105mm lens so that the depth of field is quite shallow. It is obvious that the out-of-focus pictures are a good deal more interesting than the in-focus ones. In Figure 23 is shown a colony of *E. coli* K12, the strain mainly used for experimental work in molecular biology. The in-focus picture is not enormously different from that for *Pseudomonas fluorescens* which is quite a different organism, but the out-of-focus pictures are quite distinctive. In Figure 24 we see the same set of pictures of Staphlococcus albus giving a distinctly different set of patterns. Figure 25 shows a lucite and glass model in which images photographed at various heights above the colony are mounted on a scale which is exaggerated by a factor of 4 vertically. The topmost image is in fact taken one inch above the colony and the others are in proportion as shown. The method of analysis we have used consists in measuring the optical density profile of these circular images taken across a diameter of the image. For simplicity we have mounted a fine-grained diffusing screen 0.5-inches above the agar surface and photograph the images cast on it by the colonies when illuminated from below by parallel white light. Optical density profiles of four diameters of each colony image, taken 45° apart from each other, are averaged and analyzed to obtain the first twenty Fourier coefficients characterizing the averaged profile. The results of this analysis are shown in Figure 26 for *Pseudomonas fluorescens.* The three profiles along the top are the in-focus, 0.1 inch out-of-focus and 0.5 inch out-of-focus images. Below these profiles are shown the first 20 Fourier coefficients resulting from analysis of these profiles. The bottom half of the figure shows the identical result for a second colony to give some idea how reproducible this kind of information is from colony to colony. Figure 27 shows the same data for two colonies of a strain of *E. coli* resistant to streptomycin. Again the two colonies give very similar results. Figure 28 shows results for quite a different type of organism, *Vibrio metchnikovi* which is related to the causative organism of cholera. In our present procedure each dish containing about 15 colonies is photographed in white, blue and red light making three black and white images and each colony is characterized by the diameter in blue light, the first 5 Fourier coefficients in each of the 3 colors, and the ratios of the maximum optical densities measured in blue, white, and red light, for a total of 18 attributes. About 20 seconds of computer time is required to scan and analyze each photograph in this way. From a sample of colonies of the same known strain a library of prototype colonies is constructed for each strain. An unknown colony whose identity is to be determined is then assigned to that strain in the library having the closest prototype. The effectiveness of this procedure is shown in Table 1. The first column lists the name of the bacterial species studied and the second column shows the accuracy with which the prototype library represents 500 to 1000 colonies in our learning sample of each strain. These accuracies are less than 100% because occasionally a colony belonging to one strain will be misclassified if its representative point in an 19 dimensional attribute space lies close to a cluster belonging to a different strain. The last column shows the accuracy within which an unknown colony inoculated and incubated on another day can be reclassified correctly. These results are a considerable improvement over earlier results and have been attained by improvement of the clustering and reclassification scheme and also by considerable improvement in the biological techniques. Very careful attention must be paid to uniformity of the agar, of the nutrients, of the humidity and of the temperature of the incubation, of the uniformity of illumination of the dishes during photography and other experimental parameters. The rather poor showing of three of the strains indicates a misidentification in which the colony of one strain was confused with the other two that look very similar to it. We can improve this accuracy somewhat by further improvements in biological, optical and photographic techniques and perhaps further improvements in the analysis programs, but the fact remains that these three strains are rather similar to each other and very slight changes in experimental conditions causes confusion. We are, therefore, beginning a program of photographing the same sample of bacteria incubated under two different biological conditions since different strains respond quite differently to different nutritional and thermodynamic environments. By growing colonies on two different standardized nutrient agars we hope to resolve some of the ambiguities shown in this table.* It may well be that the use of two or three distinctly different agars would allow us to reduce the precision required in the incubation and photographic steps and even simplify the analytical reclassification system. There will then be a trade-off between the number of different kinds of agar used, the number of different colored photographs taken and the number of geometric features that must be analyzed. So far our analysis has depended only on the radial optical density distribution of the patterns. It is obvious that a two-dimensional analysis of the pattern would pick up certain kinds of granularity, spoked patterns, scalloped

*Very recently we discovered that *Aerobacter aerogenes* and *Enterobacter* are two names for the same organism so that the computer was quite correct in confusing them, although they came from different sources!

edges and a variety of other features which are now ignored. With the addition of these new measurements we hope to raise our identification accuracy to well over 90% for all the strains in a library containing 30 to 50 standard organisms. That ability will be sufficient for most medical applications of this technology and will allow us to undertake many types of large scale genetic and evolution experiments.

One important development for the near future is to add a television or image dissector system which can look directly at the growing colonies without the need for photography. Using such real time observation it will be possible to add drugs and nutrients, to change the temperature, illumination and gaseous environment and to record the response of the growingfcolonies to these changes. That will increase enormously the biological information required for identifying an organism and increase the subtlety of possible biological experiments.

Acknowledgements*

This work was made possible by the imaginative technical assistance of Philip Spielman, the superb engineering work of Leif Hansen and Ronald Baker, the excellent computer hardware and software contributions of Robert Henry, Ted Fujita, Dr. James Berk, and Fraser Bonnell, and the indispensable photomicrography and administrative assistance of Mrs. Aleen Simmons.

*This work was supported in part by the U. S. Public Health Service through research grants GM13244 and GM12524 from the National Institute of General Medical Sciences.

TABLE 1

Library Strain	*Library*	*Repeat*
Staph epidermidis	92%	95%
Sal. LT-2	99	97
Herrellia	> 99	99
Serratia	93	92
Aerobacter	95	50
Enterobacter	> 99	53
E. coli Hadley	85	65
Staph aureus	98	>99

Results of automatic colony classification. About 500 colonies of each strain are used to define the standard library type represented in the memory of the computer by about 10 similar prototype colonies for each strain. All colonies in the group are represented by these prototypes with the efficiency shown in the first column. When plates are reinoculated a few days later with the same organisms and their profiles analyzed the accuracy of identification is obtained as shown in the second column. The poor showing of *Aerobacter, Enterobacter* and *E. coli* results from the similarity among these strains and the slight changes in inoculation and incubation conditions which allow them to be easily confused. Methods are described in the text for resolving these confusions. See footnote, page 144.

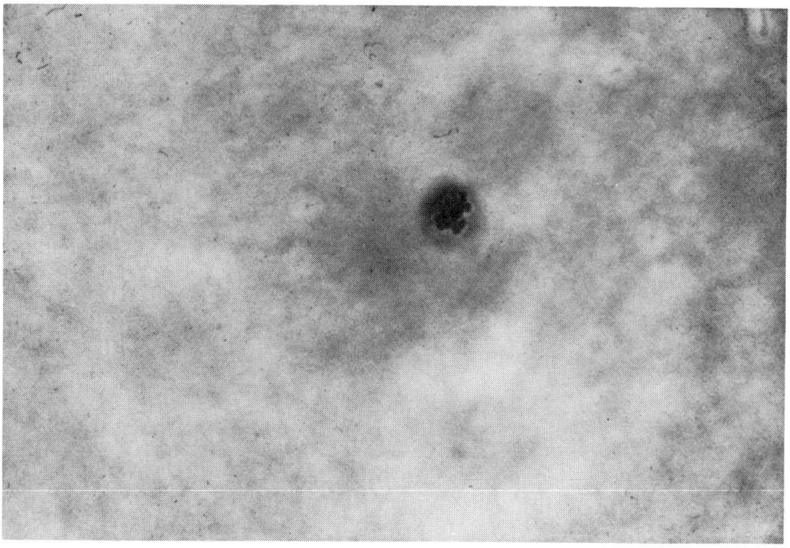

Figure 1. *Staphlococcus albus* colony incubated for 5 hours at 37°C

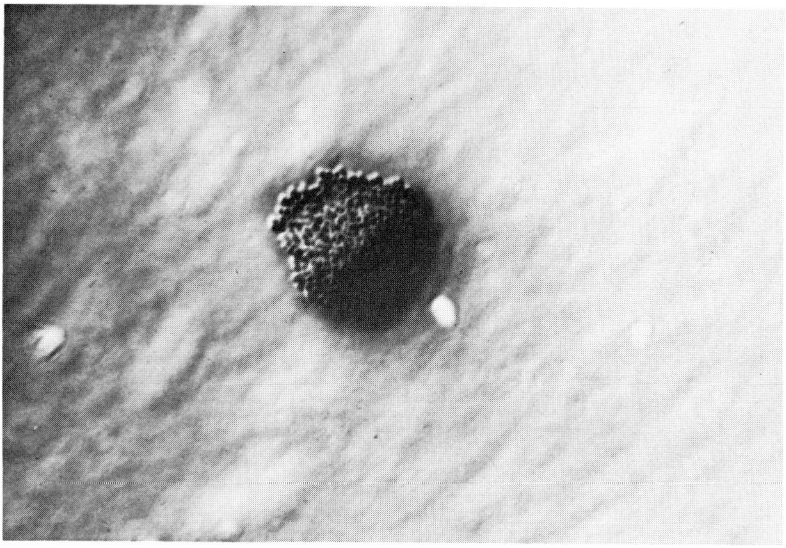

Figure 2. *Staphlococcus albus* colony incubated for 8 hours at 37°C. Individual cells are spherical, divide symmetrically and do not seem to form long chains so the colony becomes more or less circular at a rather early stage

Figure 3. *Staphlococcus albus* colony incubated 24 hours at 37°C

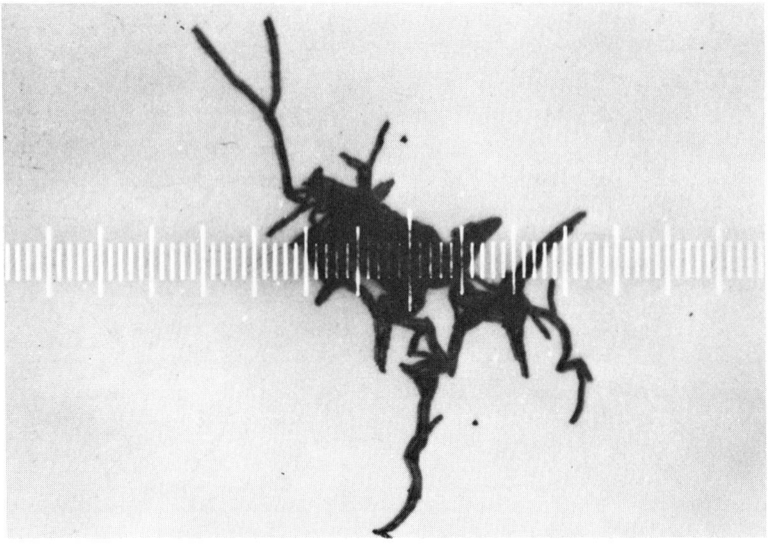

Figure 4. *Bacillus subtilis* incubated for 5 hours at 37°C. Individual cells are long, rod shaped, and tend to remain in chains in long strings even after they have divided

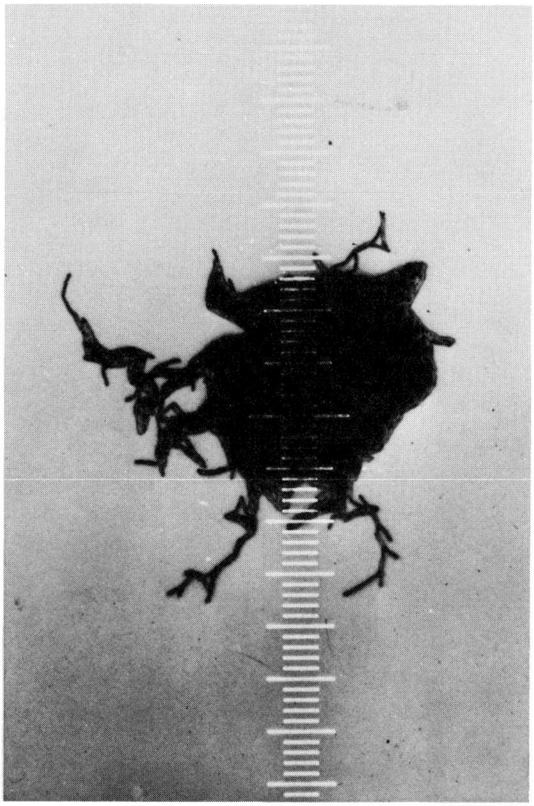

Figure 5. *Bacillus subtilis* incubated for 8 hours at 37°. The chainlike growth prevents rounding up of the colonies at this early stage

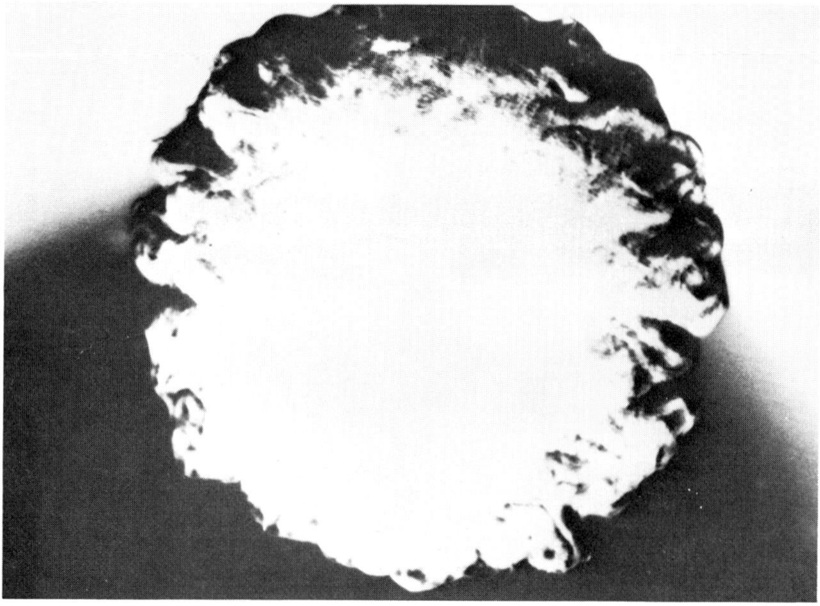

Figure 6. *Bacillus subtilis* incubated for 24 hours at 37°C. Although the colony is approximately circular its rough appearance and scalloped edges are characteristic

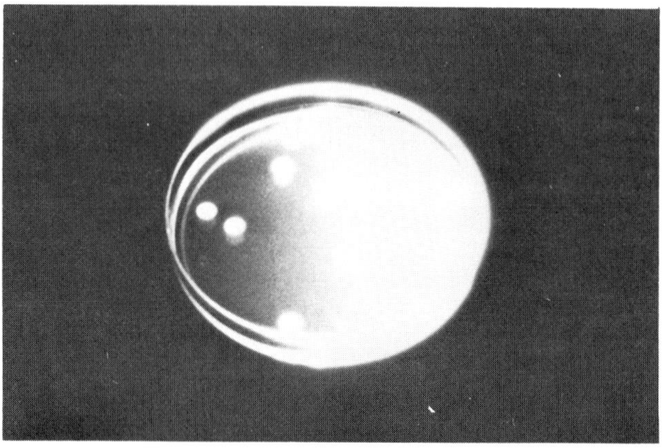

Figure 7. A disposable plastic petri dish, 100mm in diameter, sparsely inoculated for easy identification of colony morphology

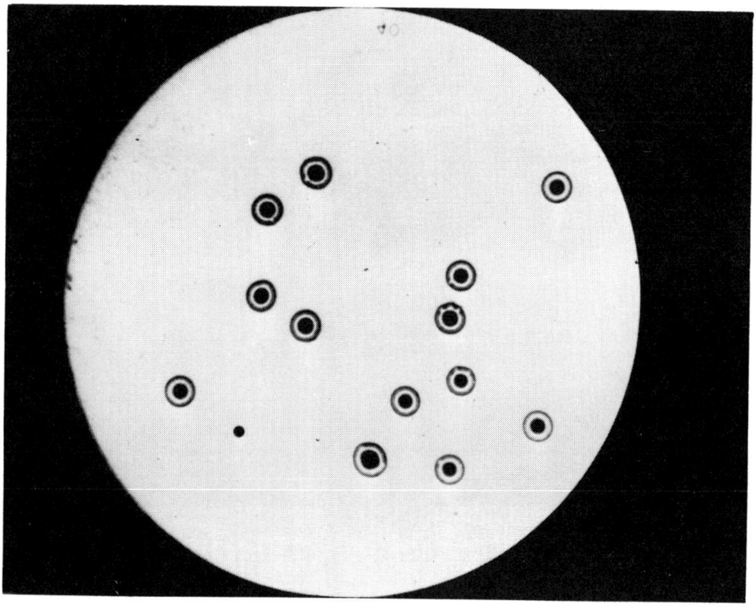

Figure 8. Twenty-four hour colonies of *Aerobacter aerogenes*

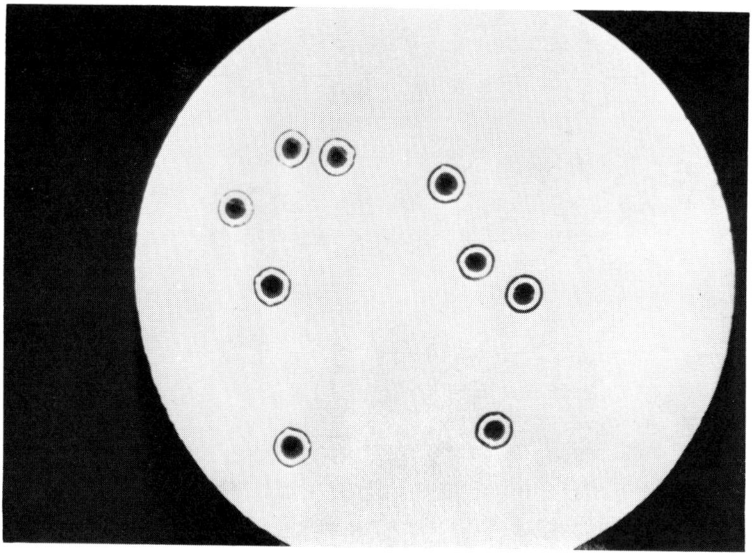

Figure 9. Twenty-four hour colonies of *E. coli* alkalescense dispar

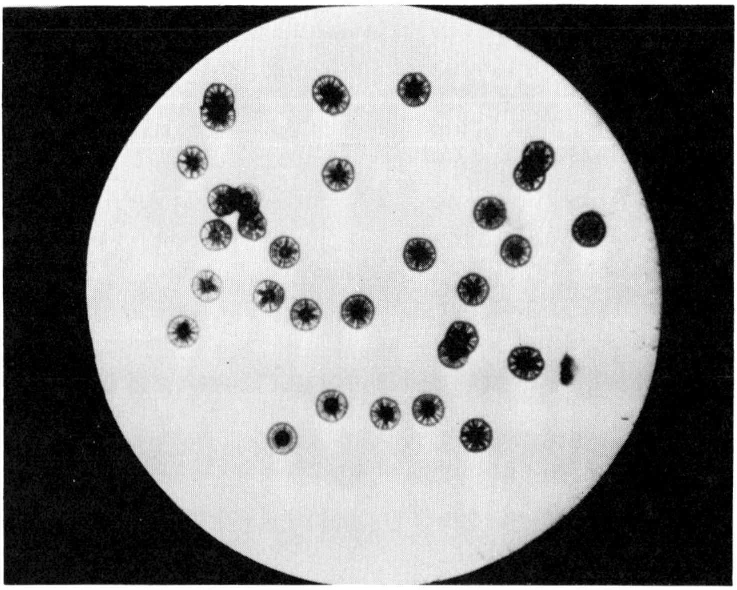

Figure 10. Twenty-four hour colonies of *Serratia marcescens* showing some overlapping and crowded colonies whose morphology is not characteristic because of the crowding. Isolated colonies show the standard pattern

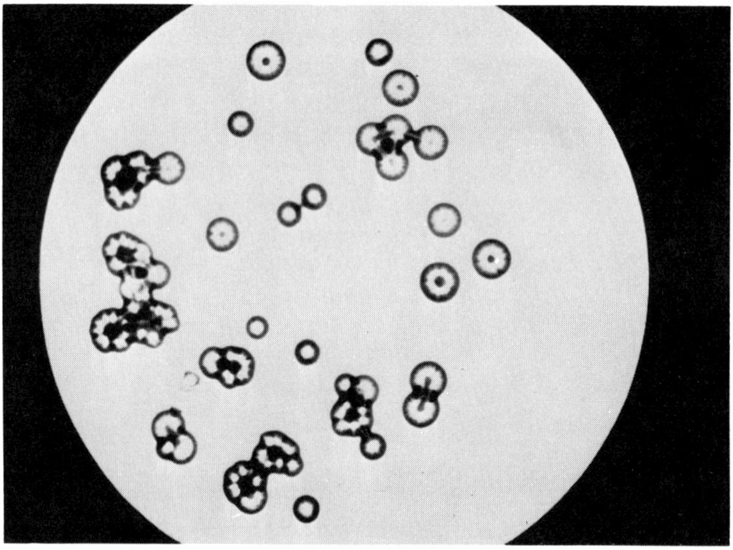

Figure 11. A black and white print of a color slide made with false color infrared film showing colonies that grew up from a drop of relatively pure pond water. Considerable variety of different organisms are seen in the picture

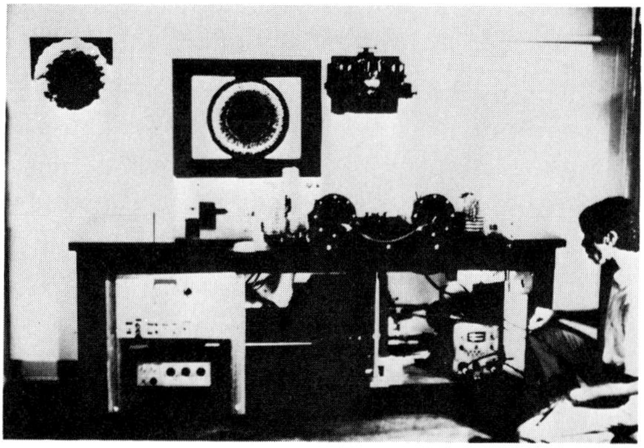

Figure 12. "Candid camera" incubator-camera projects a very well collimated beam of white light up through the bottom of the petri dish which is photographed from above with 35mm black and white film. The incubator glove box allows the operator to photograph the dishes while they are kept at growth temperature without disturbing the growth

Figure 13. "Roundabout". For photographing large numbers of petri dishes prepared in the laboratory by hand, the dishes are presented to the machine in plastic cartridges containing stacks of 20 and are photographed automatically along with identifying computer readable numbers at the rate of about 1 dish per second

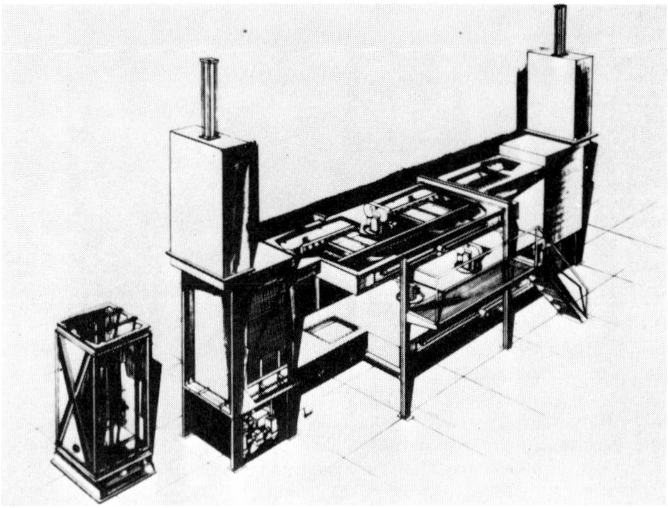

Figure 14. "Dumbwaiter". For large experiments this machine will have a capacity equivalent to 10,000 petri dishes, carried in 1 m square frames which circulated around the machine passing stations where they can be photographed and manipulated, where standard operations such as spraying with drugs and nutrients, colony picking, and restreaking and other steps can be carried out under computer control. The machine will be about two stories high and forty feet long. Stacks of frames containing 5000 dishes each can be loaded and unloaded from the machine and stored in cold rooms or warm rooms so that several parallel experiments may be carried out at one time

Figure 15. Close-up of one of the Dumbwaiter frames showing two large glass trays. These trays can accommodate 32 conventional petri dishes each or hold one large sheet of nutrient agar. The position of the trays in the machine is controlled by a PDP-8 computer which can access any point on any frame with an accuracy of 0.005 inches

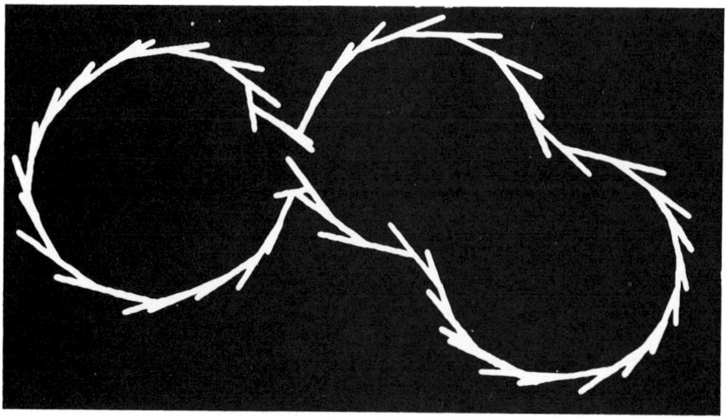

Figure 16. Computer display of the image of a 3 colony overlap figure in which tangents have been thrown down along the boundary points found by the computer

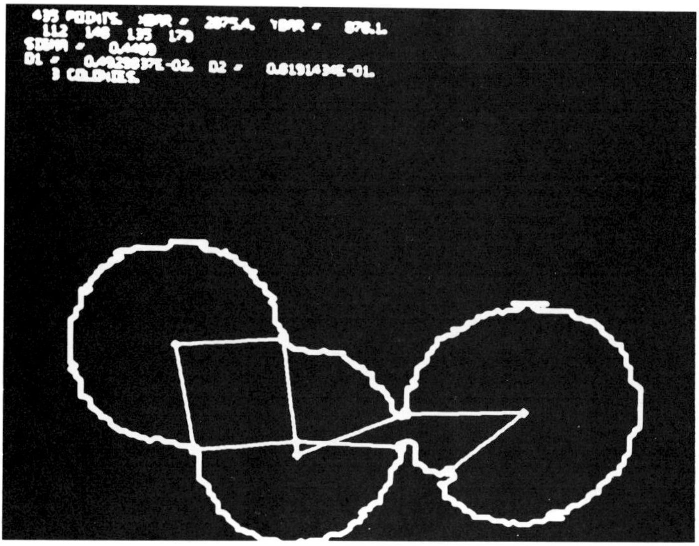

Figure 17. Cusps are located by the computer and least squares circular fits made to arcs joining adjacent cusps. When two centers are very close together the machine fuses them for getting the final colony count

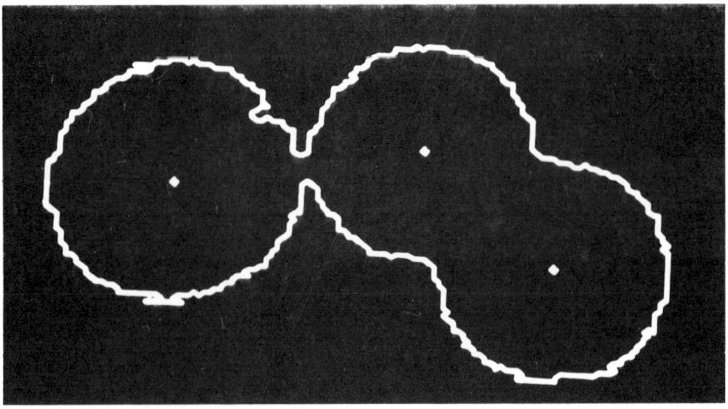

Figure 18. The computer has decided that three centers represent this figure adequately and therefore will register a count of 3 colonies for this figure

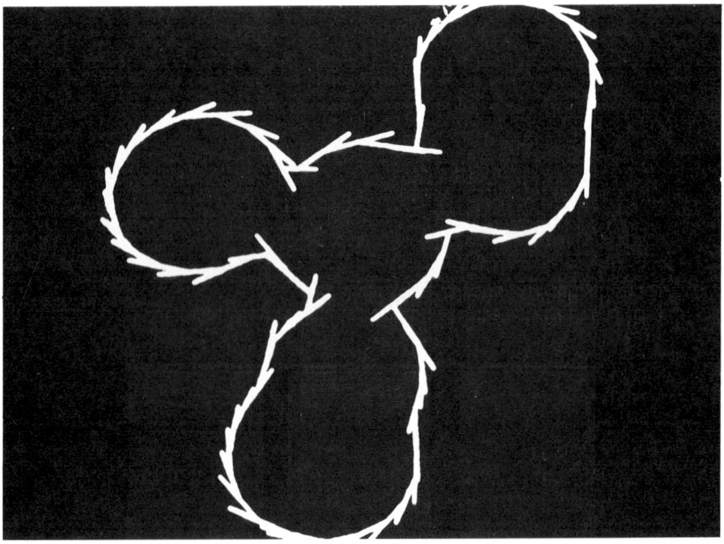

Figure 19. Boundary points and tangents on the computer display for a more complicated figure

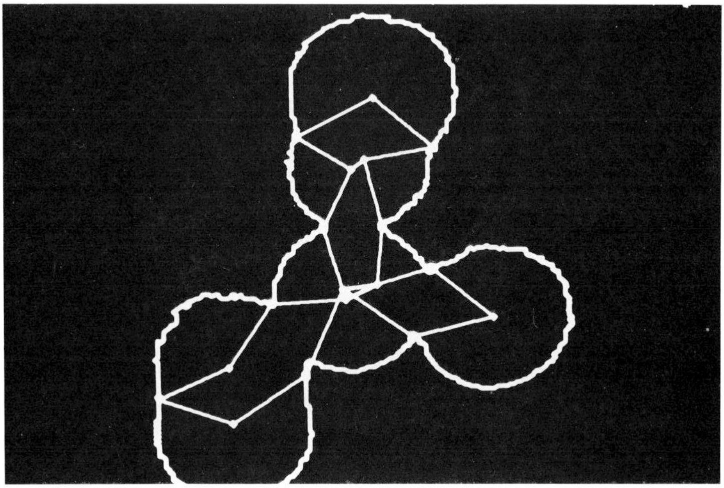

Figure 20. Cusps and centers of curvature located by the computer. Lines joining nearby centers indicate that the computer will fuse these centers

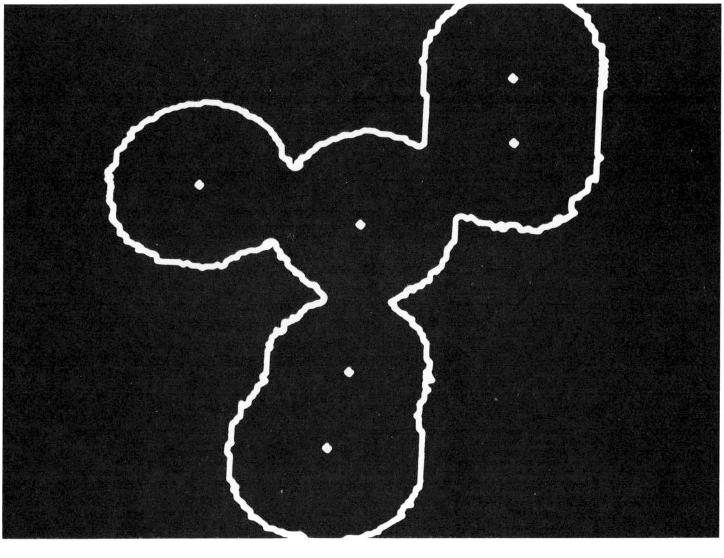

Figure 21. Final decision after fusion of arc centers showing a total count of 6 colonies

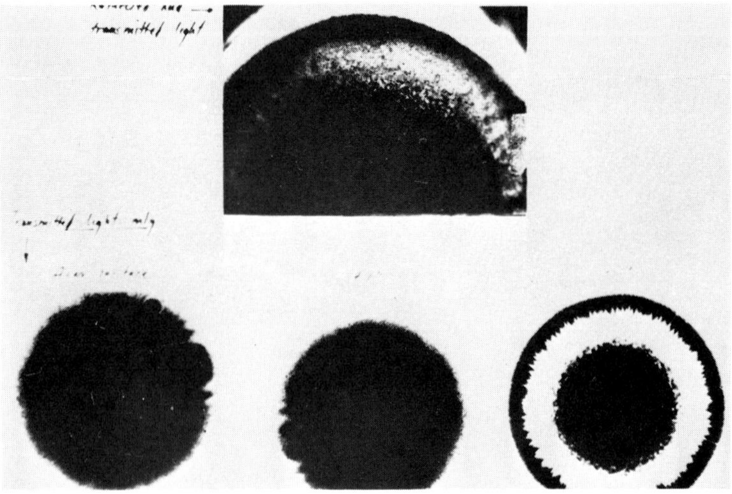

Figure 22. Single *Pseudomonas fluorescens* colony photographed (a) top center–in a combination of transmitted and reflected light, characteristic of ordinary visual inspection (b) focussed accurately on the agar surface in transmitted light (c) focussed 0.1 inches above the agar in transmitted light (d) focussed 0.5 inches above the agar in transmitted light

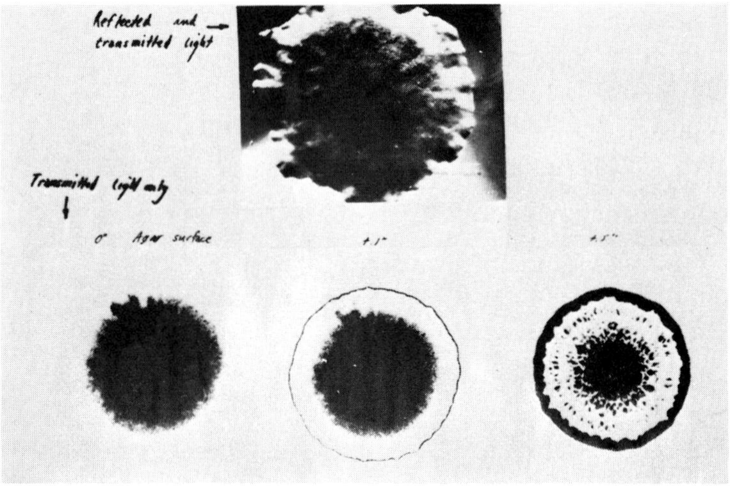

Figure 23. Single colony photographs of *E. coli* K12, an important experimental strain, photographed under the same conditions as used in Figure 22

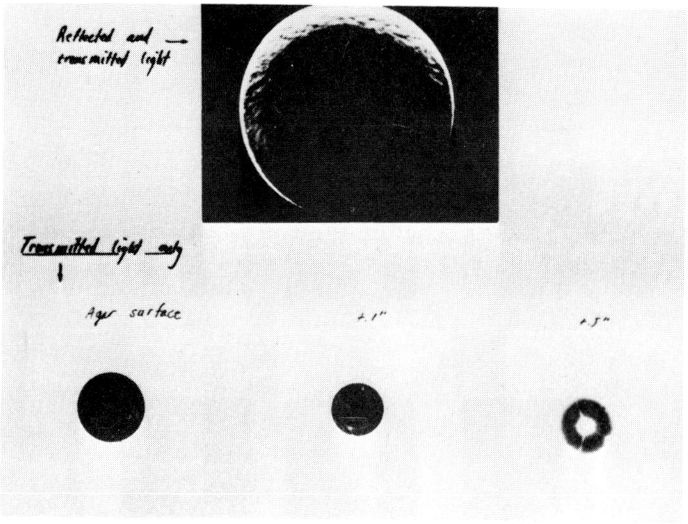

Figure 24. Single colony *Staphlococcus albus* photographed under the same conditions as in Figures 22 and 23

Figure 25. Lucite and glass model showing a composite of a number of photographs of a single colony of *Aerobacter aerogenes* taken at various heights above the agar

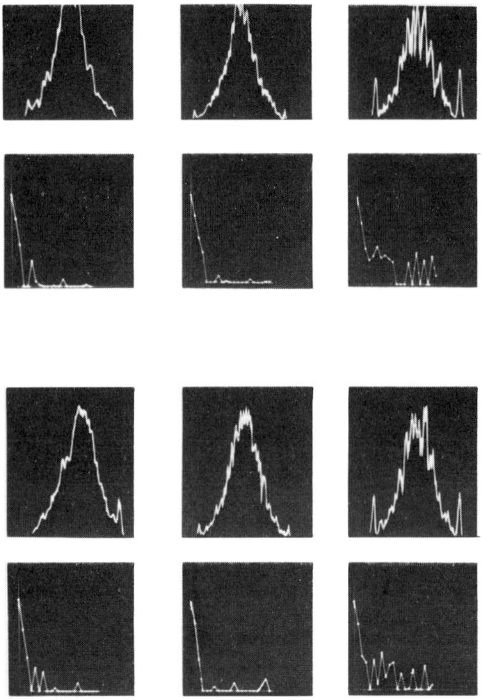

Figure 26. Colony profiles and Fourier analyses of two *Pseudomonas fluorescens* colonies showing an average diametral optical density profile for the in-focus 0.1 and 0.5 inch out-of-focus photographs, together with the Fourier power spectrum showing the first 20 Fourier coefficients for these images. The lower half of the figure shows a second colony to give quite similar results to the first one

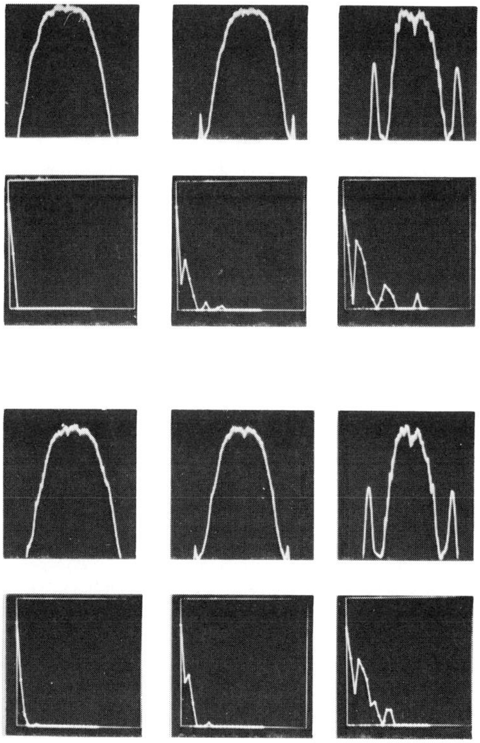

Figure 27. Profiles and Fourier spectra of 2 single colonies of *E. coli* (streptomycin resistent), rough form. The same information is contained as in Figure 26

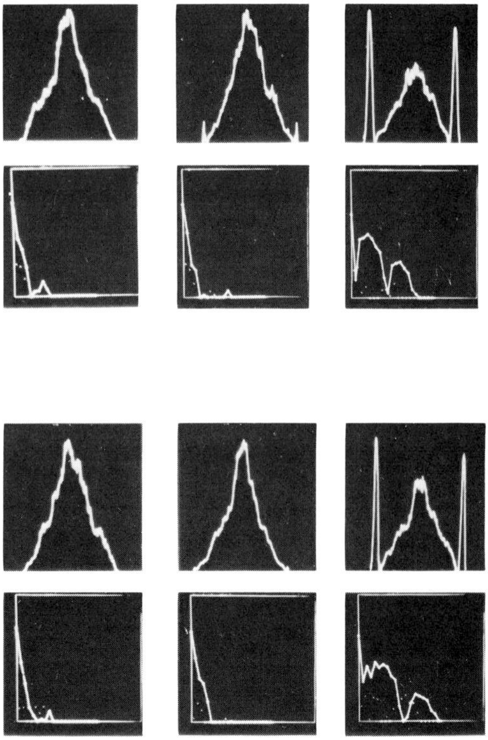

Figure 28. Optical density profiles and Fourier power spectra for 2 colonies of *Vibrio metchnikovi*. Same information as shown in Figures 26 and 27

ON LINGUISTIC, STATISTICAL AND MIXED MODELS FOR PATTERN RECOGNITION

*Laveen Kanal**

COMPUTER SCIENCE CENTER
UNIVERSITY OF MARYLAND
COLLEGE PARK, MARYLAND

*B. Chandrasekaran***

DEPARTMENT OF COMPUTER AND INFORMATION SCIENCE
OHIO STATE UNIVERSITY
COLUMBUS, OHIO

Abstract

The "pure" linguistic model is usually presented as a contrast to the "pure" statistical classification model. Neither pure model is relevant to applications. Rather, different models are appropriate for different kinds of prior information. The viewpoint espoused in this paper can be termed "heuristic complexity decomposition," which corresponds to reducing a complex problem to a set of problems of complexity of lower order. It is shown that it is hybrid linguistic-statistical models that are useful in practice. This viewpoint reconciles the dichotomy that is currently believed to exist between "structural" and "geometric" approaches.

We present a selective discussion of some aspects of linguistics, statistical and mixed approaches to pattern recognition, and consider the potential of transformational grammars, a proposed formalism for pattern analysis and recognition, and heuristic and formal procedures for inference of pattern grammars. We point out the utility of first-order predicate calculus formalism for pattern description in view of the availability of a large body of heuristic techniques for analysis.

---

*Work partially supported by subcontract to L. N. K. Corporation from Philco-Ford Corporation under Contract F 33615-69-C-1571 for the 6570th Aerospace Medical Research Laboratorv, Aerospace Medical Division, Air Force Systems Command, Wright-Patterson Air Force Base, Ohio; and in part by the Systems Command, under Grant AFOSR 71-71-1982.

**Work supported by NSF Grant GN-534.1.

I. Introduction

U. Neisser in his review [Neisser (1969)] of a book on recognizing patterns, says "Is there -- can there be -- a field of inquiry devoted to what is called 'pattern recognition'? Almost certainly not, despite the efforts of this useful and occasionally fascinating book". Since the search for regularities in the environment is the principal concern of all scientific inquiry, and since recognizing patterns is intrinsic to all intelligent activity, it would appear that the field of pattern recognition encompasses all scientific inquiry and intelligent behavior! Nevertheless, it is a mark of the present age that we are not content with just using words such as learning and pattern recognition but want to probe further and attempt to gain some understanding of what the words mean. Thus sentiments such as those expressed by Neisser have not prevented an influx of researchers into the field called pattern recognition.

An observer of the pattern recognition "scene" during the period of the last decade and a half could hardly have failed to notice the following features. In the beginning of this period there was great excitement about trainable networks. The followed considerable activity on the statistical design of categorizers. At about the same time that the activity on trainable networks was reaching its peak, arguments were advanced for a formal "linguistic" approach to pattern recognition. These arguments, together with the success of syntax-directed compilers, have persuaded many that a formal linguistic approach using pattern grammars and syntactic analysis is the answer; now this latter approach is the most prominent feature of the scene.

In order to justify or motivate a particular pattern recognition technique or contrast a proposed method against previous methods, it has been common for analytically inclined authors to make statements of the type "the pattern recognition problem is" followed by a rather specific model such as a receptor-categorizer model, an n-dimensional Euclidean space model, a structural analysis model, or formal grammar model. A little reflection shows that the use of the word "patterns" conveys meanings beyond those which can be easily handled by any single analytical framework proposed thus far.

In automatic pattern recognition, some of the most notable successes have come from focussing on specific well-defined problems and delving deeply into their solution. This is usually the approach which produces quick, tangible results in many fields. It is marked by categorization and precise isolation of phenomena in order to develop specific techniques. Examples in automatic pattern recognition are the automatic recognition of typed letters of the alphabet and the computer processing of bubble-chamber tracks.

In studying pattern recognition, the feature extraction-classification model with classification being performed according to deterministic rules, statistical methodology or fuzzy-set based algorithms, and the linguistic model using generative grammars, have been suggested by some of the evidence concerning phenomena encountered in recognizing patterns. The feature extraction-classification model has proved very useful not only in organizing and focussing efforts on the study and development of classification algorithms but also in solving a variety of real life problems in automating pattern recognition tasks. Indeed the major successes to date in automatic pattern recognition have been achieved by transforming a perception-recognition problem into a classification problem [Kanal and Chandrasekaran (1968)].

In the *pattern analysis* area, there were in the earlier phases, few models of relatively general applicability. With the passage of time, however, attempts to develop relatively general approaches, applicable to a class of problems, are perhaps irresistible. Many workers have succumbed, and today we have in our midst models of reasonable generality – in both theoretical and experimental domains. The so-called linguistic approaches are the prominent examples in the theoretical arena, while interactive, graphics-oriented, data analysis techniques are the response to demands for generality in the experimental domain.

In the following pages, we look at some aspects of the linguistic, and linguistic-statistical methods that have aroused interest in the past few years. The reader interested in a capsule summary of our views is directed to Section II.2.

II. Linguistic and Linguistic-Statistical Methods in Pattern Recognition

Good reviews of published work on the use of linguistic techniques in pattern recognition are available elsewhere [Miller and Shaw (1968), Fu and Swain (1969)]. Our intent here is to discuss certain aspects either covered very lightly or not covered by these reviews and to reconcile the existing dichotomy between what Aiserman [1969] calls "geometric" and "structural" approaches, i.e., "feature-extraction-classification" and "linguistic" approaches.

1. *Preliminaries*

In the geometric approach, each pattern is represented as a point in a multidimensional feature space, which is divided into disjoint regions, each region corresponding to a pattern class. This division might be effected on the basis of statistical or nonstatistical considerations. We will consider statistical methods as representative of techniques in the geometric approach. Note that features are left undefined within the model. As an example, consider a character in a suitably quantized two-dimensional space; the gray level in each retinal region might be a feature. Of course, if suitable preprocessors are available, one might define other features, such as a binary valued feature to indicate existence of a certain stroke, and so on.

In the structural, or 'linguistic' approach, one defines a class of patterns as satisfying a certain set of relations between suitably defined 'primitives'. The relations might be boolean expressions in a relatively simple case, or might be specifiable by a generative grammar in a more complex case. Note that here 'primitives' are left undefined within the model. Again, in the case of an alphabetic character, the set of primitives might be a 'vertical stroke', two 'horizontal strokes', etc., and the structural relationship specifies how the strokes are to be juxtaposed to qualify as a certain character. The recognition of primitives is another pattern recognition problem, albeit of a lower complexity. The term 'linguistic' is especially preferred when generative grammars are used, in obvious analogy to language analysis. Except where the context calls for great care, we use the terms 'linguistic' and 'structural' almost synonymously. (See Section II.3 for some comments on this.)

As pointed out in a later section, to some extent, the structural solution can be cast in the geometric mold. However, in most instances one description or another is clearly the more natural.

2. *A Parable and Some Theses:*

We shall introduce some of the major theses of the paper in the form of a parable, somewhat like H. Simon's parable of the watchmakers, Hora and Tempus in his excellent essay on the architecture of complexity [Simon (1969)]. Our protagonists have less colorful names, A and B, both of whom are designers of pattern recognition systems.

A attends many pattern recognition meetings, and tries to learn many new things to keep his work modern. But of late, he has not been doing very well. For one thing, he hasn't learned the lesson of hierarchical construction. He still tries to come up with completely "optimal" systems from beginning to end. He uses all the sophisticated classification techniques and sequential methods, but when some changes in the assumptions for which they are valid are made, his systems become far from optimal. In spite of his addiction to 'optimality,' or perhaps because of it, he glosses over the fact that the space over which he is looking for an optimal design, as well as the criteria of optimality, have nothing optimal about them, but were arrived at by a combination of intuition, problem knowledge, etc. More importantly, however, the recent "geometric" vs "structural" discussions in meetings have confused him. Whichever approach he adopts, on completion of the design, he is ill at ease, with the thought that he could do better, much better.

B, however, is doing precisely that: much better. In this case, he has been applying hierarchical principles in the following fashion: he first divides the problems into many subproblems. While there are no formal criteria to guide him in this task, he keeps in mind the weaknesses and strengths of the many different tools, expecially the geometric and structural tool, and attempts to design subproblems to be especially suitable to one or another of the approaches (Section II.4). Of course, in case the subproblems can be divided once again to make the matching of available solutions more promising, that possibility is allowed also. Another criterion he uses deals with the kind of a priori information which is available, or can be obtained by a careful study of the problem. Those parts of the problem for which structural relationships are available or can be deduced are isolated from the parts where much information is noisy or unavailable. In the latter certain relationships may be available in the form of conditional probabilities, which the person familiar with the problem area might want to inject into the system. It is not always profitable to let the system "learn" them by observing samples (Section II.5).

After this division he solves each subproblem either by reducing it further, or by the application of methods most appropriate for the subtask. In this manner, B views the various methods as complementary, and not as rivals.

B views formalisms as essentially economies in description, in addition to whatever virtues they might possess in capturing the physical or mathematical basis for the generation of patterns in specific instances. He has no naive hopes of writing compact generative grammars for every complex pattern analysis and recognition problem he has to solve. On the other hand, with his concept of hierarchy and subproblems, he is willing to consider that several structural subproblems in his hand can be compactly handled by formal grammars of one kind or another.

When considering generative mechanisms for any class of patterns, his hierarchical view point affords him a bonus. He develops simple grammars to describe a rather large class of patterns of which the class he is interested in is a subset, and then attempts to specify formal mechanisms of transformation, or, which is the same thing, selection rules, to precisely delineate patterns of interest. This releases him from the onerous task of producing a supercomplex formalism; instead he uses the old evolutionary idea of building complexity upon complexity to produce systems of arbitrary complexity.

Thus he is led to consideration of transformational grammars (Section III.3) which are examples of mechanisms for complex "sentences", obtained by nesting mechanisms of low complexity.

B's viewpoint can be characterized as pragmatic complexity decomposition. This simply means that the problem is divided into bite-sized pieces. Because of this position, he has some sympathy with the approach advocated by Grenander (Section III.4) in connection with deformation grammars. B views deformation grammars as devices which can be useful in some cases for describing a complex set of noisy patterns.

When he is willing to consider formalisms, B is naturally faced with the problem of inferring a grammar from a set of figures. There are several aspects and versions of the problem, ranging from very formal systems for automatic inference to interactively applicable heuristics (Section III.6).

The rest of the paper is substantially an elaboration of B's positions. We discuss several related ideas in considerable detail so that the paper also presents a selective survey of linguistic-statistical methods in pattern recognition.

3. *The Linguistic Attitude*

The linguistic approach, as the phrase is used in pattern recognition now, does not refer as much to a set of procedures as to an attitude -- that in order to be effective, pattern recognition algorithms must be based on the mechanisms that generate and deform patterns. The traces in a bubble chamber photograph do not have arbitrary shapes; they are generated by physical processes and occur only in a limited range of varieties of shapes. An algorithm which is based on the joint distributions of pattern densities at various points in the frame of the bubble chamber photograph, has a limited chance of success compared to an algorithm based on first locating the traces, recognizing their constituent parts, namely lines in various directions, circular arcs of different radii, etc., and then reconstituting them to determine if the trace of a particular kind has occurred.

The way it has been used in the literature, for a recognition procedure to be linguistic, it is not necessary that it should explicitly formulate expressions in a formal language and process it to reach the classification decision. All that is necessary is that the recognition of the pattern be based on the presence and proper juxtaposition of specific 'elements' of the pattern. Many of the commercial print readers are in this sense 'linguistic pattern recognizers' even though their designers may not be conscious of that categorization. Actually we would prefer to use the broader term *morphological* or *structural* to describe this type of pattern recognition situation and reserve the term linguistic or syntactic pattern recognition for the cases in which formal generative grammars and parsing are used, but usage of terms in the literature is not that precise.

Under the enlarged definition and usage of the term linguistic, all decision-tree recognition procedures are linguistic. The reason why there is no need in this case to formulate explicit expressions is that for any decision-tree heuristic, one can generate a corresponding expression in a suitable formal language.

Under the enlarged definition of the term linguistic are also included all generative models which leads to a differential equation model, or a functional equation model, or a stochastic model such as a finite state Markov chain model.

4. *Hybrid Systems*

Two extreme viewpoints can be illustrated as follows. Consider for simplicity two dimensional pictorial pattern recognition problems. One can propose a general "solution" by asking that class samples be obtained and class conditional pattern intensity joint distribution functions be estimated for as many points in the frame as necessary. Then the optimal decision function can be designed on the basis of the properties of these distribution functions.

Or one can propose that since patterns belonging to different classes are differentiated by different juxtapositions of elements from what can be called the set of morphs or signs, all one needs to do is to break up the patterns into the constituent morphs, and reconstitute them in a manner so as to explicitly display the interrelationship. As for the recognition of morphs themselves, they are expressed in terms of morphs at a lower level. For instance, alphabetic characters are expressed in terms of entities such as strokes and loops, and strokes and loops are expressed in terms of points in the quantized two dimensional space.

Considering the first approach, viz, that using joint distributions for points of the frame, such a direct, unstructured procedure might appear attractive because it is general. But it has serious limitations. There is no guarantee that the class conditional density functions behave well enough in a general problem for the minimum achievable error on this basis to be acceptably low. If we want the decision function to be invariant, for instance, a procedure which is not totally committed to the first approach would probably first locate the pattern in the field and normalize it by heuristic decisions (this is what is called 'registration') and then perhaps use a statistical analysis of the pattern *per se.* But a strict adherence to the first approach would not permit these heuristics and would instead require estimation of the distribution functions with class paradigms occurring in all translated positions. In the appendix we present an analysis which shows that in general the minimum error when no registration is permitted and translation invariance has to come naturally from the estimated statistical quantities, is greater than in the case where measurements for statistical analysis are made after heuristic registration. This shows the desirability of introducing non-statistical structural properties for improving performance.

If we consider the other approach mentioned, viz the strictly structural approach, we soon realize that real world patterns do not correspond to the model. Statistical decisions have to be made all along the line, not only in gap-filling and line-thinning routines for 'cleaning-up' the image, but on deciding on the presence of individual signs, as well as due to the random ways in which the signs may be put together in order to arrive at a pattern belonging to one class.

The above considerations show that the key to pattern recognition problems does not lie wholly in statistical approaches, or heuristic programming or more formal linguistic approaches. Rather, a good pattern recognition system has as an integral part, a versatile tool kit and uses statistical, linguistic and heuristic tools in various stages of the processing of the patterns, with each tool being applied at the stage for which it seems best suited. This viewpoint gives us the flexibility we need to take advantage of the special characteristics of each approach. Philosophically, it seems reasonable that most pattern recognition problems can be divided into subproblems which can be solved satisfactorily by one or the other of the approaches.

Finally, it is appropriate to note that under some conditions, the structural model can be recast as a geometric model. In the case where a finite number of relationships between a finite number of primitives characterize a pattern class, define features such that each feature indicates whether the given pattern satisfies a specified relationship. In this binary-valued feature space, then, the structural logic of classification becomes the hypersurface of separation. However, in most instances, such transformations have a ring of artificiality, and one or the other is preferred as more "natural".

5. *Relationship to A Priori Information*

Like Archimedes who said, "Give me a place to rest my fulcrum and I will move the earth", the Bayesian extremist says, "Give me enough samples, and I shall discover all the truths". If one considers that structural relationships are nothing more than special cases where certain conditional probabilities take on the value unity, it seems possible that a statistical procedure would be able to arrive at a structural description. [For an interesting experiment to discover Fortran grammatical categories by statistical procedures, see Rosenfeld, et al (1968)].

However, when structural descriptions are the basis of the decision logic, a large amount of information has been transmitted to the recognizer. On the other hand, a procedure which has to "learn" these relationships, say, in a Bayesian formulation -- will need an inordinately large number of samples. In this sense, structural methods correspond to large amounts of prior information given to the recognizer, with need for only a little further statistical processing.

This also explains why traditionally, most practical recognition systems have tended to be structure-oriented. It is much more reasonable to do intensive, problem-oriented pattern analysis and transmit this knowledge in the form of structural relationships, than to design a system whose finite-sample learning cannot generally approach this degree of compacted information. If analysis of patterns yields a residual core of uncertainty, and the obtained information can be expressed only in terms of density functions, then one uses statistical methods. In this sense, statistical methods begin where structural methods leave off. In our parable, when B divides the problem into subproblems, he is in fact matching the solution to the kind and amount of a priori information that can be imparted to the machine.

III. Formal Grammars and Syntactical Methods

Even among the adherents of structural methods in pattern recognition, there is disagreement over the desirability and utility of formal grammatical approaches. Even if one concedes that formalisms are economical means of describing things, the question remains whether current favorites such as phrase-structure grammars are necessarily the most useful for pattern recognition tasks. There have also been some disagreements over the meaning of picture syntax. In the next few sections we consider several aspects of formal grammatical methods in pattern recognition.

1. *Rationale for Using Formal Grammars for Patterns*

Narasimhan [1964] a major advocate of the formal linguistic approach to pattern recognition stated the case for this approach as follows:

> ". . . it is much more appropriate to view the so-called pattern recognition problem as really the problem of pattern analysis and description . . . the aim of any adequate procedure should be not merely to arrive at a 'yes', 'no' or 'don't know' decision but to produce a structural description of the input picture. It is our contention that no model can hope to accomplish this in any satisfactory way unless it has built into it, in some sense, a generative grammar for the class of patterns it is set up to analyze and recognize." Narasimhan further said, "This rather close analogy to

linguistic analysis is more than incidental."

All languages have items that recur throughout utterances. Linguists call the recurring items morphs and group them by various processes into morphemes. The study of the arrangement of morphemes is subdivided into Morphology, which is the study of word formation, and Syntax, which describes the use and order of words in constructions. Thus, speaking generally in terms of parts and sub-parts of patterns, one could say that almost all work on pattern recognition has been morphological or syntactical. However, formal linguistic analysis of patterns involves rather specific procedures. Patterns are viewed as statements in a formal language, sometimes a two-dimensional language [Kirsch (1964), Dacey (1970), Rosenfeld (1970)] and grammars are defined for the generation and analysis of these statements.

2. *Some Views on Picture Syntax*

Consider the following quotations:

1. "In fact, circuit diagrams have a syntax. If we want to teach a machine to read circuit diagrams, we have to tell it about their syntax. This is not the same thing as telling it about the electromagnetic theory of circuits. Picture patterns have a syntactical structure independent of the physical facts about the world which these patterns intend to denote." [Kirsch (1968)].

Commenting on the above position, Minsky [1968] said:

2. "It's risky to maintain that there is such a thing as a syntax of circuit diagrams independent of other things. Certainly there are conventions, e.g., if a thing isn't made of lines, it's not a circuit diagram. But this is not a matter of a syntax of a formal language with a phrase structure grammar or something like that; this is a matter of knowledge that the program has to have about the subject matter that it's going to deal with.

   I don't think you can make a distinction between syntactic rules and knowledge about electromagnetic theory . . .

   I'm not saying: 'That's a good distinction, but it doesn't work.' In fact, it probably does work well, up to a point. I think it can do some harm, as has happened in the case of mechanical translation. Some of these attempts had the form: 'The proper description of language is a set of 'rules'; these are to be written down, and there is to be a parsing program that uses the rules to parse the expressions in the language'. That is a good approximation for simple cases, but it's a very dangerous idea to fix on so firmly that you cannot think about it any other way.

   Certainly linguistic problems are hard, but linguists have made it very much harder for themselves. They've got themselves into situations where they can't analyze simple things said in two sentences."

M. B. Clowes [1969]:

3. "The interpretation of pictures involves a further syntactic structure of the of the event being pictorially depicted – which consitutes the semantics of the picture.

. . . we should regard the semantics of pictures as concerned with the exhibition of relationships of a nonpictorial kind. These relationships must be regarded as defining the character of the 'physical world'. Pictures express events in this physical world.

We have alluded earlier to the multiplicity of possible picture-syntactic descriptions assignable to some pictorial expression. Such a multiplicity would present an impossible task for a syntax-directed parser. If however we assume that the parser is directed not only by a picture grammar, i.e., by what pictorial relationships are computable by the parser, but also by the necessity to recover well-formed event descriptions in some world (this world being manifested pictorially), then it seems plausible that the variety of potentially assignable descriptions can be dramatically reduced.

. . . it seems appropriate to regard English sentences, nuclear equations and bubble chamber photographs all as being mappings of a single nuclear event and to that extent descriptive of *it* not of one another.

. . . it follows that the development of a machine capable of relating English sentences or equations of one kind or another, to diagrams or photographs requires the provision of at least three syntax specifications. These would be of English sentence structure, pictorial relationships, and the relational structure of the event (nuclear event, electrical circuit, etc.) being referred to in these various languages. In addition of course, rules for mapping from structures in one domain to those in another are required. It is these mapping rules together with a syntax specification of some 'object world' which are now the most pressing needs in the development of such machines."

We have included this sequence of quotations for they give a capsule presentation of the development of ideas in the linguistic approach to pattern analysis and recognition. The quotation from Clowes (see also the earlier paper by Lipkin, Watt and Kirsch) depicts an ambitious goal, using the development of various languages and formalisms for describing complex relationships.

3. *What Aspects of Language Structure are Relevant to Pattern Processing?*

Given that we desire a versatile tool kit which includes linguistic tools, what aspects of linguistic methodology are particularly relevant to pattern generation, analysis, and recognition? And which linguistic methods seem most promising and worth further investigation for pattern analysis? A number of investigators [see e.g., the survey by Fu and Swain 1969] propose that we consider context-free grammars and more powerful grammars such as context-sensitive grammars and also that we consider stochastic grammars involving various complex probabilistic mechanisms defined over the grammar. One is entitled to ask: Is this a good way to proceed at this stage in the development of syntactical pattern recognition?

Phrase structure grammars and other related grammars were motivated by the interest in describing a sentence in terms of its parts and the parts in terms of smaller parts.* Context-free grammars are inadequate for describing natural language structures and more powerful grammars such as context-sensitive grammars have not led to very informative structural descriptions and do not represent a very fruitful approach. Rather, it is *transformational grammars* that have provided deep insights into the structure of natural languages and that allow the incorporation of relations among sets of sentences. Among linguistically oriented investigators in pattern recognition, Clowes [1967, 1969] has been the major advocate of transformational grammars for pattern analysis. Transformational grammars are very useful for pattern analysis because they permit factorization of the generative mechanism into a simple base grammar which generates a certain set of patterns, and a problem-oriented set of transformations which generates from this set only the patterns we originally set out to find a generative model for. Thus, a transformational grammar can be defined as $G_\phi = (G,\phi)$, where G is a reasonably simple "base" grammar such as a context-free grammar, and ϕ is mapping which maps a structure in G, i.e., a tree, into a related tree.

In order to show the flavor of the approach, we briefly outline an example due to Joshi [1970]. Let L_p denote the set of polygons, each edge of each polygon having an integral length and each angle between adjacent edges a multiple of $\frac{\pi}{3}$. Figures with some vertices with more than two edges incident on them will be excluded. If one attempts to write a grammar for this set of figures directly, one ends up with a complicated context-sensitive grammar, which despite its complexity provides no insight.

One can however develop the following transformational grammar. Let the base grammar G have as the primitive an equilateral triangle of unit edge length as in Figure 1. Let $\bar{L}_p$ be the set of all figures generated by the primitive and the operation of placing two primitives such that they share an edge. We direct the reader to Joshi [1970] for the context-free grammar generating $\bar{L}_p$. Figure 2 is an example of an element of $\bar{L}_p$. This figure has

*We are indebted to Professor A. K. Joshi for many ideas in the ensuing discussion.

a corresponding tree representation.

As can be seen this grammar is not quite what we need. We need a mechanism, or "transformation", to erase the lines inside, just retaining the periphery of the figure. For this problem, one can define two transformations which will essentially do the job. Each transformation may have " "blocking" conditions associated with it, such that when these conditions are present, that transformation is inapplicable. Informally, the first transformation erases an edge shared by two triangles such that one is dominated by an edge of the other. (Here "dominated" is used with reference to the tree of the figure.) The second type of transformation erases an edge which is shared by two triangles where one of them is introduced arbitrarily later, relative to the other, in the derivation. In this case, the second transformation is blocked when the figure being transformed corresponds to an element in $\overline{L}_p$ in which we have retraced a primitive triangle. Further whenever a transformation is blocked, the generator abandons that element of $\overline{L}_p$ on which the transformation was attempted. This is essentially a filtering-out condition such that only a subset of $\overline{L}_p$ is mapped to L_p, the set of polygons we are interested in generating. In addition to this, a global blocking condition provides for rejecting transformations which produce a figure consisting of an element of L_p properly contained in another element of L_p.

We hope that the above example illustrates the suggestion that the pattern recognition researcher, rather than burden himself with more and more complex grammars should instead factor the problem into domains of manageable proportions, which is what transformational grammars help him do. They have a further bonus in the form of intuitively appealing suggestions for assigning probabilities to sentences in the grammars. An assignment based on the underlying representation and the transformational derivation of a sentence will be more meaningful than one based on a grammar that directly generates the set of sentences.

4. *A Formalism for Pattern Analysis and Recognition*

A formalism which attempts to combine the linguistic and statistical aspects of pattern analysis and recognition has been proposed by Grenander in a series of paper and reports [Grenander (1969 a), Freiberger and Grenander (1968) Grenander (1969 b)]. Grenander's goal is "a precise language in terms of which we shall be able to analyze and describe patterns." We give a brief description of his model [Freiberger and Grenander (1968)]. Given: a collection Σ of primitive objects called signs, divided into disjoint subsets $\Sigma_1, \Sigma_2, \ldots, \Sigma_m$ called paradigmatic classes, and a group $G = \{g_i\}$ of transformations called similarity transformations satisfying

$$g : \Sigma \rightarrow \Sigma, \text{ all } g$$
$$G\ \Sigma_i - \Sigma_i,\ i - 1, 2, \ldots, m.$$

An arbitrary n-tuple of signs $C = (s_1, \ldots, s_n)$ defines a *configuration,* and an equivalence class I of configurations is called an *image.* Let T denote the set of all admissible images generated by the grammar, admissibility being determined by a set R of syntactic rules.

The noisy image is assumed to result from the operation of a deformation mechanism on a pure image. This deformation mechanism is defined as a probabilistic mapping from the set of pure images to the set of deformed images. A probability measure is defined on the set of deformation operators D.

A recognition algorithm is a mapping from the set of deformed images to the set of pattern classes, which are G-invariant subsets of T. This mapping can be set up to minimize an average loss in the sense of decision theory. Thus images and patterns are generated on the *grammatical* level; deformed on the *probabilistic* level; and recognized on the *computational* level.

Grenander views the model essentially as a framework in which to discuss patterns and their recognition in a systematic and unified manner, and not as a tool to solve problems in special cases. He compares it to general decision theory, "which has been useful for formulating decision problems but in which each separate problem requires its own treatment." The details of the model are somewhat changed in a later report. The similarity transformations are required now to form only a semi-group, rather than a group. The definition of the pattern is also modified. We will not discuss the details here.

In considering the relevance of this abstract structure to reality, we note first that the set of objects called "signs" is taken as the set of primitives, or basic structural elements. These are rarely uniquely defined in practical applications. They must be chosen to satisfy the twin requirements of sufficiency and economy. The only thing that prevents them from being completely ad-hoc, as is the case with pure statistical classification, is that some attempt is made in this model as in all linguistic models, to have the signs be components of a generative mechanism implicit in the problem. The formalism proposed by Grenander assumes that the signs and the generation in Section III.3, different combinations of primitives and grammars can be used for the same set of patterns and some combinations can turn out to be considerably better than others.

The pure patterns of the formalism are generated by signs and *known* grammars and then subjected to probabilistic deformations. In practice, in most interesting problems it is only the deformed patterns, further corrupted by noise, that are available and the grammar or other generative mechanism must be discovered from a limited set of samples. Because there will rarely be a unique definition of primitives and generative mechanisms, there will rarely be a unique analysis as demanded by the formalism.

Of course Grenander is aware of these limitations for in the first report he had already stated: "It should not be assumed, however that a G_{prob} is always the thing to look for. It may very well happen that it does not make sense to impress any probability measure P on D, or, in case it does, it may be hard to find P. Actually this last problem (exploratory grammar) is of considerable practical interest but will not be pursued systematically here."

The analogy between Grenander's formalism and classical statistical decision theory is close indeed. The above mentioned limitations on the formalism are similar to the assumptions in statistical decision theory that all probability distributions and densities, as well as loss functions are known; the procedures that are prescribed are optimal only under these conditions. The estimation of probability densities, etc., which needs to be done in practice in order to apply statistical decision theory, has its counterparts here in the estimation of the deformation mechanism (and the learning of the mechanism which generates the pure images). In Statistical Decision Theory the estimation and learning that is done in a practical problem are prescribed by the assumed hypothesis concerning the form of the distribution functions, etc. For pattern analysis and recognition it is the build up of knowledge concerning the type of hypotheses which are meaningful for the deformation mechanisms in practical problems, that will perhaps lead to this formalism being relevant to practical problems.

As developed in his reports (1969 a), (1969 b), Grenander's formalism and most of his examples while based on the linguistic attitude do not use the methods of formal grammars and syntactical analysis mentioned in the section above. Indeed many of his examples are based on differential equations and stochastic processes as the generators of the pure images and as the generators of the deformation mechanisms. However, in one report [Grenander, (1969 c)] Grenander has suggested the possibility of defining a probability distribution over the set of syntactic rules of a context free grammar and provided theorems for defining legitimate probability measures over the set of terminating trees generated by the context free grammar. Although context-free grammars are considered, Grenander does note that "A reader interested in natural language may wish to extend the model to general phrase structure grammars, to transformational grammars, or even to very general formal systems, but this will not be discussed here." In this context we recall the remark at the end of Section III.3 that an assignment of probabilities based on the underlying representation and the transformational derivation of a sentence will be more meaningful than one based on a grammar that directly generates the set of sentence. Even for pattern recognition problems of complexity much below that of natural languages, this appears to be a more promising route.

5. *First-Order Pattern Languages*

Once a language for a certain class of pattern is chosen, then the classification problem becomes conceptually simple: given a sentence, parse it to find if it is an element of the language describing a pattern class; if it is, classify it as a member of that class.

In practice, however, the problem of efficient parsing is not solved. There are many algorithmic methods available, but few of them are guaranteed to be efficient for a reasonably large class of applications. This then makes languages for which a body of efficient heuristic techniques are available particularly appropriate candidates for pattern description.

Such a language appears to be the first-order predicate calculus. Viewed as a formal system, a suitable first-order predicate calculus must have axioms corresponding to appropriately chosen primitives, and rules of inference corresponding to ways in which complex patterns can be put together from simple patterns. Efficient analysis procedures are available from the body of knowledge accumulated by researchers in automating theorem proving, especially methods based on the resolution principle. [For a lucid introduction to resolution methods, see Nilsson (1971).] Here then, each legitimate pattern of the class will be a theorem in the corresponding first-order language. In view of the great need for efficient analysis procedures, a first-order pattern language seems a promising area of investigation.*

6. *Grammatical Inference*

In applying statistical classification models to real life problems we rarely know the parametric form of the probability distribution functions although we can often make reasonable assumptions in the light of whatever body of knowledge and samples of data are available to us. Similarly in considering generative models or generative grammars what are usually available are finite samples of patterns or strings of symbols from which we must infer the generative mechanism or the grammar. The nature of our a priori

*The paper by Burstall and Barrow (1971) in this conference considers the application of resolution methods in pattern description and analysis. They report that better methods to guide search properly are needed for successful application of these methods.

knowledge and the data available will determine how much can be assumed, what form the inference can take and how successful we are in explaining or deriving the underlying mechanism. An important consideration in how we proceed is also the goal we have in mind for the model. Some models are more suitable for some purposes than other models although both may be equally good in an abstract sense.

In this section, we consider some examples of grammatical inference for deterministic (i.e., no stochastic deformation), noise-free, line drawings [Evans (1969)], which in many ways derive from some work on grammatical inference using context-free grammars [Feldman (1967)]; we also consider some work on stochastic extensions of context-free grammars [Horning (1969)] for inferring a grammar for a formal language on the basis of finite samples of the language. We comment on the role of formalisms versus heuristics in these examples.

a. *Some Heuristic Transformations for Inferring Pattern Grammars*

Some of the processes involved in grammatical inference as applied to pattern analysis are very nicely illustrated by the examples presented by Evans [1969]. In his work, a set of terminal (lowest level) object types (what we had earlier called primitives) are assumed given, such that the input pattern can be viewed as consisting of a list of such primitives. A set of predicates expressing properties of objects and relations among them is also assumed. The primitives and predicates are chosen outside the model on the basis of the investigator's purpose and interest. This agrees with the view and approach of our earlier work on semi-automatic screening of aerial photography [Kanal and Randall (1964), Harley, Kanal and Randall (1968)] where our primitives consisted of certain statistically-designed feature blocks. Even though relationships between them were not expressed in a formal language, they were nevertheless designed to be suitable for computer processing. This successful juxtaposition of statistical and structural methods reinforces our earlier statements about the inapplicability of "pure" models in practical cases.

If the subject matter is line-drawings, reasonable primitives might be line segments, arcs, etc., and a predicate might be *left*(x;y), which will be 'true' if x is to the left of y. The grammar is a set of productions, each of which essentially defines a condition under which a given pattern might be a member of a specified class. These conditions are written in terms of available predicates. There may be a number of alternate rules for defining an object of a given class, and the rules may be recursive so that a class can be defined in terms of the rules involving itself.

This formalism allows one to go from grammars for individual scenes to a single grammar which in some sense fits all the scenes, that is, is a generalization of the individual grammars. Evans does not have theoretical measures of how good a generalization is, or how well the grammar fits the individual scenes but in the examples he presents, his procedures lead to the type of generalization that seems reasonable and are in fact, intuitively appealing.

As an illustration we use Example 4 of Evans [1969]. In this example the only terminal, i.e., primitive object type, is line segment, called seg., and there are only two predicates: *join*[x,y] and *close*[x,y]. These apply to any objects x, y, made up of a sequence of line segments, and test for the "meet at one end", "meet at both ends" situation shown in Figures 3 and 4.

In terms of this set up, using G1, G2 and G3 as nonterminals and "S" as the "sentence" symbol, the grammar for a rectangle is:

1) S → (x,y): seg (x), G1(y) : *close*[x,y]

2) G1 → (x,y): seg (x), G2(y) : *join*[x,y]

3) G2 → (x,y): seg (x), seg(y) : *join*[x,y]

which states that the "scene" S consists of two objects x, y, where x is the object type seg, and y is object type G1 with the two objects satisfying the predicate *close*[x,y], i.e., they "meet at both ends". G1 in turn consists of two objects x, y, where x is object type seg, y is object type G2 and they satisfy the predicate *join,* and finally G2 consists of two objects, both of object type seg, satisfying the predicate *join.*

In a similar manner the grammar for a triangle is:

4) S → (x,y): seg (x), G3(y) : *close*[x,y]

5) G3 → (x,y): seg (x), seg(y): *join*[x,y]

Let us take the union of these two grammars and attempt to reduce the two to a single general grammar by identifying certain nonterminals as being identical. So in the five rule grammar which is the union of the above two grammars, let us say G3 and G1 are identical. This makes rule 4 identical to rule 1, so we drop rule 4, to get the grammar:

1′) S → (x,y): seg(x), G1(y) : *close*[x,y]

2′) G1 → (x,y): seg(x), G2(y) : *join*[x,y]

3′) G2 → (x,y): seg(x), seg(y) : *join*[x,y]

4′) G1 → (x,y): seg(x), seg(y) : *join*[x,y]

Next let G2 and G1 be identified as being identical. This eliminates rule 3′ and introduces a recursive definition of G1, giving

1″) S → (x,y): seg(x), G1(y) : *close*[x,y]

2″) G1 → (x,y): seg(x), G1(y) : *join*[x,y]

3″) G1 → (x,y): seg(x), seg(y) : *join*[x,y].

This result is a reduced grammar that generalizes the two "scenes" rectangle and triangle and arrives at the concept polygon. The reduced grammar will "recognize" any polygon.

Comparing the above example with that outlined in Section III.3, we note that the identification of certain terminals and the consequent dropping of rules is akin to the erasing rule of the transformational grammar. In fact, the identification of some nonterminals as being identical is but one of the transformational rules used by Evans in inferring grammars, which generalize, from the union of individual "scene" grammars. We will not give these rules here, but direct the reader to Evans [1969].

b. *Formalisms for Grammatical Inference*

A number of the elements of Evan's strategy for inferring picture grammars were present in Feldman's (1967) proposed strategy for inferring finite-state string grammars. However, whereas Evans is largely interested in heuristic transformations, Feldman and his associates [Feldman (1967); (1969); Feldman, et al (1969); Horning (1969)] have placed primary emphasis on theoretical and formal aspects of grammatical inference.* Here we consider a representative example (Horning) in some detail, mainly as an instance of work at the other end of the scale of formalism from that of Evans.

Horning's position on formalism vs heuristics can be gauged from the following: "The present study has been motivated by the twin goals of devising useful inference procedures and of demonstrating a sound formal basis for such procedures. The former has led to the rejection of formally simple solutions involving restrictions which are unreasonable in practice; the l latter to the rejection of heuristic 'bags of tricks' whose performance is in general imponderable."

Constraining one's thinking to procedures for which a sound formal basis can be demonstrated is not always a virtue. Such procedures are suitable for problems in a man-made universe. Their success in handling natural phenomena usually depends in a crucial way or some heuristics introduced somewhere along the way (and soft-pedaled in favor of the formalism to which success is then attributed). Often the heuristics of today lead to the formalisms of tomorrow and the heresies of one generation are the theoretical foundations for the next -- witness the modern development of Bayesian processing after a period in which it was scorned.

This demurral of ours notwithstanding, Horning presents an excellent exposition on the specification of a well-formed problem in grammatical inference and the development of a formal procedure for grammatical inference within the specified framework. To obtain a well-formed problem he

*The excellent survey by Bierman and Feldman in this volume covers most of their work.

carefully specified (a) the class of grammars to be inferred. This is the hypothesis space; (b) the space of observations, i.e., the nature of the observed data; (c) the evaluation measure allowing one to objectively tell which is the best hypothesis in a given situation; and, (d) the performance criterion for an acceptable solution. The elements of the hypothesis space he chooses to work with are obtained by extending context-free grammars to stochastic grammars through the specification of a discrete probability distribution over each set of alternative productions. As, for example, is shown by the grammar G_2 defined by the following rules

$$S \rightarrow T|S + T \qquad (\frac{2}{3}, \frac{1}{3})$$

$$T \rightarrow P|T{*}P \qquad (\frac{1}{2}, \frac{1}{2})$$

$$P \rightarrow a|(S) \qquad (\frac{3}{4}, \frac{1}{4})$$

in which T and P are nonterminals, a, +, *, (,), are terminals and the probabilities over each set of alternative productions are specified on the right-hand side and add to unity (the grammar formed by deleting the alternative probabilities from each production of a stochastic grammar is termed a characteristic grammar). By restricting the alternative probabilities to rational numbers, the hypothesis space is limited to a denumerable class of stochastic grammars.

The main burden of Horning's work is to set up definitions and restrictions so that the formalism of Bayes Theorem and Bayesian Inference can be directly applied to enumerate the a posteriori probabilities, with respect to the given smaples, of elements of a denumerable class of stochastic grammars with known a priori probabilities of being the source of observed sample. The resulting procedure, which is called Enumerative Bayesian or EB procedure guesses which one of the grammars in the denumerable hypothesis space has maximum a posteriori probability given the current sample. Further treating the probabilities of a stochastic grammar as parameters to be estimated, the standard methodology of Bayesian estimation, including the use of conjugate prior, or reproducing, densities, is also brought to bear on this problem.

To cast the inference of stochastic grammars into a manageable Bayesian mold, Horning introduces the assumption that successive strings in the samples are independent random variables with identical distributions, and the observation space is taken to be the stochastic *text* presentation of the grammar – i.e., the samples provided from the languages whose grammar is to be inferred contain only valid strings as opposed to an *informant* presentation in which both valid and invalid sequence of such strings, $\{x_1, x_2 \ldots\}$

where x_i are independent, identically distributed random variables with the distribution determined by the grammar. A stochastic grammar is termed *deductively* acceptable (DA) if it assigns a non-zero probability to the current sample S_K.

Let $\{G_1, G_2 \ldots\}$ be the denumerable hypothesis space of grammars, let $P(\frac{G_i}{C})$ denote the probability that grammar G_i is true, given some context C, and let $T(\delta)$ be a computable function such that for $i > T(\delta)$, $P(\frac{G_i}{C}) < \delta$. Further let t_k denote the least integer such that G_{t_k} is deductively acceptable with respect to the current sample s_k. Also let $\delta_k = P'(\frac{G_i}{S_k'}, C) = P(\frac{G_i}{C}) \cdot P(\frac{S_k}{G_i}, C)$, and let $T_k = T(\delta_k)$. Then the Enumerative Bayes procedure computes $P'(\frac{G_i}{S_k}, C)$ for each G_i, $T_k \leq i \leq T_k$, and calls the first i in this range for which $P'(\frac{G_i}{S_k}, C)$ is maximum, the best guess, $G_{EB(K)}$. Each step of this procedure is computable so that the procedure EB is computable. It is easy to see that if at each time k, one considers only grammars which are DA with respect to the sample S_k, $G_{EB(K)}$, is unchanged since if a grammar G_i is non-DA, $P(\frac{S_k}{G_i}) = 0$ and $P'(\frac{G_i}{S_k}, C) = 0$. This helps cut down the hypothesis space somewhat. Various other theorems are introduced to help cut down the hypothesis space but the end result is still a very unmanageable enumeration problem. Thus heuristics have to be resorted to do anything at all with the EB procedure.

The case where the grammar is fixed and the probabilities are learned, is handled by a straightforward application of Bayesian estimation. For the situation in which noise is present, it is assumed that the distribution of *noise strings is known a priori.* Even with a known noise distribution, deductive acceptability with respect to the sample is no longer a relevant requirement on the grammar and if the noise distribution is not known then we encounter problems of identifiability in estimating the parameters of the stochastic grammar as well as the noise distribution. These problems of identifiability have not been touched upon in Horning's study of grammatical inference.

For the evaluation of grammars Horning uses $M(\frac{G_i}{S_j}, C) = \log P(\frac{G_i}{S_j}, C)$ as the measure of complexity of a grammar G_i, with respect to the samples S_j and the context C, and (ignoring the denominator when expressing

$P(\frac{G_i}{S_j}, C)$ by Bayes Theorem writes $M(\frac{G_i}{S}, C) = M(\frac{G_i}{C}) + M(\frac{S_j}{G_i}, C)$. The complexity of a grammar with respect to a given sample and context is thus thought of as consisting of two components. The first is termed the *intrinsic complexity* of the grammar and the second, the *relative complexity* of the sample given the grammar.

The Enumerative Bayes procedure proposed by Horning for grammatical inference completely emphasizes the probabilistic structure of the observations and the resulting formalism might just as easily have never mentioned grammars. Horning sees it as a virtue that the procedure does not rely on unique properties of grammars. We, on the other hand, feel that there has already been an overemphasis on the purely probabilistic structure of patterns and on gymnastics with Bayes theorem and that there should be an emphasis on ways to take into account the underlying structure of patterns and grammars which seem to get lost in this formalism.

The virtue of a formalism is that it provides a guide to our thinking about a problem and suggests procedures that should be attempted. The counterpart is that thinking in terms of formalisms introduces rigidity of thought and restricts the space of solutions we explore. As far as this particular enumerative procedure is concerned, the only way it can even begin to work is if strong heuristics are introduced at the very beginning to severely restrict the hypothesis space.

IV. Concluding Remarks

Our main points, presented as the virtuous qualities that we conferred on the protagonist B in the parable in Section II.2, need not be restated here. Even in a selective survey such as this one, the dynamism of the field of pattern recognition comes through quite clearly. The field of evolving to a state where the previously mostly ignored "heart of the problem", viz., pattern analysis is being attacked with increasing sophistication, mainly with linguistic tools.

The linguistic model which connotes an underlying generative grammar, while not answering the question of what primitives are best, does provide hints for discovering, as shown by the polygon transformation grammar presented in Section III.3, which set of primitives leads to a more natural (or less awkward) style of grammar for the particular patterns being generated and analyzed.

We have attempted to show that hybrid linguistic-statistical techniques are more relevant for practical problems than the pure statistical and linguistic models. The important aspect of the linguistic approach is the specification of a succinct generative mechanism and differential equations, stochastic models and dynamical systems have fulfilled this role in many pattern analysis studies. The main virtue of a generative approach is that if one feels that a generative model is a good candidate for modeling the process under study, then an investigation of the generative model can answer many detailed questions concerning the process more easily than a direct study of the process. In turn, knowledge of certain descriptive aspects of the process guides the development and refinement of the generative model. This may be termed an "analysis by synthesis" approach to the study of patterns. In work on formalisms for pattern analysis and recognition hopes for achieving significant advances are pinned on developing a precise language which can be used for analysis and description. Such a precise language will be a long time coming unless it is restricted to specific abstractions or "man-made universes" rather than being applicable to broad real world-phenomena. If past experience in various fields is any guide, it is quite likely that pre precise measures and precise language will be more useful in proving limit theorems and providing guidance on "impotence principles" and solvability questions, than in tackling specific pattern recognition problems. Thus, for example, as shown in Kanal and Harley [1969] and Harley, Kanal and Randall [1968], not having a unified theory of precise measures of complexity dod not prevent the identification of elements of complexity relevant to a specific pattern recognition problem, the allocation of problem complexity amongst these elements, and the use of these elements to judge whether or not the problem was solvable by various competing techniques. Indeed, whereas the heuristic concepts fof complexity developed in these two cited references proved very useful, none of the work on formal measures of complexity was found to be relevant.

Evans [1969] in his work on grammatical inference mentions a similar experience with the procedures for grammatical inference. Of the two examples of work on grammatical inference which we present in this report, Horning [1969] represents one extreme on the scale of formalism and Evans the other. Evans presents a set of purely heuristic transformations and intuitive measures of goodness. For grammatical inference studies in pattern analysis and modeling, the type of procedures described by Evans along with the formalism of transformational grammars, seem worth exploring. Further, for pattern analysis itself, more powerful languages with well-developed syntactic analysis techniques, such as the first-order predicate calculus, seem to offer interesting approaches.

Appendix

CLASSIFICATION ERROR OF STATISTICAL DECISION FUNCTIONS UNDER TRANSLATION INVARIANCE*

We shall make several simplifying assumptions. We assume two equally probable classes labeled 1 and 2, with probability density functions $f_1(x)$ and $f_2(x)$, where x is a, possibly scalar, measurement variable. For simplicity, however, we consider univariate measurements, occurring in the real line.

For a given set of $f_1(x)$ and $f_2(x)$, we can assume without loss of generality that a number c can be found such that the decision function takes the form

$$x < c \Rightarrow \text{class } 1$$
$$x \geq c \Rightarrow \text{class } 2$$

and such that the mean classification error is a minimum. The mean probability of error is then given by

$$P_e = \frac{1}{2} - \frac{1}{4} d(f_1, f_2)$$

where $d(f_1, f_2) = \int |f_1 - f_2| \, d\mu$ with μ the Lebesgue measure.

We introduce the notion of translation in the following manner. This is somewhat artificial, but sufficient for our purposes. Assume that the patterns can occur in only one of two positions, each with equal probability. Let $f_1(x)$, $g_1(x)$ refer to the probability density functions of class 1 patterns in these two positions and similarly $f_2(x)$ and $g_2(x)$ for class 2 patterns. We denote this translation by $(f_1 \overset{T}{\Rightarrow} g_1)$. If one were to estimate the density functions without knowing that translation has occurred, one would arrive at density functions for the composite class 1 and class 2 as

$$f_i^*(x) = \{\frac{1}{2}\} (f_i + g_i), \quad i = 1,2$$

For the decision function to be invariant to this translation, it has to be designed on the basis of $f_i^*(x)$. In this case, the probability of error P_e^* is

$$P_e^* = \frac{1}{2} - \frac{1}{4} d(f_1^*, f_2^*).$$

We also note that translation is measure-preserving and hence

$$d(f_1, f_2) = d(g_1, g_2).$$

*Analysis due to B. Chandrasekaran and K. Salter.

This means that the probability of error for density sets (f_1, f_2) and (g_1, g_2) are the same, and let it be denoted by P_e.

We need to define some terms in preparation for the statement of the theorem.

$$\text{Def: } \delta = f_1 - f_2$$
$$\sigma = g_1 - g_2$$

Note that δ and σ are real-valued summable functions on X.

$$A = \{x \in X | \delta > 0\}$$
$$B = \{x \in X | \delta < 0\}$$
$$C = \{x \in X | \sigma > 0\}$$
$$D = \{x \in X | \sigma < 0\}$$
$$E = \{x \in X | \delta + \sigma > 0\}$$
$$F = \{x \in X | \delta + \sigma < 0\}$$

Superscripted c refers to complement of the set. We can now prove the following theorem.

Theorem: The decision function invariant for the translations $(f_i \overset{T}{\Rightarrow} g_i)$, i.e., based on f_i^*, has a greater classification error than the decision functions based on the sets (f_i) or (g_i), unless the set

$$[(A \Delta C) \cap E^c] \cap [(B \Delta D) \cap F^c]$$

contains only a finite number of points, or more precisely has measure zero, in which case the probabilities are equal.

Proof: The following identities can be proven by rather tedious considerations.

$$E = (A \cap C \cap E) \cup (A \cap C^c \cap E) \cup (A^c \cap C \cap E)$$
$$F = (B \cap D \cap F) \cup ((B \cap D^c \cap F) \cup (B^c \cap D \cap F)$$
$$A = (A \cap C \cap E) \cup (A \cap C^c \cap E) \cup (A \cap C^c \cap E^c)$$
$$C = (A \cap C \cap E) \cup (A^c \cap C \cap E) \cup (A^c \cap C \cap E^c)$$
$$B = (B \cap D \cap F) \cup (B \cap D^c \cap F) \cup (B \cap D^c \cap F^c)$$
$$D = (B \cap D \cap F) \cup (B^c \cap D \cap F) \cup (B^c \cap D \cap F^c)$$

$$d(f_1 + g_1, f_2 + g_2) = \int_E (\sigma + \delta) - \int_F (\delta + \sigma)$$

$$= d(f_1,f_2) + d(g_1,g_2) + \int_{A^c\cap C\cap E} \delta - \int_{B^c\cap D\cap F} \delta$$

$$- \int_{A\cap C^c\cap E^c} \delta + \int_{B\cap D^c\cap F^c} \delta + \int_{A\cap C^c\cap E} \sigma - \int_{B\cap D^c\cap F} \sigma$$

$$- \int_{A^c\cap C\cap E^c} \sigma + \int_{B^c\cap D\cap F^c} \sigma$$

In the above $d\mu$ has been omitted for convenience.

Examine each of the integrals in the last expression,

$\int_{A^c\cap C\cap E} \delta < 0$, unless $A^c\cap C\cap E = \phi$, since in A^c, $\delta < 0$

$-\int_{B^c\cap D\cap F} \delta < 0$, unless $B^c\cap D\cap F = \phi$, since in B^c, $\delta > 0$, and so on.

Each integral contributes a nonpositive quantity to the expression. Hence, $d(f_1 + g_1, f_2 + g_2) \leq d(f_1, g_1) + d(f_2 + g_2)$ the equality being valid if and only if

$$(B\cap C\cap E) \cup (A\cap D\cap F) \cup (A\cap C^c\cap E^c) \cup (B\cap D^c\cap F^c)$$
$$\cup (A\cap D\cap E) \cup (B\cap C\cap F) \cup (A^c\cap C\cap E^c) \cup (B^c\cap D\cap F^c) = G \neq \phi$$

By noting that

$$(A\cap C^c\cap E^c) \cup (A^c\cap C\cap E^c) = [(A\Delta C) \cap E^c]$$
$$(B\cap D^c\cap F^c) \cup (B^c\cap D\cap F^c) = [(B\Delta D) \cap F^c]$$
$$(B\cap C\cap E) \cup (A\cap D\cap F) \cup (A\cap D\cap E) \cup((B\cap C\cap F)$$
$$= \{[(B\cap C) \cup (A\cap D)] \cap (E\cup F)\}$$

and that

$$A\cap C^c\cap E^c \supseteq A\cap D\cap F$$
$$A^c\cap C\cap E^c \supseteq B\cap C\cap F$$
$$B\cap D^c\cap F^c \supseteq B\cap C\cap E$$
$$B^c\cap D\cap F^c \supseteq A\cap D\cap E$$

the set G can be shown to be quivalent to $[(A\Delta C) \cap E^c] \cup [(B\Delta D) \cap F^c]$..

Further,

$$d(f_1{*}, f_2{*}) = \frac{1}{2}\, d(f_1 + g_1, f_2 + g_2)$$

$$P_e{*} = \frac{1}{2} - \frac{1}{8}\, d(f_1 + g_1, f_2 + g_2)$$

$$P_e = \frac{1}{2} - \frac{1}{4}\, d(f_1, f_2) = \frac{1}{2} - \frac{1}{4}\, d(g_1, g_2)$$
$$= \frac{1}{2} - \frac{1}{8}\, [d(f_1, f_2) + d(g_1, g_2)]$$

$$P_e^* \geq P_e <=> d(f_1 + g_1, f_2 + g_2) \leq d(f_1, f_2) + d(g_1, g_2).$$

Hence, except when the set G is empty

$$P_e^* > P_e \qquad \text{Q. E. D.}$$

The above proof is valid whether x is scalar or vector.

It is to be noted that in general G is not empty. We consider two illustrative examples below.

1. f_1, f_2, g_1, g_2 are normal distributions with identical variances differing only in their mean values. Let f_1 and f_2 intersect at $x = a$, g_1 and g_2 at $x = b$; assume without loss of generality that $b > a$. Then $f_1 + f_2$ and $g_1 + g_2$ intersect at $\frac{1}{2}(a + b)$. Then it can be shown that the G consists of $[a,b] \neq \phi$; hence in this case $P_e^* > P_e$.
2. Let f_1 and f_2 be nonoverlapping triangular distributions. Then there exist values of translation parameter a' such that $G = \phi$. In this case $P_e^* = P_e$.

Also note that translation invariance has been considered as an example. The same general deterioration in performance is true for other types of invariance in more complex situations, such as rotational invariance in two-dimensional spaces.

REFERENCES

1. Aisermann, M. A. (1969), "Remarks on Two Problems Connected with Pattern Recognition", in M. S. Watanabe (Ed.): *Methodologies of Pattern Recognition,* Academic Press, New York, 1969.
2. Biermann, A. W., and J. A. Feldman (1971), "A Survey of Results in Grammatical Inference", this volume.
3. Burstall, R. M., and H. G. Barrow (1971), "Some Techniques for Recognizing Structure", this volume.
4. Clowes, M. B. (1967), "Perception, Picture Processing, and Computers" in *Machine Intelligence 1,* N. Collins and D. Michie, (Eds.), Oliver and Boyd, Ltd., pp. 181-198, 1967.
5. Clowes, M. B. (1969), "Transformational Grammars and the Organization of Pictures", in *Automatic Interpretation and Classification of Images,* A. Grasselli (Ed.) (Ed.), Academic Press, pp. 43-77, 1969.
6. Dacey, M. F. (1970), "The syntax of a triangle and some other figures", *Pattern Recognition,* Vol. 2, pp. 11-31, January 1970.
7. Evans, T. G. (1969), "Grammatical Inference Techniques in Pattern Analysis", presented at the 3rd International Symposium on Computer and Information Sciences, Bal Harbor, Florida, December 1969. To appear in *Proc.* to be published by Academic Press in 1970.
8. Feldman, J. (1967), *First Thoughts on Grammatical Inference,* Stanford Artificial Intelligence Memo No. 55, Computer Science Dept., Stanford University, August 1967.
9. Feldman, J. (1969), *Some Decidability Results on Grammatical Inference and Complexity,* Stanford Artificial Intelligence Project Memo AI-93, Computer Science Dept., Stanford University, August 1969, AD693106.
10. Feldman, J. A., J. Gipps, J. J. Horning, S. Reder (1969), *Grammatical Complexity and Inference,* Technical Report #CS125, Memo AI-89, Computer Sciences Dept., Stanford University, June 1969, AD692390.
11. Freiberger, W., and U. Grenander (1968), "Computer-Generated Image Algebras", *Proc. IFIP Congress 68,* Edinburgh, Scotland, pp. H4-H9, August 1968.
12. Fu, K. S., and P. H. Swain (1969), "On Syntactic Pattern Recognition" presented at the 3rd International Symposium on Computer and Information Sciences (COINS 69), Bal Harbor, Florida, December 1969. To appear in the *Symp. Proc.* published by Academic Press in 1970.
13. Grenander, U. (1969a), "Foundations of Pattern Analysis", *Quarterly of Appl. Math,* Vol XXVII, No. 1, pp. 1-55, April 1969.
14. Grenander, U. (1969b), *A Unified Approach to Pattern Analysis,* Tech. Report, Brown University, Center for Computer and Information Sciences, May 1969.
15. Grenander, U. (1969c), *Syntax Controlled Probabilities,* Tech. Report., Brown University, Center for Computer and Information Sciences, July 1969.
16. Harley, J. J., L. N. Kanal and N. C. Randall (1968), "System Consideration for Automatic Imagery Screening" in G. Cheng, et al (Eds.), *Pictorial Pattern Recognition,* Thompson Book Co., Washington, D.C., pp. 15-31.

17. Horning, J. J. (1969), *A Study of Grammatical Inference,* Tech. Report CS 139, Stanford Artificial Intelligence Project Memo AI-98, Computer Science Dept., Stanford University, August 1969; AD695401.
18. Joshi, A. K. (1970), "Remarks on Some Aspects of Language Structure and Their Relevance to Pattern Analysis", Appendix to L. Kanal (1970).
19. Kanal, L. (1970), "Generative, Descriptive, Formal and Heuristic Modeling in Pattern Analysis and Classification", Report to Aerospace Medical Division, Air Force System Command, Wright-Patternson AFB, Ohio; Contract F33615-69-C-1571.
20. Kanal, L., and B. Chandrasekaran (1968), "Recognition, Machine 'Recognition', and Statistical Approaches", presented at the 1968 International Conference on the Methodologies of Pattern Recognition, Hawaii. Appears in M. S. Watanabe (Ed.), *Methodologies of Pattern Recognition,* Academic Press, New York, 1969.
21. Kanal, L. N., and T. J. Harley (1969), *The Complexity of Patterns and Pattern Recognition Systems,* Tech. Rep. AMRL-TR-69-6Z, Aerospace Medical Research Lab., Air Force Systems Command, Wright-Patterson Air Base, Ohio, November 1969.
22. Kanal, L. N., and N. C. Randall (1964), "Recognition System Design by Statistical Analysis", *Proceeding of the 19th National Conf. of the Association for Computing Machinery,* New York: pp. D2. 5-1 to D2. 5-10.
23. Kirsch, R. A. (1964), "Computer Interpretation of English Text and Picture Patterns", *IEEE Trans. on Electronic Computers,* Vol. EC–13, pp. 363-376, August 1964.
24. Kirsch, R. A. (1968), "Picture Syntax", Summary in L. Kanal (Ed.), *Pattern Recognition,* Thompson Book Co., Washington, D. C., pp. 183-184, 1968.
25. Lipkin, L. E., W. C. Watt and R. A. Kirsch (1966), "The Analysis, synthesis, and Description of Biological Images", *Annals New York Academy of Sciences,* 128, pp. 984-1012, January 31, 1966
26. Miller, W. F., and A. C. Shaw (1968). "Linguistic Methods in Picture Processing – A Survey", *Proc. 1968 Fall Joint Computer Conference,* pp. 279-290, November 1968.
27. Minsky, M. (1968), "Discussion of Kirsch's talk", in L. Kanal (Ed.), *Pattern Recognition,* Thompson Book Co., Washington, D.C., pp. 185, 1968.
28. Narasimhan, R. (1964), "Labeling Schema and Syntactac Descriptions of Pictures", *Information and Control,* Vol. 7. pp. 151-179, 1964.
29. Neisser, U. (1968). Review of *Recognizing Patterns: Studies in Living and Automatic Systems American Scientist,* Vol. 56, No. 4, pp. 464A-465A, Winter 1968.
30. Nilsson, N. J. (1971), *Problem Solving Methods in Artificial Intelligence,* Chapter 6, McGraw-Hill Book Co., 1971.
31. Rosenfeld, A., H. K. Huang, and V. H. Schneider (1968), *An Application of Cluster Detection to Text and Picture Processing,* Tech. Report 68-68, Computer Science Center, University of Maryland.
32. Rosenfeld, A. (1970), "Isotonic Grammars, Parallel Grammars and Picture Grammars", *Machine Intelligence VI,* D. Michie and B. Meltzer (Eds.), U. of Edinburgh.
33. Simon, H. (1969), *The Sciences of the Artificial.* Chapter 4, M. I. T. Press.

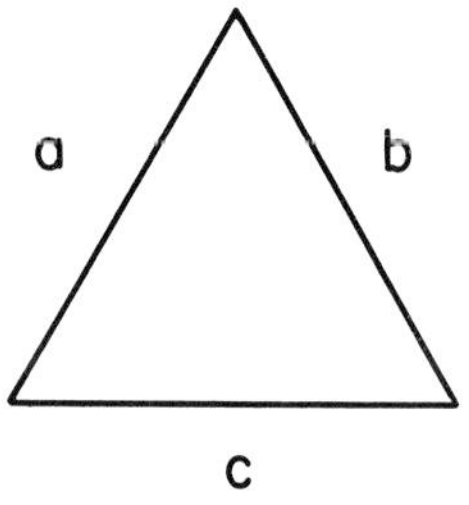

Figure 1. The primitive for the base grammar

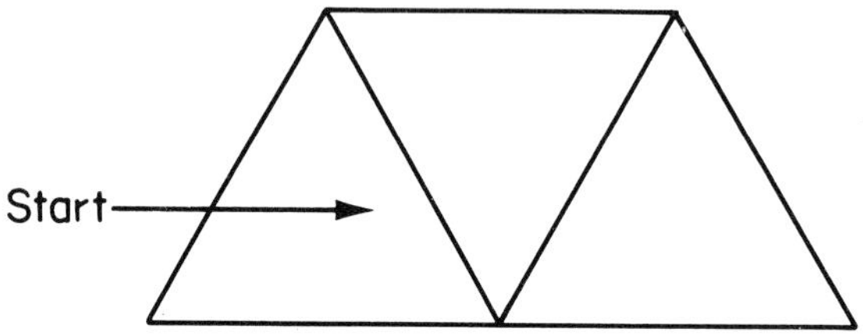

Figure 2. An element of $\overline{L}_p$

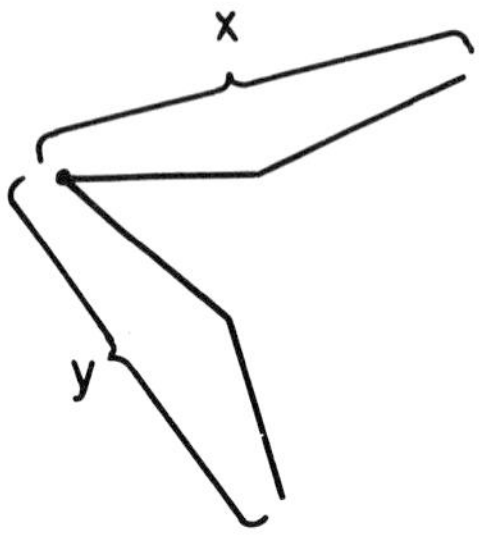

Figure 3. "Meet at one end"

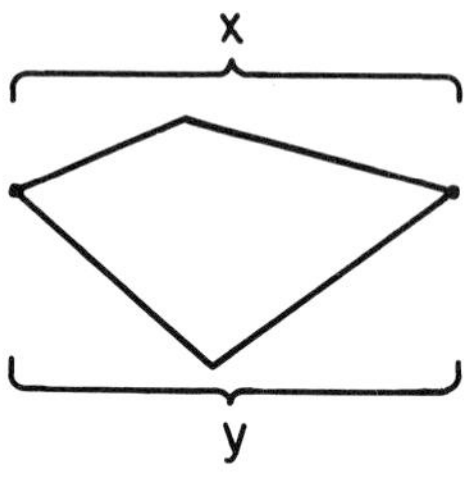

Figure 4. "Meet at both ends"

PATTERN COGNITION AND THE ORGANIZATION OF INFORMATION

S. Kaneff

RESEARCH SCHOOL OF PHYSICAL SCIENCES
THE AUSTRALIAN NATIONAL UNIVERSITY
CANBERRA, A. C. T. AUSTRALIA

1. Introduction

Developments in pattern recognition over the past decade or so have been characterized more by the proliferation of effort involving various motivations and different approaches than by concrete realization of practical working systems. The attempted application of an impressive and increasing array of mathematical techniques and psychological and philosophical theories has failed to make a fundamentally significant contribution to understanding and solution of the complex and subtle problems associated with the recognition of familiar (to us) objects and situations.

Mechanical systems (commonly employing digital computers) have been applied with the greatest degree of success to the recognition of very simple, highly stylized or simplified objects or images, particularly those for which statistical methods have most relevance, or in which a comparatively straightforward formalization of features or attributes can be made. Least success has occurred with natural or real-world objects and images whose formalization is not apparent. Reasons for this situation are numerous and complex: they include a general disinclination to face up to the problems of reality in a concerted and integrated manner—only piecemeal solutions of various facets have been attempted and expediency has apparently dictated gross over-simplification; little planning or effort appears to have been directed towards establishing adequate frameworks for research into identifying important factors and problems and in developing appropriate means for studying these and their inter-relationships. A particular feature of much work has been the application of mathematical techniques to the formulating of algorithms, followed by a search for problems which might be thereby solved, rather than the converse, and potentially more useful approach, of seeking awareness, understanding and specification of key problems, prior to attempting solution.

It has been argued elsewhere (Kaneff 1970 a) that real-world situations arise as a result of the operation of sets of constraints and certain behavioural or action capabilities, and that the study (and attempted formalization) of the end result of these processes, that is, of the patterns or situations, does not necessarily lead to understanding of the inherent key factors and their inter-relations, nor does it give any clue as to how to build systems which can handle these patterns and situations. Indeed, it is too readily possible to be misled into study of the wrong problems: this comment has particular relevance to the search for general language or picture-grammars which aim to describe situations without reference to (or concern for) the action and nature of the "machinery" which produced those situations. A major criticism of many pattern recognition studies therefore can be based on the concern for detailed but possibly irrelevant factors, in problems for which the basic fundamentals are ignored or not understood.

Unfortunately, while enlightenment on the many complex and subtle requirements for pattern recognition systems might have been expected from the disciplines of Psychology, Philosophy and Linguistics, surprisingly little contribution has been forthcoming. Instead, important advances have come from "practical" disciplines concerned with actually *building* systems (which operate in a real-world environment): thus, among the many trans-disciplinary concepts from Engineering and Information Science which are proving of great importance through advent of the digital computer, are those of models or algorithms and procedures. A potentially most important and useful philosophy introduced comparatively recently in pattern recognition studies is that of employing structural descriptions: several approaches described in the literature (for example, review by Macleod 1970) depend for their success on the articulation of the structure of patterns or situations. However, the term 'structural description' is merely an appellation and does not define any particular approach; nor does it give a guide on the production of descriptions or on what kind of descriptions are necessary or appropriate. Nevertheless, it is considered that the concept of 'structural description' provides a pointer to future progress in the solving of the many aspects of pattern recognition, including the separation of object from background, the handling of unfamiliar objects, ambiguity, fuzziness of detail, the nature of the three dimensional problem, and the many other aspects of processing natural objects and images, development of which is at present only at a very rudimentary stage.

It is noteworthy that major advances in the Physical Sciences over the past century have been due in no small measure to the richness of the developed procedures for building models (or theories) of great predictive power in a real-world environment. Our objectives are on analogous lines: to build machines which can interact with the environment through suitable action mechanisms and interfaces, with a rich capability to build models of the environment, generate hypotheses and improve their models and procedures through the interaction processes, and particularly to handle a changing environment. Our long term aim is to produce pattern recognition systems with a reasonable level of performance in a real-world environment, as contrasted to merely simulating certain cognitive and behavioural functions. Through study of specific real-world problems, it is hoped to elucidate essential factors and their inter-relationships and to provide a framework for research addressed to more general pattern recognition problems. Because of the need for operation in changing environments, there is here accordingly a pre-occupation with pattern *cognition** rather than with pattern *re*-cognition. This paper discusses factors which seem relevant to the establishment of a suitable framework for research into achieving pattern cognition systems, with attention being directed to the understanding and realization of operation in an informal, analogical, intuitive or paradigmatic (Narasimhan 1970) mode, thereby hopefully extending machine capabilities into the kind of operation in which human beings are so capable but for which machines so far have been so inept.

2. On Handling Real-World Problems

To develop insight into difficulties to be faced in developing pattern cognition systems, including the isolation of key factors and their inter-relationships, the writer's group has been studying a number of realistic problems, with attention directed more towards discovering useful philosophies, strategies, functions and required system inter-relationships, then to the short-term solution of the real-world problems themselves—this latter being, however, an ultimate aim. Such problems (discussed further in later sections) include the study of man-produced symbols, characters and objects, man-machine co-operative interaction, and the study of complex natural objects, particularly pollen and landform.

Little profound reflection on how we handle pattern cognition and recognition problems is needed to produce an awareness of the appropriateness of the view, expounded frequently, that our thinking processes and

*Subscribing to the view that our operational concepts have been acquired through a unique (and complex) set of experiences in each case, with consequent futility in attempting precise definition, it is with some reluctance that a set of various informal notions used is appended at the end of this paper.

capabilities are very much geared to our powers of interaction with the environment. (It is interesting to speculate, for example, on the capabilities of a hypothetical "independent" brain which could not interact with the environment). Awareness of our own action capabilities seems to play an important part in performance: consider, for example, the following:

(a) *Characters*

Probably as much, if not more, effort has been devoted to character recognition than to any other task in the pattern recognition field. Nevertheless, while simplified or stylized characters can be handled with comparative ease, success with 'everyday' characters—produced by hand, by different individuals at different times in different moods, by imperfect typewriters or printing machines, or with characters which have unforeseen distortions and modifications on a standard model—has been far from spectacular, and in some cases there has been abject failure in circumstances in which human performance seems relatively unaffected. In spite of various obvious imperfections, little difficulty is experienced in recognizing the characters depicted in Figure 1(a), for example. Through past experience in interacting with the environment—specifically, while writing or forming characters for themselves—human beings develop goals, intentions regarding what they are trying to achieve each time they produce a particular character; further, they achieve an awareness of their own action capabilities in forming characters and of the performance constraints applying to these capabilities, as well as of the constraints associated with particular media for producing characters. Thus, the intention or goal in producing a character for the number "two" may be simply to form a curve, convex on the right hand side, placed above a substantially horizontal straight line segment, fine details of the connection between the two being a matter of choice—possibly by a sharp junction or by a flowing closed loop, as illustrated in Figure 1(b). Similarly, the intention in depicting a character representing the number "three" may be by two curves, each essentially convex on the right hand side, placed one above the other: again, the join between the curves may be sharp or a flowing closed loop (as in Figure 1).

Through experience of the world of characters and their production, an awareness develops on the nature of variations and imperfections and their causes, including the fact that:

lines have thickness and imperfections, depending on the implements and media used for their production;

hastily produced lines have certain typical characteristics (for example often producing a tailing off of their ends as illustrated in Figure 1(a)*.

certain people take great care in producing their handwritten characters, others employ careless flourishes;
characteristic slopes for all characters are a feature of some handwriting or handprinting, while other such work appears to make no attempt to produce uniformly sloping characters;
modifications to the detail of a character may be caused by the motion of the writing implement in moving to form the next character before it has been lifted from the surface of the paper etc.— this is particularly true of hurried activity;
decoration may be employed, for example serifs; characters may be produced in any colour;
size and orientation of characters may vary considerably, so may the relative sizes of the different parts of a character,
. . . and so on.

Experimentation, particularly while learning to form characters, offers the opportunity for discovering many of the operating constraints imposed by one's own capabilities and by the environment, in relation to achieving the particular intentions or goals in question. At the same time, valuable information is gained for assessing others' performance at the same or similar tasks. Knowledge gained through experience of the effect of constraints (both on the individual's capabilities and of those imposed by the tools and other media involved) on actual performance achieved in relation to intentions or goals, therefore, appears to be one of the central factors which ensures success in character recognition tasks.

(b) *Artifacts*

Recognition of artifacts also seems to be aided by a knowledge of the "machinery" which has produced them, by handling and by using them, and especially by actually making the artifacts. A potter who has worked clay into a cup-shape, (with and without a potter's wheel), has rolled a piece of clay, formed it into a handle and attached this to the cup, has then fired the unit in an oven and has subsequently used the cup for drinking tea, achieves a substantial knowledge and awareness of the world of tea-cups—of constraints imposed by the properties of clay materials and production processes; the fragility of chinaware; the strength of such handles dependent on their cross sections and general shape; the fact that handles might break off at the point of attachment or elsewhere, depending on the nature of the joint or shape of handle; knowledge of weight, texture, heat conducting properties, and many other factors. With experimentation, a good grasp is achieved of what is possible and what is not possible in relation to size, shape, thickness, balance, and so on of tea-cups. In this way an extremely wide repertoire of understanding of the constraints applying to tea-cups and our relevant action capabilities is obtained.

In relation to intention or goals, unlike the situation with characters the production of which is a common experience, relatively few people actually construct many artifacts.* Appreciation and knowledge of the relevant constraints and action capabilities is accordingly of a somewhat different kind, appropriate to observation and use, rather than to production; nevertheless, other experience (viewing of films on pottery for example) enables an almost as good knowledge to be developed by using our cognitive functions to reconstruct processes and action capabilities mentally—this however is an imperfect substitute as the constraints imposed by materials, processes and other real-world factors and the necessary actions to effect production, may not be foreseen. A further complication may be posed by the associated intention or goals involved—the intention of the manufacturer in making a tea-cup may not be accepted by a user who may consider that the object makes an excellent paperweight (admitting, however that it could probably be used as a tea-cup): such problems are normally no practical barrier to pattern recognition except in very marginal cases where an object has useful generally accepted properties relevant to two or more applications, or is a new and substantially different instance of a particular object (a tea-cup in the form of a slipper, for example).

As in the case of characters, context plays a useful part in facilitating pattern recognition—a tea-cup, even of unusual shape, may be readily recognized as such if placed on a saucer, and forming part of a dinner setting on a dining table, whereas a tea-cup in the form of a slipper may escape detection as a tea-cup, if placed in a shoe box.

In spite of the relevance of aspects of the kind discussed above in (a) and (b), knowledge of this kind has hardly found its way into pattern recognition machines, except indirectly or in very primitive form. It appears that attention has largely been misdirected, as suggested in the previous section, to the formalizing of the patterns themselves (and not of the "machinery" which has produced the patterns); consequently, introduction of the kinds of imperfections and variations involved in real-world (instead of ideal) characters and artifacts has proved to be immensely difficult. A circle, for example, is relatively easy to describe and formalize because we know the constraints involved—note that an understanding of these constraints enables us to write a program to produce a circle—this is a case where the "machinery" has been understood and may be formalized. On the other hand, the constraints on the production of characters or artifacts, and the action capabilities necessary, that is, the mechanisms involved in producing them, are more

*Characters are considered here as being in some respects different from artifacts.

complex and not immediately transparent—however, the discussions of (a) and (b) above suggest approaches towards understanding these factors, and consequently of being able to formulate machinery, expectedly of a complex nature, for their handling.

Discussion so far has emphasized, in relation to man-produced characters and objects, the part played by experience and our knowledge of ourselves, of our environment, and the interactions between the constraints imposed on us by the environment and the constraints and action capabilities bearing on our own performance. Turning our attention now to the world of naturally-produced objects, the nature and roles of intention or goals become more elusive and speculative. Depending on philosophical attitude, the occurrence of natural objects might be considered in many ways; for example, as the directed product of natural systems; nevertheless, it is suggested that here, too, it is more profitable to attempt to elucidate the "machinery" of production than to formalize the product itself. Our observations and interactions should be directed towards discovering the appropriate constraints and action capabilities provided by the environment in producing the objects concerned; an essential part of this observation and interaction process is to develop awareness of the constraints and action capabilities regarding our own sensory and perceptive processes—for example, the kinds of cues and relationships we can use to appreciate depth in a three dimensional (3D) world, the basic factors which allow us to interpret a 2D image as the 3D object it represents, and so on. Accordingly, it is hoped to develop more effective pattern recognition systems by understanding the underlying processes which have led to the emergence of the natural objects themselves, and by understanding the constraints and action capabilities which determine our own performance in observing, reflecting on and processing the appropriate associated information.

To gain insight into the nature of the problems of handling natural objects in their full complexity, two studies representing typical complexity are being pursued by the writer's group, in the expectation that what we are able to discover and understand may generalize to other problems and situations.

(c) *Pollen*

The fascinating world of pollen is peculiar in its unfamiliarity to many, due to its inaccessibility to our normal sensory capabilities because of the extremely small size of pollen grains (of the order of a few microns in diameter, varying over some 100:1 in range of sizes). Figure 2 shows typical scanning electron micrographs of several species of pollen. It is interesting to observe that notwithstanding the novelty of this world of visual objects, human pattern recognition capabilities are such that there is an almost instantaneous correct interpretation of shape and form of the 3D objects from their 2D images: there is also the correct deduction that the objects are the product of living processes.

Motivation for selecting pollen for pattern recognition studies arises not only from the richness and variety of its species and genera, (possibly $> 10^5$) but also for a more practical reason—an extremely large number of samples usually needs to be processed: for example, specimens collected in the South West Pacific Region by the Research School of Pacific Studies of the Australian National University are not only very numerous, but contain many samples not encountered previously. The task of a human observer in identifying or classifying even a single pollen grain may take from minutes up to many hours and sometimes much longer. Collected samples awaiting classification are of the order of millions—a single slide preparation can have some 10^4 samples with 10^2 species or genera. In these circumstances, any mechanical assistance would be extremely welcome. (Macleod (1970) presents many intriguing aspects of pollen studies and outlines preliminary attempts aimed eventually at automating pollen interpretation).

Pollen identification capabilities of human observers develop substantially through practice—an experienced observer employs a strategy* in which, referring to a pollen grain, identification is carried on by a process of successive approximation based on crude observations of overall size relationships, numbers and general dispositions of apertures and projections, plus the most obvious characteristics of the surface pattern. This usually leads to possible family groups. At this stage, a *group* is chosen for more detailed searching by comparison; usually, through experience, a conscious selection is made from within the family, based on the kinds of features which experience shows are useful in differentiating within a particular group. When provisional identification has been achieved, it is confirmed by comparison of further details of structure. Most of the time the person is comparing the unknown individual with a single reference individual (actual, photographic images, or remembered) using a very *few* criteria at a time. If the criteria are accepted, further comparisons are made but the range over which they are made is defined by the identity of the individual first accepted. If, as a result of a comparison at the first level, the reference type is rejected, a return is made to the starting point and another try is attempted, usually *reducing the number of criteria* in order to widen the possible field.

The performance of a human investigator in this complex task clearly

*As noted by Professor Donald Walker (Department of Geomorphology, Research School of Pacific Studies, Australian National University), after careful observation of the work of his group—private communication.

gains from use of a planning approach as it is not usually possible to achieve recognition and classification "at a glance". This suggests that pattern cognition and recognition machines could well profit by adopting similar planning approaches, thereby placing them in the category of complex artificial intelligence systems:* this concept is developed further in section 3.

(d) *Landform*

Whereas pollen studies are directed to the identification of samples, including the cognition and classification of previously unknown species in an environment of tremendous variety and richness of samples, with processing based largely on surface features and structure, landform investigations have much broader objectives, with the additional peculiarity that the study of landform from aerial photographs is still in a largely developmental phase with as yet ill-defined objectives. Only now are there developing methods for rational description of landform for systematic survey purposes—Speight (1970). Indeed not only it is unclear how information should be processed, but doubts exist on what to process and to what purpose. These uncertainties make the problem attractive, as progress in understanding, biassed by pattern cognition concepts, may well proceed along more profitable lines.

Figure 3 shows (somewhat unusual) landform aerial photographs which, as well as more normal directly overhead views, it is hoped eventually to process mechanically to achieve objectives such as:

'The ability to record economically all those landform attributes which are likely to have value for prediction of rocks, weathering mantles, soils, drainage conditions, and to present these attributes in a useful manner for geomorphologists and others studying the natural resources of a region and planning the development of the terrain.'

It is apparent that if these objectives are to have a chance for realization, apart from required sensory, perceptual and other processing capabilities, a great deal of knowledge must be available; for example, that regarding underlying terrain structure, mechanisms for landform development and their relationships and interactions with vegetation, soils, climate and many other factors.

Natural (and artificial) scenes of the kinds just discussed are inevitably complicated by factors which appear to impose almost insurmountable difficulties: isolation and identification of objects in scenes are influenced by problems of separating object from background, by lighting, overlap, indefinite or merging boundaries and surfaces, the effects of texture, colour,

*For a useful outline of the objectives of artificial intelligence systems, see reference Project MAC (1969).

shadows and numerous other factors. In many cases, studies must be made from 2D images of 3D scenes, thereby introducing the added complication of making 3D interpretations from 2D information. Fortunately, our experience and knowledge allows us to handle such difficulties by making use of various cues, including those very factors which may appear, superficially, to be a hindrance (for example, reflections and shadows), and which give clues to shape, size, useful segmentation, articulation, and so on. Other more-general acquired knowledge, involving the manner in which things change and grow, give further clues to shape and structure—all natural objects have weight; involve 3D; growth follows particular paths; expansion in volume and structure occur in certain ways; characteristic kinds of symmetry are established and maintained; physiological processes rely on certain concepts; crystals grow in various ways. This list can be extended almost indefinitely with factors which all play appropriate parts in facilitating our pattern cognition and recognition performance.

In the language of the discussions earlier, through interaction with the real-world, we become aware of constraints and action capability of the environment and of our own sensory, perceptive and information processing powers, at least to some extent adequate for making useful segmentations and decision on natural patterns, allowing us to operate satisfactorily in the environment. Constraints and action capabilities involved appear more subtle and complex than those relevant to (a) and (b); at least they seem more remote from concepts of goal-oriented systems (natural or otherwise), and intention. With such natural systems, intention appears to have two usefully distinguishable aspects: (i) as the apparent end-result of the operation of natural systems themselves, and (ii) as the search for man-imposed order or structure which facilitates our interpretation of natural phenomena, allowing us to operate effectively, although imperfectly, in the natural environment. Thus, after adequate development, we can with relative ease segment scenes into objects, distinguish between natural and man-made objects and between living and inanimate objects, apparently irrespective of how novel the objects are in the first instance.

It seems that for success to be achieved in real-world recognition problems, certain sensory, perceptive and information processing capabilities are necessary, together with a considerable knowledge and awareness of relevant underlying mechanisms which operate, or have operated, to produce the object(s) (to be recognized) in the first instance, and a similar awareness of the nature of our own "machinery" which, in interacting with the environment, supplies the relevant information. What interactive and other capabilities are essential and what information organization is useful, are just some of the key problems which must be faced and solved before high level pattern cognition and recognition systems become a reality.

By reference to several appropriate problems, chosen for their richness and promise in producing insight, this section has considered some of the many factors which appear relevant. The next section discusses philosophical aspects bearing on the paths which might be taken in order to solve such problems.

3. Philosophical Aspects

In relation to the basic objectives of ultimately producing a machine which has pattern cognition and recognition capabilities in some respects comparable with our own, able to operate in a real-world environment, a number of factors appear, in the light of the previous discussion and for other reasons, to offer hope for further advances towards these goals. Brief discussion of some of these aspects follows.

(a) *Operation in a Real-World Environment*

The theme, already discussed in section 2, is advanced that for development of high level pattern cognition and recognition systems to progress, real-world problems should be tackled in their full complexity, in order to tease out the important factors and their relationships and thereby gain insight into the requirements of mechanized systems. Of particular concern has been the manner in which our pattern processing capabilities appear to develop, with the implication that attempts at mechanization might well profit from studying these processes.

(b) *Integrated System Approach*

By virtue of the need for (quite complex) interaction with the environment, not only must there be provision for certain action capabilities in the system, but it must be also endowed with appropriate sensory, perceptual and information processing capabilities, including the ability to construct or plan solutions and argue them through, possibly gathering further information, experimenting with the environment, and checking the results of its information processing against the real-world. Such a machine would be no less than an Artificial Intelligence System, able to operate in the natural environment or in some (still complex) subset of it: to operate at all, very careful matching of the various components for compatibility with each other, and integration of their characteristics, operation and performance, seems necessary.

In order to move towards such a system, therefore, it appears essential to adopt an integrated approach, right from the start, otherwise there is no assurance that interaction between the various components of the system will be possible, let alone practicable. This aspect is considered worthy of underlining as there appears to be a quite strong feeling in some quarters that once a system of statistical or other mathematical solutions of the problem has been outlined, the rest is merely a matter of (rather trivial) "Engineering". This writer considers the converse is more likely to be true in the solution of complex real-world problems; that is, the elucidation of the problem in all its aspects and complexity, the interactions and inter-relations between the various components concerned, and a specification of what can and must be done in order to build a complete working system to solve the problem, constitutes the major achievement: the use of mathematical tools is only one of the important factors contributing to this solution. Finally, the system must be built and proved to work before success can be claimed.

The advent of grammar-based approaches in pattern recognition, including picture languages (Narasimhan (1970b), Clowes et al. (1970)) also touches on the concept of integrated systems. The objectives of devising grammars and languages may be identified with building systems: however, they could be remote from action capabilities and outside constraints. Consequently, the internal constraints inherent or incorporated in such languages or grammars are not necessarily related to the requirements of interacting with the environment and may therefore be too restrictive or inflexible to cope with change or with novel situations. The search for context-independent grammars particularly seems remote from these problems; on the other hand, languages or grammars forming *part* of a system (syntax-assisted approach) appear to have considerable virtue when properly integrated with other elements of the system.

(c) *The Formation of Models and Concepts*

That our concepts and thinking procedures are determined by various constraints and action capabilities and are experience and environment dependent, has been already noted. Similar constraints would appear to apply to a machine designed to perform similar tasks, if it is built "in our image". Why we should seek to build machines in this way becomes a profound philosophical question which will not be argued here;* however, a number of practical reasons may be offered, a major factor being that of the need for communication (for example see Stanton (1970)), and co-operation, between man and machine. With effective communication established, it is possible to monitor and assess performance, operation and development of capabilities and information structure of a machine in fine detail, to provide

*The serious pre-occupation of various groups to build robots, provides further comment on this point.

and obtain information, to guide solution of problems, and so on.

Our own information handling capabilities seem to depend on a concept-based organization of information, which is very subjective due to experience and environment dependence. We have powers of forming our concepts from models generated as or from descriptions of the environment and can refine and update these models and concepts in the light of new experience (achieved through interaction).

The viewpoint is here proposed that successful pattern cognition and recognition systems need to be able to form a rich variety of models, including families of models (based on description) *which are problem dependent* and related to appropriate conceptual frames of reference, thereby being able to call on the full conceptual and procedural powers associated with such frames of reference in solving the problems concerned.

The question of 'understanding' seems intimately related to communication or operation which results in a mapping into a model which exists, or is formed during the process, in man or machine and in which they can operate with their existing procedural and action capabilities.

Adequate model (and concept) forming capabilities, together with a conceptual organization of information, seem crucial to the successful realization of pattern processing systems; reflecting this attitude, section 4 offers more detailed comments and discussion.

(d) *Paradigmatic and Syntagmatic Operation*

Rather than strive for the probably unattainable precise definition and formulation of our experience and environment dependent concepts, a somewhat different approach appears necessary: deliberate seeking of the most generalized model which is practicable—this implies the relaxing and/or removal of all but the absolutely essential constraints* from the description, (including implied constraints). Refinement or updating of the model or concept then involves the addition and/or removal of constraints. Within the framework of these generalized concepts, detail and precision may be introduced as facts and procedures, stored appropriately. The informal information organization, having been established, may then be considerably enhanced in performance capability by formal aspects such as the addition of procedures, algorithms, grammars, formal languages and others. The former mode of human operation has sometimes been called paradigmatic, the latter, syntagmatic (Narasimhan (1970a)).

---

*Constraints include attributes, objects and relationships, which apply.

(e) *Learning*

A vital requirement of a system operating in the real-world is the ability to handle change; coping with unfamiliar objects and situations, modifications, supplementary information, breakdown, redundancy, inadequate information, and so on, demands, apart from appropriate procedural and behavioural capabilities, the proper models in the appropriate problem-dependent conceptual frames of reference. Consequently we must strive for a machine which can learn to form and recognize models as a key requirement. Economy of information storage also appears to lead to a similar need.

Endowment with such features would then allow not only the acquiring of information, whether it be factual, conceptual, relational, structural or procedural, by 'pointing' to this information, by providing representative samples and by algorithm, but also by learning from an environment which has been structured, either naturally or deliberately by a teacher; further, learning could occur from deliberate experimentation or interaction with the environment.

While there need to be basic functions incorporated in any system on which to build through interaction, a central problem to be resolved is the useful balance to be struck between innate and learned capabilities (and structure).

(f) *Man-Machine Interaction*

Pattern processing machines which can educate themselves and acquire all necessary information to solve real-world problems seem, at present, a rather remote possibility. Closer to reality, however, are systems in which a human co-operator takes part. This allows human intervention to guide, correct and plan solutions to problems; receive information useful in (human) decision making; study and guide interaction and model building and so ensure that adequate relevant models are built up; structure the environment to facilitate machine learning; and so on. In relation to this, a machine capability worthy of inclusion is the ability to reconstruct, from the model information, that which has been modelled—human monitoring of this reconstruction holds great potential for guiding machine acquisition of concepts and models.

A man-machine co-operative interactive system should then allow the operator to define character sets; tell the machine what kind of bubble chamber tracks he wishes to be processed (by drawing type examples); indicate which features of a pollen grain are significant and which are not (facilitated by viewing a reconstruction of the current model of the pollen grain being studied); outline important landform features or unclear boundaries, and allow a vast array of other possibilities to be carried out.

(g) *Complexity*

No useful pattern cognition and recognition system seems possible in a real-world environment without considerable complexity in structure, behavioural and procedural capabilities, and a considerable knowledge of the world (or subsets of it). Pattern cognition requires a number of interdependent functional operations including learning, induction, hypothesis generation, model building, decision making, planning, and others.

Our present knowledge of these functions is extremely limited, but is expanding: continuing the theme of constraints and action capabilities in relation to these, it may be noted that in a general and detailed sense, learning and model building are involved with the learning of constraints and action capabilities and with forming representations of these in a suitable organizational structure. Planning may involve selection and operations with constraints and action capabilities, and the clever part of inductive inference seems to be the discovery of appropriate constraints, followed by the use of deduction. These absorbing aspects well warrant separate studies in themselves.

In concluding this section, it must be admitted that the above discussion has hardly scratched the surface of those factors which seem to have bearing on the problem of achieving high level pattern processing systems and which appear to merit further study. Discussion of one of the more important aspects, that of information organization, is continued in section 4.

4. Descriptions and Concepts

The ability of a pattern processing system to compile appropriate descriptions of what it may observe about the environment (or parts thereof) determines to a significant extent, its subsequent performance potential. The kind of description which may be formed, in turn, influences the model and concept building features. The need for a system to form a rich variety of models, which are problem dependent, has been expressed in the previous section. These aspects seem crucial to the development of pattern cognition and recognition systems and warrant serious attention and study.

In a sense, our patterns or concepts enjoy only tentative status at any moment and are subject to continual change. As Narasimhan (1967) has pointed out in relation to the acquisition of language behaviour, children acquire language behaviour through intimate behavioural interaction with a language community and therefore acquire by *functioning* in the language as part of the normal process of growth (they are operating in a paradigmatic mode). What is actually acquired depends on the child's body action capabilities and on the objects and actions available for perception in the visual, auditory and tactile modes—with every relationship is associated an action used to verify the validity of that action (c.f., constraints and action capabilities introduced earlier). As the child learns, its capabilities to describe or manipulate situations increase. On this argument, the concepts which an individual has will be influenced by the environmental factors encountered and by his innate and acquired procedural capabilities. The interpretation of facts or percepts by an individual (in relation to his processing powers and immediate and previous experience) leads to concepts, the nature of which is therefore determined by the exact manner in which all appropriate factors have been inter-related—the change of any one factor in the situation would have led to a (slightly) different but equally valid conceptual organization.

Experience and environment dependence, arising from the capacity to construct models of the experienced environment and to continually update models and the corresponding concepts, means that no two individuals will have exactly the same concepts, or organization of concepts: if mathematically precise definition is sought, this fact introduces formidable problems in attempts to formalize concepts; however, this feature of concepts has the overwhelming advantage of facilitating operation in a practical world of everchanging aspects, and is just the kind of capability we would like our machines to have.

That a suitable description of (part of) the environment, achieved with the help of our sensory mechanisms, forms the essential starting point for model building, concept formation and pattern recognition, seems evident. *'What kind of description?,'* is the really vital question to which, directly or indirectly, workers in pattern recognition have been addressing themselves for some time: another form of this question is, 'What kind of information is processed and stored and how is this organized?'

It is the main theme here that it may prove profitable to attempt organization of information based on patterns or concepts, devising a machine, with sensory, perceptive and organizational capabilities, which can itself process information along the following general path:

Percept → Description → Model → Concept → Conceptual Frame of Reference → Higher Frames of Reference

The essence of this scheme is in the constitution of the conceptual organization and the way in which this depends on perceptual information. Features considered relevant include:

(1) *Percepts* - that is, information obtained as a result of sensory appreciation of the environment through interaction, employing the endowed

interactive behavioural and procedural capabilities—provide the "raw" data about the world, on which all subsequent processing depends. For this reason, the more comprehensive the sensory capabilities the better the percepts in relation to information content. Furthermore, because subsequent processing may require (or gain from) reference to this data at any time in the future (for example to ascertain if there is any existing contradictory or confirmatory evidence regarding hypotheses which may be generated, to search for possible relationships between entities, to help the search for higher level concepts, and so on), for economy and effectiveness of action, there appears to be a good case for 'remembering', and retaining access to, all percepts (except those of relatively small difference which may benefit from being generalized).

(2) *Descriptions of Percepts,* that is, the form in which their information is available for the production of models, should be such that the resulting models (which might be structural descriptions) would be considered reasonable to human beings, as discussed in section 3(c), when mechanization is considered.

(3) *The nature of Descriptions* themselves (and the models which can be formed from them) is such as to allow multiple possibilities, limited only by the constraints and action capabilities associated with sensory and behavioural interaction with the environment. Thus linguistic descriptions, pictorial descriptions, electric circuit descriptions etc., may be invoked to provide cues which allow us to call on our past experience (or information) and on our procedural capabilities to build up an appropriate model of a situation which the description is aimed at producing, in order to achieve communication and understanding. The modalities used may be single (for example natural language) or one or more different languages embedded in another. There must, of course, for reasons of economy and practicability, be a useful selection of the type of description(s) to suit the occasion.

Procedural capabilities should be adequate, therefore, to achieve goal-oriented behaviour, thereby allowing the provision of proper guidance in the formation of descriptions following a recognition that particular percepts should or may be developed into models or concepts within a certain conceptual frame of reference appropriate to the task at hand. The capability for producing multiple descriptions and models, of course, is demanded to cope with problem-dependent requirements.

(4) *Concepts*

A concept is viewed as a validated model, adequately generalized to be compatible with all percepts which have been sensed and described to date, and which have been considered as belonging together in this way, possibly because the descriptions evoked match to sufficient degree to draw attention to their similarity. (This matching capability is by no means infallible—sometimes we can miss apparently close similarity while at other times notice quite obscure matching details, probably as a result of goal-oriented searching: "We see largely only that for which we are looking"). An operative feature of some importance here is the tendency to segmentation in articulating descriptions: apparently the simplest form of description in simple familiar terms is that which is usually chosen. Further, segmentation and articulation of the descriptions of unfamiliar or complex objects or scenes are usually in terms of familiar objects plus differences. This strategy of course produces an economy of models needed, with consequent reduced demands on memory capacity. Thus the pollen grains of Figure 2 need not present insuperable difficulty for description—Castanopsis, for example, may be roughly described as being, 'football shaped with a slit along the surface along a long axis meridian,' and two of the characters in Figure 1 may be described respectively as a '2' and a '3' with serifs. Some relevant problems of segmentation and other aspects of description have been covered by Macleod (1970), character-oriented descriptions have been discussed by O'Callaghan (1968), and Langridge (1971) has recently tried the difficult (to us) task of articulating the description of 'blobs'.

Relatively little effort is needed to bring to attention the considerable difficulty of articulating descriptions of even simple objects, and when this is done, descriptions seem to be in terms of relationships between other objects (or concepts), or in terms of a concept with variations on this (small differences are with advantage treated in this way, thereby removing the need for yet another new concept: for example, 'a triangle with a corner cut out' is a better description for many purposes than an attempt to re-name the new figure). Such considerations have led to the representation of structural descriptions by nodal nets in which objects (or concepts) appear at the nodes, while connecting links carry the relationships between these objects or concepts—for example, Kaneff (1970b), Winston (1970). The structural description achieves concept status when the nodes have been generalized to include all instances met with, and the relationships have been modified to reflect the generalized constants applying in these instances. These kinds of representations, although a step forward, have very severe limitations in representing conceptual organization because of the difficulty of including all relevant factors. While it is outside the purpose of the present paper to extend this theme significantly, some further comment is in order.

Consider Figure 4(a), which shows part of a zinnia pollen grain. A simple relational structure which provides a notional structural description might be as in Figure 4(b). (Note that quantization may be introduced into the description and that many versions of this description may be made). This simple description chosen makes use of the concepts of a sphere plus perturbations, in this case spines, which can themselves be particularized as having conical shape but with a bent vertical axis and with surface craters in certain position. In this way, use can be made of a knowledge of familiar objects (spheres, cones, surfaces, objects) and the corresponding conceptual and procedural capabilities and powers associated with these, in order to describe an unfamiliar object.

The structural description of Figure 4(b) can achieve the status of a concept if, through study of a number of zinnia grains, validation of the model can be achieved and it can be generalized, and constraints appropriately relaxed or tightened: for example, the relation "has" may be tightened to "must have"; spines "must have" conical shape; the cones "can have" (but not necessarily) a bent vertical axis; spines "can have" surface craters (but not necessarily); quantitative values may achieve certain ranges of tolerance–spines are separated by, say, 5μ - 8μ and may number, say, 100-120. This (notional)* concept of zinnia pollen may then be used to study a fresh sample by a matching of its structural description with the concept of zinnia pollen: the outcome of such a process might result in a matching except that one spine is truncated–the useful comment then being, 'a zinnia pollen grain with one truncated spine.'

This slight treatment of the problem has served the intention of throwing up a number of important factors:

(a) Illustration that concepts can enjoy only a tentative status at any time–they can be dismantled and assembled in a different way and in different detail as required.

(b) Incompleteness of the details of a concept in absolute terms is apparent, but a given form may be adequate for a particular

*Notional because the features included here are only approximate and illustrative, for purposes of discussion.

purpose. A concept based on Figure 4(b), for example, could be adequate for separating zinnia from castanopsis: a practical system may indeed use a strategy similar to that reported in section 2(c).

(c) Operation to produce descriptions, validation of models into concepts, and comparing new instances with these, requires considerable behavioural and procedural capability, particularly reference to deeper structures (than contained in the representation) and a considerable appropriate knowledge of the world.

(d) *Constraints and Action Capabilities* enter into the situation in several ways:

(i) As the constraints and action capabilities relating to the performance possible from the sensory, perceptive, behavioural and procedural attributes of the system which handles the percepts and makes a description, then produces higher level organizations,

(ii) As the information on constraints and action capabilities carried by the percept itself and subsequently *interpreted* by the pattern processing system,

(iii) As the concepts and relationships (the most obvious constraints) recorded in the description and in the nodal net representation of the concept in question,

(iv) As the actual procedures and other knowledge of the world invoked by the operation of the system in forming the nodal net description and the conceptual representation of the object in question.

Handling of this kind of information certainly needs better languages than normally available to digital computers. In this respect, the MIT PLANNER Language (Hewitt (1969)) is a considerable step in the right direction.

Not only do we need a knowledge of the world of concepts involving objects, but we also need to be able to conceptualize a large number of relationships, helpfully expressed as procedures for determining concepts such as 'above', 'below', 'to the left of', 'to the right of', 'inside', 'outside', 'near', 'connected to', etc., and others such as 'has', 'greater than', 'less than' and so on.

(5) *Conceptual Frames of Reference*

In concept learning studies with young children, lists of objects are sometimes presented with a request to find the 'object that does not fit'. The words, 'cow, fish, rabbit, sheep,' for example might be offered in the expectation that 'fish' will be considered as not fitting: there are many conceptual frames of reference for which such a separation is valid—on the basis of habitat, method of propulsion, and so on. However, the contradiction no longer applies if the conceptual frame of reference of "food" is remembered, thereby providing a simple instance of how conceptual frames of reference can tie together apparently unrelated objects.

The tea-cup example used earlier may also be considered as illustrating how different frames of reference may produce different viewpoints: the frames of reference of potters, artists, engineers, classical scholars and public servants will all differ as regards tea-cups.

A conceptual frame of reference may be considered as a network of concepts and their inter-relationships augmented by a group of behavioural and procedural capabilities which can operate on these concepts and inter-relationships.

Recognition that a concept may fall within the province of a particular conceptual frame of reference, then not only enables the full behavioural and procedural power associated with that frame to be applied to the concept, but also enables new light to be thrown on the associated constraints and action capabilities involved. Organization on this basis, then, appears to be an extremely desirable goal.

(6) *On Forming Concepts—To Discover Constraints*

Having established within the system a basic sensory, behavioural and procedural capability with a certain level of knowledge of the world, it would be expected that, through study of the environment, multiple descriptions of percepts could be made on the basis of a plan of action in conjunction with particular conceptual frames of reference. Once rudimentary nodal networks of the notional kind illustrated in Figure 4(b) have been obtained, a plan may be generated, employing strategies such as:

(i) Deliberately change a given constraint, noting the effect, and modifying the net in accordance with the fed-back results from the environment.

(ii) Seek further information about certain nodes or relationships.

(iii) In co-operation with a teacher, perform (i) and, on the basis of the teacher's comments, modify the net.

(iv) In co-operation with a teacher who deliberately *structures* the environment to emphasize certain constraints, (preferably one at a time, cf. Winston (1970)), develop the network further.

(v) Seek matching between the description in question and different conceptual frames of reference.

The structural network should be considered as an *active* net, in which nodes and relationships may be considered as subgoals with access, by association and by direct links, to deeper structure, procedural and behavioural, and that involving knowledge of the world—the Descriptions carry with them, in effect, a recipe or plan for further action, wherever the net is entered. A key feature is that the system is able to experiment and modify on the basis of constraints and action capabilities.

(7) *Sensory Capabilities*

While attention has been directed here largely to the organization of information, as suggested on several occasions, sensory action capabilities are also of paramount importance. This aspect will not be taken up except to indicate that in terms of the tasks represented by Figures 2 and 3, some form of optical scanning mechanism would be used to produce an organization based on picture primitives, then by iterative interaction between the system and the objects and scenes, or in this case their corresponding images, appropriate descriptions would eventually be constituted. In this way, the description of Figure 3(a) might be in terms of stream and ridge patterns, and that of Figure 3(b) might be in terms of typical slopes and drainage patterns, and so on, (retaining, however, the full image detail in case of future need for this).

This section has attempted to highlight certain features and advantages of an organization based on relational networks of concepts. To develop a system operating on this basis appears to be a desirable but an exceedingly complex task.

5. Pattern Processing System Development

Discussion in the previous sections has been centered on a number of factors considered to be important in the development of pattern cognition and recognition systems which can operate in a real-world environment. A great deal of stress has been laid on the necessity for integration of the various functions in order to be able to make effective use of the sensory, perceptive, behavioural and procedural capabilities necessary, and on adequate knowledge of the world. The advantages of a conceptual organization of information have been put forward as a good basis on which to build the requisite information, both innate and acquired through interaction with the environment.

It has been argued that because processing tasks may require the identification of sub-tasks and accordingly demand complex organizational, structural and procedural capabilities for planning solution, it seems profitable to view a pattern recognition machine as an integrated artificial intelligence system, (and benefit from progress in the development of such systems).

A large number of complex problems has been raised: the status of our understanding of such problems in a very real sense, tells us what we know about ourselves, apart from allowing us to build machines which can perform tasks which we may consider worthy of mechanization.

Acknowledgements

Helpful discussions with members of the Canberra Group working in Pattern recognition have, over a period, assisted in the formation of the viewpoints expressed in this paper.

Acknowledgement is due to Dr. I. D. G. MacLeod of the Australian National University for providing the photographs of Figure 2, and to Mr. J. A. Cavanagh of the CSIRO Division of Land Research, Canberra, for supplying the photographs of Figure 3.

6. Appendix

Some Informal Notions Used in this Paper:

Primitives: the smallest parts into which an object or situation, or their images, are subdivided for purposes of description.

Description: a report or record, in an appropriate representation, of an object or situation (or their images).

Structure: a specific arrangement and interrelation of parts or primitives of an object or situation (or their images). Structure is considered as an allotted (by man or machine) property and may be based on physical separation of parts or on a 'virtual separation'. Where structure is determined from an image, the structure is that of the object(s) represented in the image and not of the image.

Structural Description: a report or record in an appropriate representation, of the structure of an object or situation (or their images), which defines the organization imposed on the primitives

chosen to represent the object or situation.
(For example—the steel framework of a building may be described as being a structure. A structural description may be in terms of steel girders and connecting links (bolts, welds, web plates etc.)—the primitives, and their relationship to each other. A non-structural description might be in terms of the colour of materials, number of parts, weights,and sizes of members and so on).

Percept: a thing perceived—an instance of an object or situation or part thereof.

Model: a representation of a percept—this representation may (but not necessarily) be a structural description.

Concept: a validated and generalized model.

Pattern: synonymous with concept.

Fact: statement about a concept or concepts and/or their inter-relationships.

Pattern Cognition: } the original validation and generalization of a model;
Concept Formation: } the 'discovery' of a new pattern or concept.

Pattern Recognition: the allocation of a percept to an already formed concept or pattern. This term is often used in the literature synonymously with pattern cognition.

Procedure: (normally) an operation or process 'internal' to man or machine, often resulting in the definition and/or control of action capability (ies).

Action Capability: a capacity for 'external' operation—manipulating the environment or self configuration.

Constraint: a limitation of procedure(s) and/or action capability(ies).

Conceptual Frame of Reference: a related group of concepts and their inter-relationships which can usefully draw together a subset of (apparently) unrelated concepts by providing (often higher order) relationships usually more subtle than those met, learned or abstracted from common experience, and appropriate procedures. (For example, the body of knowledge for geometry, trigonometry, or subsets of them. At a lower level, for example, the body of knowledge relating the organization of picture primitives in the representation of picture objects).

Knowledge of the World: a knowledge of concepts, conceptual frames of reference, and their inter-relationships, knowledge of procedures, action capabilities, constraints and so on, relevant to all or subsets of the world. An organization of concepts, facts, procedures, action capabilities, useful for operation in a particular environment. (For example, knowledge of the world of pollen; of solving problems in geometry, trigonometry; of building houses; and so on).

REFERENCES

1. Clowes, M. B., Langridge, D. J., and Zatorski, R. J., (1970), "Linguistic Descriptions" in "Picture Language Machines", Ed. Kaneff, S., Academic Press, London and New York, pp. 87-117.
2. Hewitt, C., (1969), "PLANNER: A Language for Manipulating Models and Proving Theorems in a Robot", M. I. T. Project MAC Artificial Intelligence Memo No. 168 MAC-M-386 (Revised September).
3. Kaneff, S., (1970a), "On the Role of Learning in Picture Processing" in "Picture Language Machines", Ed. Kaneff, S., Academic Press, London and New York, pp. 213-229.
4. Kaneff, S., (1970b), "The Organization of Cartographic Information", Proceedings CSIRO and Department of National Development Study Group on Automated Cartography, Canberra, October.
5. Langridge, D. J., (1971), "On the Computation of Shape", This Conference.
6. Macleod, I. D. G., (1970), "A Study in Automatic Photo Interpretation", Ph.D. Thesis, The Australian National University, Research School of Physical Sciences, Canberra, March 1970.
7. Narasimhan, R., (1967), "An Outline of a Methodology of Behaviour with Specific Application to Language Behaviour; Part I—Language Acquisition by Children" Tata Institute of Fundamental Research, Computer Group Technical Report No. 37, Bombay, October.
8. Narasimhan, R., (1970a), "Computer Simulation of Natural Language Behaviour", in "Picture Language Machines", Ed. Kaneff, S., Academic Press, London and New York, pp. 257-290.
9. Narasimhan, R., (1970b), "Picture Languages" in "Picture Language Machines", Ed. Kaneff, S., Academic Press, London and New York, pp. 1-30.
10. O'Callaghan, J. F., (1968), "Pattern Recognition using some Principles of the Organism—Environment Interaction", Ph.D. Thesis, The Australian National University, Research School of Physical Sciences, Canberra, September.
11. Project MAC, (1969), "Progress Report VI" MIT.
12. Speight, J. G., (1970), "A System of Terrain Pattern Description for Air Photo Mapping", Proceedings CSIRO and Department of National Development Study Group on Automated Cartography, Canberra, December.
13. Stanton, R. B., (1970), "Plane Regions: A Study in Graphical Communication",

in "Picture Language Machines", Ed. Kaneff, S., Academic Press, London and New York, pp. 151-192.

14. Winston, P. H., (1970), "Learning Structural Descriptions from Examples", M. I. T. Project MAC Report MAC TR-76, September.

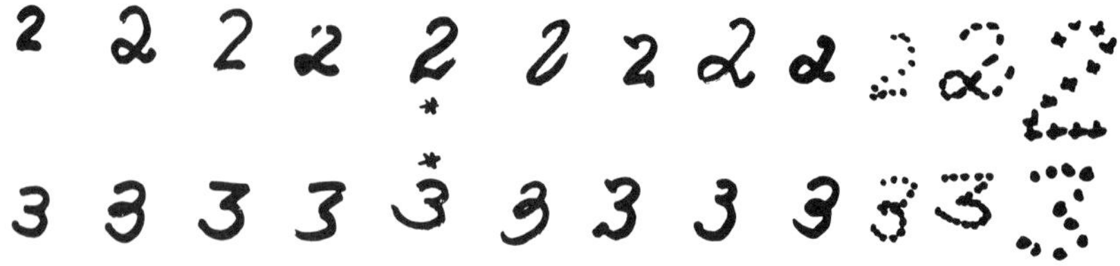

Figure 1(a). "Everyday" Characters

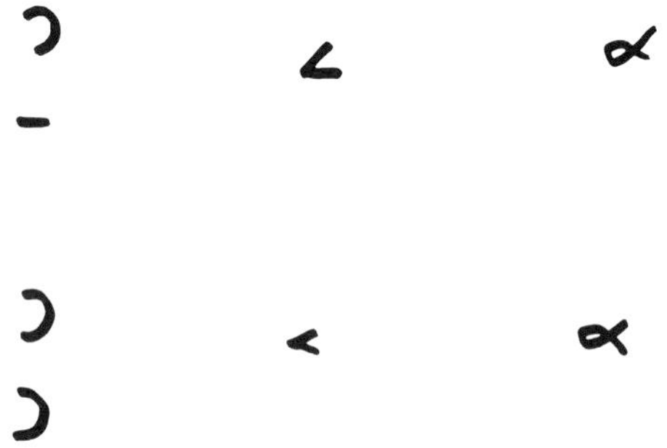

Intended Curves	Sharp Join	Flowing-Loop Join

Figure 1(b). A rationalization of Intention in producing 2's and 3's by hand

Figure 1. Hand drawn characters.

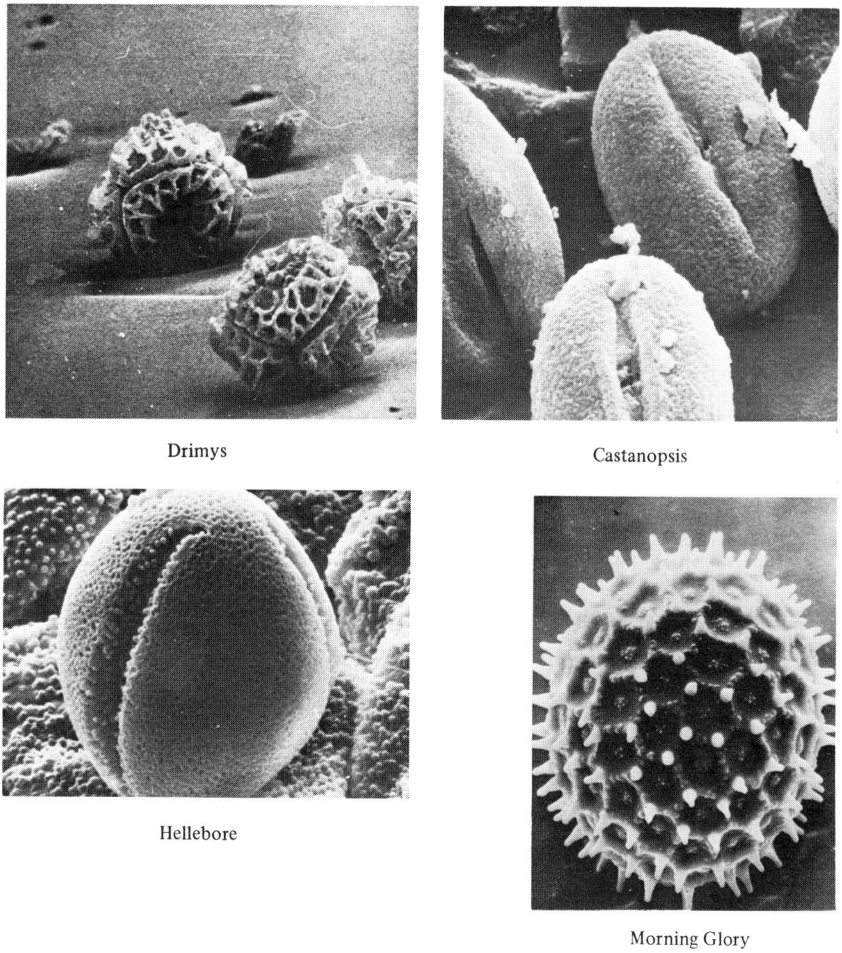

Figure 2. Typical Scanning Electron Micrographs of Pollen

Figure 3(a). Mesa Formation in Central Australia

Figure 3(b). Drainage Network in North Western Australia

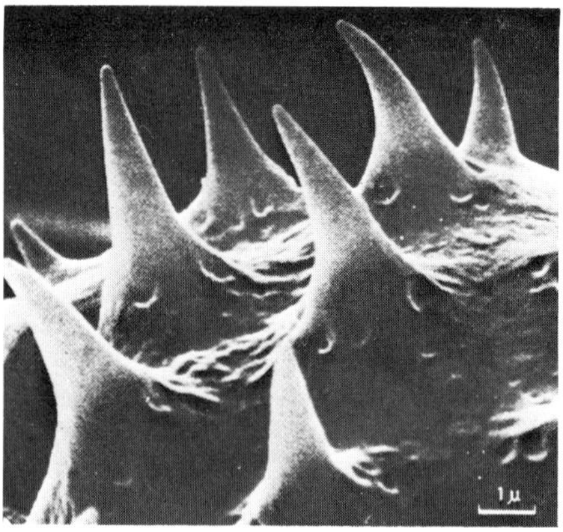

Figure 4(a). Zinnia Pollen

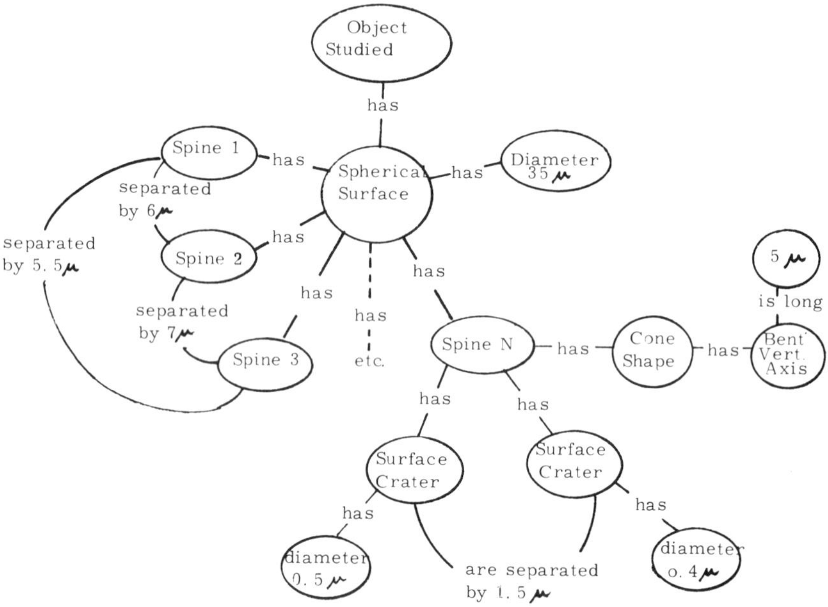

Figure 4(b). Structural Description

Figure 4. Notional Structural Description of Zinnia Pollen

EXPERIMENTS WITH AN ON-LINE PICTURE LANGUAGE

T. Kasvand

CONTROL SYSTEMS LABORATORY
DIVISION OF MECHANICAL ENGINEERING
NATIONAL RESEARCH COUNCIL
OTTAWA 7, ONTARIO

Abstract

During the investigation of diverse pattern recognition problems it has become increasingly apparent that recognition of objects in a complex picture cannot be treated as an open loop process consisting of feature extraction and classification. A paradox is encountered in that reliable features can only be extracted if the object in the picture has been recognized, but the object cannot be recognized before its features are identified.

The recognition process is better characterized by a closed-loop process containing an hypothesis testing procedure. Starting even from a single feature, which has been detected and recognized only to a certain degree as being a known feature, the machine will have to form an hypothesis as to which objects this feature may belong to and what additional information has to be gathered from the picture before the feature can be recognized with greater reliability. Only then can the machine improve on feature detection, search out other features expected to belong to the hypothesized object and decide whether its hypothesis can be maintained in the context of the given recognition problem.

Some of the problems encountered in trying to realize such a system are discussed. The proposed solutions have been tested to some degree by using an on-line picture language program. A preliminary version of the on-line picture language has been completed. By using a controllable flying spot scanner the computer has direct access to a picture of about 4000 × 4000 resolution elements. The picture is treated as a read only memory and it may contain many different objects. The entire program consists of three major subdivisions labelled (a), (b), (c).

(a) Atom Formation, Description and Recognition:

A complicated object is fragmented ("atomized") by using an algorithm which operates with or without guidance. If guided, the operator may only point out the approximate location of the atom that he proposes to the machine. The algorithm decides whether the area can be considered to be an atom and how much of the object it should include. A description of the atom is formed and normalized, before it is compared against already known "ideal" atoms. If the match is sufficiently good, the presented fragment is considered to be a realization of the best matching ideal atom. If the match is inadequate, the fragment becomes a new "ideal" atom.

(b) Teaching of Object-Inter-relationships:

When all the fragments (or a sufficient number of them) have been extracted, the operator instructs the computer how these atoms are to be interrelated for a given object. The operator can teach the machine expressions of the type:
"If you see atom a_1 (at location (x_0, y_0)), go search for atom a_2 (at location (x_1, y_1))", or "an object 0_2 consists of atoms a_1, a_2 and a_3 ($0_1 = a_1 \cdot a_2 \cdot a_3$)", or
"object 1 (0_1) is the same as object 2 (0_2), i.e., $0_1 = 0_2$".
The position, size and rotation relationships between the atoms and objects are retained.

(c) Recognition of Objects:

In the recognition part of the system, the taught relationships are used to guide the machine from the identified atoms to the expected atoms until an object of the desired class has been identified or all the usable taught relationships have been exhausted.

During running of the recognition programs the machine appeared to behave as if it "understood" the problem by going from one atom to the next in a systematic exploration of the picture. However, it also became apparent that the machine needs a goal-seeking algorithm in the recognition stage to guide it through the maze of instructions via the shortest path.

At present the object fragmentation stage (a) can be run without human interference and there appear to exist no unsurmountable programming problems to automate step (b), i.e., to allow the machine to teach itself. The present programs are written for two-dimensional objects. Extension to three-dimensional objects is conceptually simple.

Introduction

Ideally one would like to construct a machine or to write a computer program which "shows enough curiousity" so that any object in a picture which it does not recognize, it automatically analyses, forms its own descriptors for it and remembers it for future reference. This, of course, is the typical behavior of biological organisms.

From our often disappointing experiences with rather simple pattern recognition problems, the construction of such a machine would appear to be just wishful thinking. A closer examination of the problem, however, reveals that many of the details constituting such a system have already been tried experimentally. The structure, which incorporates all the necessary elements, is lacking and as a consequence experimental results are not available to indicate how close we are to solving this problem.

With these considerations in mind, a rather primitive set of computer programs was written to investigate some of the problems. The programs are operational, but each experiment points out something new (or something obvious once the problem has been isolated), so that the programs are under continuous modification. In the following, the problem is first discussed in general terms and then illustrated with results from computer programs.

Scope of Problem

The pictures considered are stationary and monochromatic, i.e., they contain gray levels only. The objects in the picture should be essentially two-dimensional or flat. There is no fundamental reason why the following arguments cannot be extended to colour pictures of three-dimensional moving objects.

The surfaces of three-dimensional objects in particular contain much texture or detail which is essentially statistical in nature and the boundary between two objects may only be detectable as a change of the local statistics. However, all objects must have boundaries which are detectable. The detection of the boundaries is easier if the objects are free of texture and have unique boundaries definable by local gray level changes. It is assumed here that the objects are essentially free of texture, but this restriction is not absolutely necessary.

Besides these restrictions, as much realism as possible is to be retained so that the pictures resemble actual images rather than their idealized versions. Consequently no restrictions are placed on the number of objects, their location, size, shape or orientation in the picture. Some noise must be expected and some objects may have missing pieces or overlap other objects.

The computer programs to be written should be able to learn or be capable of being taught various specialized pattern recognition problems and are not to be specialized for a given problem only. The amount of operator interaction with the computer should be kept to a minimum.

Picture Analysis

The picture is to be partially processed and certain features extracted before even recognition of the features is attempted. The analysis consists of extraction of "point features", object fragmentation, and the description of the fragments before fragment recognition is attempted.

A Paradox

The picture may contain an arbitrary number of objects of varying sizes and shapes, in arbitrary locations and orientations. The objects may overlap to a certain degree or some parts of the objects may be missing. Some random noise must be tolerated.

In this situation we immediately encounter a paradox, i.e., it is impossible to extract one object from the picture before the object is recognized and it is impossible to recognize the object before it is extracted, standardized for size, etc. In other words, attempts to process one complete object for recognition will not succeed. The paradox is conventionally bypassed by contour following or by various segmentation algorithms geared to specific problems. Most often this difficulty is avoided by defining that the objects are not to touch or overlap. However, the paradox is one of the fundamental problems in picture analysis, at least in the opinion of the author.

Object Fragmentation

In light of the above paradox one can only assume that an object in the picture consists of one or more "pieces" and that at least some of them are "visible" at any given instant, irrespective of noise or overlap of object. Clearly, the contrary situation is meaningless, i.e., if no part of an object is visible in the picture, the object just is not there.

The "pieces" out of which an object may be assumed to consist are in general arbitrary. Thus, if one asks a person to divide up an object into pieces, the number and types of pieces may be quite different from one attempt to the next. Hence the decision of what pieces an object consists of should not be allowed to be specified by humans. The human may only *advise* the computer which part of an object he considers to be "a piece", but the final decision should be made by an algorithm. The algorithm is, of course, conceived and programmed by a human, but all that is required is that the object pieces which the algorithm "looks for" have not been defined before the algorithm is written.

For the moment let us define that all the object pieces that the algorithm finds are to be called "atoms". The object is composed of one or more of these atoms. For the sake of clarity, let us say that a set of co-ordinates has been assigned to the picture. Each object and atom may now be referred to via these (picture) co-ordinates.

Symbolically, an object 0 in the picture may now be represented as:

$$0_p = a_{p1} u \ a_{p2} u \ \ldots \ u \ a_{pk} u \ \ldots \ u \ a_{pn} \quad (1)$$

where 0_p = object 0 in picture co-ordinates

a_{pk} = k-th atom of 0_p in picture co-ordinates.

The symbol u means "in conjunction with".

In the strictest sense u may be considered to be the logical "and" operator. The object 0_p and the atoms a_{pk} (k = 1, 2, . . . n) are now treated as logical variables (taking on the values true or false).

In practice the situation is much more flexible, since we cannot expect all the atoms of the object to be present at any one time. Some of them may for example be obscured, simply be missing or are outside of the picture. All the atoms are not of equal value or "importance" in describing the object 0 among a given set of objects to be recognized. To give an example, let us assume that it is desired to recognize only the letters R and P from all the letters of the alphabet. Obviously the most critical separating variable (atom) in this case is the "right leg" of R. If the recognition involves separating R and C then the "right leg" has less significance.

Besides the importance, the atom itself is only identified with a certain probability or reliability as being "the" ideal atom. In practice equation (1) thus takes the form

$$0_p = w_{1m} \ r(a_{p1}) \ u \ w_{2m} \ r(a_{p2}) \ u..u \ w_{km} \ r(a_{pk}) \ u \ \ldots \ u \ w_{nm} \ r(a_{pn}) \quad (2)$$

where: w_{km} = the weight or importance of the k-th atom when a certain subset m of all the objects "known" to the machine are to be recognized

$r(a_{pk})$ = the reliability with which the atom has been identified as a_{pk}.

u = addition operation.

The above ideas may be expressed in different formalisms, but one has to include the importance of each atom in a given context and the degree to which the atom is recognized as one of the "known" atoms.

Effects of Allowable Transformations

The picture co-ordinates, as assigned by some scanning device, are not very useful in the description of an atom since the objects are in arbitrary positions in the picture. On each atom one has to find a point or a small neighbourhood (e) which can be used as the origin of a new co-ordinate system. The atoms can now be described in terms of "their own" co-ordinates. Thus, the algorithm which fragments the object, each fragment being an atom, has to define the location of e with respect to the picture co-ordinates. For the moment, it is sufficient to say that

$$a_{ok} = a_{pk} + T_{pk} \tag{3}$$

where:

a_{pk} = k-th atom of object 0 described in the picture co-ordinates.
a_{ok} = k-th atom of object 0 described in "its own" co-ordinates.
T_{pk} = a translation operation which shifts the k-th atom from picture to its own co-ordinates.

Equation (3) is not very significant, since the algorithm which defines and locates the atom gives the location (x_o, y_o) of the point e with respect to picture co-ordinates. Another algorithm, which forms a description of the atom, defines everything with respect to (x_o, y_o). The translation T_{pk} $(k = 1, 2, \ldots n)$ is only necessary for defining the positional inter-relationships between the atoms.

We are used to talking about an "ideal" atom as the ideal, uncorrupted and undistorted version of the atom we actually observe in the picture. The ideal atom may be defined to exist, but is actually never observed. The ideal atom may possibly be computed from a collection of non-ideal atoms of the same kind, using their frequency of occurrence etc. This aspect of the problem has not been investigated.

We may formalize the problem, however, by saying that the atom as observed (a_{ok}) has to be scaled for gray level (G_k), scaled in size (S_k), rotated (R_k) and transformed or distorted (D_k) to a degree before it becomes the idealized atom, (a^i_{ok}), i.e.,

$$a^i_{ok} = D_k R_k S_k G_k \, a_{ok} \tag{4}$$

where: a^i_{ok} = the "ideal" k-th atom of object 0 in "its own" co-ordinates.
a_{ok} = the observable k-th atom of object 0 in "its own" co-ordinates. It is assumed that the co-ordinates for a^i_{ok} and a_{ok} are the same.
G_k = gray level transformation of k-th atom of object 0.

S_k = the size transformation for the k-th atom of object 0.
R_k = the rotation transformation for the k-th atom of object 0.
D_k = distortion or deformation of the k-th atom of object 0.

The operations T_{pk}, S_k, G_k, R_k, D_k will be called "the (allowable) transformations" in the rest of the text.

On the picture we can only hope to locate the observable version (a_{ok}) of the atom. We do not know the size of a_{ok}, we do not know its rotation, nor do we know the amount of distortion present. Initially we do not even know where the atom is located in the picture, or alternatively, we do not know which atom, if any, is in a given location in the picture.

Since we are seeking a solution to the problem in general terms, it will not be possible to put arbitrary restrictions on these transformations. Thus, we cannot specify that the objects are to be separated, in certain positions, of certain size, in a given angular direction, etc. If any one or any combination of these restrictions is a separating variable in the recognition of objects (for example M vs W) this fact is to be included in the picture language statements and is not to become the prerequisite for the initial recognition of various atoms out of which the objects are composed.

In principle, it is possible to search the picture for all the known atoms in all the positions, orientations, sizes and expected distortions. In practice this search takes too long, besides being an extremely crude way of trying to solve the problem. A closer examination of the problem reveals that there is a method which avoids most of these difficulties.

In a picture which contains some objects, it is possible to define at least two kinds of variables in terms of which to describe the objects. The first kind can be computed from the picture data irrespective of what the objects in the picture represent. These will be called the "point features". The other kind depends on the types of objects in the picture. They are called "atoms" and will be described in terms of variables of the first kind, i.e., in terms of the point features.

All the atoms in the picture are to be located, described and normalized before any recognition is attempted. Whether this is possible or not depends on the complexity of the atoms. For simple pictures and atoms no difficulties are expected. In a more complicated picture, specially when attempts have been made to confuse the objects by random or systematic noise, the formation of the description of the atom may require help from the recognition algorithm. This form of information feedback will be discussed later on.

Point Features

The point features can, by definition, be computed from the picture irrespective of what the objects are, irrespective of their size, shape, orientation etc. If possible, the point features should be independent of the allowable transformation, i.e., independent of translation, size, rotation, shade and shape of the objects. If this is not possible, their dependence on the allowable transformations must be known. Furthermore, it is desirable, but not necessary, that this dependence is decoupled, i.e., the dependence on size does not influence the dependence on rotation, etc.

Even though these requirements may appear difficult to satisfy, all the needed information is available in picture. Defining the picture in the usual way is a surface in three-dimensional space, i.e.,

$$i = f(x,y) \tag{5}$$

where i = the gray level at point x,y
x,y = picture co-ordinates

it has been proved that $f(x,y)$ is "well behaved" or sufficiently close to a regular surface (1). The treatment of (local) surface descriptors is well worked out in differential geometry (2), even though difficulties may occur in numerical calculation, specially in a noisy environment. Besides this problem, there should exist a rather close agreement between what the human visual system extracts from the picture and what is obtained by computation (3, 4, 5).

Since only the gray levels $i = f(x,y)$ are available, the computations have to start with this data. The calculations may be carried out over the entire picture, if desired or only in the local area under study. In the following discussion we assume that we are dealing with a local area. The origin of the co-ordinate system (u,v) for this area is the origin of an atom. It will be shown later how the origin is obtained.

We can compute the local spatial gradient $g(u,v)$ both in magnitude $|g|$ and direction φ. $|g|$ depends on the general gray level contrast of the area. φ depends on the rotation of the atom. One of the regions where the eye sees a contour is where the spatial gradient changes (6). The sharpness or boldness of the contour is related to the magnitude of this change. Thus, the local maximum of a function involving the gradient, the Laplacian etc. of $f(u,v)$ defines the so-called contour, $k(u,v)$. The local curvature $c(u,v)$ of the contour can now be computed from the change of direction of the gradients where the contours have been found.

To summarize:

Given the gray level $f(u,v)$ in the local co-ordinates (u,v),

$$g(u,v) = \nabla f\ (u,v) = \text{the gradient} \tag{6}$$

$$k(u,v) = \max_{s}\{\text{function } [f(u,v),\ g(u,v),\ \nabla^2\ f(u,v)]\} = \text{the "contour"} \tag{7}$$

where s = a trajectory along φ for $|g| >$ some limit.

$$c(u,v) = d(\varphi(u,v))/dt = \text{the curvature of contour} \tag{8}$$

where t = a trajectory at 90° to φ (along the contour) over a certain range. The variation of the point features as a function of the allowable transformations is discussed in connection with atom formation.

Considerable work has been done in detecting edges and their slopes, line segments, curved segments, angles etc. These have all been called features out of which an object may be constructed. They can only be defined in a small neighbourhood (η) in the picture. The above defined "point features" are more general, since each of the specialized features can be constructed of the point features in η by using a suitable co-ordinate system. The point features may be difficult to compute in practice, and are very time consuming when using a standard digital computer. To save time these calculations could be performed with specialized electronic circuits. In the following, the point features are assumed to be available, whenever necessary.

The τ Function

The point features which have been computed are, of course, "attached" to the objects and the atoms. When the objects are translated, changed in size, rotated or the general illumination level is changed, the point features change in a known way. Distortion is a somewhat different variable since, given enough distortion, one object can change into another object. We need to assume that distortion is kept within reasonable limits.

At this moment the location, size, rotation etc. of the objects is unknown, but all the point features are known or can be computed whenever necessary. The problem is how to locate the atoms of the various objects, without knowing what they are, where they are, etc. In other words, the objects have to be fragmented *before* it is known what they are or where they are.

This problem consists of two separate sub-problems, namely, locate a neighbourhood (η) in the picture which contains one and only one complete atom, and define a reasonably fixed point (e) in that neighbourhood to serve as the origin of a co-ordinate system (u,v) in which to describe the inter-relationships among the point features belonging to this atom. It has to be done with an algorithm (τ) which uses the point features over an undefined area (η) in the picture. The algorithm (τ) should be some function which has an extremum in η. The location of the extremum (e) can serve as the origin for the co-ordinate system (u,v). The requirements on the function (τ) are as follows:

(a) It should be independent of the general gray level and independent of the size, position, rotation and number of objects in the picture. Thus, it should not matter how the objects are arranged nor what they are. If an atom (a_1) is present and is observable, it should be found together with all the other observable atoms.

(b) τ should not be too sensitive to random noise. Noise which is correlated to picture content (for example ghosts on TV) or noise which has structure (for example a figure crossed out or covered with lines) is mentioned later.

(c) The local extremum (e) of τ should define a point which can serve as the origin of the co-ordinate system (u,v). The location of e should not be very sensitive to minor variations of the point features in η which are used by τ.

(d) The function τ should define the area (η) over the object which is to be considered an atom, i.e., τ should fragment the object.

One could use a whole set of algorithms, each one detecting a special type of feature. There is nothing much to be said against such a procedure if the algorithms detect the feature irrespective of size, rotation, etc. If the algorithms require constraints on size, rotation, location etc., then we have come back to mask matching, the point features may be dispensed with and it would bring us back to the beginning of the problem of selecting a suitable set of features.

Obviously it is desirable to use as few τ functions as possible. However, exactly what form these functions should take in general is at present impossible to say. Furthermore, we would prefer that the object fragments so found would correspond to object fragments which humans presumably use without being aware of them (7). In the following some examples of τ are described:

(i) By using the gray levels f(x,y) only, the "outstanding" extrema in the picture are local blackish and local whitish areas, i.e.

$$e(x_o, y_0) = \underset{\eta}{\text{extremum}} \int_{\epsilon} f(x,y) \qquad \epsilon << \eta \qquad (9)$$

where the local area η may be fixed or defined by some limit on the magnitude of the gradient $|g|$. The integration over a small area ϵ may be needed to avoid spurious noise.

(ii) The so-called elliptic, parabolic and saddle points are rather "striking" features in the picture. They may be computed from their classical definitions in differential geometry or possibly by using a modified version of equation (9).

(iii) An expression similar to equation (9) involving the gradients g(x,y) defines regions where the gradient changes are extremal.

(iv) The extrema over a region of any (combination of) point features may give usable "focal" points:
Thus, from the curvature c(x,y) of the contours, a set of very significant points is obtained, by locating

$$e(x_o, y_0) = \underset{t}{\text{extremum}}\ c(x,y) \tag{10}$$

where t = trajectory along the contour.
These are points which we call corners or points, that these points carry much information for visual perception may be inferred from the illustrations in Reference 4.

(v) An area containing a large number of corners is full of detail, while an area with few corners is relatively uniform. Such areas can be located by applying an expression of this form (equation (9)) to the results from equation (10).

(vi) Obviously, statistical considerations applied to point features in a local area can locate many types of areas in the picture, for example where there is some invariance, uniformity or extreme scatter.

(vii) The maximum of the distance transform is a relatively invariant point with respect to the contours of an object or atom, provided the effects of noise can be avoided (1).

(viii) The skeleton of a figure, specially at points where several "wave fronts" meet, is another example of invariant points on an object which are being used to describe the atoms (8).

(ix) An interesting and perhaps workable scheme of determining which points on an object a person would select as "outstanding" (e(x,y)), is to ask him to shoot at various areas of the object. The point where he aims (and hits if he is a good shot) are apparently more significant than the remaining points of the object. For a detailed study see References 7, 9, 10, 11.

The τ Function in the On-line System

If the objects to be fragmented have definite contours and the exteriors as well as the interiors of the objects are relatively free of detail (i.e. have no significant texture) then the following algorithm was found to produce acceptable results:

The program starts at an arbitrary point (x,y) in the picture. The origin of a polar co-ordinate system (r, θ) is "placed at" (x,y). There are no problems with co-ordinate conversions since the picture is "read" directly via the on-line scanner.

(i) Start a circular scan at (x,y) with radii $r_1, r_2 \ldots$ in angular directions $\theta_1, \theta_2 \ldots \theta_n$. Both r and θ are quantized.

(ii) At every point where a contour is encountered, record r, θ, $|g|$, φ, c, (i.e., radius, angle, magnitude of gradient, angle of gradient, curvature).

(iii) Ignore every θ direction during circular scan for which the 5-tuple $(r, \theta, |g|, \varphi, c)$ has been found.

(iv) Terminate scan when $\delta r/r_{av} >$ some limit, where δr = standard deviation of r, r_{av} = average value of r. This defines an area (η) bounded by contours, i.e., in this case the area of the atom is defined in terms of "raggedness".

(v) When the scan has terminated, evaluate a function of the form

$$F(\theta) = r(\theta)\, f_1(k) \,.\, f_2(\alpha), \; \theta = \theta_1, \theta_2 \ldots \theta_n \tag{11}$$

where: $f_1(k)$ = a parabolic function in the number of contours points (k) found. $f_1(0)$ = maximum ≥ 1, $f_1(n) = 1$.

$f_2(\alpha)$ = a parabolic function in $|\theta - \varphi|$ modulus 90°. $f_2(0°)$ = maximum ≥ 1, $f_2(90°) = 1$.

In words: $f_1(k)$ determines the "importance of contours", i.e., if there are contours in few θ directions, the machine should search them out by placing more emphasis on them. $f_2(\alpha)$ determines how "strongly" the ray $r(\theta)$ is "attached" to the contour. The rays $r(\theta)$ (radius values from x,y to contour in a given direction θ) may be looked upon as n radially placed rubber bands in tension. The tension of each band, in direction θ, is given by $F(\theta)$.

(vi) The center of the circular scan is moved in the direction of the resultant of $F(\theta)$, until the resultant approaches zero. This gives a new point (x ,y). Now the neighbourhood from which the 5-tuples of point features were computed has changed. The computations (i) to (vi) are repeated for (x',y') as the center until the resultant of $F(\theta) <$ some limit.

Many versions of this idea have been tried. The above formulation is a simplified version of the τ function used in the present programs.

Atom Description

As the next step in the procedure, an easily manipulable description for the atom has to be found. A "bootstrap" version of the atom description is to be constructed and normalized before recognition of the atom is attempted. The τ function has given a point for the origin of a co-ordinate system and defined, at least to the first approximation, the neighbourhood (η) in which the point features for the atom are located. The nature of the τ function is, of course, known and consequently we also know the nature of the neighbourhood (η), i.e., whether it is an area, a line segment, a junction between lines, etc.

Contour Atom

Probably the most logical atom is a segment of a contour. The origin (x_o, y_0) for its co-ordinate system is given by the extremum of curvature. The orientation of the segment is uniquely defined by the illumination gradient $g(x_o, y_0)$ at (x_o, y_0). The most convenient co-ordinate system in which to describe the inter-relationships of local curvatures (and other point features, if desired) is the so-called natural or intrinsic system, consisting of s and $c(s)$, where s = distance along segment, $c(s)$ = curvature as function of s. The only uncertain quantity is the length of contour to be included in the atom representation. A convention will have to be adopted, if the τ function does not specify the length of the contour.

For computational purposes, the segment may be represented by some approximating function, or as a list of values, i.e.,

x_o, y_0 = location of origin of intrinsic co-ordinates

φ = angle of gradient at (x_o, y_0) with respect to the (x,y) co-ordinates of the picture

$s_i, c(s_i)$ = pairs of distances along curve (s_i) and curvatures $c(s_i)$, $i = 0, \pm 1, \pm 2, \ldots$

The positive direction of s and the sign of c has to be defined consistently with respect to $g(x_o, y_0)$.

The s, $c(s)$ pairs are independent of rotation and translation. Translation is given by a change in (x_o, y_0) and rotation is given by φ. If the picture is magnified m times, then of course all curvature values are reduced by $1/m$. Normalization for the length of the contour, i.e., for size, should be determined in the procedure by which the various segments are recognized. The description of the contour segments and the inter-relationship between these segments can be used to describe an object or any part of it.

Line Atom

It is often argued that line segments, line ends, junctions between lines, corners etc. should be treated as atoms. To simplify the extraction of such atoms, the line is usually thinned to one element thickness. Assuming that a τ function locates these atoms, one finds it difficult to form a unique description of the atom before its recognition. Thus, from the origin (x_o, y_0) one, two, three, etc. lines may radiate in different tangential directions φ_t. The common denominator for these is the line end. If the end of a line is at (x_o, y_0), with tangent direction φ_t its description in terms of s, $\zeta(s)$ pairs is unique, except for the length of the line, $\zeta(s)$ = curvature at s. A line is now describable as two joined line ends, a Y junction as 3 joined line ends etc.

If the line is not thinned to a single string of elements, it may be treated as a combination of contours, or as an area.

Area Atom

The contours of an object usually form an enclosed area. A description which covers an area and includes the point features in a conveniently manipulable form will be very useful. The skeleton of the area is such a description, but a polar co-ordinate system, with its origin at the extremum point (e(x,y)) may be the simplest. In the polar co-ordinates the angular direction (θ) refers naturally to rotation and radial direction (r) is directly related to the size of the area.

In the computer, the atom may now be described as a table, for example by using equal increments in θ, i.e.

x_0, y_0 = location of extremum of τ in an arbitrary co-ordinate system covering the entire picture.

θ, r, c, φ, $|g|$, k, i = 7-tuples of numbers, giving the angular direction θ, radius to contour r, the curvature at this point c, the angle of the gradient φ, the magnitude of the gradient $|g|$, the contour "boldness" or "heaviness" k and the gray level i.

If the point features k and i are ignored, being of less significance, the 5-tuples θ, r, c, φ, $|g|$ describe the atom as a curve in a five-dimensional space. This curve, however, is usually multivalued and discontinuous.

The size of the area (or of the atom) is now given by the average value of the radial directions ($\bar{r}$). The scaling of the atom to a standard size is simple, since r is scaled directly, and c is scaled as $1/\bar{r}$. The scaling of the magnitude of the gradient $|g|$ may be performed in terms of gray level statistics computed over the entire picture, or simply by computing an average ($|\bar{g}|$) of $|g|$ and scaling the individual values accordingly. The location of the extremum (x_0,y_0) is independent of rotation and nearly independent of limited distortion of the atom. The zero reference for θ and φ may as well be the x-axis of the picture co-ordinates. Thus when the atom is rotated, the values of φ and θ change accordingly or we can rotate the object at will with respect to the r, θ co-ordinates by incrementing θ and φ. The location of the atom is of course given by (x_0,y_0), and the atom may be translated by modifying these values. An atom formed by reflecting a known ideal atom is treated as a new ideal atom.

If the area contains much texture, which produces a large number of rather poorly related point features, and if the corresponding τ function has defined the area of the atom, the θ, r, c, φ, $|g|$, k, i description becomes cumbersome, and should possibly be replaced by some statistical representations. Beyond the local statistics based on i, the author is not aware of any published experimental results.

Atom Recognition

Thus, the conditions laid down in the beginning have all been met. The object can be fragmented algorithmically, local area or atom descriptions can be obtained and these can be normalized before any recognition is attempted. The recognition of individual atoms is now quite simple.

Each of the observable or non-ideal atoms a_o of a given type have an "idealized" version a^i from which they can be derived provided the size (S), rotation (R), and distortion (D) are known. In the analysis of a picture the situation is exactly opposite. It has been possible to construct a representation of an unknown but observable atom (a_u) to a certain degree of accuracy, and it has been possible to normalize it for size, but not for rotation. However, it is known how to rotate the unknown atom a_u.

Assume that the machine "knowns" a set of "ideal" or "memory" atoms $a_1^i, a_2^i, \ldots a_k^i \ldots a_n^i$. The unknown atom a_u is normalized for size (a'_u) and compared with all the memory atoms. The comparison procedure consists of computing a weighted distance between a'_u and a_k^i, $k = 1, 2, \ldots n$, for all rotations θ, i.e.

$$d_{uk}(\theta) = \text{distance } (a'_u, a_k^i) \; ; \; k = 1, 2, \ldots n; \quad \theta = 0 \text{ to } 2\pi \tag{12}$$

The rotation angle $(\theta_k{}^*)$ which gives the minimum distance $d_{uk}{}^*$ gives the best matching orientation between a'_u and a_k^i, i.e.

$$d^*_{uk}\,(\theta_k{}^*) = \underset{(\theta)}{\text{minimum}}\,(d_{uk}(\theta)); \; k = 1, 2, \ldots n \tag{13}$$

The comparison is carried out for all the ideal atoms in the memory. The unknown atom is considered to correspond to the ideal atom which has the lowest distance $(d^*(\theta^*))$, provided this distance is below a limit d_m i.e.

$$d^*(\theta^*) = \underset{k}{\text{minimum}}\,(d_{uk}{}^*\,(\theta_k{}^*)) \tag{14}$$

This procedure selects one ideal atom a^{i*} as being the one "nearest" to the unknown atom a'_u. If $d^*(\theta^*) \leq d_m$, the unknown atom a'_u is considered to be a^{i*}, but it is rotated by an angle θ^* and it has a certain size relation (s_u/s_i) with respect to a^{i*}. (Size of $a_u = s_u$, size of $a^{i*} = s_i$, size being defined as the average radius $(\bar{r})$.). If $d^*(\theta^*) > d_m$ then the unknown atom is a new one and it is added to the machine's list of "ideal" atoms.

The recognition of "contour" and "line" atoms is even simpler, but has not been investigated by the author. The assignment of the positive direction for the measure along the curve (s) with respect to the gray level gradient, tangent or normal to the curve has to be consistent. In order to normalize these atoms some convention has to be adopted regarding the length of the line to be followed. One procedure worth trying is to follow the line half-way to the next e(x,y) point on the same line, unless the line goes on beyond some limit (or terminates). The recognition of the atoms consists of correlation and selection of the best matching ideal atom.

If the minimization procedure is replaced by an ordering procedure, then the unknown atom a_u will cause the ideal atoms to be ordered according to distance. Differently expressed, the unknown atom a_u is equivalent to a_1^i with probability p_1, equivalent to a_2^i with probability p_2,etc. This leads to procedures for allowing the machine to form its own idealized atoms, to select a suitable set of atoms and to "help itself" in atom location and formulation, provided the problem is to recognize a given set of objects from a given environment. However, it is premature to go into these speculations until at least the fundamentals of the proposed scheme have been tested experimentally.

Description of Atom Interrelationships

To describe the relationship between the various atoms that constitute an object is now relatively straightforward. The description, however, has to be "relativistic". The situation is best illustrated with an example.

Assume that an object consists of ideal atoms a_1^i and a_2^i. In the object a_1^i occurs in two different sizes and rotations, i.e., a_1^i has two present (observable) realizations a_1^1 and a_1^2. The atom a_2^i has only one present realization called a_2^1.

Thus, on the object we can find atoms a_1^1, a_1^2 and a_2^1, but let us assume that the machine has only "hit upon" and recognized a_1^1 as a_1^i in its present realization, i.e., $a_1^1 = a_1^i\ (s_1, \lambda_1)$, where s_1 = size wrt a_1^i; λ_1 = rotation wrt a_1^i. If a_1^1 is to be used as a starting point for locating another atom say a_1^2, then the distance $d_{1,2}$ and the angular direction $\psi_{1,2}$ where to find a_1^2 have to be given with respect to a_1^1. If the object is magnified by a factor m, the size (s_1) of a_1^1 is m times larger and the distance $d_{1,2}$ is also m times larger. Thus a description of where the next atom is to be located can be given in terms of $d_{1,2}/s_1$ and $\psi_{1,2}$ measured with respect to λ_1. The machine is now able to estimate the location of the next atom irrespective of the size and rotation of the object. The distortion of the object or inaccurate location of a_1^1 only introduces an error term into the estimation of where a_1^2 is to be found.

For a combination of atoms, (i.e., $0_1 = a_1 . a_2 . a_3$) the location (of 0_1) has been defined as the center of "gravity" of the individual atoms, the size taken as the average size and the direction as the vector sum, weighted for size, of individual atom directions (with respect to the ideal atoms a_1^i, a_2^i, a_3^i). The description of positional inter-relationships is now possible also for composite atoms (molecules) which are not directly locatable with the τ function.

Object Recognition

To summarize the previous discussion, we defined the existence of point features which can be computed irrespective of the contents of the picture. These point features are "attached to" the objects and are endities like contours, gradients, curvatures of contours, etc. Using an algorithm (τ), certain (more or less) stationary points (e(x,y)) on or near the objects are identified as well as the area (η) considered to contain the atom. These points (e(x,y)) serve as "focal points" where the origin of a local co-ordinate system (u,v) is placed. In this co-ordinate system (u,v) the inter-relationships between the point features in η are described. The minimum size of the neighbourhood η is defined by the τ function. The neighbourhood can be expanded under the control of the picture language. More about this later. These neighbourhood descriptions are the atoms out of which an object is composed. Only after the atom has been so described and normalized is an attempt made to recognize the atom. If the atom location and formulation is unique, the recognition problem is simple. A unique atom formulation is required, irrespective of how the objects are placed in the picture, i.e., irrespective of the allowable transforms. It is preferable to have atoms which are recognizable by humans as certain parts of objects, but this is not a necessary condition.

The necessary and sufficient conditions for this procedure to work is best described by the following example, where we want to teach the machine to recognize an object.

(a) Show the object (0) in isolation from other objects

(b) Fragment the object (0) using the (τ) algorithm and form atom descriptions

(c) Describe the inter-relationships between the atoms for this object.

Now the analysis part is complete. The machine should now be able to recognize the object (0) when it is scaled in size, rotated, translated, somewhat distorted (call it 0′) and placed among other objects which are either known or unknown to the machine.

The recognition of object $(0')$ as being 0 will be possible if the object fragmentation algorithm (τ) succeeds in locating the same atoms for $0'$ in the composite picture as it did when the object 0 was isolated. The absolute minimum requirement is that only one of the atoms in $0'$ is located and identified as an atom belonging to 0. The linguistic procedure should be able to assist in the extraction of additional atoms in $0'$ and in matching them with atoms in 0.

Structure of the On-Line Picture Language

The preliminary version of the on-line picture language was kept as simple as possible. It incorporates many display programs and allows the operator to interact with the programs. Operator interaction, however, consists only of modifying certain weights (for example, in the computation of distance between atoms) and in *advising* the machine about the selection of object fragments.

The language consists of three major parts:

(1) Object fragmentation and fragment recognition.

(2) Teaching of fragment inter-relationships.

(3) Recognition of objects.

During initial experiments, these parts are run independently, but they can be linked together.

Machine's "Memories"

The machine has four types of "memory" in which the results are retained. These "memories" contain the following data:

(a) A list of "ideal" atoms, i.e., tables representing $\overset{i}{a}_1{}^i$, $\overset{i}{a}_2{}^i$ etc. In these tables each "ideal" atom has been given a name for operator purposes and a serial number for computer use. There is also information on how the atom was obtained, its size, etc., and a list of θ, r, $|g|$, φ, c for $\theta = 0°, 15°, 30°, \ldots 345°$ for the first and second contours as seen from the origin (x_o, y_0) of the atom.

(b) A list of atom inter-relationships. In this list are entered all the taught relationships, as given by the operator. The list is fairly complex, and is handled by miniature list processors. In this list the computer can find:

(i) all the ideal atoms which it has been taught, i.e., $\overset{i}{a}_1{}^i$, $\overset{i}{a}_2{}^i \ldots \overset{i}{a}_k{}^i \ldots \overset{i}{a}_n{}^i$.

(ii) All the present (observable) realizations of each ideal atom which the machine has "seen" and which are "sufficiently different" to be worth storing. The decision of what is "sufficiently different" is obtained from a distance calculation between the present realizations or is forced onto the machine by the operator. Thus for the k-th ideal atom $a_k{}^i$, one finds a list of present realizations $a_k(s_1, \lambda_1)$, $a_k(s_2, \lambda_2)$, $a_k(s_3, \lambda_3)$ etc. where either $s_1 \# s_2$ or $\lambda_1 \# \lambda_2$ etc., s = size, λ = angle of present realization of atom wrt the ideal atom.

(iii) All the taught relationships between the present realizations. For the moment the picture language contains three operators only, which may verbally be expressed as follows:

(I) "If you see atom $a_1\ (s_1, \lambda_1)$ at location (x_0,y_0) go search for atom $a_2\ (s_2, \lambda_2)$ at location $d_{1,2}/s_1$, $\psi_{1,2}-\lambda_1$, i.e.," $a_1\ (s_1, \lambda_1, d_{1,2}/s_1, \psi_{1,2}-\lambda_1) \rightarrow a_2\ (s_2, \lambda_2)$

(II) "The object 0_1 consists of atoms a_1, a_2 and a_3, i.e.,"
$0_1\ (s, \lambda) = a_1\ (s_1, \lambda_1, d_{1,2}/s_1, \psi_{1,2}-\lambda_1)$.
$.\ a_2\ (s_2, \lambda_2, d_{2,3}/s_2\ .\ \psi_{2,3}-\lambda_2)$.
$.\ a_3\ (s_3, \lambda_3, d_{3,1}/s_3, \psi_{3,1}-\lambda_3)$

(III) "An object 0_1 is the same as an object 0_2, i.e.,"
$0_1\ (s_1, \lambda_1) = 0_2\ (s_2, \lambda_2)$.

At present the weights for each atom are set to unity, and the dot (.) represents the logical "and" operator.

(c) A list of what the machine is "seeing" at present. This is a list of present or observable realizations of the atoms which the machine has found during analysis of the picture or during recognition of an object. The teaching of atom inter-relationships is based on this list. The machine may, of course, be programmed to work out the atom inter-relationships in this list without operator intervention. When the teaching of an object has been completed, or the machine has recognized an object, this list is zeroed.

(d) A coarse image of the picture the machine is analysing. In this list all the areas that the machine has analysed are marked off. It is the simplest way of preventing the machine from analysing a given area more than once. The list is only used when the machine is extracting atoms by itself from an object presented in isolation, i.e., when the operator is not involved.

Relations Taught

The preliminary picture language only contains three operators which relate the present realizations (i.e. observable atoms) of given ideal atoms. The three operators are:

(1) The "pointing" operator ($\rightarrow$) which allows the machine operator to instruct the machine about atom inter-relationships without reference to any particular object. This operator is normally used to guide the machine from less significant atoms, which it has located, to more significant ones yet to be found. Thus, the expression $a_1{}^1 \rightarrow a_2{}^1$ means that if atom $a_1{}^1$ (an observable version of $a_1{}^1$) has been found, then one expects $a_2{}^1$ (an observable version of $a_2{}^1$) in a certain positional relationship with respect to

a_1^1 (relative to the size and orientation of a_1^1).

(2) The "and" operator (.) is used to compose present realizations of atoms into objects or parts of objects which are larger than a single atom. Assume for example that an object 0 was found to consist of two ideal atoms a_1^i and a_2^i. For a_1^i two different present realizations were found (i.e., 0 contained a_1^i in two different sizes or orientations a_1^1, a_1^2). Only one present realization (a_2^1) was found for a_2^i. The statement $0 = a_1^1 \;.\; a_1^2 \;.\; a_2^1$ specifies the composition of 0. Again, the positional relationships between atoms are described in a "relativistic" form. In the present version of the language each atom has equal weight and the string $a_1^1 \;.\; a_1^2 \;.\; a_2^1$ is treated as a logical "and" operation.

(3) The equality operator (=) is used to define equalities between atoms or between an object and a string of atoms.

The picture language allows construction of compound statements of the form $0_1 = a_1^1 \;.\; a_2^1$; $0 = 0_1 \;.\; a_1^2$; $a_1^1 \rightarrow 0_1$; $a_2^2 = 0_2$ etc. and the naming of hierarchies of objects. The observable atoms (i.e., the present realizations a_1^1, a_1^2 etc.) are on the lowest level in the hierarchy. The objects are on the higher levels. Altogether 8 hierarchy levels are possible.

Details of the Program

The programs operate essentially as follows. The machine is assumed to be completely "newborn",; i.e., it has no previous knowledge of anything, except for the programs.

(1) Object fragmentation and (fragment or) atom recognition (see block diagram # 1):

(a) The operator guides the machine to the vicinity of the desired atom or object fragment, but the operator cannot tell the machine to choose this fragment as an atom.

(b) The point features are computed, the τ algorithm locates the center of the atom and determines its extent over the object. If the fragment is not acceptable to the algorithm, the machine either calls the operator or locates a nearby fragment.

(c) The description of the atom is formed, and it is normalized for size.

(d) The machine compares this atom (a_u) with all the known ideal atoms ($a_1^i, a_2^i \ldots$) and presents the one that matches best, provided there are any ideal atoms and the match is within a given limit.

(e) If the match is not acceptable or there are no ideal atoms, the machine wants to know the name of this new atom and asks the operator. This atom is now stored as the "ideal" atom and the match is 100% correct.

(f) If the match was acceptable, the atom is considered recognized and it is stored in the list of "seen" atoms, with all the necessary descriptors for position, size etc.

The procedures (a) to (f) are repeated until an object has been fragmented sufficiently. It should be noted that the operator does not give the object fragment but simply guides the machine to a certain location in the picture. The τ algorithm decides whether this area can be considered a fragment. By using a "memory map" of the area being explored and by setting a limit on the match the procedure can be run automatically.

(2) Teaching of atom inter-relationships (see block diagram #2)

The "list of seen atoms" contains all the necessary information about the atoms in order to be able to inter-relate them and to store them in the list structure. The teaching is done by the operator and is not automated. However, there does not appear to be any reason why this step cannot be done automatically, provided the possible number of inter-relationships is kept to a reasonable limit. Since the atoms are recognized with a certain degree of reliability, one could, for example, make the less reliable atoms "point to" the more reliable atoms and only compose the object of atoms which are "more reliable" and which have not been used in a similar string for another object.

Anyway, if for example the present realizations (of the atoms for object 0) were a_1, a_2 and a_3, where a_2 is "most important", the teaching for object 0 proceeds as follows:

(g) $a_1 \rightarrow a_2$ i.e. if a_1 has been found go look for a_2
$a_3 \rightarrow a_2$, i.e., if a_3 has been found go look for a_2
$0 = a_1 \, . \, a_2 \, . \, a_3$ i.e., object 0 consists of atoms a_1, a_2 and a_3.

One may include logical "or" operations by repetition, i.e.,
$0_1 = a_1 \, . \, a_2$; $0_2 = a_3 \, . \, a_2$; $0 = 0_1$; $0 = 0_2$
One may also say
$0_1 = a_1 \, . \, a_2$; $0 = 0_1 \, . \, a_3$ etc.

This procedure is repeated until a sufficient number of logical relationships have been entered in "the list of taught relationships". It is apparent that there is no uniqueness about this procedure, and one can teach bad inter-relationships as well as good ones.

(3) Recognition of objects (see block diagram #3)

At any stage in the machines "level of learning" one may enter the recognition part of the system and determine how well the system behaves. This part of the system contains most of the programs needed to analyse the picture, but instead of just forming a list of "seen atoms", the machine continues on and uses the taught inter-relationships to guide itself from one atom to the next until this list is exhausted or one of the objects of the required hierarchy has been identified.

The problem, however, is considerably more complicated. Two of these problems are rather interesting. The first is the so-called "wrong starting assumption" and the second is created by objects belonging to the same hierarchy, but one is a part of another object.

The effect of the wrong starting assumption is easiest seen if we assume that the letter L was the object the machine tried to recognize. Let us assume that the first atom that the machine found was the top end of a vertical bar, and that the picture language now instructs the machine to find the lower right horizontal end of the bar, "thinking" that it is dealing with the letter L. If however, the letter (L) was rotated by 90° (⅃) then the machine fails to find the expected atom. There is a provision in the program which allows it to modify its "initial assumption" about the rotation of objects.

The other problem illustrates that a search for objects cannot be discontinued as soon as one object of the desired hierarchy has been found. By continuing the above example, assume that the top end of a vertical bar was found. The machine "thinks" it is dealing with the letter L and goes and looks for the lower right end of the horizontal bar. We assume that it finds this one also, the actual object, however, was an upside down T (⊥).

The program operates as follows, with the "list of seen atoms" set to zero at start:

(h) The first point in the picture where the machine "looks" may be given by the operator or may be obtained from a random number generator.

(i) The machine computes the point features and uses the τ algorithm until an atom has been located.

(j) The atom description is formed and normalized for size.

(k) This unknown atom (a_u) is compared with the ideal atoms and the best matching one is chosen as being a_u. (If the match is too poor, the machine goes back to step (h)). The atom is now entered as known (say a_1) in the list of "seen atoms". (In fact a whole string of "best matching" atoms may be chosen and ordered according to their match).

(l) The machine now checks the list of taught relationships, finds the present realizations (n = 1, 2, . . .) in this list that match a_1 best and marks these as true. (Again, the number of entries marked as "true" may be varied by modifying the match criterion and n).

(m) It also checks if by any chance the found atom is the desired object. Normally this is not the case. Anyway, the list of taught relationships is checked to see if an object of the desired hierarchy has been found.

If this is not the case the machine goes to step (n), if it is the case it checks whether the found object is a part of another, as yet undetected, object of the same hierarchy. If the answer is "no", the recognition is complete. If the answer is "yes" the machine computes the location of the first "unchecked" atom, marks this atom as "expected" or the reference to it as "used", gives the co-ordinate to the τ algorithm and returns to step (i).

(n) Based on the already found atoms, i.e., the ones that have been marked "true" in the list of taught relationships, the machine computes the location of the next atom, marks it as "expected", or marks the reference to it as "used" and returns to step (i).

Comments

It was initially thought that whenever the "expected" atom was not found, it should be marked as "false". As a consequence, any string with a false element was marked false, (i.e., $0_2 = a_3{}^F \,.\, a_4$, F = false makes 0_2 false) and any string that has become true was marked true (i.e. $0_1 = a_1{}^T \,.\, a_2{}^T$, T = true, makes 0_1 true). The process is repeated until there are no more true or false entries to be marked.

This method was found to give poor performance since an atom that was not found where it was expected to be, not because it was not there, but because of errors in locating the atom, was marked false. The machine usually found another atom in the vicinity of the expected atom. Since the expected atom was marked false, any reference to it was ignored.

A much milder effect was obtained if instead of marking the expected atom as false, the reference from the found to the expected atom was simply marked as "used". With this method the machine proceeded from atom to atom and managed to recognize objects even in the presence of programming errors.

Conclusion

This experiment is far from complete. The initial realization of the computer programs and the results they produced clarified many problems but of course generated others.

Thus it became very obvious, while watching the displays during a recognition experiment, that the machine needs a goal-seeking algorithm to guide itself through the list of taught relationships. Without such a goal-seeking procedure, as the program is at present, the machine "muddles through", it does recognize the object finally, but in so doing it checks too many atoms.

The taught relationships are "frozen" in the sense that once they have been given, the machine cannot change them. This, obviously, is not realistic. The machine should be able to modify the object relationships during recognition, i.e., it should "learn" while it is "seeing". At least counts of frequency of occurrence of atoms and atom-relationships should be included.

The construction of the description of the atom, starting from some "bootstrap" atom should be under the guidance of the ideal atoms which the machine knows about. However, care should be exersised to prevent the machine from constructing atoms which are not in the picture, i.e., to prevent "hallucinations". Objects which are intentionally confused, for example by drawing lines across them or by superimposing several transparent objects, produce a particular challenge since the atoms themselves are "well hidden". The point features can be relied upon, but many of them are "spurious", being caused by criss-crossing lines.

Appendix

An example of analysis, teaching and recognition

A practical problem, which had been studied before was chosen for the experiment. The problem is to recognize nerve-fiber cross-sections, which are the more or less circular rings in Figure 1. Its "conventional" solution is described in Reference 12. The experiment was intended to be a comparison between a linguistic recognition procedure and a specialized procedure.

The experiments are carried out on a small (8K) process control computer by linking or overlaying the programs. The computer has direct access to the picture. About 4000 × 4000 spatial resolution elements are possible by using a controllable on-line flying spot scanner. The picture is treated as a read-only memory.

Experiment 1: The behavior of the τ function

As explained before, the operator cannot specify the atoms. He can only ***advise*** as to what might be an atom by guiding the computer to a certain area in the picture. The τ algorithm will decide whether the area can become an atom. For operator convenience, the picture is scanned in coarse steps and displayed, see Figure 2.

For the first experiment, the machine was directed to "consider" various regions in the picture. The results are illustrated in Figures 3, 4 and 5.

Figure 3a shows a point (the center of the circle) where the τ algorithm was started. The circle indicates the largest area that the machine can "see". Figure 3b shows a magnified version of the area. The dots (on the circular trajectory) show contour points where the point features have been computed. The string of dots in the center shows the motion of the center point (x', y') of the τ algorithm. It moves towards the center of the fiber.

Balance is reached in the second attempt, see Figure 3c. Figure 3d shows the details of what the τ algorithm considers to be an atom. Figure 3e shows a detailed display of the area seen and passed on to the atom forming program.

Figures 4a to 4e show the same experiment for a part of an inter-fiber space that becomes an atom. Figures 5a to 5c show that a wall section can also be considered to be an atom.

In general, the τ algorithm defines as atoms the fiber centers, wall sections, parts of inter-fiber spaces, joined areas where two walls touch, etc.

Experiment 2: Guided picture analysis

At the start of this experiment all the computer "memories" have been cleared, i.e., the computer "knows nothing". Based on the results of experiment 1, the operator guides the machine to various parts of a fiber and asks for the atoms to be formed and stored.

(a) The operator guides the machine to the center of a fiber and gives control to the program. The τ algorithm finds the center and gives control to the atom forming program. The atom is formed, but since the memory was cleared, the machine asks for the name of the atom. The operator calls this atom A1 and it becomes the first "ideal" atom, see Figure 6. This "ideal" atom, as well as its "present realization" are stored.

(b) The procedure is repeated for the left-hand wall section of the same fiber. Since the wall section and the center of the fiber are very different, the comparison fails and the machine asks for the name of this atom. The operator gives W1 (wall section number 1). W1 becomes the second "ideal" atom, see Figure 7.

(c) Next the operator points out the top part of the fiber wall. The atom is formed, see Figure 8. Now, however, there is an ideal atom (W1) which matches the top wall section, see Figure 9. Thus, the presently seen atom is only another realization of an already known "ideal" atom.

(d) The operator now guides the machine to the right-hand wall section and then to the bottom wall section. In each case they are recognized as W1 and the different present realizations are stored. An "exploded" view of what the machine has "seen" is shown in Figure 10.

(e) Since atoms can include two contours, the machine is instructed to form an atom similar to A1, but including two contours. This atom is called B1 and becomes the third "ideal" atom, see Figure 11.

The fundamental steps in the analysis are now complete. The list of "ideal" atoms contains A1, W1 and B1, see Figures 6, 7, 11. The list of seen atoms contain four present realizations of W1, one realization of A1 and one of B1, i.e., $W_1\ (s_1, \lambda_1)$, $W_1\ (s_2, \lambda_2)$, $W_1\ (s_3, \lambda_3)$, $W_1\ (s_4, \lambda_4)$,

A_1 (s_5, λ_5), B_1 (s_6, λ_6), where s = size and λ = angle wrt ideal atom.

Experiment 3: On-line teaching

The list of atoms which the machine has seen, or the list of present realizations of ideal atoms is shown in Figure 10 (B1 is not included for clarity). The operator bases his teaching on this display by giving the operation number and the addresses. Thus the top wall section (W1) is at address 3 and A1 is at address 1. The "pointing operator" is represented by 1, "equality" is 2, "and" is 3. To instruct the machine that "from the top wall section you should go to A1" is accomplished by typing 1, 3, 1. The result is shown in Figure 12.

The following instructions were given:

W_1 (s_1, λ_1) $\rightarrow$ A_1 (s_5, λ_5)
W_1 (s_2, λ_2) $\rightarrow$ A_1 (s_5, λ_5) see Figure 12
W_1 (s_3, λ_3) $\rightarrow$ A_1 (s_5, λ_5)
W_1 (s_4, λ_4) $\rightarrow$ A_1 (s_5, λ_5)
A_1 (s_5, λ_5) $\rightarrow$ B_1 (s_6, λ_6)
F_1 (s_7, λ_7) = W_1 (s_1, λ_1) . W_1 (s_2, λ_2) . W_1 (s_3, λ_3) . W_1 (s_4, λ_4)
see Figure 13
F_1 (s_7, λ_7) = B_1 (s_6, λ_6)

W1, A1, B1 are at hierarchy zero, i.e., they are visible and can be treated as atoms, F_1 is set at hierarchy one, i.e., at higher level than the atoms. No mention has yet been made of inter-fiber spaces, regions where two fibers touch, specially mis-shapen fibers, black dots, etc. These cases and others encountered during recognition experiments, can be added whenever desired or when the machine gets into difficulties.

Experiment 4: Recognition

Since the machine only "knows about" wall sections (W1), the center A1) and the whole fiber (B1, F1), but nothing about inter-fiber spaces, the starting point for the experiment should be a wall section or the center of a fiber. The hierarchy of objects to be recognized is set to 1. The list of seen atoms is zeroed and the machine is guided to any wall section. The result is, of course, rather predictable in this simplified case.

(a) The machine is guided to the lower left wall section, see Figure 14. From this point onwards no human intervention occurs.

(b) The machine finds the focal point, forms the atom, compares it and identifies it as a version of W1. This information is stored in the list of seen atoms, see Figure 15, and the "closest" present realization of W1 is marked as found in the list of taught relationships. In this list it now "looks for" what to do next. It can either use a "pointing" statement or it can use the "and" statement.

In this case it uses the "pointing" statement, since it is first in the list, types "looking for A1" and goes towards the center of the fiber, see Figure 16. Due to a programming fault, the direction is about 45° in error, resulting in a rather incorrect starting point for the τ algorithm, see line in Figure 16.

(c) The τ algorithm manages to locate the center of the fiber, see Figures 17, 18, 19. The area presented to the atom forming program is shown in Figure 20.

(d) The atom is formed, identified as a version of A1 and entered in the list of seen atoms, see Figure 21.

(e) The next taught entry was A1 → B1. B1 is located and recognized, see Figure 22. The seen atoms are shown in Figure 23.

(f) Since B1 = F1, the recognition is complete and a fiber has been located.

Comment

The machine was taught to recognize inter-fiber spaces, joining fiber walls and instructed to go directly to the center of the closest fiber. When started at a random point in the picture, it appeared to "understand" the problem by "going after" the fibers. No statistically significant comparison between the "conventional program" and this program has been made, since the program is very slow. However, this program can be taught in a few hours what would take months of programming using a "conventional" method.

REFERENCES

1. Rosenfeld, A., Picture Processing by Computer. Academic Press, 1969.
2. Kreyszig, E., Introduction to differential geometry and Riemannian Geometry. University of Toronto Press, 1968.
3. Luria, A. R., Higher Cortical Functions in man. Basic Books, 1966.
4. Kolers, P. A., Eden, M. Recognizing Patterns, Studies in living and automatic systems. MIT Press 1968, pp. 14.
5. McCulloch, W. S., Embodiments of Mind. The MIT Press, 1965.
6. Ratliff, F., Mach Bands: Quantitive Studies on Neural Networks in the Retina. Holden–Day Inc., 1965.
7. Yarbus, A. L., Eye Movements and Vision. Plenum Press, 1967.
8. Blum, H., Shape and Visual Science. (to be published)
9. Noton, D., A theory of visual perception. I.E.E.E. Trans. SSC 6, No. 4, October 1970, pp. 349-357.

10. Piggins, D. J., Fragmentation of a geometrical figure viewed under intermittent illumination. Nature, Vol. 227, No. 5259, pp. 730, August 15, 1970.
11. Evans, C. R., Some studies of pattern perception using a stabilized retinal image. Brit. J. Psychol., 1965, pp. 121-133, Vol. 56, No. 2.
12. Watanabe, S., Methodologies of Pattern Recognition. Academic Press, 1969, pp. 333.
13. Sharma, O. P., A syntactic model for online realtime description, analysis and generation of handdrawn patterns. Dept. of Electrical Engineering, N.Y. University, May 1970.
14. Grasselli, A., Automatic Interpretation and Classification of Images. Academic Press, 1969, pp. 391.

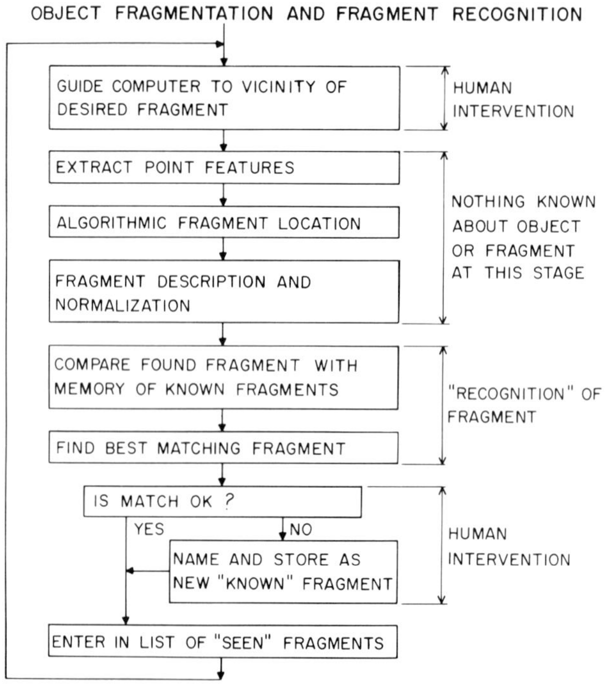

Block Diagram No. 1

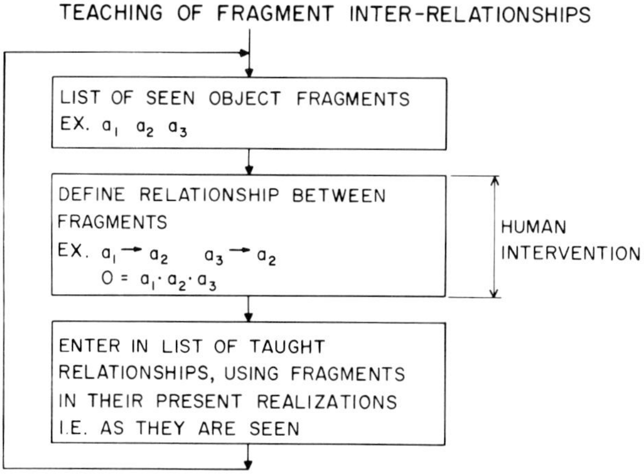

Block Diagram No. 2

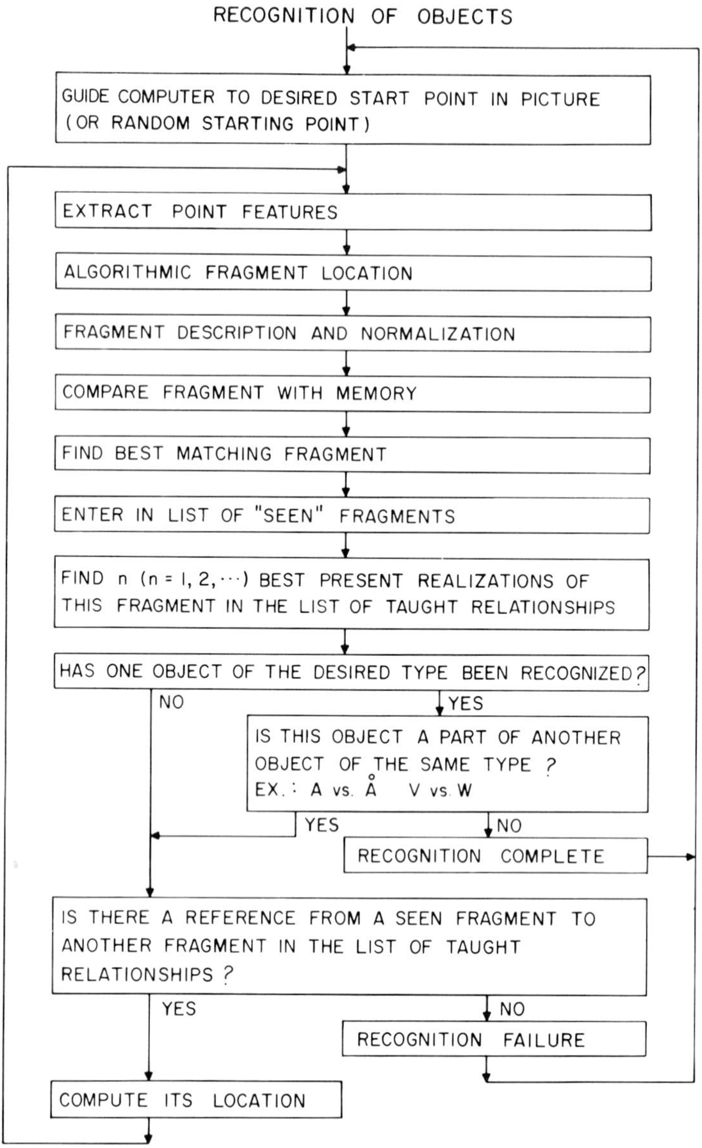

Block Diagram No. 3

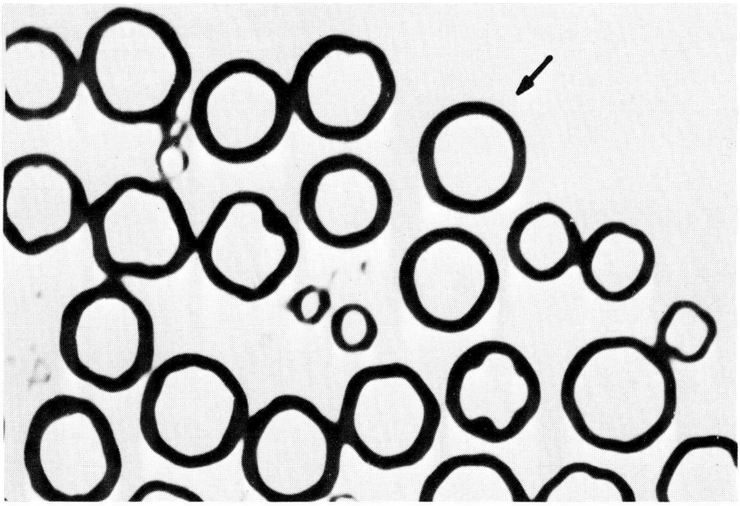

Figure 1

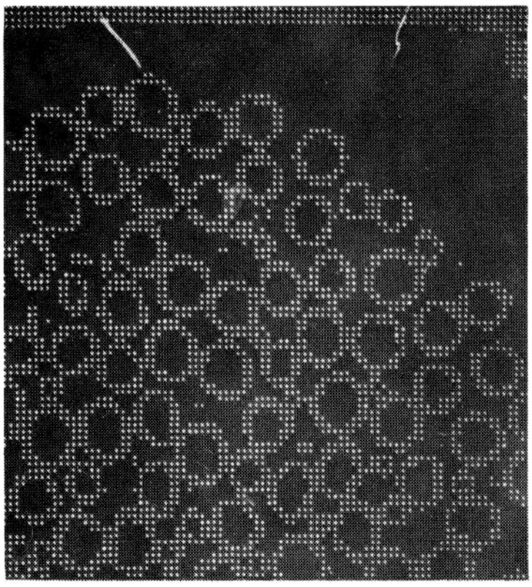

Figure 2

Figure 3a

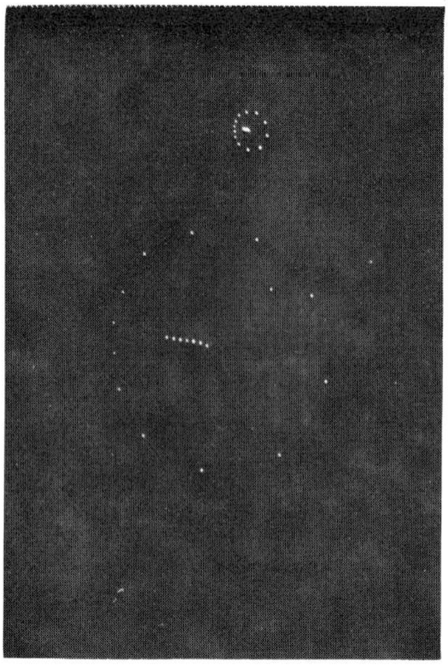

Figure 3b

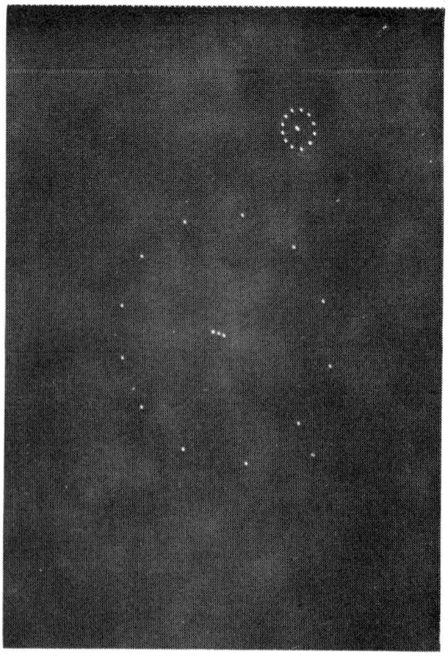

Figure 3c

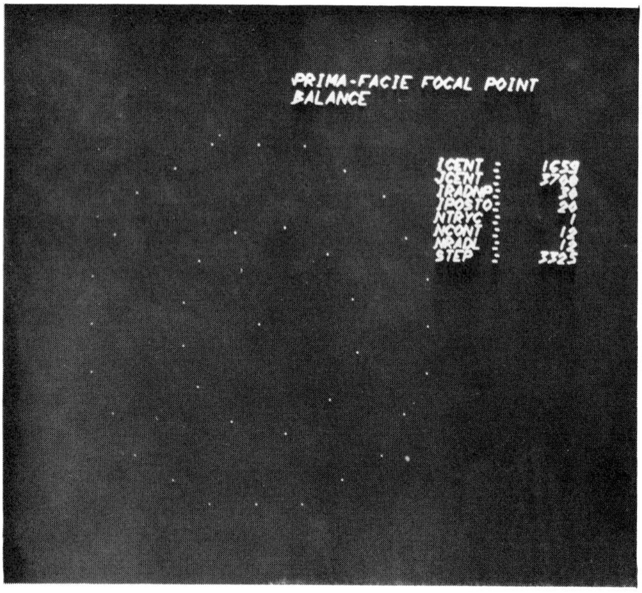

Figure 3d

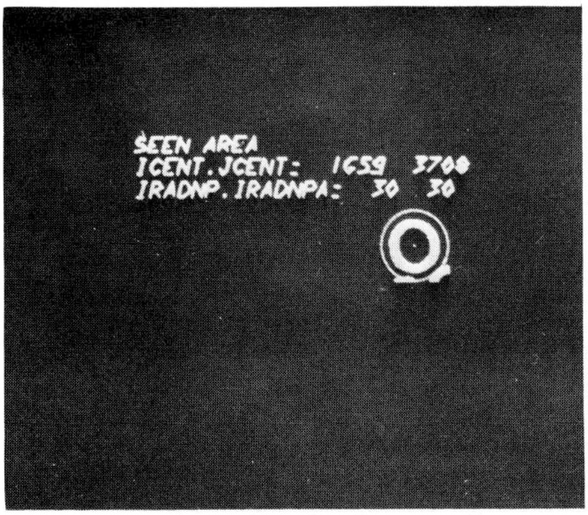

Figure 3e

Figure 4a

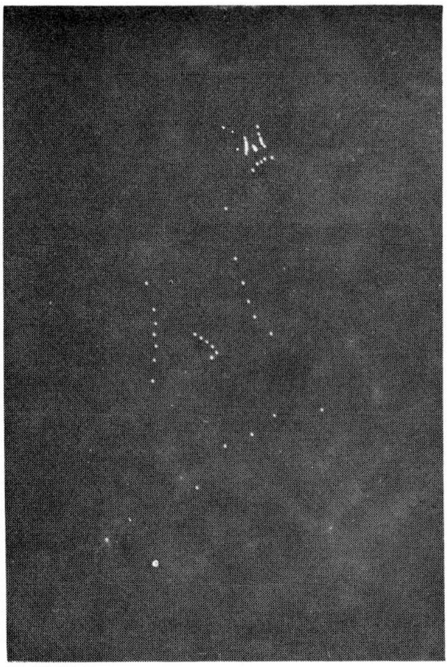

Figure 4b

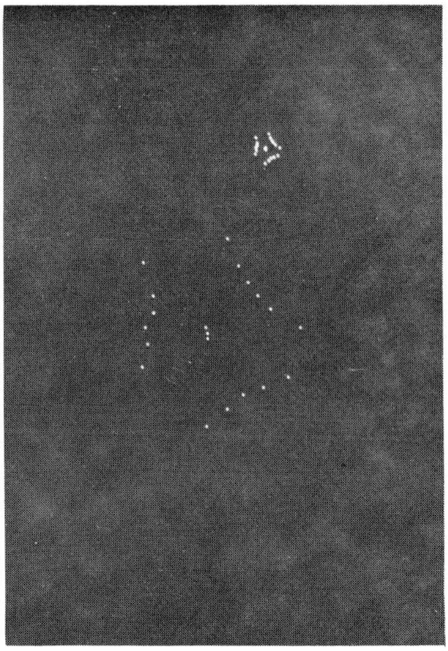

Figure 4c

Figure 4d

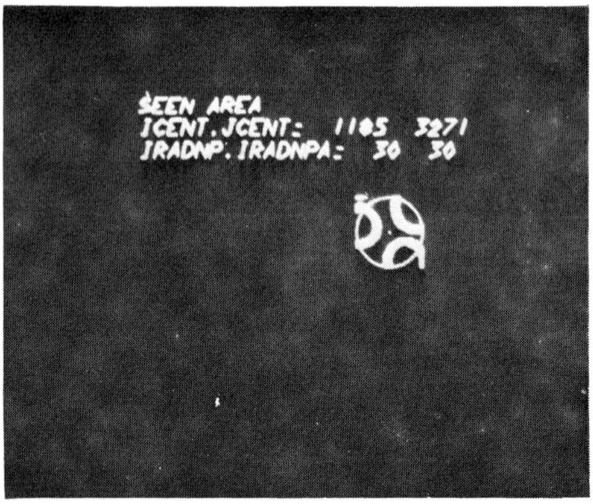

Figure 4e

Figure 5a

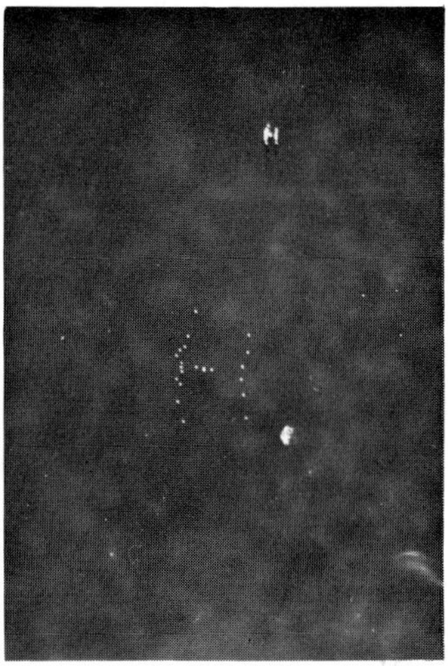

Figure 5b

Figure 5c

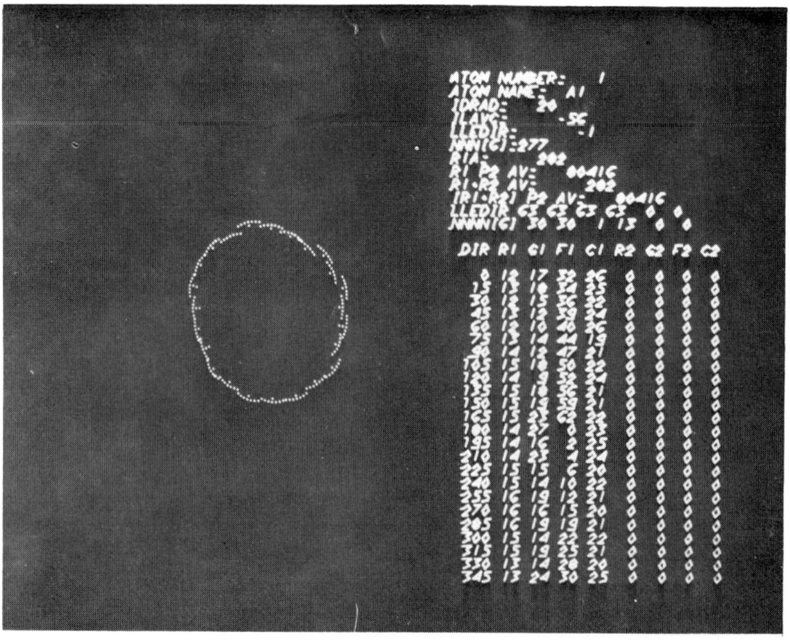

Figure 6

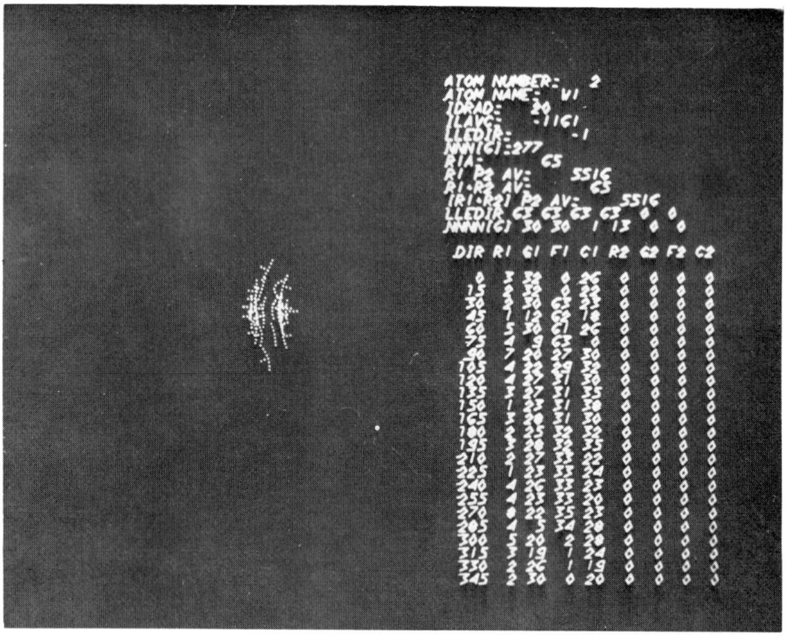

Figure 7

Figure 8

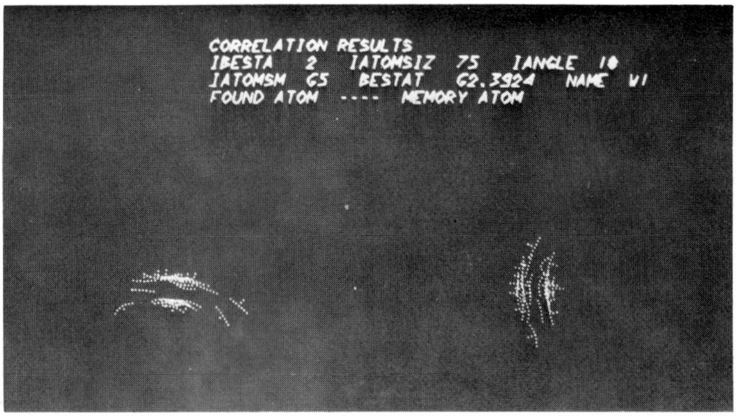

Figure 9

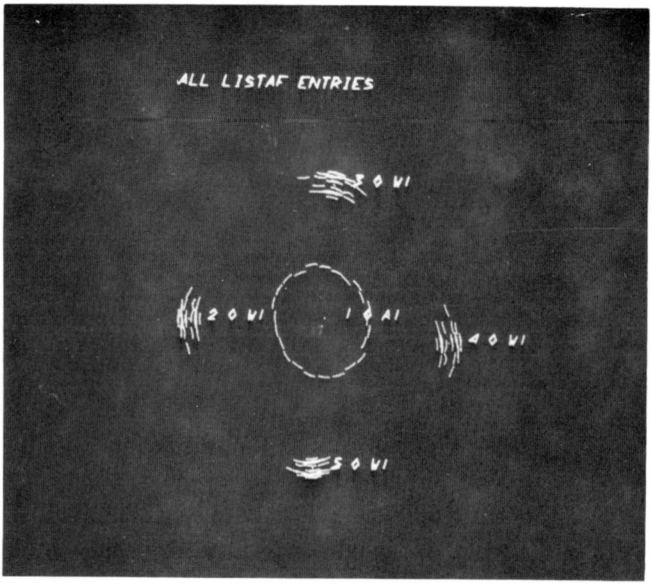

Figure 10

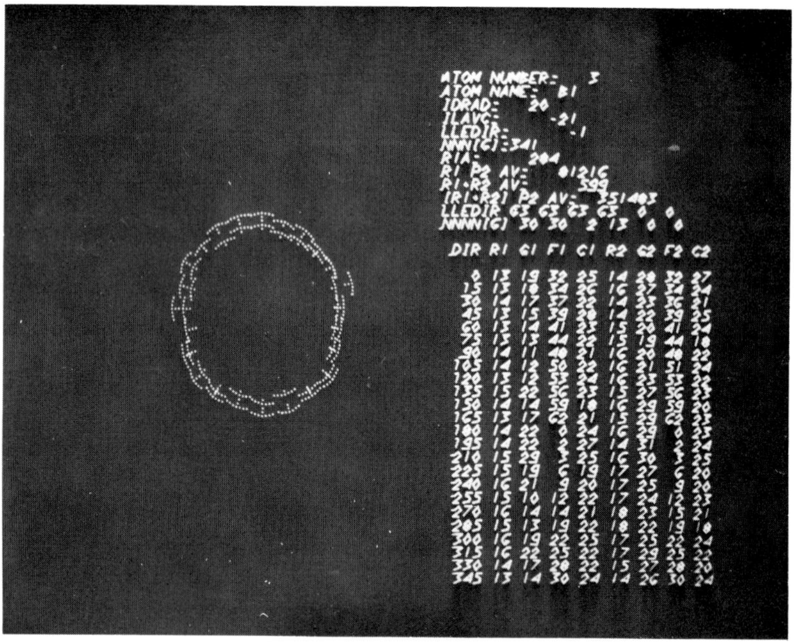

Figure 11

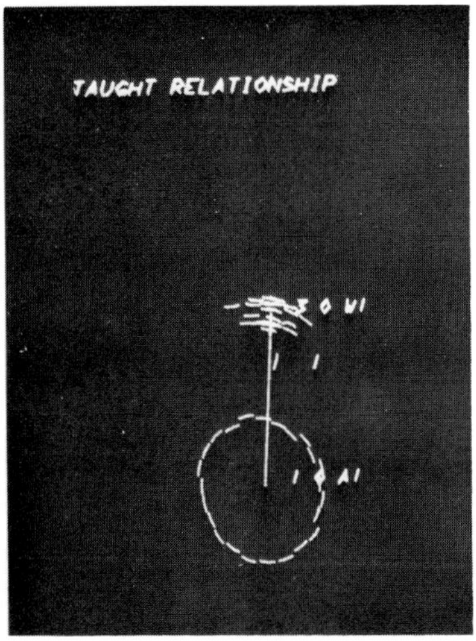

Figure 12

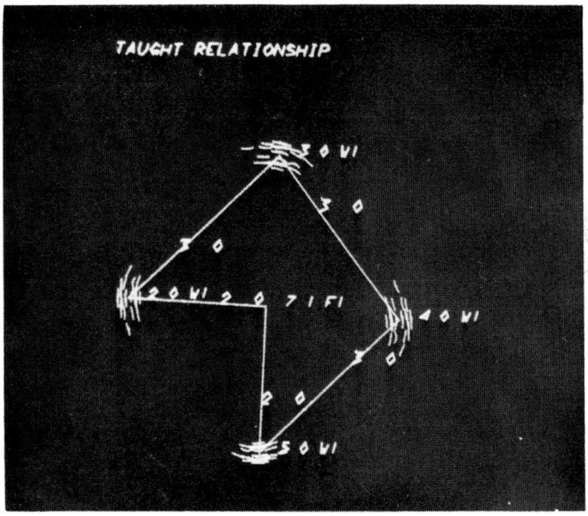

Figure 13

Figure 14

Figure 15

Figure 16

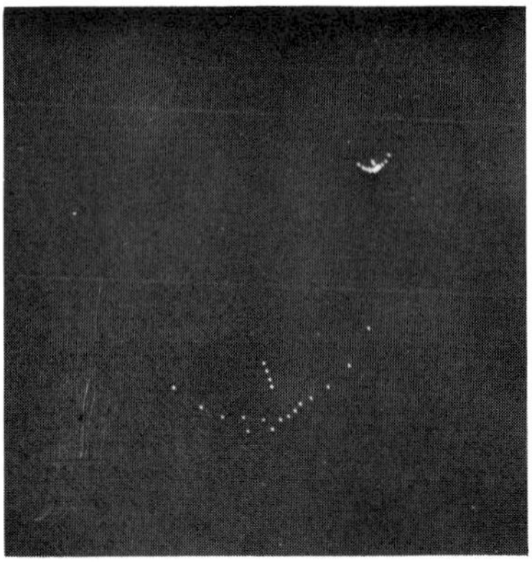

Figure 17

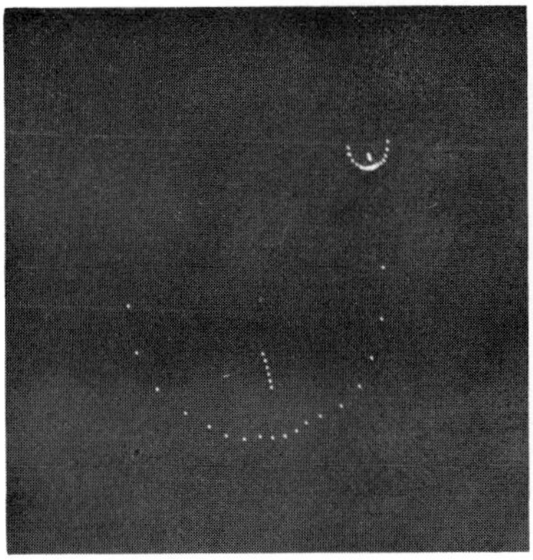

Figure 18

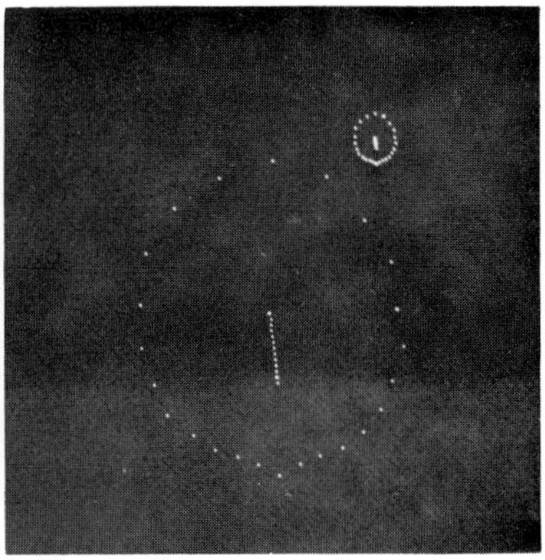

Figure 19

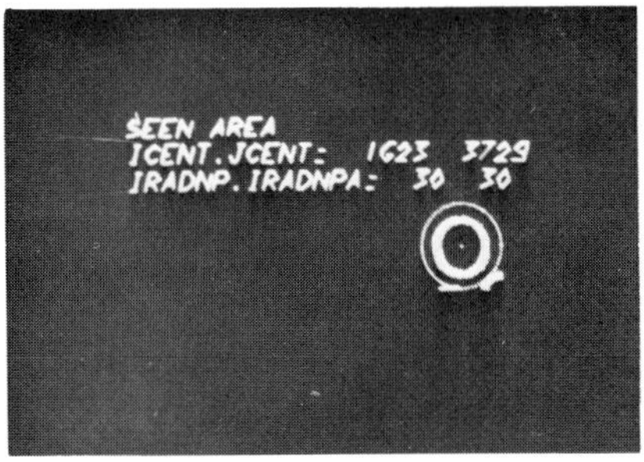

Figure 20

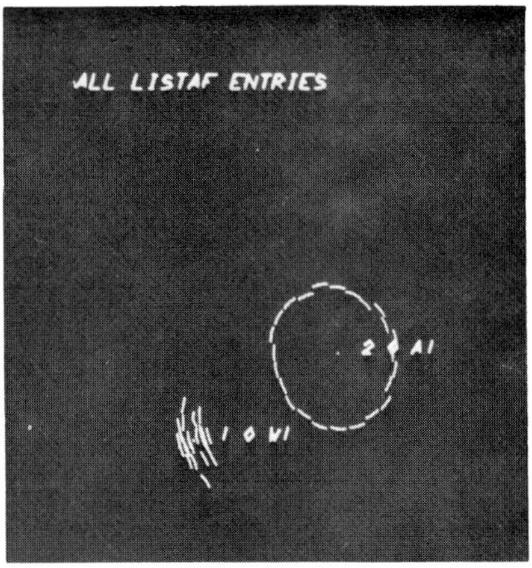

Figure 21

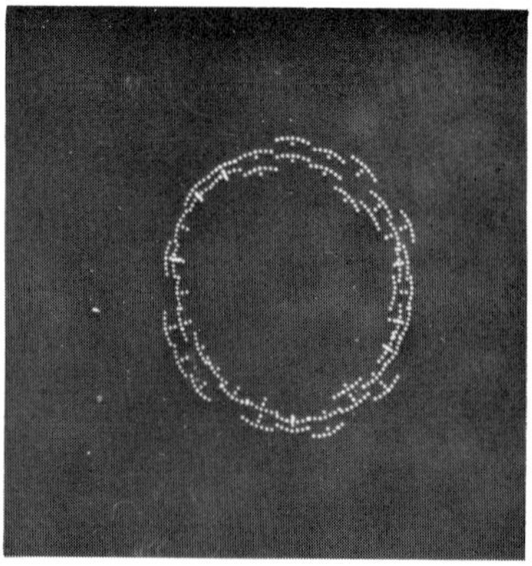

Figure 22

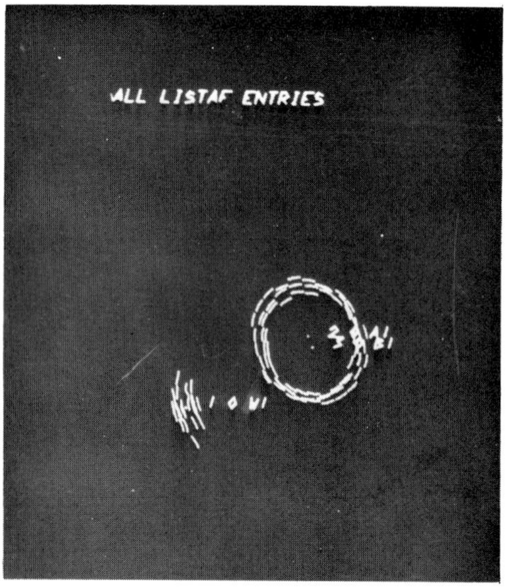

Figure 23

A BASIC STUDY ON HUMAN FACE RECOGNITION

Y. Kaya and K. Kobayashi

DEPARTMENT OF ELECTRICAL
ENGINEERING
UNIVERSITY OF TOKYO,
HONGO, BUNKYO-KU
TOKYO, JAPAN

Introduction

Human face is a pattern most familiar to us. Almost all papers in the field of pattern recognition, however, are on recognition of characters or voices but not on recognition of human faces.

It goes without saying that the ability of identifying a person by his face is indispensable to any person in his daily life. A machine possessing this ability, if realizable, may be used as a guardman of private facilities such as a factory, a parking place or a nightclub. It will help very much police activities by finding the photograph of the corresponding suspect in a pile of photographs. These needs and recent development of high speed on-line computer have forced the authors to the study on human face recognition.

It is noted at the starting point of the study that difficulties of human face recognition lie in the following two properties of human face as a pattern.

(1) Number of patterns, i.e. faces to be classified are tremendous, maybe infinite. (In case of recognition of English characters, only 26 patterns.)

(2) Almost all patterns are very similar. Any normal face has two eyes, one nose, one mouth and two ears which are similarly located in a face. (A greater part of alphabets are mutually fairly different.)

So the technique used in recognition of characters or of voices is hardly applicable to the face recognition problem, at least as it is. It suggests how difficult it is to realize machine recognition of human face. The objective of the paper is not to propose any concrete algorithm of human face recognition, but to study on basic properties of photographed human faces (front view). It will serve much to construct the foundation of human face recognition.

In sections 2 and 3 properties of the parameters characterizing a face are discussed. Geometric values about eyes, nose, mouth and outline of face are adopted as parameters. Data of the parameters are then collected from standardized photographs of 62 Japanese adults. Data of the noise inherent in parameter estimation are also collected from photographs of 8 Japanese adults. In section 4 collected statistical data in the preceding section are used to calculate the amount of information about a face carried by the parameters. Finally in section 5 an algorithm of pattern classification is proposed, of which effectiveness is also theoretically analyzed.

2. Characteristic Parameters of a Face

The ultimate objective of the study is, of course, to recognize human faces, three dimensional ever-changing patterns. Such a problem is however too hard to solve, at least at present. Throughout the paper the patterns to be recognized are assumed photographs of front views of human faces, with mouth closed, without beard and without eyeglasses, of which possessors are requested to look into the camera when the photographs are taken. This assumption makes objects of recognition two dimensional static patterns although light condition when photographs are taken and size of them may vary.

Necessary Conditions of Characteristic Parameters

There can be many kinds of candidates as parameters characterizing a face, of which choice should depend on properties necessary as characteristic parameters. They are required to have the following properties.

(P1) They can as easily be estimated from photographs as possible.

(P2) Any change of light conditions when photographs are taken, or of degrees of development of them has as little effect as possible on estimated parameter values.

(P3) Any small change of face expression has as little effect as possible on estimated parameter values.

(P4) They can carry as much amount of information about a face as possible. The meaning of (P1) to (P3) will be easily understandable. (P4) is the most essential property the parameters should have. To explain this, let **X** be a n-dimensional parameter vector of a face and **Y** be an estimate of **X**. **Y** can be written as

$$\mathbf{Y} = \mathbf{X} + \mathbf{D} \tag{1}$$

where **D** is the noise present at the stage of estimating **X**. This situation is illustrated in Figure 1. **D** consists of two components, **Di** and **Dm**, of which properties will be discussed later.

Now required is to recognize each face in a cluster of faces. It indicates that the number of classifiable patterns because of knowledge of **Y** has to be more than, or at least equal to the population of the faces under consideration. Information theory[1] tells us that the maximum number of classifiable patterns because of knowledge of **Y** is not more than the average mutual information of **X** and **Y**, I(**X**;**Y**) defined as

$$I(\mathbf{X};\mathbf{Y}) = H(\mathbf{X}) - H(\mathbf{X}|\mathbf{Y}), \qquad (2)$$

where H(**X**) is the entropie of **X** and H(**X**|**Y**) the one when **Y** is given. Once given the population of faces, N, I(X;Y) of the parameters should be greater than $\log_2 N$ bits. I(**X**;**Y**) can then be interpreted as a measure of degrees of effectiveness of parameters characterizing a face.

When both **X** and **D** and so **Y** are normally distributed and **X** is independent of D, equation (3) holds.[1]

$$I(\mathbf{X};\mathbf{Y}) = \frac{1}{2}\,(\log_2|M_X + M_D| - \log_2|M_D|), \qquad (3)$$

where M_X and M_D are the covariance matrix of **X** and that of **D** respectively. It is seen from equation (3) that the parameters, of which variances are large and those of noises are small are effective in characterizing a face.

Use of Geometric Parameters

Four properties above mentioned lead us to the decision that any parameters requiring detailed knowledge about the intensity of the photograph (a set of Fourier coefficients is a typical example of such parameters) should be deleted from list of the candidates, because intensity of a photograph and/or its distribution greatly depends on the light condition when the photograph is taken and on the technique of development.

It then stands to reason to use Euclidean distances between several singular points in a face, as characteristic parameters. This idea is supported by results of a simple experiment, in which 10 to 40 men are requested to look at photographs of 3 men for a few seconds for each and to tell their impressions on characteristics of the faces in the photographs. Results are shown in Table 1. It is seen that the characteristics of the faces they pointed out are those of geometric distances between some singular points of which values are far from the average of those. Considering that man has an excellent ability of recognizing patterns, such geometric distances may be effective ones as characteristic parameters.

In the paper parameters shown in Figure 2 are selected. Note that characteristic parameters to be proposed are parameters shown in Figure 2 divided by nose length, because otherwise parameter values would vary by variations of size of photographs and of distance between face and camera. Parameters related to shapes of hair and eye-brows are deleted because they may vary in a wide range from time to time especially in case of women's faces, although the authors recognize hair style and shape of eye-brows contribute much to characterize a face.

Professor Yamazaki, one of famous anthropologists, proposed to use the 3 angles shown in Figure 3 as characteristic parameters(2). This idea was adopted in an exhibition of Nippon Electric Company in EXPO'70 held in Osaka, in which they tried to classify faces caught by TV camera into 21 categories. The amount of information carried by these 3 angles has been estimated, and results tell us that these 3 angles are much inferior to the parameters the authors have proposed, and so any further discussion on them are omitted in the paper.

3. Analysis of Data of Characteristic Parameters

Data on the Proposed Parameters

Many anthropologists have studied on geometry of human face as a three dimensional pattern, but not on geometry of its projection onto a two dimensional surface. So the data of the parameters proposed in section 2 have to be newly collected.

62 Japanese adults aged between 20 and 30 were randomly chosen and front views of their faces was taken in photographs, exactly in the same light condition. They were requested to sit down in a fixed chair and to look at the camera. The center line through both ears was firmly fixed by using special equipment shown in Figure 4. Photographs were developed, enlarged in actual size and printed as in the same way as possible. By such consideration the noise present in estimating the parameters was very much reduced. These processes were carried out entirely by the people of National Institute of Police Science.

From the photographs thus obtained characteristic parameters were measured by hand. Average values, variances of these parameters are shown in Table 2 and the matrix of correlation coefficients in Table 3.

It is seen from Table 3 that the parameters are fairly correlated, partly because they are normalized by nose length. The data shown in Tables 2 and 3 are those of $\mathbf{Y}$, the estimate of the parameter vector $\mathbf{X}$. Noise present in estimation, however, was highly reduced in case of the data for Tables 2 and 3, so that they may be considered the data of $\mathbf{X}$ rather than those of $\mathbf{Y}$.

Principal Component Analysis of the Data

The fact that the parameters are fairly correlated indicates actual dimension of the parameter vector may be smaller than 9, the number of the parameters. Principal component analysis (for brevity call it P.C.A), of which principle is briefly described in Appendix 1, is a useful tool to see this. Table 4 is the result of P.C.A. applied to the data in Tables 2 and 3. The followings can be said from Table 4.

(1) About 96 percent of the variance of **x** is because of variations of only σ components, where **x** is the normalized X, namely

$$\mathbf{x} = \begin{pmatrix} x_1 \\ x_2 \\ x_n \end{pmatrix} = \begin{pmatrix} X_1/\sigma_1 \\ X_2/\sigma_2 \\ X_n/\sigma_n \end{pmatrix} \quad (4)$$

Parameters are equally weighted by this normalization. It means that x lies almost in a σ dimension sub-space constituted by the 9 major eigenvectors, and then that the actual dimension of x is almost σ.

(2) The variance of **x** due to variation of this component corresponding to the maximum eigenvalue, a_1 in equation (A4) in Appendix 1 is about two-thirds of the total variance. It means that **x** is strongly dominated by the principal eigenvector corresponding to the maximum eigenvalue.

(3) Components of the principal eigenvector ($\mathbf{e}_1 = \mathbf{L}_1/|\mathbf{L}_1|$ see Appendix 1) in the original parameter space are all positive and each component is not so different from another. So this vector may be named the vector of 'fatness'. The meaning of the item (3) will be understood by seeing the photographs from Figure 5 to Figure 7. The face in Figure 5 has the biggest a_1, the component along the principal axis, in all faces, while the one in Figure 6 has the smallest a_1 (the largest $|a_1|$ in the faces with negative a_1). The former looks fat and all parts in the face are concentrated in the center, while the latter looks very thin or long. The face in Figure 7, of which a_1 is nearly zero lie in the middle of these two extremes. It is also interesting that **x** of this face is almost the same as $\bar{\mathbf{x}}$, the average. The face then may be called 'average' face.

Results obtained here will contribute much not only to the study of human face recognition but also to the study of machine construction of a portrait or a montage which the authors have recently started.

Noise of Parameter Estimation

Noise **D** in Figure 1 consists of two components, the measurement noise $\mathbf{D}_m$ and the inherent noise $\mathbf{D}_i$.

$\mathbf{D}_m$ is the noise present in extracting parameters from the given photographs. $\mathbf{D}_m$ consists of the one caused by detection of ambiguous outlines of the parts of a face, quantization noise, inherent in conversion of a photograph into small picture elements of which densities are inputs to the computer, etc. Quantitative properties of $\mathbf{D}_m$ depends on characteristics of the camera and the computer algorithm for extracting the parameters from photographs, and so any detail of them can be hardly discussed at present.

$\mathbf{D}_i$ represents the variation of parameters of a face from photograph to photograph, caused by variation of face position to the camera (rotation of face around the horizontal and vertical axes), variation of face expression, etc. Variation of geometry of face itself in a short period (a day, a week or a month) is considered also a part of $\mathbf{D}_i$. Estimation of quantitative properties of $\mathbf{D}_i$ is also a hard problem, but the following experiment was made as a trial.

8 adults were selected each of whom was required to be taken a photograph almost in the same condition every two or three days until 10 photographs were obtained. From the 10 photographs of each person the parameters were measured by hand (then $\mathbf{D}_m$ is almost negligible) and the covariance matrix was calculated. The averaged variances of 8 samples are shown in Table 5, and the averaged correlation coefficient matrix in Table 6. It is interesting that the correlation coefficient matrix of $\mathbf{D}_i$ thus obtained is fairly similar to that of $\mathbf{X}$ shown in Table 3. It may indicate that the main cause of $\mathbf{D}_i$ is variation of face position to the camera.

4. Amount of Information Carried by the Parameters

The amount of information carried by the parameters is the average mutual information of the parameters $\mathbf{X}$ and their estimates $\mathbf{Y}$, $I(\mathbf{X};\mathbf{Y})$, as described in section 2. To calculate $I(\mathbf{X};\mathbf{Y})$ statistical properties of $\mathbf{X}$ and the noise $\mathbf{D}$ have to be given. In section 3 reliable data on those of $\mathbf{X}$ have been obtained, but it is very hard to obtain any reliable data on those of $\mathbf{D}$. The data in Tables 5 and 6 are only the data collected in a special experiment and are not expected to be a good estimate of $\mathbf{D}_i$, although they are all the authors have as quantative data. So $I(\mathbf{X};\mathbf{Y})$ is calculated in the following under some assumptions given on the property of $\mathbf{D}$.

Basic Assumptions

Assumption (1) $\mathbf{D}$ is independent of $\mathbf{X}$.

Assumption (2) $\mathbf{D}$ as well as $\mathbf{X}$ is normally distributed.

If the quantization noise is dominant, the assumption that $\mathbf{D}$ is uniformly distributed might be more appropriate one than assumption 2. Reasons why assumption 2 is adopted in spite of that are as follows.

(1) In case where $\mathbf{X}$ and $\mathbf{D}$ are normally distributed, it is easy to calculate $I(\mathbf{X};\mathbf{Y})$ (see equation (4)), while it is very hard when $\mathbf{D}$ is uniformly distributed, except when $\mathbf{D}$ is a scalar.

(2) Quantization noise is usually not so large. As an example consider the case where the photograph is divided into 100×100, or 10K picture

elements and the face width is about two-thirds of width of the photograph. Then the standard deviation of the quantization noise present at parameter estimation stage is about 0.02, which is comparable to the smaller components of $\mathbf{D}_i$ shown in Table 5.

(3) It is expected that the effect of probability distribution of **D** on the value of I (**X**;**Y**) is little. Shown in Figure 8 is the I (**X**;**Y**) when **X** and **D** are scalars and **D** is uniformly distributed. I (**X**;**Y**) when both **X** and **D** are normally distributed is also shown in Figure 8. It is seen that they are only slightly different. These two assumptions are basic properties of **X** and **D** and more detailed assumptions on **D** should be given to calculate I (**X**;**Y**). The value of I (**X**;**Y**) depends on the assumptions to be given. Two cases considered here.

Case I. $\mathbf{D}_m$ *is almost negligible.* This is an almost ideal case, so the one to be calculated is considered as an upper bound of I (**X**;**Y**).

Assumption (3) Let L be an orthogonal linear transformation of **X**.
i.e. L is a matrix of the form

$$L = \begin{pmatrix} L_1' \\ L_2' \\ \\ L_n' \end{pmatrix} , \tag{5}$$

where $\mathbf{L}_i$ (i=1,2, . . ,n) is the eigenvector of the covariance matrix of **X**, corresponding to the eigenvalue λ_i and (6) holds for $\{\lambda_i\,;\ i=1,2,..,n\}$.

$$\lambda_1 \geq \lambda_2 \geq \cdots\cdots \geq \lambda_n \tag{6}$$

Then L is also an orthogonal linear transformation of **D**.

This assumption is adopted by considering the fact that the correlation coefficient matrix of **X** is very similar to that of $\mathbf{D}_i$. Assumption 3 is useful not only to calculate I (**X**;**Y**), but to construct a pattern classification algorithm which will be discussed in the next section.

Under assumption 3 the following equations hold.

$$I(\mathbf{X};\mathbf{Y}) = I(\mathbf{X};L\mathbf{Y}) \tag{7}$$

$$= \frac{1}{2}\log_2\frac{|M_{LX} + M_{LD}|}{|M_{LD}|} \tag{8}$$

$$= \sum_i \frac{1}{2}\log_2 \left| 1 + \frac{\sigma_i^2}{\gamma_i^2} \right| , \tag{9}$$

where M_{LX} is the covariance matrix of LX and M_{LD} that of LD. Equation

(9) is derived from (8) by using the face that M_{LX} and M_{LD} are both diagonal. σ_i^2 in equation (9) is the variance of the i-th component of LX, and γ_i^2 is that of LD.

So

$$I_i = \frac{1}{2} \log_2 \left| 1 + \frac{\sigma_i^2}{\gamma_i^2} \right| \tag{10}$$

is the amount of information carried by the i-th component of LY. As an example the data of $\mathbf{D}_i$ in Tables 5 and 6 are used to estimate γ_i^2 (i = 1,2, . . ,9). Results of calculation are shown in Table 7. The reason that γ_2 is smaller than γ_3 and γ_4 is that the correlation coefficient matrix of **D** is not exactly the same as that of **X**. It then may be said from Table 7 that the parameters can carry at most information of 14 bits. The amount of information carried by the 3 angles by Professor Yamazaki was calculated in the same way, and found to be only about 5 bits, which are much less than 14 bits. This is the reason why the authors deleted the detailed discussion on these angles.

Case II. $\mathbf{D}_m$ *is dominant.* When $\mathbf{D}_m$ is comparable to or more than $\mathbf{D}_i$, assumption 4 should be adopted rather than assumption 3, because any component of $\mathbf{D}_m$ may be independent of another.

Assumption (4) Any component of **D** is independent of another.

The variance of i-th component of **D**

$$\rho_i^2 = \rho_{mi}^2 + \rho_{hi}^2 \tag{11}$$

where ρ_{mi}^2 is the variance of the i-th component of $\mathbf{D}_m$ and ρ_{hi}^2 that of $\mathbf{D}_i$. In the following calculation values of Table 5 are used as ρ_{hi}^2's and ρ_{mi}^2 is set to be proportional to the average value of the i-th parameter, X_i.

$$\rho_{mi}^2 \neq \bar{X}_i^2 \ ; i = 1,2, . . , 9, \tag{12}$$

where α is the constant.

Then

$$I(\mathbf{X};\mathbf{Y}) = \frac{1}{2}(\log_2 \left| M_X + \begin{pmatrix} \rho_1^2 & & 0 \\ & \ddots & \\ 0 & & \rho_9^2 \end{pmatrix} \right| - \log_2 \rho_1^2 \ldots \rho_9^2) \tag{13}$$

Results are in Table 8.

5. Pattern Classification

I (X;Y) is only an upper bound of the number of classifiable faces, and the number actually classifiable depends largely on the algorithm of pattern classification.

Proposed in the paper is the one useful when $\mathbf{D}_i$ is dominant in $\mathbf{D}$, namely in Case I described in the preceding section where assumption 3 holds.

The Algorithm

One of measures of the effectiveness of the classification algorithm is the average number of parameters used to identify a face. The smaller the number, say $\bar{n}$, the better because the number of storages for parameters of patterns to be classified can be smaller.

In Case I of the preceding section it can be said that the amount of information carried by the first component of **LY** is the biggest, then that by the second component the next biggest, and so on. So it seems effective for reducing $\bar{n}$ to use components of **LY** as the parameters and to classify a cluster of faces one by one from the first component to the 9th.

Now let the parameters **LY** of the face to be recognized be

$$\mathbf{Z}_0 = (Z_{01}, Z_{02}, \ldots, Z_{09}) \tag{14}$$

and the set of **LY**'s of faces stored in computer memory be

$$\Omega_0 = \{\mathbf{Z}_1, \mathbf{Z}_2, \ldots, \mathbf{Z}_N\}, \tag{15}$$

where $\mathbf{Z}_i$ is the **LY** of the i-th face and N is the population of the faces. Then the proposed algorithm is in the following.

Step 1. Choose the faces satisfying equation (16) from Ω_0.

$$|Z_1 - Z_{01}| < K_1, \tag{16}$$

where Z_1 is the first component of **Z** of the face concerned and K_1 is a constant.

Let the set of chosen faces by Ω_1.

Step 2. Choose the faces satisfying equation (17) from Ω_1.

$$|Z_2 - Z_{02}| < K_2, \tag{17}$$

where Z_2 is the second component of Z of the face concerned and K_2 is a constant.

And work in the same way as described above until Ω_r, the set of chosen faces at the r-th step involves only a face. The face left in Ω_r is then the one corresponding to Z_0.

There can be many ideas about the choice of $K_i (i = 1,2, \ldots)$, but a simple and farthermore effective way is to set

$$K_i = \beta \gamma_i \, ; \; i = 1,2, \ldots, \tag{18}$$

where γ_i^2 is the estimated variance of the i-th component of LD and β is an arbitrarily selected constant (An appropriate value for β may be between 1.5 and 3.0. See the numerical results of the next section.)

Theoretical Analysis of the Algorithm

In order to see how the algorithm may work the following two quantities are calculated.

(1) Probability of being able to find out the correct face, P.

(2) Expected value of the number of components of **Z**, or of the steps used until a face is extracted from N faces, $\bar{n}$.

P is calculated in the following.

Let the probability of extracting the correct face at i-th steps be P_i. Since each step is independent (assumption 3),

$$P = \sum_i P_i \tag{19}$$

It is easily seen that

$$P_i = Q_i F_i, \tag{20}$$

where Q_i is the probability that face classification ends at the i-th step and F_i the probability that the correct face can survive until the i-th step. Since **LD** is normally distributed and each component is independent, from equation (18),

$$F_i = F^i(\beta) = \left[\frac{1}{(2\pi)^{\frac{1}{2}}} \int_{-\beta}^{\beta} \mathrm{EXP}\left(-\frac{x^2}{2}\right) dx\right]^i \tag{21}$$

Q_i is calculated in Appendix 2, and the result is

$$Q_i = \left(1 - \prod_r^{i-1} G(\ell_r)\right)^N - \left(1 - \prod_r^{i} G(\ell_r)\right)^N, \tag{22}$$

where

$$G(\ell_i) = \frac{1}{2\pi} \int_{-\infty}^{\infty} dy\, \mathrm{EXP}\left(-\frac{y^2}{2}\right) \int_{y-\ell_i}^{y+\ell_i} dx\, \mathrm{EXP}\left(-\frac{x^2}{2}\right), \tag{23}$$

with

$$\ell_i = \beta \frac{\gamma_i}{\sigma_i} \quad (i=1,2,\ldots,) \tag{24}$$

σ_i is the standard deviation of the i-th component of **Z** = **LX**. It is also seen that

$$\bar{n} = \sum_i^{\infty} iQ_i \tag{25}$$

$$\simeq \sum_{i}^{9} iQ_i \tag{26}$$

The data of $\mathbf{D}_i$ in Tables 5 and 6 and those of $\mathbf{X}$ in Tables 2 and 3 are used to estimate P and $\bar{n}$. Results are shown in Figure 9 where P and $\bar{n}$ drawn as functions of N, the population of Faces, with β as parameter. It is seen from Figure 9 that when $\beta = 2.5$ the correct face can be recognized with the probability of about 92 percent from 5,000 faces, (possibly with the probability of 90 percent from 15,000 faces) and that the average number of the steps used is about 6. Considering that I(X;Y) estimated in section 4 is about 14 bits ($2^{14} \sim 16{,}000$), the algorithm may be almost satisfactory.

6. Conclusion

In the paper properties of 9 geometric parameters characterizing a face have been discussed. Amount of information carried by them have been estimated by using data of $\mathbf{X}$ and of a part of $\mathbf{D}$ and several assumptions on the property of $\mathbf{D}$. It has been found that the amount of information may range from 8 to 14 bits, depending on the amount of estimation noise. Also an algorithm for the case where the measurement noise is almost negligible has been proposed and discussed. The analysis and the data presented in the paper will, contribute much to realization of human face recognition. Recently the authors have started the study on the problem of machine drawing of a portrait or a montage, with the knowledge of characteristics of human faces above obtained. The authors expect to publish some report on this problem in the near future.

Appendix 1. Principal Component Analysis

Let A be the correlation coefficient matrix of a n-dimensional random vector $\mathbf{X}$, $\lambda_1, \lambda_2, \ldots, \lambda_n$ be eigenvalues of A ($\lambda_1 \geq \lambda_2 \geq \ldots \geq \lambda_n$) and $\mathbf{L}_1, \mathbf{L}_2, \ldots, \mathbf{L}_n$ be eigenvectors corresponding to $\lambda_1, \lambda_2, \ldots, \lambda_n$ respectively.

Furthermore, let

$$x = \begin{pmatrix} \frac{X_1}{\sigma_1} \\ \frac{X_2}{\sigma_2} \\ \frac{X_n}{\sigma_n} \end{pmatrix} \tag{A1}$$

where X_i ($i = 1,2, \ldots, n$) denotes the i-th component of $\mathbf{X}$ and σ_i^2 its variance. $\mathbf{x}$ is the $\mathbf{X}$ normalized so that its components may be equally weighted.

Sample variance of $\mathbf{x}$ is defined as

$$\sigma^2 = \frac{1}{N-1} \sum_i (\mathbf{x}_i - \bar{\mathbf{x}})' (\mathbf{x}_i - \bar{\mathbf{x}}), \tag{A2}$$

where $\mathbf{x}_1, \mathbf{x}_2, \ldots, \mathbf{x}_N$ are samples of $\mathbf{x}$, $\bar{\mathbf{x}}$ is their sample average and N is the number of samples.

Then it is easily shown that $(N-1)\lambda_i$ $(i=1,2,\ldots,n)$ is equal to the sample variance of the component of $\mathbf{x}$ along $\mathbf{L}_i$ axis. Now let

$$\mathbf{e}_i = \frac{\mathbf{L}_i}{|\mathbf{L}_i|} \quad ; \; i = 1,2,\ldots, n \tag{A3}$$

Since $\mathbf{L}_i$ $(i=1,2,\ldots n)$ is independent of $\mathbf{L}_j (j \neq i)$, $\mathbf{e}_i$ is also independent of $\mathbf{e}_j$.
Then $\mathbf{x}$ can be written as (A4).

$$x = \bar{x} + a_1 \mathbf{e}_1 + a_2 \mathbf{e}_2 + \ldots + a_n \mathbf{e}_n, \tag{A4}$$

where a_i satisfies equations (A5) and (A6).

$$E \left(a_i\right) = 0 \; ; \; i = 1,2,\ldots,n \tag{A5}$$

$$\mathrm{COV} \left(a_i a_j\right) = E \left(a_i a_j\right) = \lambda_i \delta_{ij} \; ; \; i = 1,2,\ldots,n \tag{A6}$$

From equations (A4) to (A6),

$$\sigma^2 = \frac{1}{N-1} (\lambda_1 + \lambda_2 + \ldots + \lambda_n) \tag{A7}$$

So the portron of σ^2 due to the first component of x, a_1, is $\lambda_1 / \sum^n \lambda_i$. If equation (A8) is satisfied for an arbitrary small ϵ

$$\frac{\sum^{m-1} \lambda_i}{\sum^{n} \lambda_i} < 1 - \epsilon < \frac{\sum^{m} \lambda_i}{\sum^{n} \lambda_i}, \tag{A8}$$

the dimension of $\mathbf{x}$ may be said to be m, because almost all the samples of $\mathbf{x}$ lie in the subspace constructed by the vectors $\mathbf{e}_1, \mathbf{e}_2, \ldots,$ and $\mathbf{e}_m$.

Appendix 2. Derivation of Equation (22)

Let R_k be the probability that Ω_k is a non-empty set. Then[3]

$$Q_k = R_{k-1} - R_k \; ; \; k = 1,2,\ldots \tag{A9}$$

with $R_0 = 1$. R_k is found in the following manner.

First consider the probability that a face can survive after k steps of selection, Υ_k. Since each step of selection is independent,

$$\Upsilon_k = \prod_{i=1}^{k} \text{Prob.}\ (|Z_i - Z_{oi}| < \beta \gamma_i) \qquad \text{(A10)}$$

and

$$\text{Prob.}\ (|Z_i - Z_{oi}| < \beta \gamma_i)$$

$$= \int_{-\infty}^{\infty} \text{Prob}\ (Z < Z_{oi} < Z + d_Z)\ \text{Prob}\ (|Z_i - Z_{oi}| < \beta\ _i | Z_{oi})$$

$$= \int_{-\infty}^{\infty} dZ \frac{1}{(2\pi)^{1/2}\sigma_i} \text{EXP}\left(-\frac{(Z-\overline{Z}_i)^2}{2\sigma_i^2}\right) \int_{z-\beta\gamma_i}^{z+\beta\gamma_i} dZ_i \frac{1}{(2\pi)^{1/2}\sigma_i}$$

$$\text{EXP}\left(-\frac{Z_i-\overline{Z}_i)^2}{2\sigma_i^2}\right) \qquad \text{(A11)}$$

By replacing $(Z_i - \overline{Z}_i)/\sigma_i$ by x and $(Z - \overline{Z}_i)/\sigma_i$ by y, (A11) reduces to (A12).

$$\text{Prob}\ (|Z_i - Z_{oi}| < \beta\ _i) = \frac{1}{2\pi} \int_{-\infty}^{\infty} dy\ \text{EXP}\left(-\frac{y^2}{2}\right) \int_{y-\beta\ell_i}^{y+\beta\ell_i} dx\ \text{EXP}\left(-\frac{x^2}{2}\right), \qquad \text{(A12)}$$

which is $G(\ell_i)$ defined by equation (22).
Then from (A10)

$$\Upsilon_k = \prod_{i=1}^{k} G(\ell_i) \qquad \text{(A13)}$$

The probability that none of N faces can survive after k steps of selection, which is $1 - R_k$, is $(1 - \Upsilon_k)^N$.
Then

$$R_k = 1 - (1 - \Upsilon_k)^N$$

$$= 1 - \left(1 - \prod_{i=1}^{k} G(\ell_i)\right)^N \qquad \text{(A14)}$$

Replacing (A14) into (A9) yields equation (22).

Acknowledgements

The authors express sincere thanks to Dr. K. Sakai of National Institute of Police Science and Mr. S. Goh of Sharp Electric Company for their help in taking photographs and collecting data from them. This study is supported partly by the Kawakami Foundation.

REFERENCES

1. Y. Taki and H. Miyakawa, Information theory, Iwanami Book Co., 1969.
2. K. Yamazaki, Debut of Computer Physiognomy, Chuo-Koron, July 1970, pp. 244-252.
3. A. J. Goldstein et al; Classification and Identification of Human Faces, unpublished paper.

TABLE 1 IMPRESSION ABOUT THREE FACES

FACE	IMPRESSION	NO. OF PERSONS	VALUE OF CORRESPONDING PARAMETER
A	Round face	23	Face width measured at the eye line
	Fat face	11	
	Every part in the face is relatively small	4	$\sim\hat{\mu} + 3\hat{\sigma}$
B	Thin eyes	6	Distance between centers of eyes over face width
	Small eyes	3	$\sim\hat{\mu} - 2\hat{\sigma}$
	Other characteristics	3	Eye length over external bi-ocular breadth $\sim\hat{\mu} - \hat{\sigma}$
C	Distance between nose and upper lip is long	5	Distance between nose and upper lip
	Long face	4	
	Other characteristics	4	$\sim\hat{\mu} + 2.5\hat{\sigma}$

$\hat{\mu}$; Sample average of the parameter concerned

$\hat{\sigma}^2$; Sample variance of the parameter concerned

TABLE 2 SAMPLE AVERAGES AND VARIANCES OF GEOMETRIC PARAMETERS

PARAMETERS No.	AVERAGE	STANDARD DEVIATION σ
1. Internal bi-ocular breadth	0.857	0.0946
2. External bi-ocular breadth	2.25	0.219
3. Nose breadth	0.625	0.0703
4. Mouth breadth	1.11	0.114
5. Bizygomatic breadth	3.05	0.314
6. Bigonial breadth	2.70	0.305
7. Distance between lower lip and chin	1.02	0.164
8. Distance between upper lip and nose	0.546	0.0733
9. Height of lips	0.398	0.0630

Note: Parameters are normalized with regard to nose length

TABLE 3 CORRELATION COEFFICIENT MATRIX OF GEOMETRIC PARAMETERS

Parameters \ Parameters	1	2	3	4	5	6	7	8	9
1	1.00								
22	0.81	1.00							
3	0.35	0.52	1.00						
4	0.59	0.60	0.44	1.00					
5	0.81	0.86	0.46	0.66	1.00				
6	0.77	0.81	0.47	0.65	0.96	1.00			
7	0.52	0.68	0.53	0.56	0.70	0.67	1.00		
8	0.56	0.61	0.25	0.60	0.69	0.57	0.54	1.00	
9	0.40	0.43	0.13	0.42	0.41	0.35	0.44	0.53	1.00

TABLE 4 PRINCIPAL COMPONENT ANALYSIS OF THE PARAMETER DATA

No.	Eigenvalue	Cumulative Variance Contribution* C_i	Components of the Corresponding Eigenvector 1	2	3	4	5	6	7	8	9
1	5.66	0.63	0.351	0.381	0.239	0.327	0.396	0.380	0.333	0.317	0.232
2	0.99	0.74	0.016	-0.095	-0.618	0.050	-0.058	-0.146	-0.099	0.385	0.651
3	0.72	0.82	-0.420	-0.154	0.541	0.158	-0.266	-0.280	0.373	0.035	0.439
4	0.48	0.87	-0.171	-0.256	-0.025	0.736	-0.042	-0.053	-0.220	0.393	-0.394
5	0.41	0.92	-0.373	-0.069	-0.239	-0.359	0.155	0.056	0.570	0.443	-0.349
6	0.34	0.96	0.129	0.171	0.409	-0.397	-0.04	-0.250	-0.436	0.606	-0.046
7	0.23	0.98	0.517	0.217	-0.136	0.125	-0.368	-0.555	0.398	0.009	0.222
8	0.14	1.00	-0.496	0.816	-0.157	0.139	-0.050	-0.124	-0.134	-0.082	-0.033
9	0.02	1.00	0.037	0.091	-0.010	-0.050	-0.777	0.599	0.018	0.157	-0.018

*Note: $C_i = \sum_{j=1}^{i} \lambda_j \Big/ \sum_{j=1}^{9} \lambda_j$

TABLE 5 VARIANCE OF D_i

No.	Parameter	Variance
1	Internal bi-ocular breadth	0.000625
2	External bi-ocular breadth	0.00281
3	Nose breadth	0.000620
4	Mouth breadth	0.00361
5	Bizygomatic breadth	0.00856
6	Bigonial breadth	0.00841
7	Distance between lower lip and chin	0.00323
8	Distance between upper lip and nose	0.000924
9	Height of lips	0.000361

TABLE 6 CORRELATION COEFFICIENT MATRIX OF $\mathbf{D}_i$

Parameters \ Parameters	1	2	3	4	5	6	7	8	9
1	1.00								
2	0.83	1.00							
3	0.76	0.77	1.00						
4	0.62	0.59	0.64	1.00					
5	0.87	0.88	0.81	0.63	1.00				
6	0.75	0.73	0.71	0.62	0.92	1.00			
7	0.52	0.57	0.55	0.52	0.77	0.84	1.00		
8	0.66	0.72	0.57	0.41	0.80	0.68	0.56	1.00	
9	0.41	0.50	0.39	0.30	0.50	0.51	0.46	0.50	1.00

TABLE 7 THE AMOUNT OF INFORMATION $I(\mathbf{X};\mathbf{Y})$ FOR CASE I

No. of Component	Standard Deviation of Each Component σ_i (LX)	γ_i (LD)	$I(\mathbf{X};\mathbf{Y})$
1	0.501	0.151	1.8 bits
2	0.123	0.0260	2.3
3	0.105	0.0430	1.4
4	0.0850	0.0440	1.1
5	0.0730	0.0260	1.6
6	0.0530	0.0220	1.4
7	0.0480	0.0160	1.7
8	0.0460	0.0170	1.5
9	0.0330	0.0160	1.2
		Total	14.0 bits

TABLE 8 THE AMOUNT OF INFORMATION $I(\mathbf{X};\mathbf{Y})$ FOR CASE II

α	$I(\mathbf{X};\mathbf{Y})$
0.02	9.6 bits
0.04	7.7 bits

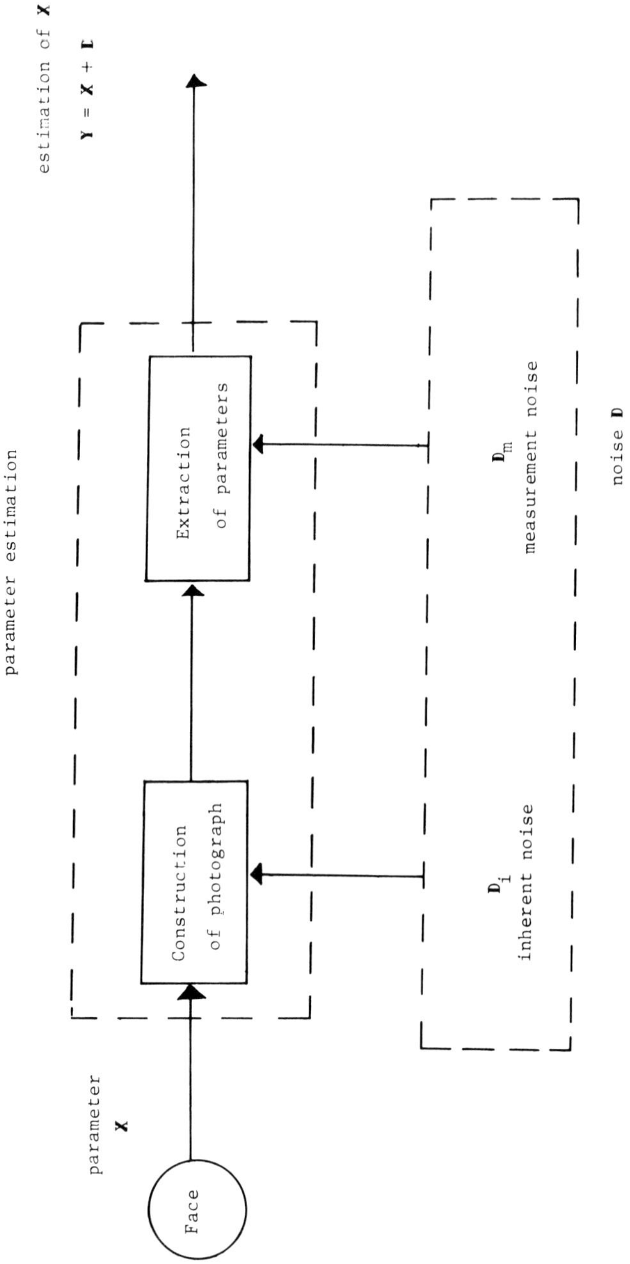
Face
parameter X
Construction of photograph
Extraction of parameters
parameter estimation
estimation of X
Y = X + E
D_i inherent noise
D_m measurement noise
noise D

Figure 1

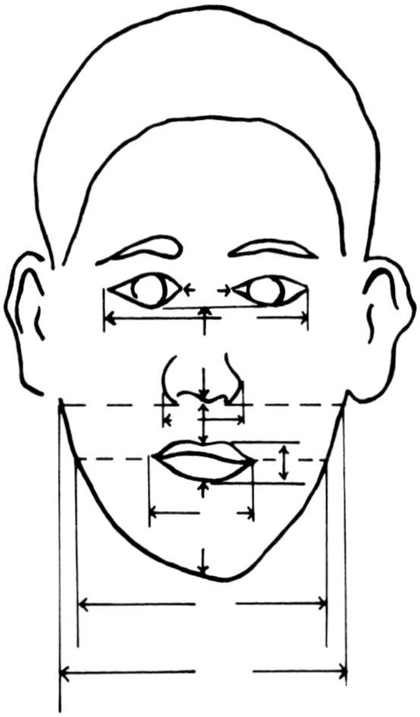

Figure 2

Parameters

1 Internal bi-ocular breadth
2 External bi-ocular breadth
3 Nose breadth
4 Mouth breadth
5 Bizygomatic breadth
6 Bigonial breadth
7 Distance between lower lip and chin
8 Distance between upper lip and nose
9 Height of lips
L; Nose length

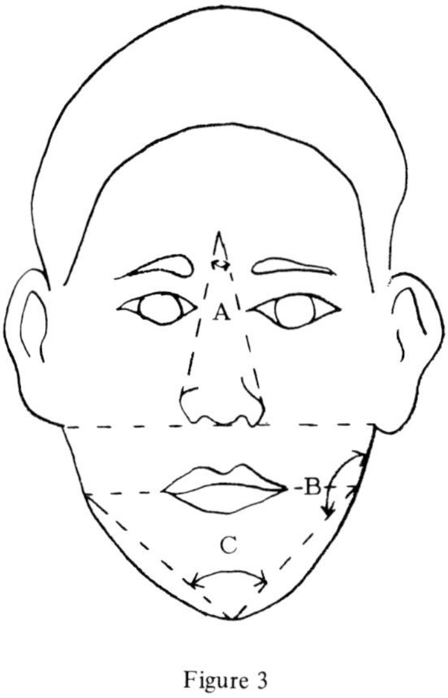

Figure 3

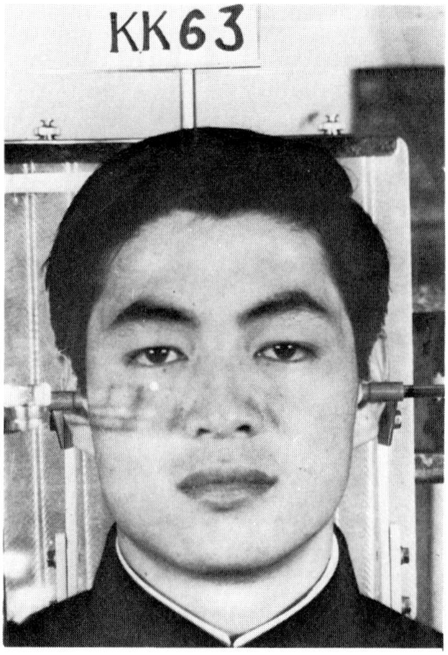

Figure 4

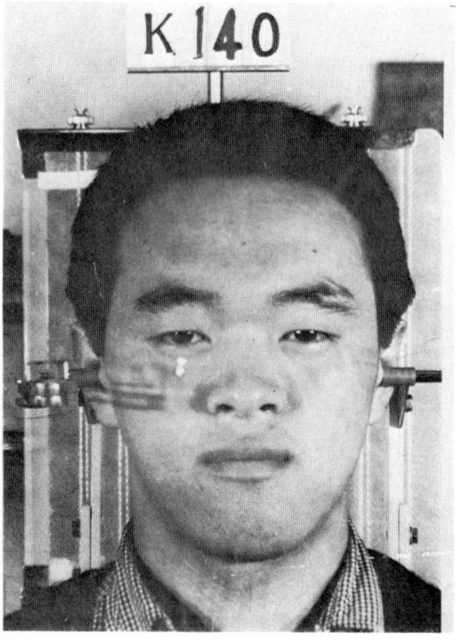

Figure 5

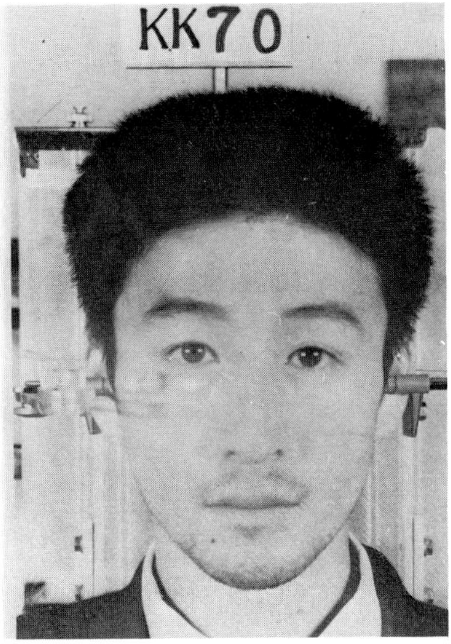

Figure 6

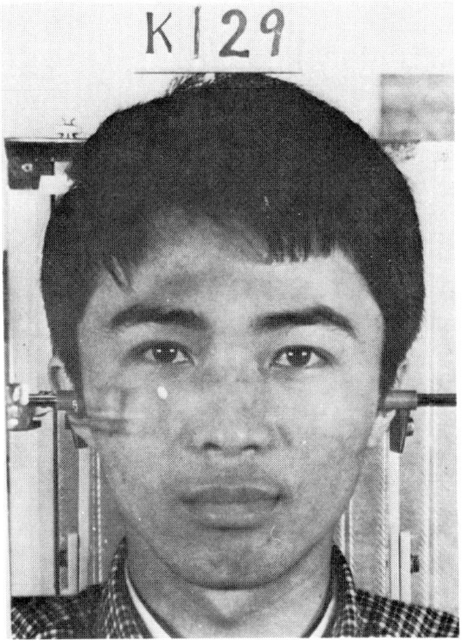

Figure 7

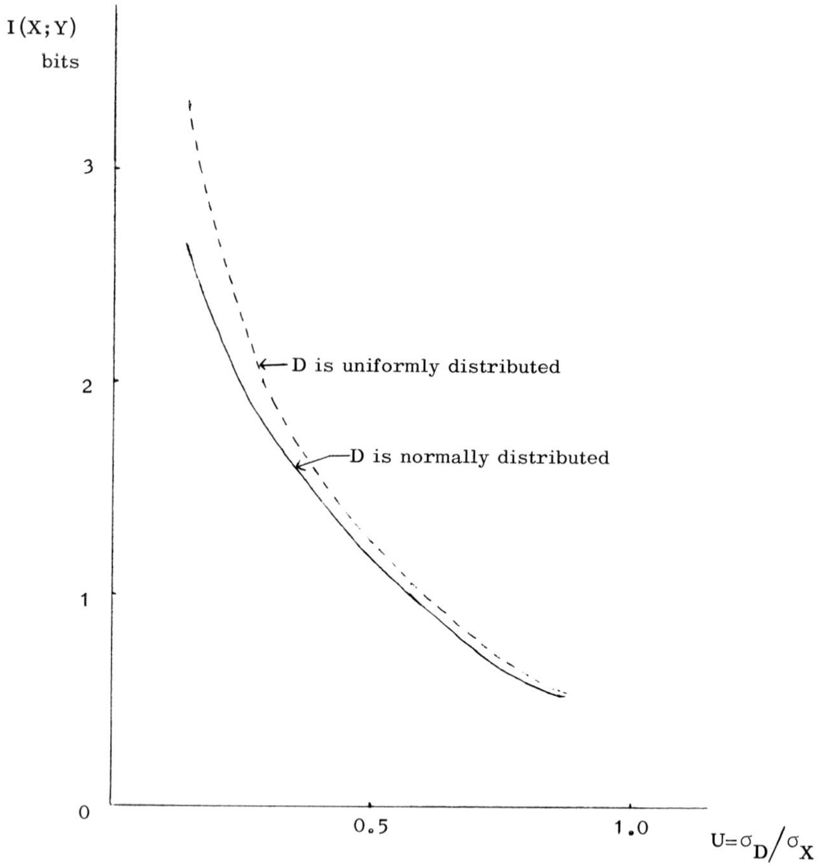
I(X;Y)
bits
3
2
1
0
D is uniformly distributed
D is normally distributed
0.5
1.0
U=σD/σX

Figure 8

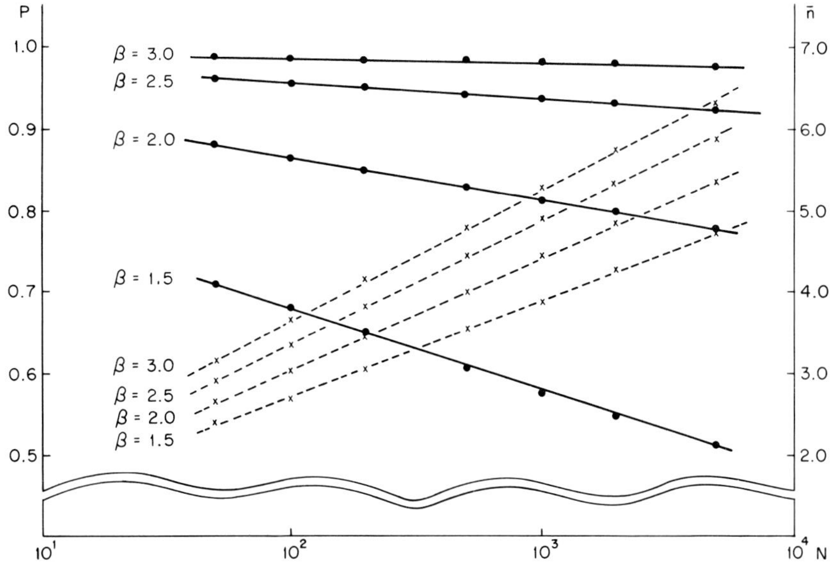
P
1.0
0.9
0.8
0.7
0.6
0.5
n̄
7.0
6.0
5.0
4.0
3.0
2.0
β = 3.0
β = 2.5
β = 2.0
β = 1.5
β = 3.0
β = 2.5
β = 2.0
β = 1.5
10¹
10²
10³
10⁴ N

Figure 9

CLUSTER ANALYSIS

M. G. Kendall

Introduction

[1] The problem with which we are concerned can be stated with specious simplicity: we are given a collection of n individuals, on each of which are observed the values of p variables, which may be continuous or classificatory. Do the individuals appear to cluster into groups or do they present the appearance of a homogeneous chaos?

[2] In tackling the subject from the statistical angle we find that in fact very little of traditional statistical theory, especially of a probabilistic kind, is applicable. There are several reasons for this:

(1) The collection of individuals may not be a sample. For example, the Moser-Scott study of the classification of British towns (1961) considered the whole population of towns over 100,000 inhabitants; and taxonomic problems of the Linnaean kind are concerned with the set of observed forms of life, regardless of what remains to be discovered.

(2) Even if the collection is a sub-set of what is known to be a larger population, we often have no reason to suppose that it is a random sample. The fact that some matter happens to radiate on a frequency which stimulates the human eye does not make the visible stars a random or representative sample of the universe.

(3) "Clustering" is very much a subjective matter. In the physical sciences we are accustomed to regard the universe and its laws as invariant under transformations of the coordinate systems by reference to which we represent them. This is, in general, not true of clustering.

(4) The number of inter-relations among a set of n individuals increases in size very rapidly with n. To tackle more than trivial problems therefore requires a computer.

[3] As I defined it above, clustering relates to the n individuals. But it is also possible to consider whether the p variables cluster in the sense of being highly correlated. Conceptually the two problems are the same, but in practice they differ, since p is rarely greater than 30 and the inter-relations of 30 points are not difficult to analyse by hand. An example is given later.

[4] The literature on the subject is rather scattered and a good many papers are to be found in non-statistical journals, e.g. those devoted to computers or biology. There is a useful review by Bolshev (1970) which contains a bibliography.

Clustering and Distance

[5] When we refer to a cluster in ordinary colloquial speech we have in mind a collection of members which are all close together; and further that the members in the middle are usually more densely distributed than those on the periphery. To refine such vague general notions to a point of precision whereat we can explain unambiguously to a computer just what it is to consider as a cluster is not easy. But however we do it, the very concept of cluster requires, in some sense, the idea of closeness, or nearness, or proximity or contiguity or neighbourhood. In short, we need a distance function, and that function must, I think, obey certain criteria. Writing $d(A, B)$ for the "distance" between objects A and B we require

$$d(A, B) = d(B, A) \qquad (1)$$

This is not trivial. In certain sociological enquiries the existence of affinity groups in a community is explored by asking each member of it whether he likes/dislikes each of the other members. It is quite possible that A likes B but B dislikes A and the emotional distance between them is not symmetrical. Having said that, I dismiss such a case from the remainder of the paper.

The variables must be scaled.

In cases where the clustering is by Euclidean distance in ordinary two- or three-dimensional space it would be absurd to measure one dimension in metres, another in centimetres and another in kilometres. In more general situations, however, the variables p do not all relate to the same kind of measurement. Towns, for example, may be measured for latitude, rainfall, rateable value and unemployment. The variables are of different kinds. If we stretch or condense the scale of one of them we may completely distort the clustering and even destroy it.

I shall therefore suppose that all variables have been standardised to unit variance. Such a condition may be relaxed if we want to give greater weight to some variables, provided that we can express that greater weight quantitatively. The variable requiring greater weight will be given smaller variance.

It is desirable (though perhaps not necessary) that the distance function should obey the triangular inequality.

$$d(A, B) \leqslant d(A, C) + d(C, B) \qquad (2)$$

I do not know of any function of distance *between points* which fail to obey this criterion, but it is as well to remember that there are probabilistic situations where it fails to hold. For example, the so-called divergence between two frequency distributions

$$\int (f_1 - f_2) \log (f_1/f_2)\, dx \qquad (3)$$

has metrical properties, but does not obey (2).

[6] I consider later in the paper the problems which arise when some of the variables are polytomous or even dichotomous. For the present I assume that they are all continuous and standardised to unit variance. The problem is then to set up a distance metric. One obvious distance is the Pythagorean sum of squares. If the variables are $x_1, \ldots x_p$ we define the square of the distance from A to B by

$$d^2\ (A,B) = \sum_{i=1}^{p} (x_{iA} - x_{iB})^2 \qquad (4)$$

The square of the distance occurs so frequently in this class of work that I shall call it the deviance.

[7] Other metrics are possible and I refer to some of them below. But (4) has two advantages which are of such great practical importance that only very powerful reasons would lead me to reject it.

For a set of n individuals there are ½n(n−1) distances between pairs. To calculate and consider them all is computationally prohibitive if n is at all large; for n = 1000 there are nearly half a million distances. However, if we denote the ith variable on the jth member of a set of n by x_{ij} we have

$$\sum_{i=1}^{p} \sum_{j=1}^{n} \sum_{k=1}^{n} (x_{ij} - x_{ik})^2 = \sum_{i=1}^{p} \sum_{j,k=1}^{n} \left\{(x_{ij} - x_i) - (x_{ik} - x_i)\right\}^2$$

where x_i is the mean of the ith variable over the set of n,

$$= \sum_{i=1}^{p} \sum_{j,k=1}^{n} \left\{(x_{ij} - x_i)^2 + (x_{ik} - x_i)^2\right\}$$

$$= 2n \sum_{i=1}^{p} \sum_{j=1}^{n} (x_{ij} - x_i)^2 \qquad (5)$$

Hence the sum of the pair-wise deviances of a set of n is 2n times the sum of deviances from the centre of gravity of the set. To find the sum of the pair-wise deviances (or their mean) we have only to compute the C.G. and the deviances of n points from it, instead of $\frac{1}{2}n(n-1)$ individual deviances. The computations are then proportional to n, not to n^2.

[8] The second advantage of the metric (7) is that it is invariant under a rotation of the axes. Thus, if we have a large number of dimensions, say 30, we can perform a component analysis and work on the scores of the principal components instead of the original variables. And if, as often happens, a few components account for nearly all the variation we can discard the others without seriously affecting the deviance. For example, in a study of the Moser-Scott data we reduced the original 57 variables to six in this way, with an enormous saving in computing time. The scores should not be rescaled to unit variance.

The Definition of "Cluster"

[9] Whatever kind of distance-metric we use, we have to decide two matters: what values constitute "closeness" and whether the definition of cluster requires that all the members are to be close to all the others. The first involves very arbitrary decisions. The only practical rule appears to be by comparison with the distances between clusters. If, for example, the deviances of a Group A from its centroid and those of B from its centroid are, on the average small compared with the distance between centroids, we might say that there exist clusters (as against the alternative hypothesis that the members are scattered more or less at random). This involves making a final decision after clusters have been identified in a provisional way.

[10] The definition of cluster itself requires some thought. The concept of the globular cluster leads to the notion that all the points should be close to *some* of the others, but not necessarily to them all. Points distributed uniformly on a circular disc, for instance, are a cluster in any sense, but those at the opposite ends of a diameter may not be close, not so close as the centre of the disc from another circular cluster of smaller radius. At the other extreme, consider a set of points distributed more or less uniformly along a straight line. Each point is close to two others (except the end points) but it is, perhaps, extending our colloquial connotation to call this a cluster. There is obviously room here for difference of opinion, and probably for difference of definition according to circumstance. I shall take as a measure of the closeness of clustering the mean deviance from the centre of gravity, as compared to the distance between centres of gravity.

[11] It would be very convenient if we could have some definition of "shape" or some measure of departure of a cluster from sphericity. Consider

a set of n points in p dimension and their convex hull. The ratio of the surface area to the volume of the hull would provide such a measure when compared to the isoperimetric values for a hypersphere. Unfortunately it is a matter of great difficulty to determine the convex hull (linear programming methods are required) and even greater difficulty to determine its volume and surface area. The best approach I have been able to think of is to perform a principal component analysis and to consider the eigenvalues of the dispersion matrix. If these are more or less equal the distribution is isotropic. If they are unequal it is elongated in some directions. A convenient summary statistic which would not involve the computations of the eigenvalues would be the determinant of the matrix divided by its mean trace to power p. This is a dimensionless number and if the eigenvalues are $\lambda_1, ..\lambda_p$, is equal to

$$\prod_{i=1}^{p} \lambda_i \Big/ \left(\frac{1}{p} \sum_{i}^{p} \lambda_i\right)^p \qquad (6)$$

This quantity is already in use as a test statistic for sphericity of a multivariate normal distribution (Kendall and Stuart, vol. 3, *42.13*). It can vary from 0 to 1, but a value of zero implies that the variation collapses into fewer dimensions. It may still have a shape in the lower space.

The Distribution of Distances

[12] Although I shall side-step the calculation of all $\frac{1}{2}n(n-1)$ deviances it is worth while considering whether any insight is to be gained into the nature of the clustering by looking at their frequency distribution. One might suppose that separation of clusters would throw up some kind of multimodality. Unfortunately this does not appear to be so. The distances are, of course, highly correlated among themselves, so that the frequency distribution is a very complex entity. But apart from that, a diagnostic interpretation of the distribution presents some peculiar difficulties.

Consider, for example, two clusters of n_1, and n_2 members which are well separated, so that the distances within clusters are small and those between clusters are large. We shall then have

$$\tfrac{1}{2}(n_1)(n_1 - 1) + \tfrac{1}{2}\, n_2\, (n_2 - 1)$$

small deviances and $n_1 n_2$ large ones. A frequency distribution would be bimodal, but the relative frequencies are very dependent on the proportion of n_1 to n_2. The difference, if fact, is

$$\tfrac{1}{2}\, n_1 (n_1 - 1) + \tfrac{1}{2}\, n_2 (n_2 - 1) - n_1 n_2$$
$$= \tfrac{1}{2}(n_1 - n_2)^2 - \tfrac{1}{2}(n_1 + n_2)$$

which will be positive if n_1 and n_2 are fairly different, but negative if they are equal. If now we suppose that the distribution of deviances in the two clusters has a substantial spread as compared to the deviances between them, we can get almost any shape of frequency distribution; and *a fortiori* for more than two clusters.

[13] An example will illustrate the effect. I took the two sets of iris, *versicolour* and *virginica* considered by Fisher in his classical paper of 1936 on discriminant analysis. There are 50 of each and I took them together as a group of 100. The distance metric used was based on ranks, because at that stage I was interested in distribution free methods, but I do not think this seriously affects the illustration. The 4,950 deviances between pairs have the following distribution

Table 1. Distribution of 4,950 deviances between pairs of iris

Deviance	Frequency	Deviance	Frequency	Deviance	Frequency
0	433	13	132	26	26
1	375	14	110	27	14
2	449	15	97	28	10
3	340	16	94	29	5
4	276	17	77	30	5
5	301	18	73	31	5
6	276	19	46	32	1
7	387	20	45	33	3
8	301	21	52	34	3
9	250	22	38	35	2
10	261	23	34	36	3
11	212	24	29	37	–
12	163	25	21	38	1
					4,950

I doubt whether an examination of this table would suggest that there are two clusters. In fact a discriminant gives a class of 44 (virginica) and 43 (versicolour with 13 cases undecided.

[14] Notwithstanding what was said above about the non-stochastic nature of many cluster problems, there is some interest in deriving the joint distribution of distances in random samples. The general problem is very unwieldly, but a brief sketch of the solution for normal distributions is given in Appendix A.

Non-Measurable Variation

[15] Consider a case where our p variables consist of continuous and classificatory types. For example, a market survey may include data on age and

income (effectively continuous) social class (in ordered categories) and some dichotomies such as sex of respondent. Elsewhere I have pointed out (Kendall and Stuart, vol. 3, *44.39*) that all these types can be reduced to common terms by ranking, even a dichotomy being representable as a heavily tied ranking. Some information for continuous variables is lost by ranking, but there seems no alternative course. To represent categories by numbers, e.g. to represent a five-fold social classification by −2, −1, 0, 1, 2, may create a certain amount of illusion as to the relative degree of separation of the classes, but again it is hard to see what else can be done.

[16] However, all is not well with the use of polytomous variables. One sees the difficulty most clearly, perhaps, in the case of multiple dichotomy. Suppose each individual bears or does not bear a value of p dichotomies, which we may represent by (0, 1) variables. If two individuals A and B have m_1 zeros and m_2 units in common, the quantity $(m_1 + m_2)/p$ is called a Similarity Index. It simply records the proportion of features in which they agree: the complementary quantity $1-(m_1+m_2)/p$ could then be regarded as a distance function. By considering the possible values on the corner of a p-dimensional hypercube we see that such a function obeys the triangular inequality.

[17] But when we try to use such a distance function to cluster we arrive at a serious difficulty. Consider the case when $p = 3$ which we can represent as in Figure 1:

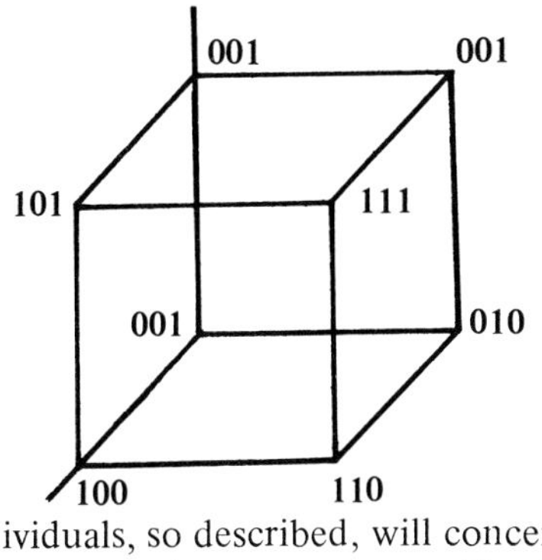

The sample of n individuals, so described, will concentrate at the corners of this cube. Individuals lying at the same corner will, of course have distance zero and in this sense we may define eight clusters, one for each corner. This may be sensible but is clearly rather trivial—any cluster merely consists of members who are all exactly alike so far as these p qualities are concerned. Suppose now that we relax the constraint and are willing to admit as a single cluster those members who have $p-1$ qualities in common. It is then easy to see on the cube that any three corners connected by edges have two qualities in common. And the resulting eight clusters are all equally valid. But they all overlap. There are eight different ways in which we can divide the members into two clusters, and there is nothing to choose between them.

The situation is worse for $p > 3$. A hypercube has 2^p corners and each is connected to p others. There will be at least $2^p/(p+1)$ ways of defining clusters with all but one quality in common.

[18] The position eases somewhat for polytomies. For example, if we consider the points on a $5 \times 5 \times 5$ lattice, there are 124 distances from one to the others and the variety of possibility is much greater. As a practical matter, then, I would admit into a cluster analysis a mixture of continuous and classificatory variables, whether reduced to common rankings or measured by pseudo-numerical methods, but should be sceptical of results obtained if the admixture of dichotomies was too high.

Probabilistic Metrics

[19] It is natural to consider whether some function such as Mahalanobis' distance could be used for continuous variables. This function, designed to measure the "distance" between two frequency distributions, is defined as

$$D^2 = \sum_{j,k=1}^{p} a_{jk} (\bar{x}_{1j} - \bar{x}_{2j})(\bar{x}_{1k} - \bar{x}_{2k}) \tag{7}$$

where a_{jk} is the inverse of the *pooled* dispersion matrix and $\bar{x}$ is the mean of the appropriate sample. The function has at least one apparent advantage, that it is scale-invariant. I have already pointed out that for many situations where clustering problems present themselves a probabilistic mechanism is quite inappropriate. To this one may add that even in a probabilistic situation it is begging the question to suppose that the clusters, if they exist, have a common dispersion matrix.

[20] Nevertheless, one jettisons the classical apparatus with some reluctance and it is, perhaps, worth considering whether there is a quadratic metric which would act as a suitable deviance other than the Pythagorean one used above. In relativity theory the field equations are derived as tensors on a four-dimensional Riemannian quadratic differential form. One might then consider a differential metric.

$$d^2 = \sum_{j,k=1}^{p} g_{jk}\, dx_j\, dx_k \tag{8}$$

I have made no progress along these lines.

The Identification of Clusters

[21] Suppose that we have set up a distance function and computed all the distances between pairs of points. Suppose further that we have decided, at

least provisionally, what limits to the deviance define "closeness". The next problem is how to determine the clusters.

One obvious way (Kendall and Stuart, loc. cit.) is to look for the closest pair, say A and B; then to look for C which is close to A and B; then to look for D which is close to A, B, C and so on. This may not give a unique answer if there are several possible pairs from which to start. The method is tedious for large n but quite convenient for clustering variables.

[22] As an example, consider Table 2. Forty-eight candidates were assessed by judges on 15 variables, each on a ten-point scale. Table 2 gives the correlations between the scores, the variables being

1. Form of letter of application.
2. Appearance.
3. Academic ability.
4. Likeability.
5. Self-confidence.
6. Lucidity.
7. Honesty.
8. Salesmanship.
9. Experience.
10. Drive.
11. Ambition.
12. Grasp.
13. Potential.
14. Keenness to join the company.
15. Suitability.

Table 2

	1	**2**	**3**	**4**	**5**	**6**	**7**	**8**	**9**	**10**	**11**	**12**	**13**	**14**	**15**
1	1.00	.24	.04	.31	.09	.23	-.11	.27	.55	.35	.28	.34	.37	.47	.59
2		1.00	.12	.38	.43	.37	.35	.48	.14	.34	.55	.51	.51	.28	.38
3			1.00	.00	.00	.08	-.03	.05	.27	.09	.04	.20	.29	-.32	.14
4				1.00	.30	.48	.65	.35	.14	.39	.35	.50	.61	.69	.33
5					1.00	.81	.41	.82	.02	.70	.84	.72	.67	.48	.25
6						1.00	.36	.83	.15	.70	.76	.88	.78	.53	.42
7							1.00	.23	-.16	.28	.21	.39	.42	.45	.00
8								1.00	.23	.81	.86	.77	.73	.55	.55
9									1.00	.34	.20	.30	.35	.21	.69
10										1.00	.78	.71	.79	.61	.62
11											1.00	.78	.77	.55	.43
12												1.00	.88	.55	.53
13													1.00	.54	.57
14														1.00	.40
15															1.00

If we regard a value of $\geqslant 0.7$ as 'close' it is seen that the closest pair is (12, 13). We can then add others to get as a cluster

$$(5, 6, 8, 10, 11, 12, 13)$$

(The correlation between 5 and 13 is 0.67 but it seems fair to condone the slight shortfall below 0.7)

It so happens that no correlation among the remaining variables exceed 0.7. We should then conclude that the other eight form distinct clusters of one.

If we relax the criterion and admit correlations $\geqslant 0.5$ as constituting closeness three further clusters appear (1, 9, 15) and (4, 7, 14). Variable 3, academic ability, remains in isolation.

[23] There is a kind of converse procedure which consists of breaking the whole set of n into two groups, then breaking these into further sub-groups and so on. But I have never seen it applied to numbers of practical size except in one dimension.

[24] The procedure which we use at Scicon for clustering of individuals is as follows:

(1) We decide on some number q, say 20, as an upper limit to the number of clusters in which we are interested.

(2) We determine in the p-dimensional space q cluster centres in some arbitrary way, say by spacing them at intervals of one standard deviation. These initially chosen points are merely for starting off on an iterative process.

(3) The observations are considered one at a time and allocated to the nearest centre. We thus define 20 "clusters".

(4) The centre of gravity of each cluster is computed.

(5) The observations are considered one at a time. An observation is moved to another cluster (or rather, the boundaries of the cluster are moved to include that point) if such a move reduces the sum of the deviances from the observations to their cluster centres *when the centres of the two clusters are simultaneously moved to their new centres of gravity.* If an observation is moved in this way the new c.g.'s are computed.

(6) The set of observations is re-scanned until no observation is moved to a new cluster. At this point we pause, having arrived at q clusters in such a way that the sum of deviances from the centres of gravity cannot be lowered by moving an observation from one cluster to another.

[25] This procedure is reasonable but it may not arrive at a set of clusters such that the overall sum of deviances from the c.g.'s is an absolute

minimum. It is conceivable that the set of clusters so obtained may depend on the starting points and the order in which the observations are considered one by one. However, if there is any serious doubt the process can be repeated with a different set of starting points. In practice we are usually working towards a smaller set of clusters than 20, and when amalgamation takes place, as described below, it usually happens in practice that even when different initial sets of 20 are chosen, they converge to agreement by the time the process has merged clusters to give, say, 10.

[26] At the next stage a pair of clusters is chosen for merging. The basis for selection is that their combination should minimize the increment in the deviances from their cluster means. When we merge two clusters some increment is inevitable. We consider all pairs of clusters and choose the one which has the smallest. This, however, is only an expedient for starting with $q-1$ clusters in an efficient way. The programme of computation then returns to the beginning and reallocates the observations to $q-1$ clusters in the manner described in paragraph 23. The calculation then proceeds to $q-2$, $q-3$, etc. clusters in turn. At each stage we compute the cluster centres, the distances between cluster centres, the sums of deviances of observations from their respective cluster centres, and finally print out the individuals in each cluster.

[27] We thus arrive at a series of answers to the problem of defining clusters, with q, $q-1$, $q-2, \ldots$ clusters. The question now is, which do we choose? A criterion suggested by my colleague E. M. L. Beale (but there may be others) is based on an analogy with the analysis of variance, though we must be careful to remember that it is an analogy only, not a formal equivalence. For c clusters we add together the c deviances from the respective cluster means. This may be regarded as a residual sum of squares, and we denote it by R_c. If it were zero, all the clusters would be condensed at their centres of gravity. If it is large the points are widely dispersed and the clustering, if any, is very loose. The criterion for choosing c clusters rather than c, depends on the ratio

$$F(c,c_1) = \frac{R_{c_1} - R_c}{R_c} \Bigg/ \left\{ \frac{n-c_1}{n-c} \left(\frac{c}{c_1}\right)^{2/p} - 1 \right\} \tag{9}$$

Heuristically, this is tested as an F-ratio with degrees of freedom

$$V_1 = p\,(c-c_1) \tag{10}$$

$$V_2 = p\,(n-c) \tag{11}$$

If this is significant then the use of more than c_1 clusters is justified. The test is not exact. If the observations were spherically and normally distributed, it would test the hypothesis that they are close enough to meld into a single spherically normal distribution. On prior grounds, however, we have no reason to suppose that the observations are either spherical or normal, or indeed that they are stochastically distributed at all. The criterion must therefore be regarded as an empirical indication only. For the deviation of the test see Beale (1969).

[28] The above procedure has been programmed for a Univac 1108 and a CDC 3200. This means, for example, that the 1108 program can handle up to 2,000 observations with up to 20 variables. And it can be redimensioned to tackle other problems of a similar overall size. The size of problem that can be tackled is larger, on any given computer, than with any method that requires the explicit calculation of the inter-point distance matrix. But the program is quite slow if the data cannot be held all in core.

Some Outstanding Questions

[29] In conclusion I refer to some outstanding questions to which it would be useful to have some answers, however partial.

The first concerns clustering when there are different probabilities of appearance at different points. Consider, for example, recorded cases of some relatively rare disease with obscure aetiology, such as multiple sclerosis. We may plot them on a map, and one question of keen interest is whether they cluster, in which case we might suspect contagion or differential environmental influence. But of course the clustering depends on the number of people at risk—it surprises no one that there are clusters in towns but not in the heart of the country. How then, do we make allowance for the numbers at risk?

Some work on this problem has been done by Merrington and Penrose (1964), Barton and David (1966) but mainly from the point of view of time-sequences. The general problem is extremely intractable. A possible approach is sketched in Appendix C.

[30] The technique for clustering variables is much simpler than component and factor analysis where rotation to meaningful variables is involved. I wonder whether we now need the latter for the identification of critical variables. In particular, the technique seems to me much more down-to-earth in dealing with problems of collinearity.

[31] There is, as yet, no method (so far as I am aware) for rejecting variables which do not effectively contribute to the clustering. In practice, having identified the clusters, I should decide this by doing a discriminant analysis and testing the coefficients in the function. The procedure is rather tedious for more than three or four clusters, and, of course, some variables may be relevant to the delimitation of one pair but not of another. There is further

work to be done here.

[32] It is hard to see, sometimes, how to deal with an observation which lies close to two clusters. It may belong to either. As I have defined the matter, clusters cannot overlap so that it cannot belong to both but sometimes, perhaps, they should. In any event, one should consult the print-out of the analysis to see whether two clusters should be regarded as having a common area.

Appendix A

Distribution of Deviance in Normally Distributed Clusters

We require an expression for the p-way integral of the exponential of a quadratic form which contains linear and constant terms. Let x_0 represent a dummy variable equal to unity and the true variables be $x_1, x_2, \ldots,$ x_p . . We require

$$\int_{-\infty}^{\infty} \cdots \int_{-\infty}^{\infty} \exp - \frac{1}{2} \left\{ \sum_{j,k=0}^{p} a_{jk}\, x_j\, x_k \right\} dx_1 \ldots dx_p, \quad a,k = a_{kj}. \tag{A.1}$$

We transform the exponent to $\sum_{j,k=1}^{p} a_{jk} (x_j - \alpha_j)(x_k - \alpha_k)$ in such a way that linear terms vanish. This gives us equations in the α's and a's typified by the vanishing of the coefficient for x_1.

$$a_{01} - a_{11}\alpha_1 - a_{12}\alpha_2 - \ldots - a_{1p}x_p = 0 \tag{A.2}$$

Let

$$M = \begin{bmatrix} a_{00} & a_{01} & a_{02} & \cdots & a_{0p} \\ a_{01} & a_{11} & a_{12} & \cdots & a_{1p} \\ a_{02} & a_{12} & a_{22} & \cdots & a_{2p} \\ \cdot & \cdot & \cdot & \cdots & \cdot \\ a_{0p} & a_{1p} & a_{2p} & \cdots & a_{pp} \end{bmatrix} \tag{A.3}$$

Then we have for the α's expressions typified by

$$\alpha_1 = M_{01} / M_{00} \tag{A.4}$$

where M_{jk} is the co-factor of a_{jk} in M.

Upon integration of the quadratic form we find, apart from constants, a value of $M_{00}^{-1/2}$. The remaining part is the exponential of

$$-\frac{1}{2} \left\{ a_{00} - \sum_{j,k=1}^{p} a_{jk}\, \alpha_j\, \alpha_k \right\}$$

$$= -\frac{1}{2M_{00}}\left\{a_{00}M_{00} - \sum_{j,k=1}^{p} a_{jk}\frac{M_{0j}M_{0k}}{M_{00}}\right\} \tag{A.5}$$

The sum $\sum_{j=1}^{p} a_{,k} M_{0j}$ vanishes unless $k = 0$ and $\sum_{j,k=1}^{p}$ is then $\sum_{j=1}^{p} a_{0,} M_{0j}$.

Hence we have simply for the whole expression $\exp -\frac{1}{2} M/M_{00}$. The integral is then a constant times

$$M_{00}^{-\frac{1}{2}} \exp\left\{-\frac{1}{2} M/M_{00}\right\}. \tag{A.6}$$

Consider now a normally distributed variable in two dimensions, with means α_1, β_1 variances σ_1^2 and τ_1^2 and correlation p_1; and a second variable with subscripts 2.

Writing

$$A_1 = \frac{1}{(1-p_1^2)\sigma_1^2}, \quad B_1 = \frac{p_1}{(1-p_1^2)\sigma_1\tau_1}, \quad c_1 = \frac{1}{(1-p_1^2)\tau_1^2}$$

with similarly expressions for the subscript 2, we have for the frequency function of a sample x_1, y_1 from the first and x_2, y_2 from the second a density functional proportional to

$$\exp -\frac{1}{2}\Big\{A_1(x_1-\alpha_1)^2 + 2B_1(x_1-\alpha_1)(y_1-\beta_1) + C_1(y_1-\beta_1)^2$$
$$+ A_2(x_2-\alpha_2)^2 + 2B_2(x_2-\alpha_2)(y_2-\beta_2) + C_2(y_2-\beta_2)^2\Big\}$$

To obtain the characteristic function of the deviance (writing θ for the imaginary parameter *it*) we have to integrate over the course of this distribution

$$\theta\left\{(x_1-x_2)^2 + (y_1-y_2)^2\right\}.$$

The result is given by (A.6) with

$$M_{00} = \begin{vmatrix} A_1 - 2\theta & B_1 & 2\theta & \theta \\ B_1 & C_1 - 2\theta & \theta & 2\theta \\ 2\theta & \theta & A_2 - 2\theta & B_2 \\ \theta & 2\theta & B_2 & C_2 - 2\theta \end{vmatrix} \tag{A.7}$$

$$M = \left|\begin{matrix} A_1\alpha_1^2 + 2B_1\alpha_1\beta_1 + C_1\beta_1^2 \\ + A_2\alpha_2^2 + 2B_2\alpha_2\beta_2 + C_2\beta_2^2 \\ -(A_1\alpha_1 - B_1\beta_1) \\ -(B_1\alpha_1 - C_1\beta_1) \\ -(A_2\alpha_2 - B_2\beta_2) \\ -(B_2\alpha_2 - C_2\beta_2) \end{matrix} \quad \begin{matrix} -(A_1\alpha_1 + \beta_1) \; -(\beta_1\alpha_1 - C_1\beta_1) \\ -(A_2\alpha_2 - B_2\beta_2) \; -(\beta_2\alpha_2 - C_2\beta_2) \\ \\ M_{00} \\ \\ \end{matrix}\right| \qquad (A.8)$$

This gives us the c.f., when we evaluate the multiplicative constant in the usual way by putting $\theta = 0$. Both (A.7) and (A.8) are quadratic functions of θ. (A.7) can be simplified but (A.8) is probably best left as it stands.

The distribution has a family resemblance to the non-central chi-squared but I have not tried to invert the c.f. If the frequency distribution were required explicitly it would probably be better to compute the c.f. and invert it by a Fourier transform.

But the same kind of argument we could obtain the c.f. of the joint distribution of deviances in random samples of $n_1, n_2, \ldots n_k$ from k multivariate normal populations of dimension p, and could, if necessary use other quadratic functions for the deviances. However, the resulting expressions would be formidable and I should not think the effort worth while unless some new and important use is found for the deviance distribution.

Appendix B

Clustering By Projection

If a set of points in p dimensions form clusters of approximately spheroidal shape, it might be supposed that this clustering effect will persist when the points are projected on to lower dimensions, and in particular when they are projected on to two dimensions. It may be thought, then, that an examination of the scatter diagrams, $\frac{1}{2}p(p-1)$ in number, would throw some light on the nature of the clustering in p dimensions.

In practice any inference of the kind is very much open to doubt. If a 2-way scatter diagram shows to the eye a clearly defined set of k clusters, there is reasonable presumption that the number of clusters in p dimensions will not exceed k. But there may not be any. Conversely, a failure in the two-way diagrams to indicate any separation into clusters does not indicate that there are none in p dimensions.

In Diagrams 1 and 2 I have graphed the 100 Iris plants (versicolour and virginica) on two of the possible six scatter diagrams. Strictly speaking, I should have reduced these measurements to a common variance, but did not consider it worth while for the purpose of this illustration. Anyone looking at these diagrams in ignorance of their origin would not, I think, suspect the existence of two clusters in the original four dimensions.

Appendix C

Geographical Clustering with Differential Background Densities

Suppose that a plane area is divided into districts for which areas and populations are known; for example, polling districts or constituencies in the United Kingdom. In considering whether the incidence of a rare condition, such as a disease or an exceptional blood-group, bears signs of clustering we have, in some way, to allow for the different densities of population at risk.

Let the population density (numbers per unit area) in the ζth district be , where ζ runs from $\alpha, \beta, \ldots$ to ω. Let n be the mean density for the whole area, so that n_ζ / n is the relative density. Consider the distance function for the two members in districts ζ, η

$$\frac{1}{n^2} \sum_{i=1}^{p} (x_{i\zeta} - x_{i\eta})^2 \, n_\zeta \, n_\eta . \qquad \text{(C.1)}$$

If all the districts have the same density this reduces to the ordinary Pythagorean deviance. Within a district ($\zeta = \eta$), it weights the distance according to the relative density of that district. The distance between a point in district ζ and one in district η may be regarded as the geometric mean of what it would have been if both points were in ζ or in η.

There are other ways of weighting the deviance (e.g. by the arithmetic mean $\frac{1}{2}(n_\zeta + n_\eta)/n$), but the form (C.1) has the advantage of preserving to some extent the relation between average deviances among pairs of points and their average deviance from a weighted centre of gravity.

It is sufficient to consider any one variable and we can drop the subscript i. Suppose there are p_ζ members observed in district ζ and a group of districts $\alpha, \beta, \ldots \theta$. Then the total contribution to the deviance for this variable is

$$\sum_{\zeta=\alpha}^{\theta} \sum_{\eta=\alpha}^{\theta} \sum_{j=1}^{p_\zeta} \sum_{k=1}^{p_\eta} (n_{j\zeta} - x_{k\eta})^2 \, n_\zeta \, n_\eta \; / \; n^2 \qquad \text{(C.2)}$$

Define a weighted mean m such that

$$m = \sum_{\zeta=\alpha}^{\theta} \sum_{j=1}^{p_\zeta} x_{j\zeta} \, \eta_\zeta \Big/ \sum_{\zeta=\alpha}^{\theta} \sum_{j=1}^{p_\zeta} n_\zeta . \qquad \text{(C.3)}$$

Then on expanding $(x_{j\zeta} - x_{k\eta})^2$ as $(x_{j\zeta} - m)^2 + (x_{k\zeta} - n)^2 - 2(x_{j\zeta} - m)(x_{k\zeta} - m)$ we find, in a familiar way, that the cross-product term vanishes on summation and (C.2) reduces to

$$2 \sum_{\zeta=\alpha}^{\theta} \sum_{j=1}^{p_\zeta} (x_{j\zeta} - m)^2 \; P \; n_\zeta / n. \qquad (C.4)$$

where P is given by

$$P = \sum_{\eta=\alpha}^{\theta} \sum_{k=1}^{p_\eta} n_\eta / n. \qquad (C.5)$$

The function of (C.1) is not invariant under a rotation of axes, but as we are concerned with only two or three dimensions the point is of no great practical importance.

REFERENCES

1. Kendall, M. G. and Stuart, A. (1968). *The Advanced Theory of Statistics,* vol. 3, 2nd edition. London, C. Griffin & Co.
2. Beale, E. M. L. (1969). Euclidean Cluster Analysis. *Bulletin of the ISI*, vol. 43, Bk. 2, pp. 92-94.
3. Merrington, M. and Spicer, C. C. (1969). Acute leukemia in New England. *Brit. J. Prev. Soc. Med.* 23, 124.
4. Merrington, M. and Penrose, L. S. (1964). Distances which involved satellited chromosomes in metaphase preparations. *Hum. Ge., Lond.* 27, 257.
5. David, F. N. and Barton, D. E. (1966). Two space-time interaction tests for epidemicity. *Brit J. Prev. Soc. Med.* 20, 44.
6. Bolshev. L. N. (1970). Cluster Analysis. *Proc. Int. Inst. Stat. London.*
7. Moser, C. A. and Scott, W. (1961). *British Towns* Oliver and Boyd. Edinburgh.

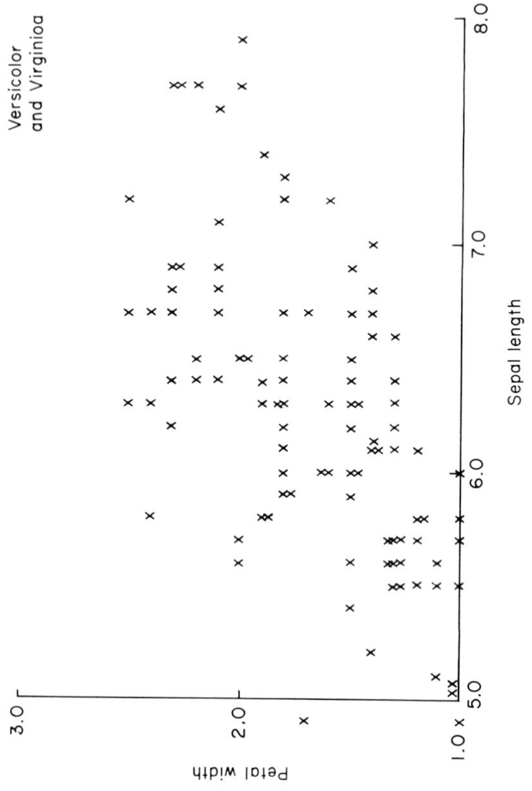
Versicolor
and Virginioa
Petal width
3.0
2.0
1.0
5.0
6.0
7.0
8.0
Sepal length

DIAGRAM 1

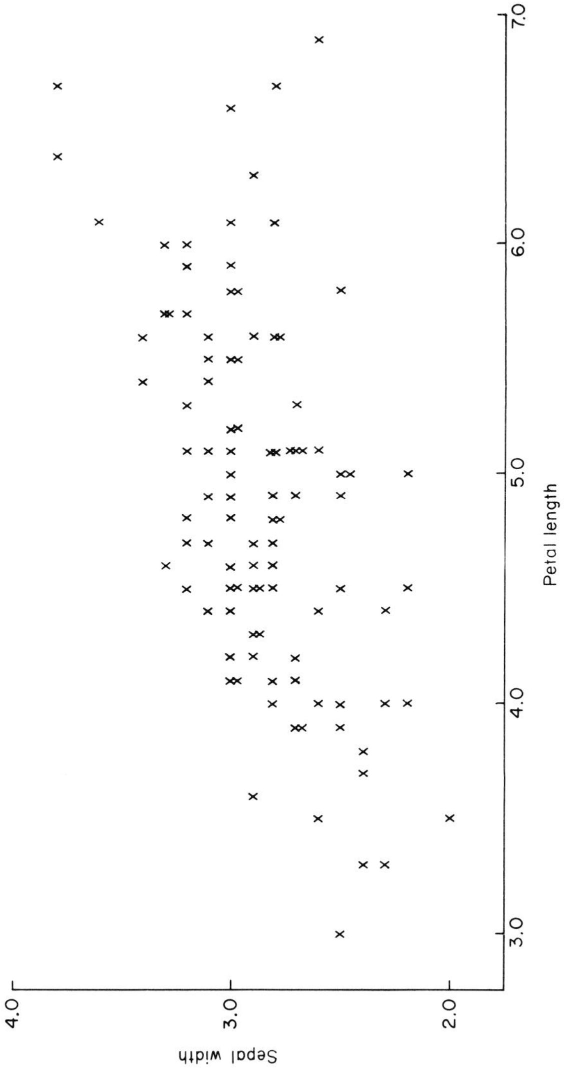

DIAGRAM 2

ADAPTIVE PATTERN RECOGNITION: A STATE-VARIABLE APPROACH

D. G. Lainiotis

DEPARTMENT OF ELECTRICAL ENGINEERING
AND ELECTRONICS RESEARCH CENTER
THE UNIVERSITY OF TEXAS AT AUSTIN
AUSTIN, TEXAS

Abstract

A state-variable approach to Bayes-optimal adaptive pattern recognition is presented for continuous data systems. Both structure and parameter adaptation, as well as supervised and unsupervised learning are considered and Bayes-optimal as well as suboptimal, recursive recognition algorithms are given. The state-variable approach consists of modeling random processes involved as the outputs of dynamic systems, linear or nonlinear, excited by white noise, and describing the systems in state-variable form. Several fundamental pattern recognition results obtained using the state-variable approach are discussed. Specifically, for the class of adaptive pattern recognition problems with signals modeled by nonlinear dynamic systems excited by white gaussian noise and observed in white gaussian noise, the following results are presented and discussed.

a) The fundamental relationship between pattern recognition and estimation is established. Namely, it is shown that pattern recognition/detection constitutes mean-square nonlinear estimation;

b) A "partition theorem" is derived that enables decomposition of the nonlinear adaptive pattern recognition system into two parts, a nonadaptive part consisting of recursive matched filters, and an adaptive part that incorporates the learning nature of the adaptive recognition system;

c) For the special class of pattern recognition problems with linear dynamic models, the "partition theorem" partitions the nonlinear adaptive recognition system into a linear nonadaptive part consisting of Kalman filters, and a nonlinear adaptive part;

d) Several simplified recursive recognition algorithms are presented with substantial computational advantages and high performance; and finally,

e) Recursive and computationally efficient algorithms are given for the on-line performance evaluation of the adaptive recognition systems.

Moreover, two special cases are considered, namely that of supervised learning, treated previously by Lainiotis, and the case of independent signalling random processes.

For the special case of independent signalling random processes, the results for continuous data are similar to those obtained by Fralick for discrete, conditionally independent data. Both deterministic decision-directed learning as well as random decision-directed learning algorithms (Agrawala's LPT) for continuous data are also obtained. Moreover, suboptimal, recursive, unsupervised learning algorithms are obtained based on approximate nonlinear estimation procedures.

I. Introduction

In this chapter, Bayesian decision theory and state-variable modelling of gaussian random processes are applied to the problem of sequential, supervised learning, pattern recognition of gaussian signals in gaussian white noise. The unsupervised learning problem arises whenever the correct classification of the sequence of previous observations is unknown and hence the system is required to learn and adapt its structure to improve classifications only on the basis of: a) the sequence of unclassified present and past observations; and, b) partial a-priori knowledge of the structure of the problem.

Specifically, the following problem is considered; decide optimally which of two hypotheses H_i, $i = 0, 1$ is active at the kth signalling interval given the continuous present and past record $\lambda_k = \{\nu_k, \nu_{k-1} \ldots, \nu_1\}$ of a realization of the m-vector observable random process $z(t)$, where $\nu_j \equiv \{z(\tau); \tau \epsilon (t_{j-1}, t_j)\}$ and

$$z(t) = \beta_j y(t) + v(t) \tag{1}$$

and $\beta_j = 1$ or 0 if hypothesis H_i or H_o, respectively is active at the j_{th} signalling interval, $j = 1,2, \ldots, k$. It is assumed, mainly for simplicity of presentation that the information source has the properties: a) it chooses the hypothesis to be active at the kth interval, independent of the sequence of past hypotheses; namely, $p(\beta_k, \beta_{k-1}) = \prod_{i=1}^{k} p(\beta_i)$; b) moreover, $p(\beta_j = 1) = p$ is known and constant for all $j = 1,2, \ldots, k$.

The signal random process $y(t)$ is assumed to be "adequately" modeled by the state-variable model

$$y(t) = H(t,\theta)\ x(t) \tag{2a}$$

and

$$\frac{dx(t)}{dt} = F(t,\theta)x(t) + G(t,\theta)u(t) \tag{2b}$$

where $x(t)$ is the n-vector signal "state" random process, $v(t)$ is a zero-mean m-vector white gaussian noise process with covariance matrix $R(t)$, $u(t)$ is a zero-mean q-vector white gaussian process, independent of $v(t)$ with covariance matrix I. $H(t,\theta)$ is the mxn observation matrix, $F(t,\theta)$ is the nxn signal dynamic matrix, and $G(t,\theta)$ is the nxq input matrix.

However, the above linear model, although considered adequate on the basis of a-priori knowledge of the particular problem under consideration, e.g. physical considerations, it is not completely known. Namely, the dynamical and statistical model is specified up to a set of unknown, time-invariant parameters denoted by the vector θ. Moreover, the state-vector dimensionality may also be unknown. The latter is herein referred to as model "structure".

The Bayesian approach to adaptive pattern recognition consists in assuming that the system generating the random processes involved is chosen at random from a collection of possible systems of state-vector dimensionality σ, σ^{th} model parameter vector value θ_σ, with known or assumed a-priori probabilities $P(\theta_\sigma,\sigma)$. It is, moreover, assumed, that the model structure is less than or equal to a fixed number n. This may be justified on the basis of physical considerations or in order to limit the complexity of the resulting system within specified constraints. In the latter,case, the problem of learning may be viewed as on-line system approximation, or constrained modeling. The assumption of an upper bound n to the system dimensionality, permits us to imbed structure adaptation into parameter adaptation by choosing the model structure as n, and determining the elements of $F(\cdot)$, $G(\cdot)$, $H(\cdot)$, etc., that are zero if the correct model structure is less than n. From here on, in view of the assumption of an upper bound n to state-vector dimensionality, only parameter adaptation will be explicitly discussed.

It is seen from the above discussion, that adaptive pattern recognition constitutes joint pattern recognition and on-line or adaptive modeling or system identification. This will be brought out further in a following section. There exists a large class of physical problems for which the adaptive formulation is suitable, several examples of which were given in Lainiotis [1], which has treated the supervised learning case only.

II. Optimal Unsupervised Learning Pattern Recognition Algorithms

In this section, optimal, recursive unsupervised learning adaptive pattern recognition algorithms are obtained. For the special case of supervised learning the algorithms reduce to the algorithm given in [1].

Specifically, the pattern recognition problem we address in this section is specified by the dynamic equations:

$$z(t) = \beta_k H(t,\theta)x(t) + v(t)$$
$$= \beta_k y(t) + v(t) \tag{3a}$$

$$\frac{dx(t)}{dt} = F(t,\theta)x(t) + G(t,\theta)u(t) \tag{3b}$$

where $\{v(t)\}$ and $\{u(t)\}$ are independent, zero-mean white gaussian random processes with covariance matrices $R(t)$, and I, respectively. The information source has the properties stated in the introduction. Moreover, $\{\beta_k\}$ is independent of $\{u(t)\}$ and of $\{v(t)\}$, as well as of θ, and $x(t_0)$. The initial state-vector $x(t_0)$ is independent of $\{v(t)\}$ and $\{u(t)\}$ for $t \geq t_0$, and it has a θ-conditional a-priori density, denoted by $p[x(t_0)/t_0, \theta]$, which is known but not necessarily gaussian. The mean and variance of this density are denoted by $\hat{x}(t_0/t_0,\theta)$, respectively. The model is completely specified by the parameter θ, which is unknown and it is random variable with a-priori probability density $p(\theta)$.

Given: a) the continuous record $\nu_k^t = \{z(\tau); \tau \epsilon (t_{k-1},t) \epsilon T_k\}$ from the current bound $T_k = \{t_{k-1}, t_k\}$ for which a decision is to be made; as well as b) the past record $\lambda_{k-1} = \{\nu_{k-1}, \nu_{k-2}, \ldots, \nu_1\}$ as summarized in the probability densities $p[x(t_{k-1})/t_{k-1},\theta]$ and $p(\theta/t_{k-1})$, the Bayes-risk minimizing decision rule as well as the minimum mean-square estimate of the state-vector $x(t)$ and the unknown parameter θ, are to be derived.

The problem stated above may be shown to be simply a nonlinear estimation problem. To see this, augment the state-vector $x(t)$ with θ and β_k, so that the augmented state-vector $x_a(t) = [x^T(t) \vdots \theta^T \vdots \beta_k]^T$. Then, the model defining equations become

$$\frac{dx_a(t)}{dt} = f_a(x_a(t),t) + g_a(x_a(t),t)\,u(t) \tag{4a}$$

$$z(t) = h_a(x(t),t) + v(t) \tag{4b}$$

where

$$f_a(x_a(t),t) \equiv [F(t,\theta)x(t) \vdots 0 \vdots 0]^T, \; g_a(x_a(t),t) \equiv [G(t,\theta) \vdots 0 \vdots 0]^T$$

and

$$h_a(x_a(t),t) \equiv \beta_k H(t,\theta)\; x(t)$$

It is apparent from the definition of $f_a(\cdot)$, $g_a(\cdot)$ and $h_a(\cdot)$, that they are nonlinear functions of $x_a(t)$. The mean-square estimate of $x_a(t)$ given ν_k^t, and $\gamma_{k-1} \equiv \{p[x(t_{k-1})/t_{k-1},\theta], p(\theta/\gamma_{k-1})\}$ is denoted by

$$\hat{x}_a(t/\nu_k^t,\gamma_{k-1}) = [\hat{x}^T(t/\nu_k^t,\gamma_{k-1}) \vdots \hat{\theta}^T(t/\nu_k^t,\gamma_{k-1}) \vdots \hat{\beta}_k(t/\nu_k^t,\gamma_{k-1})]^T \quad (5)$$

It remains to show that $\hat{x}_a(\cdot)$ contains the quantity sufficient to implement the Bayes-optimal decision rule. Lainiotis [2], was the first to point this out, namely he showed [2] that:

$$\hat{\beta}_k(t/\nu_k^t,\gamma_{k-1}) \equiv E[\beta_k/\nu_k^t,\gamma_{k-1}]$$

$$= p(\beta_k = 1/\nu_k^t,\gamma_{k-1}) \quad (6)$$

It is moreover, well-known that the Bayes-optimal decision procedure is: decide H_1 or H_0 depending on whether $p(\theta = 1/\nu_k^t,\gamma_{k-1}) \gtrless c_o$, respectively, where c_o depends on the a-priori costs for each decision. Thus, it is seen that Bayes-optimal detection consists of Bayes-optimal mean-square estimation of the indicator variable β_k, followed by a nonlinear zero-memory transformation. Namely, the optimal decision $d = C(\hat{\beta}_k - c_o)$, where $C(\omega)$ equals 1 or 0 depending on whether $\omega \gtrless 0$. From the above discussion it is apparent that detection/pattern recognition problems are simply a class of nonlinear estimation problems, with the attendant difficulties in realizing optimal nonlinear estimators [3]. Namely, the optimal, continuous data, nonlinear filter is specified, in general, by an infinite set of coupled partial differential equation [3].

In this paper, by utilizing the adaptive approach, namely by using the smoothing property of expectations, the nonlinear estimator is obtained in closed form. The desired adaptive realization is obtained by considering both the constant unknown parameter vector θ as well as the indicator variable β_k as constituting an augmented parameter vector $\alpha_k \equiv [\theta^T \vdots \beta_k]^T$ which is time-varying. The desired adaptive realization is given in the following theorems.

Theorem I:

$$\hat{x}(t/\nu_k^t,\gamma_{k-1}) = \int \hat{x}(t/\nu_k^t,\gamma_{k-1},\alpha_k)p(\alpha_k/\nu_k^t,\gamma_{k-1})d\alpha_k \quad (7a)$$

where

$$\hat{x}(t/\nu_k^t,\gamma_{k-1}) \equiv E[x(t)/\nu_k^t,\gamma_{k-1}]$$

and $$\hat{x}(t/\nu_k^t,\gamma_{k-1},\alpha_k) \equiv E[x(t)/\nu_k^t,\gamma_{k-1},\alpha_k]$$

The corresponding state-vector error covariance matrix defined as

$$P_x(t/\nu_k^t,\gamma_{k-1}) \equiv E\{[x(t) - \hat{x}(t/\nu_k^t,\gamma_{k-1})][x(t) - \hat{x}(t/\nu_k^t,\gamma_{k-1})]^T/\nu_k^t,\gamma_{k-1}\}$$

is given by

$$P_x(t/\nu_k^t,\gamma_{k-1},\alpha_k) = \int \{P_x(t/\nu_k^t,\gamma_{k-1},\alpha_k) + [\hat{x}(t/\nu_k^t,\gamma_{k-1},\alpha_k) - \hat{x}(t/\nu_k^t,\gamma_{k-1}] \cdot [\hat{x}(t/\nu_k^t,\gamma_{k-1},\alpha_k) - \hat{x}(t/\nu_k^t,\gamma_{k-1})]^T\}p(\alpha_k/\nu_k^t,\gamma_{k-1})d\alpha_k \tag{7b}$$

where

$$P_x(t/\nu_k^t,\gamma_{1-1},\alpha_k) = E\{[x(t) - \hat{x}(t/\nu_k^t,\gamma_{k-1},\alpha_k)] \cdot [\hat{x}(t) - \hat{x}(t/\nu_k^t,\gamma_{k-1},\alpha_k)]^T/\nu_k^t,\gamma_{k-1},\alpha_k\}$$

The a-posteriori probability $p(\alpha_k/\nu_k^t,\gamma_{k-1}) \equiv p(\theta,\beta_k/\nu_k^t/\gamma_{k-1})$ is given by

$$p(\alpha_k/\nu_k^t,\gamma_{k=1}) = \frac{\Lambda(\nu_k^t/\gamma_{k-1},\alpha_k)p(\alpha_k/\gamma_{k-1})}{\int \Lambda(\nu_k^t/\gamma_{k-1},\alpha_k)p(\alpha_k/\gamma_{k-1})d\alpha_k} \tag{8}$$

where

$$\Lambda(\nu_k^t/\gamma_{k-1},\alpha_k) \equiv \exp\{\int_{t_{k-1}}^t \hat{h}_a^T(x_a(\sigma),\sigma/\nu_k^\sigma,\gamma_{k-1},\alpha_k)R^{-1}(\sigma)z(\sigma)d\sigma - \frac{1}{2}\int_{t_{k-1}}^t \|\hat{h}_a(x_a(\sigma),\sigma/\nu_k^\sigma,\gamma_{k-1},\alpha_k\|^2_{R^{-1}(\sigma)} d\sigma\}$$

$$= \begin{cases} \exp\{\int_{t_{k-1}}^{t_k} \hat{x}^T(\sigma/\nu_k^\sigma,\gamma_{k-1},\theta,\beta_k = 1)H^T(\sigma,\theta)R^{-1}(\sigma)z(\sigma)d\sigma \\ \quad - \frac{1}{2}\int_{t_{k-1}}^t \|H(\sigma,\theta)\hat{x}(\sigma/\nu_k^\sigma,\gamma_{k-1},\theta,\beta_k = 1)\|^2_{R^{-1}(\sigma)} d\sigma\} & \text{for } \alpha_k = [\theta^T \vdots 1]^T \\ 1 & \text{for } \alpha_k = [\theta^T \vdots 0]^T \end{cases} \tag{9}$$

and $p(\alpha/\gamma_{k-1})$ is available from the previous baud (previous iteration).

Specifically, $p(\alpha/\gamma_{k-1})$ decomposes into

$$p(\alpha/\gamma_{k-1}) = p(\theta/\gamma_{k-1})\; p\;(\beta_k) \tag{10a}$$

where

$$p(\beta_k) = p(\beta_k = 0)\,\delta\,(\beta_k) + p(\beta_k = 1)\,\delta\,(\beta_k - 1). \tag{10b}$$

The optimal mse estimate of θ, namely $\hat{\theta}(t/\nu_k^t,\gamma_{k-1}) \equiv E[\theta/\nu_k^t,\nu_{k-1}]$ is given by

$$\hat{\theta}(t/\nu_k^t,\gamma_{k-1}) = \frac{\hat{\theta}(k-1/\gamma_{k-1}) + \rho \int \theta\, \Lambda(\nu_k^t/\gamma_{k-1},\theta,\beta_k = 1)\,p\,(\theta/\gamma_{k-1})d\theta}{1 + \rho \int \Lambda(\nu_k^t/\gamma_{k-1},\theta,\beta_k = 1)\,p\,(\theta/\gamma_{k-1})d\theta} \tag{11}$$

where $\rho \equiv \dfrac{p(\beta_k = 1)}{p(\beta_k = 0)}$ and $\hat{\theta}(k-1/\gamma_{k-1}) \equiv E[\theta/\gamma_{k-1}]$; the latter is available from the previous boud.

The optimal mse estimate $\hat{\beta}(t/\nu_k^t,\gamma_{k-1}) = p(\beta_k = 1/\nu_k^t,\gamma_{k-1})$ used for decision-making, is given by

$$\hat{\beta}\;(t/\nu_k^t,\gamma_{k-1}) = \frac{\rho \int \Lambda(\nu_k^t/\gamma_{k-1},\theta,\beta_k = 1)\,p\,(\theta/\gamma_{k-1})d\theta}{1 + \rho \int \Lambda(\nu_k^t/\gamma_{k-1},\theta,\beta_k = 1)\,p\,(\theta/\gamma_{k-1})d\theta} \tag{12}$$

where $p\,(\theta\,|\gamma_{k-1}) \equiv p\,(\theta\,|\nu_{k-1},\gamma_{k-2})$ obtained from $p\,(\theta\,|\nu_{k-1}^t,\gamma_{k-2})$ the latter evaluated at $t = t_{k-1}$. Moreover, $p(\theta\,|\,\nu_{k-1}^t,\gamma_{k-2}) = \int p(\theta,\beta_{k-1}|\nu_k^t,\gamma_{k-2})\cdot d\beta_{k-1}$ and its explicit expression is

$$p(\theta\,|\,\nu_{k-1}^t,\gamma_{k-2}) = \frac{1 + \rho\,\Lambda\,(\nu_{k-1}^t\,|\,\gamma_{k-2},\theta,\beta_{k-1} = 1)}{1 + \rho \int \Lambda\,(\nu_{k-1}^t|\gamma_{k-2},\theta,\beta_{k-1} = 1)\;p\;(\theta\,|\,\gamma_{k-2})d\,\theta}\cdot p(\theta/\gamma_{k-2}) \tag{13}$$

In the above equations t is contained in the interval $t_{k-1} \leq t \leq t_k$.

Proof: The proof is based on Lainiotis' "partition theorem" [4]. It is given in [5], and hence is omitted.

The following remarks on the interpretation, significance and meaning of the results of theorem I, as well as on their relationship to previous work, are pertinent:

a. From Equation (12) it is seen that the statistic sufficient for optimal detection, namely $\hat{\beta}(t/\nu_k^t,\gamma_{k-1})$ is given by

$$\hat{\beta}(t/\nu_k^t,\gamma_{k-1}) = \frac{\Lambda(\nu_k^t/\gamma_{k-1})}{1+\Lambda(\nu_k^t/\gamma_{k-1})} \tag{14}$$

where $\Lambda(\nu_k^t/\gamma_{k-1}) \equiv \rho \int \Lambda(\nu_k^t/\gamma_{k-1},\theta,\beta_k = 1)p(\theta/\gamma_{k-1})d\theta$ is a generalized likelihood ratio for optimal, Bayesian, multi-shot, compound detection. As such it is more general than Kailath's [6] likelihood ratio, the latter being applicable to classical hypothesis testing, namely single-shot, simple hypothesis testing without consideration of prior probabilities.

Moreover, for known θ, namely for known system models, $p(\theta/\gamma_{k-1}) = \delta(\theta - \theta^*)$ and the decision statistic takes the simple form.

$$\hat{\beta}(t/\nu_k^t,\gamma_{k-1}) = \frac{\rho\Lambda(\nu_k^t/\gamma_{k-1},\theta^*,\beta_k = 1)}{1+\rho\Lambda(\nu_k^t/\gamma_{k-1},\theta^*,\beta_k = 1)} \tag{15}$$

where the likelihood ratio $\rho\Lambda(\nu_k^t/\gamma_{k-1},\theta^*,\beta_k = 1)$ has the same functional form (given in Equation (9)) as Kailath's [6] likelihood ratio, although the former is applicable to the more general Bayesian, multi-shot detection problem.

b. The adaptive detection/pattern recognition problem, as indicated above, may be viewed as joint detection (i.e. β_k), state-estimation (i.e. $x(t)$), and system identification or modeling (i.e. θ). Moreover, it was shown that adaptive detection may be put into the framework of nonlinear estimation and hence constitutes a subclass of nonlinear estimation problems.

c. From theorem I, we note that the adaptive realization of the optimal nonlinear estimate is given in terms of the α_k-conditional (model and hypothesis conditional) state-vector estimates $\hat{x}(t/\nu_k^t,\gamma_{k-1},\alpha_k)$ and the a-posteriori model and hypothesis probability density $p(\alpha_k/\nu_k^t,\gamma_{k-1})$. The latter is in turn specified by a continuum of likelihood ratios (LR) $\Lambda(\nu_k^t/\gamma_{k-1},\theta,\beta_k = 1)$, each of which is the LR for the detection problem

$$\begin{aligned} H_1&: \; z(t) = H(t,\theta)x(t) + v(t) \\ H_0&: \; z(t) = v(t) \end{aligned} \tag{16}$$

for $\underline{\theta}$ a specified admissible value.

This leads us to the conclusion that, in essence, system identification or modeling (learning of θ) is equivalent to multi-hypothesis testing with a continuum of hypotheses, corresponding to each possible model indexed by θ. Note moreover, that these LRs' are given in the canonical causal estimator-correlator form of Kailath [6] that renders them particularly well-suited to interpretation and approximation.

d. Note that in theorem I, a performance measure, namely the conditional state-error covariance matrix, is also given. Such performance measure is very valuable. Several pertinent comments on it will be given at a more appropriate point in this section.

From Equations (8), (9), and (10), applying elementary probability operations, we obtain readily $p(\theta \mid \nu_k^t, \gamma_{k-1}), p(\theta \mid \nu_k^t, \gamma_{k-1}, \beta_k = 1) \equiv p_1(\theta \mid \nu_k^t, \gamma_{k-1})$. They are given by

$$p(\theta \mid \nu_k^t, \gamma_{k-1}) = \frac{1 + \rho \Lambda(\nu_k^t \mid \gamma_{k-1}, \theta, \beta_{k=1})}{1 + \rho \int \Lambda(\nu_k^t \mid \gamma_{k-1}, \theta, \beta_{k=1}) p(\theta \mid \gamma_{k-1}) d\theta} p(\theta \mid \gamma_{k-1}) \tag{17a}$$

and

$$p_1(\theta \mid \nu_k^t, \gamma_{k-1}) = \frac{\Lambda(\nu_k^t \mid \gamma_{k-1}, \theta, \beta_{k=1})}{\int \Lambda(\nu_k^t \mid \gamma_{k-1}, \theta, \beta_{k=1}) p(\theta \mid \gamma_{k-1}) d\theta} p(\theta \mid \gamma_{k-1})$$

Evaluation of the nonlinear estimates requires knowledge of the conditional state-vector estimates $\hat{x}(t/\nu_k^t, \gamma_{k-1}, \beta_k = 1)$, and $\hat{x}(k-1/\gamma_{k-1}, \theta)$. Algorithms for their evaluation are given in the following theorem:

Theorem II:

$$\hat{x}(t/\nu_k^t, \gamma_{k-1}, \theta, \beta_k = 1) = \hat{x}_o(t/\nu_k^t, \theta) + [\phi(t, t_{k-1}, \theta) + A(t, \theta)]$$

$$\cdot \frac{\int x_{k-1} p(x_{k-1}/\gamma_{k-1}, \theta) \exp[-\frac{1}{2} \| x_{k-1} - V(t,\theta) M(t,\theta) \|^2_{V^{-1}(t,\theta)}] dx_{k-1}}{\int p(x_{k-1}/\gamma_{k-1}, \theta) \exp[-\frac{1}{2} \| x_{k-1} - V(t,\theta) M(t,\theta) \|^2_{V^{-1}(t,\theta)}] dx_{k-1}} \tag{18}$$

where

$$\frac{d\hat{x}_o(t/\nu_k^t, \theta)}{dt} = F(t,\theta)\hat{x}_o(t/\nu_k^t, \theta) + P_o(t/\theta) H^T(t,\theta) R^{-1}(t) [z(t) - H(t,\theta)\hat{x}_o(t/\nu_k^t, \theta)] \tag{19a}$$

with initial condition $\hat{x}_o(t_{k-1}/\theta) = \hat{x}_o(t_{k-1}) = 0$

$$\frac{dP_o(t/\theta)}{dt} = F(t,\theta)P_o(t/\theta) + P_o(t/\theta)F^T(t,\theta) - P_o(t/\theta)H^T(t,\theta)R^{-1}(t)H(t,\theta)P_o(t/\theta) + G(t,\theta)G^T(t,\theta) \tag{19b}$$

with initial condition $P_o(t_{k-1}/\theta) = P_o(t_{k-1}) = 0$

and

$$A(t,\theta) = -\int_{t_{k-1}}^{t} \phi_k(t,s;\theta)P_o(s/\theta)H^T(s,\theta)R^{-1}(s)\phi(s,t_{k-1};\theta)\,ds \tag{20a}$$

$$V^{-1}(t,\theta) = \int_{t_{k-1}}^{t} [A(s,\theta) + \phi(s,t_{k-1};\theta)]^T H^T(s,\theta)R^{-1}(s)H(s,\theta)[A(s,\theta) + \phi(s,t_{k-1} + \phi(s,t_{k-1};\theta)]\,ds \tag{20b}$$

$$M(t,\theta) = \int_{t_{k-1}}^{t} [A(s,\theta) + \phi(s,t_{k-1};\theta)]^T H^T(s,\theta)R^{-1}(s)[z(s) - H(s,\theta)\hat{x}_o(s,\theta)]\,ds \tag{20c}$$

where $\phi(t,s;\theta)$ is the transition matrix of $F(t,\theta)$, and $\phi_k(t,s;\theta)$ is the transition matrix of $[F(t,\theta) - P_o(t/\theta)H^T(t,\theta)R^{-1}(t)H(t,\theta)]$.

To evaluate Equation (18) we need an expression for $p(x_{k-1}/\gamma_{k-1},\theta)$. This is given below:

$$p(x_{k-1}/\gamma_{k-1},\theta) = p(x_{k-1}/\gamma_{k-2},\theta)p(\beta_{k-1} = \theta/\gamma_{k-1},\theta) + p(x_{k-1}/\nu_{k-1},\gamma_{k-2},\theta,\beta_{k-1} = 1)\,p(\beta_{k-1} = 1/\gamma_{k-1},\theta) \tag{21}$$

where

$$p(x_{k-1}/\gamma_{k-2},\theta) = (2\pi)^{-\frac{m}{2}}|\Gamma_{k-1}(k-1,\theta)|^{-\frac{1}{2}}\int p_{r_{k-1}}(\sigma)\exp[-\tfrac{1}{2}\|x_{k-1} - \sigma\|^2_{\Gamma_{k-1}^{-1}(k-1,\theta)}]d\sigma \tag{22a}$$

$$\Gamma_{k-1}(k-1,\theta) \equiv \int_{t_{k-2}}^{t_{k-1}}\phi(t_{k-1},\tau;\theta)G(\tau,\theta)G^T(\tau,\theta)\phi^T(t_{k-1},\tau;\theta)dr \tag{22b}$$

and

$$p_{r_{k-1}}(\sigma) \equiv \frac{P_{x_{k-2}}[\phi^{-1}(t_{k-1}, t_{k-2}; \theta)\sigma]}{|\phi^{-1}(t_{k-1}, t_{k-2}; \theta)|} \tag{22c}$$

where $P_{x_{k-2}} \equiv p(x_{k-2}/\gamma_{k-2}, \theta)$, the latter given from the previous iteration (previous boud).

The a-posteriori density $p(x_{k-1}/\gamma_{k-1}, \theta, \beta_{k-1} = 1) = p(x_{k-1}/\nu_{k-1}, \gamma_{k-2}, \theta, \beta_{k-1} = 1)$ is given the closed form expression

$$p(x_{k-1}/\gamma_{k-1}, \theta, \beta_{k-1} = 1) =$$

$$= \{ | P_o^{-1}(t_{k-1}/\theta) |^{\frac{1}{2}} \int_{t_{k-2}}^{t_{k-1}} p(x_{k-2}/\gamma_{k-2}, \theta) \exp[-\frac{1}{2} \| x_{k-2} - V(t_{k-1}, \theta) M(t_{k-1},$$

$$\theta)\|^2_{V^{-1}(t_{k-1}, \theta)} - \frac{1}{2} \| x_{k-1} - \phi(t_{k-1}, t_{k-2}; \theta) - A(t_{k-1}, \theta) x_{k-2} - \hat{x}_o(t_{k-1}/\gamma_{k-1}; \theta \|_{P_o^{-1}(t_{k-1}/\theta)}]$$

$$\cdot \, dx_{k-2} \}^{-1} \{ (2\pi)^{\frac{n}{2}} \int_{t_{k-2}}^{t_{k-1}} p(x_{k-2}/\gamma_{k-2}, \theta) \exp] - \frac{1}{2} \| x_{k-2} - V(t_{k-1}, \theta) M(t_{k-1}, \theta)$$

$$\|^2_{V^{-1}(t_{k-1}, \theta)}] \, dx_{k-2} \}^{-1} \tag{23}$$

The a-posteriori probabilities $p(\beta_{k-1} = 0/\gamma_{k-1}/\theta)$ and $p(\beta_{k-1} = 1/\gamma_{k-1}, \theta)$ are obtained from Equation (8) in a straightforward fashion. They are:

$$p(\beta_{k-1} = 0/\gamma_{k-1}, \theta) = 1 - p(\beta_{k-1} = 1/\gamma_{k-1}, \theta)$$

$$= \frac{1}{1 + \rho \Lambda (\nu_{k-1}/\gamma_{k-2}, \theta, \beta_{k-1} = 1)} \tag{24}$$

Whenever t appears in the above equations, it is contained in the interval $t_{k-1} \leq t \leq t_k$.

Proof: The proof is given in detail in [5].

Utilizing theorems I-II, explicit expressions for the state-vector estimate and the corresponding error-covariance matrix $P_x(.)$ have been obtained. They are given in the next theorem:

Theorem III:

$$\hat{x}(t/\nu_k^t,\gamma_{k-1}) =$$

$$\{\int \phi(t,t_{k-1};\theta)\hat{x}(k-1/\gamma_{k-1},\theta)p(\theta/\gamma_{k-1})d\theta + \rho \int \hat{x}(t/\nu_k^t,\gamma_{k-1},\theta,\beta_k = 1)\cdot$$

$$\Lambda(\nu^t/\gamma_{k-1},\theta,\beta_k = 1)p(\theta/\gamma_{k-1})d\theta\} \{1 + \rho \int \Lambda(\nu_k^t/\gamma_{k-1},\theta,\beta_k = 1)\cdot$$

$$p(\theta/\gamma_{k-1})d\theta\}^{-1} \tag{25}$$

where $\hat{x}(k-1/\gamma_{k-1},\theta)$ is obtained using Equation (18), and it is available from the previous iteration. It is given as

$$\hat{x}(k-1/\gamma_{k-1},\theta) = \hat{x}(k-1/\gamma_{k-2},\theta)p(\beta_{k-1} = 0/\gamma_{k-1},\theta) +$$

$$\hat{x}(k-1/\gamma_{k-1},\theta,\beta_{k-1} = 1)p(\beta_{k-1} = 1/\gamma_{k-1},\theta). \tag{26}$$

The conditional state-vector error covariance matrix is given by

$$P_x(t/\nu_k^t,\gamma_{k-1}) =$$

$$\{\int \{P_x(t/\gamma_{k-1},\theta) + [\hat{x}(t/\gamma_{k-1},\theta) - \hat{x}(t/\nu_k^t,\gamma_{k-1})][\hat{x}(t/\nu_k^t,\gamma_{k-1},\theta) - \hat{x}(t/\nu_k^t,\gamma_{k-1})]^T$$

$$\cdot p(\theta/\gamma_{k-1}\} d\theta\} \{1 + \rho \int \Lambda(\nu_k^t/\gamma_{k-1},\theta,\beta_k = 1)p(\theta/\gamma_{k-1})d\theta\}^{-1}$$

$$+\{p\int \{P_x(t/\nu_k^t,\gamma_{k-1},\theta,\beta_k = 1) + [\hat{x}(t/\nu_k^t,\gamma_{k-1},\theta,\beta_k = 1) - \hat{x}(t/\nu_k^t,\gamma_{k-1})]^T[\hat{x}(t/\gamma_{k-1},\theta)$$

$$- \hat{x}(t/\nu_k^t,\gamma_{k-1})]^T p(\theta/\gamma_{k-1})\}^{-1}\cdot \{1 + \rho \int \Lambda(\nu_k^t/\gamma_{k-1},\theta,\beta_k = 1)p(\theta/\gamma_{k-1})d\theta\}^{-1} \tag{27}$$

where

$$\hat{x}(t/\gamma_{k-1},\theta) = \phi(t,t_{k-1};\theta)\hat{x}(k-1/\gamma_{k-1},\theta) \tag{28a}$$

$$P_x(t/\gamma_{k-1},\theta) = \phi(t,t_{k-1};\theta)P(k-1/\gamma_{k-1},\theta)\phi^T(t,t_{k-1};\theta) + \Gamma_k(t,\theta) \tag{28b}$$

$$P_x(t/\nu_k^t,\gamma_{k-1},\theta,\beta_k = 1) = P_o(t/\theta) + [\phi(t,t_{k-1};\theta) + A(t,\theta)]\cdot$$

$$\frac{\int x_{k-1}x_{k-1}^T p(x_{k-1}/\gamma_{k-1},\theta)\exp[-\frac{1}{2}\|x_{k-1} - V(t,\theta)M(t,\theta)\|^2_{V^{-1}(t,\theta)}]dx_{k-1}}{\int p(x_{k-1}/\gamma_{k-1},\theta)\exp[-\frac{1}{2}\|x_{k-1} - V(t,\theta)M(t,\theta)\|^2_{V^{-1}(t,\theta)}]dx_{k-1}}\cdot$$

$$\cdot[\phi(t,t_{k-1};\theta)+A(t,\theta)]^T-[\phi(t,t_{k-1};\theta)+A(t,\theta)]\cdot$$

$$\left\{\frac{\int x_{k-1}p(x_{k-1}/\gamma_{k-1},\theta)\exp[-\frac{1}{2}\|x_{k-1}-V(t,\theta)M(t,\theta)\|^2_{V^{-1}(t,\theta)}]dx_{k-1}}{\int p(x_{k-1}/\gamma_{k-1})\exp[-\frac{1}{2}\|x_{k-1}-V(t,\theta)M(t,\theta)\|^2_{V^{-1}(t,\theta)}]dx_{k-1}}\right\}$$

$$\left\{\frac{\int x^T_{k-1}p(x_{k-1}/\gamma_{k-1},\theta)\exp[-\frac{1}{2}\|x_{k-1}-V(t,\theta)M(t,\theta)\|^2_{V^{-1}(t,\theta)}]dx_{k-1}}{\int p(x_{k-1}/\gamma_{k-1})\exp[-\frac{1}{2}\|x_{k-1}-V(t,\theta)M(t,\theta)\|^2_{V^{-1}(t,\theta)}]dx_{k-1}}\right\}\cdot$$

$$[\phi(t,t_{k-1};\theta)+A(t,\theta)]^T \tag{28c}$$

and $t_{k-1}\leq t\leq t_k$.

The other quantities involved above have been defined previously. They are available either from the previous iteration or from the nonlinear state-vector filter.

Proof: The proof is given in detail in [5], and hence is omitted.

The following comments on the results of theorems II-III are pertinent.

a: From Equations (18 and 25), it is seen that the optimal nonlinear estimator has been partitioned into a linear non-adaptive part, namely that described in Equations (19), consisting of ordinary Kalman-Bucy filters matched to each admissible value of θ, and several nonlinear parts. The first is that associated with the integral part of Equation (18). This reflects the nongaussian nature of the initial state-vector $x(t_{k-1})\equiv x_{k-1}$ for the kth boud. The second nonlinear part refers to $\hat{x}(k-1/\gamma_{k-1},\theta)$ in Equation (25), where $\hat{x}(k-1/\gamma_{k-1})$ is nonlinear because of uncertainty as to which hypotheses caused the past data. Finally the last nonlinearity is introduced by the a-posteriori density weighting of the α_k-conditional estimates. The latter is best seen from Equations (7-8).

Comparing the present results for the unsupervised learning case to the supervised learning results of [1], we see that the price of unsupervised learning is increased system complexity evidenced by the additional nonlinearities, namely the first two nonlinearities mentioned above.

b: The conditional error-covariance matrix $P_x(\cdot/\cdot)$ as given in Equation (27) consists of quantities available from the adaptive estimator or from the previous iteration. As such, $P_x(\cdot/\cdot)$ is useful for the evaluation of adaptive estimator performance as well as for the comparison of adaptive vs. non-adaptive procedures. Note that $\Delta P_x(t/\nu_k^t,\gamma_{k-1},\theta) \equiv [\hat{x}(t/\nu_k^t,\gamma_{k-1},\theta,\beta_k) - \hat{x}(t/\nu_k^t,\gamma_{k-1})]$. $\Delta P_x(t/\nu_k^t,\gamma_{k-1},\theta) \equiv [\hat{x}(t/\nu_k^t,\gamma_{k-1},\theta,\beta_k) - \hat{x}(t/\nu_k^t,\gamma_{k-1})]^T$ represents a measure of performance degradation due to processing the data from a known model by an adaptive filter instead of by the Kalman-Bucy filter matched to the correct model and the correct hypothesis. Namely, $\Delta P_x(\cdot/\cdot)$ represents the price of model and hypothesis or measurement uncertainty.

III. Approximate Recursive Unsupervised Learning Algorithms

The realization of the adaptive (nonlinear) estimator and the associated computational requirements depend integrally on the range of admissible values for θ, namely on whether the range is discrete or continuous. However, in most applications the range is continuous resulting in excessive computational requirements. One approach in alleviating this problem is to approximate the continuous parameter space with a finite set of quantized points. Such quantization is reasonable in view of the fact that quantization is inevitable in any physical realization of a system, e.g. via a digital computer with its round-off errors etc. So that either because the range of θ is discrete or because of quantization of a continuous range, $p(\theta)$ is given by $\sum_i^{N_\theta} p(\theta_i)\,\delta(\theta-\theta_i)$. For such $p(\theta)$ all integrations with respect to θ in theorems I-III become sums of N_θ terms each of which corresponds to a particular value of θ, θ_i, $i = 1,2,\ldots,N_\theta$. The results for this case are summarized in the following corollary.

Corollary II:

$$\hat{x}(t/\nu_k^t,\gamma_{k-1}) = \sum_{i=1}^{N_\theta} \frac{\{\phi(t,t_{k-1},\theta_i)\hat{x}(k-1/\gamma_{k-1},\theta_i) + \rho\,\Lambda(\nu_k^t/\gamma_{k-1},\theta_i,\beta_k=1)\hat{x}(t/\nu_k^t,\gamma_{k-1},\theta_i,\beta_k=1)\}\cdot}{1+\rho\sum_{i=1}^{} \Lambda(\nu_k^t/\gamma_{k-1},\theta_i,\beta_k=1)p(\theta_i/\gamma_{k-1})}\, p(\theta_i/\gamma_{k-1}) \tag{29}$$

$$P_x(t/\nu_k^t,\gamma_{k-1} = [1+\rho\sum_{i=1}^{N_\theta} \Lambda(\nu_k^t/\gamma_{k-1},\theta_i,\beta_k=1)\,p(\theta_i/\gamma_{k-1})]^{-1}\sum_{i=1}^{N_\theta}\{[P_x(t/\gamma_{k-1},\theta_i) +$$

$$[\hat{x}(t/\gamma_{k-1},\theta_i) - \hat{x}(t/\nu_k^t,\gamma_{k-1})][\hat{x}(t/\gamma_{k-1},\theta_i) - \hat{x}(t/\nu_k^t,\gamma_{k-1})]^T] +$$

$$\rho[P_x(t/\nu_k^t,\gamma_{k-1},\theta_i,\beta_k = 1) + [\hat{x}(t/\nu_k^t,\gamma_{k-1},\theta_i,\beta_k = 1) - \hat{x}(t/\nu_k^t,\gamma_{k-1})] \cdot$$

$$\rho[P_x(t/\nu_k^t,\gamma_{k-1},\theta_i,\beta_k = 1) + [\hat{x}(t/\nu_k^t,\gamma_{k-1},\theta_i,\beta_k = 1) - \hat{x}(t/\nu_k^t,\gamma_{k-1})]^T] \cdot$$

$$\Lambda(\nu_k^t/\gamma_{k-1},\theta_i)]\}p(\theta_i/\gamma_{k-1}) \tag{30}$$

$$\hat{\theta}(t/\nu_k^t,\gamma_{k-1}) = \frac{\hat{\theta}(k-1/\gamma_{k-1}) + \rho \sum_{i=1}^{N_\theta} \theta_i \Lambda(\nu_k^t/\gamma_{k-1},\theta_i,\beta_k = 1)p(\theta_i/\gamma_{k-1})}{1 + \rho \sum_{i=1}^{N_\theta} \Lambda(\nu_k^t/\gamma_{k-1},\theta_i,\beta_k = 1)p(\theta_i/\gamma_{k-1})} \tag{31}$$

and

$$\hat{\beta}(t/\nu_k^t,\gamma_{k-1}) = \frac{\rho \sum_{i=1}^{N_\theta} \Lambda(\nu_k^t/\gamma_{k-1},\theta_i,\beta_k = 1)p(\theta_i/\gamma_{k-1})}{1 + \rho \sum_{i=1}^{N_\theta} \Lambda(\nu_k^t/\gamma_{k-1},\theta_i,\beta_k = 1)p(\theta_i/\gamma_{k-1})} \tag{32}$$

The other equations of theorems I-III, remain unchanged except that θ takes values θ_i, $i = 1,2, \ldots, N_\theta$.

Proof: The proof, based on the fact that if $p(\theta) \simeq \sum_{i=1}^{N_\theta} p(\theta_i)\delta(\theta - \theta_i)$ then $p(\theta/\gamma_{k-1}) \simeq \sum_{i=1}^{N_\theta} p(\theta_i/\gamma_{k-1})\delta(\theta - \theta_i)$ also, is straightforward. Hence it will be omitted.

It was shown earlier in this section that system identification constitutes in essence a hypothesis testing problem with a continuum of hypotheses. Parameter space quantization, however, has reduced the problem to one with a finite set of hypotheses. In this context one may view system identification as a sequence of hypothesis testing problem each corresponding to testing for the model indexed by parameter value θ_i, $i = 1,2, \ldots, N_\theta$.

It can be seen that a major difficulty with the proposed fixed quantization procedure is that the number of quantization levels increases exponentially with the dimension of the θ-space, so that fine quantization, although it results in very nearly optimal estimation, requires a large number of model conditional filters, while coarse quantization results in suboptimal extimation. To alleviate the dimensionality problem, Sengbush and Lainiotis [7] proposed recursive, on-line, quantization procedures that reduce drastically the required number of filters without sacrificing the accuracy of parameter estimation.

Another major source of computational complexity for the optimal estimator is the nonlinear term in Equation (18). This term arises from the fact that the initial state-vector x_{k-1} of the kth boud, $k = 1,2, \ldots,$ is nongaussian i.e. $p(x_{k-1}/\gamma_{k-1},\theta_i)$ is nongaussian. However, this difficulty also may be readily circumvented as follows:

Using Wiener's theorem on approximation [8], the nongaussian density $p(x_{k-1}/\gamma_{k-1},\theta_i)$ may be approximated as closely as desired by a sum of normal densities (i.e. by a "mixture" density), namely

$$p(x_{k-1}/\gamma_{k-1},\theta_i) \simeq \sum_{j=1}^{N_x} p_{k-1}(j,\theta_i) \frac{1}{(2\pi)^{\frac{n}{2}} \mid P_x(j,k-1,\theta_i) \mid^{\frac{1}{2}}} \cdot \exp\{-\frac{1}{2} \| x_{k-1} - \hat{x}_{k-1}(j,\theta_i) \|^2_{P_x^{-1}(j,k-1,\theta_i)}\}$$

where $\hat{x}_{k-1}(j,\theta_i)$ and $P_x(j,k-1,\theta_i)$ are the mean and covariance matrix of the jth normal density in the mixture and $p_{k-1}(j,\theta_i)$ is the jth "mixing" probability.

Define $\eta \equiv [\hat{x}^T_{k-1}(\theta_i) \vdots \pi_i^T]^T$, where π_i is the vector of elements sufficient to completely define $P_x(k-1,\theta_i)$. Then, to the accuracy of the above approximation, η takes values from the set $\{\eta_1, \eta_2, \ldots, \eta_{N_x}\}$, where η_j corresponds to $\{\hat{x}_{k-1}(j,\theta_i), P_x(j,k-1,\theta_i)\}$, with a-priori probability $P_{k-1}(j,\theta_i)$, $j = 1,2, \ldots, N_x$. The desired results may now be obtained by observing that the dynamical equations at the kth boud are completely defined if the value of the augmented parameter vector $\alpha \equiv [\theta^T \vdots \eta^T \vdots \beta_k]^T$ is given. Hence, by using α, the problem has been imbedded into the adaptive estimation framework. Note moreover that $\alpha \in \{\alpha_i, i = 1,2, \ldots [2N_x N_\theta]\}$, since $\beta_k \in \{1,0\}$, $\theta \in \{\theta_1, \theta_2, \ldots, \theta_{N_\theta}\}$, and $\eta \in \{\eta_1, \eta_2, \ldots, \eta_{N_x}\}$.

The desired results are given in the following corollary.

Corollary III:

$$\hat{x}(t/\nu_k^t,\gamma_{k-1}) = \sum_{i=1}^{N_\theta} \sum_{j=1}^{N_x} \sum_{\ell=0}^{1} \hat{x}(t/\nu_k^t,\gamma_{k-1},\theta_i,\eta_j,\ell) p(\theta_i,\eta_j,\ell/\nu_k^t,\gamma_{k-1}) \quad (33a)$$

and the corresponding state error-covariance matrix is

$$P_x(t/\nu_k^t,\gamma_{k-1}) =$$

$$\sum_{i=1}^{N_\theta} \sum_{j=1}^{N_x} \sum_{\ell=0}^{1} \{P_x(t/\nu_k^t,\gamma_{k-1},\theta_i,\eta_j,\ell) + [\hat{x}(t/\nu_k^t,\gamma_{k-1},\theta_i,\eta_j,\ell) - \hat{x}(t/\nu_k^t,\gamma_{k-1})] \cdot$$

$$[\hat{x}(t/\nu_k^t,\gamma_{k-1},\theta_i,\eta_j,\ell) - \hat{x}(t/\nu_k^t,\gamma_{k-1})]^T\} p(\theta_i,\eta_j,\ell/\nu_k^t,\gamma_{k-1}) \quad (33b)$$

where

$$\hat{x}(t/\nu_k^t,\gamma_{k-1},\theta_i,\eta_j,\ell) \equiv \hat{x}(t/\nu_k^t,\gamma_{k-1},\theta=\theta_i,\eta=\eta_j,\beta_k=\ell)$$

and

$$p(\theta_i,\eta_j,\ell/\nu_k^t,\gamma_{k-1}) = p(\theta=\theta_i,\eta=\eta_j,\beta_k=\ell/\nu_k^t,\gamma_{k-1})$$

$$= \frac{\Lambda(\gamma_k^t/\gamma_{k-1},\theta_i,\eta_j,\ell)}{\sum_{i=1}^{N_\theta}\sum_{j=1}^{N_x}\sum_{\ell=0}^{1}\Lambda(\nu_k^t/\gamma_{k-1},\theta_i,\eta_j,\ell)p(\theta_i,\eta_j,\ell/\gamma_{k-1})}\,p(\theta_i,\eta_j,\ell/\gamma_{k-1}) \tag{33c}$$

where

$$\Lambda(\nu_k^t/\gamma_{k-1},\theta_i,\eta_j,\ell)$$

$$\equiv \exp\left\{\int_{t_{k-1}}^{t}\hat{x}^T(\tau/\nu_k^\tau,\gamma_{k-1},\theta_i,\eta_j,\ell)\cdot\ell\cdot H^T(\tau,\theta_i)R^{-1}(\tau)z(\tau)d\tau\right. \tag{33d}$$

$$\left.-\frac{1}{2}\int_{t_{k-1}}^{t}\|\ell\cdot H(\tau,\theta_i)\hat{x}(\tau/\nu_k^\tau,\gamma_{k-1},\theta_i,\eta_j,\ell)\|^2_{R^{-1}(\tau)}d\tau\right\}$$

Moreover, the decision statistic $\hat{\beta}(t/\nu_k^t,\gamma_{k-1})$ is given by

$$\hat{\beta}(t/\nu_k^t,\gamma_{k-1}) = \frac{\rho\sum_{i=1}^{N_\theta}\sum_{j=1}^{N_x}\Lambda(\nu_k^t/\gamma_{k-1},\theta_i,\eta_j,\ell=1\,\rho_{k-1}(j,\theta_i)\rho(\theta_i/\gamma_{k-1})}{1+\rho\sum_{i=1}^{N_\theta}\sum_{j=1}^{N_x}\Lambda(\nu_k^t/\gamma_{k-1},\theta_i,\eta_j,\ell=1)\,P_{k-1}(j,\theta_i)\,P(\theta_i/\gamma_{k-1})} \tag{34}$$

and the learning algorithm consists of the recursive updating of the a-posteriori density

$$p(\theta_i/\nu_k^t,\gamma_{k-1}) = \frac{1+\rho\sum_{j=1}^{N_x}P_{k-1}(j,\theta_i)\,\Lambda\,(\nu_k^t/\gamma_{k-1},\theta_i,\eta_j,\ell=1)}{1+\rho\sum_{i=1}^{N_\theta}\sum_{j=1}^{N_x}\Lambda\,(\nu_k^t/\gamma_{k-1},\theta_i,\eta_j,\ell=1)\,P_{k-1}(j,\theta_i)p(\theta_i/\gamma_{k-1})}\,p(\theta_i/\gamma_{k-1}) \tag{35a}$$

and the corresponding mse estimate of θ is given by

$$\hat{\theta}(t/\nu_k^t,\gamma_{k-1}) = \frac{\hat{\theta}(k-1/\gamma_{k-1}) + \rho \sum_{i=1}^{N_\theta} \sum_{j=1}^{N_x} \theta_i P_{k-1}(j,\theta_i)\, \Lambda(\nu_k^t/\gamma_{k-1},\theta_i,\eta_j,\ell=1) p(\theta_i/\gamma_{k-1})}{1 + \rho \sum_{i=1}^{N_\theta} \sum_{j=1}^{N_x} \Lambda(\nu_k^t/\gamma_{k-1},\theta_i,\eta_j,\ell=1)\, P_{k-1}(j,\theta_i)\, p(\theta_i/\gamma_{k-1})} \tag{35b}$$

The conditional state-vector estimate $\hat{x}(t/\nu_k^t,\gamma_{k-1},\theta_i,\eta_j,\ell)$ and the corresponding error-covariance matrix $P_x(t/\nu_k^t,\gamma_{k-1},\theta_i,\eta_j,\ell)$ are given by the Kalman-Bucy filter relations. Namely

$$\frac{d\hat{x}(t/\nu_k^t,\gamma_{k-1},\theta_i,\eta_j,\ell)}{dt} = F(t,\theta_i)\hat{x}(t/\nu_k^t,\gamma_{k-1},\theta_i,\eta_j,\ell) + P_x(t/\nu_k^t,\gamma_{k-1},\theta_i,\eta_j,\ell)$$
$$\cdot\, \ell H^T(t,\theta_i)R^{-1}(t)[z(t) - \ell H^T(t,\theta_i)\hat{x}(t/\nu_k^t,\gamma_{k-1},\theta_i,\eta_j,\ell)] \tag{36a}$$

with initial condition $\hat{x}(k-1/\gamma_{k-1},\theta_i,\eta_j,\ell) = \hat{x}_{k-1}(j,\theta_i)$

and

$$\frac{dP_x(t/\nu_k^t,\gamma_{k-1},\theta_i,\eta_j,\ell)}{dt} = F(t,\theta_i)P_x(t/\nu_k^t,\gamma_{k-1},\theta_i,\eta_j,\ell) + P_x(t/\nu_k^t,\gamma_{k-1},\theta_i,\eta_j,\ell)$$
$$\cdot\, F^T(t,\theta_i) + G(t,\theta_i)G^T(t,\theta_i) - P_x(t/\nu_k^t,\gamma_{k-1},\theta_i,\eta_j,\ell)\,\ell^2 H^T(t,\theta_i)R^{-1}(t)H(t,\theta_i)$$
$$\cdot\, P_x(t/\nu_k^t,\gamma_{k-1},\theta_i,\eta_j,\ell). \tag{36b}$$

with initial condition $P_x(t_{k-1}/\nu_k^t,\gamma_{k-1},\theta_i,\eta_j,\ell) = P_x(j,k-1,\theta_i)$.

The above equations are to be used in the kth boud, namely for $t_{k-1} \leq t \leq t_k$.

Proof: The proof is given in [5] and hence it is omitted.

The results contained in the above corollary are very fundamental in several respects. First, it is seen that by using the "mixture" approximation of $P(x_{k-1}/\gamma_{k-1},\theta_i)$, the optimal mean-square error estimator is partitioned into a bank of linear (Kalman-Bucy) filters and a non-linear part consisting of the a-posteriori probabilities $p(\theta_i,\eta_j,\ell/\nu_k^t,\gamma_{k-1})$. Namely, the "partition theorem" form for supervised learning [1] is true also under unsupervised learning. Moreover, the approximate estimator given in corollary II may be made as close to the optimal as one wishes by appropriately increasing the number of components in the mixture, i.e. by increasing N_X. The point can also be made that the approximation made in corollary II is inevitable in view of the fact that $p(x_{k-1}/\gamma_{k-1},\theta_i)$ is a non-reproducing density and hence it does not possess a sufficient statistic. As such storage of $p(x_{k-1}/\gamma_{k-1},\theta_i)$ requires infinite memory. However, by using the gaussian mixture density approximation, the storage of $p(x_{k-1}/\gamma_{k-1},\theta_i)$ reduces to the storage of the sufficient statistic $\{\eta_1,\eta_2,\ldots\eta_{N_X}; p_{k-1}(1,\theta_i),p_{k-1}(1,\theta_i),p_{k-1}(2,\theta_i)\ldots, p_{k-1}(N_X,\theta_i)\}$.

To further reduce the complexity of the unsupervised learning algorithms a simpler approximation is used for $p(x_{k-1}/\gamma_{k-1},\theta_i)$, namely, it is approximated by a single gaussian density

$$p(x_{k-1}/\gamma_{k-1},\theta_i) \simeq (2\pi)^{-\frac{n}{2}} \,|\, P_X(k-1/\gamma_{k-1},\theta_i)\,|^{-\frac{1}{2}}$$

$$\cdot\exp\{-\frac{1}{2}\,\|\, x_{k-1} - \hat{x}(k-1/\gamma_{k-1},\theta_i)\,\|^2 P_X^{-1}(k-1/\gamma_{k-1},\theta_i)\}$$

where $\hat{x}(k-1/\gamma_{k-1},\theta_i)$ and $P_X(k-1/\gamma_{k-1},\theta_i)$ are the model conditional state-vector estimate and the related error-covariance matrix. They are available from the previous boud. Specifically, they are given by

$$\hat{x}(k-1/\gamma_{k-1},\theta_i) = \hat{x}(k-1/\gamma_{k-1},\theta_i,\beta_{k-1}=0)p(\beta_{k-1}=0,\theta_i)$$
$$+\ \hat{x}(k-1/\gamma_{k-1},\theta_i,\beta_{k-1}=1)p(\beta_{k-1}=1/\gamma_{k-1},\theta_i)$$

and

$$P_X(k-1/\gamma_{k-1},\theta_i) = \{P_X(k-1/\gamma_{k-1},\theta_i,\beta_{k-1}=0)$$
$$+\ [\hat{x}(k-1/\gamma_{k-1},\theta_i,\beta_{k-1}=0) - \hat{x}(k-1/\gamma_{k-1},\theta_i)]$$
$$\cdot\ [\hat{x}(k-1/\gamma_{k-1},\theta_i,\beta_{k-1}=0) - \hat{x}(k-1/\gamma_{k-1},\theta_i)]^T\}$$
$$p(\beta_{k-1}=0/\gamma_{k-1},\theta_i) + \{P_X(k-1/\gamma_{k-1},\theta_i,\beta_{k-1}=1)$$
$$+\ [\hat{x}(k-1/\gamma_{k-1},\theta_i,\beta_{k-1}=1) - \hat{x}(k-1/\gamma_{k-1},\theta_i)]$$
$$\cdot\ [\hat{x}(k-1/\gamma_{k-1},\theta_i,\beta_{k-1}=1) - \hat{x}(k-1/\gamma_{k-1},\theta_i)]^T\}$$
$$\cdot\ p(\beta_{k-1}/\gamma_{k-1},\theta_i)$$

where all of the above quantities are available from the previous boud.

It is seen that in this approximation, the knowledge weaned from past observations is, effectively, contained in the initial conditions, $\hat{x}(k-1/\gamma_{k-1}, \theta_i)$ and $P_x(k-1/\gamma_{k-1},\theta_i)$, namely

$$\gamma_{k-1} \equiv \{\hat{x}(k-1/\gamma_{k-1},\theta_i);\ P_x(k-1/\gamma_{k-1},\theta_i);\ i=1,2,\ldots,N_\theta\}$$

The unsupervised learning recognition algorithm utilizing the above approximation procedure, is given in the following corollary.

Corollary IV:

The optimal state-vector estimate is

$$\hat{x}(t/\nu_k^t,\gamma_{k-1}) = \sum_{i=1}^{N_\theta} \sum_{\ell=0}^{1} \hat{x}(t/\nu_k^t,\gamma_{k-1},\theta_i,\ell)\, p(\theta_i,\ell/\nu_k^t,\gamma_{k-1}) \tag{37a}$$

and the corresponding error-covariance matrix is given by

$$\begin{aligned} P_x(t/\nu_k^t,\gamma_{k-1}) = \sum_{i=1}^{N_\theta} \sum_{\ell=0}^{1} \{ & P_x(t/\nu_k^t,\gamma_{k-1},\theta_i,\ell) + [\hat{x}(t/\nu_k^t,\gamma_{k-1},\theta_i,\ell) \\ & - \hat{x}(t/\nu_k^t,\gamma_{k-1})]\,[\hat{x}(t/\nu_k^t,\gamma_{k-1},\theta_i,\ell) \\ & - \hat{x}(t/\nu_k^t,\gamma_{k-1})]^T p(\theta_i,\ell/\nu_k^t,\gamma_{k-1}) \end{aligned} \tag{37b}$$

where

$$\hat{x}(t/\nu_k^t,\gamma_{k-1},\theta_i;\ell) \equiv \hat{x}(t/\nu_k^t,\gamma_{k-1},\theta=\theta_i,\beta_k=\ell)$$

and

$$p(\theta_i,\ell/\nu_k^t,\gamma_{k-1}) \equiv p[\theta=\theta_i,\beta_k=\ell/\nu_k^t,\gamma_{k-1}]$$

Moreover

$$p(\theta_i,\ell/\nu_k^t,\gamma_{k-1} = \frac{\Lambda(\nu_k^t/\gamma_{k-1},\theta_i,\ell}{\sum_{i=1}^{N_\theta}\sum_{\ell=0}^{1}\Lambda(\nu_k^t/\gamma_{k-1},\theta_i,\ell)p(\theta_i,\ell/\gamma_{k-1})}\, p(\theta_i,\ell/\gamma_{k-1}) \tag{37c}$$

where

$$\Lambda(\nu_k^t/\gamma_{k-1},\theta_i,\ell) \equiv \exp\{\int_{t_{k-1}}^{t} \hat{x}^t(\tau/\nu_k^\tau,\gamma_{k-1},\theta_i,\ell)\cdot \ell \cdot H^T(\tau,\theta_i)R^{-1}(\tau)z(\tau)d\tau$$

$$-\frac{1}{2}\int_{t_{k-1}}^{t} \| \ell \cdot H(\tau,\theta_i)\hat{x}(\tau/\nu_k^t,\nu_{k-1},\theta_i,\ell) \|^2_{R^{-1}(\tau)} d\tau\}$$

and

$$p(\theta_i,\ell/\gamma_{k-1}) = p(\theta_i/\gamma_{k-1})p(\beta_k = \ell)$$

The conditional state-vector estimate $\hat{x}(t/\nu_k^t,\gamma_{k-1},\theta_i,\ell)$ and the corresponding error-covariance matrix $P_x(t/\nu_k^t,\gamma_{k-1},\theta_i,\ell)$ are given by the Kalman Bucy filter relations given in Equations (36a-b), with initial conditions $\hat{x}(k-1/\gamma_{k-1},\theta_i,\ell) = \hat{x}(k-1/\gamma_{k-1},\theta_i)$ and $P_x(k-1/\gamma_{k-1},\theta_i,\ell) = P_x(k-1/\gamma_{k-1},\theta_i)$ where $\hat{x}(k-1/\gamma_{k-1},\theta_i)$ and $P_x(k-1/\gamma_{k-1},\theta_i)$ are available from the previous (k−1) boud.

Moreover, the decision statistic $\hat{\beta}(t/\nu_k^t,\gamma_{k-1})$ is given by

$$\hat{\beta}(t/\nu_k^t,\gamma_{k-1}) = \frac{\rho \sum_{i=1}^{N_\theta} \Lambda(\nu_k^t/\gamma_{k-1},\theta_i,\beta_k = 1)\, p(\theta_i/\gamma_{k-1})}{1 + \rho \sum_{i=1}^{N_\theta} \Lambda(\nu_k^t/\gamma_{k-1},\theta_i,\beta_k = 1)\, p(\theta_i/\gamma_{k-1})} \tag{38a}$$

and the learning algorithm consists of

$$p(\theta_i/\nu_k^t,\gamma_{k-1}) = \frac{1 + \rho\, \Lambda(\nu_k^t/\gamma_{k-1},\theta_i,\beta_k = 1)}{1 + \rho \sum_{j=1}^{N_\theta} \Lambda(\nu_k^t/\gamma_{k-1},\theta_j,\beta_k = 1)p(\theta_j/\gamma_{k-1})}\, p(\theta_i/\gamma_{k-1}) \tag{38b}$$

and the corresponding mse estimate of θ is given by

$$\hat{\theta}(t/\nu_k^t,\gamma_{k-1}) = \frac{\hat{\theta}(k-1/\gamma_{k-1}) + \rho \sum_{i=1}^{N_\theta} \theta_i \Lambda(\nu_k^t/\gamma_{k-1},\theta_i,\beta_k = 1)p(\theta_i/\gamma_{k-1})}{1 + \rho \sum_{i=1}^{N_\theta} \Lambda(\nu_k^t/\gamma_{k-1},\theta_i,\beta_k = 1)p(\theta_i/\gamma_{k-1})} \tag{38c}$$

where $\Lambda(\nu_k^t/\gamma_{k-1},\theta_i,\beta_k = 1)$ is given by Equation 9 and $\hat{\theta}(k-1/\gamma_{k-1})$ is available estimate from the previous boud.

The above equations are to be used in the Kth boud; namely for $t_{k-1} \leq t \leq t_k$.

Proof: The proof consists of the obvious observation that this is a special case of corollary III, as such the above equations follow immediately from those of corollary III.

IV. Special Case: Supervised Learning

In this section the special case of supervised learning is considered. For supervised learning, the results of section II simplify to the results of part I [1]. The results for this special case is presented in the following corollary. To keep the paper as short as possible and because of greater applicability only the results for the case of quantized parameter spaces are given.

Corollary V (Supervised Learning)

Given: a) the continuous record $\nu_k^t = \{z(\tau);\tau \epsilon (t_{k-1},t) \epsilon T_k\}$ from the current boud $T_k = \{t_{k-1},t_k\}$ for which a decision is to be made; as well as b) the past record $\gamma_{k-1} = \{\nu_{k-1},\nu_{k-2}, \ldots ,\nu_1\}$ and the correct sequence of past hypotheses active $\sigma_{k-1} = \{\beta_{k-1} = \ell_{k-1},\beta_{k-2} = \ell_{k-2}, \ldots ,\beta_1 = \ell_1\}; \ell_i \epsilon (1, 0)$ given, where the random processes involved are given by Equations (3) with $p[x_o/\theta]$ a gaussian density. The optimal decision rule, learning algorithm, state-vector error covariance-matrices are given respectively by: The decision rule at k^{th} boud ℓ_k is given by

$$\ell_k = C[\hat{\beta}(k/\nu_k,\omega_{k-1}) - c_o] \tag{39a}$$

where $\omega_{k-1} = \{\lambda_{k-1},\sigma_{k-1}\}$ and

$$\hat{\beta}(k/\nu_k,\omega_{k-1}) = \frac{\rho \int \Lambda(\nu_k/\omega_{k-1},\theta,\beta_k=1)p(\theta/\omega_{k-1})d\theta}{1+\rho\int\Lambda(\nu_k/\omega_{k-1},\theta,\beta_k = 1)p(\theta/\omega_{k-1})d\theta} \tag{39b}$$

The learning algorithm consists of the recursive updating of the a-posteriori density

$$p(\theta/\nu_k^t,\omega_{k-1}) = \frac{1 + \rho \int \Lambda(\nu_k^t/\omega_{k-1},\theta,\beta_k=1)}{1 + \rho \int \Lambda(\nu_k^t/\omega_{k-1},\theta,\beta_k = 1)p(\theta/\omega_{k-1})d\theta} p(\theta/\omega_{k-1}) \tag{39c}$$

where

$$\Lambda(\nu_k^t,\omega_{k-1},\theta,\beta_k = 1) = \exp\{\int_{t_{k-1}}^{t} \hat{x}^T(\sigma/\nu_k^\sigma,\omega_{k-1},\theta,\beta_k = 1)H^T(\sigma,\theta)R^{-1}(\sigma)z(\sigma)d\sigma$$

$$-\frac{1}{2}\int_{t_{k-1}}^{t} \| H(\sigma,\theta)\hat{x}(\sigma/\nu_k^\sigma,\omega_{k-1},\theta,\beta_k = 1)\|^2_{R^{-1}(\sigma)} d\sigma\}$$

The optimal state-vector estimates and the corresponding error-covariance matrices are given by:

$$\hat{x}(t/\nu_k^t,\omega_{k-1}) = \sum_{i=1}^{N_\theta} \sum_{\ell=0}^{1} \hat{x}(t/\nu_k^t,\omega_{k-1},\theta_i,\ell)p(\theta_i,\ell/\nu_k^t,\omega_{k-1}) \tag{40a}$$

where $\omega_{k-1} \equiv \{\lambda_{k-1},\sigma_{k-1}\}$, $\hat{x}(t/\nu_k^t,\omega_{k-1},\theta_i,\ell) \equiv \hat{x}(t/\nu_k^t,\omega_{k-1},\theta_i,\beta_k = \ell)$

and

$$p(\theta_i,\ell/\nu_k^t,\omega_{k-1}) = p(\theta_i,\beta_k = \ell/\nu_k^t,\omega_{k-1})$$

$$= p(\theta_i,\ell/\omega_{k-1})\exp\{\int_{t_{k-1}}^{t} \hat{x}(\tau/\nu_k^\tau,\omega_{k-1},\theta_i,\ell)\,\ell H^T(\tau,\theta_i)R^{-1}(\tau)z(\tau)d\tau$$

$$-\frac{1}{2}\int_{t_{k-1}}^{t} \| \ell H^T(\tau,\theta_i)\hat{x}(\tau/\nu_k^\tau,\omega_{k-1},\theta_i,\ell)\|^2_{R^{-1}(\tau)} d\tau\}$$

$$\cdot\{\sum_{i=1}^{N_\theta} \sum_{\ell=0}^{1} p(\theta_j,\ell/\omega_{k-1})\cdot$$

$$\exp[\int_{t_{k-1}}^{t} \hat{x}^T(\tau/\nu_k^t,\omega_{k-1},\theta_j,\ell)\cdot \ell \cdot H^T(\tau,\theta_j)R^{-1}(\tau)z(\tau)d\tau$$

$$-\frac{1}{2}\int_{t_{k-1}}^{t} \| \ell \cdot H^T(\tau,\theta_j)\hat{x}(\tau/\nu_k^\tau,\omega_{k-1},\theta_j,\ell)\|^2_{R^{-1}(\tau)} d\tau\}^{-1} \tag{40b}$$

The state-error covariance matrix is given by

$$P_x(t/\nu_k^t,\omega_{k-1}) =$$

$$\sum_{i=1}^{N_\theta} \sum_{\ell=0}^{1} \{P_x(t/\nu_k^t,\omega_{k-1},\theta_i,\ell) + [\hat{x}(t/\nu_k^t,\omega_{k-1},\theta_i,\ell) - \hat{x}(t/\nu_k^t,\omega_{k-1})]$$

$$\cdot [\hat{x}(t/\nu_k^t,\omega_{k-1},\theta_i,\ell) - \hat{x}(t/\nu_k^t,\omega_{k-1})]^T\}p(\theta_i,\ell/\nu_k^t,\omega_{k-1}). \tag{40c}$$

The conditional state-vector estimates and the corresponding error-covariance matrix are given by the Kalman-Bucy filter.

$$\frac{d\hat{x}(t/\nu_k^t,\omega_{k-1},\theta_i,\ell)}{dt} = F(t,\theta_i)\hat{x}(t/\nu_k^t,\omega_{k-1},\theta_i,\ell) + P_x(t/\nu_k^t,\omega_{k-1},\theta_i,\ell)$$

$$\cdot\, \ell\, H^T(t,\theta_i)R^{-1}(t)[z(t) - \ell\, H^T(t,\theta_i)\hat{x}(t/\nu_k^t,\omega_{k-1},\theta_i,\ell)] \qquad (40d)$$

for $t \epsilon (t_{k-1},t_k)$, with initial condition $\hat{x}(k-1/\omega_{k-1},\theta_i,\ell_{k-1})$, $t_{k-1} \equiv k-1$. The above initial condition is the solution of the following equation at time $t_{k-1} = k-1$

$$\frac{d\hat{x}(t/\nu_{k-1}^t,\omega_{k-2},\theta_i,\ell_{k-1})}{dt} = F(t,\theta_i)\hat{x}(t/\nu_{k-1}^t,\omega_{k-2},\theta_i,\ell_{k-1})$$

$$+ P_x(t/\nu_{k-1}^t,\omega_{k-2},\theta_i,\ell_{k-1}) \cdot \ell\, H^T(t,\theta_i)R^{-1}(t)[x(t) -$$

$$\ell\, H^T(t,\theta_i)\hat{x}(t/\nu_{k-1}^t,\omega_{k-2},\theta_i,\ell_{k-1})] \qquad (40e)$$

for $t \epsilon (t_{k-2},t_{k-1})$ with initial condition $\hat{x}(k-2/\omega_{k-2},\theta_i,\ell_{k-2})$ and where ℓ_i takes the appropriate value 1 or 0 in each boud as dictated by $\sigma_{k-1} = \{\beta_{k-1} = \ell_{k-1}, \beta_{k-2} = \ell_{k-2}, \ldots, \beta_1 = \ell_1\}$.

The corresponding error-covariance matrix is given by

$$dP_x(t/\nu_k^t,\omega_{k-1},\theta_i,\ell) = F(t,\theta_i)P_x(t/\nu_k^t,\omega_{k-1},\theta_i,\ell)$$

$$+ P_x(t/\nu_k^t,\omega_{k-1},\theta_i,\ell)F^T(t,\theta) + G(t,\theta_i)G^T(t,\theta_i)$$

$$-P_x(t/\nu_k^t,\omega_{k-1},\theta_i,\ell)H(t,\theta_i)\,\ell^2R^{-1}(t)H(t,\theta_i)P_x(t/\nu_k^t,\omega_{k-1},\theta_i,\ell)$$

$$(40f)$$

for $t \epsilon (t_{k-1},t_k)$, with initial condition $P_x(t/\nu_k^t,\omega_{k-1},\theta_i,\ell_{k-1})$ which is the solution of the following equation at time $t_{k-1} \equiv k-1$.

Similarly

$$\frac{dP_x(t/\nu_k^t,\omega_{k-2},\theta_i,\ell_{k-1})}{dt} = F(t,\theta_i)P_x(t/\nu_{k-1}^t,\omega_{k-2},\theta_i,\ell_{k-1})$$

$$+ P_x(t/\nu_{k-1}^t,\omega_{k-2},\theta_i,\ell_{k-1})F^T(t,\theta_i) + G(t,\theta_i)G^T(t,\theta_i) -$$

$$P_x(t/\nu_{k-1}^t,\omega_{k-2},\theta_i,\ell_{k-1})R^{-1}(t)H(t,\theta_i) \cdot P_x(t/\nu_{k-1}^t,\omega_{k-2},\theta_i,\ell_{k-2}) \qquad (40g)$$

for $t \epsilon (t_{k-2}, t_{k-1})$ with initial condition $P_x(k-2/\omega_{k-2}, \theta_i, \ell_{k-2})$ where ℓ_i, $i = k-2, k-2$ takes the appropriate value 1 or 0 in each boud as indicated by σ_{k-1}. The above recursive calculations are initiated by the initial conditions at t_o, namely $\hat{x}(t_o/\gamma_o, \theta_i)$ and $P_x(t_o/\gamma_o, \theta_i)$. These are assumed to be known.

Proof: Corollary IV is a special case of corollary III, since for the supervised learning problem $p(x_{k-1}/\omega_{k-1}, \theta_i)$ is a gaussian density (degenerate mixture density), namely

$$p(x_{k-1}/\omega_{k-1}, \theta_i) = \frac{\exp\{-\frac{1}{2} \| x_{k-1} - \hat{x}(k-1/\omega_{k-1}, \theta_i, \ell_{k-1}) \|^2_{P_x^{-1}(k-1/\omega_{k-1}, \theta_i, \ell_{k-1})}\}}{(2\pi)^{\frac{n}{2}} \, | P_x(k-1/\omega_{k-1}, \theta_i, \ell_{k-1}) |^{\frac{1}{2}}} \tag{40h}$$

and the summation with respect to j in Equation (33) becomes a single term ($N_x = 1$). The proof of corollary III is straightforward, hence it will be omitted.

Several pertinent comments for this case have been made in part I [1]. Note that since $p(x_{k-1}/\omega_{k-1}, \theta_i)$ is itself a gaussian, namely a reproducing density, there was no need for approximating it by a mixture density.

V. Special Case: Independent Signalling

In this section a special case is considered that pertains to a mode of signalling such that $\{y(t); t \epsilon t_{k-1}, t_k)\}$ is independent of $\{y(\tau); \tau \epsilon (t_{j-1}, t_j)\}$ for $j = 1, 2, \ldots, k-1$. Such a situation may arise if one, for reasons of security, chooses the signalling waveform at each boud from a different random process. It is assumed that the random processes involved have identical statistics, whose dynamical and statistical models are known to remove up to an unknown but constant parameter θ. However, the correct sequence of past hypotheses active is not known. Only λ_{k-1} is given. The results for this special case are presented in the following corollary.

Corollary V (Independent Signalling)

Given: a) the continuous record ν_k^t from the current boud; and b) the past record λ_{k-1}, where the random processes involved are given by Equations (3) and are such that $\{y(t); t \epsilon (t_{k-1}, t_k)\}$ is independent of $\{y(\tau);$ $\tau \epsilon (t_{j-1}, t_j), j = 1, 2, \ldots, k-1\}$, with $p(x_o/\theta)$ a gaussian density, the optimal decision rule, learning algorithm state-vector estimates and corresponding error-covariance matrices are given respectively by:

The decision rule is

$$\ell_k = C[\hat{\beta}(k/\nu_k,\gamma_o) - c_o] \tag{41a}$$

where

$$\hat{\beta}(k/\nu_k,\gamma_o) = \frac{\rho \sum_{i=1}^{N_\theta} \Lambda(\nu_k/\gamma_o,\theta_i,\beta_k = 1)p(\theta_i/\gamma_{k-1})}{1 + \rho \sum_{i=1}^{N_\theta} \Lambda(\nu_k/\gamma_o,\theta,\beta_k = 1)p(\theta_i/\gamma_{k-1})} \tag{41b}$$

The learning algorithm is given by

$$p(\theta_i/\nu_k^t,\gamma_{k-1}) = \frac{1 + \rho\, \Lambda(\nu_k^t/\gamma_o,\theta_i,\beta_k = 1)}{1 + \rho \sum_{i=1}^{N_\theta} \Lambda(\nu_k^t/\gamma_o,\theta_j,\beta_k = 1)p(\theta_j/\gamma_{k-1})}\, p(\theta_i/\gamma_{k-1}) \tag{41c}$$

where

$$\Lambda(\nu_k^t/\gamma_o,\theta_j,\beta_k = 1) = \exp\{\int_{t_{k-1}}^{t} \hat{x}(\sigma/\nu_k^\sigma,\sigma_o,\theta_j,\beta_k = 1)H^T(\sigma,\theta_j)R^{-1}(\sigma)z(\sigma)d\sigma$$
$$-\frac{1}{2}\int_{t_{k-1}}^{t} \| H(\sigma,\theta_o)\hat{x}(\sigma/\nu_k^\sigma,\gamma_o,\theta_j,\beta_k = 1)\|^2_{R^{-1}(\sigma)} d\sigma\} \tag{42}$$

The optimal state-vector estimate and corresponding error-covariance matrice are given

$$\hat{x}(t/\nu_k^t,\gamma_{k-1}) = \sum_{i=1}^{N_\theta} \sum_{\ell=0}^{1} \hat{x}(t/\nu_k^t,\gamma_o,\theta_i,\ell)p(\theta_i,\ell/\nu_k^t,\gamma_{k-1}) \tag{43a}$$

where $\hat{x}(t/\nu_k^t,\gamma_o,\theta_i,\ell) \equiv E[x(t)/\nu_k^t,\gamma_o,\theta_i,\beta_k = \ell]$, and

$$p(\theta_i,\ell/\nu_k^t,\gamma_{k-1}) \equiv p(\theta_i,\beta_k = \ell/\nu_k^t,\gamma_{k-1})$$

$$= p(\theta_i,\ell/\gamma_{k-1}) \cdot \exp\{\int_{t_{k-1}}^{t} \hat{x}(\tau/\nu_k^\tau,\gamma_o,\theta_i,\ell) \cdot \ell \cdot H^T(\tau,\theta_j)R^{-1}(\tau)z(\tau)d\tau$$
$$-\frac{1}{2}\int_{t_{k-1}}^{t} \| \ell \cdot H^T(\tau,\theta_i)\hat{x}(\tau/\nu_k^\tau,\gamma_o,\theta_i,\ell)\|^2_{R^{-1}(\tau)} d\tau\}$$

$$\cdot \{\sum_{j=1}^{N_\theta} \sum_{\ell=0}^{1} p(\theta_j, \ell/\gamma_{k-1}) \exp[\int_{t_{k-1}}^{t} \hat{x}^T(\tau/\nu_k^\tau, \gamma_o, \theta_j, \ell) \cdot \ell \cdot H^T(\tau,\theta_j) R^{-1}(\tau) z(\tau) d\tau$$

$$-\frac{1}{2}\int_{t_{k-1}}^{t} \| \ell \cdot H^T(\tau,\theta_j)\hat{x}(\tau/\nu_k^\tau, \gamma_o, \theta_j, \ell) \|^2_{R^{-1}(\tau)} d\tau\}^{-1} \tag{43b}$$

The state-error covariance matrix is given by

$$P_x(t/\nu_k^t, \gamma_{k-1}) = \sum_{i=1}^{N_\theta} \sum_{\ell=0}^{1} \{P_x(t/\nu_k^t, \gamma_0, \theta_i, \ell) + [\hat{x}(t/\nu_k^t, \gamma_0, \theta_i, \ell) - \hat{x}(t/\nu_k^t, \gamma_{k-1})]$$

$$\cdot [\hat{x}(t/\nu_k^t, \gamma_0, \theta_i, \ell) - \hat{x}(t/\nu_k^t, \gamma_{k-1})]^T\} p(\theta_i, \ell/\nu_k^t, \gamma_{k-1}) \tag{43c}$$

The model-conditional state-vector estimate and the corresponding error-covariance matrix are given by the Kalman-Bucy filter equations:

$$\frac{d\hat{x}(t/\nu_k^t, \gamma_0, \theta_i, \ell)}{dt} = F(t,\theta_i)\hat{x}(t/\nu_k^t, \gamma_0, \theta_i, \ell) + P_x(t/\nu_k^t, \gamma_0, \theta_i, \ell)$$

$$\cdot \ell\, H^T(t,\theta_i) R^{-1}(t)]\, z(t) - \ell \cdot H^T(t,\theta_i)\hat{x}(t/\nu_k^t, \gamma_0, \theta_i, \ell) \tag{44a}$$

with initial condition $\hat{x}(k-1/\gamma_0, \theta_i, \ell) = \varphi(t_{k-1}, t_0; \theta_i)\hat{x}(t_0/t_0, \theta_i)$, and

$$dP_x(t/\nu_k^t, \gamma_0, \theta_i, \ell) = F(t,\theta_i)P_x(t/\nu_k^t, \gamma_0, \theta_i, \ell) + P_x(t/\nu_k^t, \gamma_0, \theta_i, \ell)F^T(t,\theta_i) +$$

$$G(t,\theta_i)G^T(t,\theta_i) - P_x(t/\nu_k^t, \gamma_0, \theta_i, \ell)H(t,\theta_i) \cdot \ell^2 R^{-1}(t) H(t,\theta_i) P_x(t/\nu_k^t, \gamma_0, \theta_i, \ell) \tag{44b}$$

with initial condition

$$P_x(k-1/\gamma_0, \theta_i, \ell) = \varphi(t_{k-1}, t_0, \theta_i) P_x(t_0/t_0, \theta_i) \varphi^T(t_{k-1}, t_0; \theta_i) +$$

$$\int_{t_0}^{t_{k-1}} \varphi(t_{k-1}, \tau; \theta_i) G(\tau,\theta_i) G^T(\tau,\theta_i) \varphi^T(t_{k-1}, \tau; \theta_i) d\tau \tag{44c}$$

for $t \epsilon (t_{k-1}, t_k)$, and where $\hat{x}(t_0/t_0, \theta_i)$ and $P_x(t_0/t_0, \theta_i)$ are the mean and variance of $p(x_o/\theta_i)$.

Proof: Corollary IV is also a special case of corollary II since the independent signalling case $p(x_{k-1}/\lambda_{k-1}, \theta_i)$ is not only a gaussian density but also independent of past data λ_{k-1}. So

$$p(x_{k-1}/\lambda_{k-1},\theta_i) = p(x_{k-1}/\theta_i)$$

$$\frac{\exp\{-\frac{1}{2}\| x_{k-1} - \hat{x}(k-1/\theta_i)\|^2_{P_x^{-1}(k-1/\theta_i)}\}}{(2\pi)^{\frac{n}{2}}|P_x(k-1/\theta_i)|^{1/2}}$$

Given the dynamical Equations (3), for the time-evolution of x(t), Equations (44) become apparent.

Note that the results of corollary IV are the continuous data equivalent of Fralick's results, the latter obtained for conditionally independent, discrete data.

VI. Decision-Directed Learning, Pattern Recognition Algorithms

In this section, decision-directed learning, pattern recognition algorithms are considered. Both deterministic as well as random decision-directed learning algorithms for continuous data are obtained. Deterministic decision-directed learning is based on allocating the data of past bouds to hypothesis H_1 or H_0, namely deciding $\beta_i = 1$ or 0, for i = 1,2, . . . ,k−1, by using the usual deterministic (nonrandom) Bayesian decision rule. The results for deterministic decision-directed learning are given in the following corollary.

Corollary VI (Deterministic Decision-Directed Learning)

Given: a) the continuous record ν_k^t from the current boud for which a decisioniis to be made; as well as b) the past record λ_{k-1}, and the sequence of past decisions $\hat{\sigma}_{k-1} = \{d_{k-1} = \ell_{k-1}, d_{k-2} = \ell_{k-2}, \ldots, d_1 = \ell_1\}$, where

$$\ell_i = C[\hat{\beta}(i/\nu_i,\hat{\omega}_{i-1}) - c_o]$$

where $\hat{\omega}_{i-1} \equiv \{\lambda_{i-1},\hat{\sigma}_{i-1}\}$, $C(\omega)$ equals 1 or 0, depending on whether $\omega \gtrless 0$, respectively, and c_o depends on the a-priori costs; and where the random processes involved are given by Equations (3), with $p(x_o/\theta)$ a gaussian random vector, the optimal decision rule, learning algorithm, state-vector estimate as well as state-vector error covariance matrix are given, respectively by:

$$\ell_k = C[\hat{\beta}(k/\nu_k,\hat{\omega}_{k-1}) - c_o] \tag{45a}$$

where

$$\hat{\beta}(t/\nu_k^t,\hat{\omega}_{k-1}) = \frac{1+\rho\int\Lambda(\nu_k/\hat{\omega}_{k-1},\theta,\beta_k=1)p(\theta/\hat{\omega}_{k-1})d\theta}{1+\rho\int\Lambda(\nu_k^t/\hat{\omega}_{k-1},\theta,\beta_k=1)p(\theta/\hat{\omega}_{k-1})d\theta} \tag{45b}$$

$$p(\theta/\nu_k^t,\hat{\omega}_{k-1}) = \frac{1+\rho\int\Lambda(\nu_k^t/\hat{\omega}_{k-1},\theta,\beta_k=1)}{1+\rho\int\Lambda(\nu_k^t/\hat{\omega}_{k-1},\theta,\beta_k=1)p(\theta/\hat{\omega}_{k-1})d\theta}\,p(\theta/\hat{\omega}_{k-1}) \tag{45c}$$

and

$$\Lambda(\nu_k^t/\hat{\omega}_{k-1},\theta,\beta_k=1) = \exp\{\int_{t_{k-1}}^{t}\hat{x}^T(\sigma/\nu_k^\sigma,\hat{\omega}_{k-1},\theta,\beta_k=1)H^T(\sigma,\theta)R^{-1}(\sigma)z(\sigma)d\sigma$$
$$-\frac{1}{2}\int_{t_{k-1}}^{t}\|H(\sigma,\theta)\hat{x}(\sigma/\nu_k^\sigma,\hat{\omega}_{k-1},\theta,\beta_k=1)\|^2_{R^{-1}(\sigma)}d\sigma\} \tag{46}$$

The state-vector estimates $\hat{x}(t/\nu_k^t,\hat{\omega}_{k-1})$, $\hat{x}(t/\nu_k^t,\hat{\omega}_{k-1},\theta,\ell)$, and the corresponding error-covariance matrices $P_x(t/\nu_k^t,\hat{\omega}_{k-1})$ and $P_x(t/\nu_k^t,\hat{\omega}_{k-1},\theta,\ell)$ respectively are given by Equations (38) - (40) of corollary IV, with values for ℓ_i, $i=1,2,\ldots,k-1$ dictated by $\hat{\sigma}_{k-1}$.

Proof: The proof consists of the rationale for deterministic decision-directed learning which is that the decisions of the system are going to be taken as the correct sequence of past states and consequently processing is to proceed in a "supervised learning" manner.

The random decision-directed learning algorithm, first proposed for discrete data only, by Agrawala [9] and called by him "learning with a probabilistic teacher" (LPT) is based on allocating the data of past bouds to hypothesis H_1, or H_0, namely deciding $\beta_i = 1$ or 0, for $i=1,2,\ldots,k-1$, by using a random decision rule. The continuous data random decision-directed learning (LPT), pattern recognition algorithms are given in the following corollary.

Corollary VII (Random Decision-Directed Learning)

Given: a) the continuous record ν_k^t from the current boud for which a decision is to be made; as well as b) the past record λ_{k-1}, and the sequence of past random decisions $\hat{\sigma}_{k-1} = \{d_{k-1}=\ell_{k-1}, d_{k-2}=\ell_{k-2},\ldots,d_1=\ell_1\}$, where ℓ_i has the value 1 or 0 depending on whether the outcome of an independent random experiment is 1 or 0, where

$$\mathcal{F}_i : (S_i, F_i, P_i, \text{ with } S_i = \{1,0\},$$

and probabilities $p_i(1) \equiv p(\beta_i = 1/\nu_i, \hat{\hat{\omega}}_{i-1})$ and $p_i(0) = 1 - p_i(1)$, where $\hat{\hat{\omega}}_{i-1} \equiv \{\lambda_{i-1}, \hat{\hat{\sigma}}_{i-1}\}$; and where the random processes involved are given by Equations (3) with $p(x_o/\theta)$ gaussian, the optimal decision rule, learning algorithm, state-vector estimates and error-covariance matrices are given by:

$$\ell_k = C[\hat{\beta}(k/\nu_k, \hat{\hat{\omega}}_{k-1}) - c_o] \tag{47a}$$

where

$$\hat{\beta}(t/\nu_k^t, \hat{\hat{\omega}}_{k-1}) = \frac{\rho \int \Lambda(\nu_k^t/\hat{\hat{\omega}}_{k-1}, \theta, \beta_k = 1) p(\theta/\hat{\hat{\omega}}_{k-1}) d\theta}{1 + \rho \int \Lambda(\nu_k^t/\hat{\hat{\omega}}_{k-1}, \theta, \beta_k = 1) p(\theta/\hat{\hat{\omega}}_{k-1}) d\theta} \tag{47b}$$

$$p(\theta/\nu_k^t, \hat{\hat{\omega}}_{k-1}) = \frac{1 + \rho \int \Lambda(\nu_k^t/\hat{\hat{\omega}}_{k-1}, \theta, \beta_k = 1)}{1 + \rho \int \Lambda(\nu_k^t/\hat{\hat{\omega}}_{k-1}, \theta, \beta_k = 1) p(\theta/\hat{\hat{\omega}}_{k-1}) d\theta} p(\theta/\hat{\hat{\omega}}_{k-1}) \tag{47c}$$

and

$$\Lambda(\nu_k^t/\hat{\hat{\omega}}_{k-1}, \theta, \beta_k = 1) = \exp\{\int_{t_{k-1}}^{t} \hat{x}^T(\sigma/\nu_k^\sigma, \hat{\hat{\omega}}_{k-1}, \theta, \beta_k = 1) H^T(\sigma,\theta) R^{-1}(\sigma) z(\sigma) d\sigma$$
$$- \frac{1}{2} \int_{t_{k-1}}^{t} \| H(\sigma,\theta) \hat{x}(\sigma/\nu_k^\sigma, \hat{\hat{\omega}}_{k-1}, \theta, \beta_k = 1) \|^2_{R^{-1}(\sigma)} d\sigma\} \tag{48}$$

The state-vector estimates $\hat{x}(t/\nu_k^t, \hat{\hat{\omega}}_{k-1})$, $\hat{x}(t/\nu_k^t, \hat{\hat{\omega}}_{k-1}, \theta, \ell)$, and the corresponding error-covariance matrices $P_x(t/\nu_k^t, \hat{\hat{\omega}}_{k-1})$ and $P_x(t/\hat{\hat{\omega}}_{k-1}, \ell)$, respectively are given by Equations (38) - (40) or corollary IV, with values for ℓ_i, $i = 1, 2, \ldots, k-1$, dictated by $\hat{\hat{\sigma}}_{k-1}$.

Proof: The proof consists simply of the rationale of random decision-directed learning which is that the sequence of outcomes of the independent random experiments $\mathcal{F}_i$ are taken to be the correct sequence of past states and consequently data processing proceeds in a "supervised" manner. A discussion of the validity of such rationale, the performance of recognition systems using LPT and the convergence properties of the learning algorithm can be found in Agrawala [9], although for discrete data systems only.

The above results are the continuous data equivalent of Agrawala's [9] results for discrete data. Moreover, they are more general than Agrawala's results because they pertain to the case of unknown parameter vector θ. Agrawala [9], in contrast, considered only the case of completely known discrete models.

VII. Suboptimal Nonlinear Estimation Procedures

It was shown in section II, that the unsupervised learning pattern recognition problem under consideration constitutes a nonlinear estimation problem. Specifically, for $x_a(t) = [x^T(t) \vdots \theta^T \vdots \beta_k]^T$, the model is defined by Equations (4). But as was pointed out earlier, the optimal, continuous data, nonlinear filter is specified, in general, by an infinite set of coupled stochastic partial differential equations. As such it is unrealizable. This problem was partially circumvented in section II by using an adaptive approach in conjunction with quantization of the unknown parameter space. In this section approximate nonlinear estimation algorithms are used that do not require parameter space quantization. These are based on the so-called relinearized Kalman-Bucy filter [17]. For the general nonlinear model given below

$$\frac{dx(t)}{dt} = f(x(t),t) + G(x(t),t)\,u(t)$$

$$z(t) = h(x(t),t) + v(t)$$

where, $f(\cdot)$, $g(\cdot)$, and $h(\cdot)$ are, in general, nonlinear functions of $x(t)$; and $\{u(t)\}$ are independent, white gaussian random processes, the relinearized filter is defined [10], by the following set of coupled differential equations.

$$\frac{d\hat{x}(t/t)}{dt} = f(\hat{x}(t/t),t) + P(t/t) \cdot \nabla h^T(\hat{x}(t/t),t)R^{-1}(t)[z(t)-h(\hat{x}(t/t),t)] \tag{49a}$$

$$\frac{dP(t/t)}{dt} = \nabla f(x(t/t),t)P(t/t) + P(t/t)\,\nabla f^T(\hat{x}(t/t),t) + g(\hat{x}(t/t),t)g^T(\hat{x}(t/t),t) - P(t/t)\nabla h^T(\hat{x}(t/t),t)R^{-1}(t)\nabla h(\hat{x}(t/t),t)P(t/t) \tag{49b}$$

with initial condition $\hat{x}(t_0/t_0) = E[x(t_0)/t_0]$, $P(t_0/t_0) = E\{[x(t_0) - \hat{x}(t_0/t_0)] \cdot [x(t_0) - \hat{x}(t_0/t_0)]^T\}$; where $\hat{x}(t/t) = E[x(t)/z(\tau); \tau \in (t_0,t)]$, and $\nabla h(\hat{x}(t/t),t), \nabla f(\hat{x}(t/t),t)$ are jacobian matrices of $h(\cdot)$ and $f(\cdot)$, respectively.

Specifically, for the pattern recognition model under consideration, given by Equations (4), the relinearized filter equations are given in the following theorem.

Theorem IV:

Given: a) the observation record ν_k^t from the kth boud for which a decision is desired, as well as b) the initial conditions

$$\alpha_{k-1} \equiv \{\hat{x}^T(k-1/\nu_{k-1},\alpha_{k-2}),\hat{\theta}^T(k-1/\nu_{k-1},\alpha_{k-2}),\hat{\beta}_{k-1}(k-1/\nu_{k-1},\alpha_{k-2}\}^T,$$

the relinearized filter estimate $\hat{x}_a(t/\nu_k^t,\alpha_{k-1}) \equiv [\hat{x}^T(t/\nu_k^t,\alpha_{k-1}) \vdots \hat{\theta}^T(t/\nu_k^t,\alpha_{k-1}) \vdots \hat{\beta}_k(t/\nu_k^t,\alpha_{k-1})]^T$ is given by

$$\begin{bmatrix} \dfrac{d\hat{x}(t/\nu_k^t,\alpha_{k-1})}{dt} \\ \dfrac{d\theta(t/\nu_k^t,\alpha_{k-1})}{dt} \\ \dfrac{d\hat{\beta}(t/\nu_k^t,\alpha_{k-1}}{dt} \end{bmatrix} = \begin{bmatrix} F(t,\hat{\theta}(t/\nu_k^t,\alpha_{k-1})]\,\hat{x}(t/\nu_k^t,\alpha_{k-1}) \\ 0 \\ 0 \end{bmatrix} +$$

$$+\, P(t/\nu_k^t,\alpha_{k-1}) \begin{bmatrix} \hat{\beta}_k(t/\nu_k^t,\alpha_{k-1})H^T[t,\hat{\theta}(t/\nu_k^t,\alpha_{k-1})] \\ \hat{\beta}_k(t/\nu_k^t,\alpha_{k-1})\hat{x}(t/\nu_k^t,\alpha_{k-1})\nabla H^T[t,\hat{\theta}(t/\nu_k^t,\alpha_{k-1})] \\ \hat{x}^T(t/\nu_k^t,\alpha_{k-1})H^T[t,\hat{\theta}(t/\nu_k^t,\alpha_{k-1})] \end{bmatrix} R^{-1}(t)$$

$$\cdot\, [z(t) - \hat{\beta}(t/\nu_k^t,\alpha_{k-1})H^T(t,\hat{\theta}(t/\nu_k^t,\alpha_{k-1}))\hat{x}(t/\nu_k^t,\alpha_{k-1})] \tag{50a}$$

for $t \epsilon (t_{k-1}, t_k)$, with initial conditions: $\hat{\alpha}(k-1 \mid \alpha_{k-1}) = \hat{\alpha}(k-1 \mid \nu_{k-1},\alpha_{k-2})$, $\hat{\theta}(k-1 \mid \alpha_{k-1}) = \hat{\theta}(k-1 \mid \nu_{k-1},\alpha_{k-2})$, and $\hat{\beta}_k(k-1 \mid \alpha_{k-1}) = p(\beta_{k-1}) = p$

and

$$\frac{dP(t/\nu_k^t,\alpha_{k-1})}{dt} \begin{bmatrix} F(t,\hat{\theta}(t/\nu_k^t,\alpha_{k-1})) & \nabla F(t,\hat{\theta}(t/\nu_k^t,\alpha_{k-1}) & 0 \\ 0 & 0 & 0 \\ 0 & 0 & 0 \end{bmatrix} P(t/\nu_k^t,\alpha_{k-1})$$

$$+P(t/\nu_k^t,\alpha_{k-1})\begin{bmatrix} F^T(t,\hat{\theta}(t/\nu_k^t,\alpha_{k-1})) & 0 & 0 \\ \hat{x}(t/\nu_k^t,\alpha_{k-1})\nabla F^T(t,\hat{\theta}(t/\nu_k^t,\alpha_{k-1})) & 0 & 0 \\ 0 & 0 & 0 \end{bmatrix}$$

$$+\begin{bmatrix} G(t,\hat{\theta}(t/\nu_k^t,\alpha_{k-1}))G^T(t,\hat{\theta}(t/\nu_k^t,\alpha_{k-1})) & 0 & 0 \\ 0 & 0 & 0 \\ 0 & 0 & 0 \end{bmatrix}$$

$$-P_\alpha(t\,|\,\nu_k^t,\alpha_{k-1})\begin{bmatrix} \hat{\beta}_k(t\,|\,\nu_k^t,\alpha_{k-1})H^T(t,\hat{\theta}(t\,|\,\nu_k^t,\alpha_{k-1})) \\ \hat{\beta}_k(t\,|\,\nu_k^t,\alpha_{k-1})\hat{x}^T(t\,|\,\nu_k^t,\alpha_{k-1})\nabla H^T(t,\hat{\theta}(t\,|\,\nu_k^t,\alpha_{k-1}))R^{-1}(t). \\ \hat{x}^T(t\,|\,\nu_k^t,\alpha_{k-1})H^T(t,\hat{\theta}(t\,|\,\nu_k^t,\alpha_{k-1})) \end{bmatrix}$$

$$\begin{bmatrix} \hat{\beta}_k(t\,|\,\nu_k^t,\alpha_{k-1})H^T(t,\hat{\theta}(t\,|\,\nu_k^t,\alpha_{k-1})) \\ \hat{\beta}_k(t\,|\,\nu_k^t,\alpha_{k-1})\hat{x}^T(t\,|\,\nu_k^t,\alpha_{k-1})\nabla H^T(t,\hat{\theta}(t\,|\,\nu_k^t,\alpha_{k-1})) \\ \hat{\alpha}^T(t\,|\,\nu_k^t,\alpha_{k-1})H^T(t,\hat{\theta}(t\,|\,\nu_k^t,\alpha_{k-1})) \end{bmatrix}^T P_a(t\,|\,\nu_k^t,\alpha_{k-1}) \tag{50b}$$

for $t\in(t_{k-1},t_k)$, with initial conditions $P_a(k-1\,|\,\alpha_{k-1})$ given by

$$P_a(k-1\,|\,\alpha_{k-1})\equiv\begin{bmatrix} P_x(k-1\,|\,\nu_{k-1},\alpha_{k-2}) & P_{x\theta}(k-1\,|\,\nu_{k-1},\alpha_{k-2}) & 0 \\ P_{\theta x}(k-1\,|\,\nu_{k-1},\alpha_{k-2}) & P_\theta(k-1\,|\,\nu_{k-1},\alpha_{k-2}) & 0 \\ 0 & 0 & p(1-p) \end{bmatrix} \tag{50c}$$

where $P_x(\cdot)$, $P_{x\theta}(\cdot)$ and $P_\theta(\cdot)$ are the corresponding elements of the covariance matrix $P_a(k-1\,|\,\nu_{k-1},\alpha_{k-2})$ available at the end of the previous boud, and $p = p(\beta_k = 1)$.

Proof: The proof consists of application of the relinearized filter equations to Equations 4 to obtain the stochastic differential equations (50a) and (50b). The given initial conditions are based on the fact that β_k is statistically independent of past β_i, $i = 1,2,\ldots,k-1$, and past data $k-1$, as well as of θ and as such the initial conditions at t_{k-1}, pertaining to β_k should be the a-priori ones, since the past data is irrelevant as far as β_k is concerned. Moreover, since this is not the case with $x(\cdot)$ and θ, the corresponding quantities at the end of the previous internal (i.e. t_{k-1}) are the quantities pertaining to $x(\cdot)$ and θ.

The rationale in using the relinearized Kalman filter is that it is simple, and moreover, that it works effectively in a large class of problems. The latter was demonstrated recently by Licht [10],

Conclusions

This chapter integrates the results of a series of papers on adaptive pattern recognition and its applications, using state-variable approach. It pertains essentially to optimal, unsupervised learning, adaptive pattern recognition of "lumped" gaussian signals in white gaussian noise. Specifically, optimal, recursive, unsupervised learning, pattern recognition algorithms are obtained and presented in a closed integral form as well as simplified algorithms are obtained. For the special case of supervised learning, the results are shown to reduce considerably, and for the special case of independent signalling random processes, the results for continuous data are similar to those obtained by Fralick for discrete, conditionally independent data. Both deterministic decision-directed learning as well as random decision-directed learning algorithms (Agrawala's LPT) for continuous data are also obtained. Moreover, simplified, suboptimal, recursive, unsupervised learning algorithms are obtained based on approximate nonlinear estimation procedures namely the so-called "relinearized" Kalman filter.

REFERENCES

1. D. G. Lainiotis, "Sequential Structure and Parameter Adaptive Pattern Recognition, Part I: Supervised Learning,'" IEEE Transactions on Information Theory, Vol. IT-16, no. 5, pp. 548-556, September 1970.
2. D. G. Lainiotis, "On a General Relationship Between Estimation, Detection, and the Bhattacharyya Coefficient," IEEE Transactions on Information and Theory, Vol. IT-15, no. 4, pp. 504-505, July 1969.
3. A. H. Jazwinski, *Stochastic Processes and Filtering Theory,* Academic Press, New York, 1970.
4. D. G. Lainiotis, "Optimal Adaptive Estimation: Structure and Parameter Adaptation," IEEE Transactions on Automatic Control, Vol. AC-16, no. 2, pp. 160-170, April 1971.
5. D. G. Lainiotis, "Sequential Structure and Parameter Adpative Pattern Recognition, Part II: Unsupervised Learning," To appear 1972.
6. T. Kailath, "A General Likelihood-ratio Formula for Random Signals in Gaussian Noise," IEEE Transactions on Information Theory, Vol. IT-15, no. 3, pp. 350-361, May 1969.
7. R. L. Sengbush and D. G. Lainiotis, "Simplified Parameter Quantization Procedure for Adaptive Estimation:, IEEE Transactions on Automatic Control, Vol. AC-14, no. 4, pp. 424-425, August 1969.
8. N. I. Achieser, *Theory of Approximation,* translated by C. T. Hyman, Frederick Unger Publishing Company, New York, 1956.
9. A. K. Agrawala, "Learning with a Probabilistic Teacher," IEEE Transactions on Information Theory", Vol, IT-16, no. 4, pp. 373-379, July 1970.
10. B. W. Licht, "Approximations in Optimal Nonlinear Filtering," Ph.D. Thesis, Case-Western Reserve University, January, 1970.

ON THE COMPUTATION OF SHAPE

D. J. Langridge

COMMONWEALTH SCIENTIFIC AND INDUSTRIAL RESEARCH ORGANISATION
CANBERRA, AUSTRALIA

1. Some Remarks on the Descriptive Approach

The most coherent statement of the aims of the descriptive approach to pictorial processing are to be found in two papers by Narasimhan (1969, 1970). For instance in his 1969 paper he states "a descriptive schema must assign structure to a scene in terms of occurrences of specific objects and their spatial dispositions; it must assign structure to an object in terms of occurrences of subparts and their composition; assign structures to subparts and their composition; and so on. Further, the descriptive schema must assign attribute lists to objects and their subparts and compute values for them". It is clear in this statement, that when Narasimhan talks of the structure or organisation of objects, he is referring to those structures that correspond to what a human-being would perceive in the scene under normal circumstances. Thus the goal of the descriptive approach is to provide adequate computational theories for fragments of human visual perception.

It is true that success in certain pictorial processing tasks has been achieved without this aim. However, I am one of Grasselli's pessimists, (Grasselli, 1969) and regard these as "bags of tricks". To be able to communicate with machines meaningfully, they must simulate some aspects of our behavior.

The initial section of the paper expresses disappointment in some of the developments of the descriptive approach. There appears to be an overemphasis of the linguistic aspects; and more specifically an overemphasis on the word "syntax" and its connotations.

Clowes (1969(a), 1969 (b)) presents a metalanguage based on the generalised transformation of Chomskian linguistics. The notation produced is very clumsy and difficult to follow. In neither paper is there any discussion of the possibility of a computer interpretation of the notation, even in a modified form; that is, we do not know if it is interpretable or not.

Narasimhan (1969) has strongly pointed out the danger of devising descriptive languages without consideration of their interpretation. He states, "it is not tenable to argue that specification schemata could be studied independently of action mechanisms and that, in fact,one could think in terms of setting up universal specification schema whose output could be coupled to any particular action mechanism". In this instance he is discussing picture-generation and continues, "we would still be left with the problem of having to *translate this specification* into a form that can be made use of by a given, particular action mechanism. There is no *a priori* guarantee that this could be done at all, or could be done uniformly for all action mechanisms".

The justification given by Clowes for the development of the notation was that "we need to focus attention upon the adequate description of patterns" and thus, "we are faced with the problem of devising a language in which we can express our intuitions about shape and more importantly what these intuitions *are*". In both papers we are given definitions of various pictorial relationships, for instance, join between two lines, whether two points are on the same side of some axis, the convex relation between two edges, etc. While agreeing with some of the arguments presented about the need for such relationships, I consider there is nothing profound in representing them in this notation and, in the absence of an interpreter for the language, rather a waste of time.

Evans (1969) was more successful than Clowes in that he did devise an interpreter for his descriptive language, which is somewhere between a simple phrase-structure grammar and a programming language. It allows the statement of the relationship between syntactic categories, which are implicit in phrase-structure grammar, and the creation of attribute lists within each rule, if required, for further computation. However the facilities offered could have been torn apart and the pieces embedded in a general-purpose language. Evans states most of the above himself. He gives as justification for the approach that "we must be able to generalize the notion of grammar so that we can:

(i) isolate the kind of structure we want,
(ii) do a reasonably efficient analysis of an input pattern according to it".

Evans does not discuss (i) but instead gives eight examples of his own and others work. All of them are essentially graph-theoretic, i.e. lines concatenated in various ways. None of the examples given provide any insight into pictorial organisation and basically all he demonstrates is that his pattern analysis can find a sub-graph amongst a graph or several graphs. Evans relates some shortcomings of his system with regard to (ii), "since the analyser doesn't know what predicates may be used, it is unable to take advantage of any special properties they or the input pattern may have to shorten the analysis". The only way out of this difficulty at present is to move to the programming language end of the range where the user can exert as much control as he desires over the parsing procedures. To do otherwise is to assume that we can develop problem-solving procedures that understand the nature of our problems and manipulate relationships and their computational procedures without being able to simulate a significant part of our behavior, which would include amongst other things, visual perception. At the risk of labouring the obvious, if anyone has an insight into perception then he can communicate this to his fellows by normal means, i.e. natural language, diagrams and so on. Before doing so he will probably have to test out his ideas on a machine, and thus he would translate these into some programming language. I, myself, find FORTRAN as convenient as anything else available. Hopefully, when we understand pictorial organisation better, the design of procedural picture languages i.e. those in which the statement of pictorial recovery procedures is convenient, would appear to be a necessary task. At the present time I regard it as premature.

2. General Blobs

The problem with which I am basically concerned is the computation of the shape of any blob. As a starting point I assume that the boundary of the shape has been recovered and is given by an ordered list of the coordinate values of the edge points, and that this is sufficient to compute the shape of the blob. The ordering of the points represents the nearest neighbour relation between points, taken in this paper to be in a clockwise sense. Such a list could be obtained by scanning a picture, which we will assume is black and white only, and then by applying a simple edge-following algorithm.

This type of representation, i.e. the ordered list, appears counter-intuitive in many cases. For instance in Figure 1(a), the algorithm would obtain the coordinates of the line, through all its twists and turns, far removed from the boundary of the envelope of the figure which has a triangular shape. Although we can consciously follow the line through in Figure 1(a) and 1(b) our immediate perception is of a textured region having triangular shape. Our algorithm would obtain a host of small boundaries for 1(b) and as such, is far removed from our global percept. The process that obtains the boundary of the triangular region 1(b) would, one assumes, be the same that obtains the boundary of the triangular region 1(a), and that for 1(a) depending on which level we are looking, we should really have the boundary of the triangular region, or each individual region such as in 1(c), and not the whole line. Moreover the boundary of the triangular region is a reasonable object to compute with. The boundary of 1(a) then, in its initial line form, may present us with a too arduous problem or we may, by considering it discover something useful.

Within the descriptive approach, descriptions are normally presented in terms of lines or bars that join or meet in various ways, e.g. a triangle as 3 lines joined at their ends, a "T" as a vertical bar touching the middle of a horizontal bar. To me, this type of description fails to capture the visual scene and is more suited as a string of interpretable commands to some drawing instrument. One aspect of the scene not represented in these descriptions is the ground. The conventional description of 2(a) in terms of bars or rectangles relates the edges of each bar together as in 2(b). However the largest area "grabbed" by 2(a), the triangular-shaped ground, is not represented in the description. We do usually grasp this area since if we were told to "place the circle in the corner of 2(a)," surely we would respond as in 2(c), none of the interior corners being considered. The interpretation of 2(a) is ambiguous. Another view is easily seen if the figure is rotated to 2(d) where 2(e) gives a different edge grouping. In this case we might obtain a description in terms of a "figure" triangle and a "ground" triangle. Hence a description of some scenes could involve a mixture of ambiguous views. A description of the ground appears to be essential for figures such as 3(a) where the description of the interior of the figure cannot be given in simple terms.

One way of attempting to find the ambiguous views of simple general blobs such as Figure 2(a) is to generalise an idea of Clowes (1969(b)). He proposed that "it is an essential part of this approach to picture syntax that we regard forms containing concavities of boundary as concatenations of forms which *are* convex". He gives Figure 3(b) as sole illustration of this idea saying that the underlying perceptual organisation of this is 3(c). However this idea cannot be applied to 3(a). We can generalise this approach in the following manner. Initially we compute for each nearest neighbour point pair (vector) on the boundary the relationship convex, concave, or not related, between that vector and all other vectors. The definition of this relationship is given in Figure 4. Next we find all the unique subsets of vectors such that the relationship between each and everyone is wholly convex or wholly concave. The result of applying this to Figure 2(a) would be to produce the subsets indicated in Figure 5 and these are well-suited as input to further processes that could eventually produce the descriptions previously mentioned. An important point of the effect of using this form of convex/concave is that we do not obtain any relationship at all between edge a and edge c, or b and most of e, which if it were present would be pulling together figure and ground. I believe that the primitive relation as given in

Figure 4, is an essential one for the computation of shape but the "find all" algorithm with no additional relationships is too flexible. For, consider the results obtained if we computed on Figure 3(a). We would obtain the top edge and bottom edge as subsets, which is good, but what would happen between these objects. This is illustrated in Figure 6 for one vector of the bottom edge. Each vector of the bottom edge would be responsible for a new subset, each subset being formed by extending the vector in both directions until it intersects the top edge. Thus far too many possible subsets would be obtained, for what appears to be a relatively simple figure, and I feel that at this level they should never be obtained at all. The approach must be strengthened. The methodology I have currently adopted is based on that fact that we do not know how to compute the shape of a purely convex blob, which one intuitively feels is the simplest of all blobs and that perhaps some answers may be found if we investigate these.

3. Convex Blobs

My final dissatisfaction with the descriptive approach is that in descriptions offered there is no mention of corners. Descriptions are normally given in terms of what one would interpret as sides. In attempting to describe the visual scene corners are as important as sides; both being significant attributes of any shape. I began my investigation into the shape of convex blobs believing that the initial processes should recover corners and that subsequent processes would obtain sides. Figure 7(a) is a piece of boundary and let us assume that the point labelled A, is the corner-point of this piece. A corner is an area concept, the corner-point being an attribute of the object corner. How then do we obtain the area, or domain of a corner? The following observations may help. Point A dominates this section of boundary, i.e. it appears more important, but it depends on your viewing position. In 7(b) using the axis as horizontal, point A is dominant; in 7(c) using the new axis as horizontal a point to the left of A appears dominant, but it would seem wrong to judge A from this position. These observations suggest that if we are trying to find whether a point dominates a section of the boundary, a possible constraint is that the point must be at a maximum height relative to the chord that joins the ends of the boundary fragment. This is illustrated in 7(d).

In Figure 7(e) two chords have been drawn such that point A satisfies this constraint. It is obvious that if we were to consider all possible boundary fragments, i.e. joining each point to every other, some point or points would be a maximum but in 7(e) both chords do not appear to represent "good viewing-points from which to judge A. A better point of view would be more symmetrical, and in general corners are not. However if we look at the four relationships or constraints that exist in the symmetrical situation we may be able to utilise one of them. This is presented in Figure 8. Discussion of these will be deferred for the moment.

Let us assume, for convenience, that we are using constraint 1 on Figure 9(a) for point A. We would, computationally, be drawing a series of chords across the figure, as indicated. We need to know two further criteria. Firstly, we need a criterion for saying point A dominates over each domain IJ. For example we could predicate a circle on the three points I, A and J, and use various properties of this circle to determine whether any point between I and J "sticks-out" more than A. Secondly, a criterion limiting how far around the figure this procedure should go is necessary, as it appears counter-intuitive to go the whole way around as in 9(b). A plausible limit is to continue the process half-way around the boundary in an angular sense, i.e. the external angle between the two rvectors local to I and J must be $\leq \Pi$, (ignoring the sign of the angles).

If we did this process then we would obtain for each point on the boundary two limits which give the domain of the point. Each point is thus a "corner" and minimally each point must at least dominate as far as its nearest neighbours. One further step is possible, which is illustrated by Figures 9(d) and 9(e). We would expect point A to dominate as far as I_A J_A in 9(d). Points near A, as B in 9(e), would terminate at A, i.e. A would "stick-out" more than B according to any of our circle criteria. Thus it has a small domain and this lies inside the domain of A. Perhaps then, we could remove all such "minor" corners as these and be left with the "major" corners of the figure. Organizations of the figure could then be based upon these "major" corners. However a very simple figure can be used as a counter-example to, at least, some of the details of the model proposed. In Figure 10(a) the algorithm would obtain the two large corners and the two small corners. Since points such as A are not inside any of these they would remain, and we would not say that such points are corners. Furthermore the shape is basically triangular and we can ask why the results obtained are so different from those we would get if B and C were replaced by a single point, i.e. a single sharp corner. A way out of this difficulty is, that when we use our circle criterion we do not stop when we find that "stick-out" points exist but also record which ones "stick-out" most for the left and right separately. However, I have not been successful in finding an algorithm that does this completely satisfactorily, and many approaches remain to be investigated. For a brief discussion of the anomalies of some of the methods I have used see Appendix A.

Let us assume though, that this can be done and that points between B and C, in 10(a), give B and C as side-maxima or "stick-out" points. My original views on the use of side-maxima were that if the ratio of BC to DE was smaller than some parameter, say 1/3, we could coalesce B and C together and thus this would be similar to the single-point corner situation. The following procedure is better than this. If we ignore the ratio completely and keep all side-maxima then points between A and B in Figure 10(b) would yield A and B. This corresponds to a side of the figure and within the same algorithm we would obtain both the domain of possible corners and possible sides. Furthermore we would obtain the point-pairs (C,A) and (B,D) but not the pair (D,C) due to the Π constraint, i.e. the external angle between vectors on the side BD and side CA is greater than Π. The failure to grasp the pair (D,C) is unreasonable.

Π, as noted before, is half-way around the figure in an angular sense. As an alternative we could go half-way around in a distance sence, i.e. around the perimeter. That is, the maximum domain of any point is up to one quarter of the perimeter (P/4) either side of the point and subject to one of the symmetry conditions. This distance measure is not as intuitively plausible as Π but there is one argument that demonstrates that we must compute at least as far as P/4. In Figure 10(c), for instance, if the assumption is made that we must obtain points C and A together, to denote a possible side, then the limits for points approximately in the middle of CA will be just beyond C and A as CB tends to zero. Thus it is always possible to obtain C and A with this limit.

To return now to the postponed discussion of the symmetry conditions given in Figure 8. Conditions 1 and 4 are local i.e. predicated on nearest neighbours while conditions 2 and 3 are global, and global conditions are preferable. However while all of them are plausible when attempting to find single corners, the effects of 2, 3 and 4 lead to the rejection of these conditions, at least at this stage of the computation. In Figure 11 only points between C and D can possibly obtain A and B together as side-maxima due to the P/4 condition, and for all points we would be considering boundary fragments whose chords are parallel to AB, such as IJ. Condition 1 is satisfactory as it is satisfied by all possible IJ's for all points between C and D. Condition 2 and 3 have similar effects in that as IJ moves downwards from AB each point in turn to the left from the mid-point, M, satisfy the conditions only once. This is unrealistic and there is a great danger that if the line AB was replaced by an asymmetric curve then these conditions might not be satisfied at all, and thus the pair (A,B) would not be obtained as a possible side. Condition 4 is not satisfied at all.

It may be the case that no symmetry conditions at all should be considered whilst these computations are performed and there are aspects of symmetry that cannot be accounted for by the simple local condition we are left with. However it does provide a consistent viewing position and overcomes certain difficulties that occur if it is removed, e.g. crossing chords for

for the same point. It is worthwhile now to summarise where these arguments have lead.

The type of algorithm now proposed on purely convex shapes is that firstly for each point on the boundary, say A in Figure 12, we determine the two points left and right of A that are at a distance P/4 from A, namely I′ and J. One of these points is in general further from the axis, PQ, that bisects the external angle at A, so that a further point is computed at a distance from PQ equal to the smaller, i.e. I in Figure 12. The line IJ obtained is the maximum viewing position for point A. We then apply some process between IA and AJ that finds the most significant points, i.e. side-maxima or "stick-out"points. Some algorithms would always return with a point, e.g. we could find the point with the maximum y value relative to the chord IA or AJ, although this is not recommended. For such algorithms dominance would still need to be determined. At this stage for point A we could stop, although it may prove necessary to consider further chords parallel to PQ and between IJ and A. I have a few thoughts on what to do next.

It is obvious that further relationships must be investigated. What is obtained for each point is an attributed area, AA, and I have looked at some simple relationships between these areas. These attributes are represented in Figure 13(a). I and J are the limits of the viewing position of point A, L is the left side-maximum and R is the right side-maximum. At one time I believed that the organisation of a figure would be predicated on four AA's each pair overlapping each other as in 13(b).

If all AA's that give the same side-maxima are lumped together, Figure 14(a) would give 3 sets of 4 AA's, each would have the three AA's that correspond to sides, the fourth AA in each case corresponding to a corner, indicating that 14(a) is 3 ways ambiguous, perhaps leading to three base-apex organizations. In 14(b) however, only one set of 4 would result, the three sides plus the dominant corner. Does this show the essential difference between these two types of triangle?

For 14(c) one set of AA's would be obtained from points like EFGH, each AA corresponding to a side, i.e. the parellogram view of 14(c), the other set from points ABCD, each corresponding to corners, i.e. the diamond view. I have not yet devised an algorithm that attributes these sets. The most important attribution would be the labelling of sides and corners and a representation of their organisation. For instance for 14(c), it must be decided whether DA is a side or EF is a side, etc. Another problem is that for 14(d) the sets obtained are essentially the same as those for 14(c). We would want to indicate that perhaps A and B are "privileged points" but not points that are seen as ends of sides.

There are some difficulties with the "set of 4 view" which indicate that it might not always be possible to obtain them, i.e. a total view does not exist and that we will have to settle for less; i.e. we could only represent organisations of large areas of the figure corresponding to what we would see at different orientations. All that I know is that symmetry is important, but I do not know, computationally, what symmetry is.

4. Conclusion

The descriptive approach, as currently conceived by some writers, has been criticised throughout this paper from two standpoints. If we believe that the central aim of the descriptive approach is a theory of visual perception then research into the linguistic aspect of the approach is irrelevant and the descriptions offered are inadequate.

There is no need "to devise a language in which we can express our intuitions about shape", as adequate means already exist. We need to concentrate upon the recovery of descriptions rather than the representation of descriptions, and the adoption of any "object-descriptive" language necessarily imposes constraints on the flexibility of procedures. We should use "procedure-descriptive" languages in which to write recovery procedures and general-purpose programming languages, with all their faults, are better-suited to the task.

In order to recover pictorial descriptions we must determine the pictorial relationships used at each stage of the process. Three levels of the problem of the general blob have been examined:

(1) Recovery of grcuped fragments for a general blob,
(2) Determination of the significant points of selected areas for each of these groupings,
(3) How these areas are related.

It is probable that much of the detail proposed will require modification but I believe the methodology holds promise.

Appendix A.

Some Unsatisfactory Methods for Side-Maxima

The problem is to find the most significant points of a section of boundary. As input we have the coordinate values of 3 points, A, I, and J as in Figure A1 where A has maximum y value relative to IJ. The parameters for the methods tried are given in A2. For one of the symmetry conditions a equals c and for the other 3 conditions A must lie between I and J. Two computed templates were used. The first was a circle computed as in A3, which gives the two left half cases; the second was an ellipse where all computations were performed by transforming the coordinates to the unit circle given in A4. The left section of the boundary i.e. IA, was treated separately to the right i.e. AJ.

The first property used to determine side-maxima was to find the point that had the maximum radius and to retain it if it exceeded the radius of the predicated circle. If it did not then A dominated this section. In general, the elliptical case was very good whereas the circular case was too fine i.e. many maxima could hardly be seen. However, both suffer from a major defect in that they occasionally obtain a completely wrong point, an example of this is in A5 where the point C might be found.

This defect can in general, be overcome by using angular properties of the circles. The simplest is to determine the maximum external angle, max α_ρ, subtended at any point by the chords IA and IJ, this is shown for IA in A6. The defect of this approach is given in A7 where small bumps near to the axis, such as C, are obtained, whereas a point such as B is preferable. A more complicated angular property is given in A8, based on local changes of r and θ, but while this appears to completely overcome the difficulties of the radius approach it has similar tendencies to the external angle method. In this case dominance is rarely computed as only a restricted family of curves produce no side-maxima. For the present it would be perhaps better not to worry about the threshold problem but to discover an algorithm that gives intuitively the correct points based on some global properties.

Appendix B.

Some Blobs

As a point of interest I have included some of the convex blobs that are my data. They were obtained by drawing on a CRT with a light-pen and, as it is impossible to draw purely convex blobs, subjected to an "elastic-band" algorithm to remove the concavities. This accounts for the uneven spacing of points. The first point is marked "0" and every tenth as a ".", all others as a "+". Some of these blobs are very difficult.

REFERENCES

1. Clowes, M. B. (1969a), "Transformational Grammars and the Organisation of Pictures", in Automatic Interpretation and Classification of Images. A. Grasselli (Ed.), Academic Press, pp. 43-77.
2. Clowes, M. B. (1969b), "Pictorial Relationships – a syntactic approach" in Machine Intelligence 4, (B. Meltzer and D. Michie, Eds.) Edinburgh University Press, pp. 361-383.
3. Evans, T. G. (1969), "Descriptive Pattern Analysis Techniques", in Automatic Interpretation and Classification of Images, A. Grasselli (Ed.), Academic Press, pp. 79-95.
4. Grasselli, A. (1969), Preface to Automatic Interpretation and Classification of Images. A. Grasselli (Ed.), Academic Press.
5. Narasimhan, R. (1969), "On the Description, Generation and Recognition of Classes of Pictures", in Automatic Interpretation and Classification of Images, A. Grasselli, (Ed.), Academic Press, pp. 1-42.
6. Narasimhan, R. (1970), "Picture Languages", in Picture Language Machines S. Kaneff (Ed.), Academic Press, pp. 1-30.

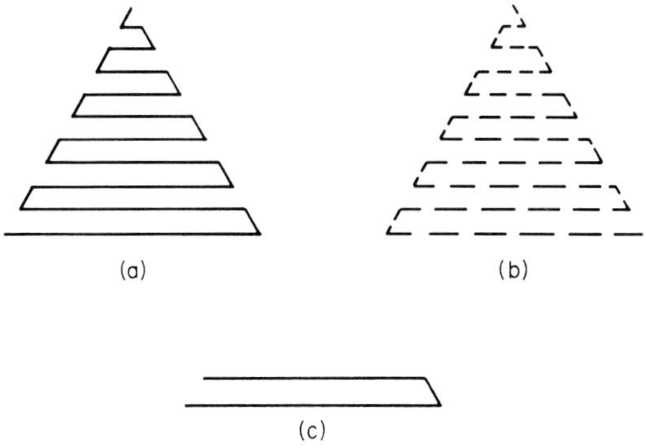

Figure 1

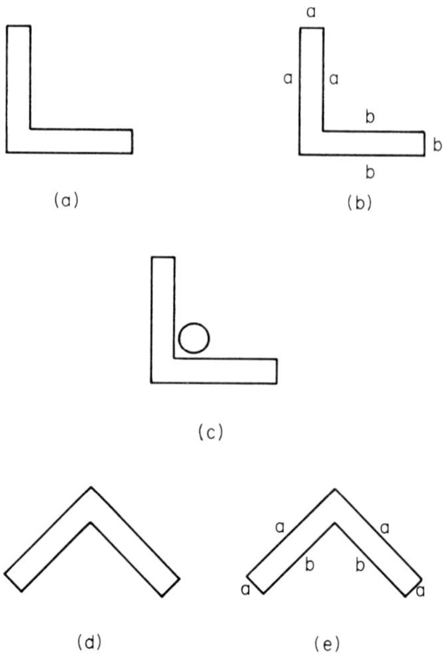

Figure 2

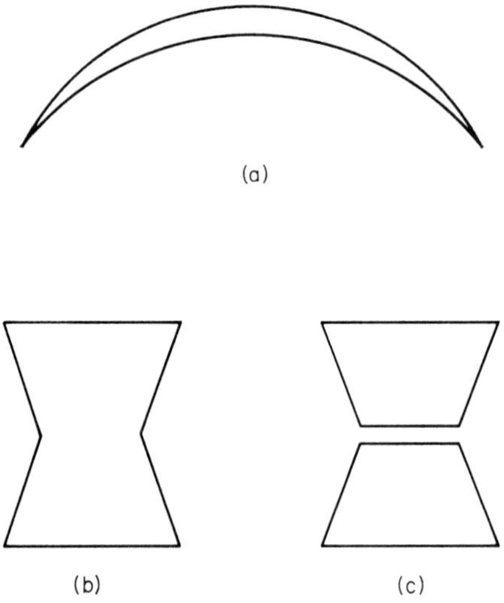

Figure 3

Convex

AXIS(I, I+1): $Y(J-1) \leq 0$, $Y(J) \leq 0$, $0 \geq \alpha \geq -2\Pi$

AXIS(J−1,J): $Y(I) \leq 0$, $Y(I+1) \leq 0$

Concave

As for convex but with signs reversed

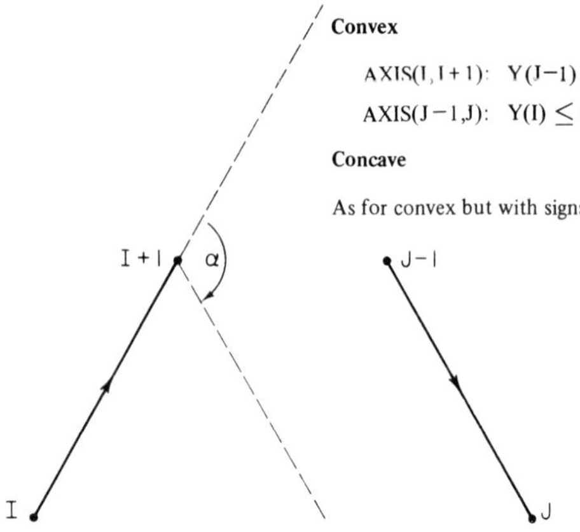

Figure 4

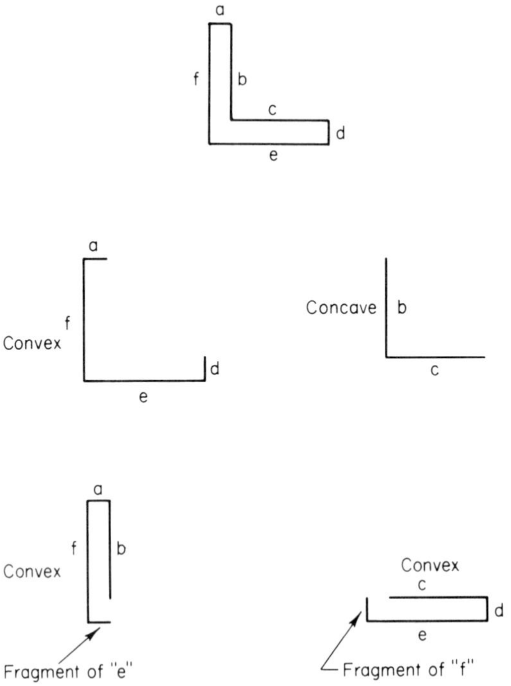

Figure 5

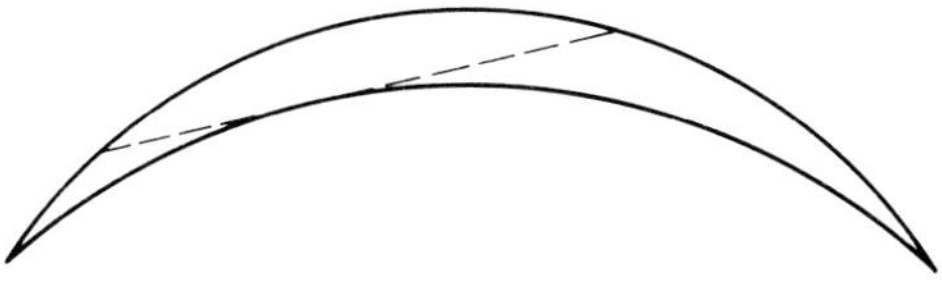

Figure 6. One of many convex fragments

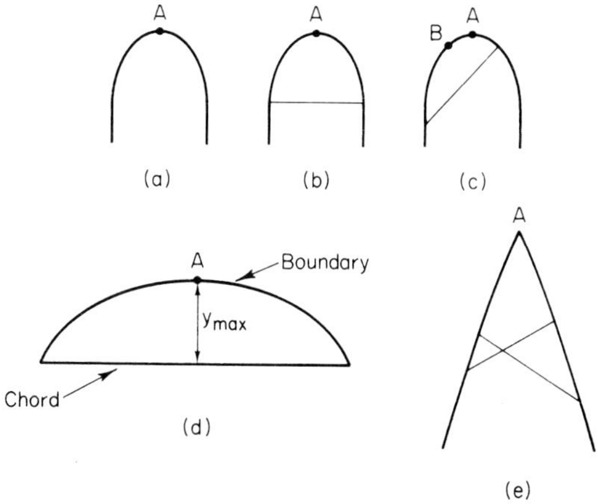

Figure 7

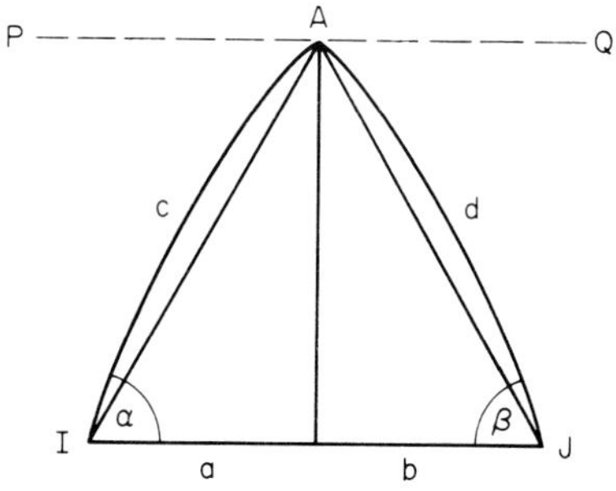

(1) IJ is parallel to PQ. PQ is the bisector of the external angle at A.
(2) c = d i.e. equal perimeter
(3) a = b or IA = AJ
(4) $\alpha = \beta$

Figure 8

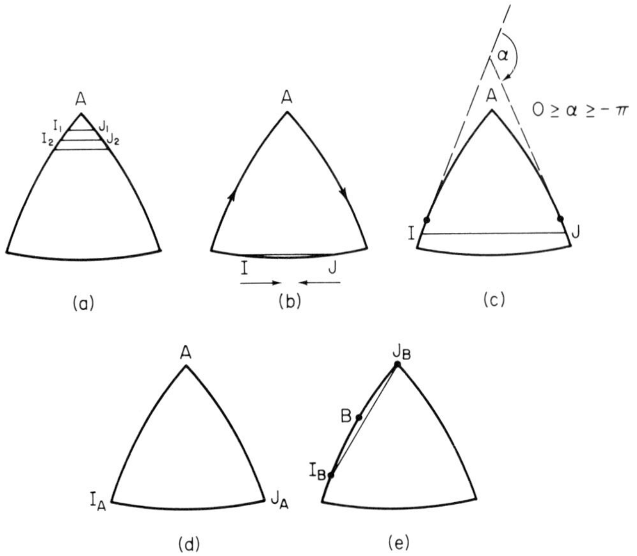

Figure 9

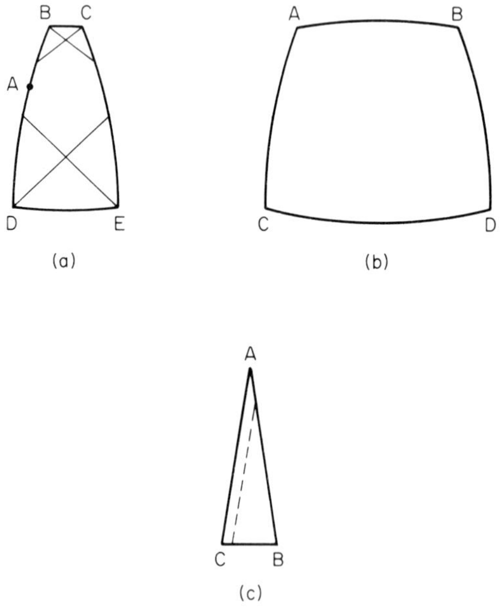

Figure 10

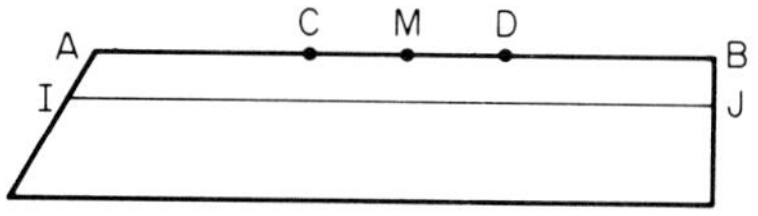

Figure 11

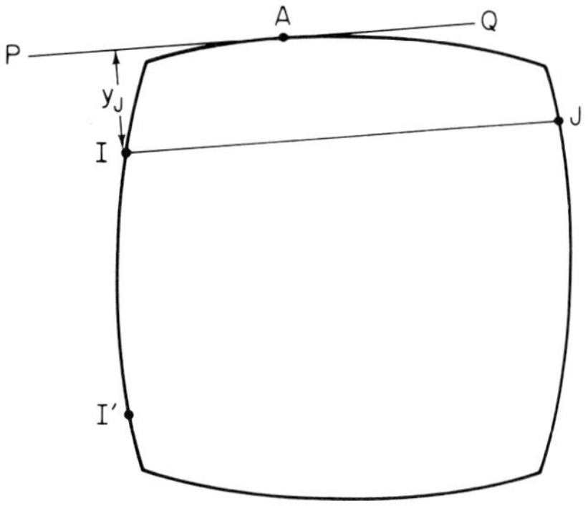

Figure 12

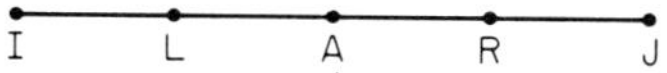

The five attributes of an AA

(a)

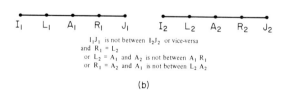

I_1J_1 is not between I_2J_2 or vice-versa
and $R_1 = L_2$
or $L_2 = A_1$ and A_2 is not between A_1 R_1
or $R_1 = A_2$ and A_1 is not between L_2 A_2

(b)

Figure 13

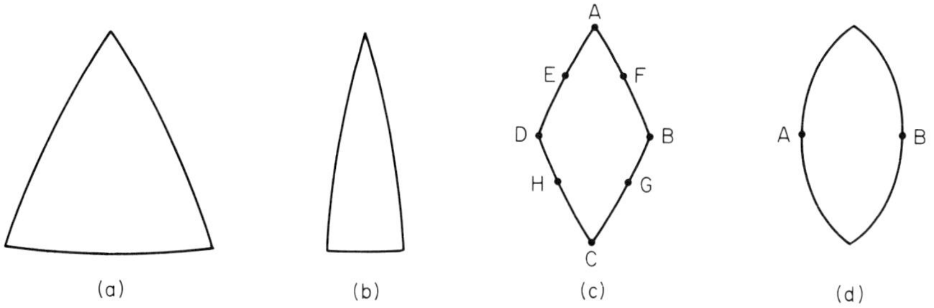

Figure 14

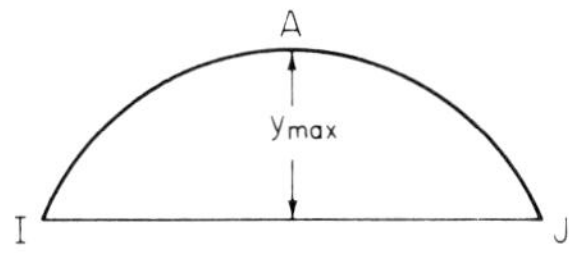

Figure A1

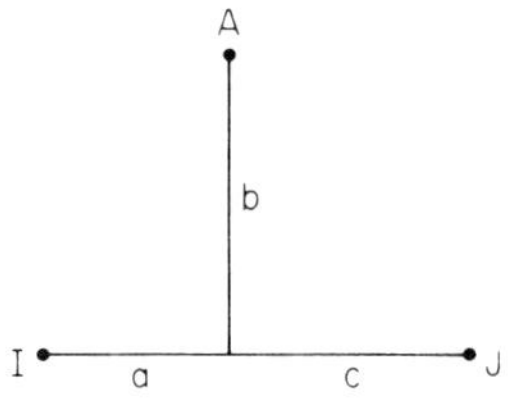

Figure A2

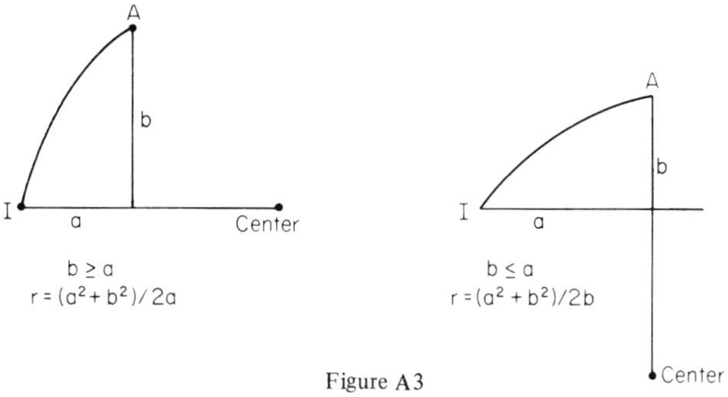

Figure A3

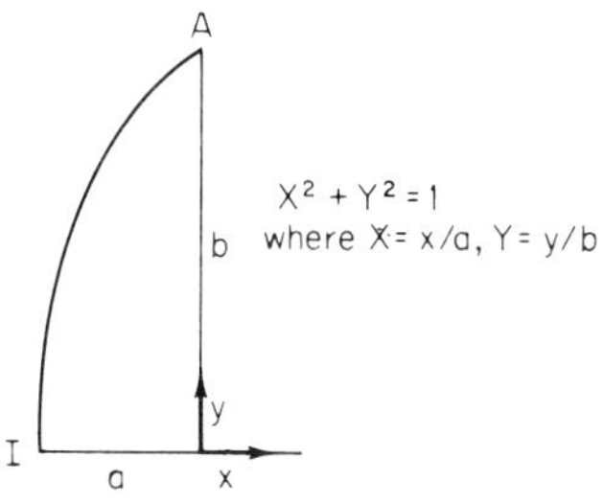

Figure A4

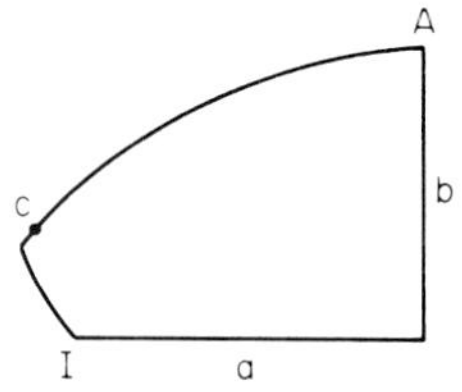

Figure A5

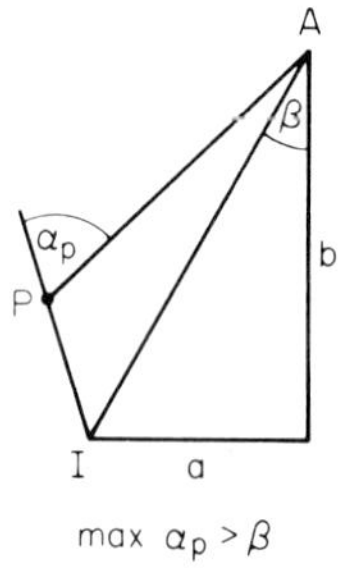

Figure A6

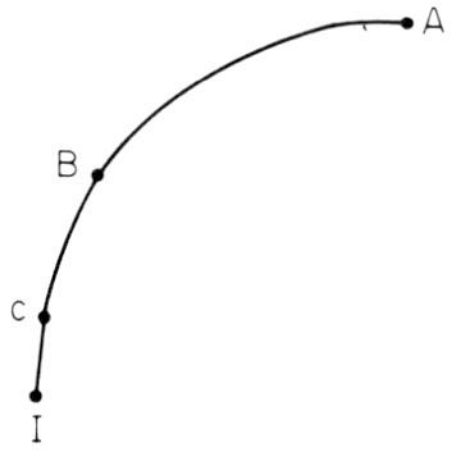

Figure A7

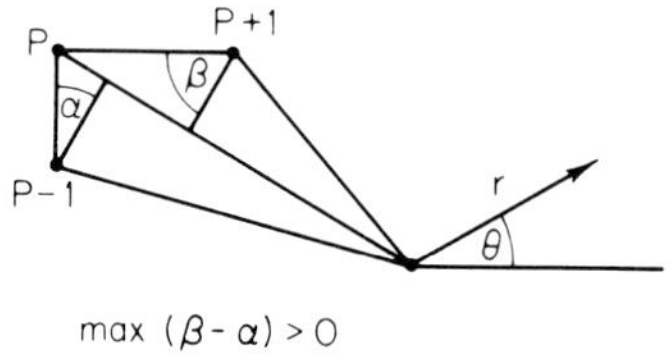

Figure A8

Some Blobs

A "CRISIS" IN THE THEORY OF PATTERN RECOGNITION*

A. Lerner

Why does the problem of pattern recognition learning arouse such interest of the part of scientists in various fields? In answering this question we could of course refer to the potential practical use of ideas and methods of pattern recognition. The solution rules obtained while training computers in pattern recognition appear very effective in medical diagnosis, epidemiology, interpretation of geophysical data, weather forecasting, character recognition, etc.

This is not, however, the attraction of the problem, which perhaps is in some unexpected, not quite understandable, and even sensational applications that are fruitful thanks to the heuristics of the algorithms used, more than to the known statements of the problem. The rules obtained in pattern recognition learning even with scarce empirical data are sometimes found to be much stronger than could be expected from the estimates which are valid for the problem stated in the sense that they yield correct solutions in the situations that have not been encountered in the training sequence. The researchers are also attracted by the unusual success of the experiments in applying pattern recognition to various fields of science by using most diverse learning algorithms.

Quite unexpected, the difficulties were encountered in the methodology of this problem.

On the Statement of the Problem

For ten years scientists have tried to comprehend what is the problem they face. Sometimes one can draw a general and thus incomplete sketch designed to fit the statement of the pattern recognition problem. With an orthodox mathematical approach to this problem one can assert that the

*This is the first manuscript submitted to the conference, but he was unable to attend the meeting. We tried to contact him to obtain the final version of the paper but we were unsuccessful.

problem is a primitive problem of searching for optimal solution rules on the basis of empirical data; primitive, because the solution rules that result from the processing of empirical evidence are surprisingly simple and are merely characteristic functions. Furthermore, they may be just linear discriminant functions.

If we share the traditional view of the mathematicians that setting the class of functions where we are searching the best one, according to a certain criterion, is the external representation of the statement of the problem, then the problem is a particular case in the problem of search for the best solution by empirical data. The mathematical tools, however were found insufficient to solve this particular problem. Therefore, certain areas of the probability theory and mathematical statistics have to be further developed such as the theory of statistical approximation, the theory of uniform convergence of the frequency of events to their probability. This need could, however, appear by itself, unrelated to the problem of pattern recognition. Moreover, if what we term as the development of tools and the theory of the learning problem can at all be separated, they are generally akin to the traditional fields of mathematics. Besides, no algorithm has yet been developed from a theory. Almost unvariably, theory followed an algorithm to justify it.

What is the novelty, then, that the researchers are after in the theory of pattern recognition? What is the specific contents that they try to introduce into the formalization of the concept of learning?

Different facets of the problem were viewed as the principal ones over the period of research in the field. Just 10 or 12 years ago when the first papers of Rosenblatt were published, learning seemed to be a mysterious phenomenon inherent to living beings and the methods of studies in learning was very much like that in the present day studies in bionics: it was assumed that we should understand the learning technology of living beings and then computerize it. Then, however, the problem was restated as one of risk minimization. As a result, a huge number of algorithms appeared and this flow is strong enough even now. Soon these algorithms were found to be based on the same ideas, either stochastic approximation or minimization of the empirical risk. This discovery immediately led some to believe that a crisis broke out in the theory of pattern recognition. Indeed, if the general principles of stochastic approximation or minimization of the statistical risk are to be used throughout, then there is nothing specific in the problem and this cannot be the object of fundamental studies.

What is then the state-of-art? What is the specific nature of the problem statement? How does this problem differ from the general problem of risk minimization? The specific features of the problem are believed to stem from the fact that the class of solving rules is exceedingly simple. It is desirable to use this class in order to find the most particular features of the risk minimization problem, the features that are inherent in this class alone and cannot be the general properties of the risk minimization methods.

Unfortunately, no statement has yet crystallized that would define the specific features of learning problems within the framework of the classical decision-making theory.

The scope of learning problems can yet be defined, but to do this we have to touch upon the general methodological problems of scientific cognition and try to sort out the criteria which are used by scientists, consciously or subconsciously, who discover the laws of nature, select the alternative hypothesis and form the picture of the world in their mind.

On the Role of Intuition

Lately the greatest number of laws, observations that can be strictly formulated were made by physicists. The pattern of physical discoveries is generally the same. There is a number of experiments or observed phenomena that cannot be explained within the framework of the old theory. Therefore, the old theory is replaced by a new one that interprets both the facts that were known before and those that puzzled the old theory. What is surprising is not the fact that a new theory is each time developed, but that this theory fits new facts (a "true" theory has been developed). Indeed, formally there are a great many laws that explain the known facts, but are incapable of predicting new facts. For Einstein to develop the theory of relativity he had to develop a theory that would contain the classical mechanics and explain two or three facts, of which the most important one was the Michaelson experiment. Formally such theories are numerous. How did Einstein find the true one?

Generally physicists offer various explanations. Some said that a theory should be beautiful, others, that it should be unusual (recall the now classical saying that the theory "is not crazy enough to be true"), still others, that a theory should be a simple rule that would explain the world. About this phenomenon Einstein said, "God is ingenious, but not evil". In other words, physicists are aware that facts alone are not sufficient to select a true theory, and a theory that would explain the world should also have an extremum property (some term this beauty, others, unusualness, still others, simplicity, etc.).

This selection has been done without any formal rules, by intuition. Therefore if we want a computer to "reasonably" select the solution rule from a set of rules which agree with the experimental evidence, the computer should have some substitute for intuition.

"Computer Intuition"

How then computer intuition should be understood? Let us have a closer look at the statement of the problem. The formal objective of learning is to find in a class of solution rules such a rule that would minimize the probability of an error, but in fact we can only select a rule that minimizes the frequency of errors (in a learning sequence). According to the classical theorem of the theory of probability the frequency reduces to the probability at infinite increase of the number of experiments.

To insure that the rule which leads to the minimal value of the frequency will be also true for the minimal value of the probability (or a value close to it), this is evidently insufficient. The frequency should converge to the probability uniformly. An offshoot in just one point, as in Figure 1, can lead to selection of exactly that solution which was represented by the point of the offshoot.

Let us consider a simple case: the set $\{S\}$ is finite and consists of N events $S_1, \ldots S_N$. For each fixed event the law of great numbers holds (the frequency V converges to the probability at infinite increase of the number of experiments). A particular case of that law is the value of the estimate for the rate of convergence to the probability P of the frequency V found by a sample of the length ℓ.

$$P(|V-P| \geqslant E) < e^{-\frac{E^2\ell}{4}} \tag{1}$$

We are, however, interested in the case of uniform convergence, or the probability that all N inequalities

$$\begin{array}{c} |P_1 - V_1| \geqslant E \\ \vdots \\ |P_N - V_N| \geqslant E \end{array}$$

will be true simultaneously. This probability can be calculated since equation (1) estimates the probability of observing each individual inequality which is

$$P(\underset{i}{\ up}\,|V_i^\ell - P_i| \geqslant E) < Ne^{-\frac{E^2\ell}{4}} \tag{2}$$

Let us require that this probability is equal to η

$$Ne^{-\frac{E^2\ell}{4}} = \eta \tag{3}$$

Solving equation (3) for E we will have

$$E = 2\sqrt{\frac{\ell n N - \ell n \eta}{\ell}} \tag{4}$$

a quantity which characterizes the reliable interval for any solution rule. What is important in equation (4) is that the lower N the smaller the deviation of the error probability from the calculated frequency can be insured. This fact enables one to answer the question, how to find the best rule from a set of rules that minimize the magnitude 0 of empirical risk.

To do this one has to order a priori the set of solution rules so that they form a system of inserted subsets with the number of elements

$$N_1 < N_2 < \ldots . < N_i$$

and try to select the solution rule from a subset with the smaller index. If the rule that minimizes the risk in the i subset, then the value of the mean risk will not exceed

$$E = \sqrt{\frac{\ell n\, Ni - \ell n\, \eta}{\ell}}$$

Consequently, the introduction of an a priori orderliness enables one to select the best rule from a set of rules that minimize the empirical risk. This is "computer intuition". What is required is to develop a theory of uniform convergence for the case where the class of solving problems consists of a concinuum of functions, and introduce an a priori order into this class. Important results in this field were obtained by V. N. Vapnik, a researcher of my laboratory.

On a World Where Intuition is Possible

With the kind of reasoning on ordering that has been presented above one would believe that to introduce the concept of order (which it is desirable to identify with complexity) is completely in our hands. Actually this is not so. When ordering, we set the class of functions by the recursive technique (by setting the rules of obtaining such functions) rather than by listing the elements. The rules for a class of a lower order should be such that the sets of the functions obtained should be introduced into the set of functions of a higher order. The rules proper for obtaining the functions are given by the constructive, and therefore relatively simple method.

How various are the ordering techniques? In what terms can this variety be defined? There is no answer to these questions thus far. The experimental fact that such apparently different algorithms as the method of generalized portrait and the CORA algorithm lead to about the same results for all problems is also hard to explain. Furthermore, those engaged in application of learning techniques firmly believe that if a problem can be solved by one algorithm, then it can be solved by many others.

I would believe that this can be explained if the concept of complexity is introduced and a model of a simple world where all phenomena have a simple functional relation is built in these terms.

On the other hand, almost all functions are complex in that the less the complexity, the lower the number of such functions in a class. For the functions of Boolean algebra this is indeed the case. To find a certain law there is no need to look for it in a class of complex functions, which is also useless for we are short of experimental evidence, because the world is simple according to the hypothesis. (Incidentally although almost all Boolean algebra functions are complex, no example of a complex function has been built).

This extremum may further be related to obtaining a "simple" solving rule. Let us note that to find a simple solving rule that would satisfy the empirical facts is much more complicated than to find any rule (we are short of simple rules!). In our human perception simplicity is intimately related to beauty. It is may be for this reason that the properties of rule such as "simplicity", "unexpectedness", "beauty", which is used by physicists to select a law represent different facets of the same functional.

Einstein's saying remains the profoundest of all. "God is ingenious" because it is hard to understand what the complexity of the world is, it is hard to get to know the world; He is not evil because the world can be comprehended with the tools available to us, although it is not so hard to imagine a world to understand which we would be eternally short of experience.

All this should probably be the subject of the science of learning.

HEURISTIC USE OF IMAGE PROCESSING TECHNIQUE FOR THEORETICAL STUDIES OF AUTOMATA

Hidenosuke Nishio

DEPARTMENT OF BIOPHYSICS
KYOTO UNIVERSITY

1. Introduction

1.1 PURPOSIVE AND EPISTEMOLOGICAL

We would like to begin by commenting upon relationship between the study of pattern recognition and the theoretical study of automata. It is two-fold: (1) Theory of automata will be a base or a background for pattern recognition. (2) Pattern recognition (processing) technique will help the theoretical study of complex systems such as cellular automata.

The field of pattern recognition has two distinct goals. One is, typically speaking, to construct an effective machine for classifying given images into certain preassigned categories. The other is to know the mechanism of image perception and pattern recognition in a human being or other living organisms. The former may be called a *purposive* study, while the latter an *epistemological* one.

In spite of efforts in the fields of psychology and physiology, the latter goal seems difficult to attain in the near future. The purposive pattern recognition, on the other hand, has enjoyed a great success in the last decade. Many practical and experimental devices have been built for various applications. Several powerful theories and methods have been developed as well. This is because the goal of the purposive study is concrete and nearer contrary to the epistemology, where to know the mechanism is a difficult and unclear question.

1.2 STUDIES ON PATTERNS AND RECOGNIZERS

In the purposive study, researchers generally investigate first the distinctive features of given images or sample patterns which might belong to each pattern category. It is not too much to refer to it as the *study of patterns*. A typical method, which has been proved effective, is the structural study of line patterns by means of the generative grammar or other structural languages. Thus the structures of various patterns have been made clearer. In this kind of studies, they consider implicitly the computer as processor of images, or little is talked about the specific structure of recognizer itself.

On the other hand, the *theory of recognizers,* living and artificial, is not so rich. In physiology for example, much experimental facts have been revealed, but an integrated theory, which depicts the whole process of pattern recognition, has not been obtained. A reason for this will be that the theory of recognizer should be of general purpose, while that of patterns is more or less of special purpose.

When we refer to the theory of recognizers, we mean concepts as follows; the physical structure of processing elements (neuron, threshold element, transistor and so on), the way of connection (uniform, random, purposive as in computer and so on), the manner and amount of memory (digital, analog, bits and so on), the learning mechanism (perceptron, PAPA), the speed of operation (serial, parallel, asynchronous), the versatility (special purpose or general purpose, single-font or multi-font and so on) and others. In my definition the present computer is universal in ability but amorphous in structure. Or better, it has a structure from engineering necessities (purposive!). Image processing languages generally have structures.

Perceptron has a structure of linear threshold logic [1]. Various variants have been devised of this category. A non-linear perceptron like structured recognizer has been originated from analogy with neuro-physiology [2]. The theory of computational geometry by Minsky and Papert [3] is a study connecting the features of patterns to the structure of the classifiers (various perceptrons in this case). They relate the complexity of patterns to the amount of memory required for classifying them. Thus theories, which take into account the structure of recognizers as well as that of patterns, have emerged.

Before going to the main subject, we must touch on the mathematical theory of classifiers. This is one of the richest areas of pattern recognition. It includes the statistical decision theory, linear and nonlinear classifiers, potential function theory [4], series expansion [5], learning with or without teacher [6] and so on.

Among these theories there are some which consider the physical structure of classifier explicitly, or can be interpreted naturally as such.

There are also such theories that are purely mathematical and could not be implemented easily. Mathematical procedures are simulated by a computer or reduced to some iterative calculation. We expect that efforts by many authors in this area will lead to such a theory that reflects naturally, or give a hint to, the mechanism of perception in living systems.

1.3 CELLULAR AUTOMATA AND PATTERN RECOGNITION

A cellular automaton is, as von Neumann first formulated [7], an array of uniformly interconnected identical finite automata. An array may be finite or infinite and 1-dimensional, 2-dimensional or so on in general. Studies on cellular automata are classified into two types. One is theoretical, such as what Burks collected [8]. The other is more purposive and includes experimentation or engineering like arithmetic circuits. Unger's work on pattern recognition using the cellular system is also purposive and directed to engineering [9]. His system is combinatorial, which is more tractable than the ordinary automaton having memory.

We are interested in such a uniform structure because of biological analogy as well as manufacturing possibility.

At present we have not much evidence that the cellular structure has definite advantage in the study (theoretical or engineering) of pattern recognition. There are only the above mentioned Unger's work, Hennie's motivation for the theory of iterative logical circuits [10], and Minsky-Papert's comment on the connectedness of patterns processed by iterative system [3]. They have payed attention to the parallel operation of the system, which might be an essential feature of the pattern recognition in living organisms.

This approach is not necessarily epistemological (like physiology) but not purposive at the same time. We want to know the mechanism of pattern recognition in terms of the structure of recognizer.

As a representative system which has a natural structure, we have chosen the cellular structure. Another structure will be the linear threshold logic or the perceptron. PAPA is a 'mathematical machine' [11].

As is well known, the basic features of behaviors and capabilities of cellular automata have been little revealed, though several topics such as self-reproduction, synchronization problem [12], have been investigated and published. We want to establish a systematic study, which will be necessary for various applications as well as for pattern recognition.

There are many fundamental concepts about the cellular structure. Among these, we explain here the *problem of information transmission* and related theme [13].

In studying this problem, we devised a theoretical tool, which, with a graphic display system, is powerful in illustrating the information processing in the system.

1.4 PATTERN RECOGNITION AND OTHER DISCIPLINES

Let's change our point of view to an application of pattern recognition. The developing image processing techniques have three ways of interaction with other disciplines.

(1) The first one is so called *on-line interaction* such as automatic mailing service and traffic control system, where the following scheme will hold: observation of images → image processing → decision making → control of devices. For this the study of patterns involved is essential.

Sakai's group has investigated this direction from various aspects [14]. It aims at constructing a multiplex integrated computer system, which is equipped with versatile input-output devices such as OCR for multi-font typewritten texts, graphic display of storage tube type, and XY pen input for line patterns, speech analysis and response unit as well as various programs for processing natural languages. One of the recent results is an application of LISP, whose processor has been implemented by this group to recognition of line patterns [15].

Sakai's motivation to the integrated system will be expressed by the statement: "Picture processing is not the research field isolated from those of transmission and control systems." The following items should be considered:

1. picture processing power, scanning speed
2. bandwidth of transmission line
3. buffer memory between transmission lines and processors
4. output (display) systems and devices
5. interrupt signals, control signals
6. interruption and modification through man-machine system.

(2) The second interaction is *on-line but not so real time,* as seen in experimental studies such as chromosome identification: observation → image processing → partial decision making → human experimenter. The procedure does not necessarily include the final decision. The goal will be that the image processing system gives the experimenter much useful information extracted from source data. We, as well as Sakai's group, have little experience of this aspect, though our newly established department of biophysics will begin some experimentation.

(3) The last one is *off-line interaction,* which is seen in theoretical studies such as automata theory, finite group theory and other combinatorial studies. In this case, contrary to the formers, the stage of observation may

be omitted, since the objects are not physical phenomena but given in the form of symbols. The procedure will be: set of symbols with or without structure → processing algorithm with pattern recognition capability → display → human researcher → change of algorithm or change of display technique → display → and so on. The final goal will be to get proof of a theorem within the brain of the researcher. Applications to various games may be classified into this category. In the case of complex games such as chess, Go and shogi, the technique of image processing is inevitable.

The above mentioned classification is a conceptual one and it is needless to say that concrete image processing techniques themselves are interchangeable among three aspects.

My point lies in the third aspect. This may also be a purposive study of pattern recognition, where the pattern is not usual. The goal is not necessarily recognition by machine but by a human being. Therefore the role of image processing is greater than that of mechanical decision.

2. Problem of Information Transmission in Cellular Automata

2.1 1-DIMENSIONAL CELLULAR AUTOMATON–NOTATION AND DEFINITION

For ease of explanation we first treat the problem for the i-dimensional cellular automata. Extension to higher dimensionality is easy.

In Figure 1 each cell A_i is the same copy of a finite automaton $A \triangleq (S,f)$, where S is the set of the internal states and f is the state transition function $S \times S \times S \rightarrow S$. A is considered to be of Moore type, i.e. its outputs to both directions are identical and identified with its internal state at the moment. That is, for the state of A_i at time t is denoted by $x_i(t)$, then

$$x_i(t+1) = f(x_{i-1}(t), x_i(t), x_{i+1}(t)) \quad \begin{array}{l} i = 1,2, \ldots, n \\ t = 0,1, \ldots \end{array}$$

where $x_0(t) = b_l$ (fixed left boundary condition) and
$x_{n+1}(t) = b_r$ (fixed right boundary condition).

A cellular automaton A(n) is determined when S,f,n (the number of cells or length of the automaton) and the boundary conditions are given. The left-most cell A_1 is defined to be the output cell of the system and then the sequence $\{x_1(t), t=0,1, \ldots\}$ is the output sequence of the system, which is determined by the initial state of each cell. If $x_i(t)=a_i, (a_i \in S$, for $i = 1,2, \ldots, n)$, then we denote like $\overline{x(t)} = (a_1, a_2, \ldots, a_n)$ or shortly α_n. A Greek letter denotes a string of symbols. When the initial state is α_n, the output sequence of A(n) is denoted by $P(\alpha_n)$. Because of autonomous behavior of the system, $P(\alpha)$ is divided into two parts: a transient part and a cyclic part which follows it. Since there is a canonical representation for such a sequence, it is easy to decide whether two output sequences are the same or not.

Let S^* be the set of all finite strings of alphabet S, and S^k be that of all strings of length k. Now we can conclude that the information about the state of the right-most cell is not transmitted to the output cell, if $P(\alpha a) = P(\alpha b)$ for $\forall \alpha \in S^{n-1}$ and $a \neq b \in S$. That is, it is impossible by observation of the output to decide whether the right-most cell had been in state a or b at the beginning. We formulate this statement precisely in the next section.

2.2 CLASSIFICATION OF 1-DIMENSIONAL CELLULAR AUTOMATA

Let the cardinality of S be denoted by $|S|$. If the set of all possible transition functions over S^3, where $|S| = m$ is denoted by F, then $|F| = m^{m^3}$.

If the boundary conditions are kept fixed, the classification of the systems A(n) can be identified with that of F. We classify F into three classes C_I, C_{II} and C_{III} as follows:

(I) $f \in C_I$ if and only if for $\exists k > 0$, $\forall \alpha_k \in S^k$ and $\forall \beta \in S^*$, $P(\alpha_k) = P(\alpha_k \beta)$.
(The smallest number k for which (I) holds is called the k-value of f.)

(II) $f \in C_{II}$ if and only if for $\exists k > 0$, $\exists \alpha_k \in S^k$ and $\forall \beta \in S^*$, $P(\alpha_k) = P(\alpha_k \beta)$ but such α_k's do not exaust S^k.

(III) $f \in C_{III}$ if and only if for $\forall \alpha_k \in S^k$ and $\exists \beta_j \in S^j$, $P(\alpha_k) \neq P(\beta_j)$.

Obviously from (I), (II) and (III),

$$F = C_I \cup C_{II} \cup C_{III} \text{ and } C_I \cap C_{II} = C_{II} \cap C_{III} = C_I \cap C_{III} = \phi$$

For any $|S|$ it can be shown that C_I, C_{II} and C_{III} are not null sets.

A short informal explanation of this classification would increase understanding: For those automata which belong to C_I, the initial state of a cell located at enough distance from the output cell never has influence upon the behavior of the latter. Contrary to C_I, C_{III} represents a class of cellular automata where the effect of an arbitrarily far cell will appear at the output cell in a time. The automaton which belongs to C_{II} behaves like C_I or C_{III} according to the initial state condition.

In other words the above classification reflects the *ability of right to left transmission of information* or *effect of the initial state condition on the output.*

2.3 A DECISION PROBLEM ON CLASSIFICATION

Given an arbitrary S and $f: S^3 \rightarrow S$, is it recursively decidable to which class f belongs?

Regretfully we have not reached the conclusion, though we formulated and proved several theorems which would pertain to classification.* Our conjecture is that it is decidable whether $f \in C_I$ or not, but not whether $f \in C_{II}$ or $f \in C_{III}$. In discussing the decidability of C_I, a computable upper bound of k-values for all functions of C_I would play an essential role. A successful approach would be to obtain some numerical estimates as well as to prove theorems. We started with the case $|S| = 2$ or the simplest non-trivial finite automaton. In this case $|F| = 256$.

We investigated each function one by one, by means of above mentioned theorems and other skillful techniques. It was made clear that even this simplest case could not be settled easily. Table 1 indicates the results obtained thus far.

C_I									C_{II}	C_{III}	?	Total
k-value	1	2	3	4	5	6	7	Total				
	64	34	19	5	1	0	1	124	46	27	59	256

Table 1 Number of classified functions, case of $|S| = 2$

Out of efforts to do the above mentioned classification, a simulation method has been formulated which will be explained in the next section.

3. Simulation Method with Unknown Variable

For ease of exposition, assume first $|S| = 2$. Then $f : S^3 \to S$ can be considered to be a three variable Boolean function. Now suppose for example, $f(0,0,0) = 1$ and $f(0,0,1) = 0$. Then it would be natural and reasonable to claim that $f(0,0,X) = \overline{X}$, where X is a Boolean variable and $\overline{X}$ is its negation. Furthermore if $f(0,0,1) = 1$ and $f(0,1,0) = 0$, then $f(0,X,\overline{X}) = \overline{X}$, and so on.

In general we can expand the domain of f or S^3 to G^3, where G is the set of all Boolean functions of X or $G = \{0,1,X,\overline{X}\}$. We denote this extended function as $\tilde{f}$. In order to realize this extension, we must define sum and product on G, which are compatible with those of S. For this we denote any element of G as follows:

$g(X) = a_1 + a_2X$, where a_1 and a_2 is 0 or 1, + is the mod.2 sum and product is the ordinary one. The correspondence with the Boolean function is given in Table 2.

*It is not the objective of this paper to show these theoretical results, which will appear elsewhere.

Boolean expression	$g(X): (a_1, a_2)$
$f(X) = 0$	$g_1 = (0,0)$
$f(X) = 1$	$g_2 = (1,0)$
$f(X) = X$	$g_3 = (0,1)$
$f(X) = \overline{X}$	$g_4 = (1,1)$

Table 2

We define sum and product in G as follows:

if $g_1(X) = a_1 + a_2X$ and $g_2(X) = b_1 + b_2X$, then

$$(g_1 + g_2)(X) = (a_1 + b_1) + (A_2 + b_2)X \text{ and}$$

$$(g_1 g_2)(X) = a_1 b_1 + (a_1 b_2 + a_2 b_1 + a_2 b_2)X.$$

On the other hand, the transition function can be also expressed in the similar form:

$$f(x,y,z) = u_1xyz + u_2xy + u_3xz + u_4yz + u_5x + u_6y + u_7z + u_8,$$

where $u_i = 0$ or 1 and x,y and z are the states of the left neighbor, the cell itself and the right neighbor respectively. This form of transition function was of course defined for S^3 but now that we have defined operations on G, we can calculate $\tilde{f}$ for G^3 by substituting x,y and z with elements of G. Thus we have obtained the extended function $\tilde{f} : G^3 \rightarrow G$.

Using this machinery we can simulate the information transmission along a 1-dimensional cellular array. If one wants to see how the initial state of the right-most cell influences the behavior of the system, he may set the state of the right-most cell to X (0 or 1 but unknown which of them) and begin simulation using the extended transition function $\tilde{f}$ instead of f. Some illustrative examples are given in Figure 2. Note that in order to use our method a conversion of function from the Boolean to ours, say g-expression is necessary. This conversion is not so difficult for programming.

Example (a) in Figure 2 indicates the case where the information of the right-most cell appears at the left-most cell and remains in the system forever. Example (b) illustrates the situation where the information is not transmitted to the end and disappears at $t = 12$. In example (c) the information does not reach the left-most cell nor disappear.

This simulation method with an unknown variable X is obviously applicable to other cases for example such as information transmission from left to right, that from the center to the ends and so on.

Extension to two unknown variables X and Y is done as follows: Any two variable function $g(X,Y) : \{0,1\}^2 \rightarrow \{0,1\}$ can be written in the form,

$$g(X,Y) = a_1 + a_2 X + a_3 Y + a_4 XY \quad (a_i = 0 \text{ or } 1).$$

There are sixteen such functions in all and the set of them is denoted by G. Operations on G are defined as the 1-variable case but with restrictions $X^2 = X$ and $Y^2 = Y$. Then extension of f to $\tilde{f}$ is done in the same manner. A computational example is given in (d) of Figure 2, where the information X of the right-most cell and Y of the center cell interfere at the right-most part of the system and produce a function X + Y [Boolean] which is changed into $\overline{X} \cdot \overline{Y}$ by '1'. In later time the informations X and Y propagate in the system in the form of those functions but never appear at the output cell and finally disappears from the system at $t = 79$.

As seen from examples the information transmission property of a cellular automaton varies according to the length n and the initial state condition. Though we have kept fixed the boundary condition, classification may heavily depend on it.

Now we consider more complex automaton, or the case $|S| > 2$. In order to apply the above mentioned method to it, we must assume that $|S|$ be power of a prime number, or $|S| = p^n$. Then S can be considered to be $GF(p^n)$. A function $g(X): GF(p^n) \rightarrow GF(p^n)$ can be written as follows;

$$g(X) = a_1 X^{q-1} + a_2 X^{q-2} + \ldots + a_p n,$$

where $q = p^n$ and $a_i \in GF(p^n)$. There are q^q such functions and the set of them is denoted by G. The two operations which give G the structure of field are mod.q sum and product with $X^q = X$. (Note the case n = 1 relates to the Fermat's law $X^p = X$).

The transition function $f: S^3 \rightarrow S$ is written in the form;

$$f(x,y,z) = u_1 x^{q-1} y^{q-1} z^{q-1} + u_2 x^{q-1} y^{q-1} z^{q-2} + \ldots$$

$$\ldots + u_{q^3-1} x + u_{q^3} \quad (u_i \in GF(q)).$$

The coefficients u_i $(i = 1, 2, \ldots, q^3)$ are uniquely determined when f is given. Extension of f to $\tilde{f}: G^3 \rightarrow G$ is the same as in the case $|S| = 2$.

Cases with more than one unknown variables can be treated in a similar way. The only thing to do is to have expressions of function of many variables $g(X,Y,Z, \ldots)$.

If $|S| \neq p^n$, the above mentioned formulation can't be applied and another method would be required. We have one which is not smart but do not enter this problem any further.

4. Interactive Graphic Display System for 2-dimensional 2-state Cellular Automata

4.1 FORMULATION

As is shown in Section 3, we can visualize the information transmission using the method of unknown variable. Since 1-dimensional automaton was used for explanation there, we must here formulate the problem for 2-dimensional case.

Let $S = \{0,1\}$, therefore $|S| = 2$. The transition function is defined as follows: $f: S^5 \to S$ and

$$f(x,y,z,u,v) = w_1 xyzuv + w_2 xyzu + \ldots + w_{31} x + w_{32} \qquad (w_i = 0 \text{ or } 1)$$

If f is given, say in the form of a 5 variable Boolean function, the coefficients w_i $(i = 1,2, \ldots 32)$ can be calculated by solving a set of linear equations.

If we are going to simulate the effect of the initial state of an arbitrary cell or the information transmission, the above mentioned method is applicable. In this case $G = \{0,1,X,\overline{X}\}$. The extended transition function $\widetilde{f}$ is obtained as in 1-dimensional case. This procedure can be easily programmed and it is quite practical for this simple case to calculate $\widetilde{f}$ for all combinations of G^5 beforehand and to store the results in the form of an array (of FORTRAN) in the core memory. It increases the speed considerably.

4.2 EQUIPMENTS

We are using the graphic display system installed at the Data Processing Center, Kyoto University. It consists of a FACOM 270-30 computer and a CRT display console with 4 kw buffer memory. The display console is connected with the computer through data channel, which has a 32 kw core memory and a 256 kw magnetic drum. A word is 16 bits. The CRT console has a 1024 × 1024 points display screen and a light pen. A function keyboard belongs to the console. Program and main data are read by a card reader, while modification and addition of data are performed with light pen and keyboards. The system has a line printer to get a hard copy of displayed objects and two magnetic tape units to store displayed data for later processing.

The cycle time of the main core memory is 0.9 μsec and that of the buffer memory is 4.2 μsec. The display is of refreshing type, whose highest refreshing rate is 40 frames per second and when the contents to be displayed are too much the image on the screen flickers. This disturbs experimentation of a long time very much.

The software system is a job monitor with a special routine for attention handling of the display console and FORTRAN compiler with a set of system subroutines called GSP for controlling the display system by user program. GSP contains routines for generating a vector, a string of characters, a circle and so on, those for displaying such images generated on the memory or extinguishing them, those for informing the programmer of the status of interruption raised by light pen and keyboard and so on.

A post graduate student of Sakai's laboratory, who has a similar classification problem as in Section 2, has made experimentation using the graphic display system installed there and obtained a definite result. In his study the method of unknown variable is essential. He used the graphic system of storage tube type, which seemed favorable for our purpose.

(By the way, E. F. Codd seems to have used an on-line simulator and analyser for his study of self-reproducing 2-dimensional cellular automata [16].)

4.3 INTERACTIVE PROGRAM

Since we are studying unknown area of cellular automata, it is impossible to program all procedures beforehand. We prepare, therefore, an interactive program and use it in a heuristic way. We should modify and add routines when necessary.

Our requirements to the program are as follows:

1. Mathematical analysis of state transition diagram.
   Display of the diagram itself, number of isolated subdiagrams, number of Garden of Eden, periods of cyclic parts, shape of subdiagrams (ring, tree)
   (Program of 1-dimensional case was finished)
2. Simulation of the state transition as well as the information transmission.
   Comfortable simulation speed
3. Image processing
   Extraction of necessary and sufficient information memory and identification of specified patterns search for specified patterns
4. Display of patterns
5. Filing of data
6. Simple operation
7. Fail soft for incorrect operation
8. Documentation or hard copy of results

Considering these points, we made a program of the first version last summer, which was never satisfactory. Routines for 1-dimensional casc arc rather rich but those for 2-dimensional case should be improved. The simulation routine seems to be effective, thought the image processing power is yet poor.

Explanation of program

Input data:

(1) Initialization of the program

(2) Cards of the transition functions labelled with names, which are stored in drum and accessed by name by means of keyboard.

(3) Cards of initial conditions of the array, which are also stored and accessed by name.

Function keyboard with 32 buttons specified:

(1) Stop simulation for changing the boundary condition, the state of arbitrary cells and so on, and restart it.

(2) Store the displayed images in magnetic tape and access them.

(3) Start and stop the 16 mm camera.

(4) Change the display time.

(5) Print the displayed image on line printer.

Light pen is the pointer of the following light buttons:

(1) Change of initial state

(2) Change of boundary condition

(3) Change of states of cells

(4) Choice of full symbols or variables only

(5) Specifying the position of the cell to be changed

Number of states of each cell = 2

Size of the array = 23×23

States $0,1,X,\bar{X}$ are represented by "blank", ".", "X" and "0".

Figure 4 shows examples of the displayed images.

4.4 SOME EXAMPLES ILLUSTRATING THE SYSTEM

As mentioned in Section 2.3, our goal is to classify the set of functions F into three classes. Contrary to 1-dimensional case where there are 256 functions, it is impossible to investigate all functions one by one, since there are $2^{2^5} = 2^{32}$ functions in this case. In addition to this we have not probably grasped all phenomena related to the information transmission and may expect to find new ones by means of this system. For these reasons, we have begun experimentation with rather arbitrary functions. It seems natural to choose the threshold functions at first, because it has been investigated very much in the theory of logical functions and in relation to the neural nets as well as to pattern classifiers. Among the simplest threshold functions, there are $f = x + y + z + u + v$, $f = \bar{x} + y + z + u + v$ and so on, where the functions are expressed in the Boolean expression. For such functions with adequate boundary and initial conditions, interesting phenomena of information transmission have been observed.

An unknown variable X is injected usually at the center of automata. It propagates to a fixed direction or in four directions symmetrically, or disappears and so on. The 16 mm film, which will be shown soon, gives some interesting examples.

5. Conclusions

Our classification problem is new in the study of cellular automata. The interactive graphic display system with image processing ability seems effective in this study, though definite results have not yet been obtained. The simulation method using unknown variables has been newly devised for visualizing the information transmission. New theoretical results are expected from this kind of man-machine communication, and from two-fold relationship between pattern recognition and theory of automata.

Acknowledgements

The author expresses his thanks to Professor Sakai for encouragement and recommendation. He appreciates very much the contributions of Mr. Kobuchi in theoretical discussion and those of Mr. Kamei in writing the computer program. His thanks are also due to Mr. Nishihara of the Data Processing Center for his help in making the animation film, which was screened at the conference.

REFERENCES

[1] Rosenblatt, F. (1962), *Principles of Neurodynamics.*

[2] Fukushima, K. (1970), A Feature Extractor for Curvilinear Patterns: A Design Suggested by the Manmmalian Visual System, Kybernetik *7*, 153-160.

[3] Minsky, M. and Papert, S. (1969), *Perceptrons.*

[4] Aiserman, A. (1969), Remarks of Two Problems Connected with Pattern Recognition, *Methodologies of Pattern Recognition,* ed. Watanabe.

[5] Watanabe, S. (1965), Karhunen-Loéve Expansions and Factor Analysis, Proc. of 4th Conf. of IT.

[6] Cooper, P.W. (1969), Fundamentals of Statistical Decision and Learning, *Automatic Interpretation and Classification of Images,* ed. Grasselli.

[7] Von Neuman, J. (1966), *Theory of automata:* Construction, Reproduction, Homogeneity, ed. A. Burks.

[8] Ed. A. Burks (1970), *Essays on Cellular Automata.*

[9] Unger, S. H. (1963), Pattern Recognition Using Two-Dimensional Iterative Logic Networks, Information and Control *6*.

[10] Hennie, F. C. (1961), *Iterative Arrays of Logical Circuits.*

[11] Gamba, A. (1961), Proc. IRE, 49, 349-350.

[12] Waksman, A. (1966), An Optimum Solution to the Firing Squad Synchronization Problem, Inf. and Control, *9*.

[13] Nishio, H. (1970), On Studies of Cellular Automata, (in Japanese) Seibutsu-butsuri (biophysics), 10.

[14] Sakai, T. (1970), Adaptive System of Pattern Recognition, *Methodologies of Pattern Recognition,* ed. Watanabe.

[15] Sakai et al. (1971), Matching of straight line patterns by means of LISP, (in Japanese), Report if IECE of Japan.

[16] Codd, E. F. (1968), *Cellular Automata.*

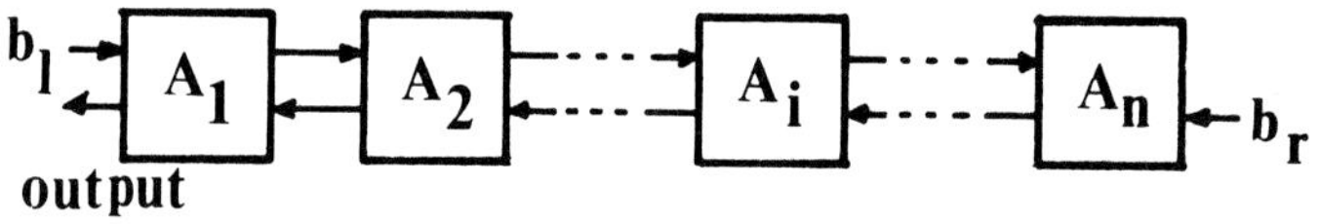

Figure 1. 1-dimensional cellular automaton

$b_1 = b_r = 1$

$f = x\bar{y} + (x\bar{z} + \bar{x}z)y$ [Boolean]
$= x + yz$ [g-expression]

(i) $n=5$
0 0 1 1 +
1 0 1 − −
1 1 − + 0
0 + 1 − +
→ 1 + 1 1 1
− − − 0 0
+ 0 − − 0
. . .
. . .
1 1 − 0 +
— 0 + 1 − +

$r=4$
$p=30$

(a)

(ii) $n=9$
1 1 1 0 1 1 1 1 +
0 0 1 1 1 0 0 − −
1 0 1 0 1 1 0 − 0
1 1 0 1 1 1 1 0 −
0 1 1 1 0 0 1 1 −
1 1 0 1 1 0 1 + +
0 1 1 1 1 1 + − 0
1 1 0 0 0 − 1 + −
0 1 1 0 0 − 1 1 1
1 1 1 1 0 − + 0 0
0 0 0 1 1 0 − + 0
1 0 0 1 1 1 0 − +
1 1 0 1 0 1 1 0 1
→ 0 1 1 0 1 1 1 1 1
. . . . .
. . . . .
1 0 0 1 1 1 0 1 0
— 1 1 0 1 0 1 1 0 1

$r=14$
$p=10$ (b)

(iii) $n=9$
1 1 1 0 1 1 1 0 +
0 0 1 1 1 0 1 1 +
1 0 1 0 1 1 1 − −
1 1 0 1 1 0 + + 0
0 1 1 1 1 1 + + +
1 1 0 0 0 − − 0 0
0 1 1 0 0 − − − 0
1 1 1 1 0 − 0 − −
0 0 0 1 1 0 − − 0
1 0 0 1 1 1 − − −
1 1 0 1 0 + + 0 0
0 1 1 0 1 + + + 0
1 1 1 1 + − 0 + +
→ 0 0 0 − 1 + − + 0
. . . . .
. . . . .
0 1 1 0 + 1 1 1 −
— 1 1 1 1 + − 0 + +

$r=14$
$p=10$ (c)

\+ denotes X,
− $\bar{X}$.

	(iv) $n=17$ (2-variables)
1	0 0 0 0 0 0 0 Y 0 0 0 0 0 0 X
2	1 0 0 0 0 0 0 0 Y 0 0 0 0 0 X
3	1 1 0 0 0 0 0 0 0 Y 0 0 0 0 X
4	0 1 1 0 0 0 0 0 0 0 Y 0 0 0 X
5	1 1 1 1 0 0 0 0 0 0 0 Y 0 0 X
6	0 0 0 1 1 0 0 0 0 0 0 0 Y 0 X
7	1 0 0 1 1 1 0 0 0 0 0 0 0 Y X
8	1 1 0 1 0 1 1 0 0 0 0 0 0 α β
9	0 1 1 0 1 1 1 1 0 0 0 0 0 0 γ
10	1 1 1 1 1 0 0 1 1 0 0 0 0 0 γ
11	0 0 0 0 1 1 0 1 1 1 0 0 0 0 γ
12	1 0 0 0 1 1 1 1 0 1 1 0 0 0 γ
13	1 1 0 0 1 0 0 1 1 1 1 1 0 0 γ
14	0 1 1 0 0 1 0 1 0 0 0 1 1 0 γ
15	1 1 1 1 0 0 1 0 1 0 0 1 1 1 γ
16	0 0 0 1 1 0 0 1 0 1 0 1 0 δ δ
17	1 0 0 1 1 1 0 0 1 0 1 0 1 δ 0
18	1 1 0 1 0 1 1 0 0 1 0 1 δ 1 δ
.	
.	
31	0 0 0 δ 1 1 δ 1 1 1 δ 0 γ 1 0
32	1 0 0 δ γ γ γ γ 0 γ 1 δ γ γ 1
.	
.	
78	1 1 0 1 0 1 1 0 0 1 0 1 0 δ γ
79	0 1 1 0 1 1 1 1 0 0 1 0 1 0 1
80	→ 1 1 1 1 1 0 0 1 1 0 0 1 0 1 1
.	. . . .
89	— 0 1 1 0 1 1 1 1 0 0 1 0 1 0 1

$r=80$, $p=10$

α denotes XY,
β $X\bar{Y} + \bar{X}Y$,
γ $X+Y$,
δ $\bar{X}\bar{Y}$, [Boolean]

(d)

symbols: + indicates X
- indicates $\bar{X}$

r = length of transient part
p = length of cyclic part of the transition diagram

boundary condition:
$b_1 = b_r = 1$

Figure 2. Computational results

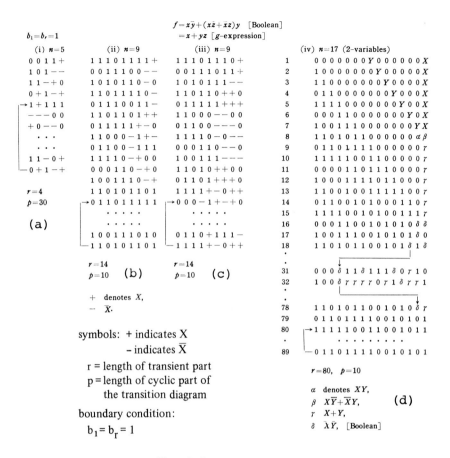

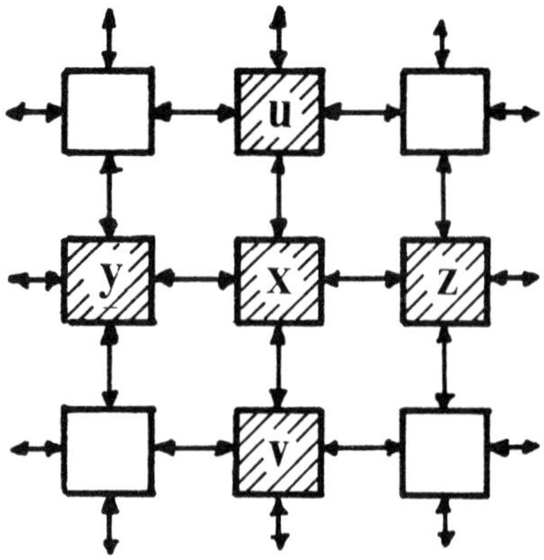

Figure 3. Neighbors in 2-dimensional case

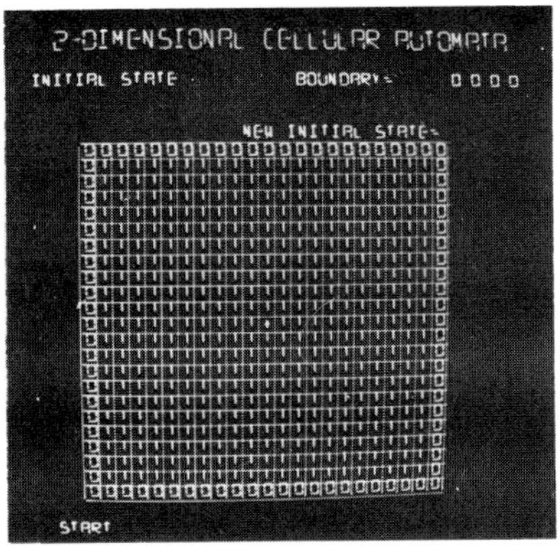

(a) Initial states are all "1" with X in the center. Light buttons are seen

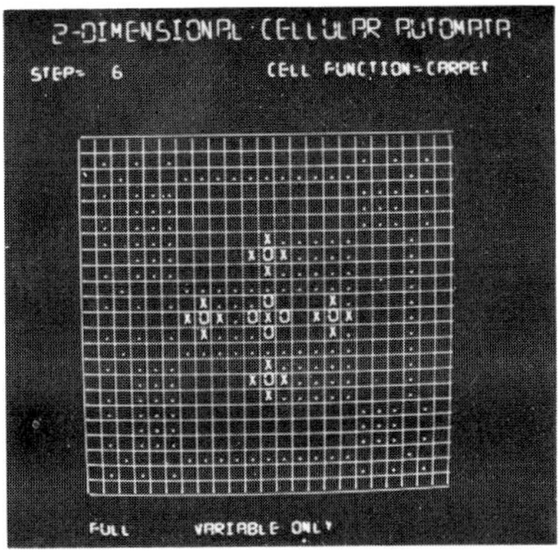

(b) States of cells; "blank", ".", "X", "O"

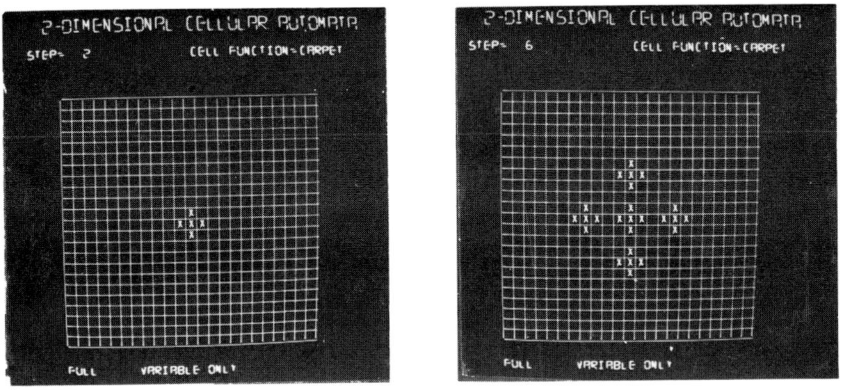

(c) "Self-reproduction" of patterns, t=2 and 6

Figure 4. Displayed images on the screen

RELATIONSHIP BETWEEN ORGANIZING CAPABILITY AND INFORMATION UTILIZED FOR SYSTEM ORGANIZATION

Shoichi Noguchi, Shingo Tomita and Takashi Watanabe

RESEARCH INSTITUTE OF ELECTRICAL COMMUNICATION
TOHOKU UNIVERSITY
SENDAI, JAPAN

Summary

This paper presents the fundamental properties of the typical parametric organizers for the supervised and the nonsupervised classification and makes clear the relationship between the organizing capability and the information which is utilized for the system organization.

In the supervised case, the system performance is evaluated uniformly by means of the concept of the information processing capacity and the percent information processing capacity under the assumption that the pattern is distributed according to the multivariate normal distribution.

The typical organizers considered here are (1) the minimum distance organizer, (2) the Bayes organizer, (3) the regression organizer, (4) the linear admissible organizer, (5) the multi-regression organizer, (6) the partial Bayes organizer, (7) the modified Fisher organizer and (8) the modified regression organizer.

In the nonsupervised case, two basic organizing methods are considered. The one is the nonsupervised organizer by a stochastic approximation method, and the other is by the Karhunen-Loéve orthogonal system.

For the first case, two basic algorithms are considered on the typical criterions. The one is the criterion to minimize the distance between the mean values of two categories, and the other is to minimize the average distance between the hyperplane and the sample patterns for each category. We also discuss the relationship between the organizing capability and the information which is utilized for its system organization.

For the second case, in order to organize the system, number of trials are required utilizing the Karhunen-Loéve orthogonal system, but it is proved that there exists a dichotomy which converges to the Bayes solution by increasing the number of samples, if the mixture distribution is identifiable and some conditions are satisfied.

[I] Supervised Organizer

1. Basic Assumption

Our basic assumptions are as follows:

(a) The pattern is represented by an N dimensional vector $\underline{X}$ and each $\underline{X}$ is distributed according to the multivariate normal distribution.

(b) In two categories problem, each category has a member of $\frac{M}{2}$ sample patterns and for R categories problem, each one has a member of M sample patterns. (The various cases of different sample patterns in each case can also be obtained with slight modification.)

(c) The sample covariance matrix is assumed to be full rank.

2. The Typical Statistical Organizers

The typical organizers treated in this section are as follows:

(1) The minimum distance organizer, (2) the Bayes organizer, (3) the regression organizer, (4) the linear admissible organizer, (5) multi-regression organizer, (6) partial Bayes organizer, (7) the modified Fisher organizer and (8) the modified regression organizer. We treat the two categories problems for (1) – (6) and the R categories problems for (7) and (8).

We evaluate the capability of the organizers under the assumption that the covariance matrices in each category are the same except (4).

3. The System Organization of the Typical Statistical Organizers

For convenience, we denote the sample mean and the sample covariance matrix for each category by $\underline{\overline{X}}^{(1)}$ and $\underline{S}_{(1)}$ (1 = 1, 2) and the difference of the sample means and the total sample covariance matrix by $\underline{\delta}$ and $\underline{S}$ respectively.

3.1 THE MINIMUM DISTANCE ORGANIZER

The decision function which decides the region of classification into category ω_1, R_1 and into ω_2, R_2 is given as follows:

$$R_1 : g(\underline{x}) = \underline{\delta}^T \underline{X} - \frac{1}{2} \underline{\delta}^T (\underline{\overline{X}}^{(1)} + \underline{\overline{X}}^{(2)}) \geq 0, \quad R_2 : g(\underline{x}) < 0$$

3.2 THE BAYES ORGANIZER[1]

If the loss function $\lambda(j\,|\,i)$ is given by $(1-\delta_{ij})$, the decision function is given as follows:

$$R_1 : g(\underline{x}) = \underline{X}^T\underline{S}^{-1}\underline{\delta} - \frac{1}{2}(\underline{\overline{X}}^{(1)} + \underline{\overline{X}}^{(2)})^T\underline{S}^{-1}\underline{\delta} \geq 0,\ R_2 : g(\underline{x}) < 0$$

3.3 THE REGRESSION ORGANIZER[1]

The decision function is obtained as follows:

$$R_1 : \underline{W}^T X + \underline{W}_o \geq 0,\quad R_2 : \underline{W}^T X + \underline{W}_o < 0$$

where $\underline{W}^T$ and $\underline{W}_o$ are obtained as the function of $\underline{\overline{X}}$, $\underline{S}$ and the desired output.

3.4 THE LINEAR ADMISSIBLE ORGANIZER

When the covariance matrices are different in each category, the optimal classifier becomes non-linear, but the linear classifier can be organized in the admissible way.

Putting $\underline{A} = t_1\underline{S}_1 + t_2\underline{S}_2$, $\underline{W} = \underline{\delta}^T\underline{A}^{-1}$

and $C = \underline{W}^T(\underline{\overline{X}}^{(1)} + \underline{\overline{X}}^{(2)}) + t_1\underline{W}^T\underline{S}_1\underline{W} - t_2\underline{W}^T\underline{S}_2\underline{W}$,

the admissible linear decision function is obtained as follows:

$$R_1 : \underline{W}^T\underline{X} - C \geq 0,\qquad R_2 : \underline{W}^T\underline{X} - C < 0$$

3.5 THE MULTI REGRESSION ORGANIZER

If some components of $\underline{\delta}$ are almost zero, the over all system organization can be simplified by organizing the system neglecting the zero components of $\underline{\delta}$ positively, and can decrease the dimension of the organizer. We divide each $\underline{X}^{(1)}$ and $\underline{\delta}$ as follows:

$$\underline{X}_{1\alpha}^{(1)T} = (\underline{X}_{2\alpha}^{(1)T},\ \underline{X}_{2\alpha}^{(1)T}),\ \underline{\delta}^T = (\underline{\delta}_1^T,\ \underline{\delta}_2^T),$$

where $\underline{X}_{2\alpha}^{(1)}$ and $\underline{\delta}_2$ are k dimensional vectors and zero components of $\underline{\delta}$.

Putting $\underline{S} = \begin{pmatrix}\underline{S}_{11} & \underline{S}_{12}\\ \underline{S}_{21} & \underline{S}_{22}\end{pmatrix}$, $\underline{B} = \underline{S}_{12}\,\underline{S}_{22}^{-1}$ and $\underline{y}^{(1)} = \underline{X}_{1\alpha}^{(1)} - \underline{B}\,\underline{X}_{2\alpha}^{(1)}$, and denoting the mean value and the covariance matrix of $\underline{y}^{(1)}$ as $\underline{\overline{y}}^{(1)}$ and $\underline{S}_y$ respectively, the decision function is obtained as follows:

$$R_1 : g(\underline{y}) = (\overline{\underline{y}}^{(1)} - \overline{\underline{y}}^{(2)})^T \underline{S}_y^{-1} (\underline{y} - (\underline{y}^{(1)} + \underline{y}^{(2)})/2) \geq 0, \quad R_2 : g(\underline{y}) < 0$$

3.6 THE PARTIAL BAYES ORGANIZER[2]

Divide the input $\underline{X}^{(1)}$ into s blocks as follows:

$$\underline{X}^{(1)T} = (\underline{X}_1^T, \underline{X}_2^T, \ldots, \underline{X}_s^T)$$

Putting $\overline{\underline{X}}_i^{(1)}$ as sample mean and $\underline{S}_{ii}$ as the sample covariance matrices of each block for each category, the decision function which utilizes the partial information of the covariance matrices is obtained as follows:

$$R_1 ; \ g(\underline{x}) = \sum_{i=1}^{s} (\overline{\underline{X}}_i^{(1)} - \overline{\underline{X}}_i^{(2)})^T \ \underline{S}_{ii}^{-1} \ \{\underline{X}_i - (\overline{\underline{X}}_i^{(1)} + \overline{\underline{X}}_i^{(2)})/2\} \geq 0,$$

$$R_2 : \ g(\underline{x}) < 0$$

3.7 THE MODIFIED FISHER ORGANIZER[2]

The decision function $g_j(\underline{x})$ and its rule for j category is given as follows:

$$R_j ; \qquad |g_j(\underline{x})| \leqq |g_i(\underline{x})| \qquad (j \neq i, \ i = 1 \sim R),$$

where $g_j(\underline{x}) = \overline{\underline{X}}^{(j)T} \underline{S}_j^{-1} (\underline{X} - \overline{\underline{X}}^{(j)})$,

$$\overline{\underline{X}}^{(j)} = \frac{R}{M} \sum_{i=1}^{M/R} \underline{X}_{(i)}^{(j)} \quad \text{and} \quad \underline{S}_j = \frac{R}{M-R} \sum_{i=1}^{M/R} (\underline{X}_{(i)}^{(j)} - \overline{\underline{X}}^{(j)}) (\underline{X}_{(i)}^{(j)} - \overline{\underline{X}}^{(j)})^T$$

3.8 THE MODIFIED REGRESSION CLASSIFIER[2]

This system is organized so that input patterns are nearly on the same hyperplane for each category by the moderate linear transformation. The decision function is the same as the previous organizer.

4. The Evaluation of the Organizing Capability of the Organizer

When the input patterns are distributed according to the normal distribution, the output of every organizer discussed in the preceding section becomes an uninormal distribution.

It is also proved[1],[2] that the correct recognition probability R of each organizer is expressed in the following form;

$$R = \Phi \{ f(d) \},$$

where Φ is an error function and d is some kind of a statistical distance and distributed according to some distribution.

The function f and the form of the distribution of d are decided by each organizer respectively.(1),(2)

From these considerations, the probability density function of the correct classification is determined theoretically as the function of M, N, and the statistical parameters.

But in order to have an insight in the gross, we simplify the problem by considering the representative parameters of the distribution, and define the average recognition probability $\bar{R}$ as follows; $\bar{R} = \Phi\ \{f(\bar{d})\}$ where $\bar{d}$ is the mean value of d.

Then, the evaluation of the organizing capability of each organizer is obtained by the concept of the information processing capacity $\underline{I}_n$ and the percent information processing capacity $\underline{I}_n$ (a %).(1)

These parameters mean the average number of patterns which are classified by one dimension of the weight vector under the condition that the average recognition probability is 1 for the former case and a % for the latter case respectively. These are defined as follows:

$\underline{I}_n \triangleq (M/N)$; when the average recognition probability is 1,

$\underline{I}_n (a\%) \triangleq (M/N)$; when the average recognition probability is a %.

As the difficult case for the classification, we consider when both patterns belong to the same normal distribution $N(\underline{0},\underline{\Sigma})$ except (4). (If there is a difference between the mean value in each category, the same consideration is also possible with slight modification(1), (2)).

4.1 THE MINIMUM DISTANCE ORGANIZER(1)

$$\bar{R}_m = \Phi\left(\frac{1}{2}\sqrt{\bar{d}_m}\right), \quad \bar{d}_m = \frac{4N}{M}$$

$$\underline{I}_n = 0, \qquad \underline{I}_n(99\%) \cong 0.184 \tag{1.1}$$

4.2 THE BAYES ORGANIZER(1)

$$\bar{R}_b = \Phi\left(\frac{1}{2}\sqrt{\bar{d}_b}\right), \quad \bar{d}_b = \frac{4N}{M-N-3}$$

$$\underline{I}_n = 1, \qquad \underline{I}_n(99\%) \cong 1 + 0.184 \tag{1.2}$$

4.3 THE REGRESSION ORGANIZER

$$\bar{R}_r = \Phi\left(\sqrt{\frac{\bar{d}_r}{2-\bar{d}_r}}\right), \quad \bar{d}_r = \frac{2N}{M}$$

$$\underline{I}_n = 1, \quad \underline{I}_n\,(99\,\%) \cong 1 + 0.184 \tag{1.3}$$

4.4 THE LINEAR ADMISSIBLE ORGANIZER

In this case, we consider when the sample distributions are given as follows;

$$R_I;\ N(\underline{0}, \underline{\Sigma}), \qquad R_{II};\ N(\underline{0}, \lambda^2\underline{\Sigma})$$

$$\bar{R}_A = \Phi\left(\frac{1}{\lambda+1}\sqrt{\bar{d}_a}\right), \quad \bar{d}_a = 2(\lambda^2+1)\frac{1}{\frac{M}{N}-1}$$

$$\underline{I}_n = 1 \tag{1.4}$$

$\bar{R}_A$ becomes minimum at $\lambda = 1$, but shows a slight increase with the change of λ.

4.5 MULTI REGRESSION ORGANIZER

$$\bar{R}_M = \Phi\left(\frac{1}{2}\sqrt{\bar{R}_M}\right), \quad \bar{R}_M = \frac{r}{\frac{M}{N}-1}\left[1 + \frac{1-r}{\frac{M}{N}-(1-r)}\right]$$

where $r = \frac{P}{N}$ and P is the dimension of $\underline{\delta}_1$,

$$\underline{I}_n = 1 \tag{1.5}$$

4.6 THE PARTIAL BAYES ORGANIZER[2]

$$\bar{R}_P = \frac{1}{2}\Phi\left(2\sqrt{\bar{d}_p^{\,2}}\right), \quad \bar{d}_p^{\,2} = \sum_{i=1}^{m}\frac{N}{M}\,\frac{1}{M-N_i-3}$$

$$\underline{I}_n = {}^{n_s}/N, \quad \underline{I}_n(99\,\%) \cong ({}^{n_s}/N) + 0.184 \tag{1.6}$$

where n_s is the maximum rank of $\underline{S}_{ii}$.

4.7 THE MODIFIED FISHER ORGANIZER

In this case, the classifiers organize the decision functions for each category.

$$\overline{R_F} = 1 - \frac{2}{R} \sum_{i \neq j} \sum \Phi \left(\sqrt{\frac{\overline{d_{ij}}}{2}} \right) \left(1 - \Phi \left(\sqrt{\frac{\overline{d_{ij}}}{2}} \right) \right)$$

$$\overline{d_{ij}} = \frac{R}{\frac{M}{N} - R}$$

$$\underline{I}_n = R, \quad \underline{I}_n(99\,\%) = 2.150 \quad (\text{for } R = 2) \qquad (1.7)$$

4.8 THE MODIFIED REGRESSION ORGANIZER

This organizer shows the same characteristics as 4.7.

5. The Relation Between the Organizing Capability and the Total Information Which Is Utilized for the System Organization

The organizers described in section 3 are classified into five types in the following way from the point of the information utilization.

(1) The organizer which utilizes the sample means; the minimum distance classifier.

(2) The organizer which utilizes the sample means and the partial sample covariance matrices; the partial Bayes organizer.

(3) The organizer which utilizes the partial sample means and the total sample covariance matrices; the multi-regression organizer.

(4) The organizer which utilizes the mean values and the covariance matrices; the Bayes organizer and the regression organizer.

(5) The organizers which utilize mean values and covariance matrices for each category; the modified Fisher organizer and the modified regression organizer.

In any case, there is a very distinct relationship between the organizing capability and the information which is utilized for the system organization.

For case (1), $\underline{I}_n = 0$.

For case (2), $\underline{I}_n = \frac{n_s}{N}$, where n_s is the maximum rank of the subcovariance matrix.

For cases (3) and (4), $\underline{I}_n = 1$, but the $\underline{I}_n(a\%)$ of (3) is inferior compared to case (4).

For case (5), $\underline{I}_n = R$.

But it must be mentioned that the number of the weighting element required for the system organization is also $R \cdot N$.

6. Computer Simulation

In order to check the theoretical results, several kinds of computer simulation are made for the organizing capability for each organizer using the random patterns.

These results coincide well with our theoretical ones. In Figure 1, we show the theoretical curves and the experimental results for the minimum distance organizer, the Bayes organizer and the partial Bayes organizer. The same results are also obtained for other cases.

[II] Nonsupervised Organizer

For the nonsupervised organizer we have not yet succeeded to obtain the quantitative relationship between the organizing capability and the utilized information for the system organization as in the supervised case.

But we have a clear qualitative relationship between them as is seen in this section 1.

1. Self-organization by the Stochastic Approximation.[3]

1.1 BASIC ASSUMPTION

Let a pattern be represented by an N-dimensional column vector $\underline{X} = (x_1, x_2, \ldots, x_N)^T$ where T denotes the transposition. The pattern class is represented by $\omega_k (k = 1,2)$. We discuss the two-category problems and suppose that the discriminant functions used here classify the given pattern into the class according to their values being positive or negative. It is assumed that $\underline{X}$ is a random vector having the mixture distribution

$$H(\underline{X}) = P_1 F(\underline{X}|\omega_1) + P_2 F(\underline{X}|\omega_2), \tag{1.1}$$

where $P_k (k = 1,2)$ is the unknown prior probability of receiving a pattern which belongs to ω_k and $F(\underline{X}|\omega_k)$ is the unknown conditional distribution function of the patterns of ω_k.

1.2 NONSUPERVISED LEARNING ALGORITHMS BASED ON THE CRITERION $K(\underline{u}_1, \underline{u}_2)$

Let us define a self-corrective criterion $K(\underline{u}_1, \underline{u}_2)(\underline{u}_1, \underline{u}_2 \in R^N)$ which is easily shown to be equivalent to one proposed by E. M. Braverman,[4] as follows;

$$K(\underline{u}_1, \underline{u}_2) = E[\sum_{k=1}^{2} d_k(\underline{X}; \underline{u}_1, \underline{u}_2) \, \| \underline{X} - \underline{u}_k \|^2], \tag{1.2}$$

$$d_1(\underline{X}; \underline{u}_1, \underline{u}_2) = \begin{cases} 1 & \text{if } g(\underline{X}; \underline{u}_1, \underline{u}_2) \leqq 0 \\ 0 & \text{if } g(\underline{X}; \underline{u}_1, \underline{u}_2) > 0, \end{cases} \tag{1.3}$$

$$d_2(\underline{X}; \underline{u}_1, \underline{u}_2) = 1 - d_1(\underline{X}; \underline{u}_1, \underline{u}_2), \tag{1.4}$$

where E represents the expectation with respect to $\underline{X}$ and the function $g(\underline{X}; \underline{u}_1, \underline{u}_2)$ is the discriminant function such that

$$g(\underline{X}; \underline{u}_1, \underline{u}_2) = 2(\underline{u}_2 - \underline{u}_1)^T \underline{X} - (\underline{u}_2 + \underline{u}_1)^T (\underline{u}_2 - \underline{u}_1). \tag{1.5}$$

The unknown vectors $\underline{u}_1$ and $\underline{u}_2$ of the function $g(\underline{X}; \underline{u}_1, \underline{u}_2)$ are chosen to minimize $K(\underline{u}_1, \underline{u}_2)$, which are the solutions of the equations;

$$E[d_k(\underline{X}; \underline{u}_1, \underline{u}_2)(\underline{X} - \underline{u}_k)] = 0 \quad (k = 1, 2). \tag{1.6}$$

We obtain the following algorithm from the equations (1.6) by the Robbins-Monro procedure,

$$\begin{aligned} &\text{(i) if } g(\underline{X}_n; \underline{u}_{1(n'-1)}, \underline{u}_{2(n''-1)}) \leqq 0 \\ &\quad \underline{u}_{1(n')} = \underline{u}_{1(n'-1)} - {}_1C_{n'} (\underline{u}_{1(n'-1)} - \underline{X}_n), \\ &\text{(ii) if } g(\underline{X}_n; \underline{u}_{1(n'-1)}, \underline{u}_{2(n''-1)}) > 0 \\ &\quad \underline{u}_{2(n'')} = \underline{u}_{2(n''-1)} - {}_2C_{n''} (\underline{u}_{2(n''-1)} - \underline{X}_n), \\ &\quad (n = n' + n''), \end{aligned} \tag{1.7}$$

where $\{\underline{X}_n\}$ is a set of the training sample vectors and $\{{}_kC_n\}$ $(k = 1, 2)$ are sequences of the nonnegative numbers satisfying the conditions

$$\sum_{n=1}^{\infty} {}_kC_n = \infty, \quad \sum_{n=1}^{\infty} {}_kC_n^2 < \infty \quad (k = 1, 2). \tag{1.8}$$

Theorem 1.1

If $E\left[\|\underline{X}\|^2\right] < \infty$, then the sequences $\{\underline{u}_{1(n')}\}$ and $\{\underline{u}_{2(n'')}\}$ converge to some vectors $\underline{u}_1^*$ and $\underline{u}_2^*$ that satisfy the equations (1.6) with probability one respectively.

It must be mentioned that the system is self-organized by utilizing only the mean values of the sample patterns respectively.

But this procedure can extend to general multicategory problems easily, where the extended criterion $K(\underline{u}_1, \underline{u}_2, \ldots, \underline{u}_m)$ $(m > 2)$ is used.

1.3 NONSUPERVISED LEARNING ALGORITHMS BASED ON THE CRITERION $J(\underline{B}, b)$

In order to apply this criterion, it is necessary to translate the mean vector $E[\underline{X}]$ to the original point of the pattern space. But it is easily shown that this imposes no restriction on the nonsupervised learning. Let us define a self-corrective criterion $J(\underline{B},b)$ $(\underline{B} \in R^N,\ b \in R)$, as follows;

$$J(\underline{B},b) = E[(\underline{B}^T\underline{X} + b - a(\underline{X};\underline{B},b))^2], \tag{1.9}$$

$$a(\underline{X};\underline{B},b) = \begin{cases} 1 & \text{if} \quad \underline{B}^T\underline{X} + \geqq 0 \\ -1 & \text{if} \quad \underline{B}^T\underline{X} + < 0 \end{cases} \tag{1.10}$$

The vector $\underline{B}^T$ and the scalar b which define the discriminant function $f(\underline{X};\underline{B},b) = \underline{B}\ \underline{X} + b$ are chosen to minimize $J(\underline{B},b)$ and are the solutions of the equations;

$$E[(\underline{B}^T\underline{X} + b - a(\underline{X};\underline{B},b))\underline{X}] = 0, \tag{1.11}$$

$$E[\underline{B}^T\underline{X} + b - a(\underline{X};\underline{B},b)] = 0. \tag{1.12}$$

We obtain the following algorithm from the equations (1.11) and (1.12) by using the Robbins-Monro procedure under the assumption $E[\underline{X}] = 0$,

$$\underline{B}_n = \underline{B}_{n-1} - {}_1C_n(\underline{B}_{n-1}^T\underline{X}_n - a(\underline{X}_n; \underline{B}_{n-1}, b_{n-1}))\underline{X}_n, \tag{1.13}$$

$$b_n = b_{n-1} - {}_2C_n(b_{n-1} - a(\underline{X}_n; \underline{B}_{n-1}, b_{n-1})). \tag{1.14}$$

Theorem 1.2

Let $E[\|\underline{X}\|^4] < \infty$, then the sequences $\{\underline{B}_n\}$ and $\{b_n\}$ converge to some values $\underline{B}^*$ and b^* with probability one, respectively, which satisfy the equations;

$$\underline{B} = 2q_1q_2\ E[\underline{X}\underline{X}^T]^{-1}(\underline{u}_1 - \underline{u}_2), \quad b = q_1 - q_2, \tag{1.15}$$

where $q_k = \int_{\underline{X}^{(k)}} dH(\underline{X})$, $\underline{u}_k = (1/q_k)\int_{\underline{X}^{(k)}} \underline{X}dH(\underline{X})$ $(k = 1, 2)$,

$\underline{X}^{(1)} = \{\underline{X}; \underline{X} \in R^N,\ \underline{B}^T\underline{X} + b \geqq 0\}$ and $\underline{X}^{(2)} = \{\underline{X}; \underline{X} \in R^N,\ \underline{B}^T\underline{X} + b < 0\}$.

It must be mentioned that the system is self-organized by utilizing the second moment and the mean values of the sample patterns, that is, $f(\underline{X}; \underline{B}, b)$ is organized utilizing higher moment than $g(\underline{X}; \underline{u}_1, \underline{u}_2)$. By this consideration it may be estimated that the discriminant function $f(\underline{X}; \underline{B}, b)$ shows the much higher capability than $g(\underline{X}; \underline{u}_1, \underline{u}_2)$.

And this relation is clearly proved in the following theorems and the computer simulations.

1.4 CAPABILITY OF THE SYSTEM ORGANIZED ON $K(\underline{u}_1, \underline{u}_2)$

Let us take the case where the patterns are distributed according to the mixture distribution composed of the two normal distributions with the same covariance matrices $\underline{\Sigma}$ and the mean vectors $\bar{\underline{u}}_k (k = 1, 2)$ and the same prior probabilities.

In this case we obtain the following theorem.

Theorem 1.3

The Bayes discriminant function $D(\underline{X})$[9] is a solution of the equations (1.6) if and only if the vector $(\bar{\underline{u}}_1 - \bar{\underline{u}}_2)$ is an eigen-vector of the covariance matrix $\underline{\Sigma}$.

Corollary

If $\underline{\Sigma} = \sigma^2 \underline{I}$, then $D(\underline{X})$ is a solution of the equations (1.6) where $\underline{I}$ denotes the identity matrix and σ^2 is a positive number.

1.5 CAPABILITY OF THE SYSTEM ORGANIZED ON $J(\underline{B}, b)$

Again let us consider the case where the patterns are distributed according to the mixture distribution composed of the two normal distributions with the same covariance matrices $\underline{\Sigma}$ and the mean vectors $\pm \bar{\underline{u}}$ and the same prior probabilities. In this case we obtain the following theorem.

Theorem 1.4

The Bayes discriminant function $D(\underline{X})$ is a solution of the equations (1.15) if and only if the equation

$$\int_{D(\underline{X}) > 0} \underline{X} dH(\underline{X}) = a\bar{\underline{u}} \qquad (a \in R)$$

is satisfied.

Corollary 1

If $\underline{\Sigma} = \sigma^2 \underline{I}$, then $D(\underline{X})$ is a solution of the equations (1.15).

Corollary 2

If the vector $\underline{\bar{u}}$ is an eigenvector of the covariance matrix $\underline{\Sigma}$, then D(X) is a solution of the equations (1.15).

Corollary 3

If the norm $2\|\underline{\bar{u}}\|$ is large enough compared with the covariance matrix $\underline{\Sigma}$, then $D(\underline{X})$ is approximately a solution of the equations (1.15).

By the theorems given in 1.3 and 1.4, it is proved that the learning procedure based on $J(\underline{B}, b)$ yields the discriminant function having the much higher capability than that based on $K(\underline{u}_1, \underline{u}_2)$ by means of utilizing the information of the covariance matrix of the sample patterns.

1.6 EXPERIMENTAL RESULTS

We have performed the numerical experiments with the two nonsupervised learning procedures based on $K(\underline{u}_1, \underline{u}_2)$ and $J(\underline{B}, b)$.

The experimental results for two examples are represented in Figures 2 and 3, where the partitionings of the pattern space by the functions $g(\underline{X}; \underline{u}_1, \underline{u}_2)$ and $f(\underline{X}; \underline{B}, b)$ are shown compared with the partitioning by the Bayes discriminant function $D(\underline{X})$. The sample patterns used in the experiments were obtained by pseudorandom numbers which were distributed according to the mixture distribution composed of the two normal distributions listed in Table 1, where all the prior probabilities of the classes were equal, that is $\frac{1}{2}$.

The results show that the procedure based on $J(\underline{B}, b)$ yields a more suitable discriminant function than that based on $K(\underline{u}_1, \underline{u}_2)$ does.

1.7 AFFINE TRANSFORMATION $\mathfrak{A}$

As the extension of the algorithm given in (1.2) we obtain the following learning procedure.

Let us consider the two normal populations $N(\underline{\bar{u}}_1, \underline{\Sigma}_1)$ and $N(\underline{\bar{u}}_2, \underline{\Sigma}_2)$ with the prior probabilities p_1 and p_2, respectively. An affine transformation $\mathfrak{A}$ from a random vector $\underline{X}$ to a random vector $\underline{Y}$ is defined, as follows;

$$\underline{Y} = \mathfrak{A}(\underline{X}) = \underline{A}(\underline{X} - E[\underline{X}]), \tag{1.16}$$

where the matrix $\underline{A}$ satisfies the relation such that

$$\underline{A}E[(\underline{X}-E[\underline{X}])(\underline{X}-E[\underline{X}])^T]\underline{A}^T = d\underline{I} \quad (d>0). \tag{1.17}$$

By this transformation $\mathfrak{A}$ the normal population $N(\underline{\bar{u}}_k, \underline{\Sigma}_k)$ $(k = 1, 2)$ is transformed to the new normal population $N(\underline{\hat{u}}_k, \underline{\hat{\Sigma}}_k)$ where the new mean vector $\underline{\hat{u}}_k$ and the new covariance matrix $\underline{\hat{\Sigma}}_k$ are given by

$$\underline{\hat{u}}_k = A\underline{\bar{u}}_k - \underline{A}E[\underline{X}], \quad (p_1\underline{\hat{u}}_1 + p_2\underline{\hat{u}}_2 = 0), \tag{1.18}$$

$$\underline{\hat{\Sigma}}_k = \underline{A}\,\underline{\Sigma}_k\underline{A}^T \quad (k = 1, 2). \tag{1.19}$$

Theorem 1.5

If $\underline{\Sigma}_1 = a\underline{\Sigma}_2 (a > 0)$, then the new mean vector $\underline{\hat{u}}_1 \left(= -\frac{p^2}{p_1}\underline{\hat{u}}_2\right)$ is an eigenvector of the new covariance matrix $\underline{\hat{\Sigma}}_1 (= a\underline{\hat{\Sigma}}_2)$.

Consequently, it is proved that both of the nonsupervised learning algorithms based on the criteria $k(\underline{u}_1, \underline{u}_2)$ and $J(\underline{B}, b)$ yield the Bayes discriminant function by using the affine transformation $\mathfrak{A}$ under the assumption that the patterns are distributed according to the mixture distribution composed of the two normal distributions with the same covariance matrices and the same prior probabilities.

And it must be mentioned that both systems utilize the information of the mean values and the covariance matrix.

2. Self-organization by Karhunen-Loéve Orthogonal System

In this system, the information of the mean value and the covariance matrix are utilized for each trial, so a lot of the information are required for the system organization.

But it is proved that there exists a dichotomy which converges to the Bayes solution by increasing the number of samples under some conditions.

2.1 THE KARHUNEN-LOÉVE ORTHOGONAL SYSTEM

Let us explain the outline of the Karhunen-Loéve orthogonal system.

Let a pattern on the N-dimensional space $\underline{R}_N$ be $\underline{X}$ and a normal and orthogonal system on $\underline{R}_N$ be $\underline{a}$. Then a pattern $\underline{X}$ is expanded by $\underline{a}$ as follows:

$$\underline{X} = \xi_1^X(\underline{a})\,\underline{a}_1 + \xi_2^X(\underline{a})\,\underline{a}_2 + \ldots + \xi_N^X(\underline{a})\,\underline{a}_N, \text{ where } \xi_\nu^X(\underline{a}) = \underline{a}_\nu^T\underline{X},$$

$$\underline{a}_i^T\underline{a}_j = \delta_{ij} \text{ and } \underline{a} = (\underline{a}_1, \underline{a}_2, \ldots, \underline{a}_N).$$

Let the mean square of coefficients of $\underline{X}$ be $\xi_\nu(\underline{a}) = E[\xi_\nu^X(\underline{a})^2]$ ($\nu = 1,2,\ldots,N$), where $E[*] = \int * dG(\underline{X})$ is the distribution of patterns. Suppose that all $\xi_\nu(\underline{a})$'s are ordered as follows: $\xi_1(\underline{a}) \geqq \xi_2(\underline{a}) \geqq \ldots \geqq \xi_N(\underline{a})$. The sum, $\xi(\underline{a}, m) = \Sigma_{\nu=1}^{m} \xi_\nu(\underline{a})$, is defined as a quantity of features extracted by $\underline{a}_1, \underline{a}_2, \ldots, \underline{a}_m$.

Let the autocorrelation of a set of patterns $\underline{X}$ be $E[\underline{X}\underline{X}^T]$, then an eigenvalue λ_ν and the eigenvector $\underline{t}_\nu$ corresponding to λ_ν is obtained by the equation $E[\underline{X}\underline{X}^T]\,\underline{t}_\nu = \lambda_\nu \underline{t}_\nu$. Let the normal and orthogonal system be $\underline{t} = (\underline{t}_1, \underline{t}_2, \ldots, \underline{t}_N)$, then $\lambda_\nu = \xi_\nu(\underline{t})$ and $\xi(\underline{t}, m) = \mathrm{Max}\{\xi(\underline{a}, m) \mid \forall \underline{a}\}$ are proved respectively.

The above normal and orthogonal system is called the Karhunen-Loève orthogonal system[5] or simply the KL system.

2.2 CLASSIFICATION ALGORITHM AND BASIC PROPERTIES

Let an asymmetric finite mixture distribution of patterns be $G(\underline{X}) = pF(\underline{X}|\omega_1) + qF(\underline{X}|\omega_2)$, where $q + p = 1$, $p, q > 0$ and ω_1 and ω_2 are the given two categories. Let the two vectors and two matrices be defined as follows;

$$\underline{M} = \frac{1}{2}\{E[\underline{X}|\omega_1] + E[\underline{X}|\omega_2]\},\ \underline{\alpha} = \frac{1}{2}\{E[\underline{X}|\omega_1] - E[\underline{X}|\omega_2]\},\ \Lambda =$$

$$\frac{1}{2}\{E[(\underline{X} - E[\underline{X}|\omega_1])(\underline{X} - E[\underline{X}|\omega_1])^T|\omega_1] + E[(\underline{X} - E[\underline{X}|\omega_2])(\underline{X} -$$

$$E[\underline{X}|\omega_2])^T|\omega_2]\},\ \underline{\Sigma} = \frac{1}{2}\{E[(\underline{X} - E[\underline{X}|\omega_1])(\underline{X} - E[\underline{X}|\omega_1])^T|\omega_1] -$$

$$E[(\underline{X} - E[\underline{X}|\omega_2])(\underline{X} - E[\underline{X}|\omega_2])^T|\omega_2]\},\ \text{where } E[*|\omega_i] = \int * \, dF(\underline{X}|\omega_i).$$

Then, $E[\underline{X}\underline{X}^T|\omega_1] = \underline{E} + \underline{D}$, $E[\underline{X}\underline{X}^T|\omega_2] = \underline{E} - \underline{D}$, where $\underline{E} = \underline{\Sigma} + \underline{M}\underline{M}^T + \underline{\alpha}\underline{\alpha}^T$, $D = \Lambda + \underline{\alpha}\underline{M}^T + \underline{M}\underline{\alpha}^T$.

Suppose that Rank $E[\underline{X}\underline{X}^T] = N$, then there exists a matrix $\underline{S}$ such that $\underline{S}E[\underline{X}\underline{X}^T]\,\underline{S}^T = \underline{I}$, where $\underline{I}$ is a unit matrix. Let all patterns generated from the distribution $G(\underline{X})$ transform by $\underline{S}$, and denote them by the same symbol $\{\underline{X}\}$, then $E[\underline{X}\underline{X}^T|\omega_1] = \underline{I} + 2q\underline{D}$, $E[\underline{X}\underline{X}^T|\omega_2] = \underline{I} - 2p\underline{D}$.

The two quantities of features corresponding to ω_1 and ω_2 extracted by the KL system are proved to be the eigenvalues of $E[\underline{X}\underline{X}^T|\omega_1]$ and $E[\underline{X}\underline{X}^T|\omega_2]$ respectively, so $\lambda_\nu^{(1)}$ and $\lambda_\nu^{(2)}$ are two quantities of features corresponding to ω_1 and ω_2. $\lambda_\nu^{(i)}$ is obtained by the following equation:

$$E[\underline{X}\underline{X}^T|\omega_i]\,\underline{t}_\nu^{(i)} = \lambda_\nu^{(i)}\,\underline{t}_\nu^{(i)} \quad (i = 1, 2;\ \nu = 1, 2, \ldots, N).$$

Let $\underline{D}\,\underline{t}_\nu = \lambda_\nu \underline{t}_\nu$ ($\nu = 1, 2, \ldots, N$) and $\lambda_1 \geqq \lambda_2 \geqq \ldots \geqq \lambda_N$, then $\lambda_\nu = \dfrac{\lambda_\nu^{(1)} - 1}{2q} = \dfrac{1 - \lambda_\nu^{(2)}}{2p}$ by the following relations: $\underline{t}_\nu = \underline{t}_\nu^{(1)} = \underline{t}_\nu^{(2)}$ ($\nu = 1, 2, \ldots, N$).[6]

In order to classify a set of given patterns into two true categories, we introduce a parameter to evaluate the extent of the correct classification and adopt the parameter ρ such that

$$\rho = \sqrt{\Sigma_{\nu=1}^{N}\ (\lambda_\nu^{(1)} - \lambda_\nu^{(2)})^2}.$$

ρ is defined as the difference of features.

Although the mixture distribution $G(\underline{X})$ is given, ρ is not determined uniquely in general. But if $G(\underline{X})$ is identifiable, ρ is determined uniquely. So we obtain the following theorem.

Theorem 2.1

If the asymmetric finite mixture distribution $G(\underline{X})$ is identifiable, then the difference of features ρ is determined uniquely by $G(\underline{X})$.

Let ω_1^* and ω_2^* be two sets of patterns which are decided by some dichotomy, then the conditional probability $P(\omega_j | \omega_i^*)$ satisfies the following formula; $P(\omega_1 | \omega_1^*) + P(\omega_2 | \omega_1^*) = P(\omega_1 | \omega_2^*) + P(\omega_2 | \omega_2^*) = 1$.

Moreover let p^* and q^* be defined as follows: $p^* = P(\omega_1 | \omega_1^*) + P(\omega_2 | \omega_2^*)$, $q^* = P(\omega_2 | \omega_1^*) + P(\omega_1 | \omega_2^*)$. If $p^* > 1$ then q^* is defined as an evaluated error value, if $p^* < 1$, then p^* is defined as an evaluated error value. For a set of patterns ω_i^*, we suppose that

$$P(\underline{X} | \omega_i^*) = P(\underline{X} | \omega_1) P(\omega_1 | \omega_i^*) + P(\underline{X} | \omega_2) P(\omega_2 | \omega_i^*), \tag{2.1}$$

is satisfied. Then we have $F(\underline{X} | \omega_i^*) = F(\underline{X} | \omega_1) P(\omega_1 | \omega_i^*) + F(\underline{X} | \omega_2) P(\omega_2 | \omega_i^*)$. Consequently,

$$E[\underline{X}\underline{X}^T | \omega_i^*] = E[\underline{X}\underline{X}^T | \omega_1] P(\omega_1 | \omega_i^*) + E[\underline{X}\underline{X}^T | \omega_2] P(\omega_2 | \omega_i^*) \tag{2.2}$$

For two sets of patterns ω_1^* and ω_2^*, the difference of features is defined as follows:

$$\rho^* = \sqrt{\Sigma_{\nu=1}^{N}\ (\lambda_\nu^{*(1)} - \lambda_\nu^{*(2)})^2},$$

where $\lambda_\nu^{*(i)}$ is the eigenvalue of the autocorrelation $E[\underline{X}\underline{X}^T | \omega_i^*]$ and $\lambda_\nu^{(1)}$ is ordered in the following way:

$$\lambda_1^{*(1)} \geqq \lambda_2^{*(1)} \ldots \geqq \lambda_N^{*(1)} \text{ and } \lambda_\nu^{*(2)} \text{ is vice versa.}$$

From the formula (2.2) we obtain the important relation between ρ and ρ^* such that $\rho^* = |1 - q^*|\rho$.

If two dichotomies are executed, then two differences of features ρ^* and ρ^{**} are decided respectively. And let q^*, q^{**} be evaluated error probabilities, then $\rho^{**} - \rho^* = (q^* - q^{**})\rho$.

Condition A: $G(\underline{x})$ is identifiable, ρ is not zero and the formula (2.1) is satisfied.

Theorem 2.2

$\rho^{**} > \rho^*$ if and only if $q^{**} < q^*$ under the condition A.

If the dichotomy getting the maximum difference of features is equal to decreasing the evaluated error value q^* into zero, then $P(\omega_i|\omega_j^*) = \delta_{ij}$ or $1 - \delta_{ij}$.

Theorem 2.3

Let the condition A be satisfied. Then

$$P(\omega_i|\omega_j^*) = \delta_{ij} \text{ if and only if } P(\underline{X}|\omega_i) = P(\underline{X}|\omega_j^*).$$

From the result of theorem 2.3, it is possible to estimate the true distributions corresponding to each given category, if it is possible to decrease the evaluated error value q^* into zero.

Let the ideal decision function be $D(\underline{X}) = P(\omega_1|\underline{X}) - P(\omega_2|\underline{X})$ and a decision function be $D^*(\underline{X}) = P(\omega_1^*|\underline{X}) - P(\omega_2^*|\underline{X})$ when ω_1^* and ω_2^* are given.

Suppose that the specified two sets of patterns are $\hat{\omega}_1$ and $\hat{\omega}_2$ which are obtained by some dichotomy, and let the difference of features and the decision function corresponding $\hat{\omega}_1$ and $\hat{\omega}_2$ be $\hat{\rho}$ and $D(\underline{X})$ respectively. If $D(\underline{X}) = \pm D(\underline{X})$, then $P(\hat{\omega}_1) \neq 0$, $P(\hat{\omega}_2) \neq 0$.

Then the following theorem is obtained.

Theorem 2.4

Suppose that the condition A is satisfied. Then

$$\hat{\rho} = \rho \quad \text{if and only if } \hat{D}(\underline{X}) = \pm D(\underline{X}).$$

Let the true distance of means between the two categories ω_1 and ω_2 be $r = \| E[\underline{X}|\omega_1] - E[\underline{X}|\omega_2] \|$, and a distance of means between ω_2^* and ω_2^* be $r^* = \| E[\underline{X}|\omega_1^*] - E[\underline{X}|\omega_2^*] \|$, where $\| \cdot \|$ is a norm of a vector.

Then $r^* = |1 - q^*|\, r$.

Theorem 2.5

Suppose that the condition A is satisfied and $E[\underline{X}|\omega_1] \neq E[\underline{X}|\omega_2]$. Then

$$\rho^{**} > \rho^* \quad \text{if and only if } r^{**} > r^*.$$

Let the symmetric finite mixture distribution $G(\underline{X})$ be defined as the special form such that

$$G(\underline{X}) = pF(\underline{X} - \underline{\alpha}) + qF(\underline{X} + \underline{\alpha}),\ p + q = 1, p, q > 0.$$

The two mean vector corresponding ω_1 and ω_2 are defined respectively as follows: $E[\underline{X}|\omega_1] = \int \underline{X} dF(\underline{X} - \underline{\alpha})$, $E[\underline{X}|\omega_2] = \int \underline{X} dF(\underline{X} + \alpha)$, where $\underline{\alpha}$ is an unknown parameter.

Let the mean vector of ω_i^* be $E[\underline{X}|\omega_i^*]$, then $E[\underline{X}|\omega_i^*] = E[\underline{X}|\omega_1]P(\omega_1|\omega_i^*) + E[\underline{X}|\omega_2]P(\omega_2|\omega_i^*)$ is satisfied under the formula (2.1).

Suppose that the specified vector $\underline{\alpha}^*$ is defined as follows: $\underline{\alpha}^* = \frac{1}{2}\{E[\underline{X}|\omega_1^*] - E[\underline{X}|\omega_2^*]\}$. Then from theorem 2.5, the following corollary[7] is obtained.

Corollary: $\rho^* = \rho$ if and only if $\underline{\alpha}^* = \pm \underline{\alpha}$ under the condition A.

Suppose that the distribution $G(\underline{X})$ satisfies the following condition B.

Condition B: For any small $\epsilon > 0$, there exists a large positive number K such that

$$\left| \int_{-\infty}^{-K} x_i x_j \, dG(\underline{X}) \right| < \epsilon \quad \text{and} \quad \left| \int_{K}^{\infty} x_i x_j \, dG(\underline{X}) \right| < \epsilon,$$

where $\underline{X}^T = (x_1, x_2, \ldots, x_N)$.

Let a set of finite patterns be $\{\underline{X}^{(\nu)}\}^{2n+1}$ or $\{\underline{X}^{(-n)}, \underline{X}^{(-n+1)}, \ldots, \underline{X}^{(n)}\}$ and $\{\underline{X}^{(\nu)}\}^{2n+1}$ satisfy the following condition.

Condition C: For any small $\epsilon > 0$, there exists a large integer n such that

$$P\left\{ \left| x_i^{(\nu)} x_j^{(\nu)} - x_i^{(\nu-1)} x_j^{(\nu-1)} \right| < \frac{1}{2n+1} \right\} \geqq 1 - \epsilon$$

for some positive number A, where $\underline{X}^{(-n)T} = (-K, -K, \ldots, -K)$, $\underline{X}^{(n)T} = (K, K, \ldots, K)$.

The autocorrelation of $\{\underline{X}^{(\nu)}\}^{2n+1}$ is defined as follows:

$E[\underline{X}\underline{X}^T] = \frac{1}{2n+1} \Sigma_{\nu=-n}^{n} \underline{X}^{(\nu)} \underline{X}^{(\nu)T}$. $E[\underline{X}\underline{X}^T]$ is a symmetric matrix, so there exists a normal matrix $\underline{S}^{(n)}$ such that $\underline{S}^{(n)}\, E[\underline{X}\underline{X}^T]^{(n)}\, \underline{S}^{(n)T} = \underline{I}$.

Let all patterns $\{\underline{X}^{(\nu)}\}^{2n+1}$ transform by $\underline{S}^{(n)}$, and denote them by the same symbol $\{\underline{X}^{(\nu)}\}^{2n+1}$, and two sets of patterns which are obtained by a dichotomy from $\{\underline{X}^{(\nu)}\}^{2n+1}$ be $\omega_1^{*(n)}$ and $\omega_2^{*(n)}$ respectively.

The autocorrelation of a set of patterns ω_i^* is defined as follows:

$E[\underline{X}\underline{X}^T \mid \omega_i^{*(n)}] = \frac{1}{n_i} \sum_{\nu} \underline{X}^{(\nu)}\underline{X}^{(\nu)T}$, where n_i^* is a number of $\omega_i^{*(n)}$ $n_1^* + n_2^* = 2n + 1$.

Let the difference of features $\omega_1^{*(n)}$, $\omega_2^{*(n)}$ be $\rho^{*(n)}$ and $\omega_1^{(n)}$, $\omega_2^{(n)}$ be $\rho^{(n)}$ respectively, where $\omega_i^{(n)}$ satisfies the following equations: $P(\omega_1^{(n)} \mid \omega_j^{*(n)}) + P(\omega_2^{(n)} \mid \omega_j^{*(n)}) = 1$. Then the following theorem is obtained.

Theorem 2.6

Suppose that all of the conditions A, B and C are satisfied. Then

(i) $P\{\lim_{n\to\infty} \rho^{*(n)} = \rho\} = 1$ if and only if $P\{\lim_{n\to\infty} D_n^*(\underline{X}) = \pm D(\underline{X})\} = 1$, where $D_n^*(\underline{X}) = P(\omega_1^{*(n)} \mid \underline{X}) - P(\omega_2^{*(n)} \mid \underline{X})$.

(ii) Let the maximum difference of features be defined as follows:

$$\rho^{(n)}_{max} = \mathrm{Max}\ \{\rho^{*(n)} \mid \forall\, \omega_1^{*(n)},\ \forall\, \omega_2^{*(n)}\}.$$

Then $P\{\lim_{n\to\infty} \rho^{(n)}_{max} = \rho\} = 1$.

2.3 SUMMARY OF PROPERTIES AND CAPABILITY OF THIS SYSTEM

Under the certain conditions, we obtain the summary as follows.

(A) If the asymmetric finite distribution of patterns is identifiable, increasing the difference of features is equivalent to decreasing the error probability of classification, and obtaining the maximum difference of features is equivalent to estimating the true distributions of given categories.

(B) To obtain the maximum difference by some dichotomy is equivalent to getting the Bayes solution and to get the maximum distance of means between two categories, if the two means of categories is not equal.

(C) There exists a dichotomy with probability one to get the maximum difference of features by increasing the number of samples and this dichotomy converges to the Bayes solution with probability one.

2.4 RESULTS ON A COMPUTER

Let a 2-dimensional normal distribution with the mean vector $\underline{M}_O$ and the covariance matrix $\underline{\Sigma}_O$ be $N(\underline{X} : \underline{M}_O, \underline{\Sigma}_O)$ and the mixture of two normal distribution be $G(\underline{X}) = pN(\underline{X}:\underline{M}_0 + \underline{\alpha}_0, \underline{I}) + qN(\underline{X}:\underline{M}_0 - \underline{\alpha}_0, \underline{I})$, where $\underline{M}_0^T = (1, 1)$, $\underline{\alpha}_0^T = (\alpha, 0)$, $\alpha > 0$ and $\underline{I}$ is a unit matrix of 2×2.

To compare our method with a classification with teacher, the decision function $D(\underline{X})$ by the Bayes law is adopted as follows: $D(\underline{X}) = \log P(\omega_1 | \underline{X}) - \log P(\omega_2 | \underline{X})$, where $P(\underline{X} | \omega_i) = \frac{1}{2\pi} |\Sigma_i|^{-1/2} \exp\{-\frac{1}{2}(\underline{X} - \underline{E}_i)^T \Sigma_i^{-1} (\underline{X} - \underline{E}_i)$, $\underline{E}_1 = \underline{M}_0 + \underline{\alpha}_0$, $\underline{E}_2 = \underline{M}_0 - \underline{\alpha}_0$, $\Sigma_1 = \Sigma_2 = \underline{I}$. In this case, the decision function $D(\underline{X}) = \log \frac{p}{q} + 2(\underline{X} - \underline{M}_0)^T \underline{\alpha}_0$ .... (2.3)

The dichotomy is as follows: If $D(\underline{X}) > 0$, then $\underline{X} \epsilon \omega_1$, if $D(\underline{X}) < 0$, then $\underline{X} \epsilon \omega_2$. To simulate the mixture of normal distributions, random numbers are generated from the normal distribution with mean value zero and the variance value one. The uniform distribution with the interval [0, 1] are used, and the classification based on theorem 2.6 and formula (2.3) are executed on a digital computer.

The results on a computer are shown in Figure 4 and Table 2 in the case of $p = q = \frac{1}{2}$ and $M = 800$, where M is a number of samples. In Figure 4 and Table 2, four symbols are as follows:

C: Classification with teacher based on $D(\underline{X})$

C*: Classification without teacher based on theorem 2.6

Div: Divergence reported by Kullback[(8)]

ϵ^*: Absolute error rate. $\epsilon^* = \text{Min}\{\|\underline{\alpha}^* - \underline{\alpha}_0\| / \|\underline{\alpha}_0\|, \|\underline{\alpha}^* + \underline{\alpha}_0\| / \|\underline{\alpha}_0\|\}$

Conclusion

The fundamental properties of the typical parametric organizers are considered for the supervised and the nonsupervised cases.

The relationship between the organizing capability and the information which is utilized for the system organization are made clear theoretically and experimentally.

For the supervised case, the properties and the organizing capability are analysed systematically by means of the information processing capacity and the percent information processing capacity.

By these considerations, we have found that there exists a very distinct relationship between the organizing capability and the information which is utilized for the system organization.

For the nonsupervised case, the concrete quantitative relationship between the organizing capability and the utilized information for the system organization is not yet obtained as the supervised case.

But we obtained a clear qualitative relationship between them.

We adopt two basic organizing methods; one is self-organization by a stochastic approximation method and the other is by the Karhunan-Loéve orthogonal method.

For the stochastic approximation method two basic algorithms are considered; one is the self-organization which utilizes the mean value of sample patterns, and the other the mean value and the second moment.

We obtain a clear qualitative relationship between them and show that the latter organizer has higher capability compared with the former one by the theoretical and the experimental results.

For the Karhunen-Loéve orthogonal method the number of trials are required for the system organization.

This means that the information of the mean values and the covariance matrix are utilized for each trial. So, in this case, a lot of the information is utilized for system organization but it is proved that there exists a dichotomy which converges to the Bayes solution by increasing the number of samples if the mixture distribution is identifiable and certain conditions are satisfied.

Acknowledgements

The authors gratefully acknowledge Professor Juro Oizumi, Tohoku University, for the support of this work.

REFERENCES

(1) S. Noguchi, K. Nagasawa and J. Oizumi: "The evaluation of the statistical classifier," Methodologies of Pattern Recognition, 1969, Academic Press, New York.

(2) S. Noguchi and J. Oizumi: "Proceeding of Conference on Artificial Intelligence," May 7-9, 1969.

(3) T. Watanabe, S. Noguchi and J. Oizumi: "On nonsupervised learning for Pattern classification," Four Hawaii International Conference on System Sciences, January, 1971.

(4) E. M. Braverman: "The method of potential functions if the problem of training machines to recognize patterns without a trainer," Automation and Remote Control, vol. 27, pp. 1748-1170, 1966.

(5) S. Watanabe: "Knowing and Guessing," Wiley Book, 1969.

(6) K. Fukunaga, W. L. Koontz: "Application of the Karhunen-Loéve expansion to feature selection and ordering," IEEE Trans. C-19, 1970.

(7) D. B. Cooper, R. J. Schwartz: "On suitable condition for statistical pattern recognition without supervision," SIAM Appl. Math. 17, 1969.

(8) S. Kullback: "Information theory and statistics," Dover, 1968.

(9) T. W. Anderson: "An introduction to multivariate statistical analysis," Wiley Book, 1958.

Table 1. Pattern statistics

	Fig. 2	Fig. 3
Covariance matrix	$\begin{bmatrix}1 & 0\\0 & 1\end{bmatrix}$	$\begin{bmatrix}1 & 0\\0 & 4\end{bmatrix}$
Mean vector	$\begin{bmatrix}1\\1\end{bmatrix}, \begin{bmatrix}-1\\-1\end{bmatrix}$	$\begin{bmatrix}2\\2\end{bmatrix}, \begin{bmatrix}-2\\-2\end{bmatrix}$

Table 2 Results of the comparison

a	3.0	2.0	1.0	0.75	0.5	0.25
Div	72.0	32.0	8.0	4.5	2.0	0.5
ϵ^*	0.012	0.057	0.103	0.350	0.599	0.863
ρ_{max}	1.978	1.910	1.594	1.391	1.104	0.735

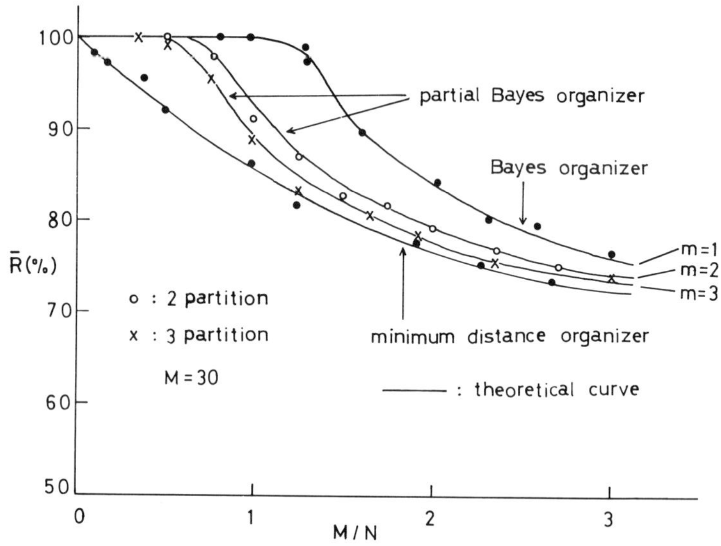

Figure 1. The relation between $\bar{R}$ and M/N

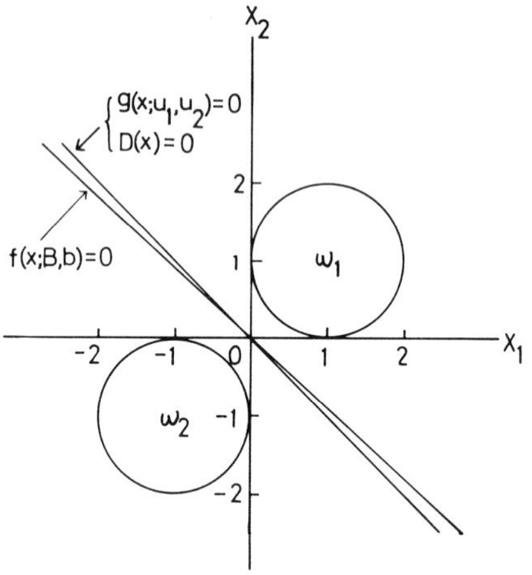

Figure 2. Decision surface after 5000 iterations

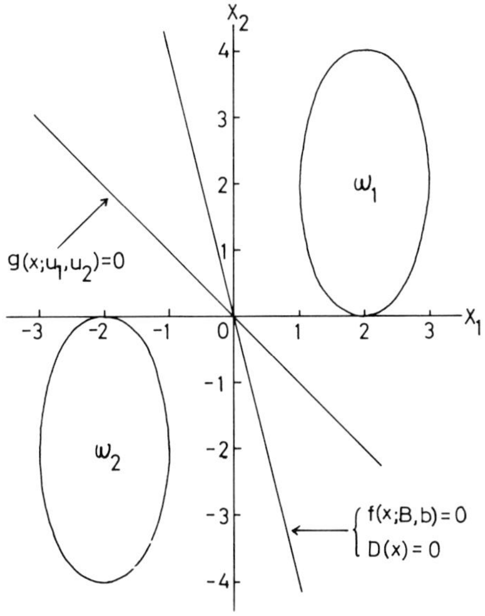

Figure 3. Decision surface after 50000 iterations

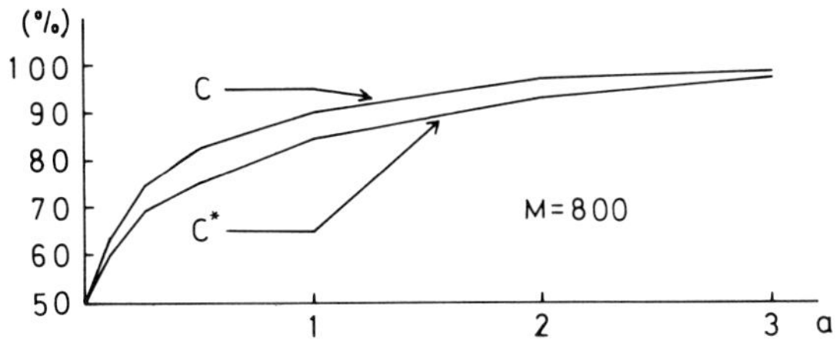

Figure 4. Results of the comparison

A PRIORI PROBLEM KNOWLEDGE AND TRAINING SAMPLES

Edward A. Patrick

SCHOOL OF ELECTRICAL ENGINEERING
PURDUE UNIVERSITY
LAFAYETTE, INDIANA

The usual notation of the Bayes framework for decision making will be used. Denote by χ the measurement space with $\underset{\sim}{x} = [x_1, x_2, \ldots, x_L]$ The Bayes decision rule requires knowledge of

$$f(\underset{\sim}{x} \mid i)\ P_i, \quad i = 1, 2, \ldots, M \tag{1}$$

where M is the number of classes, $f(\underset{\sim}{x} \mid i)$ the i-th class conditional probability density function, and P_i the a priori class probability for class i. The unknowns can be any $f(\underset{\sim}{x} \mid i)$, P_i, and M.

Two approaches to solving the above implied problem are the parametric approach and the nonparametric approach [1]:

PARAMETRIC

$$(\ f(\underset{\sim}{x} \mid i)\ )_n = \int f(\underset{\sim}{x} \mid i, \underset{\sim}{b}_i)\ f(\underset{\sim}{b}_i \mid \dot{\underset{\sim}{x}}_n)\ d\underset{\sim}{b}_i \tag{1a}$$

$$\dot{\underset{\sim}{x}}_n = [\underset{\sim}{x}_1, \underset{\sim}{x}_2, \ldots, \underset{\sim}{x}_n].$$

NONPARAMETRIC

$$(\ f(\underset{\sim}{x} \mid i)\ )_n = \frac{v_i}{(n_i + 1)\ \phi_i}, \quad \begin{array}{l} v_i \text{ number of samples} \\ \text{in region with volume} \\ \phi_i \text{ about } \underset{\sim}{x}\ . \end{array} \tag{1b}$$

In (1a), $\underset{\sim}{b}_i$ is a point in the parameter space characterizing class i, $\underset{\sim}{x}_1, \underset{\sim}{x}_2, \ldots, \underset{\sim}{x}_n$ is a sequence of training samples, possible unclassified. It is assumed that "the family of functions $f(\underset{\sim}{x} \mid i, \underset{\sim}{b}_i)$ is known a priori". In (1b), a region about $\underset{\sim}{x}$ is formed for each class at the time sample $\underset{\sim}{x}$ is to be recognized. Both approaches can be shown to converge as $n \to \infty$ to minimum risk decision rules under certain conditions.

In practice, there are several possible situations as suggested below:

Possible Situations

(a) Man knowns $f(\underset{\sim}{x} | i)\ P_i$, $i = 1, 2, \ldots, M$ and puts them in computer.

(b) Man has $\underset{\sim}{x}_1^1, \underset{\sim}{x}_2^1, \ldots, \underset{\sim}{x}_{n_1}^1$

$$\underset{\sim}{x}_1^2, \underset{\sim}{x}_2^2, \ldots, \underset{\sim}{x}_{n_2}^2$$

$$\vdots$$

$$\underset{\sim}{x}_1^M, \underset{\sim}{x}_2^M, \ldots, \underset{\sim}{x}_{n_M}^M$$

and puts them in computer.

(c) Man has knowledge about $f(\underset{\sim}{x} | i)$, P_i, $i = 1, 2, \ldots, M$

Man has samples $\underset{\sim}{x}_s^i \left\{ {n_i \atop s=1} \right\}$, $i = 1, 2, \ldots, M$.

It is appropriate to define a relationship space which contains relationships among $x_1, x_2, \ldots, x_L$ for each suspected class. It is well known that samples $\underset{\sim}{x}_1, \underset{\sim}{x}_2, \ldots, \underset{\sim}{x}_n$ can be supplied by data (*data samples*) or people (*people samples*). *Relationships* can be supplied by people:

Concerning (c)

A priori Knowledge about $f(\underset{\sim}{x} | i)$ is available in *measurement space* χ and *Relationship space.* Relationship space contains relationships among $x_1, x_2, \ldots, x_L$ for each *suspected class.* It is well known that "data" samples and "People" samples in χ are equivalent. Because of Man's field of knowledge in a special problem area, he creates relationships. In the a posteriori Bayes spirit, man can measure how well samples match different sets of relationships he has supplied. Then he can pick the best set of relationships; furthermore, he can adapt the relationships to accommodate "odd samples."

Theoretically, relationships can be estimated as $n \to \infty$. But, the pragmatic problem is to determine the a priori knowledge which will result in a specified performance for a given n.

The curves in Figure 1 suggest that to achieve performance P_e with 1000 training samples requires a certain amount of a priori knowledge.

To illustrate the importance of a priori supplied relationships, answer how many clusters there are in Figure 2. The answer, given relationship among dimensions corresponding to hypercoils, is that there are two clusters as shown in Figure 3.

Conclusion

We need a facility to

(a) Put a priori relationships for each suspected class into a computer. These relationships reflect correlations and in general hyper-objects.

(b) For classes with overlapping hyper-objects, probability density is attached to the hyper-object.

(c) Training samples update these probability densitities. Further, they are observed by man and he adapts the relationships defining the hyper-objects.

(c) The concept includes waveforms and Pictures as measurement vectors but obviously is more complex.

REFERENCES

[1] E. A. Patrick, *Fundamentals of Pattern Recognition,* Prentice Hall, February 1972.

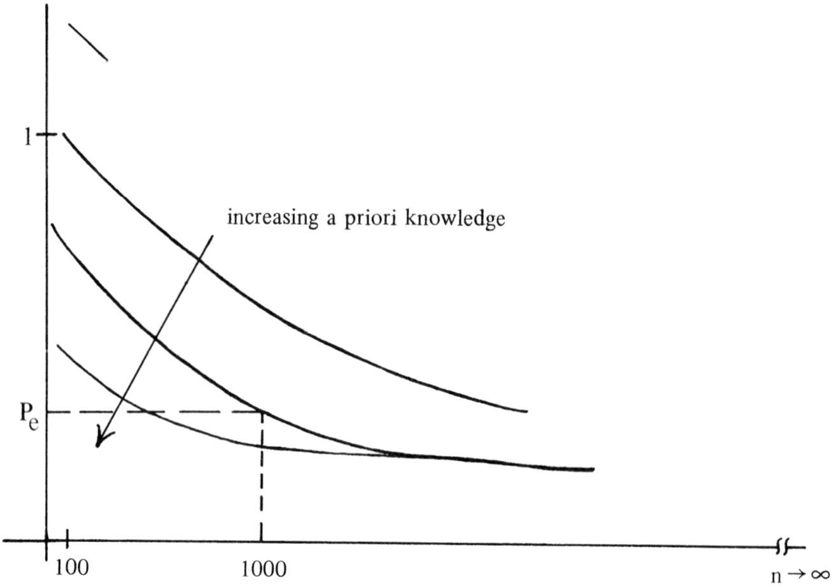

Figure 1. How much A priori Knowledge is Required?

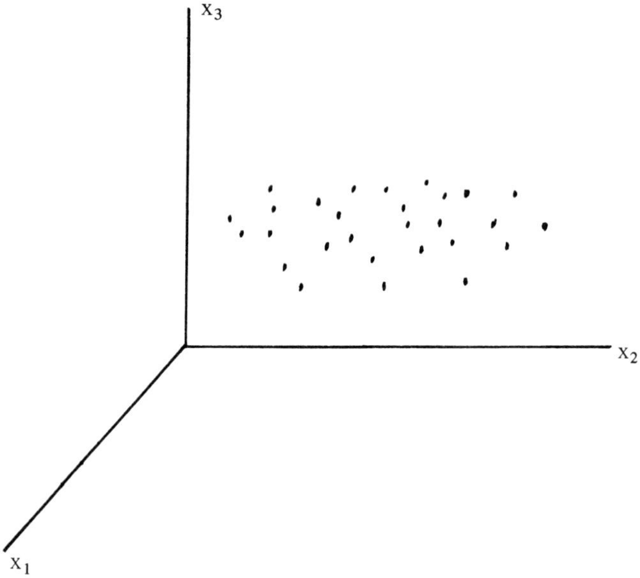

Figure 2. How Many Clusters?

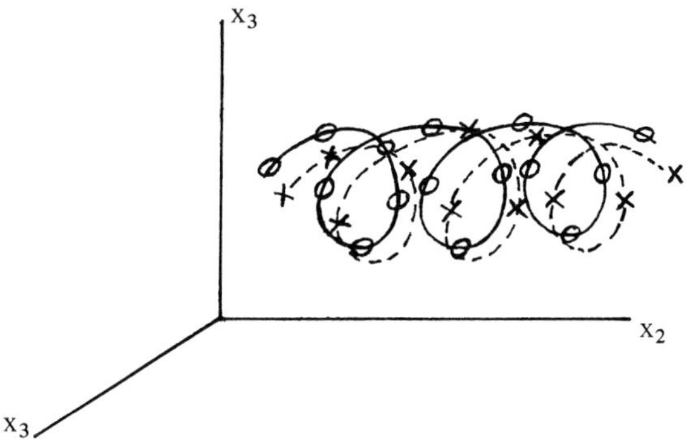

Figure 3. Answer: two Hypercoil Type Clusters

STRUCTURAL PATTERN RECOGNITION: PRIMITIVES AND JUXTAPOSITION RELATIONS*

Theodosios Pavlidis

DEPARTMENT OF ELECTRICAL ENGINEERING
PRINCETON UNIVERSITY

I. Introduction

Research in pattern recognition deals usually either with general classification techniques, independent of applications, or with techniques strongly dependent on specific applications as typewritten character recognition, chromosome classification, etc. The major exception to this trend are linguistic methods dealing with picture processing [1,2]. A number of authors have considered the class of "thin line pictures" and have proposed various methods for dealing with such patterns [eg., 3-7]. This paper considers a wider class of problems, namely the ones involving visual shape recognition. This includes printed or handwritten text, many biomedical pictures, recognition of objects in photographs through their "silhouettes", certain types of wave-forms and, of course, all "thin line" pictures. It does not include recognition of faces in photographs or other similarly complex tasks (e.g., recognizing all 1968 models of Buick in a picture of a parking lot). Of course there are a number of problems whose membership in this class is uncertain. Cloud pictures are such an example.

Our main effort will be to show how such pictures can be expressed in terms of simpler pictures and the juxtaposition relations of the latter. The end result will be a labeled graph. Further analysis of the graph can be made in a number of ways which will depend mostly on the specific problem. This is to some extent the opposite of the classical receptor/categorizer approach where the classifier was independent of the application and the receptor strongly application dependent. It offers the advantage of a common "preprocessor" for many applications. The algorithms for classification

*This work was supported by NSF Grant GK-13-622.

will have in general as a common input a labeled graph. The only exceptions are cases where the classification will be based on the output of an intermediate step of the preprocessor. Although this approach is obviously structural [8] it is not necessarily linguistic. The use of a phrase structure grammar to analyze the resulting graphs will depend strictly on the particular application.

At their present form the procedures involved require considerable computational effort and it is possible that for any given case special purpose techniques will do better. We feel, however, that an effort towards the development of a general analytical theory for shape recognition is worth such a price. A likely possibility is that one may always implement approximations to the general method as it is often done in many fields of physics and engineering (one does not use directly the Maxwell equations to analyze a simple RLC circuit). This was done successfully for early versions of this method [9-11]. Thus at this time we choose to ignore speed and memory constraints imposed by commercial applications (e.g., requiring the recognition of 1200 characters per second). We take, however, into account constraints involving the realizability of the proposed procedures in modern computers (e.g., the analysis of a simple picture can be done within a few seconds in an IBM 360-91 computer by using a high level language like PL/1).

This paper emphasizes the general features of our approach and its connection to other methods rather than the analytical details involved. Some of these have been already published elsewhere [9, 10, 12, 13] and others will be described in forthcoming papers. An example of the latter is described in the Appendix. One can distinguish three basic steps in the processing of a picture involving the recognition of the shape of objects in it:

The first step is to distinguish the object from its background. This is certainly easy in the case of typewritten text or line drawings, but more difficult in the case of aerial photographs or biological data. Figure 1 also shows another case where the distinction is easy for a human observer but requires a special computer program. In some applications this is also the most crucial part of the problem, e.g., recognizing a wheat field from a lake on a satellite photograph. These do not involve strictly speaking shape recognition but they can be considered as distinguishing objects from their background. A further discussion of this subject can be found in Section II.

The results of this step will be a collection of subsets of the plane. If they are of "regular" shape or their individual shape is not of great importance one can proceed directly in an examination of their juxtaposition relations. If they are of "irregular" shape then some further effort is needed in order to express them in terms of primitive sets or sets of "regular" shape. From a practical viewpoint the sets which are the output of the first step can be classified into two categories: "thin line" and "full" sets. One rigorous definition of this distinction is the following:

Definition 1: A nonempty subset S of the Euclidean plane is *thin* if it coincides with its boundary.

Obviously for practical applications this definition must be modified, e.g., the maximum circle contained in S is of diameter less than some prescribed constant δ. Another method has been described by Narasimhan [3]. However, the important thing is not so much the algorithm used for the distinction but the decision to treat a set as thin and describe it as union of curves and lines. A special case of thin sets are waveforms. These are characterized by the fact that the thin lines forming them contain no Y configurations. The same property is also shared by boundaries of polygons and other sets. Thus we may use a special name to characterize such thin sets.

Definition 2: A *slim* set is a thin set with the property that for each one of its points there exist a circle divided in at most two parts by the set.

In contrast to thin sets we define now full sets as following:

Definition 3: A subset of the Euclidean plane is *full* if its boundary is slim and it has a nonempty interior.

In Figure 2 set A is full, set B is slim, set C is thin, but not slim while set D is neither full nor thin.

It is obvious that an "irregularly" shaped thin set can be described as an aggregate of "regularly" shaped segments of curves or, at least, it can be approximated by such a collection. There is an abundance of such examples in the literature (1-7). On the other hand, there is no obvious form of representation for full sets. One possible way is to reduce them in thin sets by using their directed boundary. (It is well known that such a boundary characterizes a set uniquely.) This may be an acceptable approach for certain cases, but one can think of situations where a description in terms of "regularly" shaped full sets is desirable. The development of such a representation is the subject of Section III.

Suppose now that in some way a set S is represented as the union of the "regular" sets $S_1, S_2, \ldots, S_n$. The next question is how such a representation can be used for the description of S. In the case of thin sets there is an obvious possibility: Describe adjoining segments as a concatenation of symbols. If A is a concatenation operator then a slim set S can be described as $S_{i_1} A S_{i_2} A S_{i_3}, \ldots S_{i_n}$ for a permutation $i_1, i_2, \ldots i_n$ of the indices $1, 2, \ldots n$. In general, such expressions will involve also parentheses, especially for sets which are not slim. There are a number of systematic exposures of this approach in the literature of linguistic pattern recognition [1-7]. However, concatenation operators are not as easily defined for full sets. We discuss this problem in detail in Section IV.

Finally in Section V we give a brief description of how the resulting representation might be used for pattern recognition.

II. Segmentation of the Domain of Functions of Two Variables

Every "black and white" picture can be represented as a function of two variables g(x,y) denoting the gray scale level at the point x-y. There is considerable literature on the processing of such pictures in general and on methods for dividing the domain of g(x,y) into regions where the functions can be approximated by a constant [14,15].

We will discuss here only such patterns which are characterized by the shape of subsets of the domain of g(x,y). However, it is not necessary that these subsets be characterized by the fact that g(x,y) has an approximately constant value. Such a restriction would have excluded such interesting cases as the one shown in Figure 1. These can be taken into account by introducing a more general segmentation procedure. Indeed, let $\mathcal{F}$ be a family of transformations mapping the set of all real valued functions of two variables into itself.

Definition 4: An F-segmentation of the domain of g(x,y) is a subdivision of that domain into regions where f(x,y)= F[g(x,y)] for some $F \epsilon \mathcal{F}$ is approximately constant.

Of course the latter term must be defined rigorously in any implementation of the segmentation. Depending on choice of $\mathcal{F}$ the class of patterns which are characterized by the shape of the regions of an F-segmentation can be quite large. Actually one may argue that for any class of patterns there might exist an appropriate F-segmentation. In practice $\mathcal{F}$ is chosen to include a rather small class of transformations. Usually one assumes that besides the identity transformation $\mathcal{F}$ contains differentiation operators and operators which determine the texture or granularity of various parts of the picture [16-18]. One transformation which would achieve the obvious segmentation for the example of Figure 1 is the following:

$$f(x,y) = \int_{x-\Delta}^{x+\Delta} \left| \int_{y-\Delta}^{y+\Delta} \int_{w-\Delta}^{w+\Delta} g(\xi,\eta)\ (\xi - w) d\xi d\eta \right| dw$$

where Δ equals the width of the stripes. Obviously for points within the region of horizontal stripes at a distance from the boundary at least equal to Δ the integral with respect to ξ is always zero. Hence f(x,y) = 0 over most of the region with horizontal stripes. On the other hand its value over most of the region with vertical stripes equals $c \cdot \Delta^3$ (where c is a constant).

Another interesting example is provided by the division of the domain into regions where the gradient of the function is approximately constant.

This has been used for storing in a reduced form topographical data [19] but it has obvious applications in pattern recognition. One such problem is the detection of the faces of a solid object from a two-dimensional picture [20]. There segmentation according to constant values of g(x,y) results in too many segments. On the other hand, a segmentation according to gradient corresponds more closely to the faces.

A more extensive discussion of this subject is beyond the scope of this paper and in the sequence we will simply assume that the application of an appropriate algorithm, possibly with editing [20] resulted in a segmentation of the domain into m disjoint regions $D_1^{k_1}, D_2^{k_2}, \ldots, D_m^{k_m}$. k_i denotes the value of f(x,y) associated with the ith region. For many applications this may be the final non-trivial step. For others this is only the beginning. We have two classes of such problems.

In one the exact shape of some of the regions is of importance and they can be considered as the main entities again some background. If the shape is irregular then it must be described in terms of simpler shapes. This type of analysis is discussed in the next section. If it is "regular", then the various regions can be used directly as primitives. Typical problems of this type are recognition of written text, analysis of certain types of biological images, detection of objects in aerial photographs (e.g., tanks), etc.

In another class the relative positions of the regions are more important than their exact shape. One cannot really talk about objects against a background, but rather as a total scene with various interrelated parts. Then the definition of juxtaposition relations becomes crucial. Examples of such problems can be found in the analysis of 3-dimensional scenes [20-22] and maps [23]. We will discuss some of these topics in Section IV.

III. Segmentation According to Shape

This section deals with ways of representing an "irregularly" shaped subset S of the Euclidean plane by "regularly" shaped plane sets. Usually such sets are also subsets of S and the process of determining them is referred to as segmentation. Up to this point the terms "irregularly" and "regularly" shaped have been used in an informal way. Their formal definition will be the subject of a substantial part of this section.

Quite often the subsets of S with "regular" shape are identified as deformations of some other sets which are called primitives [1,2,6] or signs [24,25]. Thus S is thought of being generated by assembling deformed images of the primitives. (In Grenander's terminology this assumes that the deformations are both covariant and homorphic [24].) Then an abstract description of S can be obtained through a list of those primitives and the way in which they are assembled.

There are probably as many ways of defining and identifying the primitives as researchers in this field. However, some basic lines of approach may by distinguished. In one the set S is searched for subsets which would fit the description of a priori chosen primitives. This is exemplified by Narasimhan's labeling algorithm [3]. In another S is first decomposed in "regularly" shaped subsets which in turn are identified with primitives. This is exemplified by the decomposition algorithms described by Pavlidis [9,10]. One important feature of such a method is that it does not require an a priori definition of the primitives. Instead one can determine them inductively by examining a collection of "regularly" shaped sets obtained from the analysis of a family of "typical" pictures. This can be done through the use of similarity measures [9,10].

However, this is not the only way of structural representation. One may use a very small number of primitives and then generate more sets not only through deforming transformations, but also through the application of certain structural rules on them. (This type analysis does not necessarily require the assumptions of covariance and homomorphism for the deformations [24].) In this case it is also important to subdivide the set S into the subsets which are deformed images of the ones formed directly by the primitives. Thus regardless of the formalism one is faced with the task of segmenting S into some kind of "regularly" shaped subsets.

For thin sets there are some rather obvious choices for shape "regularity": Linear segments, circular arcs, etc. [1-7]. This is not the case, however, for full sets. Because of this difficulty a number of investigators [26,27] reduced them first into slim sets by considering their directed boundary as we mentioned in the introduction. Finding the boundary of a set is an easily programmable operation and the required time depends only linearly on the size of the plane set which contains the picture. The boundary then can be described as a chain of simpler elements. For some types of problems this is a good approach. For example, one might be searching for local features like the existence of an indentation or he might be interested in a general property like roughness or smoothness. On the other hand there are situations where this approach does not seem very appropriate. Figure 3a illustrates such a case. A boundary description of the rectangle requires at least four components, while a similar description of the L-shaped polygon requires six. In order to bring out our intuitive characterization of the boundary it is necessary to do some further processing or editing of the original description. We will show how this is in some ways equivalent to a segmentation of S into full subsets. However, before proceeding into that we should say a few words about another method for reducing full sets into thin sets, the medial axis transformation [28-31]. The medial axis of a set is defined as the locus of points which have a non unique closest neighbor on the boundary of the set. There are also many alternative definitions which emphasize the intuitive motivation of the method [28]. Figure 3b shows the medial axes for the sets of Figure 3a. Again it is obvious that such description is quite complex. This is especially true if one takes into account that the medial axis does not define uniquely a picture, but it is necessary to add to it a distance function [28,31]. For the rectangle one needs five linear segments and since the distance functions are linear one must define their values at only six points. For the L-shaped figure one needs seven linear segments and two parabolic arcs. The distance function must be defined in 10 points. In spite of these disadvantages the method has been used to pattern recognition because it is rather simple computationally [32,33].

Let us look now for "regularly" shaped full sets. There are a number of attributes which are desirable for such sets:

1. They must conform with our intuitive notions of "simpler" components of a "complex" picture. This is very important because our aim is shape recognition.

2. They must have a well defined mathematical characterization. This is necessary in order to be able to provide algorithms for determining them.

3. Their characterization must be subject independent, i.e., regardless of the nature of the picture from which S was derived.

4. The complexity of representing the set S through them should be comparable to the original description of S.

5. When a full set is reduced to a thin set by some type of limiting processes the "regularly" shaped components should be reduced to "regularly" shaped thin components.

Obviously some of them tend to be incompatible (e.g., the first two) and thus one must reach a compromise. One choice which seems to possess these attributes in a great degree is maximal convex subsets. Quite often an untrained human observer will describe a "silhouette" through such components. Typical examples are chromosome and letter recognition. Convexity is a well defined mathematical property and so is the notion of maximal convex subsets. Moreover, aggregates of convex sets possess many interesting mathematical properties [10,34-36]. It is also obvious that such a characterization has the third attribute listed above. In the limit (when their width tends to zero) convex sets reduce to linear segments and thus they possess the fifth attribute. They seem only to lack the fourth attribute because, in general, a set has an infinite number of maximal subsets. Not only that, but some sets require an infinite number of them for a cover. Figure 4 shows one example for each case. In (a) the sets (ABDE) and (EFGH) form a cover, but not in (b).

Thus we must impose some additional restrictions besides convexity and maximality. One is to restrict the sets under consideration only to polygons. This does not really result in any loss of generality because any full set S can be approximated by a polygon P with as high a degree of accuracy as desired. As a matter of fact some of the algorithms mentioned in the previous section segment the original picture directly into polygons [19]. In the sequence we will consider only polygons and when we talk about the set represented by a polygon we will actually mean the class of all sets S which are approximated by that polygon. The restriction to polygons now allows us to introduce some modifications in our original choice. We will consider the class E of convex subsets which are formed by extensions of the sides of the polygon and in particular only those which are maximal in E. In Figure 4a the only sets satisfying this restriction are (ABDE) and (EFGH). Although such sets are also maximal convex subsets, this is not always the case. Figure 5a shows a counterexample.

In many instances the cover formed by maximal elements of E is minimal, but this is not always true. Figure 5b shows a counterexample. However, in either case the complexity of representation has not increased substantially. The modified definition seems also to possess the other desired attributes, at least in the same degree as the original. It is also obvious that such a cover is invariant under translation, rotation, dilation or contraction and indexing of the vertices and the sides of the polygon. These are certainly desirable properties from a pattern recognition viewpoint. We can introduce now some formal definitions.

Definition 5: A polygon P will be *oriented* if all its sides have been assigned a direction in a clockwise manner (Figure 6).

Definition 6: A *primitive halfplane* (ph) of the oriented polygon P is a halfplane defined by the right side of the extension of a directed polygon side (Figure 6).

This definition is equivalent to an earlier one [9,10].

Definition 7: A *Q-subset* of an (oriented) polygon P is a nonempty convex subset of it formed by an intersection of some of its primitive halfplanes.

Definition 8: The *fundamental graph* of an (oriented) polygon is the directed graph formed by the extensions of its sides (Figure 6).

Definition 9: A *convex circuit* of the fundamental graph is a circuit where the (directed) angle between any two successive branches is less or equal to 180° (in Figure 6 ABICDEKLNA is not a convex circuit, while ABICDENA is).

A direct consequence of these definition is:

Proposition 1: A Q-subset is equivalent to a convex circuit of the fundamental graph.

Definition 10: The *formative list* of a Q-subset of A is a list of the indices of the halfplanes which are required to form A through their intersection and only of those. The *exclusion list* of A is a list of the indices of all halfplanes which if added to the above intersection would change the form of A.

Definition 11: A primary subset of an (oriented) polygon P is a maximal Q-subset (or a maximal convex circuit of the fundamental graph).

Definition 12: A nucleus of an (oriented) polygon P is a minimal Q-subset (or a minimal convex circuit of the fundamental graph).

It has been proven elsewhere [10] that:

Theorem: The union of the primary subsets of a polygon P equals P.

From these definitions it is clear that the construction of the primary subsets and the nuclei is in a sense equivalent to an editing of a representation by boundary segments. This process involves a rather complicated graph analysis problem since finding the circuits of a graph is not always simple [37]. An alternative construction algorithm has been described elsewhere [10] and it has also been implemented through a PL/1 program. Figures 7 and 8 show the output of the program. It gives a list of the primary subsets (PCS), the nuclei contained in each one of them and the formative lists of the primary subsets. (This is sufficient information to reconstruct the polygon.) For display purposes each primary subset is assigned a number equal to a power of 2 and to each point of the polygon a number is assigned equal to the sum of the nubmers of the primary subsets containing it. The labeling of the printout uses letters of the alphabet to denote numbers greater than 9 (A = 10, B = 11, etc.). The analysis of each polygon required about 3 seconds of IBM 360-91 time.

An obvious restriction in Figures 7 and 8 is that the sides of the polygons are either vertical or horizontal. This is due to the difficulties of discretizing lines at other angles for the original representation of the polygon and not to any limitations of the algorithm. The use of the fundamental graph can circumvent this limitation if one uses algebraic equations for describing the lines. However, important as these steps are in the implementation of the algorithm they do not affect the basic development of the theory. One may proceed by using a *"draftsman algorithm"* which is a sequence of geometric constructions resulting in the primary subsets. This circumvents the difficulties associated with discrete graphics. Figures 9 and 10 illustrate additional examples analyzed by such an algorithm.

It is also easy to verify that in the case of thin "polygonal" sets primary subsets correspond to the branches of the resulting graph or to the unions of branches lying on the same straight line. The nuclei correspond to the nodes of such a graph. Figure 11 illustrates this case. If one uses the nuclei to "subdivide" the primary subsets then this description is identical with the ones commonly used [1-7]. Thus the present approach contains as a special case the analysis of thin sets.

IV. Representation of Full Sets by Graphs

We have seen how a scene or an object S can be described as a union of subsets $S_1, S_2, \ldots S_n$ of the Euclidean plane. A list of these sets together with their determining parameters* describes S as completely as it is allowed by the accuracy of the various preprocessing algorithms. However, such a description contains most of the interesting information in an implicit form rather than explicit and additional analysis is required. One may argue that this should be done only in connection with a particular application and therefore, general analysis ends with the determination of the subsets $S_1, S_2, \ldots S_n$. It seems, however, that it is possible to proceed further without a significant loss of generality. As a matter of fact two very different types of problems accept quite similar formal representations. One is shape recognition and the other scene analysis. We will proceed with the first and come back to the second later.

There are a number of fundamental questions which one may ask in a shape recognition problem. Is the set S connected? Does it contain any holes? Does it contain, for example, two bars at right angle, etc.? None of this can be answered readily from a list of its primary subsets or for that matter from any other subdivision. This can be done only by considering the relative location or the juxtaposition relations among the primary subsets. Although for thin sets it is easy to define adjacency operators [36] the situation is more complicated for full sets. For this reason there have been attempts to describe the structure of S without using any such operators. This can be done by using a system of coordinates which is either fixed or relative to S (e.g., its origin might be at the lower left hand corner of S). Then the location of each primary subset can be defined by the coordinates of a prespecified point of it (e.g., its lower left hand corner). This method has been used for the recognition of alphabetic characters [7] and in a different context for the analysis of mathematical formulas [38].

Again one may require considerable computation before answering questions about the connectivity of S. Thus a coordinate description lacks in comparison to properly defined adjacency relations.

*In the case of primary subsets, their formative lists.

An obvious juxtaposition relation is set intersection. In the analysis described in the previous section this information is obtainable during the construction of the primary subsets and thus one can express S in terms of a graph whose nodes correspond to primary subsets and whose branches connect nodes corresponding to intersecting sets. Figure 12a shows a polygon and Figure 12b its corresponding graph. It is obvious that the resulting graphs are identical for both a Y and a Δ configuration. This may be avoided if a list of the nuclei is added and connections are established only between intersecting nuclei and primary subsets, but not between intersecting primary subsets. (It is easy to see that two nuclei have always an empty intersection.) We can introduce now certain formal definitions.

Definition 13: The *primary graph* of a set S is labeled graph whose nodes correspond to the primary subsets of S (These will be called *P-nodes*) and to the nuclei of S (these will be called *N-nodes*) and the branches connect only differently labeled nodes corresponding to intersecting subsets.

Figure 11c shows the primary graph for the polygon of Figure 12a.

Definition 14: A *completely labeled primary graph* is one whose nodes contain also the formative and exclusion lists of the corresponding subsets.

Obviously a polygon is uniquely characterized by a completely labeled primary graph while for a given primary graph there exist many different polygons. Thus the simple graph P-N-P corresponds to all polygons formed by the union of two intersecting convex polygons.

A similar form of graph definition for full sets can be used with other types of segmentation even if the various components are disjoint. A graph with nodes corresponding to the subsets $S_1, S_2, \ldots, S_n$ and branches connecting adjoining subsets will suffer from the same defects as the representation of Figure 12b. However, if $T_1, T_2, \ldots, T_m$ denote the connected components of all intersections of the closures of $S_1, S_2, \ldots, S_n$ then they can play the role of the nuclei and use as nodes of a graph those very similar to a primary graph. However, the form of "complete labeling" required will be in general different.

In the case of thin sets primary subsets correspond to line segments and nuclei to their intersections. If a thin set is such that no line extends through an intersection (i.e., no T-shaped formations exist, but only Y-shaped) then no primary set contains more than 2 nuclei. Then all P-nodes are of degree at most 2 and subgraphs of the form -P- or P- can be considered as single branches. Thus we have the classical formulations as mentioned in the previous section.

The algorithm for the construction of nuclei and primary subsets allows the recognition of another form of relation between such sets. Figure 13 shows an example where a nucleus (N1) is contained in just one primary subset (P1), but is formed by extensions of the sides of another (P3). In the primary graph we may add "broken line" connections between these nodes (N1 and P3). Such a primary graph will be called *extended* and connections of this type will be called *extensions*.

Up to this point we have considered only two extreme cases. The primary graph without any labeling except for the P and N nodes and the completely labeled graph. The first contains explicitly topological information, but there may still be many "hidden features". Actually representing a set by a labeled graph offers the attractive possibility that there may exist different levels of labeling depending on how much one wants to know about the picture. Thus "intermediate labeling levels" may be introduced besides the P or N label and the formative and exclusion lists. Such a procedure produces in effect a hierarchical ordering of the features of the set. Thus depending on the nature of the problem one may look at different levels of labeling either throughout the primary graph or in a subgraph of it only. Considering different levels at different parts of the primary graph is equivalent to looking at a greater or a lesser detail in different parts of a picture depending on the context. We will illustrate this point later by an example, but first we must describe some intermediate labeling levels.

Let $P_1, P_2, \ldots P_k$ be all the primary subsets containing a nucleus N. Let V be their common intersection. Note that although $N \subset V$ it is not always true that $N = V$. The relation of the boundaries of V and the primary subsets provides some interesting information about the configuration they form. Let now f_i and e_i be the formative and exclusion lists of P_i and f_v and e_v the corresponding lists for V. Then one can define the following two variables:

$$\sigma_i = |f_i \cap f_v|$$

and

$$\tau_i = |e_i \cap f_v|$$

where a list intersection means a list containing the common members of the two lists and $|\ell|$ denotes the number of members of the list ℓ. Because $V \subset P_i$ it is also true that

$$e_i \cap e_v = e_v$$

Because there is a unique nucleus N included in V the branches of the primary graph between N and $P_1, P_2, \ldots P_k$ can be labeled by the pair (σ_i, τ_i). This establishes a new type of juxtaposition relation. Its importance can be readily illustrated for the case of a subgraph of the form P1-N-P2 where P1 and P2 may be connected to other nuclei but N is connected only to P1 and P2. It is obvious that in this case there are three basic types of configurations: L, T or X shaped as shown in Figure 14. In the Appendix it is shown that the following simple algorithm allows the discrimination between these three types:

S1. Is $\tau_1 = 1$? If yes go to S3. If no proceed to S2.
S2. Is $\tau_1 + \tau_2 < |f_v|$? If yes return (T-type).
If no return (X-type).
S3. Is $\tau_2 = 1$? If yes return (L-type).
If no return (T-type).

Another level of labeling involves the nodes. Indeed let $\sigma(B,A)$ be a similarity distance defined-over the set G of equivalence classes of convex sets under a set of similarity transformations T. Examples of such measures have been discussed elsewhere [9,10]. Let H be a countable subset of G such that for any $A \epsilon G$ there exists at least one $B \epsilon H$ such that $\sigma(B_k,A) < \epsilon$ for some specified positive constant ϵ. Then each node can be labeled with the index k of its closest neighbor in H.

If T includes translations, rotations and scaling then it is obvious that the graph so labeled is going to be the same for all polygons which are equivalent under the above transformations. For example, it would offer no distinction between the four configurations shown in Figure 15a. Figure 15b shows the common graph where k is assumed to be the index for a rectangle and j the one for a square. If rotation information is to become available then two steps should be taken: one is to remove rotation from the set of similarity transformations. This will, of course, increase the size of H. The other is to mark the relative orientation of a primary subset with respect to the nuclei. Thus if a scan from left to right meets the primary set before the nucleus an index 1 or 3 is assigned to the branch. Otherwise 2 or 4. If a scan from top to bottom meets first the primary set then an index 1 or 2 is assigned. Otherwise 3 or 4. Figure 15c shows the labeled graphs for the case of Figure 15a (k_1 denotes a vertical rectangle while k_2 a horizontal rectangle).

In practice it is desirable to preserve in the same graph both types of information, invariant under T and describing the effect of T. This can be achieved by a proper indexing of the members of H. Suppose for example, that H contains only rectangles and let it be indexed according to the ratio of their greater side to the smaller:

$$H_1(1:1),\ H_2(2:1),\ H_3(3:1),\ H_4(3:2),\ H_5(4:1),\ H_6(4:3)\ \ldots$$

Let now $\phi_1, \phi_2, \ldots, \phi_n$ denote a set of values of the angle of the greater side with the horizontal. Then each member of H generates n more others indexed as H_{jk} where j represents the ratio of the sides of k the angle. One can use a single index instead of two by using a Gödel scheme

[39]. Thus H_{jk} could be given the index $2^j 3^k$.

It is easy to construct lists describing the labeled graph for its storage in computer memory and also organize them to provide labeling flexibility and efficient information retrieval. Many of the standard techniques described in the literature [40] are readily applicable.

We may discuss now the scene analysis problem. An important special case is the identification of solid objects from two dimensional pictures [20-22]. Guzman has developed a program which performs this task on the basis of a primitive representation involving polygonal regions and vertices (but not edges) [22]. Figure 16a shows a simple example of such a scene where numbers denote regions (6 is the background) and letters denote vertices. Figure 16b shows a labeled graph corresponding to the scene. Its nodes correspond either to regions (R-nodes) or to vertices (V-nodes) and branches connect nodes of different types corresponding to adjacent entities. Again the numbers and the letters associated with the graph are not part of the labeling but simply help for the reader in identifying the components of the graph with the original scene.

The branches of the graph are labeled with the angle formed by the region at the corresponding vertex. From this graph one can proceed to higher orders of labeling. Thus the FOOP and KIND lists used by Guzman [22] correspond to the minimal circuits around an R-node or a V-node respectively. The labels of the branches incident at a V-node provide the "type" information (fork, arrow, etc.) (*ibid.*).

There is at least a formal similarity between this graph and primary graphs and it will be an interesting study to investigate grammars generating such graphs and compare them with grammars generating primary graphs (9). It seems that this similarity is actually due to certain common properties of the types of primitives used. The nodes of a primary graph correspond to maximal and minimal subsets of S. The same can be said here: Regions are in a sense maximal subsets and vertices minimal. A description using edges does not have this property.

V. Structural Description and Recognition of Patterns

The labeling of primary graphs can be considered as a form of syntactic analysis (in determining the σ and τ parameters) or feature extraction (in labeling P-nodes according to their similarity to members of a "basis"). Although one can provide additional labels than those discussed in the previous section it is obvious that he must stop at some point and start looking for descriptions directly connected with the classes of patterns of particular interest.

In the past the most popular method has been the description of the patterns in terms of formal grammars [1-4,7,23,26,41,42]. More often than not such grammars are context sensitive [*ibid.*] and therefore require complex parsing algorithms [43]. Moreover it is very difficult to infer a grammar from a finite number of samples, a problem crucial in the context of pattern recognition [44-46].

There is one point which should be emphasized here. The discrimination among, say, n classes of patterns requires n grammars $G_1, G_2, \ldots G_n$ with disjoint languages $L_1, L_2, \ldots L_n$. It is not necessary that all the members of anyone of these languages be meaningful patterns. If C_i is the collection of linguistic representations from all the members of ith class then it is sufficient that C_i is a subset of L_i. Such an embedding allows, in general, grammars of simpler form then otherwise. For example, suppose that all patterns in one class are of the form $a^n b^n c^n b^n$ $(n > 0)$ while all patterns in another are of the form $a^n c^n b^n$ $(n > 0)$. Although context sensitive grammars are required to produce each class the discrimination can be achieved by a finite automaton accepting all strings containing the substring ac for the second class.

This brings us back to the old question of feature selection. It may be easy to determine grammars with the property $L_i = C_i$, but they will be, in general, too cumbersome. In terms of the classical approach this corresponds to the use of a very large number of features. On the other hand using simpler grammars with $L_i \supset C_i$ and $L_i \cap L_j = \phi$ for $i \neq j$ it is equivalent to choosing a small number of discriminating features. Thus the use of formal languages offers no real advantages by itself. It is the structural description which makes things easier because if properly done, it produces a mathematical structure corresponding to the important attributes of the pattern. It is in a sense an implicit feature selection procedure. If this is achieved then the formal classification method is of secondary interest.

In this context we may compare primary graphs to descriptions of patterns directly in terms of chain-link encoding of their boundary [12,13,27]. These components are very close to the "raw data" and therefore they cannot be described in terms of any reasonably simple grammar. On the other hand, both the construction and the labeling of a primary graph involves in essence a syntactic analysis of an original description of the boundary through linear segments. Thus it may be possible to characterize classes of patterns in a simple way, for example if their primary graphs contain always a particular subgraph (different for each class, of course). Then they can be described either through finite state languages or, in terms of the classical approach, through masks.

We may also point out that there are a number of other properties which do not lend themselves readily to a linguistic description.

Connectedness of the set S (corresponding to the connectedness of the primary graph) and the existence of holes (related to the existence of circuits in the primary graph) are such examples.

We will illustrate these points through an example. Figure 17 shows ten samples of polygonal approximaties of capital letters with their primary sets and nuclei superimposed. Figure 18 shows the corresponding primary graphs with the values of τ_i expresses through multiple lines. A P-node is labeled H for a horizontal bar, V for a vertical bar, DP for a bar at an angle of 45° with the horizontal, DN for a bar at an angle of 135° with the horizontal, T for a triangle, S for a square and X for all other shapes. The labels P1, P2, . . . ,N1, N2, ...etc. are simply for helping the reader and are not part of the formal labeling scheme.

Polygons a-e can be classified visually as A's, f and g as R's, h and i as H's and j as P. The design of a classifier involves an inspection of the primary graphs for common properties. This can be guided by the intuitive characterizations of the letters and in practice it should be done through interactive programming. In this case some of the common properties involve subgraphs. The following algorithm achieves classification. (The notation P . . . .N stands for a "do not care" connection, i.e., any value of τ_i. The notation N. . . .? or P. . . .? stands for an optional connection with other parts of the graph.) In brackets are the polygons which satisfy each condition.

S1. Is there a circuit with at least three primary subsets, none of them labeled T? If yes proceed to S2. [a-g,j]. If no return (H). [h,i]

S2. Look for the subgraph

```
==N. . . .P (≠V). . . .N==
  :                    :
  : ?                  : ?
```

If present then proceed to S3. [a-f]
Else go to S5 [g,j]

S3. Look for the subgraph

```
==N---P. . . . .
```

If present then proceed to S4 [e,f]
Else return (A) [a-d]

S4. Check the label of P in subgraph of S3.
If it is DN then return (R) [e,f]
else return (A)

S5. Look for the subgraph

```
. . .P(V)==N. . .P
           :
           P (DP)
```

If present then return (R) [g]
else return (P) [j]

The only error is character "e" (it is called an R) which certainly is ambiguous even in visual classification.

Instead of the above algorithm one could define predicates x_i which take the value 1 when the condition in step Si is true. Then the following set of discriminant functions would achieve the same classification.

$$\varphi A = x_1 \cdot x_2 (\bar{x}_3 + x_3 \bar{x}_4)$$

$$\varphi H = \bar{x}_1$$

$$\varphi R = x_1 \bar{x}_2 \bar{x}_5$$

$$\varphi R = x_1 (x_2 x_3 x_4 + \bar{x}_2 x_5)$$

Note that this procedure has not required any normalization of size, thickness, slant, etc.

VI. Discussion

We have presented a method for automatic recognition of shape. It is based on the assumption that expressing a "silhouette" through some of its convex subsets can make shape recognition easier. This seems to be justified, at least to the extent that character recognition can be done successfully through such subsets as illustrated by the example of the previous section and earlier approximate implementation of the method [11]. There have been additional recent reports about using convextiy in order to recognize both letters [47] and chromosomes [48].

Regardless of the extent to which the specific formalism of the method will prove useful in the future we believe that we have presented at least an example of a systematic approach to the problem. It is probably too optimistic to expect that mathematical techniques developed for other applications (e.g., statistical communication, theory of formal languages) will provide a solution to the problem of shape recognition. What is needed is the development of a mathematical model for that problem and then attempt its solution. It also seems necessary to isolate this particular problem from the general problem of building machines which can recognize patterns. For example, we should distinguish the development of geometrical constructions for shape analysis (draftsman's algorithms) from their implementation on a digital machine. The digitization of picture poses certain unique problems [49-52] and we should at least separate them from the mathematical modeling of shape recognition. Successful mechanical pattern recognition must wait for advances in both areas (and others as well) but we should at least be aware where we do stand with respect to each one of these problems.

Appendix

In Section IV an algorithm was described for distinguishing various configurations corresponding to the graph P-N-P. We will give here the proof of that algorithm and certain other related results.

It is obvious that the boundary segments of V are also parts of the boundary segments of $P_1, P_2, \ldots, P_k$. If the latter do not have any common segments then each boundary segment of V will be counted only once while forming the variables $\sigma_1, \sigma_2, \ldots, \sigma_k$. Thus their sum should equal $|f_v|$. This is illustrated in Figure 19a where $|f_v| = 5$ and $\sigma_1 = 1$, $\sigma_2 = 2$, $\sigma_3 = 2$. On the other hand, if the primary subsets have common boundaries some of the boundaries of V will be counted more than once while forming the variables $\sigma_1, \sigma_2, \ldots, \sigma_k$. Thus their sum should be greater than $|f_v|$. This is illustrated in Figure 19b where $|f_v| = 5$ and $\sigma_1 = 2$, $\sigma_2 = 3$, $\sigma_3 = 1$, $\sigma_4 = 2$ and $\sigma_5 = 3$. Note that even if the redundant sets P_4 and P_5 are omitted (a minimal cover consists only of P_1, P_2 and P_3) still $\sigma_1 + \sigma_2 + \sigma_3 = 6 > 5$. An arrangement as shown in Figure 19a may be called an X-type configuration. We summarize these observations as:

Proposition A-1: $\sigma_1 + \sigma_2 + \ldots + \sigma_k \geq |f_v|$ with equality occuring if and only if the primary subsets form an X-type configuration.

In any configuration, for a given primary subset P_i, the boundary segments of V are either parts of the boundary of P_i or they are contained within P_i and therefore the corresponding primitive halfplanes are part of the exclusion list of P_i. Therefore we have:

Proposition A-2: Always $\sigma_i + \tau_i = |f_v|$.

As a direct consequence of the above results we have:

Proposition A-3: For $k = 2$ the following are true:

(a) An X-type configuration is characterized by any of the following (equivalent) relations:

(i) $\sigma_1 + \sigma_2 = |f_n|$

(ii) $\tau_1 + \tau_2 = |f_n|$

(iii) $\sigma_1 = \tau_2$

(iv) $\sigma_2 = \tau_1$

(b) An L or T-type configuration is characterized by any of the following (equivalent) relations:

(i) $\sigma_1 + \sigma_2 > |f_n|$

(ii) $\tau_1 + \tau_2 < |f_n|$

We still do not know how to distinguish L from T-type configurations. However, it is easily seen that in an L-type both τ_1 and τ_2 should equal 1 (Figure 19c). In a T-type at least one of them must be greater than 1 (sets (1) and (2) in Figure 13b) and in an X-type both (sets (2) and (3) in Figure 19a).

Proposition A-4: In an L-type configuration:

(a) $\tau_1 = \tau_2 = 1$

In an T-type configuration:

(b) $\tau_1 \geq 1$, $\tau_2 > 1$ or ($\tau_1 > 1$, $\tau_2 \geq 1$)

In an X-type configuration:

(c) $\tau_1 > 1$, $\tau_2 > 1$

Note that (b) and (c) cannot be used to distinguish an X from a T-type configuration because it is possible that both inequalities in (b) be strict. The algorithm of Section IV uses Proposition A-4 (a) (ii) to distinguish between an X-type and a T-type configuration.

REFERENCES

1. Miller, W. F. and A. C. Shaw, "Linguistic Methods in Picture Processing–A Survey," *Proc. Fall Joint Computer Conference,* 1968, pp. 279-290.
2. Fu, K. S. and P. H. Swain, "On Syntactic Pattern Recognition," *Software Engineering,* (J. Tou, editor), Academic Press, 1971, v. 2, pp. 155-182.
3. Narasimhan, R., "Labeling Schemata and Syntactic Description of Pictures," *Inform. & Control,* Vol. 7, 1964, pp. 151-179.
4. Feder, J., "Languages of Encoded Line Patterns," *Information and Control,* v. 13, 1968, pp. 230-244.
5. Knoke, P. J. and R. G. Wiley, "A Linguistic Approach to Mechanical Pattern Recognition," *Proc. IEEE Computer Conference,* Sept. 1967, pp. 142-144.
6. Shaw, A. C., "Parsing of Graph-Representable Pictures," *J. ACM,* v. 17, June 1970, pp. 453-481.
7. Shaw, A. C., "A Formal Picture Description Scheme or a Basis for Picture Processing Systems," *Information and Control,* v. 14, 1969, pp. 9-52.
8. Aizerman, M. A., "Remarks on Two Problems Connected with Pattern Recognition," *Methodologies of Pattern Recognition,* (S. Watanabe, editor), Academic Press, 1969.
9. Pavlidis, T., "On the Syntactic Analysis of Figures," *Proc. ACM National Conference,* 1968, pp. 183-188.
10. Pavlidis, T., "Analysis of Set Patterns," *Pattern Recognition*, v. 1, November 1968, pp. 165-178.

11. Pavlidis, T., "Computer Recognition of Figures through Decomposition," *Information & Control,* v. 14, May-June 1968, pp. 526-537.
12. Pavlidis, T., "Computer Analysis of Figures into Primary Convex Subsets," *Proc. Systems Science and Cybernetics Conference,* 1968, pp. 55-60. [This paper contains a listing of PL/1 program for finding the primary subsets of a figure.]
13. Pavlidis, T., "Representation of Figures by Labeled Graphs," *Pattern Recognition* (in press).
14. Rosenfeld, A., *Picture Processing by Computer,* Academic Press, 1969, Chapter 8.
15. Kirsch, R. A., "Computer Determination of the Constitutent Structure of Biological Images, Part I," *N. B. S. Report No. 10173,* December 1969.
16. Julesz, B., "Visual Pattern Discrimination," *IRE Trans. on Inform. Theory,* February 1962, pp. 34-92.
17. Rosenfeld, A. and E. B. Troy, "Visual Texture Analysis," *Tech. Report. 70-116,* Computer Science Center, University of Maryland, June 1970.
18. Rosenfeld, A. and M. Thurston, "Visual Texture Analysis – 2," *Tech. Report 70-129,* Computer Science Center, University of Maryland, September 1970.
19. Pavlidis, T., "Piecewise Approximation of Functions of Two Variables and Its Applications in Topographical Data Reduction," *Tech. Report No. 86,* Computer Science Laboratory, Princeton University, September 1970.
20. Brice, C. R. and C. L. Fennema, "Scene Analysis Using Regions," *SRI Art. Intell. Group, Tech. Note 17,* April 1970.
21. Roberts, L. G., "Machine Perceptions of Three-Dimensional Solids," *Optical and Electrooptical Information Processing* (J. T. Tippett et al., editors), M.I.T. Press, 1965.
22. Guzman, A., "Decomposition of a Visual Scene into Three-Dimensional Bodies," *Proc. Fall Joint Computer Conference,* 1968, pp. 291-304.
23. Rosenfeld, A. and J. P. Strong, "A Grammar for Maps," *Software Engineering* (J. Tou, ed.) Academic Press, 1971, v. 2, pp. 227-233.
24. Grenander, U., "Foundations of Pattern Analysis," *Quart. Applied Mathematics,* v. 27, 1969, pp. 1-55.
25. Grenander, U., "A Unified Approach to Pattern Analysis," *Advances in Computers,* v. 10 (W. Freiberger, Guest Editor), Academic Press, 1970, pp. 175-216.
26. Ledley, R. S. et al., "FIDAC: Film Input to Digital Automatic Computer and Associated Syntax-Directed Pattern Recognition Programming System," *Optical and Electrooptical Information Processing* (J. T. Tippett, et al., editor) M.I.T. Press, 1965.
27. Gallus, G., "Contour Analysis in Pattern Recognition for Human Chromosome Classification," *Applicazioni bio-mediche del calcolo electtronico,* n. 2, 1968, pp. 95-108.
28. Blum, H., "Transformation for Extracting New Description of Shape," *Symp. Perception of Speech and Visual Form,* M.I.T. Press, 1964.
29. Rosenfeld, A. and J. L. Pfaltz, "Sequential Operations in Digital Picture Processing," *J. ACM,* v. 13, 1966, pp. 471-494.
30. Rosenfeld, A. and J. L. Pfaltz, "Distance Functions on Digital Pictures," *Pattern Recognition,* v. 2, 1968, pp. 33-81.
31. (staff) "Study of the Mathematical Foundations of the Medial Axis Transformations," *Final Report Contract No. AF19(628)-5711,* Parke Mathematical

Laboratories, Inc., One River Road, Carlisle, Mass., August 1968.
32. Philbrick, O., "A Study of Shape Recognition Using the Medial Axis Transformation," *Report No. 288,* Air Force Cambridge Research Laboratories, November 1966.
33. Hilditch, J., "An Application of Graph Theory in Pattern Recognition," *Machine Intelligence,* Amer. Elsevier Publishing Company, v. 3, 1968, pp. 325-347.
34. Valentine, F. A., *Convex Sets,* McGraw-Hill, New York, 1964.
35. Ewald, G., "Von Klassen Konvexer Korper Erzeugte Hilbertraume," *Math. Ann.,* v. 162, 1966, pp. 140-146.
36. Ewald, G. and G. C. Shephard, "Normed Vector Spaces Consisting of Classes of Convex Sets," *Math. Zeitschr.,* v. 91, 1966, pp. 1-19.
37. Tiernan, J. C., "An Efficient Search Algorithm to Find the Elementary Circuits of a Graph," *Comm. ACM,* v. 13, 1970, pp. 722-726.
38. Anderson, R. H., "Syntax-Directed Recognition of Hand Printed Two Dimensional Mathematics," *Ph.D. Dissertation,* Harvard University, January 1968.
39. Minsky, M., *Computation: Finite and Infinite Machines,* Prentice-Hall, 1967.
40. Knuth, D. E., *The Art of Computer Programming,* v. 1., Addison-Wesley, 1968, Chapter 2.
41. Rosenfeld, A.,and Pfaltz, J. L., "Web Grammars," *Proc. Joint International Conference on Artificial Intelligence,* Washington, D. C., 1969.
42. Montanari, U., "Separable Graphs, Planar Graphs and Web Grammars," *Information & Control,* v. 16, (May 1970), pp. 243-267.
43. Hopcroft, J. E. and J. D. Ullman, *Formal Languages and Their Relation to Automata,* Addison-Wesley, 1969.
44. Feldman, J., "Some Decidability Results on Grammatical Inference and Complexity," *Memo AI-93,* Stanford Artificial Intelligence Project, August 1969.
45. Horning, J. J., "A Study of Grammatical Inference," *Tech. Report CS139,* Computer Science Department, Stanford University, August 1969.
46. Evans, T. G., "Grammatical Inference Techniques in Pattern Analysis, "Software Engineering (J. Tou, editor), Academic Press, 1971, vol. 2, pp. 183-202.
47. Sammon, J. W. and J. H. Sanders, "Handprinted Character Recognition Using Convexity Decomposition," *Proc. Symposium on Feature Extraction and Selection,* Argonne National Laboratory, October 1970.
48. Klinger, A., A. Kochman and N. Alexandridis, "Computer Analysis of Chromosome Patterns: Feature-Encoding for Flexible Decisions Mating," *Proc. Symposium on Feature Extraction and Selection,* Argonne National Laboratory, October 1970.
49. Rosenfeld, A.,"Connectivity in Digital Pictures," *J. ACM,* v. 17, 1970, pp. 146-160.
50. Montanari, U. G., "On Limit Properties in Digitization Schemes," *J. ACM,* v. 17, 1970, pp. 348-360.
51. Mylopoulos, J. and T. Pavlidis, "On the Topological Properties of Quantized Spaces: 1. The Notion of Dimension," *JACM,* v. 18, April 1971, pp. 239-246.
52. Mylopoulos, J. and T. Pavlidis, "On the Topological Properties of Quantized Spaces: 2. Connectivity and Order of Connectivity," *JACM,* v. 18, April 1971, pp. 247-254.

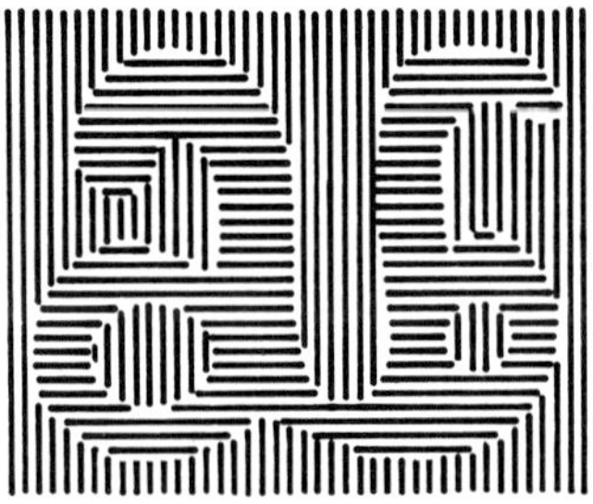

Figure 1. An example illustrating the need for special segmentation routines in order to separate the two letters from their background

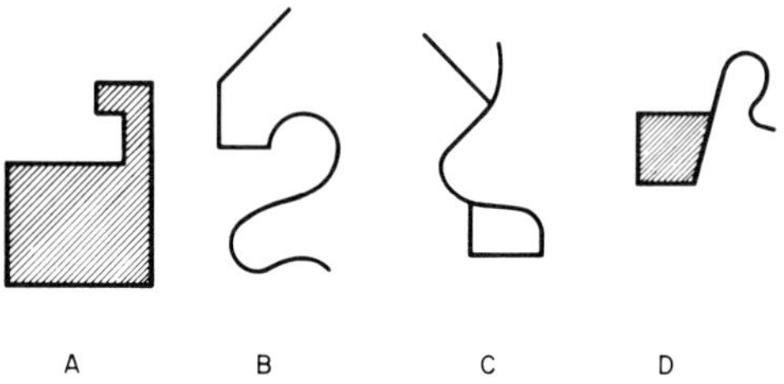

Figure 2. Illustration of Definitions 1-3. Full, Slim and Thin sets and one not belonging to any one of these categories

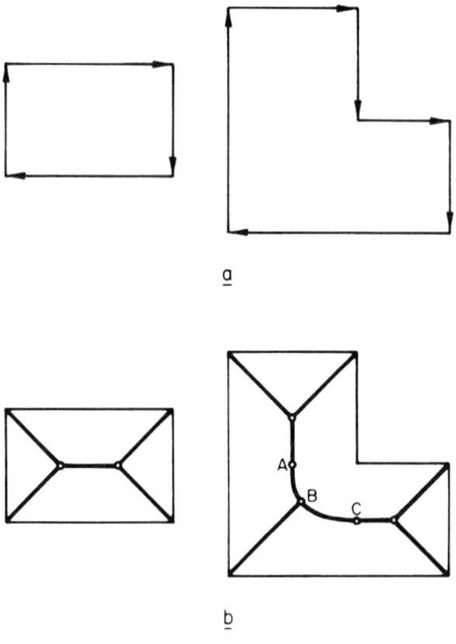

Figure 3. Two simple full sets (a) and their medial axes (b). AB and BC are parabolic arcs

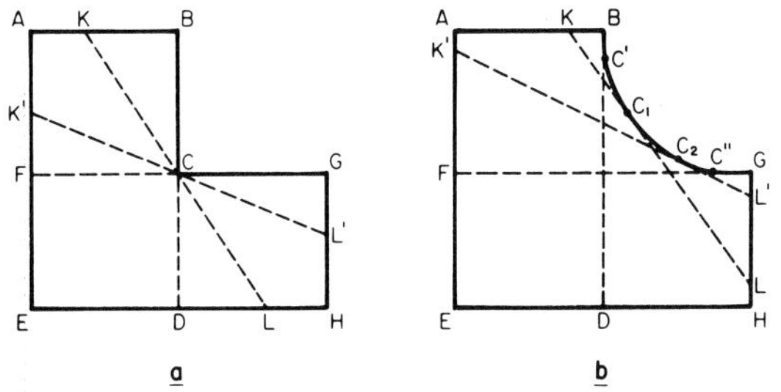

Figure 4. Illustration of maximal convex subsets. In (a) these are all subsets with one side through C: (KLEA), (K′L′HE), (ABDE), (FGHE), etc. The last two form a cover. In (b) the maximal convex subsets are all subsets with one side tangent on the curve C′C″: (KLEA), (K′L′HE), (ABDE), (FGHE), etc. Obviously there is no finite cover

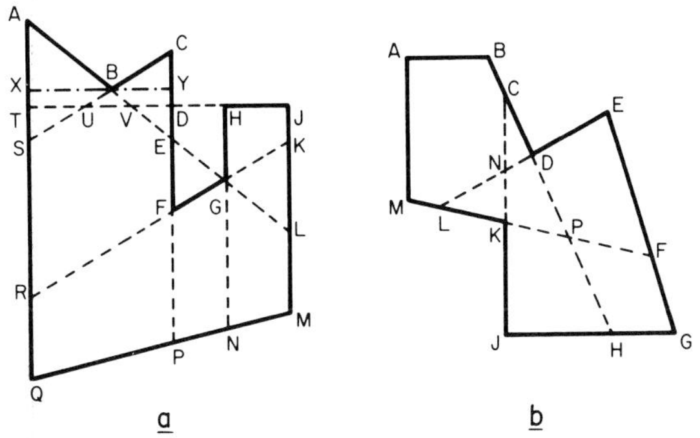

Figure 5. Maximal sets in E are not always maximal convex subsets. In (a) (TDPQ) is maximal in E, but it is a subset of (XBYRQ). They do not always form a minimal cover. Not only (TDPQ) is redundant in (a), but also (CHJ) and (LEF) in (b) which are actually maximal convex subsets

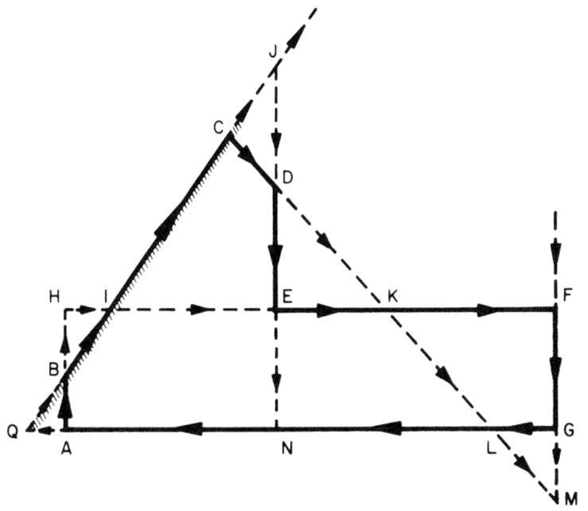

Figure 6. (ABCDEFG) is an oriented polygon. The hatching indicates the primitive halfplane defined by side (BC). The fundamental graph has as its nodes all the points marked by a letter

```
ALL TREES SEARCHED.DEVELOP SYNTAX NOW:


SYNTACTIC ANALYSIS:
PCS #  1 JOINS NUCLEI #  1  3          IT IS THE INTSCT OF HPLS #  3,  6,  9, 10,
PCS #  2 JOINS NUCLEI #  1  2          IT IS THE INTSCT OF HPLS #  5,  6,  7, 10,
PCS #  3 JOINS NUCLEI #  2  4  6         IT IS THE INTSCT OF HPLS #  1,  6,  7,  8,
PCS #  4 BELONGS TO NUCLEUS#  3         IT IS THE INTSCT OF HPLS #  3,  4,  9, 11,
PCS #  5 JOINS NUCLEI #  5  6          IT IS THE INTSCT OF HPLS #  1,  2,  7, 12,
    5 PRIMARY SETS FOUND


REPRESENTATION OF FIGURE BY PRIMARY SETS


         MMGGGGGGGGGGGGGG
         MMGGGGGGGGGGGGGG
         44
         44
         44
         44
         44
         44    99888
         44    99888
         44    99888
         44    99888
         44    99888
         44    99888
         44    11
         44    11
         44    11
         6622233
         6622233


REGULAR TERMINATION
*********************
```

Figure 7. Primary subsets and nuclei of a polygon approximating the letter G produced by a PL/1 program

```
ALL TREES SEARCHED.DEVELOP SYNTAX NOW:


SYNTACTIC ANALYSIS:
PCS #  1 JOINS NUCLEI #   1  2          IT IS THE INTSCT OF HPLS #  5,  6,  7, 10,
PCS #  2 JOINS NUCLEI #   1  3  5          IT IS THE INTSCT OF HPLS #  1,  6,  9, 10,
PCS #  3 JOINS NUCLEI #   2  4  6          IT IS THE INTSCT OF HPLS #  1,  6,  7,  8,
PCS #  4 JOINS NUCLEI #   3  4          IT IS THE INTSCT OF HPLS #  3,  4,  7, 10,
PCS #  5 JOINS NUCLEI #   5  6          IT IS THE INTSCT OF HPLS #  1,  2,  7, 10,
    5 PRIMARY SETS FOUND


REPRESENTATION OF FIGURE BY PRIMARY SETS


          MMMGGGGGGGGGGGGKKKK
          MMMGGGGGGGGGGGGKKKK
          MMMGGGGGGGGGGGGKKKK
          444            2222
          444            2222
          444            2222
          444            2222
          CCC888888888888AAAA
          CCC888888888888AAAA
          444            2222
          444            2222
          444            2222
          444            2222
          5551111111111113333
          5551111111111113333
          5551111111111113333


REGULAR TERMINATION
***********************
```

Figure 8. Primary subsets and nuclei of a polygon approximating the letter A produced by a PL/1 program

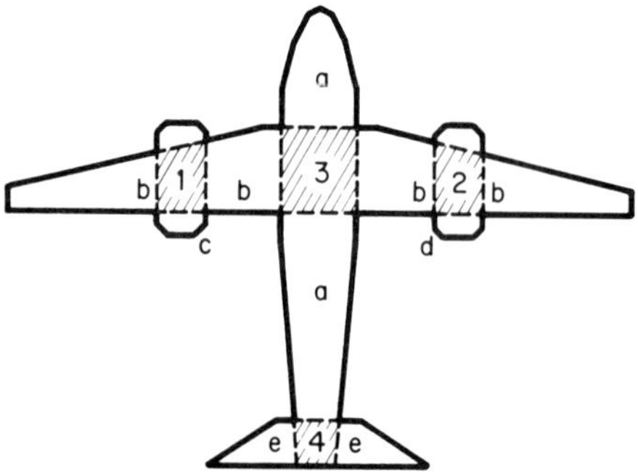

Figure 9. Computer printout showing the primary subsets (and nuclei) of a polygon approximating the silhouette of an airplane

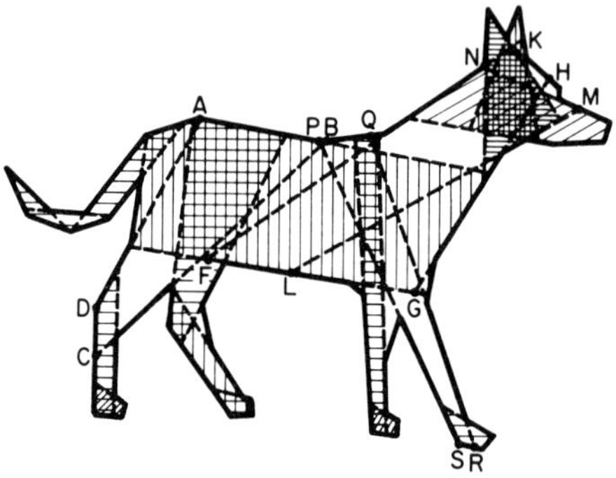

Figure 10. Computer printout showing some of the primary subsets of a polygon approximating the silhouette of a dog. Each p.s. is designated by hatching at different angle. (ABCD), (FGHK), (FLMN) and (PQRS) are some additional p.s.

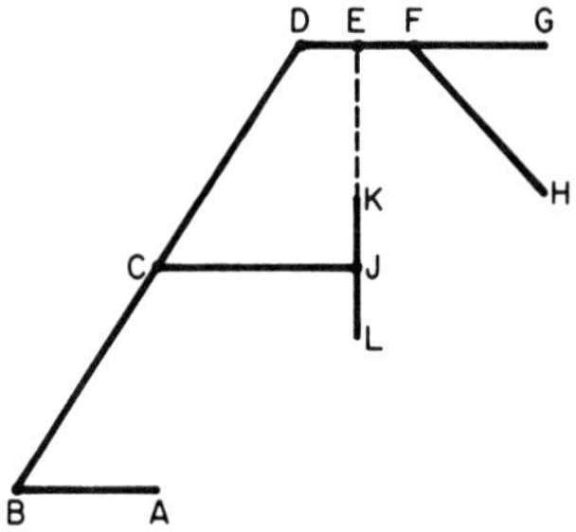

Figure 11. An example of a thin set: (AB), (BD), (DG), (FH), (CJ) and (KL) are primary subsets, while B,C,D,E,F and J are nuclei

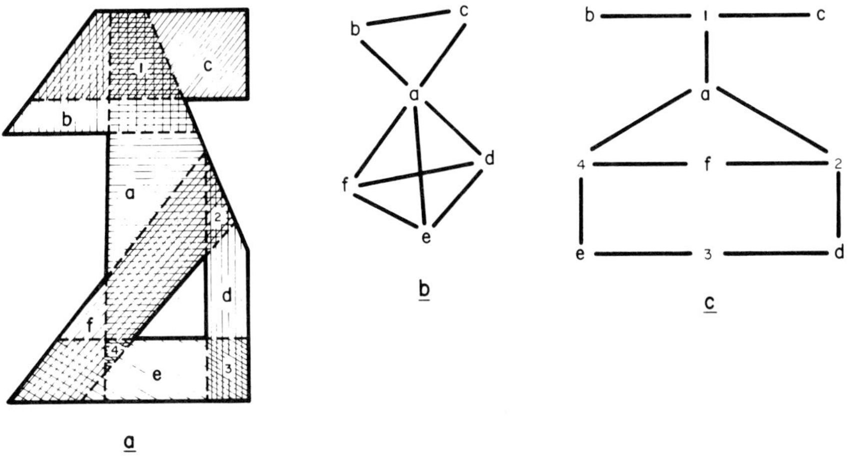

Figure 12. (a) A polygon where the primary subsets are shown through different hatching and lower case letters. The nuclei are shown by numbers and heavier cross-hatching. (b) An adjacency graph of the primary subsets. (c) A graph involving both nuclei and primary subsets

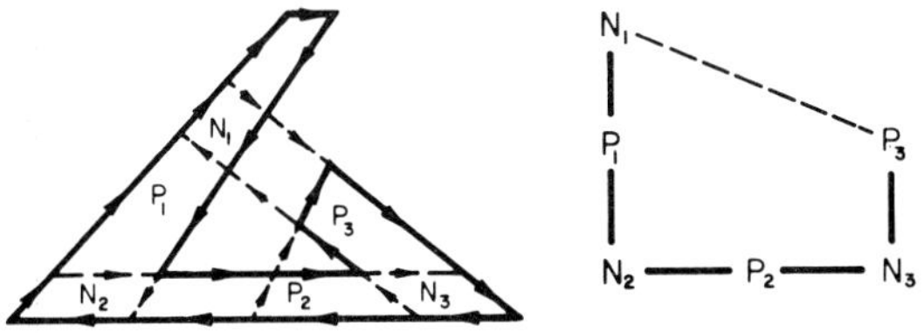

Figure 13. Illustration of a polygon resulting to an extended primary graph

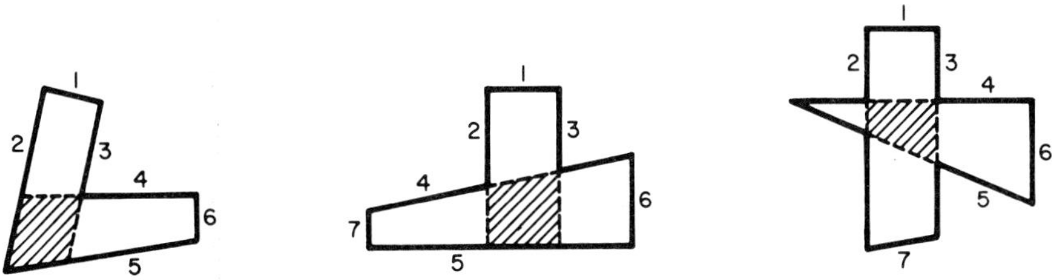

Figure 14. The three basic configurations corresponding to the primary graph P-N-P (a) an L-type, (b) a T-type (c) an X-type

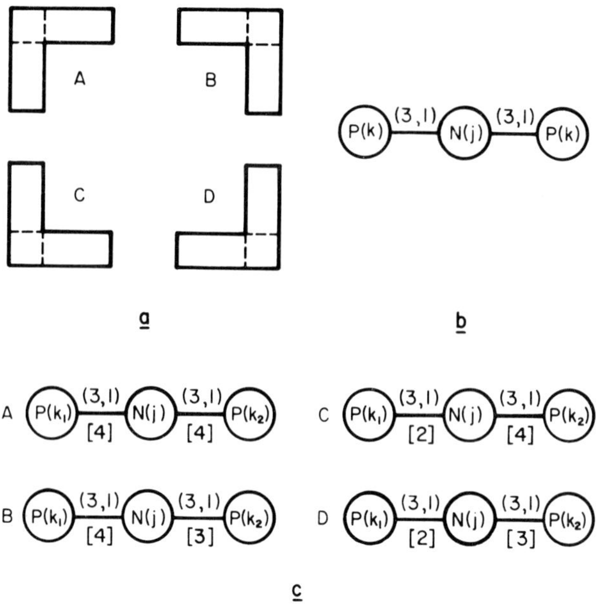

Figure 15. Removal of rotation invariance: (a) Four polygons equivalent under rotation, (b) A primary graph showing only rotation invariance properties, (c) A set of primary graphs containing angle orientation information

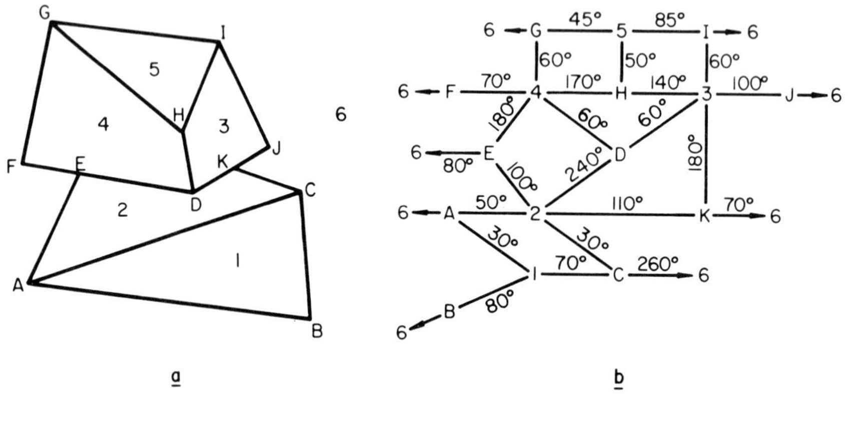

Figure 16. A two dimensional illustration of 3-dimensional objects (a) and the corresponding labeled graph (b)

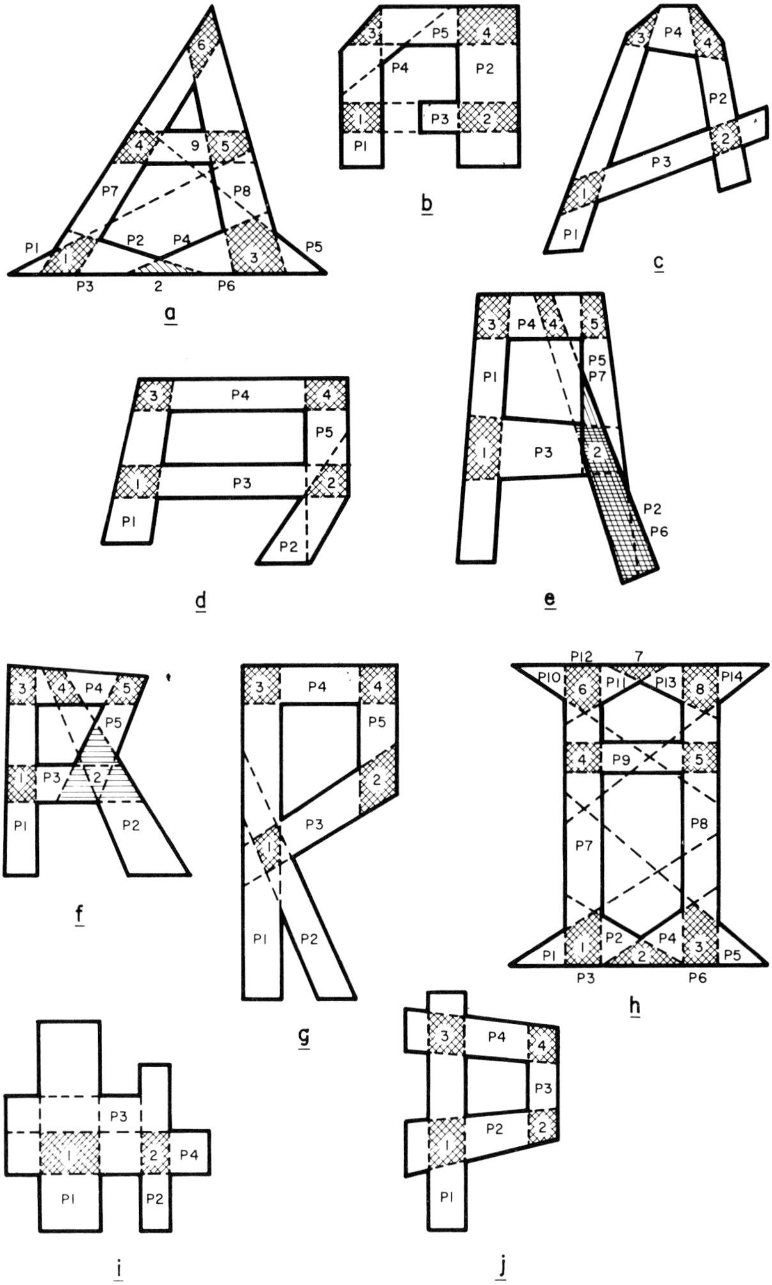

Figure 17. Polygons approximating the shapes of capital letters. The primary subsets are hatched only in cases of ambiguity. The nuclei are all crosshatched

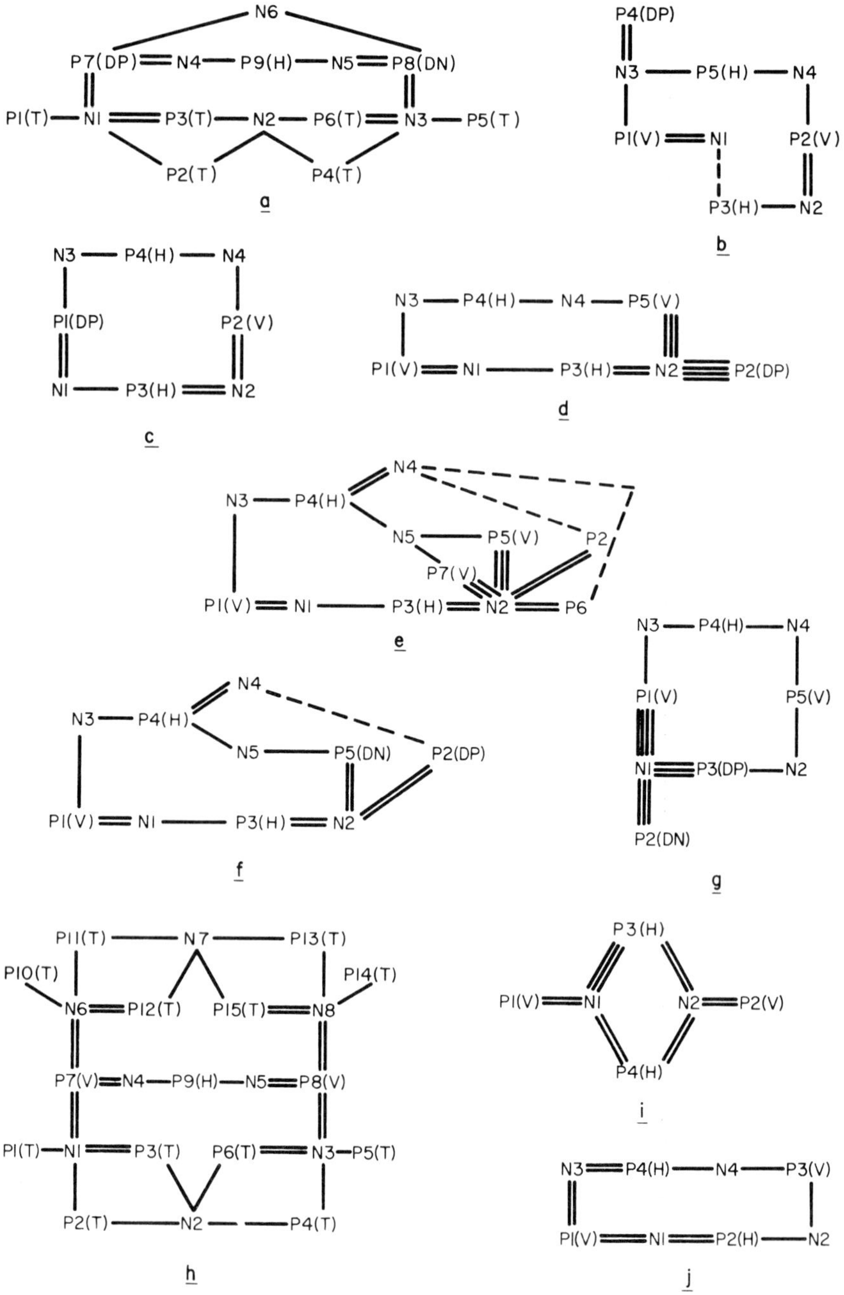

Figure 18. Primary graphs of the polygons of Figure 17

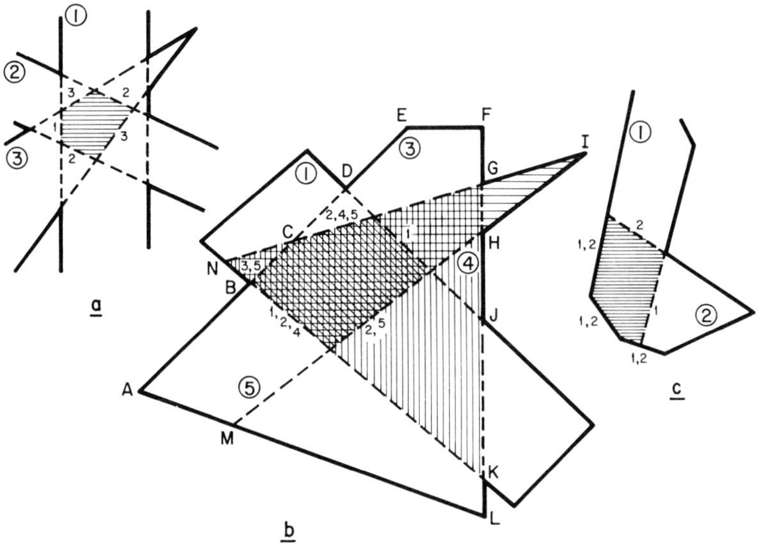

Figure 19. Various configurations of intersections of convex polygons. The numbers next to each side of the intersection denote the primary subsets which share the boundary. In (b) set (2) is denoted by horizontal hatching and (4) by vertical. Primary set #3 is (AEFL) #4 is (NGK) and #5 is (ACIM)

PATTERN RECOGNITION AND GROUP THEORY

J. M. Richardson

SCIENCE CENTER, NORTH AMERICAN
ROCKWELL CORPORATION
THOUSAND OAKS, CALIFORNIA

1. Introduction

The purpose of this paper is the discussion of several ways in which group theoretical concepts can be combined with pattern recognition. The main emphasis is on graphic patterns defined on continuous sets of points in xy-space. The first part of the paper will be devoted to preliminaries: types of groups involving geometrical and/or gray-scale transformations, the role of pattern functions as operands of group representations, preservation of area in xy-space, etc. Then attention will be devoted to several areas in which pattern recognition and group theory interact.

The first area of interaction is the study of invariant properties of graphic patterns. For any group of transformations defined by a finite set of parameters there is of course an infinite number of functionally independent invariant properties of patterns represented by continuous functions and consequently our attention must be confined to invariant properties of restricted type. Examples will be given of invariant polynomial functionals of the pattern function for a few typical groups. Examples of more complex invariant properties will be exhibited. A brief consideration will be given to the problem of determining a complete set of functionally invariant properties for a specified group and to its significance for pattern recognition. Explicit results will be presented for the case of the translation group.

The second, and to the writer most important, area of interaction is the formulation of mathematical models of classes in pattern space, where the concept of a group can sometimes be a powerful means for providing compact descriptions. For example, the class of all triangles can be described in terms of a single prototype triangle and the affine group. Some results will be presented concerning the geometrical properties of such classes in pattern space using a conventional metric. Attention is then directed to classes defined by stochastic models. An example of this is obtained when a single prototype is replaced by a statistical distribution of prototypes. Other examples are classes composed of invariant random processes. Next, a discussion is given to the relation between the invariance properties of the classes and the impossibility of separation by various kinds of surfaces.

A final, and somewhat separate, area of interaction is one in which group theory is applied to the Karhunan-Loeve expansion using techniques closely analogous to the application of group theory to Schrödinger's equation in quantum mechanics.

2. Objects to be Transformed

In the application of group theory there immediately arises the question about what is to be transformed. There emerges the related question about whether the entity or object to be transformed is actually the operand of a set of operators (linear or otherwise) that constitute a particular realization of a specified group.

Graphic patterns presented in shades of gray are represented by functions in a 2-dimensional plane (the Euclidean space R^2). A point in this space is described by the 2-dimensional vector r where

$$r = \binom{x}{y} \tag{1}$$

and the above function or pattern density is represented by $\rho(r)$, $\zeta(r)$, $\sigma(r)$, etc., in the domain D of r-space. The domain D represents the frame or retina of the graphic pattern.

In many cases of interest the pattern itself is the operand of the transformation operator, i.e.

$$0\rho(r) = \rho'(r) \tag{2}$$

where 0 is an operator representing, for example, translation, rotation, grayscale renormalization, etc. In the case of geometrical transformations we encounter the problem of the choice of the domain D. For rotations about the origin one can choose a finite domain with a circular boundary with its center at the origin. In the case of translations the domain can somewhat artificially be chosen to be a finite parallelogram if it is required to have the topology of a torus. One can combine 2–, 3–, 4–, and 6-fold rotations with translations and still have a finite domain. In general most of the transformations considered later will require infinite domains in r-space.

In the case of patterns defined on an infinite domain but observed through a finite window, the observable pattern is not a suitable operand. The transformations must be applied to the mostly unobservable pattern.

Thus these transformations could be involved in the formulation of a mathematical model describing all possible observable patterns belonging to a given class. In such a case as this it would be impossible, for example, to extract invariant properties of observable patterns.

3. Transformations

There exist two basic types of transformations of graphic patterns: a) geometrical transformations entailing changes of the elements of the pattern in r-space and b) transformations involving changes of the gray scale. Clearly, both types can occur simultaneously as well as separately.

We start our discussion of geometrical transformations by considering the transformation of points in r-space. The treatment here will be limited to the case of an infinite domain in r-space; the problem of finite domains, will be dealt with whenever it arises in later parts of this paper. A transformation of a point in r-space is defined by the substitution.

$$r \rightarrow \mathrm{T}r \tag{1}$$

where T denotes some operation (not necessarily linear) to be performed on r. Examples of such transformations are:

(a) Translation

$$r \rightarrow r + a$$

(b) Rotation

$$r \rightarrow R(\theta) \cdot r$$

where

$$R(\theta) = \begin{pmatrix} \cos\theta & -\sin\theta \\ \sin\theta & \cos\theta \end{pmatrix}$$

(c) Magnification

$$r \rightarrow \xi r$$

(d) Shear

$$r \rightarrow R(-\theta) \cdot S(\lambda) \cdot R(\theta) \cdot r$$

where

$$S(\lambda) = \begin{pmatrix} e^{\lambda} & 0 \\ 0 & e^{-\lambda} \end{pmatrix}$$

(e) Affine Transformation

$$r \rightarrow A \cdot r + a$$

where A is a general 2×2 matrix (or second order tensor) and a is a 2-vector (as in (a) above). An affine transformation may be regarded as the result of the sequence of operations: translation, rotation, magnification and uniform shear. More complex transformations in r-space are clearly possible.

Geometrical transformations of a point in r-space (denoted in the general case by the symbol T) can be classified into two subcategories: measure-preserving (in r-space) transformations and otherwise. A transformation is said to be measure preserving if

$$J(Tr/r) = 1 \tag{2}$$

where $J(r'/r)$, the Jacobian of r' (regarded as a function of r) with respect to r, is defined by

$$J(r'/r) = \mathrm{Det}(\partial r'/\partial r) = \begin{vmatrix} \partial x'/\partial x & \partial x'/\partial y \\ \partial y'/\partial x & \partial y'/\partial y \end{vmatrix} \tag{3}$$

In the earlier examples, (a), (b), and (d) are measure-preserving, and (e) is also measure-preserving if Det $(A = 1$. On the other hand (c) is not measure preserving and neither is (e) if $\mathrm{Det}(A \neq 1$.

To each transformation T of a point in r-space there corresponds a transformation τ_ν of the pattern density $\rho(r)$. We define the transformation τ_ν by the expression

$$\rho(r) \to \tau_\nu \rho(r) \triangleq |J(T^{-1}r/r|^\nu \rho(T^{-1}r) \tag{4}$$

where ν is a fixed exponent.

We note that τ_ν is always a linear operator while T is not in general.

We turn now to a discussion of the exponent ν. On the case of measure-preserving transformations we have $J(T^{-1}r/r) = 1$ by definition and hence

$$\tau_\nu \rho(r) = \rho(T^{-1}r) \tag{5}$$

Thus here the choice of ν is immaterial. In the case of transformations not preserving measure the situation is, or course, otherwise. The considerations already given in this section provide no basis for the choice of ν and we must invoke certain external considerations for its determination. One such consideration is the requirement that $\int d^2r\, \rho^\mu(r)$ be invariant in which case we must set $\nu = 1/\mu$. The case of $\mu = 1$ $(\nu = 1)$ corresponds to the preservation of the total integrated pattern density. If one wishes to regard the pattern density as a set of points in the limit of a very large total number, then the last condition is equivalent to the requirement that the total number of points be preserved.

In the case of a function of two points in r-space the definition of the transformation can be extended as follows

$$\tau_\nu^{(12)} f(r_1,r_2) = |J(T^{-1}r_1/r_1) J(T^{-1}r_2/r_2)|^\nu f(T^{-1}r_1, T^{-1}r_2) \tag{6}$$

Corresponding operations on functions of 3 and more points in r-space can be readily defined.

The discussion to this point has been devoted solely to geometrical transformations. We turn now to a brief consideration of gray-scale transformations. In general, a gray-scale transformation is defined in terms of the substitution

$$\rho(r) \rightarrow f(\rho(r)) \tag{7}$$

where $f(\rho(r))$ is a function of the value of $\rho(r)$ at the point r – we are not considering a general transformation here. If the transformation is to be one-to-one, we must require that the function f be either monotone increasing or decreasing. Simple examples of gray-scale transformations are represented by the substitutions

$$\begin{aligned} \rho(r) &\rightarrow \lambda\ \rho(r) \\ \rho(r) &\rightarrow \lambda\ \rho(r) + \mu \end{aligned} \tag{8}$$

The multiplication of $\rho(r)$ by λ can be interpreted as a change in contrast and addition of μ to $\rho(r)$ as a change in brightness. Other examples are given by

$$\begin{aligned} \rho(r) &\rightarrow \kappa\rho^2(r) + \lambda\rho(r) + \mu, \\ \rho(r) &\rightarrow a \log \rho(r) + b, \\ \rho(r) &\rightarrow \frac{\lambda\rho(r) + \mu}{\lambda'\rho(r) + \mu'} \end{aligned} \tag{9}$$

4. Groups (Finite)

In the present section we present only those aspects of group theory that are necessary in dealing with the problems occurring in later parts of this paper. For a fuller discussion the reader is urged to consult a standard treatise.[1]

A finite group is a set of transformations $T_1, \ldots, T_h$ (e.g., the transformations defined by (3.1))satisfying the following postulates:

[1] For example: E. P. Wigner, *Group Theory* (English translation), New York (1959); H. J. Zassenhaus, *The Theory of Groups,* New York (1958); E. M. Patterson and D. E. Rutherford, *Elementary Abstract Algebra,* Edinburgh and London (1965).

(a) The set is closed with respect to repeated transformation; that is, for every pair of transformations T_i and T_j belonging to the set there exists a T_k also belonging to the set such that

$$T_i T_j = T_k \tag{1}$$

(b) The associative law holds for repeated transformations, i.e.

$$T_i(T_j T_k) = (T_i T_j) T_k \tag{2}$$

(c) The set contains the identity transformation I defined by

$$T_i I = I T_i = T_i \tag{3}$$

for all i. If the T_i are transformations exemplified by (3.1) then $I = \begin{pmatrix} 1 & 0 \\ 0 & 1 \end{pmatrix}$.

(d) Every transformation has an inverse, namely for every T_i in the set there exists a T_j also in the set such that

$$T_i T_j = T_k \equiv I \tag{4}$$

We will write the solution of the above equation $T_j = T_i^{-1}$.

It follows as an immediate corollary that

$$T_i T_i^{-1} = I$$

implies

$$T_i^{-1} T_i = I$$

Now we turn to the consideration of the transformations on functions of r. We assert that using the definition (3.4) these transformations have the group property, more specifically, that if $\tau_{\nu 1}$ corresponds to T_1 and $\tau_{\nu 2}$ corresponds to T_2 then $\tau_{\nu 1}\ \tau_{\nu 2}$ corresponds to $T_1 T_2$. Applying the operations $\tau_{\nu 2}$ and $\tau_{\nu 1}$ in sequence to $\rho(r)$ we obtain

$$\begin{aligned} \tau_{\nu 1}\tau_{\nu 2}\rho(r) &= \tau_{\nu 1}[\,|J(T_2^{-1}r/r\,|^2\rho(T_2^{-1}r)] \\ &= |J(T_1^{-1}r/r)|^2 J(T_2^{-1}T_1^{-1}r/T_1^{-1}r)|^2\rho(T_2^{-1}T_1^{-1}r) \\ &= |J(T_2^{-1}T_1^{-1}r/r)|^2\rho(T_2^{-1}T_1^{-1}r) \\ &= |J((T_1T_2)^{-1}r/r)|^2\rho((T_1T_2)^{-1}r) \end{aligned} \tag{5}$$

thus demonstrating the above assertion. This property implies that if T_1 and T_2 are members of a group then $\tau_{\nu 1}$ and $\tau_{\nu 2}$ are members of a group. These two groups are not the same but may be regarded as different realizations of the same *abstract* group. Since the transformation $\tau_{\nu i}$ are linear operators, they are *representations* of the abstract group. Clearly, the transformation $\tau_\nu^{(12)}$ given in (3.6) is also a representation of the same abstract group.

An important operation is group averaging as applied to a function of appropriate type. For example in the case where $\nu = 1$ we may define $\nu = 1$

$$E_G f(r) \triangleq \frac{1}{n} \sum_{i=1}^{n} f(T_i^{-1} r) \tag{6}$$

In terms of the linear operators τ_i defined by an expression of the type (3.4) with $\nu = 0$ or $J = 1$ we can write E_G also as a linear operator:

$$E_G \triangleq \frac{1}{n} \sum_{i=1}^{n} \tau_i \tag{7}$$

Multiplication on the left by any member τ_i of the group gives

$$\tau_j E_G = \frac{1}{n} \sum_{i=1}^{n} \tau_j \tau_i = \frac{1}{n} \sum_{k=1}^{n} \tau_k = E_G \tag{8}$$

thus demonstrating that E_G is unchanged by multiplication on the right by a group element. It then follows directly that

$$E_G^2 = E_G \tag{9}$$

and therefore E_G is also a projection operator.

5. Groups (Continuous)

The most interesting transformations of graphic patterns are members of continuous sets. Therefore, it is desirable to consider the continuous generalization of discrete groups.[2]

A continuous group is a continuous set of transformations satisfying a set of postulates obtained by suitable limiting processes from those for finite groups.

$$G: \{T(\alpha)\}_{\alpha \epsilon D_\alpha} \tag{1}$$

[2] See for example N. Jacobson, *Lie Algebras*, Wiley (Interscience), New York (1962).

where $\alpha = (\alpha_1, \ldots, \alpha_p)$ is a p-dimensional vector. The domain D_α of α-space will be assumed here to be a single contiguous region although not necessarily singly connected. We further require $T(\alpha)$ to be a continuous function of α in the sense that as $\alpha' \to \alpha$, $T(\alpha')r \to T(\alpha)r$ for all r. For a given continuous group the dimensionality p of α-space is dictated by the continuity requirement.

The first group postulate can be re-stated for the present case as follows: given $T(\alpha)$ and $T(\alpha')$ where $\alpha, \alpha' \epsilon D_\alpha$ then

$$T(\alpha)\, T(\alpha') = T(\alpha'') \tag{2}$$

where $\alpha'' \epsilon \cdot D_\alpha$.

We turn to a discussion of infinitesimal transformations. As a convention let us define the origin of α-space to correspond to the identity transformation, i.e.

$$T(0) = I \tag{3}$$

Then if α is sufficiently near the origin $T(\alpha)$ represents an infinitesimal transformation, that is $T(\alpha)r$ is only slightly different from $T(0)r(=r)$. Assuming that $T(\alpha)r$ is not only a continuous function of α but also has continuous derivatives, we can write for α small

$$T(\alpha)r = r + \sum_{s=1}^{p} \alpha_s \left[\frac{\partial}{\partial \alpha_s}(T(\alpha)r)\right]_{\alpha=0} \tag{4}$$

where it is to be emphasized that the derivative of $T(\alpha)r$ is not the same as the derivative of $T(\alpha)$ (given that this has meaning) operating on r if $T(\alpha)$ is a nonlinear operator. Introducing the operator U_s (which may be nonlinear) defined by

$$\left[\frac{\partial}{\partial \alpha_s}(T(\alpha)r)\right]_{\alpha=0} = U_s r \tag{5}$$

we can then express $T(\alpha)$ in the form

$$T(\alpha) = I + \sum_{s=1}^{p} \alpha_s U_s \tag{6}$$

The product of two transformations, both labelled by small α's, is given by

$$T(\alpha')T(\alpha) = (I + \sum_{s=1}^{p} \alpha'_s U_s)(I + \sum_{s=1}^{p} \alpha_s U_s)$$

$$= I\ (I + \Sigma\alpha_s U_s)_s = 1 + \Sigma\alpha'_s U_s(I + \Sigma\alpha_s U_s) \tag{7}$$

$$= I + \Sigma(\alpha_s + \alpha'_s)U_s + 0(\alpha^2)$$

a result of the same form as that obtained in the case of linear operators even though $T(\alpha)$ and U_s may be nonlinear. An immediate consequence of the last result is (again, for small α)

$$T^{-1}(\alpha) = T(-\alpha) \tag{8}$$

If $T(\alpha)$ is a linear operator we may write

$$U_s = [\frac{\partial}{\partial\alpha_s} T(\alpha)]_{\alpha=0} \tag{9}$$

The operator U_s, defined by (5) or (9), is called the infinitesimal generator. associated with the group parameter α_s.

We turn now to the consideration of the linear operator $\tau(\alpha)$ defined by the relation

$$\tau_\nu(\alpha)\rho(r) = |J(T^{-1}(\alpha)r/r)|^\nu \rho(T^{-1}(\alpha)r) \tag{10}$$

Again requiring the origin of α-space to correspond to the identity operator ℓ associated with the operand $\rho(r)$ and assuming that $J(T(\alpha)r/r)$ is always positive, we can write the following expression for small α:

$$\begin{aligned} \tau_\nu^{-1}(\alpha)\rho(r) &= (1 + \nu\Sigma\alpha_s \nabla\cdot h_s)(\rho + \Sigma\alpha_s h_s \cdot \nabla\rho) \\ &= \rho + \Sigma\alpha_s[\nu(\nabla\cdot h_s)\rho + h_s\cdot\nabla_\rho] \end{aligned} \tag{11}$$

or alternatively

$$\tau_\nu(\alpha) = \ell + \Sigma\alpha_s v_{s,\nu} \tag{12}$$

where the infinitesimal operator v_s is defined by

$$v_{s,\nu} = -\nu\ \nabla\cdot h_s - h_s \cdot \nabla \tag{13}$$

The vector function h_s is given by

$$h_s = h_s(r) = [\frac{\partial}{\partial\alpha_s} T(\alpha)r]_{\alpha=0} \tag{14}$$

In the case where the transformations are measure-preserving in r-space, i.e. $J(T(\alpha)r/r) = 1$, we have

$$\nabla \cdot \boldsymbol{h}_s = 0 \tag{15}$$

and thus $\boldsymbol{h}_s(r)$ is a solenoidal vector field in r-space.

Where the operands are two-point functions $f(r_1, r_2)$ the direct generalization of $\tau(\alpha)$ is defined by

$$\tau_\nu^{(12)}(\alpha) f(r_1, r_2) = |J(T^{-1}(\alpha)r_1/r_1) J(T^{-1}(\alpha)r_2/r_2)| \times f(T^{-1}(\alpha)r_1, T^{-1}(\alpha)r_2) \tag{16}$$

If α is small we can write

$$\tau_\nu^{(12)}(\alpha) = \ell^{(12)} + \Sigma\alpha_s(\upsilon_{s,\nu}^{(1)} + \upsilon_{s,\nu}^{(2)}) \tag{17}$$

where

$$\upsilon_{s,\nu}^{(q)} = -\nu \nabla_q \cdot h_s(r_q) - h_s(r_q) \cdot \nabla_q \tag{18}$$

The generalization to the case of higher many-point functions is straight-forward.

Before terminating the present discussion of continuous groups, we must consider the continuous version of group averaging. In terms of the $\tau_\nu(\alpha)$ we may write

$$E_G = \frac{\int d\mu(\alpha)\tau_\nu(\alpha)}{\int d\mu(\alpha)} \tag{19}$$

where $d\mu(\alpha)$ is the differential invariant measure in α-space. The latter quantity may be written in terms of the invariant density $w(\alpha)$ as follows

$$d\mu(\alpha) = w(\alpha) d^p\alpha \tag{20}$$

The invariant measure must be consistent with the relation

$$\upsilon_{s,\nu} E_G = 0 \tag{21}$$

Here we will not discuss the determination of the invariant density $w(\alpha)$ in explicit detail. In the case of elementary groups, the invariant density assumes a very simple form. For example, the invariant density associated with the translation group is a constant if the vector parameter is taken to be the two dimensional displacement vector a. It can be shown that $d\mu(\alpha)$ or $w(\alpha)$ depends only upon the form of abstract group and not upon the particular realization (e.g., $T(\alpha)$, $\tau_\nu(\alpha)$, $\tau_\nu^{(12)}(\alpha)$, etc.) chosen.

6. Invariant Configuration Subspaces

Let us consider a 2m-dimensional space R^{2m} whose coordinates are $(r_1, \ldots, r_m)$. The point $(r'_1, \ldots, r'_m)$, where

$$r'_n = T(\alpha) r_n, \tag{1}$$

is a continuous function of the p-dimensional vector parameter α. As α ranges over its domain D_α it generates a p-dimensional subspace in R_{2m}.

This is true only if no two of the vectors $r_1, \ldots, r_m$ are equal, a condition then also satisfied by the $r'_1, \ldots, r'_m$ for almost all α. If, say, $r_1 = r_2$, then $r'_1 = r'_2$ for all α and almost all r_1 because the two vectors are transformed in precisely the same way. We will apply the term "degenerate" to cases in which two or more such vectors are equal for all α.

This subspace can be represented by setting a certain set of 2m-p functions

$$\Phi_1(r_1, \ldots, r_m), \ldots, \Phi_{2m-p}(r_1, \ldots, r_m) \tag{2}$$

equal to constants.† Clearly, such quantities must be invariants since their values do not change as a point moves on the surface, i.e. as

$$(r_1, \ldots, r_m) \to (T(\alpha) r_1, \ldots, T(\alpha) r_m). \tag{3}$$

Assuming no redundancy in the above representation of this subspace, no one of Φ's can be a function of the others; thus the Φ's constitute a set of *elementary* invariants.

We thus have shown that a continuous group involving p parameters can have only 2m-p elementary invariants in 2m-dimensional space defined by the coordinates $(r_1, \ldots, r_m)$ if $2m > p$.

If $p = 2m$, the subspace generated by the transformation $T(\alpha)$ will of course have the same dimensionality as R^{2m}. The only function that will constant over this subspace will be independent of $r_1, \ldots, r_m$, that is, it will be a constant. Thus, there are no invariants to infinitesimal transformations.

†In some cases these conditions must be amended by inequality constraints (e.g. r_i must lie in first quadrant for $i = 1, \ldots, m$).

If $p > 2m$, as α ranges over D_α the same 2m-dimensional subspace will be traced out several times over. Here, we led, *a fortiori,* to the same conclusion that there are no invariants.

7. Invariant Functions

In the present section we give a brief discussion of invariant properties of patterns. We consider two kinds of invariance:

a) to various groups of geometrical transformations and
b) to certain rudimentary groups of gray-scale transformations.

As a first step toward the derivation of invariant properties of the first type, we consider the invariance of functions of various numbers of points in r-space, e.g. $f(r)$, $f(r_1,r_2)$, ... We consider a specified continuous group G; which in the case of single-point transformations is the set $\{\tau_\nu(\alpha)\}_{\alpha \epsilon D_\alpha}$ where $\tau_\nu(\alpha)$ is defined by (5.10) but now with $f(r)$ replacing $\rho(r)$. The invariance of $f(r)$ is expressed by the relation

$$\tau_\nu(\alpha)f(r) = f(r) \tag{1}$$

In the case of two-point transformations we must deal with $\tau_\nu^{(12)}(\alpha)$ defined by (5.16). The invariance of $f(r_1,r_2)$ is then given by

$$\tau_\nu^{(12)}(\alpha)f(r_1,r_2) = f(r_1,r_2) \tag{2}$$

The generalization to the case of higher many-point functions is obvious.

There are two distinct approaches to the derivation of invariant properties of the above type. One such approach is to compute the group average of an arbitrary function $f(r_1, \ldots, r_m)$. A second, and usually more expedient, approach is find functions that are invariant to the infinitesimal transformations. In the case of one-, two-, . . . , and m-point functions we require that

$$\begin{aligned} &v_{s,\nu} f(r) = 0 \\ &(v^{(1)}_{s,\nu} + v^{(2)}_{s,\nu} f(r_1,r_2)\ 0 \\ &(v^{(1)}_{s,\nu} + \cdots + v^{(m)}_{s,\nu})f(r_1, \ldots, r_m) = 0 \end{aligned} \tag{3}$$

where $v^{(q)}_{s,\nu}$ is defined by (5.18). It must be emphasized that a function of a specified number of points must simultaneously satisfy p equations ($s = 1, \ldots, p$) where p is the dimensionality of the group parameter space (α-space) or, equivalently, the number of independent infinitesimal transformations. These equations are partial differential equations that can be solved by standard methods.

In treating the invariance to infinitesimal transformations it is essential to distinguish two cases: (a) the transformations are measure-preserving

$(J(T(\alpha)r_i/r_i) = 1,\ i = 1, \ldots, m)$ or the exponent ν vanishes, or both, and (b) the complementary case, i.e. the transformations are not measure preserving and the exponent ν does not vanish.

In the first case, namely (a) above, the p equations (with $\nabla \cdot h_s = 0$) to be satisfied by an m-point function can be solved by the method of characteristics if $2m > p$ with the result

$$f(r_1, \ldots, r_m) = F(\Phi_1, \ldots, \Phi_t) \tag{4}$$

where the functions $\Phi_k = \Phi_k(r_1, \ldots, r_m)$, $k = 1, \ldots, t$ constitute a complete set of *functionally independent* elementary invariants and where F is an arbitrary function. The number t can be shown by the geometrical arguments of Section 6 to be given by

$$t = 2m - p \tag{5}$$

Solutions of the type will be called normal solutions.

As shown in Section 6, if $2m \leqslant p$ the solutions are of the form

$$f(r_1, \ldots, r_m) = \text{const.}, \tag{6}$$

that is, the only invariants are constant functions. Solutions of this type will be called trivial solutions.

There exist additional invariant functions that belong to neither of the above categories. These functions correspond to the degenerate cases discussed in Section 6 and can be avoided by prohibiting situations in which $r_i = r_j$.

In Table I we present examples of elementary invariants for three groups. The first column gives the number m of points in r-space, the second gives sets of elementary invariants, and the third gives the number t of elementary invariants. A blank entry in the second column denotes that no normal invariants exist (only trivial constant invariants). Finally, a blank entry in the third column implies that $2m \leq p$.

The symbol r_{12} is defined by

$$r_{12} = r_2 - r_1 \tag{7}$$

and the magnitude $|r_{12}|$ is denoted by r_{12}.

In the case where $\nu \neq 0$ and the transformations do not preserve measure (i.e., $J(T(\alpha)r_i/r_i) \neq 1,\ i = 1, \ldots, m$), we must deal with the more complex situation in which $\nabla \cdot h_s \neq 0$.

TABLE I. EXAMPLES OF ELEMENTARY INVARIANTS

G: Translation
(J = 1)

m	{Φ}	t
1	- - - -	0
2	r_{12}	2
3	r_{12}, r_{13}	4
4	r_{12}, r_{13}, r_{14}	6

G: Translation and Rotation
(J = 1)

m	{Φ}	t
1	- - - -	–
2	r_{12}	1
3	r_{12}, r_{13}, r_{23}	3
4	$r_{12}, r_{13}, r_{14}, r_{23}, r_{34}$	5

G: Translation, Rotation, and Magnification
($J \neq 1$, $\nu = 0$)

m	{Φ}	t
1	- - - -	–
2	- - - -	0
3	$r_{23}/r_{12}, r_{13}/r_{12}$	2
4	$r_{13}/r_{12}, r_{14}/r_{12}, r_{23}/r_{12}, r_{34}/r_{12}$	4

A general m-point invariant must then satisfy the equation

$$\sum_{i=1}^{m} \upsilon_{s,\nu}^{(i)} f(r_1, \ldots, r_m) = 0 \qquad (8)$$

The solution can be written in the form

$$f(r_i, \ldots, r_m) = \psi_\nu(r_1, \ldots, r_m) g(r_1, \ldots, r_m) \qquad (9)$$

where ψ_ν and g must satisfy the conditions

$$\left(\sum_{i=1}^{m} \upsilon_{s,\nu}^{(i)}\right) \psi_\nu = 0, \; s = 1, \ldots, p \qquad (10)$$

$$\left(\sum_{i=1}^{m} \upsilon_{s,o}^{(i)}\right) g = 0, \; s = 1, \ldots, p \qquad (11)$$

It is sufficient to choose the simplest form of ψ_ν satisfying (10) whereas g is an arbitrary function of elementary invariants, i.e.

$$g(r_1, \ldots, r_m) = F(\Phi_1, \ldots, \Phi_t) \qquad (12)$$

A further simplification of ψ_ν involves the fact that one may write

$$\psi_\nu = (\psi_1)^\nu \qquad (13)$$

where ψ_1 satisfies (10) with $\nu = 1$.

8. Invariant Functionals

We turn now to the consideration of invariant functionals of $\rho(r)$ – i.e., invariant properties of patterns. A functional, i.e.

$$x = F(\{\rho(r)\}). \qquad (1)$$

is invariant if it is unchanged by the substitution

$$\rho(r) \rightarrow \tau_\nu(\alpha)\rho(r) \qquad (2)$$

for all pattern densities $\rho(r)$.

There exist such a large number of types of invariant functionals that to discuss a significant fraction of all possible types would require for more space than is available here. We will, however, devote some explicit discussion to simple power functionals. Such a functional of the m-th degree is

$$F(\{\rho(r)\}) = \int \prod_{i=1}^{m} [d^2 r_i \rho(r_i)] f(r_1, \ldots, r_m) \qquad (3)$$

where the function $f(r_1, \ldots, r_m)$ must satisfy conditions to be determined. Making the substitution (2) in (3), we obtain

$$\begin{aligned} &F(\{\tau_\nu(\alpha)\rho(r)\} \\ &= \int \prod_{i=1}^{m} [d^2 r'_i \,|J(T^{-1}(\alpha)r_i/r_i)|\nu\rho(T^{-1}(\alpha)r_i)|f(r_1, \ldots, r_m) \\ &= \int \prod_{i=1}^{m} [d^2 r'_i \,|J(T(\alpha)r'_i/r_i)|]^{1-\nu} \rho(r'_i)] f(T(\alpha)r'_1, \ldots, T(\alpha)r'_m \\ &= \int \prod_{i=1}^{m} [d^2 r_i \rho(r_i)] [\tau_{1-\nu}^{(1,\ldots,m)}(\alpha)]^{-1} f(r_1, \ldots, r_m) \end{aligned} \qquad (4)$$

Since the last line of the above formula must be identical to the right hand side of (3) we obtain the result

$$\tau_{1-\nu}^{(1,\ldots,m)}(\alpha) f(r_1, \ldots, r_m) = f(r_1, \ldots, r_m) \qquad (5)$$

In particular, if $\nu = 1$ it follows that

$$f(r_1, \ldots, r_m) = G(\Phi_1, \ldots, \Phi_t) \qquad (6)$$

The discussion of invariant functionals is not complete without including the consideration of gray-scale transformations. We consider two such transformations

$$\rho(r) \rightarrow \lambda\rho(r) \qquad (7)$$

and

$$\rho(r) \rightarrow \lambda\rho(r) + \mu. \qquad (8)$$

Other transformations exist but only the above ones form groups with a finite set of parameters. Any homogeneous functional of degree 0 is invariant to (7). The simplest such functional is:

$$\frac{\rho(r)}{[\int_D d^2 r \rho^2(r)]^{1/2}} \qquad (9)$$

For the transformations (8), we obtain the somewhat more elaborate functional

$$\frac{\rho_1(r)}{[\int_D d^2r\, \rho_1^2(r)]^{1/2}} \tag{10}$$

where

$$\rho_1(r) = \rho(r) - \frac{1}{A} \int_D d^2r\, \rho(r) \tag{11}$$

in which A is the area of the domain D or r-space.

9. Elementary Invariant Functionals

In Sections (6) and (7), we considered the elementary invariants $\Phi_i(r_1, \ldots, r_m)$, $i = 1, \ldots, 2m-p$. These have the property that they are functionally independent (in the sense that no one of them can be expressed as a function of the others) and are complete in the sense that any invariant function of $r_1, \ldots, r_m$ can be expressed as a function of them and them alone. It is interesting and important to consider the possibility of constructing in the same sense a set of elementary invariant functionals of $\zeta(r)$. A solution to this problem has been achieved for a restricted case.

Let us consider, for example, the translationally invariant functionals of $\zeta(r)$. For simplicity let us assume that $\zeta(r)$ is doubly periodic in the sense that

$$\begin{aligned} \zeta(r+a) &= \zeta(r) \\ \zeta(r+b) &= \zeta(r) \end{aligned} \tag{1}$$

where a and b are not parallel. To simplify matters still further, let $|a| = |b| = 2\pi$ and let a point in the positive x direction and b, in the positive y direction. Then $\zeta(r)$ in the periodicity domain D_p defined by the inequalities

$$D_p: \begin{cases} 0 \leqslant x < 2\pi \\ 0 \leqslant y < 2\pi \end{cases} \tag{2}$$

is periodically replicated over all of space in order to represent the full $\zeta(r)$.

Clearly, the Fourier series representation of $\zeta(r)$ is

$$\zeta(r) = (2\pi)^{-2} \sum_k \zeta_k \exp(ik \cdot r) \tag{3}$$

where the spatial frequency vector takes values on the lattice defined by

$$k = e_x n_x + e_y n_y \tag{4}$$

where e_x and e_y are unit vectors in the positive x and y directions, respectively, and where n_x and n_y are integers taking positive and negative values including 0. The Fourier coefficients are

$$\zeta_k = \int_{D_p} dr\, \zeta(r) \exp(-ik \cdot r) \tag{5}$$

Translations defined by

$$\zeta(r) \rightarrow \zeta(r + d) \tag{6}$$

will be confined to $d \in D_p$ since every translation with $d \notin D_p$ is identical to one with $d \in D_p$ in view of the periodicity of $\zeta(r)$. The Fourier coefficients transform in the corresponding manner

$$\zeta_k \rightarrow \zeta_k \exp(ik \cdot d) \tag{7}$$

A product of the form

$$\prod_{i=1}^{q} \zeta_{k_i} \tag{8}$$

is invariant to translations (6) for all $d \in D_p$ if and only if

$$\sum_{i=1}^{q} k_i = 0. \tag{9}$$

Thus, any functional of $\zeta(r)$ that can be expanded in a sum of products of the form (8) is a translational invariant if each product satisfies (9).

In attacking the derivation of a set of elementary translational invariants it is convenient to confine our attention to invariant products of the form (8).

Let us write

$$\zeta_k = |\zeta_k| \exp(i\Theta_k). \tag{10}$$

It follows from the reality condition that the substitution $\vec{k} \rightarrow -\vec{k}$ leaves $|\zeta_k|$ unchanged but changes the sign of $\Theta_k (\Theta_0 = 0)$, and thus any invariant product of the form (8), in which the spatial frequencies obey the condition (9), can be expressed as a function of the amplitudes

$$\zeta_0, |\zeta_k|, k \in S_{1/2} \tag{11}$$

and the phase triplets

$$\{k_1,k_2\} \triangleq \Theta_{k_1} + \Theta_{k_2} + \Theta_{k_3} \tag{12}$$

where

$$k_3 = k_1 - k_2 \tag{13}$$

The set $S_{1/2}$ is the half space defined by the inequalities

$$\begin{aligned} k_y &\geqslant 0 \text{ when } k_x < 0 \\ k_y &> 0 \text{ when } k_x \geqslant 0 \end{aligned} \tag{14}$$

It can be shown without difficulty that (11) represents a complete functionally independent set of quantities of its restricted type; that is, the most general phase and translationally invariant product can be written as a function of them. However, this kind of question remains to be answered in connection with the phase triplets (12).

It can be shown by counting arguments applied to the case of bandwidth limited patterns that there are two many phase triplets unless further restrictions are imposed on the spatial frequency vectors.

The problem is to find the minimal set of phase triplets in terms of which any arbitrary sum of phase triplets can be represented by super-position with coefficients ±1.

Using arguments too complicated to present here it is possible to prove that one such minimal set of phase triplets is

$$\begin{aligned} &\{\pm e_x n_x, e_y n_y\},\ n_x,n_y = 1,2,\ldots \\ &\{e_x, e_x n_x\},\ n_x = 1,2,\ldots \\ &\{e_y, e_y n_y\},\ n_y = 1,2,\ldots \end{aligned} \tag{15}$$

Clearly, this set is not unique.

10. Geometry of Pattern Space

The space of all possible patterns, i.e. pattern space, is clearly a function space. Although, metric properties of such a space are not always motivated by the pattern recognition problem, it is useful to introduce them nevertheless. We are thus led to consider a common realization of Hilbert space with the inner product

$$(u,v) = \int_D dr\ u^*(r)v(r), \tag{1}$$

and the norm $||u|| = (u,u)^{1/2}$. The other axioms of Hilbert space will be assumed. In certain special problems special inner products arise naturally, for example

$$(u,v) = \int_{R^2} dr_1 \int_{R^2} dr_2\ u^*(r_1)\ K(r_1-r_2)v(r_2) \tag{2}$$

where $K(r_1-r_2)$ is an inverse correlation function.

Using the definition (1) it can be shown that

$$(\tau_{1/2}(\alpha)u,\ \tau_{1/2}(\alpha)v) = (u,v) \tag{3}$$

which is usually true with $D = R^2$ and is true with more restricted forms of D for certain special groups. Of course, in the case of transformations preserving measure in r-space the index ν, which assumes the value ½ in (3), is irrelevant. In any case, the above relation implies directly that $\tau_{1/2}(\alpha)$ is unitary, which is equivalent to the preservation of metric properties in Hilbert space. Thus a constellation of points in this space rotates like a rigid body as α is varied. It is clear that the origin is always a possible center of rotation. But there may be other simultaneous centers of rotation. Let us consider an arbitrary point $\zeta(r)$ subject to the transformation $\tau_{1/2}(\alpha)$ and a point $\sigma(r)$ that is invariant to this transformation. The distance between these points is given by

$$||\tau_{1/2}(\alpha)\zeta-\sigma|| = ||\zeta-\tau_{1/2}^{-1}\sigma|| \tag{4}$$

and consequently the distance is invariant. Thus the question of the number of centers of rotation reduces to the question of the nature of the set of invariant functions.

However, we hasten to say that the requirement that a center of rotation be an invariant can be considerably weakened if α is limited to a subset of D_α, namely D'_α. Equation (4) can be rewritten in the form

$$||\tau_{1/2}(\alpha)\zeta-\sigma||^2 = ||\zeta||^2 + ||\sigma||^2 - (\tau_{1/2}(\alpha)\zeta,\sigma). \tag{5}$$

Thus we are concerned only with the invariance of the inner product of $\tau_{1/2}(\alpha)\zeta$ and σ. Let us assume that ζ vanishes beyond the finite domain D' in r-space. The domain D'' is defined by the relation

$$T^{-1}(\alpha)r \in D'' \text{ if } r \in D' \text{ and } \alpha \in D'_\alpha \tag{6}$$

It is further assumed that D′ and D'_α are chosen so that D″ is finite. It follows that a sufficient condition for the invariance of $\|\tau_{1/2}(\alpha)\zeta - \sigma\|$ for $\alpha \epsilon D'_\alpha$ is that σ be an invariant function in the domain D″ of r-space. Outside of this domain σ can take any form that insures that it is quadratically integrable.

Now let us consider the case of transformations preserving area in r-space. In this case the index ν (taking the value ½ in the above discussion) is irrelevant and thus can be dropped temporarily. If p (the dimensionality of group parameter space) is 1, then all that is required for the invariance of (5) for $\alpha \epsilon D'_\alpha$ is that in the domain D″ σ be a function of a single elementary invariant $\Phi(r)$ corresponding to the given group. There are clearly an infinite number of such functions.

If $p \geqslant 2$, then by the arguments of Section 6 the invariance of (5) for $\alpha \epsilon D'_\alpha$ requires that the function σ be a constant in D″. In the restricted Hilbert space composed of functions defined on the domain D″, the set of all such constant functions form a straight line (a linear 1-dimensional subspace) or axis passing through the origin.

11. Invariance and Separability

Let us consider two classes defined by the stochastic models

$$\begin{aligned} \rho(r) &= \tau_\nu(\alpha)\sigma_1(r) \qquad \text{(class 1)} \\ \rho(r) &= \tau_\nu(\alpha)\sigma_2(r) \qquad \text{(class 2)} \end{aligned} \tag{1}$$

where $\tau_\nu(\alpha)$ belongs to a specified continuous group G and where the distribution (cumulative) of α is proportional to $\mu(\alpha)$. The *a priori* probabilities of the classes are assumed to be P_1 and P_2 ($P_1 + P_2 = 1$).

Further, let us consider the discriminant function

$$\Delta(\{\rho\}) = \int_D dr_1 \ldots \int_D dr_m f(r_1, \ldots, r_m) \prod_{\alpha=1}^{m} g_i(\rho(r_i)). \tag{2}$$

It is to be understood that $g_i(\rho(r_i))$ is a function of the value of $\rho(r)$ at the point $r = r_i$. Extending the Minsky and Papert[3] definition of order to the case of possibly continuous functions defined on continuous sets, we say discriminant function is of the nth order. If $g_i(u) = u$ for all i, the discriminant function is of the nth degree.

We are interested in determining the adequacy of $\Delta(\{\rho\})$ in distinguishing between the two classes defined above. Alternately we can think of

[3]Minsky, M. and S. Papert, *Perceptrons,* The MIT Press, Cambridge, Massachusetts and London, England (1969).

$\Delta(\{\rho\})$ = const. defining a separating surface which attempts to separate the two classes from each other.

We will employ the difference of the means of the discriminant functions for the two classes, namely

$$M_{12} = (\Omega'_\alpha)^{-1} \int_{D'_\alpha} d\mu(\alpha)[\Delta(\{\tau_\nu(\alpha)\sigma_2(r)\}) - \Delta(\{\tau_\nu(\alpha)\sigma_1(r)\})], \tag{3}$$

where

$$\Omega'_\alpha = \int_{D'_\alpha} d\mu(\alpha) \tag{4}$$

as a criterion of separability. This is not a wholly acceptable criterion for determining quantitatively varying degrees of imperfect separability since it is not appropriately normalized with a suitable denominator (e.g., as in the case of Mahalanobis distance). However it is acceptable for our more limited purposes as long as M_{12} does not vanish by virtue of the terms (associated with the classes 1 and 2) individually vanishing. In the definition of M_{12} we have used a finite subdomain D'_α of α-space in order to leave room for certain limit processes that must be used later.

Let us consider the case of an area preserving (in r-space) continuous group with p parameters for which the domain D_α is finite. We can easily deduce that M_{12} (with $D'_\alpha = D_\alpha$) is given by

$$M_{12} = \int_D dr_1 \ldots \int_D dr_m \, \bar{f}(r_1, \ldots, r_m)[\prod_{i=1}^{m} g_i(\sigma_2(r_i)) - \prod_{i=1}^{m} g_i(\ _1(r_i))] \tag{5}$$

where

$$\bar{f}(r_1, \ldots, r_m) = (\Omega_\alpha)^{-1} \int_{D_\alpha} d\mu(\alpha) f(T(\alpha)r_1, \ldots, T(\alpha)r_m) \tag{6}$$

If $p \geqslant 2m$ it follows from the arguments of Section 6 that $\bar{f}(r_1, \ldots, r_m)$ is a constant function† whose value is λ. If f is bounded and the domain D of r-space is finite it follows that $0 < \lambda > \infty$. The separability measure reduces to

$$M_{12} = \lambda \int_D dr_1, \ldots \int_D dr_m [\prod_{i=1}^{m} g_i(\sigma_2(r_i)) - \prod_{i=1}^{m} g_i(\sigma_1(r_i))] \tag{7}$$

†We limit the present discussion to the cases in which the invariant functions must be constant over all of D, not merely piecewise constant.

This quantity is completely independent of the shapes of the functions $\sigma_1(r)$ and $\sigma_2(r)$; more specifically it depends upon a set of areas, each one of which is the total area enclosed by the isodensity contours corresponding to each density level. Thus a discriminant function of nth order cannot distinguish between two classes on the basis of shape if each of the classes is invariant to a given continuous group of transformations with p parameters if $p \geqslant 2m$.

Let the prototypes, σ_1 and σ_2, of the identically normalized with respect to gray-scale in the sense that

$$\int dr\, H(\sigma_1(r)-\kappa) = \int dr H(\sigma_2(r)-\kappa) \tag{8}$$

for all positive values of the constant κ. In (8) H(x) is the unit step function. In this case it is easy to show that if $p \geqslant 2m$ then $M_{12} = 0$, i.e. the classes cannot be distinguished at all by an mth order discriminant.

In the case where D_α and D are infinite the previous arguments break down. However, if f and g_i vanish outside of limited domains and if we consider a finite subdomain D'_α of α-space, certain useful results can be obtained. Let $f(r_1, \ldots, r_m) = 0$ if $(r_1, \ldots, r_m \notin D_m$ and $\pi g_i(\sigma_c(r_i)) = 0$ for $(r_1, \ldots, r_m) \notin D_m$, c = 1,2. If $\alpha \notin D_\alpha$ implies that $(T(\alpha)r_1', \ldots, T(\alpha)r_2) \notin D_m$ when $(r_1, \ldots, r_2) \in D_m$, then we can write

$$M_{12} = \int dr_1 \ldots \int dr_m \hat{f}(r_1, \ldots, r_m)] \pi_i g_i(\sigma_2(r_i))$$

$$- \pi_i\; g_i(\sigma_1(r_i))] \tag{9}$$

where

$$\hat{f}(r_1, \ldots, r_m) = (\Omega_\alpha^1)^{-1} \int_{D_\alpha} d\mu(\alpha) f(T(\alpha)r_1, \ldots, T(\alpha)r_2) \tag{10}$$

It is understood that the above integrations on $(r_1, \ldots, r_m)$ extend over all of this space. It is to be emphasized that the domain D_α corresponds to the complete group and is now assumed to be infinite in extent. Clearly the results (9) and (10) depend upon the above set relations being consistent with a finite domain D'_α.

In any case, if 2m = p $\hat{f}$ will be a constant† and we thereby obtain a result identical to (7) except that D now corresponds to all of r-space and the constant λ is different.

For $p > 2m$, a finite D'_α consistent with D'_m and D''_m is frequently impossible. In this situation one can first integrate on a subgroup generated by 2m infinitesimal operators thereby deducing that $\hat{f}$ is constant: Completing the averaging process over the original group involves no convergence

†See footnote on previous page.

difficulties.

12. Karhunan-Loéve Expansion

Let us consider a random process u(x) where x is q-dimensional vector and where u(x) has zero mean. The Karhunan-Loéve[4] (KL) expansion is defined by

$$u(x) = \sum_{n}^{\infty} a_n \Psi_n(x) \tag{1}$$

where the a_n are random variables satisfying the relations

$$E a_n^* a_m = \lambda_n \delta_{nm} \tag{2}$$

and where

$$\int d^q x\, \Psi_n{}^*(x) \Psi_m(x) = \delta_{nm}. \tag{3}$$

It follows that

$$E\, u(x')u(x) \triangleq C(x,x') = \sum_{n=1}^{\infty} \lambda_n \Psi_n(x') \Psi_n^*(x) \tag{4}$$

from which we deduce that

$$\int d^q x'\, C(x,x') \Psi_n(x') \triangleq C\Psi_n(x) = \lambda_n \Psi_n(x), \tag{5}$$

i.e. the $\Psi_n(x)$ and λ_n are the eigenfunctions and eigenvalues of the operator C. From the general properties of the correlation function C(x,x′) it follows that the eigenvalues λ_n are real and non-negative. It is conventional to require the ordering: $\lambda_1 \geqslant \lambda_2 \geqslant \lambda_3 \cdots$.

Now let us assume that the random process u(x) is invariant to a group G of transformations τ_i, i = 1, . . . ,h, in the sense that $\tau_i u(x)$ possesses the same statistical properties as u(x). If the τ_i are also unitary, it then follows that they all commute with the operator C. The same results hold for continuous groups.

Here we have an opportunity to apply the same group theoretical arguments that are frequently applied to Schrödinger's equation in quantum mechanics. The time-independent version of this equation has the same general form as the one we are dealing with in the KL problem.

For example, in the case of an Abelian group (the τ_i commute with each other) we can simplify the KL problem by using the common

[4] K. Karhunen, Ann. Acad. Sci. Fennicae, Ser. AI *37* (1947).

eigenfunctions of the τ_i, i.e. the complete orthonormal set $\phi_\mu(x)$, $\mu = 1,2,...$ The commutation of τ_i and C can then be expressed in the matrix form

$$(\tau_{i\mu} - \tau_{i\nu})C_{\mu\nu} = 0 \tag{6}$$

where the $\tau_{i\mu}$, $\mu = 1,2,\ldots,$ are the eigenvalues (complex with moduli 1) of τ_i and the $C_{\mu\nu}$ are the matrix elements of C in the ϕ_μ representation. In the case $\mu \neq \nu$, $C_{\mu\nu}$ must vanish if for any i $\tau_{i\mu} \neq \tau_{i\nu}$. There exist groups of infinite order in which the latter condition is always satisfied. If G is such a group, then the matrix $C_{\mu\nu}$ is diagonal; in other words, the common eigenfunctions of the group operators τ_i are also the eigenfunctions of the operator C. Thus, in this case, one need consider only the common eigenfunctions of the τ_i. The eigenvalues λ_n are then obtained by calculating the diagonal matrix elements of C.

A familiar case in one in which u(x) (with x 1-dimensional) is a stationary random process, i.e. it is invariant to the continuous group of translations $u(x) \rightarrow \tau_d\, u(x) \triangleq u(x-d)$ in the sense that u(x) and u(x−d) have the same statistical properties. In this case th eigenfunctions of τ_d, i.e. $(2\pi)^{-1/2} e^{ikx}$ with k integral, are also the eigenfunctions of C. It is assumed that the domain of x has the length 2π and has the topology of a circle.

In the case where the group is non-Abelian there will in general exist irreducible representations of dimensionality larger than 1. The eigenfunctions of C associated with any such irreducible representation will have in common a degenerate eigenvalue whose multiplicity is equal to the dimensionality of the irreducible representation.

This subject is a fully developed one and consequently an exhaustive review is hardly appropriate for this present paper. Readers wishing to go into this matter further are urged to consult the extensive literature on the application of group theory to quantum mechanics.[5]

Because of the relation between the KL expansion and factor analysis[6] it is clear that the above group-theoretical techniques can be applied to the latter discipline.

---

[5] See E. Wigner, ref. (1).

[6] S. Watanabe, Proc. Conf. Inform. Theory 4th Prague 1965.

BOUNDS ON THE COMPLEXITY OF GRAMMARS †

Azriel Rosenfeld
UNIVERSITY OF MARYLAND
COLLEGE PARK, MARYLAND

James W. Snively, Jr.
SUN OIL COMPANY
PHILADELPHIA, PENNSYLVANIA

Introduction

Given a language L (i.e., a recursively enumerable set of strings of symbols), how simple can a phrase-structure grammar which generates L be? This paper considers questions of this type in terms of three measures of the complexity of a grammar: λ, the length of the longest member in any rewriting rule; ν, the size of the vocabulary; and ρ, the number of rules. Any language has grammars in which any one of these measures has a low value, but this can in general be achieved only at the expense of increasing one or both of the other two measures. Bounds on ν as a function of λ are obtained in a number of cases; in most of these cases the grammars are required to be context free.

The following terminology and notation are used in this paper: A *phrase-structure grammar* is a 4-tuple $G = (V, \Sigma, P, S)$, where V is a nonempty finite set of symbols, called the *vocabulary* of G; Σ is a nonempty subset of V, called the *terminal vocabulary* of G; P is a set of ordered pairs (α,β) of strings of elements of V (where the string α is non-null), called the *productions* or *rewriting rules* of G; and $S \in V-\Sigma$ is a special nonterminal symbol, called the *initial symbol* of G. (For any set A, the set of strings of elements of A will be denoted by A^*[1]; the null string will be denoted by ϵ; if γ is any string the length of γ will be denoted by $|\gamma|$.) It is assumed

†This paper is based on part of J.W. Snively's Ph.D. dissertation. The support of the Information Systems Branch, Office of Naval Research, under Contract Nonr-5144(00), is gratefully acknowledged.

[1]If A is any finite set, the cardinality of A will be denoted by $||A||$.

that no rule rewrites terminal symbols; in other words, if (α,β) is a rule and $\alpha = \xi_0\eta_1\xi_1 \ldots \eta_n\xi_n$, where the ξ's are in Σ^* and the η's in $(V-\Sigma)^*$, then $\beta = \xi_0\zeta_1\xi_1 \ldots \zeta_n\xi_n$, where the ζ's are in V^*. It is also assumed that Σ contains a special symbol #, called the *endmarker*, which is never created by any rule.

The rule (α,β) is usually written $\alpha \rightarrow \beta$. If γ,δ are strings in V^*, and there exists a rule $\alpha \rightarrow \beta$ and strings τ,ω in V^* such that $\gamma = \tau\alpha\omega$, $\delta = \tau\alpha\omega$, then δ is said to be derived from γ in one step (notation: $\gamma \Rightarrow \delta$). If there exist strings $\varphi_0, \varphi_1, \ldots, \varphi_r$ in V^* such that $\gamma = \varphi_0$, $\delta = \varphi_r$, and $\varphi_{i-1} \Rightarrow \varphi_i$ $(1 \leq i \leq r)$, then δ is said to be *derived* from γ (notation: $\gamma \overset{*}{\Rightarrow} \delta$) and $\varphi_0, \ldots, \varphi_r$ is called a γ-derivation of δ. A string of terminal symbols $\xi \in \Sigma^*$ such that $\#S\# \Rightarrow \#\xi\#$ is called a *sentence* of G; the set of all sentences of G is called the *language* generated by G (notation: L(G)).

G will be called *monotonic* (an m-grammar), if $|\alpha| \leq |\beta|$ for each rule $\alpha \rightarrow \beta$ of G; *context sensitive* (a cs-grammar), if each rule of G is of the form $\varphi T \Psi \rightarrow \varphi \theta \Psi$, where $T \in V-\Sigma$ and $\theta \in V^*$, $\theta \neq \epsilon$, $\theta \neq T$; *context free* (a cf-grammar), if each rule is of the form $T \rightarrow \theta$; and *finite state* (an fs-grammar), if each rule is of the form $T \rightarrow \xi X$ or $T \rightarrow \xi$, or each rule is of the form $T \rightarrow X\xi$ or $T \rightarrow \xi$, where $X \in V-\Sigma$ and $\xi \in \Sigma^*$, $\xi \neq \epsilon$. The language generated by an m− (cs−, ef, fs−) grammar will be called an m−(cs−, cf−, fs−) language.

1. Rule Length, Vocabulary Size, and Number of Rules

One can study various measures of the *complexity* of a grammar; this paper is concerned with three such measures–rule length, vocabulary size, and number of rules. As will be seen in this section, any language has grammars for which each of these measures individually has a low value. A more difficult problem is that of finding a grammar that has minimum complexity with respect to two or more of the measures; some results on this problem, for the pair of measures (rule length, vocabulary size), are presented in the remaining sections.

For any grammar $G = (V, \Sigma, P, S)$, let λ denote the length of the longest member of any rule of G, i.e., $\lambda = \max(|\alpha|, |\beta|)$ for all $(\alpha,\beta) \in P$. Feldman [2] has studied a related property, the sum of the lengths of the rules of G.

If $\lambda = 1$, clearly only strings of length 1 can be derived (ignoring the endmarkers), so that $L(G) \subseteq \Sigma$ is finite. On the other hand, Chomsky [1] has shown that any cf-language has a cf-grammar with $\lambda = 2$, and Kuroda [6] has shown that any cs-language has a cs-grammar with $\lambda = 2$. A straightforward modification of Kuroda's proof can be used to show that

Proposition 1. Any language has a grammar with $\lambda = 2$.

Proof Let $G = (V, \Sigma, P, S)$ be a grammar for L with $\lambda \geq 3$. It will be shown that there exists a grammar for L of length $\lambda - 1$, from which the proposition follows by induction. To this end let $G' = (V, \Sigma, P, S)$ be a grammar formed from G as follows: Replace all terminal symbols $a_i \neq \#$ in the rules of P by corresponding new non-terminals A_i and add terminating rules of the form $A_i \to a_i$. If $\varphi \to \psi$ is a rule of the resulting grammar of length less than λ let it be a rule of G'. Otherwise, if $|\varphi| < |\psi|$ suppose $\psi = AB\psi'$, let B' be a new nonterminal, and let $\varphi \to AB'$, $B' \to B\psi'$ be rules of G'.[1] Similarly, if $|\varphi| > |\psi|$, suppose $\varphi = CD\varphi'$, let D' be a new nonterminal, and use $CD \to D'$, $D'\varphi' \to \psi$ as rules of G'.[2] Finally, if $|\varphi| = |\psi|$, suppose $\varphi = CD\varphi'$, $\psi = A\psi'$, let D' be a new nonterminal, and use $CD \to AD'$, $D'\varphi' \to \psi'$. The grammar thus defined has length $\lambda - 1$ and evidently generates L, since the new nonterminal cannot be rewritten except by "completing" the rewriting of φ as ψ.

Let $\nu = \|V - \{\#\}\|$ denote the number of symbols in the vocabulary of G, not counting the endmarker. Gruska [4] has studied the problem of minimizing ν for cf-grammars; he has shown that for any n, there exist cf-languages on two terminal symbols for which any cf-grammar must have $\nu > n+2$. If the grammar is not required to be cf, on the other hand, one can always make $\nu = \sigma + 1$ (where $\sigma = \| \Sigma - \{\#\}\|$ is the size of the terminal vocabulary; evidently this is the best possible result, since $S \in V - \Sigma$):

Proposition 2. Any cf-language has a grammar (not necessarily cf) with $\nu = \sigma + 1$.

Proof Greibach [3] has shown that any cf-language has a grammar whose rules are all of the forms $A \to a$, $A \to aB$, $A \to aBb$, or $A \to aBbC$ where $A,B,C \in V - \Sigma$ and $a,b \in \Sigma$. Let $G = (V, \Sigma, P, S)$ be such a grammar for L and let $f: V - \Sigma \to N$ be a one-to-one mapping of the non-terminals of G into the natural numbers such that $f(S) = 1$. Let $G' = (\Sigma \cup \{S\}, \Sigma, P, S)$ where for each rule $A \to \omega$ of P and each pair x,y of terminals, P' has the rule $xS^{f(A)}y \to x\omega'y$ where ω' is formed from ω by replacing each occurrence of a non-terminal B by the string $S^{f(B)}$. As before $L(G') = L(G)$ since the transformation which produces the rules of P' from those of P transforms #S#-derivations of strings in L(G) into #S#-derivations of the same

[1] If φ ends in #, let $\varphi = \varphi'\#$, and use the rules $\varphi' \to AB'$, $B'\# \to B\psi'$. (By the conventions in Section 1.1, φ cannot be # alone; nor can it be ##, so that φ' cannot be # alone.)

[2] If φ begins with #, i.e., C = #, use $\#D \to \#D'$, $D'\varphi' \to \psi$.

strings in L(G′). Conversely, since the only strings of S's which can be rewritten by G′ are those enclosed between terminals, it follows that the inverse transformation takes #S#-derivations for strings in L(G′) into #S#-derivations for the same strings in L(G).

We can do nearly as well for arbitrary languages:

Proposition 3. Any language has a grammar with $\nu = \sigma + 2$.

Proof Let $G = (V, \Sigma, P, S)$ be a grammar for L and let $f: V - \Sigma \rightarrow N$ be a one-to-one mapping of the nonterminals of G into the natural numbers. Let $G = (\Sigma \cup \{S,T\}, \Sigma, P, S)$ be a grammar for L where P′ consists of the rule $\#S\# \rightarrow \#TS^{f(S)}T\#$ and the rules formed from those of P by replacing each occurrence of each non-terminal A by the string $TS^{f(A)}T$. Clearly L(G′) = L(G) since the transformation which produces rules of P′ from P transforms a #S#-derivation for $\omega \in L(G)$ into a #TST#-derivation for $\omega \in L(G')$. Conversely, since the only strings of S's which can be rewritten by G′ are those enclosed between T's, it follows that the inverse transformation produces #S#-derivations for $\omega \in L(G)$ from #TST#-derivations for $\omega \in L(G')$.

Finally, let $\rho = \|p\|$ denote the number of rules of G. Gruska [5] has shown that for any n, there exist cf-languages (in fact, fs-languages) for which any cf-grammar has $\rho > n$. It is easily seen that there exist languages such that $\rho \geq \sigma$ for any grammar; for example, any grammar for $L = \{\#x\# \mid x \in \Sigma - \{\#\}\}$ must have, for each x, a rule that creates an x but no other terminals. Our final results provide bounds on ρ for arbitrary languages:

Proposition 4. Any finite language has a grammar with $\rho = 3\sigma + 6$.

Proof Let $L = \{\omega_1, \ldots, \omega_n\}$ and let ω_k^* denote ω_k with each terminal a_i replaced by a non-terminal A_i. Let G′ denote the grammar defined by the following $3\sigma + 6$ rules:

(1) $S \rightarrow WE\omega_1^*E\omega_2^*E \cdots E\omega_n^*EZ$
(2) $WE \rightarrow W$
(3) $WA_i \rightarrow W \qquad (1 \leq i \leq \sigma)$
(4) $WE \rightarrow X$
(5) $XA_i \rightarrow a_iX \qquad (1 \leq i \leq \sigma)$
(6) $XE \rightarrow Y$
(7) $YA_i \rightarrow Y \qquad (1 \leq i \leq \sigma)$
(8) $YE \rightarrow Y$
(9) $YZ \rightarrow \epsilon$

This grammar creates a string consisting of all the sentences of L in non-terminal form separated by E's; it then erases all but at most one of these and changes that one into terminal form.

Proposition 5. If a language has a grammar with vocabulary size ν, it has a grammar with $\rho = \nu^2 + 5\nu + \sigma + 5$.

Proof Let $V = \{A_1, \ldots, A_\nu, \#\}$ with $S = A_1$, and let $P = \{(\alpha_i, \beta_i) \mid 1 \leq i \leq \rho'\}$. Let (α'_k, β'_k) denote (α_k, β_k) with each A_i replaced by a non-terminal $A'_i (1 \leq i \leq \nu)$,[1] and let A^*_i be other non-terminals $(1 \leq i \leq \nu)$. Let γ denote the string $L\alpha'_1 M\beta'_1 L\alpha'_2 M\beta'_2 \cdots L\alpha'_{\rho'} M\beta'_{\rho'} L$. Let $G' = (V', \Sigma, P', S)$ be the grammar defined by the following rules:

(1) $S \to S^*\gamma$

This rule creates a string consisting of non-terminal images of all the rules of the given grammar together with an image of the initial symbol; the members of the rules are separated by the non-terminal symbols L and M. Next, for $1 \leq i,j \leq \nu$, let

(2) $A^*_i L \to LA^*_i$
(3) $A^*_i M \to MA^*_i$
(4) $A^*_i A'_j \to A'_j A^*_i$
(5) $\gamma A^*_i \to A^*_i \gamma$

These $\nu^2 + 3\nu$ rules let the A^*'s move through γ to the right and jump back to its left end, but not cross one another.

Further, let

(6) $LA^*_i A'_i \to A'_i X$

(7) $XA^*_i A'_i \to A'_i X$

(8) $XM \to MY$
(9) $YA'_i \to A^*_i A'_i Y$
(10) $YL \to L$

These $3\nu + 2$ rules will operate without blocking provided that, for some rule $\alpha_j \to \beta_j$, the symbols of α^*_j alternate with those of α'_j, and no starred symbols occur between the symbols of β'_j. Under these circumstances these rules will erase the α^*_j and create a β^*_j with its symbols alternating with those of β'_j. Finally, let

(11) $\gamma \to Z$
(12) $ZA^*_i \to A_i Z$ for those i's such that A_i is a terminal symbol
(13) $Z \to \epsilon$

[1] It can be shown that no (α_k, β_k) need involve # [8].

These $\sigma + 2$ rules can erase γ and remove the stars from the starred terminal symbols. Thus they can create a terminal string provided that the starred symbols present are all copies of terminals.

Corollary 6. Any language has a grammar with $\rho = \sigma^2 + 11\sigma + 21$.

Corollary 7. Any cf-language has a grammar (not necessarily cf) with $\rho = \sigma^2 + 9\sigma + 12$.

2. Vocabulary Size vs. Rule Length

In this section we examine the tradeoff between vocabulary size and rule length for a class of one-symbol cf-languages, $\Sigma = \{a,\#\}$.

For $b \epsilon N$ and $d \epsilon I$, let $L_{b,d} \equiv \{a^{b+md} \mid b+md \geq 0, m \epsilon N\}$. Such a set will be called an *arithmetic progression.* In particular $L_{b,0} \equiv L_b = \{a^b\}$. It is an easy consequence of Parikh's Theorem [7] that if L is a cf-language on one symbol then L is a finite union of arithmetic progressions. It follows readily that all one-symbol cf-languages are fs-languages.

A set Λ_k of natural numbers will be called a *λ-partition of k* (assuming $\lambda, k \geq 2$) if 1 and k are in Λ_k, and for each $1 \neq k_0 \epsilon \Lambda_k$ there exist $k_1, \ldots, k_m$ in Λ_k, where $k_0 \geq k_1 \geq \ldots \geq k_m$ and $m \leq \lambda$, such that $k_0 = k_1 + \ldots + k_m$. Let $k = \sum_{j=0}^{\eta-1} \delta_j \lambda^j$ be the base λ representation of k. Denote by $\eta = \eta_\lambda(k)$ the number of digits in this representation, and by $\delta = \delta_\lambda(k) = \sum_{j=0}^{\eta-1} \delta_j$ the sum of the digits in this representation. Let $\mu = \nu_\lambda(k) = \min(\|\Lambda_k\|)$ for all λ-partitions Λ_k of k.

Lemma 8. $\quad \mu < \eta + \dfrac{\delta-1}{\lambda-1} + 1$

Proof It suffices to exhibit a λ-partition of k which has fewer than $\eta + \dfrac{\delta-1}{\lambda-1} + 1$ elements. Let $\Lambda_k = \{1, \lambda, \ldots, \lambda^{\eta-1}, a_1, \ldots, a_m, k\}$ with the a's defined as follows: Let $\sum_{j=0}^{\eta_i-1} \delta_j + \delta'_{\eta_i} = \lambda + (i-1)(\lambda-1)$, where $0 \leq \delta'_{\eta_i} < \delta_{\eta_i}$, for each i such that $\lambda + (i-1)(\lambda-1) < \delta$. If m is the greatest such i, then readily $m < \dfrac{\delta-1}{\lambda-1}$. Let $a_i = \sum_{j=0}^{\eta_i-1} \delta_j \lambda^j + \delta'_{\eta_i} \lambda^{\eta_i}$, $1 \leq i \leq m$. Clearly a_1 is the sum of $\lambda = \sum_{j=0}^{\eta_i-1} \delta_i + \delta'_{\eta_1}$ powers of λ, while for $1 < i \leq m$, each a_i is the sum of a_{i-1} together with at most $\lambda - 1$ powers of λ. Similarly, k is the sum of a_m together with at most $\lambda - 1$ powers of λ. Thus Λ_k is a λ-partition of k, and has $\eta+m+1 < \eta + \dfrac{\delta-1}{\lambda-1} + 1$ elements.

Note that even if the base λ digits of k are all $(\lambda-1)$'s, their sum δ is only

$\eta(\lambda-1)$, so that $\dfrac{\delta-1}{\lambda-1} < \eta$. Thus the lemma implies $\mu < 2\eta + 1$.

Lemma 9. If $\delta = 1$, then $\mu = \eta$; if $\delta > 1$, then $\mu \geq \eta + 1$.

Proof Let $\Lambda_k = \{k_1, \ldots, k_\mu\}$ be a minimal λ-partition of k, where $1 = k_1 < \ldots < k_\mu = k$. Since each k_i is the sum of at most λ smaller k's, it follows that $k_i \leq k_{i-1}(2 \leq i \leq \mu)$. In particular $\eta_\lambda(k_i) \leq \eta_\lambda(k_{i-1}) + 1$, so that $\eta = \eta_k(k) \leq \mu$. Moreover, if $\delta > 1$, there must be a least i such that $\delta_\lambda(k_i) > 1$, and clearly for this i the number of digits cannot increase; thus $\delta > 1$ implies $\eta \leq \mu - 1$. On the other hand, for $\delta = 1$ the bound $\eta = \mu$ is taken on, using $\Lambda_k = \{1, \lambda, \ldots, \lambda^{\eta-1}\}$.

Theorem 10. If G is a cf-grammar for $L_{b,d}$ of length λ and size ν, then $\nu \geq \nu_\lambda(b)$.

Proof Let $G = (V, \Sigma, P, S)$ be a ν-optimal cf-grammar of length λ for $L_{b,d}$. If $A \in V - \Sigma$ then $A \overset{*}{\Rightarrow} a^j$ for some $j > 0$, since otherwise A could be eliminated from G without affecting L(G), contradicting ν-optimality. If $d \geq 0$, let $k(A) = \min \{j \in N \mid A \overset{*}{\Rightarrow} a^j\}$; if $d \leq 0$, let $k(A) = \max \{j \in N \mid A \overset{*}{\Rightarrow} a^j\}$. (The two definitions must agree if $d = 0$, since otherwise strings other than a^b could be generated.) Note that $k(S) = b$, since $S \overset{*}{\Rightarrow} a^b$, and if $S \overset{*}{\Rightarrow} a^j$ then $d \geq 0$ implies $j \geq b$, while $d \leq 0$ implies $j \leq b$. Finally, define $k(a) = 1$.

Let $\Lambda_{b,d} = \{k(A) \mid A \in V - \{\#\}\}$; thus $\Lambda_{b,d}$ contains 1 and b. For any $A \in V - \Sigma$, let $A \Rightarrow A_1 \ldots A_m$ be the first step in an A-derivation of a $a^{k(A)}$. Then clearly there exist k_i, $1 \leq i \leq m$, such that $A_i \overset{*}{\Rightarrow} a^{k_i}$ and $\sum_{i=1}^{m} k_i = k(A)$. Thus for $d \geq 0$ it follows that $\sum_{i=1}^{m} k(A_i) \leq \sum_{i=1}^{m} k(A)$, and by the minimality of $k(A)$ this implies $k(A_i) = k_i$, $1 \leq i \leq m$, so that $k(A) = \sum_{i=1}^{m} k(A_i)$; and analogously for $d \leq 0$. This proves that $\Lambda_{b,d}$ is a λ-partition of b, so that $\nu \geq \| \Lambda_{b,d} \| \geq \nu_\lambda(b)$.

We next exhibit cases where the lower bound of Theorem 10 is attained for $d = 0$.

Proposition 11. If $1 < \delta_\lambda(b) \leq \lambda$, then there exists a cf-grammar of length λ and size $\eta_\lambda(b) + 1$ for L_b. If $\delta_\lambda(b) = 1$, then there exists such a grammar of size $\eta_\lambda(b)$.

Proof Let the base λ representation of b be $\delta_{\eta-1}\lambda^{\eta-1} + \ldots + \delta_1\lambda + \delta_0$, where $\eta = \eta_\lambda(b)$. Let $V = \{S, A_1, \ldots, A_{\eta-1}, a, \#\}$, and let P consist of rules $S \rightarrow A_{\eta-1}^{\delta_{\eta-1}} \ldots A_1^{\delta_1} a^{\delta_0}$ and $A_i \rightarrow A_{i-1}^{\lambda}$ $(1 \leq i \leq \eta - 1)$, where $A_0 = a$. Then $G = (V, \{a, \#\}, P, S)$ is a grammar for L_b, with $\nu = \eta + 1$, which by Lemma

9 is the smallest possible value for ν if $\delta > 1$. Moreover, if $\delta = 1$, then $b = \lambda^{\eta-1}$, and L_b has a grammar with the rules $A_i \to A_{i-1}^{\lambda}$ $(1 \leq i \leq \eta-1)$, where $A_{\eta-1} = S$ and $A_0 = a$; this grammar has $\nu = \eta$, which by Lemma 9 is again optimal.

Proposition 12. If $b = m^n$, where $m > 1$, then any cf-grammar for L_b of length m has size $\geq n+1$, and any such grammar of length $< m$ has size $> n+1$.

Proof For $\lambda = m$ this follows from Lemma 9 since m^n has $n+1$ digits and sum of digits 1 in base m. But if $\lambda < m$, the base λ representation of m^n has at least $n+1$ digits; and if its sum of digits is 1, i.e., $m^n = \lambda^k$, then $k > n$ since $\lambda < m$, so that it has more than $n+1$ digits. Thus by Lemma 9 $\nu > n+1$ in either case.

These results about $L_{b,d}$ and L_b can be applied to yield bounds on the complexities of grammars for other languages whose sentences have properties involving b as a parameter. Suppose that L_b has a cf-grammar of *type* (λ, ν, ρ), i.e., of rule length λ, vocabulary size ν, and ρ rules. Then it is not difficult to prove

Proposition 13.

1) If $0 < d < \lambda$, then $L_{b,d}$ has a cf-grammar of type $(\lambda, \nu, \rho+1)$.
2) $L_{b,-1}$ has a cf-grammar of type (λ, ν, ρ^*), where $\rho^* \leq \rho + \lambda(\nu-1)$.
3) Let $E_b = \{a^{b^m} \mid m \in N\}$, the set of strings of a's whose lengths are powers of b; then E_b has an m-grammar of type $(\lambda, \nu+5, \rho+5)$.
4) Let M_b be the set of strings on $\{0,1\}$ which contain exactly b 1's (readily, M_b is an fs-language); then M_b has a cf-grammar of type $(\lambda, \nu+2, \rho+3)$. [Conversely, it is not difficult to show that if M_b has a grammar of type (λ, ν, ρ), then L_b has a grammar of type $(\lambda, \nu, \rho+1)$.]
5) Let C_b be the set of strings on $\{0,1\}$ which contain exactly b runs of 1's (this too is readily an fs-language); then C_b has a cs-grammar of type $(\max(\lambda,4), \nu+2, \rho+12)$. [Here we assume $b > 1$; the given grammar for L_b can be cs. Conversely, if C_b has a grammar of type (λ, ν, ρ), then L_b has a grammar of type $(\max(\lambda,3), \nu+1, \rho+7)$.]
6) Let Q_b be the set of strings that are concatenations of b identical substrings on σ terminal symbols. (Chomsky [1] cites Q_2 as an example of a cs-language which is not cf; his argument readily extends to arbitrary b.) If L_b has an m-grammar of type (λ, ν, ρ),

then Q_b has an m-grammar of type $(\max(\lambda,4),\ \nu+4\sigma,\ \rho+4\sigma^2+6\sigma)$.

3. (Length, Size) - Minimality

Let $(\pi_1, \ldots, \pi_n)$ be properties of a grammar that can take on positive integer values; the n-tuple of these values for a given grammar will be called its $(\pi_1, \ldots, \pi_n)$-type. A grammar G for the language L will be called $(\pi_1, \ldots, \pi_n)$-minimal if $\pi_i(G') \leq \pi_i(G)$, $1 \leq i \leq n$, and $L(G') = L(G)$ imply $\pi_i(G') = \pi_i(G)$, $1 \leq i \leq n$. It is easily shown that any language has grammars of only finitely many $(\pi_1, \ldots, \pi_n)$-minimal $(\pi_1, \ldots, \pi_n)$-types.

For example, by Proposition 12, the grammar for L_{mn} in the last part of Proposition 11 is (λ, ν)-minimal. In particular, let $n = 1$; then since the resulting grammar for L_m has only one rule $S \rightarrow a^m$, it is evidently (λ, ν, ρ)-minimal. Determining *all* the minimal grammars for a given language is more difficult; in this section we do so for two cf-languages, the palindromes and the parenthesis strings.

If $\epsilon \neq \omega \epsilon \Sigma^*$ let ω^{-1}, the *reversal* of ω, be defined as follows: If $\omega = a_1 a_2 \cdots a_n$ with $a_i \epsilon \Sigma$ for $1 \leq i \leq n$ then $\omega^{-1} = a_n a_{n-1} \cdots a_1$. The set of strings $R = \{\omega \mid \omega \epsilon \Sigma^*, \omega = \omega^{-1}\}$ is called the set of *palindromes*[1] over Σ. It will be assumed that $\sigma \geq 2$.

Let $G = (V, \Sigma, P, S)$ where $V = \{S\} \cup \Sigma$ and P contains the rules

(1) $S \rightarrow aSa$

(2) $S \rightarrow a$

(3) $S \rightarrow a^2$

for $a \epsilon \Sigma$. Then G is a cf-grammar for R of type $(3, \sigma+1, 3\sigma)$.

Let $G' = (V', \Sigma, P', S)$ where $V' = V \cup \{A_a \mid a \epsilon \Sigma\}$ and P' contains the rules

(1) $S \rightarrow aA_a$

(2) $A_a \rightarrow Sa$

(3) $S \rightarrow a$

(4) $S \rightarrow a^2$ (or $A_a \rightarrow a$)

for $a \epsilon \Sigma$. Then G' is a cf-grammar for R of type $(2, 2\sigma+1, 4\sigma)$.

---

[1] If $\sigma = 1$ then $R = \Sigma^* - \{\epsilon\}$, and so has a grammar of type $(2, \sigma+1, 2)$, e.g., having rules $S \rightarrow aS$, $S \rightarrow a$. In the case $\sigma = 2$ Chomsky [1] cites R as an example of a cf-language which is not an fs-language.

Proposition 14. The cf-grammars G and G′ defined above are (λ, ν)-minimal cf-grammars for R. Conversely, any (λ, ν)-minimal cf-grammar for R either has $\lambda = 2$, $\nu = 2\sigma+1$ or $\lambda = 3$, $\nu = \sigma+1$.

Proof Let $G = (V'', \Sigma, P'', S)$ be a cf-grammar for R with $\lambda = 2$, and suppose that $V'' - \Sigma = \{S, A_1, \ldots, A_n\}$ with $n < \sigma$. It may be assumed without loss of generality that V'' contains no superfluous nonterminals and P'' contains no superfluous rules—in other words, that $X \overset{*}{\Rightarrow} \omega$ (where $\omega \in \Sigma^*$) for all $X \in V''$, and that any rule in P'' occurs in a derivation of some sentence in R.

Let $S \to XY$ be any rule which rewrites S; then neither X nor Y can be S. Indeed, suppose that $X = S$ and $Y \overset{*}{\Rightarrow} \omega$, where $\omega = \omega' a$; then since $S \overset{*}{\Rightarrow} b$ for any $b \neq a \in \Sigma$, it would follow that $S \to XY \overset{*}{\Rightarrow} b\omega' a$, which is not a palindrome.

Suppose next that $S \to X_a Y_a$ is the first rule used in a derivation of a^3. Clearly X_a and Y_a cannot both be a's (and certainly neither can be any terminal $\neq a$); thus at least one of them is an A_i. Since there are σ different a's and only $n < \sigma$ different A's, there must exist two different terminals a,b such that the same A_i occurs at the first step in derivations of both a^3 and b^3. Suppose, for example, that $S \to X_a A_i \overset{*}{\Rightarrow} a^3$ and $S \to X_b A_i$ (or $A_i Y_b$) $\overset{*}{\Rightarrow} b^3$. But then $A_i \overset{*}{\Rightarrow}$ a or a^2, while X_b (or Y_b) $\overset{*}{\Rightarrow}$ b or b^2, so that here again a nonpalindrome could be derived from S, contradiction.

It has thus been shown that $\lambda = 2$ implies $\nu \geq 2\sigma + 1$, so that $(2, 2\sigma+1)$ is (λ, ν)-minimal. On the other hand, ν always $\geq \sigma + 1$, and since $(2, \sigma+1)$ is impossible as just shown, it follows that $(3, \sigma+1)$ is also (λ, ν)-minimal. Moreover, if (λ, ν) is minimal, either $\lambda = 2$ and $\nu \geq 2\sigma + 1$, or else $\lambda \geq 3$ (and evidently $\nu \geq \sigma + 1$), so that these two are the only possible minimal (λ, ν)-types for a cf-grammar for R.

Let G_1 be the grammar (V_1, Σ, P_1, S) where $V_1 = \{S, (,), \#\}$, $\Sigma = \{(,), \#\}$, and P_1 consists of the rules $S \to SS$, $S \to (S)$, and $S \to ()$. The language W of G_1 is called the set of well-formed *parenthesis strings.* It may be verified that W also has the grammar $G_2 = (V_2, \Sigma, P_2, S)$ where $V_2 = V_1 \cup \{A\}$ and P_2 consists of the rules $S \to SS$; $S \to (A; A \to S)$; and $S \to ()$. Note that G_1 has type (3,3,3) and G_2 has type (2,4,4).

Proposition 15. The cf-grammars G_1 and G_2 just defined are (λ, ν)-minimal grammars for W. Conversely, any (λ, ν)-minimal grammar for W either has $\lambda = 2$, $\nu = 4$, or $\lambda = 3$, $\nu = 3$.

Proof It suffices to show that $\lambda = 2$, $\nu = 3$ is impossible. Suppose that

G were a grammar for W with $\lambda = 2$, $\nu = 3$, i.e., $V = \{S, (,), \#\}$. Note first that no rule of G can have left member #S, since the right member would then have to be #S,#(, or #); the first of these is a superfluous rule, while the other two yield ill-formed terminal strings. Similarly, no rule can have left member S#; thus the only rules that can rewrite the initial S must have left members consisting of S alone.

Let $S \to XY$ be any such rule; clearly $X \neq)$ and $Y \neq ($. Suppose that $XY = (S$. Since $S \overset{*}{\Rightarrow} ()$, and no rule of this derivation uses the left endmarker, it would follow that $S \Rightarrow (S \overset{*}{\Rightarrow} (()$, which is ill-formed; and similarly $XY \neq S)$. Thus $XY = ()$ or SS, and since () is not the only string in W, $S \to SS$ must be a rule of G.

By a similar argument, the only possible rules with left member SS are $SS \to \epsilon$, $SS \to S$, $SS \to SS$ (all superfluous), and $SS \to ()$; the latter rule can be replaced, if necessary, by the cf rule $S \to ()$, so that these rules add nothing to L(G). It follows that the only strings derivable from SS in G are those of the form $\gamma\delta$, where γ and δ are each derivable from S in G. In particular, there is no way to derive the well-formed string (( )) in G, so that G cannot be a grammar for W.

REFERENCES

[1] Chomsky, N. (1959), "On Certain Formal Properties of Grammars", *Info. Control,* 2, 137-167.

[2] Feldman, J. (1969), "Some Decidability Results on Grammatical Inference and Complexity", *Stanford Artificial Intelligence Project Memo AI-93,* AD693106.

[3] Greibach, S. A. (1965), "A New Normal-Form Theorem for Context-Free Phrase Structure Grammars", *J. Assoc. Comp. Mach.,* 12, 42-52.

[4] Gruska, J. (1967), "On a Classification of Context Free Languages", *Kybernetika,* 3, 22-29.

[5] Gruska, J. (1969), "Some Classifications of Context-Free Languages", *Info. Control,* 14, 152-179.

[6] Kuroda, S. Y. (1964), "Classes of Languages and Linear Bounded Automata", *Info. Control,* 7, 207-223.

[7] Parikh, R. (1966), "On Context-Free Languages", *J. Assoc. Comp. Mach.,* 13, 570-581.

[8] Rosenfeld, A. (1970), "Isotonic grammars, parallel grammars, and picture grammars", *Machine Intelligence VI,* Edinburgh University Press, 1971, 281-294.

PICTURE GRAPHS, GRAMMARS, AND PARSING*

Alan C. Shaw **

DEPARTMENT OF COMPUTER SCIENCE
CORNELL UNIVERSITY
ITHACA, NEW YORK

Abstract

This paper is concerned with the syntactic description and analysis of pictures when graphs are employed as the primary description formalism. The present state of development, a number of significant open problems, and the advantages and limitations of this approach are discussed under the following three headings:

(a) representation of pictures by graphs,
(b) graph languages and grammars, and
(c) parsing of graphs and pictures.

In (a) we investigate transformations from pictures to graphs based on n-ary relations ($n \geq 1$) that exist among picture components, both at the primitive pattern level and among higher level subpictures; n-ary relations are reduced when $n > 2$ or expanded when $n = 1$ to binary relations. Several grammatical schemes for generating graph descriptions are then evaluated with respect to their descriptive adequacy, complexity, and practical and theoretical tractability. Syntax-directed analysis of graphs and pictures is treated from two points of view -- how to parse efficiently and how to enlist the descriptive mechanism as an aid in the difficult lower level pattern recognition tasks. The latter point is particularly emphasized with the aim of promoting a more systematic approach to contextual recognition.

*This work was supported in part by The National Science Foundation grant GJ-108.
**Present address: Computer Science Group, University of Washington, Seattle, Washington.

I. Introduction

This paper examines the use of graph representations for the description and analysis of "structured" pictures. Examples of structured pictures are particle trajectories produced in high energy particle physics experiments, circuit schematics, flow charts, organic chemistry molecules, architectural drawings, some biomedical pictures, and natural scenes. A linear list of the features, primitives, or objects contained in one of these pictures is usually not an adequate description; it is the *relationships* among the components that often provide the key to understanding and that require extended processing beyond standard pattern classification.

It is convenient to define pictures independently of any specific viewing or generation machine (e.g. flying spot scanner or plotter). At the lowest and most primitive level, we can use an extension of Rosenfeld's picture function (Rosenfeld, 1969; pp. 1-2):

A picture α is a vector-valued function f of several real variables x; i.e.

$$f(x) = (f_1(x), \ldots, f_k(x)),\ x = (x_1, \ldots, x_n),$$

where k is the number of attributes of α, f_i represents the value associated with the ith attribute, n is the dimension of α, and x is a point in n-space. Typical attributes are intensity or "gray level", colour, and opaqueness or transparency. n = 2, 3 is the normal situation but higher dimensions or n = 1 need not be excluded.

Descriptions at higher levels serve several purposes. They define encodings and classifications of pictures that allow humans and machines to comprehend and conveniently process them; from a slightly different point of view, they permit a useful articulation of the interesting parts of pictures while eliminating "noisy" or irrelevant components. Descriptions may also be employed to drive picture analyzers or generators. In the analysis case, this implies the existence of a grammar or set of rules that define the picture class of interest. Picture analysis then becomes a problem of *deriving* descriptions while generation involves the *evaluation* of descriptions.

The possible levels of description can be arranged in a hierarchy, where level i + 1 is derived from level i by some set of picture processing operations:

Level 0: $f_0(x)$, the lowest level mathematical description as discussed above.

Level 1: $f_1(x)$, a machine's view of f_0.
This is normally a quantization of f_0 over a regular array.

Level 2: $f_2(x)$, the result of "preprocessing" f_1.
Noise removal and image enhancement are typical preprocessing goals.

Level 3: $\{F_i\}$, a set of the features F_i of f_2.
Examples are line segments and edges.

Level 4: $\{P_i\}$, a classification of all the primitive objects P_i in the picture represented by Level 3.

Level 5: $\{R_i\}$, the relations R_i existing among the primitives.

Level 6-m: higher level groupings and their relationships.

Level $m+1$: C, the highest level.
This generally consists of a simple classification C.

The hierarchy is illustrated in Figure 1. We are mainly interested in describing pictures at levels 4 to $m+1$ and employing these descriptions as an aid in transforming pictures from level i to $i+1$ or $i+1$ to i for $i=0,1,\ldots,m$.

Most description schemes that have been implemented or proposed use a generative grammar of some form which defines a picture language; this approach has been termed "linguistic" because of the analogy to natural and programming language specification and analysis. Picture grammar and language notations have been based on arrays, list structures, (relation, object list) pairs, predicate calculus, set theory, and graphs (Miller and Shaw, 1968; Fu, 1970).

Graph representations have been particularly attractive because of the natural interpretation of graphs in terms of objects, relations, and concatenations, and because of the large body of graph theory and algorithms that is available. In the next section, we investigate the general problem of representing pictures by graphs. Section III examines the virtues and limitations of several graph languages and grammars that have been developed. The following section discusses algorithms for parsing graphs and pictures emphasizing problems of efficiency and the use of contextual information. Throughout the paper, we list a number of problems and directions for future research.

II. Representation of Pictures by Graphs

The composition of a picture α can often be specified hierarchically as a set S of subpictures, the relationships among the elements of S, and a number of attribute-value pairs for α and each subpicture. (The notation of Evans (1969) is complete in this sense). An n-ary relation R $(n \geq 1)$ satisfied by the objects $X_1, \ldots, X_n$ will be denoted $R(X_1, \ldots, X_n)$; an attribute-value pair will be designated by $<a,v>$.

Consider the subscripted variable A_N of Figure 2, interpreted as a picture α. One possible description of α is:

$\alpha = \{A,N\}$ *where* SUBSCRIPT (A,N)

$$A = \{DP_1, DP_2, H, DM_1, DM_2\} \textit{ where } CAT(DP_1, DP_2) \wedge CAT(DP_1, H) \wedge CAT(DP_2, DM_2) \wedge CAT(DM_2, DM_1) \wedge CAT(H, DM_1)$$

$$N = \{V_1, DM, V_2\} \textit{ where } CAT(V_1, DM) \wedge CAT(DM, V_2)$$

Let each object above have an ordered pair of points $<t,h>$ by which it may be connected to other objects; then CAT(X,Y) means that h_X is concatenated to t_Y. t and h will be referred to as the tail and head points respectively.

There are several ways to map the description to a graph. The most common and straightforward representation is a *labelled node*-oriented *directed* graph, where nodes represent objects and edges denote (binary) relations* (Figure 3 (a)). The unlabelled edges describe the "contains" relation C; for example, C(α,A) means that the object α contains A. (It is this relation that may define the levels in a description hierarchy). Note that all edges and nodes are implicity or explicity labelled ("coloured") and that the root and interior nodes decompose into graphs at lower levels. An edge-oriented graph can also be used in many cases (Figure 3 (b)). Nodes represent the tail and head points of concatenation, each object is denoted by a labelled directed edge pointing from its tail node to its head node, and all (binary) relations other than concatenation are treated as "invisible" objects and defined as edges. Here it is not necessary to label the nodes. While the latter type of graph is less general than the node-oriented form and leads to ambiguous interpretations in some instances – for example, if we had CAT(X,Y), CAT(W,Y), C(X,A), and C(W,B) – , it has the virtues of simplicity and processing convenience for those pictures where component concatenations are the primary relations (Shaw, 1969a, 1970).

The above example was contrived to involve only binary relations. However, picture descriptions frequently also require the expression of unary relations (properties) and n-ary relations for $n > 2$. For example, it might be more useful to describe an "A" as:

(1) $$A = \{L_1, L_2, L_3, L_4, L_5\} \textit{ where } TRIANGLE(L_2, L_3, L_4) \wedge HORIZONTAL(L_3) \wedge ABOVE(L_3, L_2) \wedge \ldots$$

where the ternary relation TRIANGLE is satisfied by the lines L_2, L_3, and L_4, and L_3 has the property relation HORIZONTAL. A graph-representable description is obtained by mapping all relations to binary ones. A unary relation R(X) can be changed to the binary one $\tilde{R}(X,\Lambda)$ where Λ denotes the "null" object. $R(X_1, \ldots, X_n)$ $(n > 2)$ can be transformed to a composition of binary relations, for example,

*If a relation is symmetric, it can be designated by an undirected edge.

$R_1(X_1, R_2(X_2, \ldots, R_{n-1}(X_{n-1}, X_n) \ldots))$, or to a conjunction of binary relations $R_1(X_{11}, X_{12}) \wedge R_2(X_{21}, X_{22}) \wedge \ldots \wedge R_k(X_{k1}, X_{k2})$, or to a combination of these. TRIANGLE(L_2, L_3, L_4) could be transformed into either the following equivalent relations:

$$CAT(L_2, L_3) \wedge CAT(L_3, L_4) \wedge CAT(L_4, L_2) \text{ or}$$

$$\Delta(L_3, CAT(L_2, L_4))$$

where $\Delta(X,Y)$ means that the line X is connected to form a triangle with the object Y consisting of two concatenated segments. Replacement of an n-ary relation with binary ones using composition requires the introduction of more levels (more C(X,Y) relations) in the description; description (1) could be mapped to:

(2) $$A = \{L_1, L_3, ANGLE, L_5\} \textit{ where } \Delta(L_3, ANGLE) \wedge HORIZ(L_3, \Lambda) \wedge ABOV(L_3, ANGLE) \wedge \ldots$$

$$ANGLE = \{L_2, L_4\} \textit{ where } CAT(L_2, L_4) \wedge \ldots$$

The node-oriented graph of (2) is given in Figure 4. To complete the graph descriptions, <a,v> pairs may be associated with each object or higher level structure and included as part of the node or edge label. For example, "A" might have the attributes <HEIGHT, 0.75″>,<WIDTH, 0.5″>. In summary, we can completely describe any picture as a labelled directed graph by mapping all relations to binary ones and labelling the nodes and edges with relations, object names, and <a,v> pairs.

Two disadvantages of this approach are:

1. it is sometimes awkward to describe pictures by binary relations only, and
2. the graph representation can be unnecessarily complex when compared with other description methods.

The examples given by Minsky (1961) are a good illustration of the second point. There are 8 closed curves $X_0, \ldots, X_7$ which are related according to the following description:

(3) $$\Theta(X_0 \rightarrow (\Theta(X_1, \downarrow(X_2, X_3)), \Theta(X_4, \nabla(X_5, X_6, X_7))))$$

where $\Theta(X,Y)$ means Y is inside of X,
$\rightarrow(X,Y)$ means that Y is to the right of X,
$\downarrow(X,Y)$ means that Y is below X, and
$\nabla(X,Y,Z)$ means that Y is to the right of X and Z is underneath and between them.

The corresponding graph is awkward and messy compared with (3). We have also assumed that descriptions can always be arranged in a "tree" hierarchy. This is not always possible as the following example demonstrates:

Let a picture consist of 4 objects A,B,C,D with the relations $R_1(A,B)$, $R_2(C,D)$, $R_3(A,C)$, $R_4(B,D)$, $R_5(W,X)$, and $R_6(Y,Z)$, where $W = \{A,B\}$, $X = \{C,D\}$, $Y = \{A,C\}$, and $Z = \{B,D\}$. Figure 5 portrays the relations.

The characterization of pictures by graphs seems natural and useful when the subpictures within a level in a description hierarchy are significantly related to one another and when there do not exist many interlevel relations. In this case, graph manipulation algorithms, and the model and results of graph theory can be (and have been) applied successfully in theoretical studies and experiments in picture processing. Section III and IV mention some of these applications. It is, however, still not generally clear under what circumstances graph representations are useful, nor is it evident -- despite the examples in this section -- how to generally transform a picture to a graph.

III. Graph Languages and Grammars

Both a set of pictures and a set of graphs may often be described by a grammar G generating a graph language L(G); each sentence $x \in L(G)$ specifies, up to isomorphism, a unique graph g_x, which in turn, is an abstract representation of a set P_{g_x} of one or more pictures. The purpose of such a grammar are:

1. to precisely define, by finite means, an infinite set of graphs (and pictures),
2. to impose a hierarchic structure on each $x \in L(G)$, g_x, and member of P_{g_x} (i.e. the C(X,Y) relation), and
3. to assist in the recognition, analysis, and interpretation of graphs and pictures through syntax-directed processing.

Several different notations and formalisms for graph languages and grammars have been developed and applied in experimental settings. Figures 6, 7, and 8 contain simple examples of grammars for the most prominent of these. The notation of Narasimhan (1966), formalized by Feder (1969) as "plex" grammars, describes the connectivity of picture components by using explicit lists of labelled concatenation points in each rule. Each of Feder's grammar rules, in the context-free case, is of the form:

$$A \; \Delta_A \rightarrow x \; \psi_x \; \Delta_{xA}$$

where x is an ordered list of symbols identifying primitive objects or higher level subpictures, ψ_x is a list of "joints" or connections among points of elements of x, Δ_{xA} establishes a correspondence between points of x and attachment point labels to be associated with A, and Δ_A specifies a list of attachment points for A. While the sentences generated by these grammars are not directly graphs, they can be so transformed by either assigning labelled nodes to both objects and concatenation points as suggested by Pfaltz and Rosenfeld (1969) or by mapping picture objects to nodes and concatenations to labelled edges (Figure 6(b)). The cited references apply this notation to the description of English characters, flow charts, chemical diagrams, particle trajectories in bubble chambers, and electrical circuits.

The PDL notation (Shaw, 1969a; Miller and Shaw, 1968) (Figure 7) is also based on concatenations but uses a set of binary operators, much like the CAT(X,Y) of the last section to specify connections; the original notation restricted each primitive object to two concatenation points but this restriction was eliminated in further work (Shaw, 1969b). In the figure, the network component α could be, for example, an electrical circuit element such as a resistor; the operator + indicates head to tail concatenation in a PDL description, * defines both a tail to tail and a head to head connection, and higher level structures described by $(S_1 \; \theta \; S_2)$ have tails and heads defined recursively as tail(S_1) and head(S_2) respectively. A complete set of operators for local tail/head concatenations, tail/head reversal, and "rewriting" over the graph is specified in PDL; the notation allows the description of any directed edge-labelled graph. PDL has been applied to roughly the same sets of pictures as the plex grammars (but not to chemical diagrams yet) as well as pages of text and spark chambers photographs.

The web grammars of Pfaltz and Rosenfeld (1969) (Figure 8) explicitly employ node labelled graphs ("webs") in the rewriting rules; each production describes the rewriting of a graph α into another graph β and also contains an "embedding" rule E which specifies the connection of β to its surrounding graph (host web) when α is rewritten. In the above reference, web grammars were presented for directed trees, directed two-terminal series-parallel networks (TTPSN's), directed triangles of graphs, and "Pascal's triangles"; later work has contained grammars for various classes of planar graphs and simulated neural nets (Montanari, 1969; Pfaltz, 1970). The formalism of web grammars has been mathematically analyzed to a greater extent than any of the other mentioned above and seems theoretically more pleasing. All of the notations appear to be formally equivalent but this fact has not been proven; it is not difficult, however, to map PDL grammars into plex grammars and plex grammars into web grammars.

The main limitations of Feder's description scheme are the awkwardness of the connection point lists and the difficulty of specifying relations other than concatenation. The virtue of the PDL scheme is its simplicity but it too suffers from several defects. The notation is edge-oriented and the discussion of this type of representation given in the last section is applicable. Nodes can also be labelled in PDL but not in a very clean manner. Relations are described through the use of "blank" primitives which is adequate, at least, for simple relations and graphs but can be ambiguous in more general situations. The PDL scheme, as defined, used a context-free grammar form which could generate non-graphs; this problem can probably be resolved by allowing a straightforward form of context-sensitive rule. Both of the above notations are linear strings and it may be argued that a multi-dimensional notation would be more natural. Finally, the authors of these schemes have concentrated primarily on picture description and analysis, as opposed to a deeper theoretical study of their formalisms; more work is required in this latter area.

Web grammars are the most recent of the notations. As specified, they are node-oriented with no labels on edges which means that only one relation can be specified; however, it appears as if the rules and embeddings could be extended to include labelled edges. The embedding part of each grammar rule has been given in a mixture of set theory and English; a formal language for describing these embeddings would be useful. At this point, it is not clear how convenient web grammars will be for describing pictures; some picture and graph classes seem to require grammars that are not as natural as, for example, PDL grammars. The last two points are illustrated by the examples in Figures 7 and 8.

None of the schemes provide facilities for expressing relations, other than the C(X,Y), among higher level sub-pictures. Attributes are not included in any general way but these could be obtained by associating an interpretation or "semantic" rule with each grammar rule (e.g. Knuth, 1968). The next section examines graph languages and grammars in the context of picture analysis.

IV. Parsing of Graphs and Pictures

The analysis of a set of pictures or graphs described by a grammar G can be formulated as a parsing and graph-matching process. The parse of a graph g occurs by attempting to find a sentence $x \in L(G)$ such that g_x is isomorphic to g; a picture α is parsed by looking for an $x \in L(G)$ such that $\alpha \in P_{g_x}$. On a successful parse, the resulting $x \in L(G)$ and the sequence of grammar rules that derive x comprise a syntactic description and classification of the input graph and/or picture. The rationale for this particular model is that it offers a systematic method for picture analysis that is amenable to mechanization.

The analysis of sentences in a linear string language can be inefficient (even in the context-free case) when it cannot be determined whether a substring u which matches the right part of some rule can be reduced until substrings immediately surrounding u are first examined. The same problem exists in the graph case and is further complicated by the multi-dimensional nature of the objects described; in addition, a combinatorial explosion can occur when determining graph isomorphisms (the entire n! different matchings of two n node graphs must be tried in the worst case). Clearly, one is interested in classifying sets of graphs and pictures in terms of their underlying grammars and the complexity of the "machines" required to parse or "accept" them.

A second point concerning parsing techniques is the issue of sequential versus parallel processing. There is evidence of both types in animals. A reasonable conclusion from past experiments in picture processing in machines and animals is that recognition of all primitive objects in pictures and processing within individual primitives can be done in parallel but establishing relations among primitives and building higher level structures can best be accomplished in a primarily sequential manner. The main advantage of parallel operations is, of course, speed;* one of the chief disadvantages, even at the primitive level, is that it is difficult to use contextual information to assist in recognition. A parsing approach that combines some of the best points of both types of processing is to analyze serially but attempt several different parses (paths through the grammar) in parallel. Pfaltz (1970) argues for extending the parallel approach as far as possible through a parse and relying on sequential analysis only when the former "fails". Future experiences on parallel machines, hopefully, will resolve this controversy.

A final consideration relates to the question of "who does the dirty work"; i.e. is the classification of picture primitives, the "lexical" analysis, to be done within the parsing system or as a preprocessing phrase? The main argument for performing this recognition within the parsing is that the grammar generally contains a wealth of contextual information that can potentially be employed to simplify this task; the past and current rationale for doing this externally is that parallel operations or different grammars or *ad hoc* procedures can often be used to perform the recognition more efficiently.

The author (1970) has specified a general parsing algorithm for pictures and graphs based on PDL descriptions, built an experimental system for a subset of PDL, and applied the lattern to the analysis of digitized spark chamber photographs. The algorithm is analogous to a goal-oriented top-down linear string analyzer where a tabular or list representation of the

*This assumes that a parallel machine is available.

grammar directs the parse; instead of a single one-dimensional string pointer, we employ two graph or picture pointers—one for the tail node and one for the head node. One of the aims of this work is to simplify the primitive pattern classification tasks. During a parse, the partially completed analysis in conjunction with the concatenation operators in the grammar rules tell the system where to look and what to look for; the primitive pattern recognition part of the system is directed to look for a particular primitive satisfying given tail/head constraints. Analysis was successful and efficient (despite the back-tracking) in the spark chamber application but no systematic study of other non-trivial classes of pictures or graphs has been made.

Feder (1969) has applied plex grammars in an experimental system and analyzed pictures from classes of "houses," leaf vein patterns, and bubble chamber trajectories. In his system, a plex language representation of a picture α is first obtained by analyzing a chain-encoding (Freeman, 1961) of α in terms of a given set of chain pattern languages. The next stage then parses the resulting plex according to a given plex grammar. (The plex grammar notation was put in tabular form and extended to include both parameters associated with terminal symbols and relationship subroutines). Feder's experiments with the bubble chamber photographs are impressive and further demonstrate the potential benefits of syntax-directed picture processing; it would be interesting to see whether some of the recognition errors could be reduced if the primitive classification were done within the plex grammar parse instead of during a preceding analysis stage.

The web grammar group has recently published the results of two experiments in picture and graph parsing (Pfaltz, 1970). One dealt with graphs of two terminal series parallel networks (TTSPN's) and the other analyzed simulated pictures of neural networks. In each case, a specific parsing algorithm was devised based on the web grammar of the picture class. The parsing scheme for TTSPN's is bottom-up and takes advantage of the properties of that particular class of graphs; to determine whether a node n is part of a reducible subweb, it is only necessary to examine nodes in the immediate vicinity of n. The neural network analysis was also bottom-up. Perhaps the most interesting part of this experiment was the use of parallel recognition for both primitives and (whenever possible) the higher level syntactic components. While recognition of each component of a right part of a grammar rule cannot be done generally in parallel – Pfaltz illustrates this point even in the string case (see also Rosenfeld, 1971) – there nevertheless still exists much parallelism that can be exploited.

The above works suggest several important problems that are unsolved. Of most theoretical and practical significance is the classification problem mentioned at the end of the second paragraph of this section. Such a systematic characterization of graphs and pictures should permit one to answer related questions such as:

What is the context "surrounding" a particular subgraph or subpicture α that must be examined before it is known that α can be reduced as a unit during a parse?,

What parts of the parse for a given grammar and/or language can be done in parallel?, and

What are the machine time and space requirements to analyze a given set of pictures or graphs?

Some generalization of the string language notions of "bounded-context" or "LR(k)" (e.g. Feldman and Gries, 1968), would be useful. It is perhaps significant to note that none of this work employs any probability theory or statistics, probably because of the difficulties in formulating and using "stochastic" grammars (Fu, 1970).

V. Conclusions

The development of systematic methods for describing and analyzing structured pictures is still at an early stage. The work on picture graphs, grammars, and parsing has demonstrated that many interesting and non-trivial classes of pictures can be naturally described in terms of graph languages, and that syntax-directed analysis of pictures and graphs is feasible and promising. The purpose of this paper has been to examine some past and current work in the field and to suggest problems for future work.

REFERENCES

1. Evans, T. G. (1969). A grammar-controlled pattern analyzer. In Information Processing 68, Proc. IFIP Congr. 1968, Morell, A. J. H. (Ed.), Vol. 2, pp. 1592-1598 (North-Holland, Amsterdam, 1969).
2. Feder, J. (1969). Linguistic specification and analysis of classes of line patterns. Technical report no. 403-2, Dept. of Electrical Engineering, New York University (April).
3. Feldman, J. and Gries, D. (1968). Translator writing systems. *Comm. ACM 11,* 2 (Feb.), 77-113.
4. Freeman, H. (1961). On the encoding of arbitrary geometric configurations. *IRE Trans. Electron. Comp., EC-10,* 2 (June), 260-268.
5. Fu, K. S. and Swain, P. H. (1970). On syntactic pattern recognition. In *Software Engineering,* Academic Press, N.Y. (to be published).
6. Knuth, D. E. (1968). Semantics of context-free languages. *Math. Systems Theory 2,* 2 (June), 127-145.

7. Miller, W. F. and Shaw, A. C. (1968). A picture calculus. Proc. Conf. on Emerging Concepts in Computer Graphics, University of Illinois. W. A. Benjamin Press, New York.
8. Miller, W. F. and Shaw, A. C. (1968). Linguistic methods in picture processing–a survey. Proc. AFIPS 1968 Fall Joint Computer Conference, Vol. 33, pp. 279-290 (Thompson Books, Washington, D.C.).
9. Minsky, M. (1961). Steps Forward artificial intelligence. *Proceedings of the IRE 49,* 1 (Jan.), 8-30.
10. Montanari, U. (1969). Separable graphs, planar graphs, and web grammars. *Inform. Contr.* (May), 243-268.
11. Narasimhan, R. (1966). Syntax-directed interpretation of classes of pictures. *Comm. ACM 9,* 3 (March), 166-173.
12. Pfaltz, J. L. and Rosenfeld, A. (1969). Web grammars. Proc. Joint International Conference on Artificial Intelligence, Washington, D.C. Tech. Report 69-84, Computer Science Center, University of Maryland (Jan.).
13. Pfaltz, J. L. (1970). Web grammars and picture description. Tech. Report 70-138, Computer Science Center, University of Maryland (Sept.).
14. Rosenfeld, A. (1969). *Picture Processing by Computer.* Academic Press, New York.
15. Rosenfeld, A. (1971). Isotonic grammars, parallel grammars, and picture grammars. In *Machine Intelligence VI,* Elsevier Press.
16. Shaw, A. C. (1969a). A formal picture description scheme as a basis for picture processing systems. *Inform. Contr. 14,* 1 (Jan.), 9-52.
17. Shaw, A. C. (1969b). On the interactive generation and interpretation of artificial pictures. SLAC–PUB–664, Stanford Linear Accelerator Center, Stanford (Sept.). Presented at the 1969 ACM/SIAM/IEEE Conf. on Math. and Computer Aids to Design, Anaheim.
18. Shaw, A. C. (1970). Parsing of graph-representable pictures. *J. ACM 17,* 3 (July), 453-481.

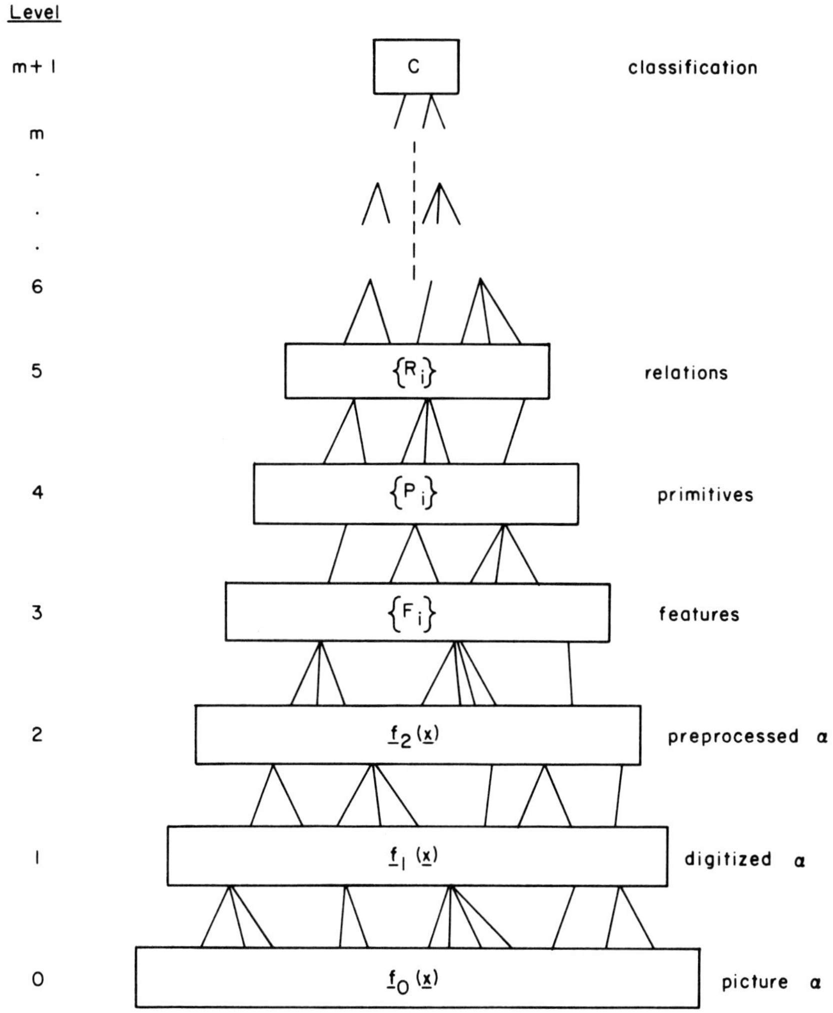

Figure 1. Levels of Picture Description

(a)

Figure 2(a). Picture of a Subscripted Variable

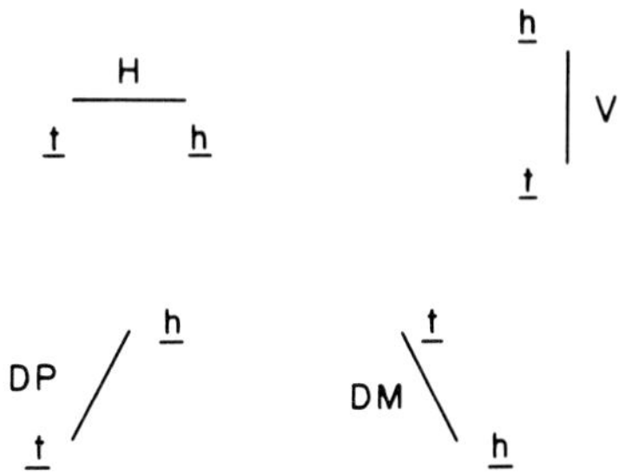

(b)

Figure 2(b). Primitive Objects

Figure 2. Simple Picture Example

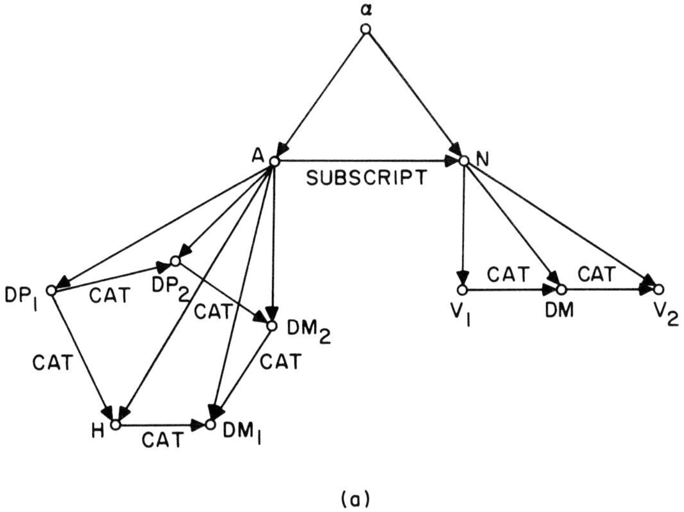

Figure 3(a). Node-Oriented Graph

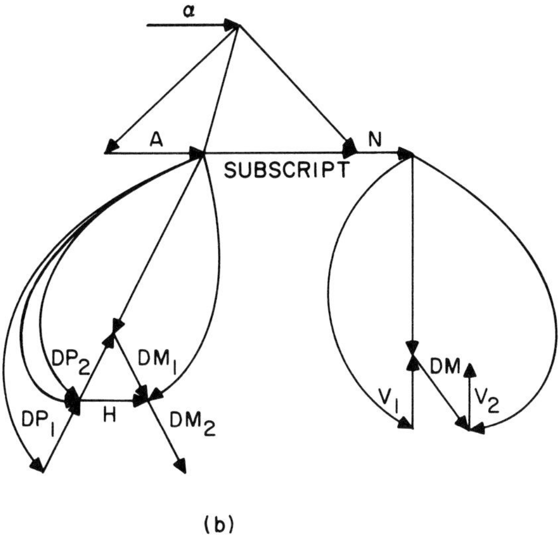

Figure 3(b). Edge-Oriented Graph

Figure 3. Graph Representations of Figure 2(a)

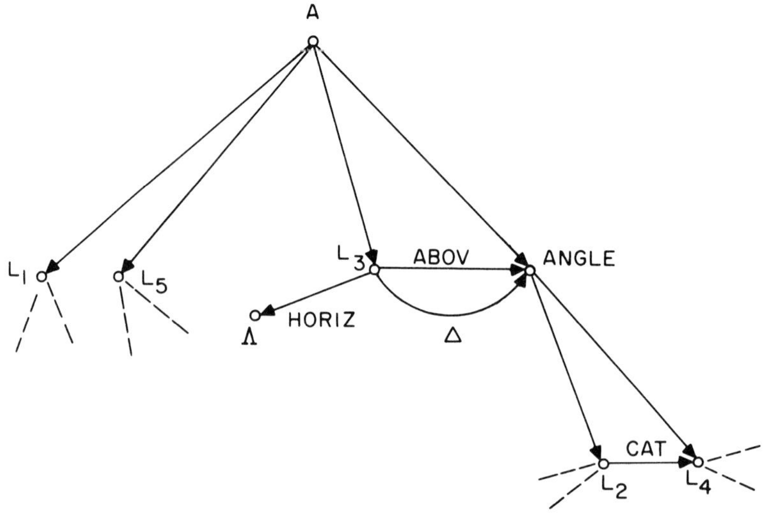

Figure 4. n-ary Relations as Binary Relations

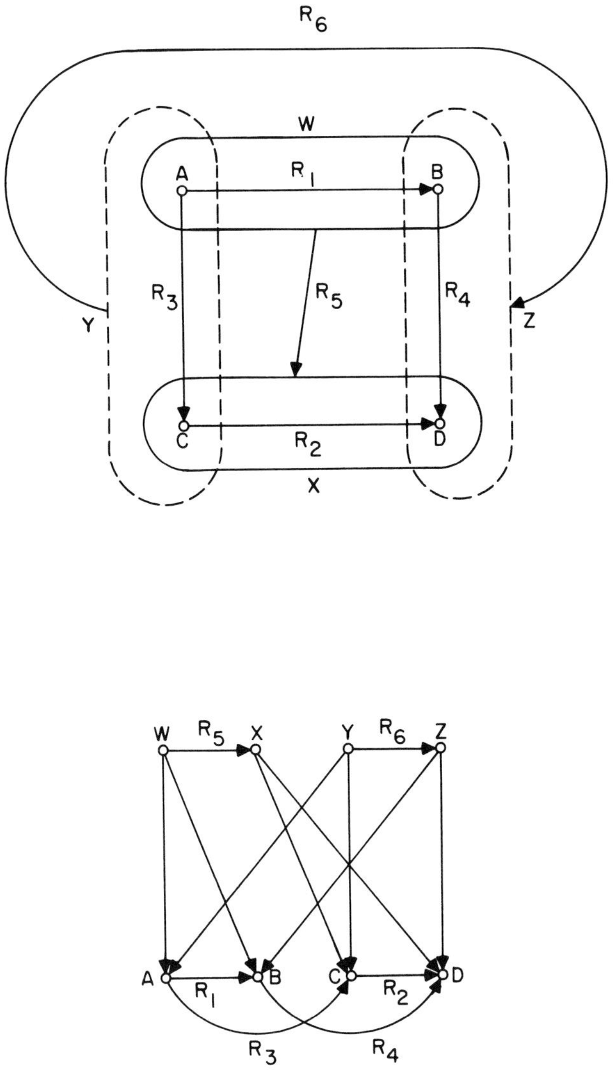

Figure 5. Example Where a Tree Hierarchy is not Possible

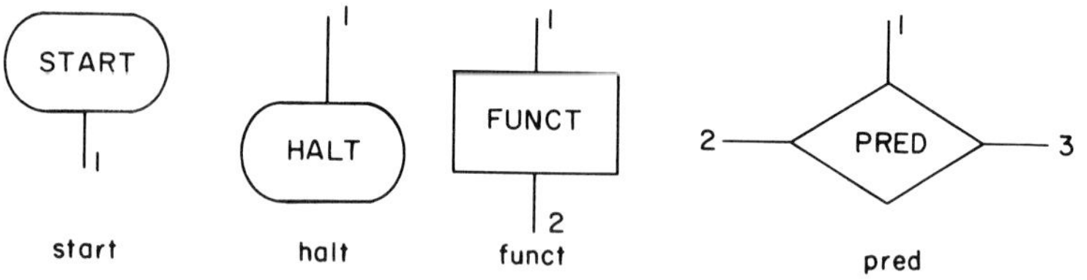

1. <PROG> → start <P> halt (110,021)

2. <P> (1,2) → funct () (1,2) | funct <P> (21) (10,02) |
pred <P> (21,12) (12,30) |
pred <P> <P> (210,301,022) (100,022)

Grammar rules

(a)

Figure 6(a). Flow Charts with Simple Nested Loops

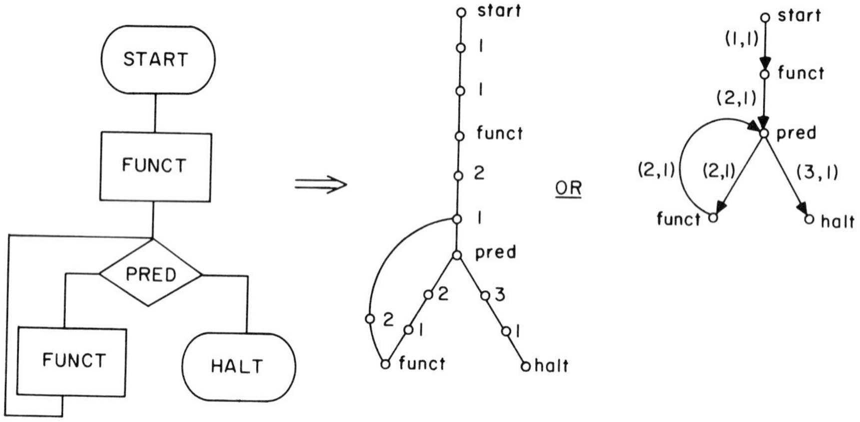

(b)

Figure 6(b). Mapping Plexes to Graphs

Figure 6. Plex Grammars (Feder, 1969) and Graphs

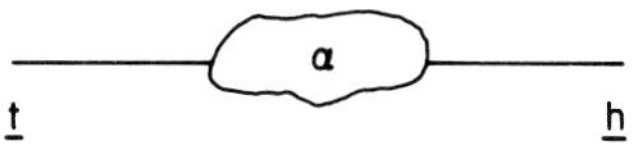

Primitive Object a

S → a | (S * S) | (S + S)

Grammar

(a)

Figure 7(a). Grammar for Series-Parallel Networks

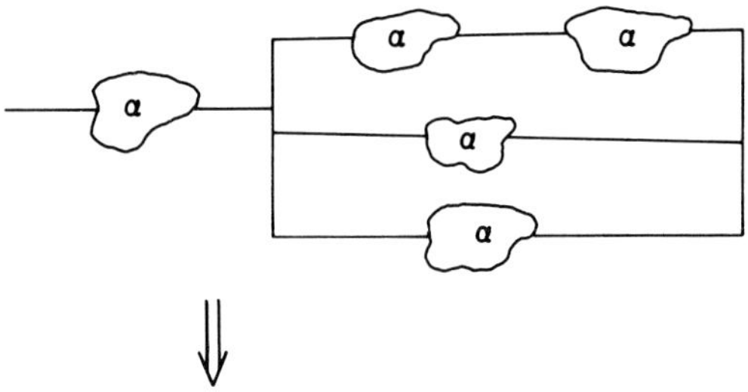

(a + (((a + a) * a) * a))   PDL description

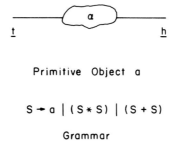

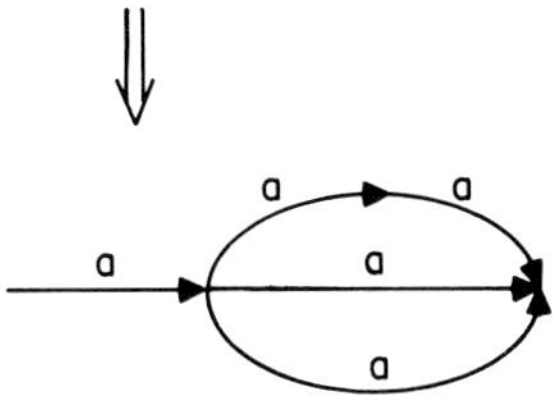

graph

(b)

Figure 7(b). Mapping Pictures to PDL to Graphs

Figure 7. PDL Grammars (Shaw, 1969a)

Initial Webs

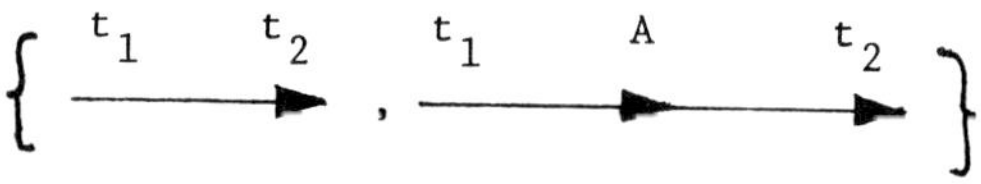

Grammar Rules:

(1) $\underset{A}{\bullet} ::= \underset{A_1}{\bullet}\!\longrightarrow\!\underset{A_2}{\bullet}$; $E = \{(p,A_1) \mid (p,A) \text{ an edge in the host web}\} \cup \{(A_2,q) \mid (A,q) \text{ an edge in the host web}\}$

(2) $\underset{A}{\bullet} ::= \begin{matrix} \bullet A \\ \bullet A \end{matrix}$ provided there exists unique p and q such that (p,A) and (A,q) in the host web;

$E = \{(p,A) \mid (p,A) \text{ an edge in the host web}\} \cup \{(A,q) \mid (A,q) \text{ an edge in the host web}\}$

(3) $\underset{A}{\bullet} ::= \underset{a}{\bullet}$; E same as in (2).

(a)

Figure 8(a). Web Grammar for TTPSN's (context-sensitive)

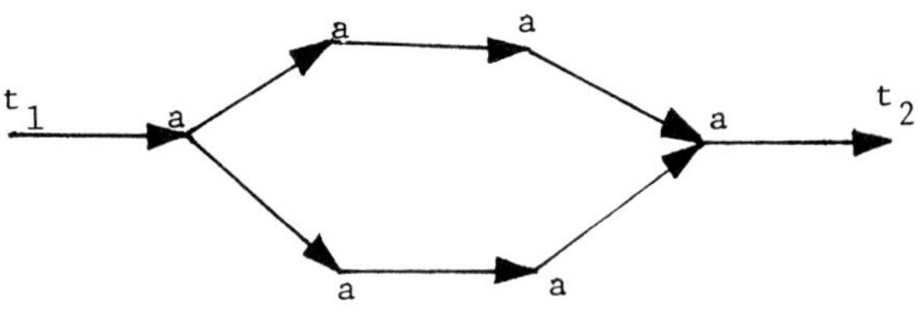

(b)

Figure 8(b). Example of a TTPSN

Figure 8. Web Grammars (Pfaltz and Rosenfeld, 1969)

SAMPLE SET CONDENSATION FOR A CONDENSED NEAREST NEIGHBOR DECISION RULE FOR PATTERN RECOGNITION

C. W. Swonger

COMPUTER RESEARCH DEPARTMENT
CORNELL AERONAUTICAL LABORATORY, INC.
BUFFALO, NEW YORK

Abstract

In this paper, an iterative algorithm for selecting a "consistent subset" (in the terminology of Hart) of samples for use in a condensed nearest-neighbor decision rule is described. This algorithm is designed to provide several practical advantages over those previously reported.

Results are presented of applying the sample set condensation algorithm to a sample set of 275 dimensional binary feature vector samples for mixed-quality mixed-font alphanumeric characters from mail addresses and other machine-imprinted material. The recognition performance experimentally obtained using the algorithm is presented and its behavior is discussed.

1. Introduction

The K-nearest neighbor decision rule of Fix and Hodges (1,2) has been examined (3,4,5,6) and reformulated and modified (7,8) in several directions. One direction is that toward the goal of increasing the rule's practical usefulness by reducing the storage requirements for reference sample points. A condensed nearest neighbor rule (CNN) was introduced by Hart (8) and, as stated therein, "no theoretical properties of the CNN rule have been established."

In this paper, an iterative algorithm for selecting a "consistent subset" (in the terminology of Hart) of samples for use in a condensed nearest-neighbor decision rule is described. This algorithm is designed to provide several practical advantages over those previously reported. The intended and empirically confirmed features of the algorithm include:

*This research was supported by internal funds of Cornell Aeronautical Laboratory, Inc.

1. The capacity to accomodate a moderate amount of "wild data" (e.g., incorrectly identified training samples) without resort to a K-nearest neighbor rule, the latter being more costly of both memory and computing time.
2. The capability to delete (as well as acquire) points from the condensed subset toward the end of obtaining a more nearly minimum consistent set.
3. The capacity to tolerate inseparable situations where two or more identical samples are encountered having different identified classes.
4. Convergence characteristics which permit termination of subset acquisition prior to achieving a perfectly consistent subset in order to affect desirable cost-performance trade-offs.

2. Characterization of the Pattern Recognition Problem

For the purposes of the following development, the pattern recognition problem is considered as follows: A design or training set of m sample patterns [X] is given. Each sample pattern X_i is in the form of a vector in an n-dimensional space. That is $X_i = (X_{i_1}, X_{i_2}, \ldots, X_{ij}, \ldots, X_{in}), (1 \leq i \leq m)$. For each design vector X_i, a defined correct classification C_i is given, where C_i is a positive integer in the interval $1,2,3, \ldots, t \ldots T-1, T$ and T is the number of defined existing classes. Similarly, an indefinite number of patterns [Y] exist for which no defined class is available.

A set [R] of K reference vectors $R_l (1 \leq l \leq K)$ is made available to the pattern classifier (through application of a design process such as that to be described below). With each R_l is associated a defined correct class $B_l (1 \leq B_l \leq T)$ (this class also being obtained through the design process).

The components X_{ij}, R_{lj} of the vectors X_i and R_l are scalars presumably representing measurements or features derived from some source for each of the corresponding sample patterns. For the purposes of any specific practical application, the scalar components X_{ij}, R_{lj} may be restricted to some set of permissible values, such as all real numbers or the binary values 0 and 1.

The condensed nearest neighbor decision rule performs pattern classification by assigning each pattern Y_i to the class B_l of that reference vector R_l in the set [R] which is nearest to Y_i in the sense of some defined positive scalar distance measure $d_{B_l}(Y_i, R_l)$ which is computable for all possible Y_i, R_l and B_l. The distance measure may be unique for each of the possible T classes of reference vectors. For example $d_{B_l}(Y_i, R_l)(1 \leq B_l \leq T)$)may be a function of only a subset $[h]$ of the n components of Y_i, R_l. That is, nearness to reference vectors of each particular class t may be measured in a subspace S_t of the entire available vector space. In order that distances so measured may be comparable, it is necessary that the range of all distance measures $d_{B_l}(1 \leq B_l \leq T)$ be identical. It is hereafter assumed that this range is $O \leq d_{B_l} \leq Pn$ for all d_{B_l}, Y_i and R_l where P is any real positive constant.

Optionally, the pattern classifier discussed here may assign a pattern to a "reject" class for any specified set of values of the measured distar.ces to all the references points [R].

3. The Design Problem

The design of a particular pattern classifier which will apply the condensed nearest neighbor type rule* to unknown pattern vectors is considered to consist of selecting a subset of the design set sample vectors [X] for use as the reference vector set [R]. That is $m \geq K$ in the above notation. Correspondingly, the defined classes C_i of the selected subset of [X] are used for the corresponding defined classes of the set [R].

The objectives of each specific design are assumed to include:

a. Minimization of the number K of reference vectors R_l.
b. Minimization of the number of vectors X_i (or Y_i) misclassified using the classifier, the reference vectors [R] and the corresponding defined correct classes.

It is further assumed that the given design sample vector set [X] and corresponding defined classes may be distributed in any manner through the range of the vector space and defined existing classes and may include some erroneous vectors and defined classifications (or "noisy data"). A corollary objective of the design is therefore to accommodate multimodal and sparse distributions of the set [X] over the vector space.

4. The Iterative Condensation Algorithm (ICA)

The algorithm described below was designed to avoid compilation of statistical data about the distribution of samples in the feature vector space and to iteratively construct a reference sample vector set [R] during repeated passes through the design sample set [X]. Further, consideration has

*It is noted here that Hart (8) uses the term "condensed nearest neighbor rule" or "CNN rule" to describe both a classifier structure and a condensation algorithm for selecting the particular design parameters for any application of that structure. This paper describes a different condensation algorithm for particularizing designs of the same form of classifier. This author believes the term "condensed nearest neighbor classifier (or rule" properly applies to the classifier structure and not to the process for selecting its design parameters.

been limited to strict selection of vectors specifically occurring in [X] without permitting derivation of other vectors (such as by interpolation, statistical computations, etc.) which may or may not be included in the population of possible patterns [Y]. From pass to pass, the size or precise composition of the design set [X] need not be fixed, though if its distribution varies rapidly, difficulty in convergence will be encountered.

The general logic flow of the iterative condensation algorithm is illustrated in simplified terms in Figure 1. During each major iteration the design set [X] is sequentially processed using the classifier operating upon a current interim reference vector set $[\hat{R}]$ and each X_i is classified, correctly or otherwise.* For the purposes of the design algorithm, the following information is also concurrently computed *for each of the* X_i:

a. $D_{min} = \underset{l}{\text{Minimum}} \left[d_{B_l}(X_i, \hat{R}_l) \right]$

b. l_{mn} = Index number of first $\hat{R}_l$ in the interim set $[\hat{R}]$ such that $d_{B_l}(X_i, \hat{R}_l) = d_{min}$

c. $D_2 = \underset{(\hat{R}_l \neq \hat{R}_{l_{min}})}{\text{Minimum}} \left[d_{B_l}(X_i, \hat{R}_l) \right]$

d. l_2 = Index number of first $\hat{R}_l$ in the interim set $[\hat{R}]$ but excluding $\hat{R}_{l_{min}}$ such that $d_l(X_i, \hat{R}_l) = d_2$

e. $D_a = \underset{\hat{R}_l \text{ such that } B_l = c_i}{\text{Minimum}} \left[d_{B_l}(X_i, \hat{R}_l) \right]$

f. $D_b = \underset{\hat{R}_l \text{ such that } B_l \neq c_i}{\text{Minimum}} \left[d_{B_l}(X_i, \hat{R}_l) \right]$

Thus the distance, the specific reference vectors (and the corresponding classes $B_{l_{min}}$ and B_{l_2}), of the *two* nearest vectors to each X_i are successively obtained** for the interim reference set $[\hat{R}]$. The distance from X_i to the nearest reference vector of class c_i and of all other classes combined is also obtained.

*A *starting* set of reference vectors is required to initiate operation of the algorithm. Discussion of the alternative choices for such a starter set is not the main point of this paper, but almost any set having at least one reference vector for every existing class will suffice. The most frequently occurring vector for each class has been used experimentally by the author.

**In the event of ambiguities or tie situations among reference vectors of different classes, the "incorrect" classes and vectors are treated as closest to promote further improvement of the design by the algorithm

In addition, the *Margin of Misclassification* F_i, is defined and computed as:

$$F_i = D_a - D_b$$

which is negative for incorrectly classified vectors and positive for correctly classified vectors. Finally, the *predominant reference vector* R_{p_i} with index p_i is defined. Unless *both* of the *two* nearest reference vectors are in the class c_i of the vector X_i, the nearest vector is designated as predominant. If $l_{min} = l_2 = c_i$ then the *joint* predominance of $\hat{R}_l$ and $\hat{R}_{l_{min}}$ is recorded for later resolution.

From these quantities, during each pass through the design set [X], the *one* sample vector *from each class* t is noted and recorded (along with its defined class) for which F_i is maximum. At the end of each pass then, the "most misclassified" sample of each class in [X] is known. In addition, during each pass, each reference vector $\hat{R}_l$ in the interim set $[\hat{R}]$ is designated as the predominant reference point for G_{a_l} samples of class B_l and for G_{b_l} samples of other classes. At the end of each pass, this compiled information and the number of errors in classification for each class are used in a two-phase process by which some reference vectors in $[\hat{R}]$ are discarded and some new references vectors are added to $[\hat{R}]$. This two-phase process will now be described.

A. DISCARDING OF REFERENCE VECTORS

Reference vectors are generally discarded at the end of each pass during the design process when they are not necessary for the correct classification of any samples in the set [X]. Further, as a last step in the design process, vectors may be discarded which appear to cause more misclassifications than correct classifications. The previously discussed compilation of values G_{a_l} and G_{b_l} for each reference vector $\hat{R}_l$ provides the basis for such discarding. However, prior to discarding reference vectors, the joint predominance of certain pairs of reference vectors referred to above is resolved. The objective of this process is to detect redundant reference vectors, either one of which alone would suffice to correctly "cover" the vectors in [X] over which they currently predominate. This type of process appears vital for the evolution of a near-minimum reference vector set.

Each pair of reference vectors $(R_{l_{min}}, R_{l_2})$ which have been recorded as jointly predominant for one or more design samples X_i are examined along with their individual predominance data $G_{a_{l_{min}}}$ and $G_{a_{l_2}}$. If $G_{a_{l_{min}}}$ or $G_{a_{l_2}}$ is zero, then the corresponding vector $\hat{R}_{l_{min}}$ or R_{l_2} is not needed for the correct classification of any design sample *as long as* the other vector in the pair is retained. But if both $G_{a_{l_{min}}}$ and $G_{a_{l_2}}$ are non-zero, then they are not completely redundant in that sense. Therefore if $G_{a_{l_{min}}}$ or $G_{a_{l_2}}$ is zero, the algorithm discards the corresponding vector and credits the other retained reference vector of the pair with all the joint predominances of the pair (adds them to G_a for the retained vector). If both $G_{a_{l_{min}}}$ and $G_{a_{l_2}}$ are non-zero the joint predominance which occurred are each credited to the nearest vector of the pair and both are retained.

Following resolution of possible reference vector pair redundancy, all reference vectors $\hat{R}_l$ for which $G_{a_l} = 0$ are discarded. On the last design iteration vectors may also be discarded under the more likely condition that $G_{a_l} \leq G_{b_l}$.

B. ACQUISITION OF ADDITIONAL REFERENCE VECTORS

Having discarded unnecessary vectors, new vectors are added to the set $[\hat{R}]$ toward the end of reducing the number of classification errors. For each class in which any errors occurred, the Iterative Condensation Algorithm selects the one vector (previously recorded) for which the margin of misclassifications F_i was maximum. Use of these new vectors will correct some misclassifications and perhaps cause some new misclassifications. However it should be intuitively obvious that for any case which is separable (by any realizable operation on the feature vectors whatsoever) a sufficient reference set will eventually be acquired.

5. Accommodation of Inseparable Cases

The Iterative Condensation Algorithm adds reference vectors as needed to reduce errors for as many iterations as it is operated or until perfect classification of the set [X] is achieved. If, however, the design set [X] contains two sample vectors which are identical but which have different defined correct classes, the algorithm in its most simple form would eventually acquire both samples as reference vectors. However, to accommodate such situations the algorithm detects the occurrence of identical vectors of different classes as it passes over the design sample set and constructs a table of such vectors. All vectors which are candidates for acquisition are then screened against this table and rejected as reference vectors if they have been noted as conflict vectors in this sense. Clearly a reasonable alternative policy (which the author has not yet experimentally evaluated) would be to assign each such vector to the class having maximum empirical conditional probability.

6. Implementation of the Algorithm

The Iterative Condensation Algorithm for a condensed nearest neighbor classifier has been implemented on the IBM 360/65 computer facility at Cornell Aeronautical Laboratory, Inc. The generality of the implementation is that of the problem characterized in Section 2 of this paper with the qualification that the vector storage data formats and distance measurement subroutines are modified when desired as a recompilation operation to provide maximum computing speed for specific choices of vector precision and distance measures. The algorithm has been applied to binary vectors of up to 275-dimensions and design sets of up to approximately 10,000 samples. The algorithm requires approximately 131,000 bytes of storage including storage for 400 reference vectors, ancillary vector lists, and all peripheral library routines. Computing time of the algorithm is a function of the vector dimensionality, design sample set size and problem complexity as it affects the number of reference vectors required. The required processing is approximately 45 seconds for one complete pass over 900 275-dimensional design samples with 90 275-dimensional reference vectors on the above facility.

7. Experimental Evaluations

The Iterative Condensation Algorithm (ICA) has been applied to a problem in mixed font mixed quality alphanumeric character recognition. An 8-class problem called for discrimination of L, I, i, 2, Z, E, B, 3 was selected as the subject of investigation.

275-dimensional vectors of features selected using an algorithm employing an information content criterion (Reference 9) were employed as inputs to a condensed nearest neighbor classifier. For each class, the classifier used the Hamming distance in a subspace of the 275-dimension complete vector space as shown in Table 1, the subspaces varying from 150 to 225 dimensions. A growing design sample set was employed which reached a size of 867 samples. A separate set of 9,785 sample vectors was used to test the resulting classifier after completion of the design process.

Table 2 illustrates the results of one of these experiments. Samples of about every 5th design iteration are shown. Note that the number of samples is growing. The distance units are normalized to a range of 0 to 1,800. The results of testing the condensed nearest neighbor classifier after design is shown in Table 3.

The algorithm described here is not a mode-seeking algorithm. Instead, it tends to acquire and retain reference vectors which are near to the appropriate decision boundaries between the various class distributions. Figure 2 illustrates the distinction between this type of operation and mode seeking.

Generally, as illustrated by Table 1, the algorithm as now implemented is characterized by slow convergence (since only one reference vector may be added per class per design pass) though obvious modifications are possible to speed up that convergence. It can also be seen that convergence of the algorithm is not necessarily monotonic–in fact, monotonic convergence will almost certainly not occur unless highly separated distributions exist in the feature space. As new reference vectors are added corresponding to the "most misclassified" vectors of each class, the most nearby sample vectors of other classes will likely become misclassified–until reference points have been located by a sequence of passes such that a satisfactory decision boundary is fit between the "front lines" of the several class distributions defined.

The treatment of the occasional spurious or "wild" data vector (which occurs in almost all significant real problems) is of interest. The iterative condensation algorithm does not incorporate any attempt to arbitrarily categorize an isolated reference vector, though it may be located well within the main distribution of another class, as spurious. It instead builds, with one new reference vector per class per pass, a collection of reference points of that distribution, which partially or completely surround the (possibly) spurious vector in the hyperspace as necessary to achieve the *defined* correct classification. If, however, the design process is terminated arbitrarily prior to achieving complete convergence, any insufficiently-surrounded isolated vectors are discarded.

The test results of Table 2 show a moderately high level of recognition given the extent of features employed on this alphanumeric character data base. The total memory implied by the 87 stored subspace reference vectors of the designed classifier is 588 32-bit words. Based upon other experiments with this data, it is known that the errors experienced are largely due to the use of only 867 samples of the 9578-character design base in which script and other unusual fonts occur late in the design and test sets.

8. Conclusions

The Iterative Condensation Algorithm described above appears to provide an effective means for the design of condensed nearest neighbor classifiers using an iterative approach which is non-parametric and economical of computer memory. The algorithm condenses a design sample set of vectors into a suitable reference vector set by a process of selection only. Further work is planned on improvements to processing speed and convergence acceleration.

9. Acknowledgements

The author wishes to thank Dr. F. P. Fischer II for his valuable ideas and technical assistance in the investigation of the algorithm described herein.

REFERENCES

1. E. Fix and U. L. Hodges, Jr., "Discriminatory Analysis, Nonparametric Discrimination, Consistency Properties," Project No. 21-49-004, Report No. 4, Contract No. AF41(128)-31. USAF School of Aviation Medicine.
2. E. Fix and J. L. Hodges, Jr., "Discriminatory Analysis: Small Sample Performance," Project No. 21-49-004, Report No. 11, USAF School of Aviation Medicine, Randolph Field, Texas, August 1952.
3. G. Sebestyen, "Decision-making Processes in Pattern Recognition," The Macmillan Company, New York, 1962.
4. Nils, J. Nilsson, "Learning Machines," McGraw-Hill Series in Systems Science, 1965.
5. T. M. Cover and P. E. Hart, "Nearest Neighbor Pattern Classification," IEEE Transactions on Information Theory, Vol. IT-13, No. 1, January 1967.
6. T. M. Cover, "Estimation by the Nearest Neighbor Rule," IEEE Transactions on Information Theory, Vol. IT-14, No. 1, January 1968.
7. E. A. Patrick and F. P. Fischer II, "Introduction to the Performance of Distribution Free, Minimum Conditional Risk Learning Systems," Purdue University, Naval Ship Systems Command Contract N00024-67-C-1162, TR-EE 67-12, July 1967.
8. P. E. Hart, "The Condensed Nearest Neighbor Rule," IEEE Transactions on Information Theory, Vol. IT-14, No. 3, May 1968.
9. C. W. Swonger, "Property Learning in Pattern Recognition Systems Using Information Content Measurements," Presented at the IEEE Pattern Recognition Workshop, Las Croabas, Puerto Rico, 24-26 October 1966.

Table 1
ITERATIVE CONDENSATION ALGORITHM EXAMPLE RESULTS

TRAINING RESULTS

CYCLE NO.	CLASS NO.	NO.OF REF.PTS	MAX. MRGN	MAX. D	ERRORS NUMBER	ERRORS PERCENT	NO. OF REF. PTS. ELIMD	NO. OF REF. PTS. ADDD	NO. OF REF. PTS. LEFT
1	1	1	-68	588	0	0.000	0	0	1
	2	1	86	558	1	6.667	0	1	2
	3	1	-225	288	0	0.000	0	0	1
	4	1	120	656	1	5.556	0	1	2
	5	1	232	536	2	33.333	0	1	2
	6	1	257	640	2	11.111	0	1	2
	7	1	400	640	1	8.333	0	1	2
	8	1	96	488	4	28.571	0	1	2

NUMBER OF PATTERNS CLASSIFIED 100
TOTAL NUMBER OF ERRORS 11
TOTAL NUMBER OF REJECTS 0

TRAINING RESULTS

CYCLE NO.	CLASS NO.	NO.OF REF.PTS	MAX. MRGN	MAX. D	ERRORS NUMBER	ERRORS PERCENT	NO. OF REF. PTS. ELIMD	NO. OF REF. PTS. ADDD	NO. OF REF. PTS. LEFT
5	1	1	-225	456	0	0.000	0	0	1
	2	3	-27	369	0	0.000	0	0	3
	3	1	261	432	2	40.000	0	1	2
	4	4	-80	312	0	0.000	0	0	4
	5	4	160	392	5	29.412	0	1	5
	6	4	48	320	11	28.205	0	1	5
	7	4	-24	216	0	0.000	0	0	4
	8	2	24	392	1	2.857	0	1	3

NUMBER OF PATTERNS CLASSIFIED 243
TOTAL NUMBER OF ERRORS 19
TOTAL NUMBER OF REJECTS 6

TRAINING RESULTS

CYCLE NO.	CLASS NO.	NO.OF REF.PTS	MAX. MRGN	MAX. D	ERRORS NUMBER	ERRORS PERCENT	NO. OF REF. PTS. ELIMD	NO. OF REF. PTS. ADDD	NO. OF REF. PTS. LEFT
10	1	1	0	504	0	0.000	0	1	2
	2	4	141	504	22	18.333	0	1	5
	3	2	99	315	2	12.500	0	1	3
	4	5	88	392	3	2.439	0	1	6
	5	9	88	392	4	7.843	2	1	8
	6	8	280	504	28	23.529	0	1	9
	7	6	64	336	6	6.897	0	1	7
	8	6	176	320	8	7.339	0	1	7

NUMBER OF PATTERNS CLASSIFIED 737
TOTAL NUMBER OF ERRORS 73
TOTAL NUMBER OF REJECTS 22

Table 1 (Continued)
ITERATIVE CONDENSATION ALGORITHM EXAMPLE RESULTS

TRAINING RESULTS

CYCLE NO.	CLASS NO.	NO.OF REF.PTS	MAX. MRGN	MAX. D	ERRORS NUMBER	ERRORS PERCENT	NO. OF REF. PTS. ELIMD	ADDD	LEFT
15	1	2	-69	504	0	0.000	0	0	2
	2	6	-18	441	0	0.000	0	0	6
	3	7	-27	261	0	0.000	0	0	7
	4	10	32	392	5	3.472	0	1	11
	5	12	0	368	0	0.000	0	1	13
	6	13	64	440	27	19.286	0	1	14
	7	10	8	264	2	1.961	1	1	10
	8	11	32	280	5	3.817	0	1	12

NUMBER OF PATTERNS CLASSIFIED 867
TOTAL NUMBER OF ERRORS 39
TOTAL NUMBER OF REJECTS 18

TRAINING RESULTS

CYCLE NO.	CLASS NO.	NO.OF REF.PTS	MAX. MRGN	MAX. D	ERRORS NUMBER	ERRORS PERCENT	NO. OF REF. PTS. ELIMD	ADDD	LEFT
20	1	2	-69	504	0	0.000	0	0	2
	2	6	-18	441	0	0.000	0	0	6
	3	7	-27	261	0	0.000	0	0	7
	4	15	8	392	1	0.694	0	1	16
	5	13	56	368	1	1.639	0	1	14
	6	16	16	440	9	6.429	0	1	17
	7	11	32	264	1	0.980	0	1	12
	8	10	8	328	1	0.763	0	1	11

NUMBER OF PATTERNS CLASSIFIED 867
TOTAL NUMBER OF ERRORS 13
TOTAL NUMBER OF REJECTS 10

TRAINING RESULTS

CYCLE NO.	CLASS NO.	NO.OF REF.PTS	MAX. MRGN	MAX. D	ERRORS NUMBER	ERRORS PERCENT	NO. OF REF. PTS. ELIMD	ADDD	LEFT
25	1	2	-69	504	0	0.000	0	0	2
	2	6	-18	441	0	0.000	0	0	6
	3	7	-27	261	0	0.000	0	0	7
	4	16	-8	392	0	0.000	0	0	16
	5	14	-8	368	0	0.000	0	0	14
	6	20	0	384	0	0.000	0	1	21
	7	12	-8	264	0	0.000	0	0	12
	8	11	-16	328	0	0.000	0	0	11

NUMBER OF PATTERNS CLASSIFIED 867
TOTAL NUMBER OF ERRORS 0
TOTAL NUMBER OF REJECTS 3

Table 1 (Continued)

ITERATIVE CONDENSATION ALGORITHM EXAMPLE RESULTS

TRAINING RESULTS

CYCLE	CLASS	NO.OF	MAX.	MAX.	ERRORS		NO. OF REF. PTS.		
NO.	NO.	REF.PTS	MRGN	D	NUMBER	PERCENT	ELIMD	ADDD	LEFT
27	1	2	-69	504	0	0.000	0	0	2
	2	6	-18	441	0	0.000	0	0	6
	3	7	-27	261	0	0.000	0	0	7
	4	16	-8	392	0	0.000	0	0	16
	5	14	-8	368	0	0.000	0	0	14
	6	20	-8	384	0	0.000	1	0	19
	7	12	-8	264	0	0.000	0	0	12
	8	11	-16	328	0	0.000	0	0	11

NUMBER OF PATTERNS CLASSIFIED 867
TOTAL NUMBER OF ERRORS 0
TOTAL NUMBER OF REJECTS 0

Table 2
EXAMPLE TEST RESULTS FOR CONDENSED NEAREST NEIGHBOR CLASSIFIER USING ITERATIVE CONDENSATION ALGORITHM

CONFUSION MATRIX

		CLASSIFIED AS								
		UL	UI	LI	N2	UZ	UE	UB	N3	RJ
	UL	1361	5	12	0	0	3	0	0	0
	UI	18	1583	17	0	0	1	0	0	6
	LI	11	27	171	0	0	0	0	3	2
TRUE CLASS	N2	0	0	0	1457	78	8	16	2	20
	UZ	2	3	0	38	617	1	1	2	17
	UE	6	6	0	25	28	1483	71	4	21
	UB	0	0	0	24	0	25	1070	18	9
	N3	0	9	2	18	6	3	14	1448	13

CONFUSION MATRIX

		CLASSIFIED AS								
		UL	UI	LI	N2	UZ	UE	UB	N3	RJ
	UL	98.6	0.4	0.9	0.0	0.0	0.2	0.0	0.0	0.0
	UI	1.1	97.4	1.0	0.0	0.0	0.1	0.0	0.0	0.4
	LI	5.1	12.6	79.9	0.0	0.0	0.0	0.0	1.4	0.9
TRUE CLASS	N2	0.0	0.0	0.0	92.2	4.9	0.5	1.0	0.1	1.3
	UZ	0.3	0.4	0.0	5.6	90.6	0.1	0.1	0.3	2.5
	UE	0.4	0.4	0.0	1.5	1.7	90.2	4.3	0.2	1.3
	UB	0.0	0.0	0.0	2.1	0.0	2.2	93.4	1.6	0.8
	N3	0.0	0.6	0.1	1.2	0.4	0.2	0.9	95.7	0.9

NUMBER OF PATTERNS	=	9785		
NUMBER OF REJECTS	=	88	=	0.90 %
NUMBER OF CORRECTLY CLASSIFIED PATTERNS	=	9190	=	93.92 %
NUMBER OF UNDETECTED ERRORS	=	507	=	5.23 %

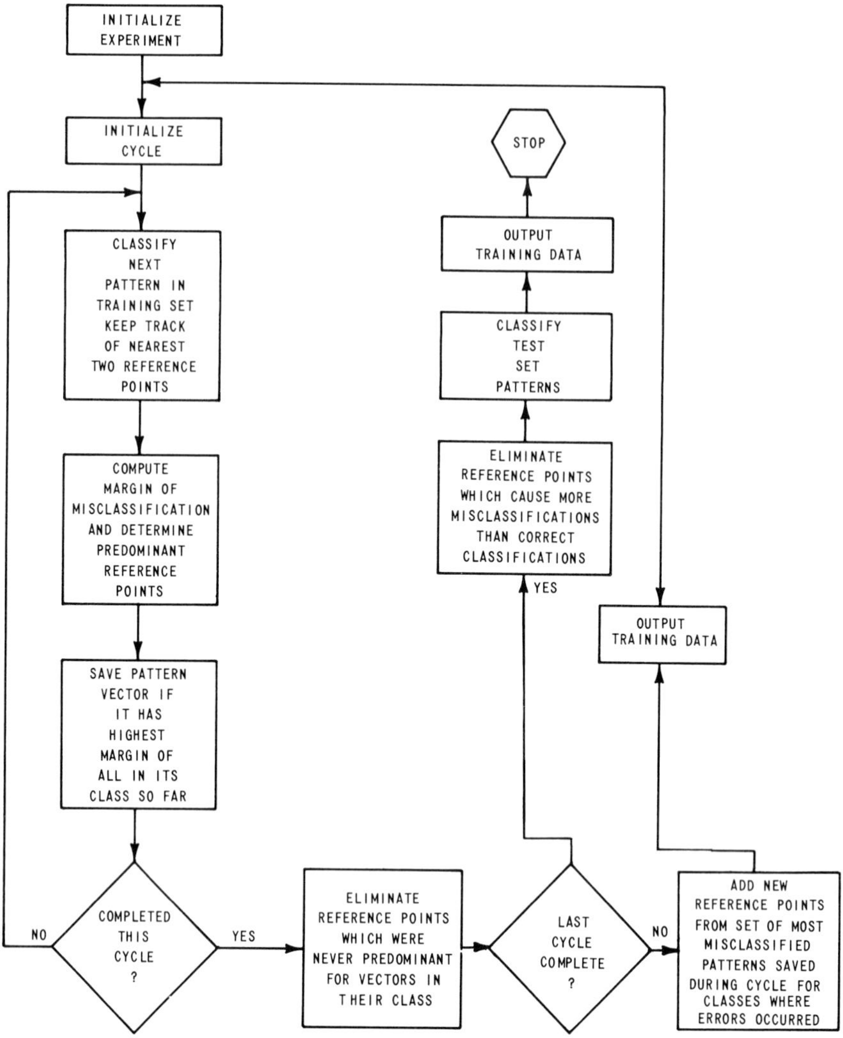

Figure 1. Simplified Flow of Iterative Condensation Algorithm

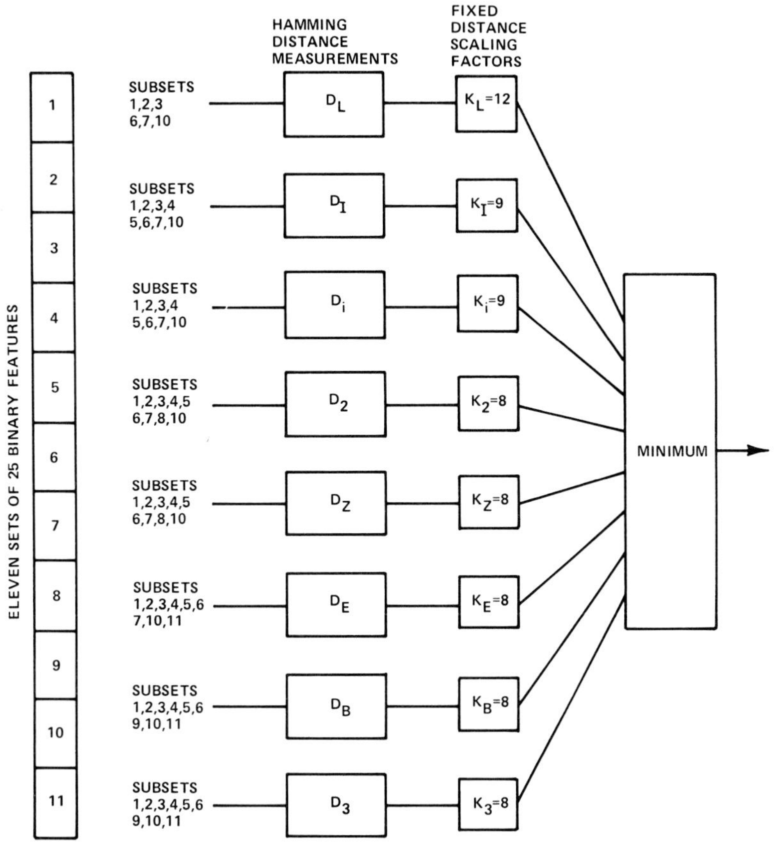

Figure 2. Condensed Nearest Neighbor Classifier Structure Used in Experiments

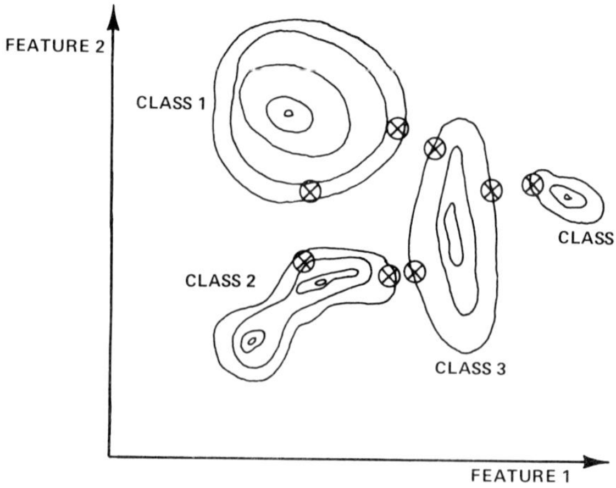

a) ITERATIVE CONDENSATION ALGORITHM

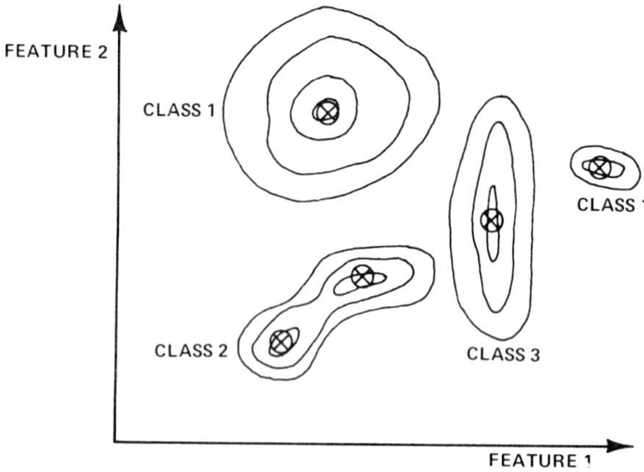

b) TYPICAL MODE SEEKING ALGORITHM

Figure 3. Alternative Condensed Nearest Neighbor Condensation Results

LEARNING ALGORITHMS OF PATTERN RECOGNITION IN NON-STATIONARY CONDITIONS

Ya. Z. Tsypkin
INSTITUTE OF CONTROL SCIENCE
PROFSOIUZNAYA 81
MOSCOW, U.S.S.R.

Introduction

Many papers are devoted to the problem of learning in pattern recognition under stationary conditions. A rather complete outline of these papers is contained in [1-3]. Essentially, the solution of the problems of learning in pattern recognition under stationary conditions lies in real, iterative algorithms, coinciding in their basis with stochastic approximation type algorithms [4,5].

Together with these considerations there often arise problems in which it is necessary to achieve recognition learning under non-stationary conditions. In such cases objects which are to be recognized change with time and of course, the usual iterative algorithms, discussed above, become inapplicable.

The number of papers dealing with pattern recognition learning under non-stationary conditions is not great. These include papers about the basis of the dynamic stochastic approximation method [6], its development [7,8], and some applications [9-11]. A few other approaches to parameter evaluation under non-stationary conditions are discussed in [12].

In all these papers learning algorithms are presented on the basis of heuristic understanding, and then their convergence is shown. The general approach, permitting one to obtain various learning algorithms, and to establish the relation between them, was presented in [13]. This general approach is a development of the adaptive approach for learning under non-stationary conditions, presented in [3,4] for learning under stationary conditions.

At this stage the question of recognition under non-stationary conditions is formulated and its solution is found at different stages of information, that is, at different stages of completeness of a priori information. This solution is obtained by considering learning algorithms on the basis of the general approach to learning under non-stationary conditions [13].

I. Background of the Problem

Let us consider randomly occurring patterns characterized by the vectors $\underline{x} = (x_1, \ldots, x_M)$, which belong to one of the unknown classes $\underline{\bar{X}}_k^0$ $(k=1, \ldots, k)$ of the space of patterns $\underline{\bar{X}}$.

The question of pattern recognition is reduced to the question of the best partitioning of the space $\underline{\bar{X}}$ in the region $\underline{\bar{X}}_k$ $(k=1, \ldots, K)$, according to which we can judge the affiliation of the pattern x to this or another class $\underline{\bar{X}}_k^0$ $(k=1, \ldots K)$. Without loss of generality we can consider the number of classes to be two $(K=2)$.

For a more precise definition of the concept of best partition we will define losses, which occur when a pattern $\underline{x}$ of class $\underline{\bar{X}}_k^0$ is associated with class $\underline{\bar{X}}_m^0$ $(k, m=1,2)$, or, in other words, when a pattern of class $\underline{\bar{X}}_k^0$ falls in the region of $\underline{\bar{X}}_m$ $(k, m=1,2)$.

Let us introduce the loss functions

$$F_{km}(\underline{x}, \underline{\vec{c}}, t) \qquad\qquad k, m=1,2 \qquad (1.1)$$

Here $\underline{\vec{c}} = (\underline{c}_1, \underline{c}_2)$ is the composite vector of the parameters. The loss functions (1.1) differ from those usually used in the theory of statistical decisions [12] in that they are assigned specifically to the composite vector of parameters and not according to the number of previously known classes and decisions but to the number of observed patterns. Besides this, the loss functions depend on the time t, in the general case.

We will define by $p(\underline{x}, t/k) = p_k(\underline{x}, t)$ and $P_k(t)$ $(k=1,2)$ the conditional density of the distribution and the a priori probability characterizing the patterns $\underline{x}$. Then the quality of recognition of the pattern $\underline{x}$ can be evaluated with average risk

$$R(t) = \int_{X_1} F_{11}(\underline{x},\underline{\vec{c}},t)P_1(t)p_1(\underline{x},t)d\underline{x} + \int_{X_1} F_{21}(\underline{x},\underline{\vec{c}},t)P_2(t)p_2(\underline{x},t)d\underline{x} + \int_{X_2} F_{12}(\underline{x},\underline{\vec{c}},t)P_1(t)p_1(\underline{x},t)dx + \int_{X_2} F_{22}(\underline{x},\underline{\vec{c}},t)P_2(t)p_2(\underline{x},t)dx \qquad (1.2)$$

The decision rule can be found from the conditions of minimum average risk. Simultaneously with the decision rule, the optimal values of the parameter vector are obtained

$$\underline{\vec{c}}(t) = \underline{\vec{c}}^*(t) \qquad (1.3)$$

which, in the non-stationary case being considered, are functions of time.

The method of obtaining the decision rule and $\underline{c}(t)$ depends on the degree of completeness of the a priori information. If $P_k(t)$ and $p_k(\underline{x},t)$ $(k=1,2)$ are known previously, then it is possible, at least, to essentially calculate the average risk $R(t)$ and then to define the decision rule, minimizing this average risk. If, however, $P_k(t)$ and $p_k(\underline{x}, t)$ are not known previously, then the preliminary calculation $R(t)$ is not possible. Precisely in this case it is necessary to allow learning according to the observed patterns $\underline{x}$ and to define the decision rule by the loss functions $F_{km}(\underline{x}, \vec{\underline{c}}, t)$. This possibility is realized by learning algorithms which, after a period of learning, define a decision rule. Thus, the problem of pattern recognition learning resolves itself into the establishment of learning algorithms.

II. The Decision Rule

The conditions which define a decision rule are the conditions of the minimum average risk (1.2).

We will assume that $\vec{\underline{c}}(t)$ can be written in the form

$$\vec{\underline{c}}(t) = \Psi(t)\underline{\alpha} \tag{2.1}$$

where $\underline{\alpha} = (\alpha_1, \ldots, \alpha_N)$ is an unknown parameter vector and

$$\Psi(t) = \| \psi_{\mu\nu}(t) \| \qquad \begin{matrix} \mu = 1, \ldots, M \\ \nu = 1, \ldots, N \end{matrix} \tag{2.2}$$

is an $M \times N$ matrix whose elements are the functions $\psi_{\mu\nu}(t)$. Inserting (2.1) in (1.2), we obtain the expression for average risk

$$\begin{aligned} R(t) &= R(\vec{\underline{c}}(t)) = R(\underline{\alpha},t) = \\ &\int_{X_1} F_{11}(\underline{x},\Psi(t)\underline{\alpha},t)P_1(t)p_1(\underline{x},t)d\underline{x} + \int_{X_1} F_{21}(\underline{x},\Psi(t)\underline{\alpha},t)P_2(t)p_2(\underline{x}t)d\underline{x} + \\ &\int_{X_2} F_{12}(\underline{x},\Psi(t)\underline{\alpha},t)P_1(t)p_1(\underline{x},t)d\underline{x} + \int_{X_2} F_{22}(\underline{x},\Psi(t)\underline{\alpha},t)P_2(t)p_2(\underline{x},t)d\underline{x} \end{aligned} \tag{2.3}$$

The conditions of the minimum $R(\underline{\alpha},t)$ (2.2) are found by known methods [4,5] in the following form:

$$\begin{aligned} &\int_{X_1} [\nabla_{\underline{\alpha}} F_{11}(\underline{x},\Psi(t)\underline{\alpha},t)P_1(t)p_1(\underline{x},t) + \nabla_{\underline{\alpha}} F_{21}(\underline{x},\Psi(t)\underline{\alpha},t)P_2(t)p_2(\underline{x},t)]\, d\underline{x} + \\ &\int_{X_2} [\nabla_{\underline{\alpha}} F_{12}(\underline{x},\Psi(t)\underline{\alpha},t)P_1(t)p_1(\underline{x},t) + \nabla_{\underline{\alpha}} F_{22}(\underline{x},\Psi(t)\underline{\alpha},t)P_2(t)p_2(\underline{x},t)]\, d\underline{x} = 0 \end{aligned} \tag{2.4}$$

and

$$f(\underline{x},\underline{\alpha},t) - [F_{11}(\underline{x},\Psi(t)\underline{\alpha},t) - F_{12}(\underline{x},\Psi(t)\underline{\alpha},t)]\, P_1(t)p_1(\underline{x},t) + [F_{21}(\underline{x},\Psi(t)\underline{\alpha},t) - F_{22}(\underline{x},\Psi(t)\underline{\alpha},t)]\, P_2(t)p_2(\underline{x},t) = 0 \tag{2.5}$$

The condition (2.4) can be rewritten in a more convenient form for future use

$$M_X\{\phi(\underline{x},\Psi(t)\underline{\alpha},t)\} = 0 \tag{2.6}$$

where M is the symbol for mathematical expectation and

$$\phi(\underline{x},\Psi(t)\underline{\alpha},t) = \begin{cases} \nabla_\alpha F_{11}(\underline{x},\Psi(t)\underline{\alpha},t), & \text{if } \underline{x} \text{ is the pattern of class } \underline{\overline{X}}_1^0, \text{ but associated with } \underline{\overline{X}}_1^0 \\ \nabla_\alpha F_{21}(\underline{x},\Psi(t)\underline{\alpha},t), & \text{if } \underline{x} \text{ is the pattern of class } \underline{\overline{X}}_2^0, \text{ but associated with } \underline{\overline{X}}_1^0 \\ \nabla_\alpha F_{12}(\underline{x},\Psi(t)\underline{\alpha},t), & \text{if } \underline{x} \text{ is the pattern of class } \underline{\overline{X}}_1^0, \text{ but associated with } \underline{\overline{X}}_2^0 \\ \nabla_\alpha F_{22}(\underline{x},\Psi(t)\underline{\alpha},t), & \text{if } \underline{x} \text{ is the pattern of class } \underline{\overline{X}}_2^0, \text{ and associated with } \underline{\overline{X}}_2^0 \end{cases} \tag{2.7}$$

From the expression (2.5) follows the decision rule $\underline{x} \in \underline{\overline{X}}_1$, that is, it is associated with class $\underline{\overline{X}}_1^0$ if

$$f(\underline{x}, \underline{\alpha}, t) < 0 \tag{2.8}$$

and $\underline{x} \in \underline{\overline{X}}_2$, that is, it is associated with class $\underline{\overline{X}}_2^0$ if

$$f(\underline{x}, \underline{\alpha}, t) > 0 \tag{2.9}$$

The vector $\underline{\alpha}$, entering into $f(\underline{x}, \underline{\alpha}, t)$, is defined from (2.4) or (2.6).

The established decision rule (2.8), (2.9) differs from the usual decision theory in that in it there figure not fixed loss functions but loss functions assigned specifically to the parameter vector $\underline{\vec{c}}$, depending, because of this, on time and not on the fixed probability P_k or the distribution density $p_k(\underline{x})$, but on their time dependent versions.

We will now use the equations we have obtained in the solution of the problem of pattern recognition under non-stationary conditions.

III. Supervised Learning

We will choose loss functions independent of the vectors $\underline{x}$ and $\underline{\alpha}$

$$F_{12}(\underline{x},\Psi(t)\underline{\alpha},t) = \omega_{12}(t) > 0, \quad F_{11}(\underline{x},\Psi(t)\underline{\alpha},t) = \omega_{11}(t) \leq 0$$
$$F_{21}(\underline{x},\Psi(t)\underline{\alpha},t) = \omega_{21}(t) > 0, \quad F_{22}(\underline{x},\Psi(t)\underline{\alpha},t) = \omega_{22}(t) \leq 0 \qquad (3.1)$$

Then equation (2.4) is satisfied identically, and from (2.5) we obtain a partitioning function defining rule (2.7), (2.8) in the form

$$f(\underline{x},t) = [\omega_{11}(t) - \omega_{12}(t)]\,P_1(t)p_1(\underline{x},t) + [\omega_{21}(t) - \omega_{22}(t)]\,P_2(t)p_2(\underline{x},t) \qquad (3.2)$$

If the a priori information is complete, that is, if $P_k(t)$ and $p_k(\underline{x},t), k = 1,2$ are known, then learning is unnecessary, and the structural scheme of the system, shown in Figure 1, accomplishes recognition according to the decision rule (2.8), (2.9) [14]. The need for learning arises if $P_k(t)$ and $p_k(\underline{x},t)$ are unknown. In this case the partitioning function (3.2) is not completely defined. We will approximate it with the help of

$$\hat{f}(\underline{x}, \underline{c}, t) = \phi^T(\underline{x})\,\vec{\underline{c}}(t) \qquad (3.3)$$

where $\underline{\phi}(\underline{x}) = (\phi_1(\underline{x}), \ldots, \phi_N(\underline{x}))$ is a vector-function whose components are orthonormal.

Using (2.1) we will rewrite (3.3) in the form

$$\hat{f}(\underline{x}), \underline{\alpha}, t) = \underline{\phi}^T(\underline{x})\Psi(t)\underline{\alpha} \qquad (3.4)$$

We will write the functional, characterizing the error of the approximation

$$J(\underline{\alpha},t) = \int_X [f(\underline{x},t) - \underline{\phi}^T(\underline{x})\Psi(t)\underline{\alpha}]^2 d\underline{x} \qquad (3.5)$$

and define the vector $\underline{\alpha}$, which minimizes the functional. The equation of the minimum (3.5) leads to the relation

$$\nabla_{\underline{\alpha}} J(\underline{\alpha},t) = -2 \int_X [f(\underline{x},t) - \underline{\phi}^T(\underline{x})\Psi(t)\underline{\alpha}]\,\Psi^T(t)\underline{\phi}(\underline{x})d\underline{x} = 0 \qquad (3.6)$$

We note that because of the orthonormality of the components of the vector of the function $\phi(\underline{x})$,

$$\int_X (\underline{\phi}^T(\underline{x})\Psi(t)\underline{\alpha})\Psi^T(t)\underline{\phi}(\underline{x})d\underline{x} = \Psi^T(t)\Psi(t)\underline{\alpha} \tag{3.7}$$

We write equation (3.6) in the form

$$\int_X f(\underline{x},t)\Psi^T(t)\underline{\phi}(\underline{x})d\underline{x} = \Psi^T(t)\Psi(t)\underline{\alpha} \tag{3.8}$$

or, after substitution in (3.8) of $f(\underline{x}, t)$ from (3.2)

$$M\{z(t)\Psi(t)\underline{\phi}(\underline{x})\} = \Psi^T(t)\Psi(t)\underline{\alpha} \tag{3.9}$$

where

$$z(t) = \begin{cases} \omega_{11}(t) - \omega_{12}(t), \text{ if } x \in X_1^0 \\ \omega_{21}(t) - \omega_{22}(t), \text{ if } x \in X_2^0 \end{cases} \tag{3.10}$$

Writing (3.9) in the form of a regression equation

$$M\{\Psi(t)\Psi(t)\underline{\alpha} - z(t)\Psi^T(t)\underline{\phi}(\underline{x})\} = 0 \tag{3.11}$$

and applying to it the general adaptive approach, we obtain learning algorithms in the form

$$\begin{aligned} \underline{\alpha}[n] = \underline{\alpha}[n-1] - \Gamma[n]\,\{\Psi^T[n]\,\Psi[n]\underline{\alpha}[n-1] - \\ z[n]\,\Psi^T[n]\underline{\phi}(\underline{x}[n])\} \end{aligned} \tag{3.12}$$

where $z[n]$ is defined from (3.10) for $t=n$.

In this algorithm $\Gamma[n]$ is a matrix, in the general case. It is significantly more convenient to have learning algorithms associated with $\underline{\vec{c}}[n]$. With this aim we premultiply both sides of (3.12) by the matrix $\Psi[n]$. Then we obtain

$$\begin{aligned} \Psi[n]\underline{\alpha}[n] = \Psi[n]\underline{\alpha}[n-1] - \\ \Psi[n]\Gamma[n]\,\{\Psi^T[n]\,\Psi[n]\underline{\alpha}[n-1] - \\ z[n]\,\Psi^T[n]\underline{\phi}(\underline{x}[n])\} \end{aligned} \tag{3.13}$$

We will designate, in agreement with (2.1), that

$$\underline{\vec{c}}[k] = \Psi[k]\underline{\alpha}[k], \qquad k = n-1,n \tag{3.14}$$

and we will assume that matrix $\Psi[n]$ satisfies the relation

$$\Psi[n] = B(\Psi[n-1])\Psi[n-1] \tag{3.15}$$

where $B(\Psi[n-1])$ is the null matrix. Then (3.13) can be written in a simpler form

$$\vec{\underline{c}}[n] = B(\Psi[n-1])\vec{\underline{c}}[n-1] - \Gamma_1[n]\left\{B(\Psi[n-1])\vec{\underline{c}}[n-1] - z[n]\underline{\phi}(\underline{x}[n])\right\}, \tag{3.16}$$

where

$$\Gamma_1[n] = \Psi[n]\Gamma[n]\Psi^T[n] \tag{3.17}$$

In agreement with (3.3) the approximation of the partitioning function is found from the expression

$$\hat{f}(\underline{x},\vec{\underline{c}}[n],n) = \underline{\phi}^T(\underline{x}[n])\vec{\underline{c}}[n] \tag{3.18}$$

The structural scheme of the system yielding the algorithms (3.16), (3.18) is shown in Figure 2. This system is capable of learning with time to accept decisions under uncertainty and under non-stationary conditions, when the conditions of convergence are complete [13]. These lead to the requirement of the condition that as n grows, the norm of the matrix $B(\Psi[n-1])$ approach unity and the corresponding conditions that the elements of $\Gamma_1(n)$ approach zero.

The approach described above is an expansion of the Bayes adaptive approach [5,15] under non-stationary conditions. Several other approaches are possible to the learning of a decision rule which is an expansion of the traditional adaptive approach under non-stationary conditions.

We will designate the value of the partitioning function as before, $\hat{f}(\underline{x},\underline{c},t)$. The limits of the partitioning function define the region

$$\begin{aligned} X_1 &= \underline{x}:\ \hat{f}(\underline{x},\underline{c},t) < 0 \\ X_2 &= \underline{x}:\ \hat{f}(\underline{x},\underline{c},t) < 0 \end{aligned} \tag{3.19}$$

We will further define by y an additional instruction teaching about the affiliation of the pattern to class $\overline{X}_1^0$ or $\overline{X}_2^0$

$$y = \begin{cases} -1 & \text{if } \underline{x} \in X_1^0 \\ 1 & \text{if } \underline{x} \in X_2^0 \end{cases} \tag{3.20}$$

The accepted solutions will be true if

$$y\hat{f}(\underline{x},\underline{c},t) > 0 \tag{3.21}$$

and false if

$$y\hat{f}(\underline{x},\underline{c},t) < 0 \tag{3.22}$$

Let us examine some convex function of the difference between y and $\hat{f}(\underline{x},\underline{c},t)$, that is,

$$F(y - \hat{f}(\underline{x}, \underline{c},t) > 0 \tag{3.23}$$

We choose in the form of a loss function such functions that

$$\left.\begin{aligned} F_{11}(\underline{x},\underline{c},t) &= F(y - \hat{f}(\underline{x},\underline{c},t)\ ), \quad \text{if } y = -1 \\ F_{22}(\underline{x},\underline{c},t) &= F(y - \hat{f}(\underline{x},\underline{c},t)\ ), \quad \text{if } y = 1 \end{aligned}\right\} \text{ and } y\hat{f}(\underline{x},\underline{c},t) > 0 \tag{3.24}$$

and

$$\left.\begin{aligned} F_{21}(\underline{x},\underline{c},t) &= F(y - \hat{f}(\underline{x},\underline{c},t)\ ), \quad \text{if } y = 1 \\ F_{12}(\underline{x},\underline{c},t) &= F(y - \hat{f}(\underline{x},\underline{c},t)\ ), \quad \text{if } y = -1 \end{aligned}\right\} \text{ and } y\hat{f}(\underline{x},\underline{c},t) < 0 \tag{3.25}$$

Then the average risk is written thus

$$\begin{aligned} R(\underline{c},t) &= \int_X F(y - \hat{f}(\underline{x},\underline{c},t)p(\underline{x},t)d\underline{x} \\ &= M\{F(y - \hat{f}(\underline{x},\underline{c},t)\ )\} \end{aligned} \tag{3.26}$$

where

$$p(\underline{x},t) = P_1(t)p_1(\underline{x},t) + P_2(t)p_2(\underline{x},t) \tag{3.27}$$

is the joint density of the distribution.

The expression of minimum average risk in (2.6), (2.7) including (3.4) is written in the form

$$M\{\phi(\underline{x},\underline{\alpha},t)\} = 0 \tag{3.28}$$

where

$$\begin{aligned} \phi(\underline{x},\underline{\alpha},t) &= \nabla_{\underline{\alpha}} F(y - \underline{\phi}^T(\underline{x})\Psi(t)\underline{\alpha}) \\ &= -F'(y - \underline{\phi}^T(\underline{x})\Psi(t)\underline{\alpha})\Psi^T(t)\underline{\phi}(\underline{x}) \end{aligned} \tag{3.29}$$

It is not necessary to use the second condition of the minimum (2.5) now since we derived the partitioning function $\hat{f}(\underline{x}, \underline{c}, t)$, which is defined from

(4.10) on the basis of the adaptive approach. Indeed, from (3.28) there follows the learning algorithm

$$\underline{\alpha}[n] = \underline{\alpha}[n-1] + \Gamma[n]F'(y[n] - \underline{\phi}^T(\underline{x}[n])\Psi[n]\underline{\alpha}[n-1]\Psi^T[n]\underline{\phi}(x[n])) \tag{3.30}$$

Premultiplying (4.12) by $\Psi[n]$ and calculating the equations (3.14), (3.15) and (3.17), we obtain the algorithm corresponding to $\underline{c}[n]$,

$$\underline{c}[n] = B(\Psi[n])\underline{c}[n-1] + \Gamma_1[n]F'(y[n] - \underline{\phi}^T(\underline{x}[n])B(\Psi[n-1]\underline{c}[n-1])\,\phi(\underline{x}[n]) \tag{3.31}$$

As before, from (3.3) we have

$$\hat{f}(\underline{x},\underline{c}[n],n) = \underline{\phi}^T(\underline{x})\underline{c}[n] \tag{3.32}$$

The structural scheme of the system, resulting in algorithms (3.31), (3.32), is shown in Figure 3.

This system is capable of learning to accept with time decisions in the presence of uncertainty and under non-stationary conditions when the conditions of convergence enumerated before are fulfilled, if the order of growth of $F(\cdot)$ with $\underline{c}$ is not more than quadratic [13]. We note that the algorithm in form (3.31) was obtained in [8] in several other forms. Into the obtained learning algorithms, (3.16) as well as (3.31), there enters a teaching instruction about the affiliation of a shown pattern to one class or another. Therefore, these algorithms comprise supervised learning.

IV. Unsupervised Learning

We will assume now that information about the affiliation of a pattern to one class or another is lacking.

We choose loss functions equal to

$$\begin{aligned} F_{11}(\underline{x},\vec{\underline{c}},t) &= F_1(\underline{x},\vec{\underline{c}},t) \\ F_{22}(\underline{x},\vec{\underline{c}},t) &= F_2(\underline{x},\vec{\underline{c}},t) \end{aligned} \tag{4.1}$$

and

$$F_{12}(\underline{x},\vec{\underline{c}},t) = F_{21}(\underline{x},\vec{\underline{c}},t) = 0 \tag{4.2}$$

The loss functions (4.1) are defined for every unknown region $\overline{\underline{X}}_k$ (k = 1,2). Then the average risk (1.2) under the assumption that the regions intersect, and with the calculation of (3.27), is written in the form

$$R(\underline{\vec{c}},t) = \int_{X_1} F_1(\underline{x},\underline{\vec{c}},t)p(\underline{x},t)d\underline{x} + \int_{X_2} F_2(\underline{x},\underline{\vec{c}},t)p(\underline{x},t)d\underline{x} \tag{4.3}$$

From the conditions of minimum average risk (2.4) and (2.5) we obtain

$$\int_{X_1} \underline{\alpha}F_1(\underline{x},\Psi(t)\underline{\alpha},t)p(\underline{x},t)d\underline{x} + \int_{X_2} \underline{\alpha}F_2(\underline{x},\Psi(t)\underline{\alpha},t)p(\underline{x},t)d\underline{x} = 0 \tag{4.4}$$

$$\hat{f}(\underline{x},\underline{\alpha},t) = F_1(\underline{x},\Psi(t)\underline{\alpha},t) - F_2(\underline{x},\Psi(t)\underline{\alpha},t) = 0 \tag{4.5}$$

because $p(\underline{x},t) > 0$.

Equation (4.4) can be written in an equivalent form

$$M\{\theta_1(\underline{x},\underline{\alpha},t)\nabla_{\alpha}F_1(\underline{x},\Psi(t)\underline{\alpha},t) + \theta_2(\underline{x},\underline{\alpha},t)\nabla_{\alpha}F_2(\underline{x},\Psi(t)\underline{\alpha},t)\} = 0 \tag{4.6}$$

where

$$\theta_1(\underline{x},\underline{\alpha},t) = 1 - \theta_2(\underline{x},\underline{\alpha},t) = \begin{matrix} 1, \text{ if } \underline{x} \in X_1^0 \\ 0, \text{ if } \underline{x} \in X_2^0 \end{matrix} \tag{4.7}$$

Taking into consideration that

$$\nabla_{\underline{\alpha}}F_k(\underline{x},\Psi(t)\underline{\alpha},t) = \Psi^T(t)\nabla F_k(\underline{x},\Psi(t)\underline{\alpha},t), \quad k = 1,2 \tag{4.8}$$

we obtain from (4.6) and (4.4) on the basis of the adaptive approach the following algorithm for self-learning

$$\underline{\alpha}[n] = \underline{\alpha}[n-1] - \Gamma_1[n]\Psi^T[n] \nabla F_1(x[n],\Psi[n]\underline{\alpha}[n-1],n) \tag{4.9}$$

if

$$\hat{f}(\underline{x}[n],\underline{\alpha}[n-1],n-1) = F_1(\underline{x}[n],\Psi[n-1]\underline{\alpha}[n-1],n-1) - F_2(x[n],\Psi[n-1]\underline{\alpha}[n-1],n-1) < 0 \tag{4.10}$$

and

$$\underline{\alpha}[n] = \underline{\alpha}[n-1] - \Gamma_2[n]\Psi^T[n] \nabla F_2(\underline{x}[n],\Psi[n]\underline{\alpha}[n-1],n) \tag{4.11}$$

if

$$\hat{f}(\underline{x}[n],\underline{\alpha}[n-1],n-1) > 0 \tag{4.12}$$

Premultiplying the self-learning algorithm (4.8) (4.10) by $\Psi[n]$ and calculating equations (3.14) (3.15), we find the self-learning algorithm associated with $\vec{c}[n]$

$$\underline{\vec{c}}[n] = B(\Psi[n-1]\underline{\vec{c}}[n-1] + \Gamma_{11}[n] \nabla F_1(\underline{x}[n], \Psi[n]\underline{\alpha}[n-1], n) \tag{4.13}$$

if

$$\hat{f}(\underline{x}[n], \underline{\vec{c}}[n-1], n) =$$

$$F_1(x[n], \vec{c}[n-1], n-1) - F_2(x[n], \vec{c}[n-1], n-1) < 0 \tag{4.14}$$

and

$$\vec{c}[n] = B(\Psi[n-1]\vec{c}[n-1] + \Gamma_{21}[n] \nabla F_2(x[n], \Psi[n]\alpha[n-1], n) \tag{4.15}$$

if

$$\hat{f}(x[n], \vec{c}[n-1], n) > 0 \tag{4.16}$$

where the algorithms (4.13) (4.15)

$$\Gamma_{11}[n] = \Psi[n]\Gamma_1[n]\Psi^T[n], \; \Gamma_{21}[n] = \Psi[n]\Gamma_2[n]\Psi^T[n] \tag{4.17}$$

The structural scheme of the self-learning system, resulting in algorithms (4.13) -- (4.16) is shown in Figure 4.

The choice of suitable concrete loss functions for algorithms of supervised (3.16), (3.31) and unsupervised learning allows us to obtain various learning algorithms under non-stationary conditions. With the choice of learning algorithms

$$B(\Psi[n-1]) = I \tag{4.18}$$

where I is the unity matrix we of course arrive at the usual pattern recognition learning algorithm under stationary conditions.

Conclusion

In this article there was presented a general method for establishing pattern recognition learning algorithms for both supervised and unsupervised learning under non-stationary conditions. The algorithms are learning systems which are capable, with time and after training, of accomplishing recognition of presented patterns.

Learning systems of a similar nature allow us to study the behavioral aspect of pattern recognition.

REFERENCES

1. Nagy, G., State of the art in pattern recognition. Proceedings of the IEEE, 1968, Vol. 56, No. 5, pp. 836-862.
2. Ho, Y. C., Agrawala, A. K.,"On pattern classification algorithms. Introduction and Survey." Proceedings of the IEEE 1968, Vol. 56, No. 12, pp. 2101-2114.
3. Fu, K. S., Learning control systems. Review and Outlook, IEEE, Transactions on Automatic Control, 1970, Vol. AC-15, No. 2, pp. 211-221.
4. Tsypkin, Ya. Z., Adaptation and learning in control systems. Academic Press, New York, 1970.
5. Tsypkin, Ya. Z., The foundations of the theory of learning systems, Nauka, Moskow, 1970.
6. Dupac, V. A dynamic stochastic approximation method. Annalen of the Mathematical statistics, 1965, Vol. 36, No. 6, pp. 1695-1702.
7. Fu, K. S., Sequential methods pattern recognition and machine learning. Academic Press, New York, 1968.
8. De Figueiredo, R. J. P., Convergent algorithms for pattern recognition in nonlinearly evolving nonstationary environment. Proceedings of the IEEE, 1968, Vol. 56, No. 2, pp. 188-189.
9. Pearson, J. B., A note on nonlinear filtering. IEEE Transactions on Automatic Control, 1968, Vol. AC-13, No. 1, pp. 103-105.
10. Chien, Y. T., Fu, K. S., Stochastic learning of time-varying parameters in random environment. IEEE Transactions on Systems Science and Cybernetics, 1967, Vol. SSS-5, No. 3, pp. 237-246.
11. Sugiyama, H., Uosaki, K., On application of the stochastic approximation processes to the Control systems with a time-varying parameters. Journal of the Japan Association of Automatic Control Engineers, 1969, Vol. 13, No. 8, pp. 529-536.
12. Albert, A. E., Gardner, L. A., Stochastic approximation and nonlinear regression. The MIT Press, 1967.
13. Tsypkin, Ya. Z., Kaplinskii, A. I., Larionov, K. A., Algorithms of adaptation and learning under non-stationary conditions, Izviestiya AN U.S.S.R., Technicheskaya Kibernetika, 1970, No. 5, pp. 9-21.
14. Middleton, D., An introduction to statistical communication theory. McGraw-Hill Book Co., New York, 1960.
15. Tsypkin, Ya. Z., Kelmans, G. K., Adaptive Bayes approach, Problems of Translating information, 1970, No. 1, pp. 52-59.

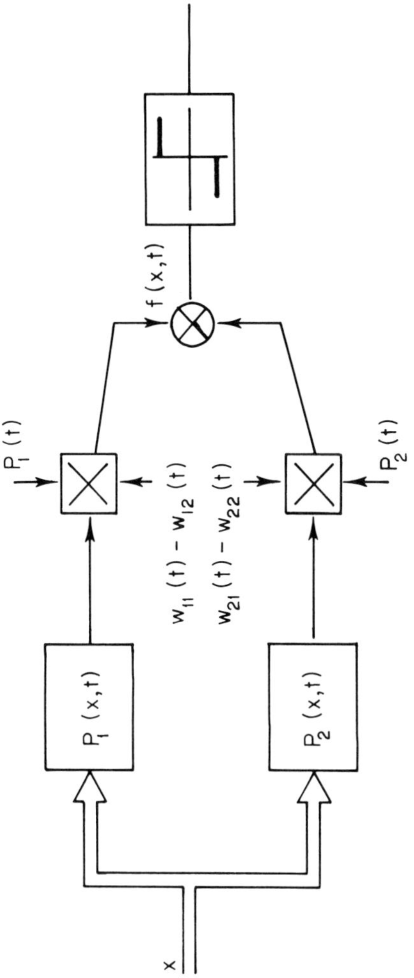

Figure 1

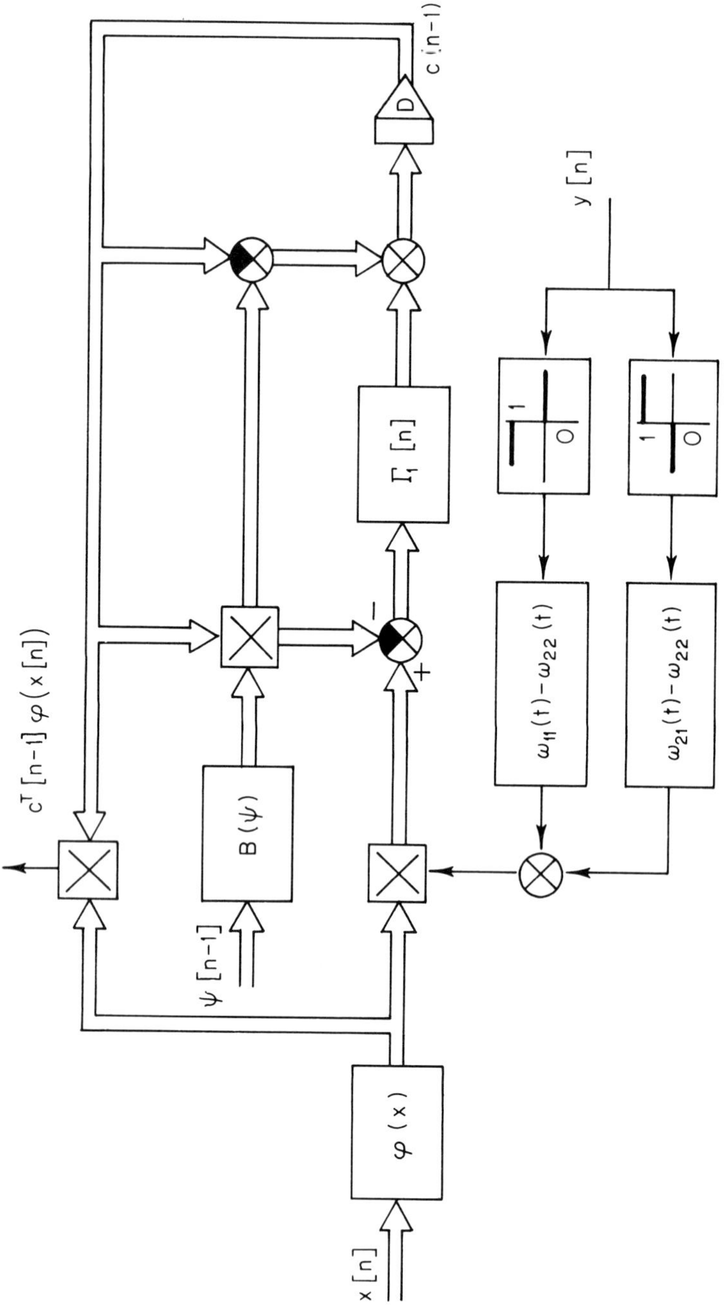

Figure 2

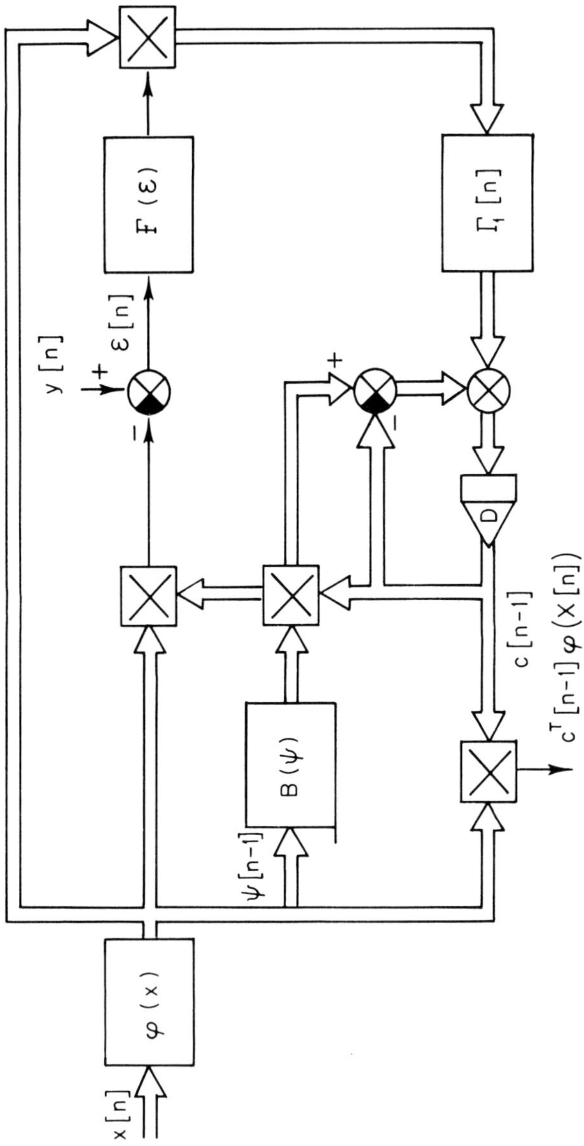

Figure 3

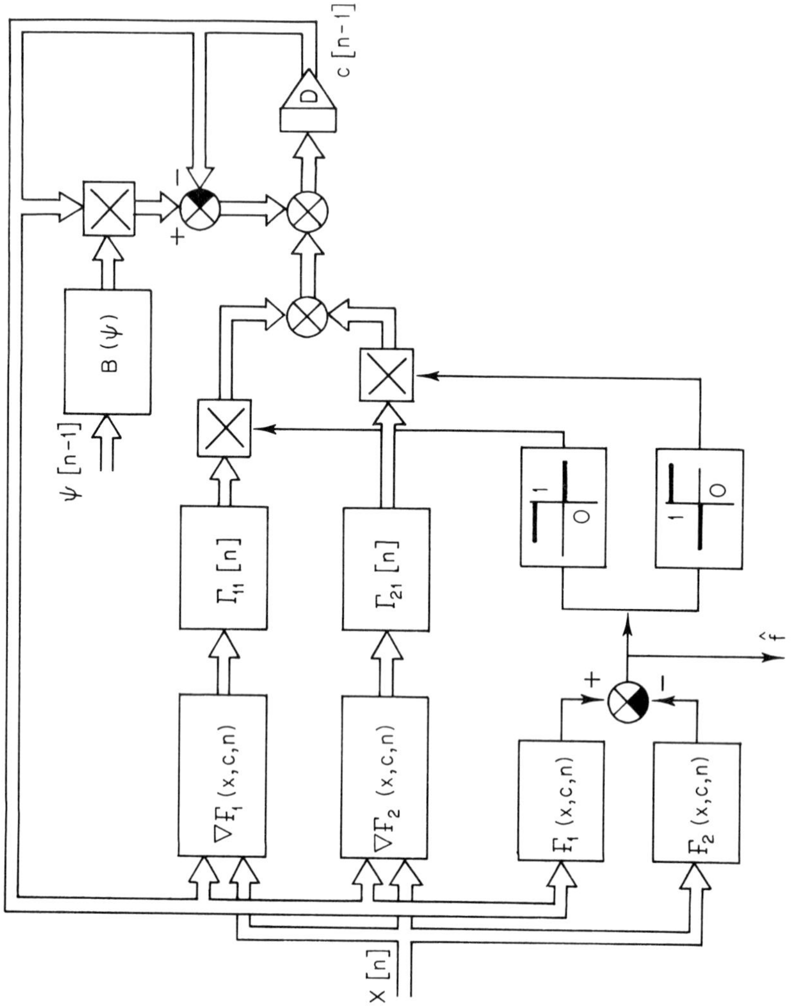

Figure 4

IDEALISED PATTERN RECOGNITION

J. R. Ullmann

DIVISION OF COMPUTER SCIENCE
NATIONAL PHYSICAL LABORATORY
TEDDINGTON, MIDDLESEX, ENGLAND

Abstract

In many successful character recognition systems, a character is first normalised (e.g. aligned in position), then preprocessed, (e.g. by feature extraction), and then classified. To say that a three-stage machine of this sort could recognise unconstrained hand-printed 0, . .9,A, . .Z is to state an hypothesis. In 1971 this is an hypothesis and not a proven fact. Scientifically, this hypothesis is not allowable, since it can never be disproved. To disprove it we would have to try out all possible normalisation schemes, all possible preprocessors and all possible classifiers, which is of course impossible. Therefore,it is possible that the usual methodology in which we concentrate either on normalisation, or on preprocessing, or on classification, will never lead to a machine which reliably recognises unconstrained hand-printed 0, . . 9,A, . . Z and if this is true we shall never find out that this is true. This consideration, and the fact that much work has already been based on the three-stage hypothesis, has prompted a search for an alternative approach to character recognition, wherein we do not divide the recognition machine *a priori* into functional blocks whose details are to be worked out later. Instead, system development is to be broken down into manageable steps by other means. According to the following suggestion, the recognition problem is idealised, as a first step.

Besides varying in position, size, orientation, and to a limited extent in general perspective, hand-printed characters are subject to variations which we cannot exactly specify *a priori*. Because of the limitations of a human's grasp of complexity, we may not wish to provide a machine with a specification of these details by means of intuitive trial and error, but instead by means of an automatic process based on training sets. If this automatic process is to be successful when characters are subject to non-trivial variations, then it should work also when characters are subject only to variations in position. It is suggested that we should not use our knowledge of variation in position in designing the machine, but instead, as a preliminary exercise, we should make the machine learn to recognise variations in position in the same way that it will (we hope) learn non-trivial variations which we are unable to specify. In character recognition it is usual to eliminate variations in position by normalisation (alignment), and then to concentrate on non-trivial variations. The present paper suggests the reverse of this: that as a first step we eliminate non-trivial variations by considering an hypothetical idealised problem in which characters belonging to any given recognition class vary only in position. This suggestion has not yet lead to good practical recognition performance, but it has contributed towards the achievement of a very limited experimental demonstration of transference of learning between recognition classes. If training sets of the letters A, . .Z are used to improve the recognition of numerals 0, . .9, this exemplifies transference of learning.

To be specific, let us consider 20×20 bit binarised hand-printed characters. Out of the 2^{400} possible 20×20 bit binary patterns, only a small proportion are patterns which we would like a machine to recognise as '2'. But even so, the number of 20×20 bit patterns which we would like a machine to recognise as '2' is a large number, perhaps of the order of 10^{10}. 10^{10} is just a very rough guess. All 2's do not have equal (a priori) probabilities of occurrence, and it is reasonable to expect many 20×20 bit 2's to occur extremely infrequently (e.g. 10^{-10}).

A recognition machine must use some sort of specification or definition of what it is to recognise. The classical methods of defining a set are *intensive* and *extensive*. Extensive definition of an astronomical number (e.g. 10^{10})of 2's does not appear to be a practical proposition. To make an intensive definition, we must specify a property shared by all 2's and not shared by 0, 1, 3, 4, . . Z. If, as seems to be the case, we cannot clearly and immediately specify any such property, then we must find one by the well-tried scientific procedure of hypothesis formation and testing. A suitable property cannot be deduced from anything: arriving at a suitable property must be an experimental scientific rather than a non-experimental mathematical process.

Since extensive definition of practical recognition classes is generally impractical, existing machines must be using intensive definitions. Let us illustrate this with a few examples. As a first example, an important commercial multifont print recognition technique intensively defines 'H' as any character for which a Boolean function such as

$$(b_1 v b_2).(b_3 b v_4).(b_5 v b_6).(b_7 v b_8).(b_9 v b_{10}).(b_{11} v b_{12}).(b_{13} v b_{14}).(b_{15} v b_{16}).w_{17}.w_{18} \ldots\ldots (1)$$

is true, where b_1 is *true* if not less than 80% of the bits in region 1 in Figure 1 are black, b_2 is *true* if not less than 80% of the bits in region 2 are black, and so on. w_{17} is *true* if not more than 20% of the bits in region 17 are black, and w_{18} is defined similarly. (See for example references 20 and 15). It is fairly obvious

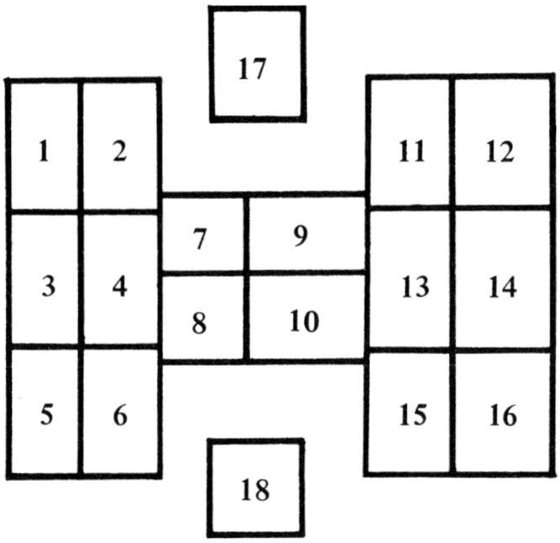

Figure 1: Regions for the letter 'H'

that (1) will recognise some H's. It may be possible to improve recognition by altering the size, shape and position of the regions 1, . . . 18, and by altering the Boolean condition (1). In practice each suggested alteration is tested on thousands of H's, and may turn out to give a big improvement or perhaps a worsening of error rates. The process of suggesting and testing alterations, and indeed of suggesting and testing (1) in the first place, is a process of hypothesis formation and testing, although an engineer may perhaps not think of it in these terms. By this process the fine details of the recognition condition for 'H' are worked out. For instance an 80% threshold may not finally be used for all regions, but instead a threshold which varies from region to region; and moreover the bits within a region may not all be weighted equally. Good weights and thresholds are found by trial and error.

Many techniques are known for determining separating surfaces automatically.[13] For simplicity let us start by considering application of such techniques directly to binary characters, and return later to the important question of preprocessing.

One of the simplest ideas is to assume that bits are statistically independent[26]. This leads to a linear discriminant system in which hyperspace is partitioned into regions. A machine using the independence assumption is based on the hypothesis that the independence assumption leads to regions such that each region contains patterns belonging to only one recognition class. This hypothesis can be validated or invalidated only by experiment. (Note that this hypothesis may turn out to be valid even if pattern bits are not statistically independent). If this hypothesis is valid, the intensive property of a recognition class (or subclass) is the property of lying within a particular region in hyperspace.

Similarly, a machine using the assumption of normality is based on the hypothesis that the normality assumption leads to hyperspace regions such that each region contains patterns belonging to only one class. (Again, this hypothesis may experimentally be found valid even if the patterns belonging to a recognition class are not normally distributed.) Perhaps these simple examples will suffice to illustrate the hypothetical basis of the application of statistical techniques in character recognition. That the basis is hypothetical has been pointed out by Sebestyen[21] and Arkedev and Braverman.[2]

In deterministic error correcting techniques, surfaces are found so as to give zero error, or at least minimum error according to some criterion, on a training set. Suppose for instance that zero error is achieved on a training set. It is usual simply to hope-for-the-best that zero error will also be achieved on patterns not belonging to the training set. In other words, it is usual to hypothesise that a classifier which learns to recognise a training set with minimum error will also recognise a further test set with minimum error. Stochastic error correcting methods,[10,23] if we do not require fast convergence, determine minimum-error surfaces not just for training sets but for open ended recognition classes. As in deterministic methods, the question whether, for given data, substitution and reject rates will be tolerably low can only be answered experimentally.

For recognition of hand-printed characters, experimental experience has dictated the interposition of a preprocessor between the raw input pattern and a statistical or error correcting classifier. Perhaps one reason for this arises from the (supposed) fact that many patterns have extremely low probabilities of occurrence. Even if a classifier is designed from a training set of one million 20×20 hand-printed characters per class, this system will be required to recognise an astronomical number of patterns not belonging to the training set, and perhaps not 'close to' members of the training set. However large the training set, it never seems to be sufficiently representative of the vast population from which it is taken.[13]

A recognition system designed in detail by a human designer does not depend only on specimen patterns which he has seen, but also, as Andrews et al[1] have remarked, on specimens which he has *imagined.* The designer does not have to wait for unusual variations of characters to occur in the design data: he can imagine them. By interposing an intuitively designed preprocessor between an input pattern and a classifier, Munson,[12] for example, has provided himself with an opportunity to use his imagination and intuitive knowledge of character shape in order to reduce pattern variability prior to classification.

Whether normalisation, e.g. size normalisation, should be regarded as one of the jobs of the preprocessor or as a separate job which should be done before a pattern reaches the preprocessor is of course a terminological question. Let us arbitrarily put 'normalisation' and 'preprocessor' in separate boxes in Figure 2. Figure 2 is a well-known outline scheme which characterises many contemporary recognition systems.

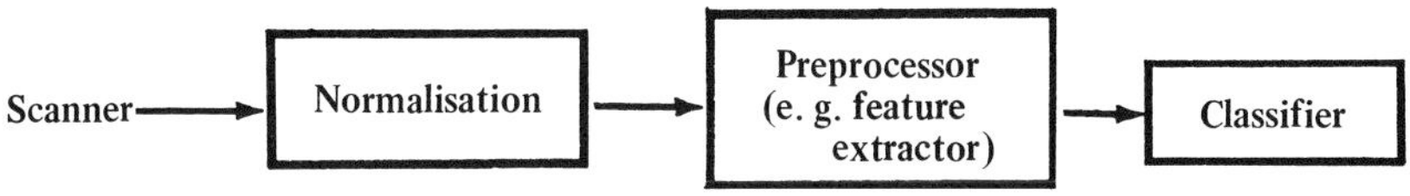

Figure 2: Classical block diagram for a recognition machine

This scheme is important because it has been successful, and it has the advantage of being simple. Figure 2 breaks down the recognition machine into three boxes, and leads to the commonly practiced methodology of designing the machine box-by-box.

If we suggest that a system conforming to Figure 2 could recognise unconstrained hand-printed characters 0, . . 9, A, . . Z, then we are making an hypothesis. An advantage of making this hypothesis is that it allows us to concentrate on one (at a time) of the three boxes in Figure 2. A disadvantage is that if this hypothesis is in fact wrong, then we shall *never* find out. To disprove this hypothesis we would have to try out all possible detailed designs for the three boxes, which is of course impossible. Since this hypothesis cannot in practice be disproved, it is not an *allowable* hypothesis, according to the precepts of natural science, but this does not mean that it is necessarily *false.*

At this juncture it may be appropriate to outline a recognition system which does not conform to Figure 2. Parks[18] has built hardware which detects features akin to Bomba's,[6] specifically, various orientations of L,T,V, Y,X features, an obtuse angle, and line-ends. Various decision making processes have been tried, and one of these is a tree process. For instance the first node might ask "is the lowermost feature in the character a downward pointing line end?". If the answer is *yes*, the next node might ask "is there an 'L' feature positioned within a 5 × 5 box centred at (−10,8) relative to the exact position of the lowermost line-end?" If the answer is *yes*, the next node might ask "is there an upward pointing line-end positioned within a 6 × 8 box centred at (0,10) relative to the exact position of the 'L' found at the second node?", and so on. The idea is that the exact position where each feature is found is used to position the zone of search for the next feature. This idea has been subject of many elaborations. For instance, the *separation* of two successive features can be used to position and *scale* the zone in which the next feature is looked for. In this case a character need not be size normalised before being 'interrogated' by the tree, and recognition is now not a three stage process as in Figure 2, but a two stage process as in Figure 3 (apart from locating the first feature in the chain of features.)

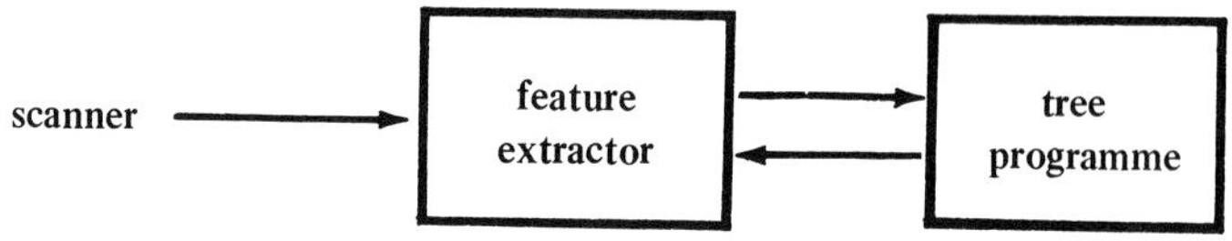

Figure 3: A two-box recognition system

Bomba[6] also used a tree, but his nine zones were fixed in advance. The Boolean recognition conditions implemented in Bomba's tree could be implemented instead in a practical parallel system conforming to Figure 2; but this is not true of Parks' system because the exact location of each feature determines the zone of search for the next.

If we suggest that a system conforming to Figure 3 could recognise unconstrained hand-printed characters 0, . .9,A, . .Z, we are making an hypothesis which is just as non-allowable as the corresponding hypothesis concerning Figure 2. The underlying difficulty with the hypotheses is not specific to Figures 2 and 3, but is surely general to any approach wherein we divide the recognition machine *a priori* into functional blocks whose details are to be worked out later. To prove that the functional block diagram was *wrong* it would be necessary to try out a hopelessly large number of detailed designs of each block.

There is strong commercial incentive for the design of a recognition machine which recognises unconstrained hand-printed 0, . .9,A, . .Z and ultimately unconstrained cursive script and speech. The fact that no such machine is yet available implies that the requisite intensive definitions of recognition classes are not yet available. Since we do not yet know such definitions we cannot be sure that a machine with a functional block diagram as in Figure 2 will ever recognise unconstrained hand-printed

0, . .9, A, . .Z; nor can we be sure that such a machine will never recognise these characters. In view of this uncertainty, surely there is something to be said for exploring alternative methodologies in which the recognition machine is not split up *a priori* into functional blocks, but instead, recognition machine development is broken down into manageable steps by other means. Before making a specific suggestion, let us consider a line of thought which has conditioned the details of this suggestion.

Some of the most successful contemporary machines for recognising highly variable characters, e.g. the IBM 1287 and 1975, have been intuitively designed. In spite of this, it seems likely that reliance on intuitive design, and the non-availability of superior automatic design techniques, is one of the factors which is impeding progress along the road towards unconstrained, unrestricted, character recognition. One reason why this may be the case is that even with the help of computer aided design, a human designer cannot intuitively grasp a design of which the complexity is unlimited. Fully automatic design, if only we knew how to accomplish it, might be more successful in unconstrained character recognition because it might not be limited in complexity. For recognizing many millions of variants of each of many different characters, it may be essential to escape from limitations of complexity of the design of the recognition machine.

Besides varying in position, size, orientation, and to a limited extent in general perspective, hand-printed characters are subject to variations which we cannot exactly describe *a priori.* Because of the limitations of a human's intuitive grasp of complexity, we do not wish to arrive at a specification of these variations by intuitive trial and error, but instead by an automatic process based on training sets. We wish to design a machine which, given training sets of the characters to be recognised, can work out the details of its own design so as to recognise further characters. In saying this we are regarding the preprocessor (if any) as part of the machine.

If this machine is to work when characters are subject to non-trivial variations which are neither known nor specified by the designer, then it should work also when characters are subject to variations only in position, even if these variations are not specified by the human designer. Conversely, a machine which does not work in the special case where characters belonging to any given recognition class vary only in position cannot be expected to work in the general case where character variations are non-trivial.

These assertions have been based on the *hypothesis* that the position-only case is, in a useful sense, a trivial case of the general class of variations to which real characters are subject. Since no proper definition of this general class of variations is yet available, we cannot *prove* that position-only is in fact a limiting case. The position-only case might be a separate problem whose solution would throw no light at all on the class of variations to which real characters are subject. In many contemporary recognition machines, position variation is dealt with by alignment, and non-trivial variations are dealt with by the preprocessor and classifier: thus position-only and non-trivial variations are treated as separate problems. The idea that the position-only case is a special case is, as we have said, no more than an hypothesis; but we suggest that this hypothesis is intuitively strongly plausible. For instance, consider three 2's, each made up of 20 ·'s. Their shape can be be made to vary non-trivially by moving some of the ·'s. relative to others. Moving all the ·'s *equally* is a special case of this.

The methodology of tackling a difficult problem by tackling its special cases first has been well tried. For example, a study of heat engines usually starts with a study of the Carnot cycle, which is an idealised special case in that it is frictionless. An obvious approach to character recognition is by tackling first the special case where characters in any given recognition class vary only in position, with the restriction that the designer must pretend that he knows as little about 'variations in position' as he knows about the non-trivial variations to which real characters are subject. If his machine cannot find out for itself what variation in position consists of, then surely it cannot find out for itself what non-trivial variations consist of. So we propose a methodology in which a machine is designed so that it works in the position-only case. If this machine does not work without modification in the general case, we abandon it and design another machine which works in the position-only case. If this does not work without modification in the general case we abandon it, and so on. When we arrive at a design which works in the general case, we *then* propose to start worrying about the cost of it.

This proposal requires clarification. Let $D_0, D_1, \ldots D_Z$ be classes of characters such that in each class the characters vary only in position. For instance, the patterns belonging to D_0 might be the same '0' shifted into different positions. The patterns belonging to D_1 might be the same '1' shifted into different positions, and so on. To recognise $D_0, \ldots D_Z$, a machine could store one specimen each of $D_0, \ldots D_Z$ and recognise an input pattern by shifting it into all possible alignments with the stored specimens and testing for exact match in each alignment. The shifting could be done by the well known shift register technique which is used, for example, in the IBM 1418.[9] Our knowledge of 'difference in position' allows us to specify exactly the shift operation and the rule whereby characters *match* if their corresponding bits are the same. The proposed methodology requires that, as a preliminary exercise, we should not make use of this knowledge in designing the machine. For instance we should not make use of this knowledge that 01101000 and 00011010 differ only in position and that 01101000 and 01110010 do not. Instead we should make use of as little prior knowledge as possible.

If all the members of each of the classes $D_0, \ldots D_Z$ were used as a training set, conventional automatic techniques could find hypersurfaces to separate all pairs of these classes. If, on the other hand, only a small proportion of each of the classes $D_0, \ldots D_Z$ were used as a training set, conventional methods would not guarantee that members of $D_0, \ldots D_Z$ not belonging to training sets would be reliably recognised. We wish to devise a system in which characters *not* belonging to the training sets would be reliably recognised. (The various solutions to Problem 2, below, are examples of machines which reliably recognise patterns *not* included in training sets. But Problem 2 is a highly idealised recognition problem.)

Note that

```
0 1 1 0 1 0 0 0  and  0 0 1 0 1 0 0 0  and  0 1 0 1 1 0 0 0  etc.
0 0 0 1 1 0 1 0       0 0 0 0 1 0 1 0       0 0 0 1 0 1 1 0
```

are all pairs of patterns differing only in position, and one of these pairs of patterns can be changed into another by altering pairs of bits enclosed between successive dotted lines. The pairs of patterns

```
0 1 1 0 1 0 0 0  and  0 1 1 1 0 0 0 0  and  0 0 0 1 1 0 0 0  etc.
0 1 1 1 0 0 1 0       0 1 1 1 1 1 0 0       0 0 0 0 1 1 1 0
```

differ roughly is size, and one of these pairs can be changed into another by altering sets of bits enclosed between successive dotted lines. These simple examples involve pairs of patterns, and let us say that in each pair the bits of one pattern are located in an array S of bit locations, and in the bits of the other pattern are located in an array T of bit locations. The dotted lines in our examples indicate mapping of bit locations, e.g.

S
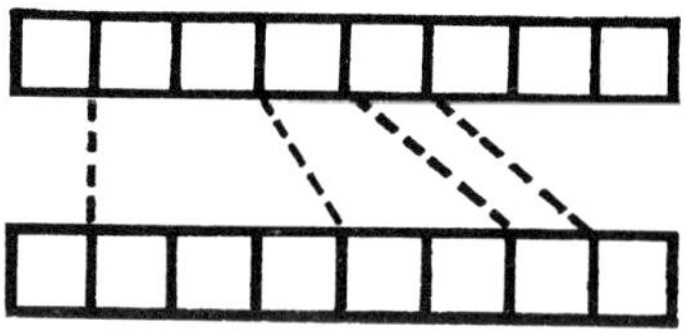
T

and the different pairs of patterns arise from different assignments of '1' and '0' to locations in the mapped subsets of S and T. When two patterns vary not only in size and position but are also subject to noise, it may be expedient to regard

0 1 1 0 1 0 0 0
0 1 0 1 0 0 1 0 , for example,

as variations of the same pattern. In cases such as this, the bits in mapped subsets of S and T are not restricted to being all 1's or all 0's.

If we are not to use our detailed knowledge of 'difference in position', we must surely use some less specific, more abstract, knowledge (or hypothesis) instead. We have mentioned examples of similar pairs of patterns in order to introduce the following suggestion as to what logical structure could reasonably be assumed. In suggesting what assumptions should be made, we are in fact formulating a recognition problem.

Problem 1

Let U be the union of S and T, and let U be partitioned into σ disjoint subsets $U_{11}, U_{12}, \ldots U_{1k}, \ldots U_{1\sigma}$, whose union is U, and let $\{U_{11}, \ldots U_{1\sigma}\} = U_1$. For $k = 1, \ldots \sigma$, let A_{1k} be a set of m alternative assignments of '0' or '1' to every bit location in U_{1k}. For instance if $m = 2$, the two members of A_{1k} might be

S
T
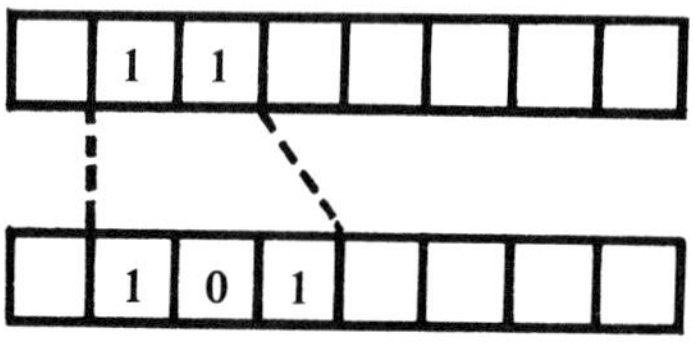

and
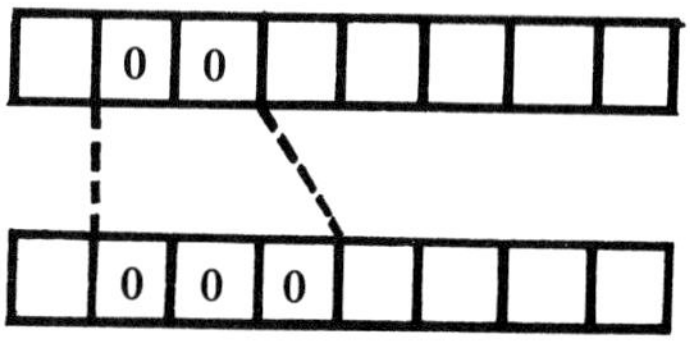

Let $A_1 = A_{11} \cup A_{12} \cup \ldots \cup A_{1k} \cup \ldots \cup A_{1\sigma}$. Let B_1 be the set of m^σ pairs made up of one member of A_{11} and one member of A_{12} and one member .... and one member of $A_{1\sigma}$.

Let U_2 be a second partition on U, A_2 be assignments of '0' and '1' to the subsets of U_2, and B_2 be the set of m^σ pairs of patterns on S and T made up from combinations of members of A_2. Let $B_3, B_4, \ldots$ be defined similarly, and let $C = B_1 \cup B_2 \cup B_3 \cup \ldots\ldots\ldots\ldots$ Problem 1 is:

to design a machine which, given some members of C as data, can automatically determine whether any further pair of patterns, one on S and one on T, is a member of C. This determination is to be made only from the given members of C, without $U_1, U_2, \ldots$ and $A_1, A_2, \ldots$ being given explicitly.

Before discussing Problem 1, let us consider a simplification:

Problem 2

A pattern on S is an assignment of '0' of '1' to every location in S. A *subpattern* is a subset of the 1's and 0's which constitute a pattern. Let S be partitioned into σ disjoint subsets $S_1, \ldots S_k, \ldots S_\sigma$ whose union is S, and let us write $\{S_1, \ldots S_a\} = S'$. A subpattern on S_k is an assignment of '0' or '1' to every location in S_k. Let A be a set of subpatterns, such that A contains m alternative subpatterns on each of $S_1, \ldots S_\sigma$. Let B be the set of all m^σ possible combinations of subpatterns belonging to A, such that each combination is a unique pattern on S. The problem is to design a machine which, given some members of B as data, can automatically determine whether any further pattern is a member of B. This determination is to be made only from the given members of B, without S′ or A being given explicitly. Let us say that the given members of B constitute a subset B_G of B. (c.f. Problem 1 in reference 24).

n-tuple Rule

Any n-element subset of S is an *n-tuple*. Let H be the set of *all* n-bit subpatterns such that each member of H is included in at least one member of B_G. The n-tuple rule is: decide that an unknown pattern X belongs to B if and only if on *every* n-tuple the n-bit subpattern which occurs in X belongs to H. When n = 2 we call the n-tuple rule the *2-tuple rule*. (The n-tuple rule requires that *all* n-bit subpatterns in X belong to H, whereas Bledsoe and Browning's method[3] works with *majorities.*)

Theorem 1

If none of the subsets $S_1, \ldots S_\sigma$ contains more than n locations, then the n-tuple rule never assigns to B a pattern X which does not belong to B.

Proof Consider a set Σ of n-tuples such that for all $k = 1, \ldots \sigma$, S_k is, or is included in, a member of Σ. If X contains a member of H on every n-tuple, then X contains a member of H on every member of Σ. A subpattern, on a member of Σ, which belongs to H is, or includes, a member of A. Therefore if X contains a member of H on every n-tuple, then X is made up exclusively of members of A, and therefore X belongs to B.

Theorem 2

If $m \leqslant n$, then the n-tuple rule never assigns to B a pattern X which does not belong to B.

Proof Let us first consider the case where $n=2$. Let us assume that the n-tuple rule assigns X to B. On any subset S_k of S', let $e_{11},..e_{1i},..e_{1Z}$ and $e_{21},..e_{2i},..e_{2Z}$ be subpatterns belonging to A, and let $e_{X1},...e_{Xi},...e_{XZ}$ be the subpattern of S_k in X. Let us assume that $e_{11},...e_{1Z} \neq e_{X1},...e_{XZ} \neq e_{21},...e_{2Z}$. In this case there must exist i such that $e_{Xi} \neq e_{1i}$ and j such that $e_{Xj} \neq e_{2j}$, and thus $e_{1i}e_{1j} \neq e_{2i}e_{2j}$. This contradicts our original assumption that the n-tuple (i.e. 2-tuple) rule assigns X to B, and thus proves Theorem 2 for the case where $n = 2$. The proof for $n > 2$ is an obvious extension of this:

Again let us consider a pattern X which the n-tuple rule assigns to B. On any subset S_k of S', let

$$\begin{matrix} e_{11},...e_{1Z}, & \text{be subpatterns belonging to A,} \\ e_{21},...e_{2Z} & \\ \vdots & \\ e_{m1},...e_{mZ} & \end{matrix}$$

and let us assume that none of these subpatterns is identical to the subpattern $e_{X1},...e_{XZ}$ on S_k in X. In this case there must exist i such that $e_{Xi} \neq e_{mm}$, and thus neither $e_{1i},e_{1j},..e_{1m}$ nor $e_{2i},e_{2j},..e_{2m}$ nor ..... nor $e_{mi},e_{mj},..e_{mm}$ is identical to $e_{Xi},e_{Xj},...e_{Xm}$. This means that, if $m \leqslant n$, the n-tuple rule does not assign X to B, and thus Theorem 2 is proved by contradiction.

Intersection Rule. The *intersection* of two patterns is the set of bits common to both of these patterns. For example, the intersection of 11001100 with 01011010 is −10−1−−0. Let I be the set of subpatterns such that the intersection between every pair of patterns in B_G belongs to I, and I contains no other subpatterns. Let I_X be the subset of I such that each member of I_X is completely included in an unknown pattern X. The intersection rule decides that X belongs to B if every bit in X belongs to a member of I_X.

Theorem 3

If the intersection rule assigns X to B, then the 2-tuple rule also assigns X to B.

Proof The proof is by contradiction. We assume that the intersection rule assigns X to B and that the 2-tuple rule does not assign X to B.

Assignment of X to B by the intersection rule implies that for *any* i there must exist α,β such that $e_{\alpha i} = e_{\beta i} = e_{xi}$ where $e_{\alpha i}$ and $e_{\beta i}$ are the ith bits in the αth and β^{th} members of B_G respectively, and e_{xi} is the ith bit in X. If the 2-tuple rule does not assign X to B there exists i, j such that $e_{\alpha i}e_{\alpha j} \neq e_{xi}e_{xj} \neq e_{\beta i}e_{\beta j}$. But $e_{\alpha i} = e_{\beta i} = e_{xi}$, and therefore $e_{\alpha j} = e_{\beta j}$. Therefore $e_{\alpha i}e_{\beta j}$ belong to the same member of I. Since $e_{\alpha i}e_{\alpha j} \neq e_{xi}e_{xj}$ the member of I which includes $e_{\alpha i}, e_{\alpha j}$ is not completely included in X, so that the intersection rule does not assign X to P. This contradicts our original assumption and thus proves Theorem 3.

Converse of Theorem 3. The converse of Theorem 3 does not hold. For instance if B_G = {0110, 0000, 0011, 1100, 1111, 1001} and X=1010, then the 2-tuple rule assigns X to B and the intersection rule does not.

General Solution to Problem 2

Theorems 1 and 2 tell us that the n-tuple rule provides a solution to Problem 2 if either the number of elements in S_k is not greater than n or $m \leqslant n$. In general, Problem 2 has no solution. To see this, suppose for example that the subpatterns in A on S_k are 111, 100, 010, 001. Unless all or nearly all the members of B are given in B_G, there is no way of deciding whether S_k in fact consists of three one-bit subsets, so that subpatterns such as 101, 000 can occur on S_k in members of B. In other words, 111, 100, 010, 001 may be the B'_G for a set B′ of 8 3-bit patterns: Problem 2 is intractable because it nests.

Determination of A

Let us consider Problem 2 in the restricted case where either $m \leqslant n$ or the number of subpatterns per S_k is not greater than n. In this case the n-tuple rule allows a machine to recognise members of B without having determined the members of A explicitly. An advantage of this is that it circumnavigates the problem of determining the members of A, and a disadvantage is that it involves using the set H which has many members, all of which must be stored explicitly. Similarly the intersection rule allows recognition of members of B without determination of A but at the cost of storing all the members of I. If A can be determined, members of B can be recognised by machine which stores only the members of A, and storage of the members of H or I is then unnecessary.

In the case where $m \leqslant 2$, a machine can easily determine a set A* of subpatterns and use A* in the same way that it would use A if A were known. A* would not have many more members than A. One procedure for determining A* is as follows. Arrange the patterns in B_G as the rows of a matrix, and let $V_1, \ldots V_i, V_j, \ldots V_N$ be the columns of this matrix.

Assign the first location in S to a subset S_1^* of S. Assign to S_1^* every element of S such that the corresponding V_i is identical or complementary to V_1. (1001 and 0110 are *complementary*). If the second location in S has not already been assigned to S_1^*, assign it to a subset S_2^* of S. Assign to S_2^* every element of S such that the corresponding V_i is identical or complementary to V_2. (If the second location in S has been assigned to S_1^*, assign the third, and all others whose vectors are identical or complementary to V_3, to S.). If the second location in S has been assigned to S_2^* and the third location in S has not yet been assigned to a subset, assign the third to a subset S_3^*. Assign to S_3^* every element of S such that the corresponding V_i is identical or complementary to V_3. Continue this procedure until all elements of S have been assigned to one of the subsets S_1^*, $S_2^*, S_3^*, S_4^*, \ldots$. The partition $\{S_1^*, S_2^*, S_3^*, \ldots\}$ partitions each pattern in B_G into subpatterns. Let A* be the set which contains all such (and no other) subpatterns, and let us call the following rule the A* rule: assign X to B if X is made up exhaustively of subpatterns belonging to A*. It is easy to prove that in the case where $m \leqslant 2$, the A* rule never assigns to B a pattern X which does not belong to B. But for $m > 2$, the A* rule may assign to B a pattern which does not belong to B. The A* rule has the advantage that the number of members of A* is generally less than the number of members of H, but the disadvantage of restrictions to $m \leqslant 2$.

(Our procedure for determining A* is a trivial ternary version of Nagy's[14] binary feature extraction programme. Block, Nilsson and Duda have described algorithms for determining sets analogous to A*, using multiple intersections.[4] It is interesting to compare these algorithms with the intersection rule given above.)

Discussion

Our brief study of Problem 2 has been intended to introduce a discussion of Problem 1. We have formulated Problem 1 because $U_1, U_2, \ldots$ and $A_1, A_2, \ldots$ can be chosen so that C consists exclusively of pairs of patterns differing only in position. For instance U_1 might be

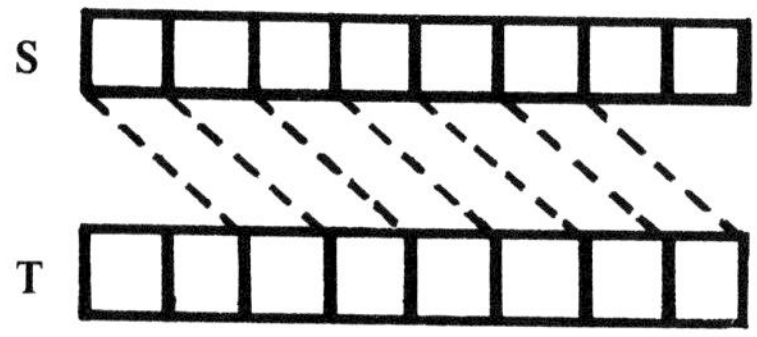

where bit locations between successive dotted lines belong to the same subset of U_1. Each subpattern belonging to A_1 would consist either exclusively of 1's or exclusively of 0's. If C consists exclusively of pairs of patterns differing only in position, a machine which is a solution to Problem 1 is a machine, which, given as data a set of pairs of patterns such that in each pair the two patterns differ from each other only in position, can determine whether or not a further pair of patterns differ from each other only in position . In the idealised case where all characters belonging to any given recognition class differ from each other only in position, the training set of members of C can consist of pairs of training-set patterns such that in each pair both of the patterns belong to the same recognition class, but in different pairs the patterns may belong to different recognition classes. If an unknown pattern X paired with a reference member of the rth class is found to belong to C, then X should be assigned to the rth class. In other words, if X is found to differ only in position from a reference pattern belonging to the rth recognition class, then X should be assigned to the rth class.

A machine which recognised characters in this way would count as a successful completion of the first step of our proposed methodology. This machine would *learn* to recognise patterns varying only in position: the machine would find out for itself which of all possible S/T mappings were those corresponding to shift. The machine designer would not have used his exact knowledge of what is meant by variation *only in position*, because the machine would not have been 'told' which of all possible choices of $U_1,U_2.$ $U_1,U_2, \ldots$ and $A_1,A_2, \ldots$ had actually been made. The position-only case is just one of the possible choices.

So far as our proposed methodology is concerned, the next question would be whether the differences between pairs of patterns, such that in each pair the two patterns belonged to the same real non-idealised recognition class, corresponded to a choice of $U_1,U_2, \ldots$ and $A_1,A_2, \ldots$. If same-class pairs of patterns were used as the training set of members of C, and X was assigned to the rth class if X paired with a reference member of the rth class was found to belong to C; and if reliable recognition was achieved this way, then the answer to the question which we have just asked would be affirmative.

This discussion of Problem 1 has been carefully phrased in conditional terms "if. ." and ". . would . . " because Problem 1 has a snag: it is generally intractable. To make Problem 1 tractable, we must restrict it. For instance it might be helpful to restrict members of $A_1,A_2, \ldots$ to consist exclusively of 1's or exclusively of 0's. Further, it might be helpful to work with overlapping subsets of U instead of non-overlapping subsets. These suggestions have influenced exploratory work in which transference of learning has been demonstrated experimentally but only marginally.

To see how the possibility of transference arises, let us consider a collection of (ordinary non-idealised) recognition classes. Let C' be the set of *all* pairs of characters belonging to these recognition classes, such that in each pair belonging to C' the two patterns belong to the same recognition class, but in any two pairs the patterns in one pair may belong to a different class to the patterns in the other pair. By pairing members of the training sets of the recognition classes, we can obtain a training set of pairs belonging to C'. Let us assume that a machine is available which, given a training set of pairs belonging to C', can determine whether any further pair of patterns belongs to C'. If this machine decides that an unknown pattern X paired with a reference member of the rth class constitutes a pair belonging to C', then X should be assigned to the rth class. This rule may be used in recognising a member of the rth class even if no member of the rth class is included in any member of the training set of C'. In this case, *transference* is exhibited, since recognition of a member of the rth class is facilitated by the use of training sets of other classes. According to this, it might for example be possible to use 2's and 3's to facilitate the recognition of 8's.

If , for example, training sets of 2's and 3's could be used to facilitate recognition of 8's, the final result would be the same as it a larger training set of 8's had been used. This sort of virtual increase in training set size could perhaps be valuable, because, without transference of learning, training sets have often been found experimentally to be too small.[13]

It is tempting to speculate that when a human designer *imagines* unusual shapes of e.g. '8', he is in fact using knowledge of shape derived from experience of other classes.

Transference may eventually prove to be useful in automatic recognition of complete words or syllables. There have been two main conventional approaches to the recognition of written or spoken words:

(i) Via segmentation into letters,[8] phonemes[16,19] or other segments.[22,5]

(ii) Recognition of a word as a single unsegmented two dimensional pattern. This approach is examplified in the work of Denes and Mathews[7] and King and Tunis[11].

Approach (ii) has the disadvantage that a separate training or design set is required for each word to be recognised, and this disadvantage obviously weighs more heavily the greater the number of different words to be recognised. Approach (i) has the disadvantage that segmentation is a source or error. Furthermore, in cursive script and in speech it is not reasonable to assume that the precise shape of a character, or the precise accoustics of a phoneme, are independent of the recognition classes of adjacent characters or phonemes. In this case, even if segmentation could reliably be achieved, recognition of words would involve more than a simple multiplication of probabilities of segments.

The requirement of approach (i) for a training or design set of words belonging to each word-class could perhaps be reduced by transference of learning between word-classes. Suppose for instance that the training set for the rth word-class consisted of only one specimen word. It might be possible to recognise an input word belonging to the rth word-class by transference of learning from two or three specimens of each of several thousand different word-classes. Having thus overcome the main disadvantage of approach (i), it would be unnecessary to resort to approach (ii), so that segmentation and its attendant difficulties would be avoided.

Acknowledgements

Theorems 2 and 3 and their proofs originated from Michael J. C. Gordon while he was working with me during August 1969.

REFERENCES

1. D. H. Andrews, A. J. Atrubin, and K. C. Hu. "The IBM 1975 Optical Page Reader. Part III: Recognition Logic Development", IBM J. Res. and Dev. Vol. 12, pp. 364-371, September, 1968.
2. A. G. Arkadev and E. M. Braverman. "Teaching Computers to Recognise Patterns", Academic Press, London and New York, 1967.
3. W. W. Bledsoe and I. Browning. "Pattern Recognition and Reading by Machine". 1959 Proc. Eastern Joint Computer Conf., Boston, Mass., Dec. 1-3, 1959, pp. 225-232.
4. H. D. Block, N. J. Nilsson, and R. O. Duda. "Determination and Detection of Features in Patterns". In "Computer and Information Sciences", J. T. Tou and R. H. Wilcox Eds. Spartan Books 1964, pp. 75-110.
5. D. G. Bobrow and D. H. Klatt. "A Limited Speech Recognition System". Proc. EJCC, 1968, pp. 305-318.
6. J. S. Bomba. "Alpha-Numeric Character Recognition Using Local Operators". 1959, Proc. EJCC, pp. 218.
7. P. Denes and M. V. Mathews. "Spoken Digit Recognition Using Time-Frequency Pattern Matching. JASA, Vol. 32, No. 2, Nov. 1960, pp. 1450-1455.
8. R. O. Duda and P. E. Hart. "Experiments in the Recognition of Hand-printed Text: Part II – Context Analysis. AFIPS Conference Proceedings, Vol. 33, FJCC 1968. Thompson Books. pp. 1139-1149.
9. E. C. Greanias. "Some Important Factors in the Practical Utilisation of Optical Character Readers". In "Optical Character Recognition", Fischer, Pollock, Raddack and Stevens, Eds., Spartan Books 1962, pp. 129-146.
10. R. L. Kashyap, C. C. Blaydon and K. S. Fu. "Stochastic Approximation", in

"Adaptive, Learning and Pattern Recognition Systems," J. S. Mendel and K. S. Fu, Eds., Academic Press, 1970, pp. 329-355.

11. J. H. King Jr. and C. J. Tunis. "Some Experiments in Spoken Word Recognition". IBM J. Res. & Dev., Vol. 19, No. 1, Jan. 1966, pp. 65-80.
12. J. H. Munson. "Experiments in the Recognition of Hand-Printed Text: Part I. "Character Recognition".
13. G. Nagy. "State of the Art in Pattern Recognition." Proc. IEEE, Vol. 56, No. 5, May 1968, pp. 836-862.
14. G. Nagy. "Feature Extraction on Binary Patterns." IEEE Trans. on Systems Science and Cybernetics. Vol. SSC5, No. 4, Oct. 1969, pp. 273-278.
15. National Cash Register Company. U. K. Pat. No. 1, 132, 548; 1968.
16. A. L. Nelson, M. B. Hersher, T. B. Martin, H. J. Zadell, and J. W. Falter. "Accoustic Recognition by Analogue Feature Abstraction Techniques". In "Models for the Perception of Speech and Visual Form", W. Wathen-Dunn, Ed., MIT Press 1967, pp. 428-440.
17. N. J. Nilsson. "Learning Machines". McGraw Hill 1965.
18. J. R. Parks. "A Multifont System of Analysis for Mixed Font and Hand-Blocked Printed Characters Recognition." In "Automatic Interpretation and Classification of Images." A. Grasselli, Ed., Academic Press, 1969, pp. 295-322.
19. D. R. Reddy. "Computer Recognition of Connected Speech." JASA, Vol. 42, No. 2, August 1967, pp. 329-347.
20. Scan-Data Corporation. "Improvements in or Relating to Character Recognition Systems or Apparatus." U.K. Pat No. 1, 129, 572, Oct. 1968.
21. G. S. Sebestyen. "Decision Making Processes in Pattern Recognition." Macmillan, 1962.
22. P. N. Sholtz and R. Bakis. "Spoken Digit Recognition Using Vowel-Consonant Segmentation." JASA, Vol. 34, No. 1, Jan. 1962, pp. 1-5.
23. Ya. Z. Tsypkin. "Use of the Stochastic Approximation Method in Estimating Unknown Distribution Densities from Observations". Automation and Remote Control, Vol. 27, No. 3, March 1966, pp. 432-434.
24. J. R. Ullmann. "Some Problems in Artificial Intelligence". In "Progress in Brain Research, Vol. 17", N. Wiener and J. P. Shade, Eds., Elsevier, 1965, pp. 102-117.
25. J. R. Ullmann. "Transference of Learning between Recognition Classes." Available from IEEE Computer Group Repository.
26. R. W. Weeks. "Rotating Faster Character Recognition System." AIEE Transactions, Vol. 80, Part I, Communication and Electronics, Sept. 1961, pp. 353-359.

PATTERN RECOGNITION AS INFORMATION COMPRESSION

Satosi Watanabe

UNIVERSITY OF HAWAII
HONOLULU, HAWAII

Abstract

Pattern recognition is considered as a case of information compression. This aspect of pattern recognition is characterized by the following facts: (1) The larger the information compression in one stroke, the better it is, but the larger the information compression, the more difficult the task is. (2) If the information compression is to be made in steps, it is desirable that the burden of information compression be distributed more or less evenly over different steps. Both the vectorial approach and the grammatical approach are examined.

1. Pattern Recognition as Classification

In this paper, we take the viewpoint that the task of pattern recognition lies in classification. We consider a set A of N possible objects and a set of its subsets $B_i \subset A$, $(i = 1,2, \ldots, M)$ such that usually $B_i \cap B_j = \emptyset$ $(i \neq j)$ and $A = \bigcup_{i=1}^{M} B_i$. Each subset or class B_i is characterized by some conditions on its members, but sometimes one of them is a meaningless catch-all subset. The task is to place a given object, member of A, into one of the subsets B's, according to the characterization of the subsets. If we use Hartley's information which is logarithm of possible alternatives, the information that an object is a particular member of the entire set A is log N and the information that the object belongs to a particular one of the subsets B_i is log M.* The necessary information compression is log N/M. This means that the classification aims to extract a "useful" information in the amount of log M from the given information in the amount of log N.

It is sometimes contended that the descriptive or grammatical approach to pattern recognition is not concerned with classification. But this contention is ill-founded because a particular structural or grammatical description does not in general specify every detail of an object, hence it corresponds to a small group of objects. Assignment of a structural description to an object therefore amounts to placing it in a subset or class.

2. Four Kinds of Classification

A class can be defined either by its extension or by its intension. The extension is the list of all the names of the individual members that form the class. The intension is the list of all the properties or predicates that are shared by all the members of the class. Corresponding to these two possibilities, there are two elementary kinds of data processing: list-look-up and (intensional) sorting. A data card representing an object may be carrying the identification number or name of the object, and the memory device may be stored with the membership list of a class. The card can be classified either as a member or a non-member according as its identification number is found in the stored list or not. This is the list-look-up process. The data card representing an individual object may be carrying (other than its identification number) the list of properties satisfied by the object. The card-sorter can be so adjusted that those cards that have a certain selection of properties are sorted out. This very common kind of card-sorting is an intensional sorting.

Logicians define a class either by its intension or by its extension. But a mother teaches to her child the class of dogs simply by pointing to a few samples of dogs. She may show a few non-dogs. The child will be able to tell the next time whether a new animal is a dog or not. This is a case of what may be called "paradigm-oriented classification." This is the kind of classification that human intelligence is specially good at. What is usually called pattern recognition in the engineering terminology is a paradigm-oriented classification.

*The entropy $-\sum_{j=1}^{N} p_j \log p_j$ becomes log N if $p_j = 1/N$. This quantity represents the amount of "ignorance" if it is not known which one of the N alternatives is the case. If this is made known, the ignorance becomes zero, providing information in the amount of log N.

From the logical point of view, it is obvious that a few paradigms of a class cannot define the class uniquely. Any set of objects that include the given paradigms could be the answer. The intension of such a class can be any arbitrary predicate that is implied by the conjunction of all the common properties of its given paradigms. In other words, the arbitrariness inherent in inductive generalization is inevitable also in the paradigm-oriented classification. The ultimate goodness and badness of an answer depends on the utility of the resulting classification. Human intuition has a certain feeling as to what predicates are more desirable to be used in generalization, and more likely to lead to a useful classification. This intuition of course cannot be an unfailing guide. See Reference 1 for more on the inductive arbitrariness in pattern recognition. Recently, some authors have started also to talk about the importance of intuition or of a priori knowledge or problem-oriented judgement in pattern recognition. These are signs of new awareness of inductive arbitrariness.

The fourth kind of classification is what is known as clustering problem. In this case we are not even given paradigms, and are asked to generate classes among the given objects with known properties in such a way that the members of a class cohere together strongly to one another due to similarity or due to some higher-order relationship. Clustering is subject to a larger extent of inductive arbitrariness than paradigm-oriented pattern recognition. See Reference 1 where paradigm-oriented pattern recognition and clustering are respectively characterized as double induction and abduction.

It is very important to note that when an answer is given in paradigm-oriented pattern recognition or clustering, the remaining task becomes that of sorting, because the class is now specified by its intension.

3. Types of Class-Intension

The main difference between the structural or grammatical approach and the vector space approach is found in the difference in the mode of description of class-intensions. In the grammatical approach, a class is characterized by a predicate of the type: consists of such and such elementary components (primitives) which are arranged in such and such manner. The vectorial approach divides itself in two. In the conventional "zone" method, a class is characterized by a predicate of the type: belongs to such and such volume in the (n-dimensional) representation space. In the "subspace" method, a class is characterized by a predicate: belongs to such and such subspace in the (n-dimensional) representation space.[2]

The structural description and vectorial descriptions are not so irreconcilably different as they might appear. If we introduce a convention determining a way to assign a numerical label (scalar or vector) to each structure description, the description becomes vectorial although the concept of nearness may not reflect the frequency of actual errors. Conversely, each vector component (or an expansion coefficient of a function) may be considered as a primitive and the ordered sequence of coefficients representing the strength of components can be considered as describing the relations among the primitives. Similarly, the binary vector expression of a black and white picture can be considered either as a vectorial representation or as a structural description whose primitives are black and white.

The papers along the line of structural description approach give the impression that this approach has nothing to do with a paradigm-oriented classification or a clustering. This is due to the fact that the authors have an inclination towards deductive exposition and they start directly with a list of terminal terms (primitives) and production rules. As stated earlier, once the primitives and the grammatical rules have been decided, we can derive and define all possible classes, hence the entire task becomes a sorting. In reality, the authors have a concrete set of patterns in mind, and their lists of primitives and production rules are a result of clustering effort. This truly inductive side is usually kept untold in the papers. It is another example of mathematicians' customary untruthful way of reporting their results, omitting the inductive aspect of their thinking.

4. Pattern Recognition as Information Compression

As pointed out in Section 1, the task of pattern recognition is classification and classification implies information compression. Indeed, the raw data about an object contain a tremendous amount of information that is irrelevant to the classificatory predicate. The essence of a pattern recognition technique lies in its capability of eliminating irrelevant and redundant information taking advantage of some regularities that exist in the problems under consideration. In other words it is an information compression. If the classificatory predicate contains inductive ambiguity, so does the notion of relevance. If we define the compression index of an operation by the difference between the information before and after, the compression index for the entire pattern recognition is log N/M, which is usually very large compared with the useful information log M. As a consequence, the entire information compression in many cases is executed in several steps.

From observation of actual cases of pattern recognition, one may probably summarize the situation as follows: (1) The larger the information compression in one step, the better it is, but the larger the information compression, the more difficult the task is. (2) If the information compression is to be made in steps, it is desirable that the burden of information compression be distributed more or less evenly over different steps.

The ideal information compression is one which does not lose any relevant portion of information, but this is not always guaranteed, and a certain compromise is bound to be made between preservation of relevant information and feasibility or ease of the operation.

5. Vectorial Description

Suppose that the set A of possible objects occupies the volume L^n in an n-dimensional space and that points within an elementary volume h^n are experimentally undistinguishable. The dimension n is the number of measured quantities about objects. Then the number of possible alternative N is $(L/h)^n$ which is usually enormously large compared with the number M of classes. One stroke compression $\log[(L/h)^n/M]$ is usually very difficult not because it is difficult to find a solution or a dividing surface satisfying the paradigms, but because there is too much arbitrariness. This necessitates preprocessing effecting a dimensionality reduction. If we first reduce the dimensionality from n to n', (we assume the same order h of indistinguishability in the new space) the information compression is done in two steps. The first step amounts to $\log[(L/h)^n/(L/h)^{n'}] = (n - n') \log(L/h)$ and the second step amounts to $\log[(L/h)^{n'}/M]$. Although the total is the same as before, this division in two steps usually makes the task considerably easier.

The SELFIC (self-featuring-information-compression) method[2] can be used for the purpose of this first stage dimensionality reduction, and the resulting new space in this case is a subspace of the original space. Instead of considering all possible vectors in the space, consider all the available paradigm points of different classes together. It is usually the case that these points are lying, within very small errors, within a subspace whose dimensionality is considerably smaller than that of the original space. The SELFIC method allows us to obtain such a subspace.

The SELFIC method can also be explained as one of maximal information compression provided we adopt a slightly different definition of information. Let the weight p_i of the i-th coordinate be defined as being proportional to the sum (over paradigms) of the squares of the i-th components of paradigm vectors of all classes subject to $\Sigma p_i = 1$. This p_i can be regarded as representing the measure to which the i-th coordinate axis is used to represent the paradigm points. If we define the entropy S by these p's, we may consider S as the average information that a particular coordinate axis carries if an object is represented by that axis. If p's are spread out rather evenly over many axes, the information carried by a single axis becomes large. This is similar to the fact that if vectors are spread out evenly over a volume, the information carried by an elementary volume becomes large. This S however depends on the coordinate system. If we rotate the coordinate system S changes. If we follow the principle that we should aim at the maximum information compression, we should rotate the axes until S becomes minimum. This is precisely what the SELFIC method does. The dimensionality reduction is then effected by just truncating those axes whose p's are small. A parallel algorithm in the "volume philosophy" instead of the "sub-space philosophy" would be to cut away those volumes where the paradigm points are scarce.

In the CLAFIC (class-featuring-information-compression)[2], we take the paradigms of a single class and determine by the same method as SELFIC the subspace in which most of the paradigm vectors of the class are lying within a small errors. This subspace is the result of the maximal information compression as explained above, only this time referring to a single class.

6. Structural Description

We next consider the case of structural description and see how the information compression is taking place. Instead of arguing in purely abstract terms, let us rather consider a simple concrete case. The object consists of a picture drawn on a tape which is a one-dimensional sequence of L "positions." Each position consists of $n \times n$ meshpoints which can be either white or black. Any arbitrary distribution of black and white meshpoints in a position is conceivable, but in a "correct" picture appears only one of the μ primitives (terminal terms), or a nonsense distribution. Each primitive belongs to one or the other of ν intermediate terms. Any concatenation of length L of ν intermediate terms is conceivable but in a "correct" picture appears only one of the M types due to the grammatical rules.

The total information compression is $\log N/M$ where N is $(2^{n^2})^L$ because each meshpoint can be either one of the two colors and there are n^2 points in a position and there are L positions. In other words the initial information is Ln^2. Due to the fact that there are only μ possibilities in each position, the entropy is reduced from Ln^2 to $L \log \mu$. Next due to the fact that some primitives are grouped together so that there are only ν intermediate terms, the entropy changes from $L \log \mu$ to $L \log \nu$. This last expresses the fact that there could be ν^L different types of strings in terms of the intermediate terms. Finally, due to the grammatical rules only M out of ν^L can happen, which changes entropy from $L \log \nu$ to $\log M$.

This sequence of operations is a successive information compression because

$$Ln^2 > L \log \mu > L \log \nu > \log M$$

The first step compression is done by the specification of primitive components. The second step compression is done in virtue of the substitution rules which change intermediate terms to terminal terms. The third step compression is done by the main syntactical part of the grammar which consists of the rules which substitute a group of intermediate terms for an intermediate term or for a starting term.

It is quite possible that the same collection of pictures can be produced by more than one grammar. Since the total information compression is constant, probably the most desirable type of grammar is the one which has a well-balanced distribution of information compression over different steps.

A grammar which uses a small number of primitives has to have a very complicated grammar. Such a grammar has to use a small value of n and the result is that we do not gain much at the first stage compression. The extreme case is one where $n = 1$ and $\mu = 2$, i.e. the case where a position consists only of one meshpoint which have two alternatives. In such a grammar, there is no information compression at the first stage, as a result a tremendous burden of compression is shifted to the second and third stages.

The other extreme case is the one where the entire domain of Nn^2 meshpoints is considered as a single position, and there are M primitives (which is the largest possible value of μ). Here we do not need any grammar but a tremendous burden is placed on the first stage. It should be noted that the first stage has anyway to be carried out by some non-structural type of pattern recognition. If we rely too much on this stage, the approach can no longer be called structural. In this connection it should be emphasized that any structural pattern recognition method depends on the non-structural method for recognition of primitives. The important thing is to find a good balance between the structural and non-structural parts.

REFERENCE

1. S. Watanabe, "Pattern Recognition as Inductive Process" in S. Watanabe (ed.), *Methodologies of Pattern Recognition,* Academic Press, New York, 1969, pp. 521-533.

2. S. Watanabe, P. Lambert, et al., "Evaluation and Selection of Variables in Pattern Recognition" in J. Tou (ed.), *Computer and Information Sciences -- II,* Academic Press, New York, 1967, pp. 91-122.

SCENE UNDERSTANDING SYSTEMS

Patrick H. Winston

THE ARTIFICIAL INTELLIGENCE LABORATORY
MASSACHUSETTS INSTITUTE OF TECHNOLOGY
CAMBRIDGE, MASSACHUSETTS

For a number of years, M.I.T.'s Artificial Intelligence Laboratory has been investigating the problems surrounding computer vision and computer manipulation. This has been a large effort, involving a great deal of engineering as well as basic research. The problems fully justify the attention, however, because the design and implementation of a system that perceives and manipulates structures is a way of approaching the serious problems inherently involved in designing big image understanding systems with lots of knowledge. This set of problems now seems central to the further development of a theory of intelligence adequate enough to support the design of machines with general intelligence rivaling that of us humans.

One particular standard of expertise that we have worked toward is the ability to copy configurations like those which small children construct with their toy blocks. This ability was first demonstrated by our system in late 1970. The machine became capable of handling scenes consisting of blocks of any manipulable size arrayed together in front of and on top of one another. Figure 1 illustrates this sort of configuration. The machine can now copy such scenes routinely, using a warehouse of spare parts previously shown to it.

Now some of the principal modules in our system are the following:

1. the line finder
2. the bookkeeper
3. the body finder
4. the body relation finder
5. the body position finder
6. the body dimension finder
7. the construction planner

The line finder is charged with the difficult job of producing a straight line drawing from a million or so noisy intensity samples. The bookkeeper uses the resulting line drawing to produce a data base for the use of the remaining programs. The body finder in turn determines how many bodies are probably represented by the drawing and stores information as to which regions belong to each. Once this is done, the position finder determines the XYZ coordinates of each object, the dimension finder calculates the size, and the construction planner establishes an orderly sequence of arm motions capable of copying the now fully analyzed structure.

Curiously none of these modules are deeply rooted in mathematical theory. There is little appeal to statistical ideas in the line finder and there is certainly no hint of the increasingly popular syntactic-style line drawing theories in the other modules. This is not because of an aversion to theory on our part, but rather reflects our feeling that the analytic procedures themselves should be thought of as theories. After all, in some sense theories are simply descriptions, and in many cases, an actual program is the most desirable description.

A straightforward system using a set of good modules for each of the listed tasks cannot be expected to work very well. In addition, a big system must have mechanisms for coping with the errors that good, but not perfect, modules must occasionally make. That is to say, the system must not only have good modules, it must also have an understanding of how those modules fail, it must have tests for developing suspicion, and it must be able to back away from errors by repealing some previous decision and examining alternatives.

Let me illustrate by discussing our two schemes for monocular XYZ position determination and how they interact. The first method works through optimizing focus. A procedure written by B. K. P. Horn moves the camera lens to a position that maximizes a measure of the high frequency portion of the spatial intensity spectrum. This can always be expected to locate a vertex to within an inch, but with our present equipment, this method is not capable of the kind of accuracy we need to pick up an object.

I developed another method that works through heuristics that determine the supporting object or objects for the one whose coordinates are to be determined. If the supporting structure is the table itself, then we can use the two dimensional pair of camera coordinates together with the prior knowledge about the table's position to fully determine the object's XYZ position.

If instead there is a series of objects between the table and the object to be located, one need only apply the process iteratively, working from the table up, measuring the height of each object as it is encountered. These heights establish a series of horizontal supporting planes of known height that give the third required constraint for determining the XYZ coordinates of the successive objects.

It is clear then that a way of finding the supports for each object in the scene is a prime requirement. The presence of T-type vertexes, as illustrated in Figure 2, often suggests when one object obscures another, but does not indicate whether the reason is because the nearer one is in front of or rather on top of the object further away.

The basic heuristic program we use tries to answer the question by a two part process. First the program attempts to find all the lines forming the bottom border of each object, the so-called bottom lines. This first part of the program rarely errs. Figure 3 illustrates the sort of results to be expected.

The second portion of the program identifies all bodies with faces that share these bottom lines and judges such bodies to be underneath the body that supplies these lines. This works in the six examples of Figure 4, but tends to do poorly when confused by large background objects, as in the case shown in Figure 5. There the problem is that the large background object shares a bottom line with the supported object in the foreground because the standing brick elevates that supported object into the line of sight.

We have augmented our basic scheme with refinements that prevent some support-hypothesizing mistakes of this type, but errors still can be expected. When this method works, it is very good, accurate to within an eighth of an inch or so. But the errors resulting from incorrect hypothesizing of support relations cause chaos. Errors of several inches or more are likely.

Our total system in some sense understands the capabilities and kinds of failure characteristic of the two position finders. The result is a position finding faculty much better than could be expected from either module working separately or from any weighted average of the two module's opinions.

The way this happens is straightforward. The position-through-structure method proposes or hypothesizes a position. This position is checked by the position-through-focus method. If the results are compatible, we can be quite confident of a set of accurate coordinates. If the answers differ by an inch or more, the system realizes that the support-deducing programs have probably erred. This initiates backup into the structure-hypothesizing program to a point where a wrong decision may have been made. An alternative is selected, in this case a different guess about support, and the position-through-focus critic is again tried.

I hope this illuminates why we feel that it is bad to expend a lot of effort in polishing already good methods. It is better to work toward a system that knows how to use many less than perfect methods in a harmonious and cooperative way.

But this point of view in turn forces us to broaden any tendencies we might have toward traditional thinking about system organization. We must think not only of the flow of control and the processing of data, but also about channels that carry complaints, suggestions, requests for help, demands for backup from error, and probably other things yet unimagined. Through experiments with these concepts in our vision laboratory we hope to discover the inadequacies in existing computer languages and ways of thinking about systems. It is in facing these that we develop ideas that I feel will have significant influence in practical pattern recognition situations.

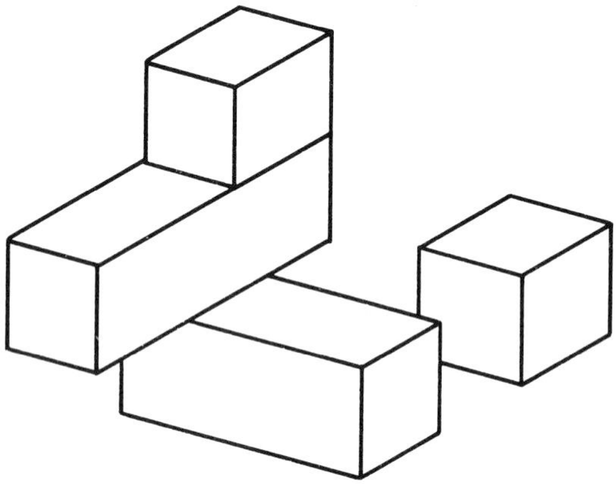

Figure 1. A scene typical of those understood by the M. I. T. robot

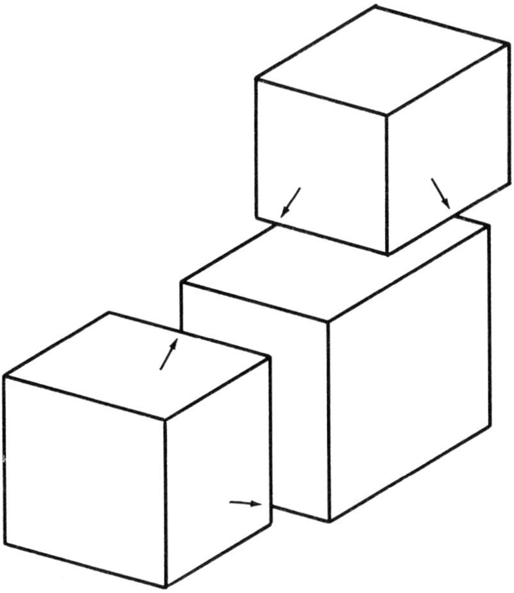

Figure 2. T-type vertexes suggest that one object obscures another

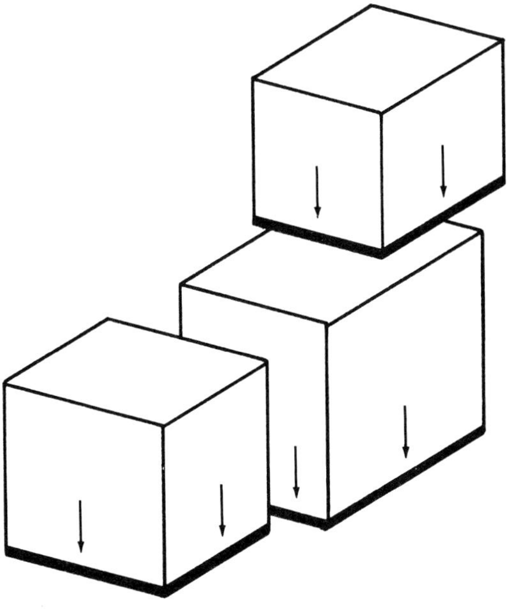

Figure 3. The supports for each object are found by a program that first identifies each object's bottom border

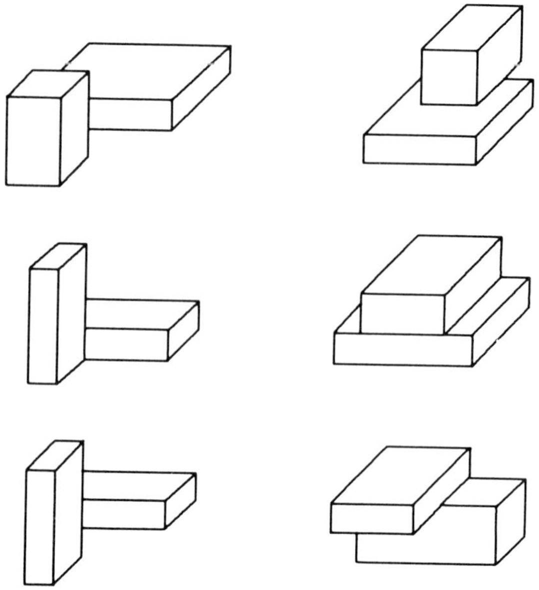

Figure 4. The program that finds each object's supports has no difficulty with these configurations

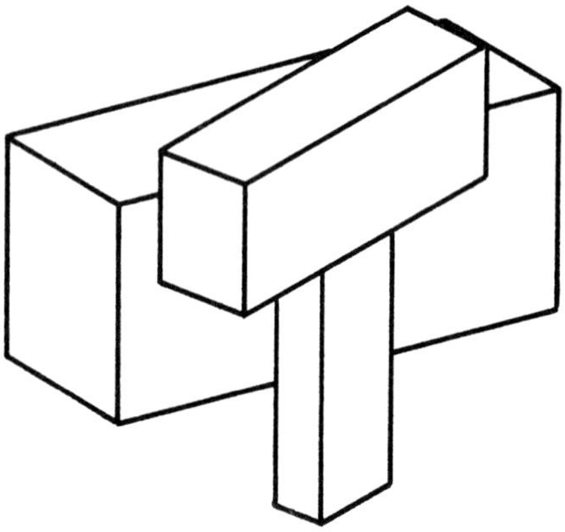

Figure 5. Large objects in the background can confuse the program that tries to find each object's supports

LEAST-MEAN-SQUARE APPROACH TO PATTERN CLASSIFICATION*

S. S. Yau[1] *and J. M. Garnett*[2]

NORTHWESTERN UNIVERSITY
EVANSTON, ILLINOIS

I. Introduction

The least-mean-square error (LMS) criterion provides a standard for assessing the quality of an approximation to an arbitrary function. In statistical pattern classification, there have been a number of techniques whose learning algorithms are based on the LMS criterion. The main advantages of using this criterion are that each of these algorithms assumes no a priori knowledge of the probability distribution of patterns (i.e. nonparameteric), yields a unique optimal solution and the pattern classifier is either a linear machine or its generalization, a Φ machine [1]. In this paper we will present a unification of these algorithms and provide some generalization in certain cases.

Let $\underline{x} = [x_1, x_2, \ldots, x_n]^t$ be the pattern vector, where x_i, $i = 1, 2, \ldots, n$, is the ith measurement of the pattern, and the superscript t denotes the transpose. Let E^n denote the n-dimensional Euclidean space, called the *pattern space,* which consists of all possible $\underline{x}$'s. Let

$$\underline{\Phi}(\underline{x}) = [\Phi_1(\underline{x}), \Phi_2(\underline{x}), \ldots, \Phi_d(\underline{x})]^t, \tag{1}$$

where $\Phi_i(\underline{x})$, $i = 1, 2, \ldots, d$, are linearly independent, real, single-valued functions of the components of $\underline{x}$. The corresponding space for $\underline{\Phi}(\underline{x})$ is E^d. To simplify our notation, we shall use $\underline{\Phi}(\underline{x})$ throughout this paper. For

*The work reported here is supported in part by U.S. PHS Grant No. 2 PO1 GM 15418-09.

[1] Departments of Electrical Engineering and Computer Sciences and Biomedical Engineering Center.

[2] Department of Electrical Engineering.

instance, a linear machine has $d = n + 1$, $\Phi_i(\underline{x}) = x_i$, $i = 1,2, \ldots, n$, and $\Phi_{n+1}(\underline{x}) = 1$. With a predetermined $\underline{\Phi}(\underline{x})$, the mean-square error for approximating a vector-valued function $\underline{f}(\underline{x})$ by a linear function of $\underline{\Phi}(\underline{x})$ becomes

$$E(\underline{W}) = \int_{E^n} |\underline{f}^t(\underline{x}) - \underline{\Phi}^t(\underline{x})\, \underline{W}|^2\, p(\underline{x})\, d\underline{x} \tag{2}$$

where $\underline{W}$ is the matrix of coefficients of the linear function of $\underline{\Phi}(\underline{x})$, and $p(\underline{x})$ is the probability density function of all the patterns in the pattern space E^n.

Application of the LMS criterion consists of finding $\underline{W}$ which minimizes $E(\underline{W})$. This process is fairly straightforward and will be presented in Section II. The resultant expression of $\underline{W}$ involves quantities which depend on $\underline{f}(\underline{x})$. In Section III it will be pointed out that several of the learning algorithms of the existing pattern classification techniques [2,3,4] differ basically in their choices of the function $\underline{f}(\underline{x})$, and thus the general LMS criterion provides a unification of these algorithms. For each choice of $\underline{f}(\underline{x})$, the resultant expression for $\underline{W}$ contains quantities which are dependent on unknown probability density functions $p(\underline{x}/\theta_i)$. There are several methods of approximating these quantities depending on the type of data available [5,6,7,8] and some of these methods will be considered in Section IV. Section V will briefly review several pattern classification methods [3,4,9] which are based on the LMS criterion, but are not simply special cases of applying our general formulation. In Section VI, a well known case of application of the LMS criterion [2] will be extended to provide a solution to a slightly more general class of problems.

II. The General Solution

We would like to find $\underline{W}$ which minimizes (2). There is a natural isomorphism between the set $\{\underline{W}\}$ of all possible matrices $\underline{W}$ and E^{dd_1}, where d_1 is the dimension of the range of $f(\cdot)$. The vector in E^{dd}, corresponding to $\underline{W}$ is $\underline{V}(\underline{W})$, where $\underline{V}(\underline{W})$ is a column vector which consists of the columns of $\underline{W}$ stacked on top of each other. $E(\underline{W})$ can be shown to be a convex function of $\underline{W}$ and hence has a unique minimum. Thus, to minimize $E(\underline{W})$ we set its gradient with respect to $\underline{V}(\underline{W})$ to zero. This yields

$$0 = \int_{E^n} [-2\underline{\Phi}(\underline{x})\underline{f}^t(\underline{x}) + 2\underline{\Phi}(\underline{x})\,\underline{\Phi}^t(\underline{x})\underline{W}]\; p(\underline{x})\, d\underline{x} \tag{3}$$

and

$$[\int_{E^n} \underline{\Phi}(\underline{x})\, \underline{\Phi}^t(\underline{x})\, p(\underline{x})\, d\underline{x}]\, \underline{W} = \int_{E^n} \underline{\Phi}(\underline{x})\, \underline{f}^t(\underline{x})\, p(\underline{x})\, d\underline{x}. \tag{4}$$

We denote

$$\underline{B} = \int_{E^n} \underline{\Phi}(\underline{x})\, \underline{\Phi}^t(\underline{x})\, p(\underline{x})\, d\underline{x} \tag{5}$$

and call this the *dispersion matrix* of $\underline{\Phi}(\underline{x})$ with respect to the probability density function $p(\underline{x})$. It is noted that

$$\underline{B} = \underline{\Gamma} + \underline{\mu}\, \underline{\mu}^t, \tag{6}$$

where $\underline{\Gamma}$ is the covariance matrix and $\underline{\mu}$ is the mean vector of $\Phi(x)$ with respect to the probability density function $p(\underline{x})$. Furthermore, for all practical purposes $\underline{B}$ is nonsingular. If this is not so, then it would have been possible to use fewer of the functions $\{\Phi_i(\underline{x})\}$ in defining $\underline{\Phi}(\underline{x})$. Finally, with $\underline{B}$ being nonsingular, we have a general solution matrix based on the LMS criterion given by

$$\underline{W} = \underline{B}^{-1} \int_{E^n} \underline{\Phi}(\underline{x})\, \underline{f}^t(\underline{x})\, p(\underline{x})\, d\underline{x}. \tag{7}$$

III. Choice of f(x)

Chaplin and Levadi [2] considered choosing a set $\{\underline{\alpha}_i\}$ of R points, one assigned to each pattern category, in R-1 dimensional Euclidean space E^{R-1}. The points were chosen so that all were equidistant from the origin and the distance between every pair of points was the same. The matrix $\underline{W}$ was determined such that the patterns in each category were mapped to the assigned category point with minimum overall mean-square error. The function minimized was

$$\varepsilon_{C-L} = \sum_{i=1}^{R} q_i \int_{E^n} p(\underline{x}/i)\, |\underline{\alpha}_i^t - \underline{\Phi}^t(\underline{x})\, \underline{W}|^2\, d\underline{x}, \tag{8}$$

where q_i is the a priori probability of Category i and $p(\underline{x}/i)$ is the conditional probability density function of pattern vectors from Category i. Obviously,

$$\sum_{i=1}^{R} q_i\, p(\underline{x}/i) = p(\underline{x}). \tag{9}$$

Setting the gradient of (8) to zero, the $\underline{W}$ minimizing (8) is found to be

$$\underline{W} = \underline{B}^{-1} [\sum_{i=1}^{R} q_i\, \underline{\mu}_i\, \underline{\alpha}_i^t]\,. \tag{10}$$

This result is identical to that obtained by substituting

$$\underline{f}(\underline{x}) = \sum_{i=1}^{R} p(i/\underline{x})\, \underline{\alpha}_i \tag{11}$$

in the general solution (7).

Yau and Lin [3] considered finding a weight matrix for a linear transformation which approximated the set of Bayes discriminant functions

$$\underline{D}(\underline{x}) = [D_1(\underline{x}), D_2(\underline{x}), \cdots D_R(\underline{x})]^t, \tag{12}$$

where

$$D_i(\underline{x}) = -\sum_{j=1}^{R} L(i/j)\, p(j/\underline{x}) \tag{13}$$

and $L(i/j)$ is the loss incurred when a Category j pattern vector is classified as being in Category i. The optimal Bayes decision rule is to categorize $\underline{x}$ into the category corresponding to the largest element of $\underline{D}(\underline{x})$. The function minimized by Yau and Lin was equation (2) with $\underline{f}(\underline{x}) = \underline{D}(\underline{x})$. If this is used in (7) the result is

$$\underline{W} = \underline{B}^{-1}\left[-\sum_{j=1}^{R} q_j\, \underline{\mu}_j\, L(1/j), \ldots, -\sum_{j=1}^{R} q_j\, \underline{\mu}_j\, L(R/j)\right] \tag{14}$$

which is identical to that in [3].

Meisel [4] considered a function defined in terms of a finite sample set. His result can be obtained by using a mass function for $\underline{f}(\underline{x})$. $\underline{f}(\underline{x})$ has a mass at each $\underline{x}$ for which there is a sample vector located at $\underline{x}$. The vector-valued mass is $\underline{e}_i$ if the sample vector at $\underline{x}$ is from Category i. Here, $\underline{e}_i$ is the standard basis vector for E^R which has a 1 in the ith component and zeros elsewhere. This mass function converts the integral of (7) into a summation over the sample set. The final result becomes

$$\underline{\widetilde{W}} = \underline{\widetilde{B}}^{-1}[\widetilde{q}_1 \underline{\widetilde{\mu}}_1, \widetilde{q}_2 \underline{\widetilde{\mu}}_2, \ldots, \widetilde{q}_R \underline{\widetilde{\mu}}_R], \tag{15}$$

where the tilde over each quantity indicates the estimate of the corresponding quantity based on the sample set.

IV. Estimation of Statistics

We have obtained three different matrices (10), (14), and (15) for the linear transformation $\underline{W}$ from the general LMS criterion. Each of these yields a result identical to that obtained by the corresponding previous method [2-4]. It is noted that (15) was derived from a fixed finite sample set, and (10) and (14) can be used only when the actual means and dispersion matrix can be estimated. Actually, the problem of obtaining estimates of statistics for use in such formulae is a significant problem in itself. Several authors [5-8] have attacked this problem. We shall now present a few of these techniques here.

It is obvious that with a finite sample set, the dispersion matrix $\underline{B}$, the mean vectors $\underline{\mu}_i$, and the a priori probabilities q_i, $i = 1,2, \cdots, R$, can be estimated for use in (10) and (14). Iterative algorithms based on a finite sample set which converge to (14) for the symmetric loss functions, $L(i/i) = 0$, $L(i/j) = 1$ for $i \neq j$, have been studied in [5] and [6]. These algorithms can be formulated as iterative approximations to the product of the generalized inverse of one matrix with another matrix. This is done by putting (14) in its matrix form. Let $\underline{A}$ be the matrix

$$\underline{A} = [\underline{\Phi}(\underline{x}^{(1)}), \underline{\Phi}(\underline{x}^{(2)}), \cdots, \underline{\Phi}(\underline{x}^{(N)})]^t, \tag{16}$$

where $\underline{x}^{(h)}, h = 1,2, \ldots, N$, are all the sample pattern vectors and N is the total number of sample patterns. Let $\underline{\theta}$ be a matrix of R columns and N rows whose entries θ_{hj} are defined by

$$\theta_{hj} = \begin{cases} 1 & \text{if } \underline{x}^{(h)} \text{ is a sample from Category j,} \\ 0 & \text{otherwise.} \end{cases} \tag{17}$$

Let $\underline{L}$ be an $R \times R$ matrix whose entries ℓ_{ij} are defined by

$$\ell_{ij} = -L(j/i). \tag{18}$$

Then, let $\underline{\widetilde{W}}$ be the estimate of $\underline{W}$ based on the estimates $\underline{\widetilde{B}}, \underline{\widetilde{\mu}}_i, \widetilde{q}_i$. We find that

$$\underline{\widetilde{W}} = \underline{\widetilde{B}}^{-1}[-\sum_{j=1}^{R} \widetilde{q}_j \underline{\widetilde{\mu}}_j L(1/j), \cdots, -\sum_{j=1}^{R} \widetilde{q}_j \underline{\widetilde{\mu}}_j L(R/j)] = \underline{A}^+ \underline{\theta}\, L, \tag{19}$$

where $\underline{A}^+$ is the generalized inverse of $\underline{A}$. Wee [10] has discussed the LMS criterion in terms of the generalized inverse. The algorithms in [5] and [6] converge to $\underline{\widetilde{W}} = \underline{A}^+\underline{\theta}$. For classification purposes this can easily be shown to be equivalent to (19) for symmetric loss. The algorithms could have been stated so that they converged to (19) for any L and we will state them in that form here. The first iterative algorithm for finding $\underline{\widetilde{W}}$ is called the *many pattern LMS algorithm* and can be stated as follows: Starting from an arbitrary $\underline{\overline{W}}(0)$,

$$\underline{\overline{W}}(k) = (\underline{I} - \delta \underline{A}^t \underline{A})\, \underline{\overline{W}}(k-1) + \delta \underline{A}^t \underline{\theta}\, \underline{L}, \quad k = 1,2, \ldots \tag{20}$$

This is based on the idea of adding to $\underline{\overline{W}}(k-1)$ an incremental component in the direction opposite the gradient of $E[W(k-1)]$. This algorithm makes $\underline{\overline{W}}(k)$ converge to $\underline{\widetilde{W}}$ if $0 < \delta < 2/\lambda$, where λ is the largest eigenvalue of

$\underline{A}^t\underline{A}$. The other algorithm, called the *single pattern LMS algorithm,* consists of using the pattern vectors cyclically as follows: Starting from an arbitrary $\overline{\overline{\underline{W}}}(0)$,

$$\overline{\overline{\underline{W}}}(k) = (\underline{I} - \delta\ \underline{\Phi}(\underline{x}^{(\bar{k})})\underline{\Phi}^t(\underline{x}^{(\bar{k})}))\ \overline{\overline{\underline{W}}}(k-1) + \delta\ \underline{\Phi}(\underline{x}^{(\bar{k})})\underline{\theta}^t_{i_{\bar{k}}}\ \underline{L},\ k=1,2,\ldots \tag{21}$$

where $\bar{k} \equiv k \pmod N$, $i_{\bar{k}}$ is the index of the category of $\underline{x}_{\bar{k}}$ and $\underline{\theta}^t_{i_{\bar{k}}}$ is the $i_{\bar{k}}$th row of $\underline{\theta}$ defined in (17). This algorithm makes $\overline{\overline{\underline{W}}}(k)$ converge to $\widetilde{\underline{W}}$ if $0 < \delta < 1/\max_h \underline{\Phi}^t(\underline{x}^{(h)})\ \underline{\Phi}(\underline{x}^{(h)})$.

In [7] an *accelerated* convergence form of the many pattern LMS algorithm for computing $\underline{A}^+\underline{D}$ for arbitrary $\underline{D}$ was considered. Letting $\underline{D}=\underline{\theta}\ \underline{L}$, this accelerated algorithm yields a result which converges to (19). This algorithm can be stated as follows:

$$\begin{aligned}
&0 < \delta < \lambda \\
&\overline{\underline{W}}_p(1) = \delta\ \underline{A}^t\underline{\theta}\,\underline{L} \\
&\underline{T}(1) = \underline{I} - \delta\ \underline{A}^t\underline{A} \\
&\underline{M}(k) = \sum_{\ell=0}^{p-1} \underline{T}^{\ell}(k) \\
&\underline{T}(k+1) = \underline{I} + \underline{M}(k)[\underline{T}(k) - \underline{I}] \\
&\overline{\underline{W}}_p(k+1) = \underline{M}(k)\ \overline{\underline{W}}_p(k).
\end{aligned} \tag{22}$$

It can be shown that, if in (20) $\overline{\underline{W}}(0) = \underline{0}$, then

$$\overline{\underline{W}}_p(k) = \overline{\underline{W}}(p^{k-1} - 1), \tag{23}$$

where $\overline{\underline{W}}(p^{k-1} - 1)$ is the result of $p^{k-1} - 1$ iterations of (20), and p is called the *order* of the algorithm. Recall that R is the number of columns in $\underline{\theta}\,\underline{L}$, d is the dimension of the sample vectors $\underline{\Phi}(x)$, and that N is the number of samples in the sample set (and hence also the number of rows of $\underline{A}$). Let m(k,d,N,R) be the number of multiplications required in k iterations of (20), and m(k,d,N,R) the number of multiplications required in k iterations of (22). It can be shown [7] that

$$m(k,d,N,R) = d[(k+1)dR + (R+d)(N+1)] \tag{24}$$

and

$$m_p(k,d,N,R) = d[kd^2(p-1) + (k+1)dR + (d+c)(N+1)]. \tag{25}$$

Because for (20) to produce an iterant beyond the kth iterant of (22) requires $p^{k-1} - 1$ iterations, we are interested in determining when

$$m_p(k,d,N,R) \leq m(p^{k-1} - 1,d,N,R). \quad (26)$$

(26) is satisfied when

$$kd(p-1) + kR \leq Rp^{k-1} - 1. \quad (27)$$

Thus, for any $p \geq 2$ the above inequality is satisfied for all k beyond some finite integer. But for all possible $p \geq 2$ in (21), which value of p is optimal in minimizing $m_p(k,d,N,R)$? It is shown in [7] that the optimal p is given by

$$p = 2 \quad \text{for } 0 < R/d \leq .71$$
$$p = 3 \quad \text{for } .71 \leq R/d \leq 1. \quad (28)$$

For $R/d > 1$, there is a dual algorithm to (22) which requires fewer multiplications [7].

In [8], stochastic approximation is studied as a method of estimating $\underline{W}$ in (10). This method is based on using an infinite *random* sequence of classified samples. It can be stated as choosing an arbitrary $\underline{W}'(0)$,

$$\underline{W}'(k+1) = \underline{W}'(k) - a_k \, \underline{\Phi}(\underline{x}_k)[\underline{\Phi}^t(\underline{x}_k)\underline{W}'(k) - \underline{\alpha}^t_{i_k}], \quad (29)$$

where i_k is the index of the category of $\underline{x}_k$ and a_k, $k = 1,2,---$, satisfy the conditions that $a_k > 0$, $\sum_{k=1}^{\infty} a_k = \infty$ and $\sum_{k=1}^{\infty} a_k^2$ is finite.

V. Combination of the LMS Criterion with Other Ideas

Up to this point we have discussed the mathematical form of linear least-mean-square approximations to functions, the methods of estimating these mathematical approximations, and their use in pattern recognition problems. In this section we shall review several approaches which incorporate the least-mean-square approximation with some other ideas.

In [3] straightforward estimates of $\underline{B}$, $\underline{\mu}_i$ and q_i are used in (14). They proposed that this result be the initial $\underline{W}$ in an iterative procedure which proceeds as follows. At each iteration, form a subset of the original sample set which consists of all the sample pattern vectors within a certain distance of the decision boundary generated by the current value of $\underline{W}$. Alter $\underline{W}$ in a manner analogous to the many pattern LMS algorithm (20), but with $\underline{A}$ in that algorithm replaced by a matrix whose rows consist of the subset of $\{\underline{\Phi}(\underline{x})\}$ generated above. The intuitive justification for this procedure is that if a small change in $\underline{W}$ will improve the performance of the classifier, then only those patterns which can be affected by such a small change should be used in generating the change. The change at each iteration tends to produce a weight matrix which satisfies an estimate of (14) based on those patterns near its own decision boundary.

Meisel [4] has independently suggested this same idea of deleting sample vectors far from decision boundaries, but he apparently intended to simply re-estimate the needed quantities based on the resulting sample subset. He also suggested two other ways of altering a finite sample set based on $\underline{W}$ obtained in the last iteration. In one case he proposed using a monotonically increasing function to alter the function being approximated at each step, and applied the function to the outcome of the classification process [i.e. to $\underline{\Phi}^t(\underline{x})\underline{W}$] to generate a new function to be approximated on the following iteration. The new function is again the mass function but the point mass is now $[\underline{\Phi}(\underline{x})\underline{W}_i] e_i$ when $\underline{x}$ is a training sample pattern vector in class i. Here $\underline{W}_i$ is the ith column of $\underline{W}$ from the last iteration. His final suggestion is to reweight each sample in the training set by increasing a fixed increment, the weight of incorrectly classified samples.

In [9], a sequence of matrices based on the vertex mapping procedure is determined for use in a sequential classification algorithm [11]. In sequential pattern classification, the components of $\underline{\Phi}(\underline{x})$ are determined sequentially, and at each step, a decision is made either to classify the pattern to one of the possible categories or to continue by determining the next component. If the cost of the acquisition of the components of $\underline{\Phi}(\underline{x})$ represents a sufficiently large percentage of the total cost of the classification process, then the sequential procedure can be less expensive than a procedure which uses all components simultaneously. This happens because a well designed sequential procedure acheives a percentage of correct classification which is almost as good as the procedure which uses all components of $\underline{\Phi}(\underline{x})$ while on the average it uses fewer components. The sequential procedure in [9] uses, at each step, a decision rule based on a linear function of the components of $\underline{\Phi}(\underline{x})$ determined up to that step. The resultant classifier is called a *linear sequential classifier* (LSC). For the description of the classification process it will be assumed that the order in which the components of $\underline{\Phi}(\underline{x})$ are determined is the same as the order in which they appear in the vector $\underline{\Phi}(\underline{x})$. Selection of a good order is one of the problems considered in [9] and will be discussed further below. Let $\underline{\Phi}_k(\underline{x})$ denote the vector in E^k which consists of the first k components of $\underline{\Phi}(\underline{x})$. Let $\underline{A}_k$ be the submatrix which consists of the first k columns of A, where A is defined by (16). Let $\underline{W}_k$ be the matrix minimizing (2), when the augmented pattern vector is $\underline{\Phi}_k(\underline{x})$ and $\underline{f}(\underline{x})$ is given by (11). Then, it follows from (10) that $\underline{W}_k$ becomes

$$\underline{W}_k = \underline{B}_k^{-1} [\sum_{i=1}^{R} q_i \underline{\mu}_{ik} \underline{\alpha}_i^t], \tag{30}$$

where $\underline{B}_k$ is the dispersion matrix of $\underline{\Phi}_k(\underline{x})$ relative to $p(\underline{x})$ and $\underline{\mu}_{ik}$ is the mean vector of $\underline{\Phi}_k(\underline{x})$ relative to $p(\underline{x}/i)$. If $\underline{W}_k$ is estimated from the finite sample set represented by $\underline{A}$, we obtain

$$\widetilde{\underline{W}}_k = \underline{A}_k^+ \underline{\theta} \underline{A} \tag{31}$$

where $\underline{\theta}$ is given by (17) and

$$\underline{A} = [\underline{\alpha}_1, \underline{\alpha}_2, \cdots, \underline{\alpha}_R]^t. \tag{32}$$

The linear sequential decision procedure may be stated as follows:

1) Set $s > 0$. The selection of s will be discussed later.
2) Determine the first component of $\underline{\Phi}(\underline{x})$, and set $k = 1$.
3) Determine $\underline{\nu}_k = \widetilde{\underline{W}}_k^t \underline{\Phi}_k(\underline{x})$.
4) Determine k_1 and k_2 for which $\underline{\alpha}_k$ is the nearest $\underline{\alpha}$ to $\underline{\nu}_k$ and $\underline{\alpha}_{k_2}$ is the second nearest $\underline{\alpha}$ to $\underline{\nu}_k$.
5) If $|\underline{\nu}_k - \underline{\alpha}_{k_2}| - |\underline{\nu}_k - \underline{\alpha}_{k_1}| \geq s$ or if $k = d$, classify the pattern in Category k_1 and terminate the algorithm. If $|\underline{\nu}_k - \underline{\alpha}_{k_2}| - |\underline{\nu}_k - \underline{\alpha}_{k_1}| < s$ and $k < d$, add 1 to k,,form $\underline{\Phi}_{k+1}(\underline{x})$ by determining the next component of $\underline{\Phi}(\underline{x})$, and go the Step 3).

The threshold, s, set in Step 1) causes no classification to be made at the kth cycle if $\underline{\Phi}_k(\underline{x})$ is mapped by $\widetilde{\underline{W}}_k$ to a point within a distance s of a decision boundary in E^{R-1}. The magnitude of s directly determines how heavily the evidence must be in favor of one category over all others in order to have a decision be made in the kth cycle of the algorithm, when $k < d$.

The order in which the components of $\underline{\Phi}(\underline{x})$ are to be determined depends on the LMS error achievable by the optimal $\underline{W}_k$ in the sense of minimizing (2). When $\underline{W}_k$ is estimated by $\widetilde{\underline{W}}_k$ from (31) and an estimate of $\mathcal{E}(\widetilde{\underline{W}}_k)$ for (2) is obtained from the same finite sample set, we have

$$\widetilde{\mathcal{E}}(\widetilde{\underline{W}}_k) = |\underline{\theta} \underline{A} - \underline{A}_k \widetilde{\underline{W}}_k|^2, \tag{33}$$

which depends on the ordering of the components of $\underline{\Phi}(\underline{x})$. The procedure used in [9] for determining the order was:

(a) Determine the first component such that $\widetilde{\mathcal{E}}(\widetilde{\underline{W}}_1) = |\underline{\theta} \underline{A} - \underline{A}_1 \widetilde{\underline{W}}_1|^2$ is minimized.

(b) Determine the kth component for $k = 2, \cdots, d$ such that (33) is minimized for the kth component taken with the $k-1$ components already determined.

Since each $\underline{\widetilde{W}}_k$ depends on the generalized inverse $\underline{A}_k^+$ of $\underline{A}_k$, it is possible to use an algorithm due to Greville [12] in the process of generating the $\underline{\widetilde{W}}_k$. The algorithm is

$$\underline{A}_k^+ = \begin{bmatrix} \underline{A}_{k-1}^+ - \underline{d}_k \underline{b}_k \\ \underline{b}_k^t \end{bmatrix} , \tag{34}$$

where $\underline{a}_k$ is the kth column of $\underline{A}$,

$$\underline{d}_k = \underline{A}_{k-1}^+ \underline{a}_k , \tag{35}$$

and $\underline{b}_k$ depends on $\underline{C}_k = \underline{a}_k - \underline{A}_{k-1} \underline{d}_k$ as follows:

$$\begin{aligned} &\text{If } \underline{C}_k \neq \underline{0}, \ \underline{b}_k^t = \underline{C}_k^+ = (\underline{C}_k^t \underline{C}_k)^{-1} \underline{C}_k^t ; \\ &\text{If } \underline{C}_k = \underline{0}, \ \underline{b}_k^t = (1 + \underline{d}_k^t \underline{d}_k)^{-1} \underline{d}_k^t \underline{A}_{k-1}^+ . \end{aligned} \tag{36}$$

Recall that at the kth cycle of the algorithm for determining the kth component, $\underline{A}_{k-1}$ has been determined and hence (34) can be applied to all the remaining components to determine the best component based on minimizing (33). When the kth component is determined, $\underline{A}_k^+$ is saved for use in the $(k+1)^{th}$ cycle and for generating $\underline{\widetilde{W}}_k$ by (31). Use of Greville's algorithm, thus, reduces the amount of computation required in determining the component order and the weight matrices $\underline{\widetilde{W}}_k$.

VI. Vertex Mapping Algorithm Extended to Arbitrary Loss Functions

The vertex mapping idea of Chaplin and Levadi [2] is equivalent to the least-mean-square approximation to the optimum Bayes discriminant functions with a symmetric loss matrix. In this section we shall extend this method so that the result can be applied to the case with an arbitrary loss matrix.

Our extension involves choosing two sets of R vertices in E^{R-1}. We map the training set into clusters around the first set of vertices in the LMS sense. For classification we determine the nearest member of the second set and classify the unknown pattern into that category whose index is the same as this nearest vertex. The two sets of vertices can be picked in such a way that this procedure is equivalent to the LMS approximation to the Bayes discriminant functions. After training, the first set of vertices is discarded and hence results in the same storage requirements as with the original vertex mapping algorithm.

For the LMS approximation to the Bayes discriminant functions we need to store Rd weight components. In vertex mapping (R−1)d weight components and (R−1)R vertex components need to be stored. If $R^2 - R < d$, then

$$(R-1)d + (R-1)R = Rd - d + R^2 - R < Rd, \tag{37}$$

and hence the vertex mapping method uses less storage.

Define $\underline{F}$ as follows:

$$\underline{F} = \begin{cases} \underline{L} & \text{if } \underline{L} \text{ is singular} \\ b\underline{L} - \underline{C}\,\underline{e}^t & \text{if } \underline{L} \text{ is nonsingular} \end{cases} \tag{38}$$

where $\underline{L}$ is given by (18), $b = \underline{e}^t \underline{L}^{-1} \underline{C}$, and $\underline{C}$ is any R-dimensional vector such that $b > 0$. Now, we have the following proposition:

Proposition: $\underline{F}$ has the rank at most R−1.

Proof: To show this, all we need to prove is that $\underline{F}$ is singular. If $\underline{L}$ is singular, then $\underline{F} = \underline{L}$. If $\underline{L}$ is nonsingular, then let $\underline{z} = \frac{1}{b}\underline{L}^{-1}\underline{C}$, which is a nonzero vector. Then,

$$\begin{aligned} \underline{F}\,\underline{z} &= [b\underline{L} - \underline{C}\,\underline{e}^t]\left(\frac{1}{b}\underline{L}^{-1}\underline{C}\right) \\ &= \underline{C} - \underline{C} = \underline{0}. \end{aligned} \tag{39}$$

Hence, $\underline{F}$ is singular. This completes the proof of the proposition.

Since $\underline{F}$ is singular, we can find an $R \times (R-1)$ matrix $\underline{F}_1$ and an $(R-1) \times R$ matrix $\underline{F}_2$ such that $\underline{F} = \underline{F}_1\underline{F}_2$. Let

$$\underline{F}_1 = \begin{bmatrix} \underline{\beta}_1^t \\ \vdots \\ \underline{\beta}_R^t \end{bmatrix} \tag{40}$$

and

$$\underline{F}_2 = [\underline{\gamma}_1, \underline{\gamma}_2, \cdots, \underline{\gamma}_R], \tag{41}$$

where $\underline{\beta}_i$ and $\underline{\gamma}_i$ all lie in the R−1 dimensional Euclidean space E^{R-1}. In the existing vertex mapping algorithm, we find $\{\underline{\alpha}_1, \underline{\alpha}_2, \cdots, \underline{\alpha}_R\}$ such that $\underline{\alpha}_i^t\underline{\alpha}_j = \underline{\alpha}_i^t\underline{\alpha}_k$ for all i,j,k and $\underline{\alpha}_i^t\underline{\alpha}_i = 1$ for all α_i. Then, we find $\underline{W}$ which minimizes

$$\sum_{i=1}^{R} q_i \int_{E^n} |(\underline{\Phi}^t(\underline{x})\,\underline{W} - \underline{\alpha}_i^t)|^2\ p(\underline{x}/i)\ d\underline{x}. \tag{42}$$

Finally, for an unknown pattern $\underline{x}$, we classify $\underline{x}$ into Category i for which $[\underline{\Phi}^t(\underline{x})\,\underline{W} - \underline{\alpha}_i^t]^2$ is minimum. Since $\underline{\alpha}_i^t\underline{\alpha}_i = 1$ for all i, this is the same as classifying $\underline{x}$ into category i for which $\underline{\Phi}^t(\underline{x})\,\underline{W}\,\underline{\alpha}_i$ is maximum.

In our generalization we will find $\underline{W}$ which minimizes (2) with

$$\underline{f}(\underline{x}) = \sum_{i=1}^{R} p(i/\underline{x})\underline{\beta}_i \tag{43}$$

where $\underline{\beta}_i$'s are defined by the matrix $\underline{F}_1$. Then, we will classify an unknown pattern x into Category i for which $\underline{\Phi}^t(\underline{x})\,\underline{W}\,\underline{\gamma}_i$ is maximum. Substituting (43) into (7) yields

$$\underline{W} = \underline{B}^{-1}\underline{U}\,\underline{F}_1, \tag{44}$$

where $\underline{U} = [q_1\underline{\mu}_1, q_2\underline{\mu}_2, \cdots, q_R\underline{\mu}_R]$. Since we classify $\underline{x}$ into Category i for which $\underline{\Phi}^t(\underline{x})\,\underline{W}\,\underline{\gamma}_i$ is maximum, this is the same as choosing the maximum component of $\underline{\Phi}^t(\underline{x})\underline{W}\,\underline{F}_2$. But,

$$\begin{aligned}\underline{\Phi}^t(\underline{x})\,\underline{W}\,\underline{F}_2 &= \underline{\Phi}^t(\underline{x})\underline{B}^{-1}\underline{U}\,\underline{F}_1\underline{F}_2 \\ &= \underline{\Phi}^t(\underline{x})\underline{B}^{-1}\underline{U}\,\underline{F}.\end{aligned} \tag{45}$$

For the approximation to the Bayes discriminant functions, we have from (14) that

$$\underline{W} = \underline{B}^{-1}\,\underline{U}\,\underline{L}, \tag{46}$$

and the decision rule is to select the category whose index maximizes $\underline{\Phi}^t(\underline{x})\underline{W}$. Now our generalized vertex mapping procedure is equivalent to (14) if the ranking of the components of $\underline{y}^t\,\underline{L}$ is the same as the ranking of the components of $\underline{y}^t\,\underline{F}$ for all $\underline{y}$. If $\underline{L} = \underline{F}$, this is true. If $\underline{F} = b\underline{L} - \underline{C}\,\underline{e}^t$, then $(\underline{y}^t\underline{L})_i - (\underline{y}^t\underline{L})j > 0$ implies that

$$\begin{aligned}(\underline{y}^t\underline{F})_i - (\underline{y}^t\underline{F})_j &= [(b\underline{y}^t\underline{L})_i - \underline{y}^t\underline{C}] - [(b\underline{y}^t\underline{L})_j - \underline{y}^t\underline{C}] \\ &= b[(\underline{y}^t\underline{L})_i - (\underline{y}^t\underline{L})_j] > 0,\end{aligned} \tag{47}$$

where $(\underline{y}^t\underline{L})_i$ and $(\underline{y}^t\underline{F})_i$ are the ith components of $\underline{y}^t\underline{L}$ and $\underline{y}^t\underline{F}$ respectively.

VII. Conclusion

In this paper we have presented a unification of several learning algorithms for statistical pattern recognition based on the LMS criterion, and provided some generalization in certain cases. From experience, the least-mean-square approach has been shown to yield linear pattern classifiers with very good performance. However, except for very special cases, so far it is impossible to obtain analytical results on the expected loss of the pattern classifiers based on the least-mean-square approach. This problem seems to be the most well-known unsolved problem in this area.

REFERENCES

[1] N. J. Nilsson, *Learning Machines,* New York: McGraw-Hill, 1965.

[2] W. G. Chaplin and V. S. Levadi, "A generalization of the linear threshold decision algorithm to multiple classes," *Proc. 2nd Symp. on Computer and Information Science,* New York: Academic Press, 1967, pp. 337-355.

[3] S. S. Yau and T. T. Lin, "Linear decision functions for pattern classification," *Proc. of the 2nd Annual Princeton Conference on Information Sciences and Systems,* Princeton University, Princeton, New Jersey, pp. 448-452, March, 1968.

[4] W. S. Meisel, "Least-square methods in abstract pattern recognition," *Information Sciences,* vol. 1, pp. 43-54, December, 1968.

[5] B. Widrow, "Generalization and information storage in networks of Adaline 'neurons'," *Self Organizing Systems,* M. C. Yovits, G. T. Jacobi and G. D. Goldstein, eds., Spartan Books, Washington, D.C., 1962, pp. 435-461.

[6] T. M. Whitney and R. K. Meany, "Two algorithms related to the method of steepest descent," *SIAM Jour, on Numer. Anal.,* vol. 4, no. 1, pp. 109-118, March, 1967.

[7] J. M. Garnett, A. Ben-Israel, and S. S. Yau, "A hyperpower iterative method for computing matrix products involving the generalized inverse," *SIAM Jour. on Numer. Anal.,* vol. 8, no. 1, March, 1971.

[8] S. S. Yau and J. M. Schumpert, "Design of pattern classifiers with the updating property using stochastic approximation techniques," *IEEE Trans. on Computers,* vol. C-17, no. 9, pp. 861-872, September, 1968.

[9] S. E. Smith and S. S. Yau, Linear sequential pattern classification," submitted for publication.

[10] W. G. Wee, "Generalized inverse approach to adaptive multiclass pattern recognition," *IEEE Trans. on Computers,* vol. C-17, no. 12, pp. 1157-1164, December, 1968.

[11] K. S. Fu, *Sequential Methods in Pattern Recognition and Machine Learning,* New York: Academic Press, 1968.

[12] T. N. E. Greville, "Some Applications of the Pseudoinverse of a Matrix," *SIAM Review,* vol. 2, no. 1, pp. 15-22, January, 1960.

CLOSING REMARKS

by Azriel Rosenfeld

Anyone who attempts to do some form of cluster detection on the topics of the papers presented at this conference will soon discover that pattern recognition is a very multi-dimensional subject. Though—as the local chairman, Professor Michael S. Watanabe, took pains to point out in his paper—all pattern recognition research may have the single goal on information reduction, the methods used to achieve this reduction vary considerably. Some of the principal axes, along which the variance in the field is maximal, will be discussed heuristically (not statistically) below.

There was much talk at the conference about the split between "linguistic" and "statistical" approaches to pattern recognition; but the conference itself provided evidence that this particular split may be healing fast, since there were several papers dealing with the interface between the two approaches, as embodied in such topics as stochastic grammars and grammatical inference. Presumably, the linguistics/statistics gap has proved bridgeable because the two approaches are both basically mathematical. This suggests that it will be much harder to bridge another gap which was very much in evidence at the conference: that between "heuristic" methods on the one hand, and linguistic and/or statistical methods—shall we say, mathematical methods in general?—on the other.

There is a rumor in circulation that the proponents of heuristic methods of pattern recognition (as embodied principally in work on scene analysis) have forbidden their students to use mathematics. Be this as it may, it is certainly true that one heuristician at this conference pointed with pride to the fact that the most complex mathematical operation used by his scene analysis program was a square root. Where, on the other hand, would either linguists or statisticians be without mathematics? We are faced with a dilemma: If we take the heuristic route, we can create some very smart computer programs that "know all about" certain types of scenes—what to look for, what to do if something fails, and so on. However, since we lack a formalism, it is hard to transfer the knowledge gained by writing such a program to other people, or to apply this knowledge to other problems. And yet if we get involved with formalisms, the temptation becomes overpowering to start proving theorems in the formal system and quickly lose sight of the real-world problems that inspired the formalism. (But is this so bad? Must we all be applied? Can't some of us be pure?) This dilemma was debated by Kirsch and Minsky at the First Pattern Recognition Workshop in Puerto Rico in 1966, and it seems no closer to a solution today.

It may, however, soon become very important to bring the mathematicians and heuristicians together. Most scene analysis work to date has dealt with very simple or very stylized scenes (blocks on a table; children's coloring books). What do we do when we get to more complex scenes? Surely the complete bags of tricks of the image processor and the pattern recognizer may barely suffice to find "primitives" in such scenes on which the heuristic analysis can base itself. The real-life primitives may be very ambiguous, so that simple bottom-up analysis with a minimum of backtracking becomes totally impractical. Furthermore, the real primitives may be amorphous sorts of blobs which have to be dissected into various types of basic pieces, and such dissection can be highly nontrivial, as at least two papers at this conference testified. A still more intriguing possibility, also touched on at the conference, is that of using pattern recognition techniques to recognize *relations* among parts of a scene. And ultimately, we will need some sorts of paradigms for doing minimum-risk scene analysis using contextual models.

One last "recognition gap" which was apparent at the conference also deserves mention: the gap between those working on "cooperative", man-made patterns—the character recognizers, in particular—and those working on "stubborn" natural scenes. The OCR people are much concerned these days, it seems, with standardization activities. How nice it would be if we could standardize the scenes that our robots are allowed to look at!

AUTHOR INDEX

A

B

C

AUTHOR INDEX

AUTHOR INDEX

SUBJECT INDEX

M

N

O

P